Algebra 2
Concepts & Connections

Ron Larson

Paul Battaglia

Erie, Pennsylvania
BigIdeasLearning.com

Big Ideas Learning, LLC
1762 Norcross Road
Erie, PA 16510-3838
USA

For product information and customer support, contact Big Ideas Learning at **1-877-552-7766** or visit us at ***BigIdeasLearning.com***.

Cover Image:
NASA, ESA, CSA, STScI

Copyright © 2025 by Big Ideas Learning, LLC. All rights reserved.

No part of this work may be reproduced or transmitted in any form or by any means, electronic or mechanical, including, but not limited to, photocopying and recording, or by any information storage or retrieval system, without prior written permission of Big Ideas Learning, LLC unless such copying is expressly permitted by copyright law. Address inquiries to Permissions, Big Ideas Learning, LLC, 1762 Norcross Road, Erie, PA 16510.

Big Ideas Learning is a registered trademark of Larson Texts, Inc.

Printed in the U.S.A.

ISBN 13: 979-8-88803-075-2

1 2 3 4 5 6 7 8 9—27 26 25 24 23

Why Big Ideas Learning?

Because Math Is What We Do!

With a singular focus on mathematics, we are uniquely qualified and committed to supporting you at every step along your journey. Written by renowned author, Dr. Ron Larson, and his expert authorship team, this program is a seamless and comprehensive curriculum with cohesive math progressions.

Ron Larson, Ph.D., is a highly acclaimed and award-winning math textbook author whose K–12, plus Higher Ed, student-friendly programs are known for their clarity, focus, coherence, rigor, and student self-reflection. Ron's enduring commitment to making math accessible and relevant to all students is his singular purpose.

Ron Larson

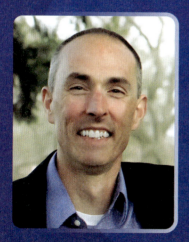

Paul Battaglia holds a Masters degree in Curriculum and Instruction and has taught high school math for 25 years. In addition to teaching, he is an educational consultant, award-winning textbook author, and is regularly invited to speak at national and international conferences. Paul's work involves efforts to inject relevance into the classroom so teachers can connect and engage more deeply with all students. For his efforts, Paul has been nominated for the Princeton Prize for Distinguished Secondary School Teaching.

Paul Battaglia

Meet the Team!

Get to know the amazing authorship team through exclusive online videos. The authors discuss many topics including their inspiration, proudest moment as an educator, and the meaning behind this program. Learn more online about the educators, experts, and community members who informed this program and how they support all aspects of the learning experience.

BigIdeasLearning.com

What Does Your Math Journey Look Like?

Investigate & Learn

Watch a STEM Career Video
Begin every chapter discovering a National Geographic Explorer's STEM research. Hear from each Explorer in the *Everyday Explorations Videos*.

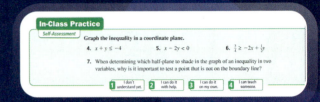

Try It and Self-Assess
Try *In-Class Practice* with feedback to help guide your learning. Rate your understanding along the way.

Think About the Big Idea
Relate the *Big Idea of the Chapter* with an investigative real-life data context.

Investigate
Work with a partner to *investigate* concepts that you will be learning in each section.

Get Ready
Refresh the skills you will need for the chapter before you begin.

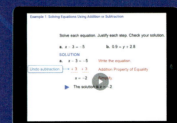

Learn and Build
Learn *Key Concepts* and interact with Examples to build your conceptual understanding.

The Road Doesn't End Here!

This program is more than just pages in a textbook. Go online to explore all the additional tools that will help you learn math this year. Watch videos of real people like an astronomer, engineer, scientist, and biologist describing how they use math every day. The learning doesn't have to stop once you leave the classroom, with online activities to get you and your family involved with your journey at home!

BigIdeasLearning.com

Connect the Big Ideas
As you learn math, you are building and connecting ideas across different pathways of thinking. Each chapter is part of your bigger math journey.

Connect to Real Life
See how the math connects to the world around you.

Get Vocabulary Help
Access vocabulary *Flash Cards* and a *Multi-Language Glossary* to strengthen your language skills.

Find Support
Access solution videos, math tools, extra practice, and more.
Calc Chat and **Calc View**

Revisit the STEM Career
Analyze a real-life data display in the field of the National Geographic Explorer and apply chapter concepts in the *Performance Task*.

Practice
Apply the concepts you are learning and connect them to a data display in the *Practice and Interpreting Data*.

Practice & Apply

1 Linear Functions

Chapter Opener 0
    CAREER: *Electrical Engineer*
    Big Idea of the Chapter: *Understand Linear Functions* 1
    Getting Ready for Chapter 1 with Calc Chat 2
Section 1.1   Parent Functions and Transformations 3
Section 1.2   Transformations of Linear
                 and Absolute Value Functions 11
Section 1.3   Modeling with Linear Functions 19
Section 1.4   Solving Linear Systems 27
Chapter Review with Calc Chat 35
Performance Task: *Flying Robot Design* 38

2 Quadratic Functions

Chapter Opener 40
    CAREER: *Data Scientist*
    Big Idea of the Chapter: *Understand Quadratic Functions* 41
    Getting Ready for Chapter 2 with Calc Chat 42
Section 2.1   Transformations of Quadratic Functions 43
Section 2.2   Characteristics of Quadratic Functions 51
Section 2.3   Focus of a Parabola 61
Section 2.4   Modeling with Quadratic Functions 69
Chapter Review with Calc Chat 77
Performance Task: *Stargazing* 80

3 Quadratic Equations and Complex Numbers

Chapter Opener 82
    CAREER: *Nuclear Engineer*
    Big Idea of the Chapter: *Relate Quadratic Equations and Complex Numbers* 83
    Getting Ready for Chapter 3 with CalcChat 84
Section 3.1   Solving Quadratic Equations 85
Section 3.2   Complex Numbers 95
Section 3.3   Completing the Square 105
Section 3.4   Using the Quadratic Formula 115
Section 3.5   Solving Nonlinear Systems of Equations 125
Section 3.6   Quadratic Inequalities 133
Chapter Review with CalcChat 141
Performance Task: *Radioactive* 144
Connecting Big Ideas: *Inflation!* 146

Nuclear Engineering
In the Performance Task, students investigate how the number of operable nuclear reactors has changed over time.

4 Polynomial Functions

Chapter Opener 148
    CAREER: *Wildlife Ecologist*
    Big Idea of the Chapter: *Understand Polynomial Functions* 149
    Getting Ready for Chapter 4 with CalcChat 150
Section 4.1   Graphing Polynomial Functions 151
Section 4.2   Adding, Subtracting, and Multiplying Polynomials 159
Section 4.3   Dividing Polynomials 167
Section 4.4   Factoring Polynomials 173
Section 4.5   Solving Polynomial Equations 181
Section 4.6   The Fundamental Theorem of Algebra 189
Section 4.7   Transformations of Polynomial Functions 199
Section 4.8   Analyzing Graphs of Polynomial Functions 205
Section 4.9   Modeling with Polynomial Functions 213
Chapter Review with CalcChat 219
Performance Task: *Thrown to the Wolves* 224

Wildlife Conservation
In the Performance Task, students will study the effects wolves have on the elk population in Yellowstone.

5 Rational Exponents and Radical Functions

Chapter Opener	226
CAREER: *Acoustic Biologist*	
Big Idea of the Chapter: *Understand Rational Exponents and Radical Functions*	227
Getting Ready for Chapter 5 with CalcChat	228
Section 5.1 *n*th Roots and Rational Exponents	229
Section 5.2 Properties of Rational Exponents and Radicals	235
Section 5.3 Graphing Radical Functions	243
Section 5.4 Solving Radical Equations and Inequalities	251
Section 5.5 Performing Function Operations	259
Section 5.6 Composition of Functions	265
Section 5.7 Inverse of a Function	271
Chapter Review with CalcChat	281
Performance Task: *The Sounds of Music*	284

Sound Art
In the Performance Task, students compare the sounds of notes in different octaves. Explain properties of the sound waves that produce those notes.

6 Exponential and Logarithmic Functions

Chapter Opener 286
       CAREER: *Archaeologist*
    Big Idea of the Chapter: *Relate Exponential and
                        Logarithmic Functions* 287
    Getting Ready for Chapter 6 with CalcChat 288
Section 6.1   Exponential Growth and Decay Functions 289
Section 6.2   The Natural Base *e* 297
Section 6.3   Logarithms and Logarithmic Functions 303
Section 6.4   Transformations of Exponential
                and Logarithmic Functions 311
Section 6.5   Properties of Logarithms 319
Section 6.6   Solving Exponential and Logarithmic Equations 327
Section 6.7   Modeling with Exponential
                and Logarithmic Functions 335
Chapter Review with CalcChat 343
Performance Task: *Carbon Dating* 346
Connecting Big Ideas: *Patented* 348

Andean Prehistory
In the Performance Task, students use carbon dating to approximate the age of an ancient manuscript made from a plant called papyrus.

7 Rational Functions

Chapter Opener 350
    CAREER: *Computer Scientist*
    Big Idea of the Chapter: *Reason About Rational Functions* 351
    Getting Ready for Chapter 7 with CalcChat 352
Section 7.1   Inverse Variation 353
Section 7.2   Graphing Rational Functions 359
Section 7.3   Multiplying and Dividing Rational Expressions 367
Section 7.4   Adding and Subtracting Rational Expressions 375
Section 7.5   Solving Rational Equations 383
Chapter Review with CalcChat 391
Performance Task: *3-D Printing* 394

8 Data Analysis and Statistics

Chapter Opener 396
    CAREER: *Volcanologist*
    Big Idea of the Chapter: *Understand Data Analysis* 397
    Getting Ready for Chapter 8 with CalcChat 398
Section 8.1   Using Normal Distributions 399
Section 8.2   Populations, Samples, and Hypotheses 407
Section 8.3   Collecting Data 415
Section 8.4   Experimental Design 423
Section 8.5   Making Inferences from Sample Surveys 429
Section 8.6   Making Inferences from Experiments 439
Chapter Review with CalcChat 445
Performance Task: *The Ring of Fire* 448
Connecting Big Ideas: *Word Games* 450

9 Trigonometric Rations and Functions

Chapter Opener 452
    CAREER: *Anthropologist*
    Big Idea of the Chapter: *Understanding Functions of Angles* 453
    Getting Ready for Chapter 9 with Calc Chat 454
Section 9.1   Right Triangle Trigonometry 455
Section 9.2   Angles and Radian Measure 463
Section 9.3   Trigonometric Functions of Any Angle 471
Section 9.4   Graphing Sine and Cosine Functions 479
Section 9.5   Graphing Other Trigonometric Functions 489
Section 9.6   Modeling with Trigonometric Functions 499
Section 9.7   Using Trigonometric Identities 507
Section 9.8   Using Sum and Difference Formulas 513
Chapter Review with Calc Chat 519
Performance Task: *Smooth Sailing* 524

10 Sequences and Series

Chapter Opener 526
    CAREER: *Chef*
    Big Idea of the Chapter: *Using Sequences and Series* 527
    Getting Ready for Chapter 10 with Calc Chat 528
Section 10.1   Defining and Using Sequences and Series 529
Section 10.2   Analyzing Arithmetic Sequences and Series 537
Section 10.3   Analyzing Geometric Sequences and Series 545
Section 10.4   Finding Sums of Infinite Geometric Series 553
Section 10.5   Using Recursive Rules with Sequences 559
Chapter Review with Calc Chat 569
Performance Task: *Walleye Stocking* 572

11 Matrices

Chapter Opener 574
    CAREER: *Photographer*
    Big Idea of the Chapter: *Use Matrices* 575
    Getting Ready for Chapter 11 with CalcChat 576
Section 11.1   Basic Matrix Operations 577
Section 11.2   Multiplying Matrices 585
Section 11.3   Determinants and Cramer's Rule 593
Section 11.4   Inverse Matrices 603
Chapter Review with CalcChat 611
Performance Task: *Food Webs* 614
Connecting Big Ideas: *World Population* 616

Selected Answers A1
English-Spanish Glossary A47
Index A59
My Guide to the Standards for Mathematical Practice ... A73
My Guide to Problem Solving A74
Quick Reference A75

1 Linear Functions

- **1.1** Parent Functions and Transformations
- **1.2** Transformations of Linear and Absolute Value Functions
- **1.3** Modeling with Linear Functions
- **1.4** Solving Linear Systems

NATIONAL GEOGRAPHIC EXPLORER
Robert Wood ELECTRICAL ENGINEER

Electrical engineer Robert Wood is an expert in tiny robots called microrobots. Microrobots are about the size of a bee. He leads a team that invents and develops entirely new classes of microrobots. For years, the team has focused on creating flying microrobots called RoboBees that can be sent on missions that are too dangerous for humans.

- A RoboBee has a 3-centimeter wingspan and a mass of 60 milligrams. Compare these measurements to the wingspan and mass of an actual honey bee.
- On what types of assignments might RoboBees be sent?

PERFORMANCE TASK
Robots can be used for a wide variety of applications. In the Performance Task on pages 38 and 39, you will design a flying robot and determine how fast it needs to flap its wings to be able to take flight.

Robotics

Big Idea of the Chapter

Understand Linear Functions

Linear functions are all transformations of the function f(x) = x. You can use linear functions to model quantities that grow by equal amounts over equal intervals.

Microrobotics is the field of miniature robotics. Microrobots are mainly used today in the biotech industry, although they have also been used for many other applications such as environmental monitoring, search and rescue, engine inspection, and agricultural research.

The graph shows the number of research articles containing the words "microrobot" or "nanorobot" in a database each year from 2000 to 2021.

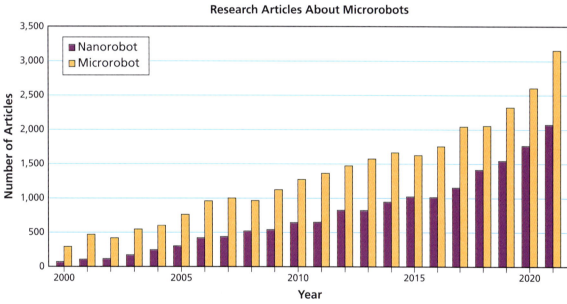

1. Consider the articles containing the word nanorobot.

    a. Write a linear model that you can use to approximate the data.

    b. Use your model to approximate when the total number of publications containing the word nanorobot will exceed 3,000.

2. Repeat Exercise 1(a) for the word microrobot. Then use your model to approximate when the total number of publications containing the word microrobot will exceed 4,000.

Getting Ready for Chapter 1

Evaluating Expressions

EXAMPLE 1 Evaluate the expression $36 \div (3^2 \times 2) - 3$.

$$36 \div (3^2 \times 2) - 3 = 36 \div (9 \times 2) - 3 \quad \text{Evaluate the power within parentheses.}$$
$$= 36 \div 18 - 3 \quad \text{Multiply within parentheses.}$$
$$= 2 - 3 \quad \text{Divide.}$$
$$= -1 \quad \text{Subtract.}$$

Evaluate.

1. $5 \cdot 2^3 + 7$
2. $4 - 2(3 + 2)^2$
3. $48 \div 4^2 + \frac{3}{5}$
4. $50 \div 5^2 \cdot 2$
5. $\frac{1}{2}(2^2 + 22)$
6. $\frac{1}{6}(6 + 18) - 2^2$

Transforming Figures

EXAMPLE 2 Reflect the black rectangle in the *x*-axis. Then translate the new rectangle 5 units to the left and 1 unit down.

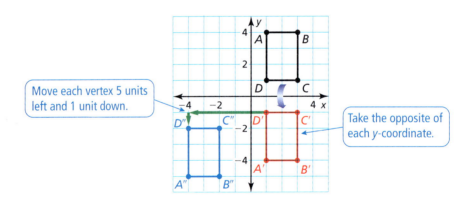

Graph the transformation of the figure.

7. Translate the rectangle 1 unit right and 4 units up.

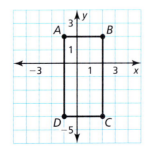

8. Reflect the triangle in the *y*-axis. Then translate the image 2 units left.

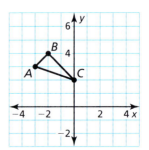

1.1 Parent Functions and Transformations

Learning Target: Graph and describe transformations of functions.

Success Criteria:
- I can identify the function family to which a function belongs.
- I can graph transformations of functions.
- I can explain how transformations affect graphs of functions.

INVESTIGATE Identifying Basic Parent Functions

Work with a partner.

1. Graphs of six basic parent functions are shown below. Classify each function as *constant*, *linear*, *absolute value*, *quadratic*, *square root*, or *exponential*. Justify your reasoning.

   a.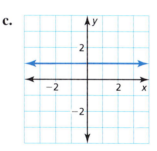

   b.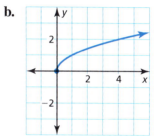

   c.

   d.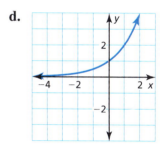

   e.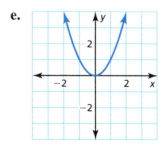

   f.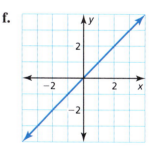

2. Sort the parent functions in Exercise 1 into groups. Explain how you grouped the functions.

3. What are the characteristics of the graphs of some of the basic parent functions?

Vocabulary
parent function
transformation
translation
reflection
vertical stretch
vertical shrink

Identifying Function Families

Functions that belong to the same *family* share key characteristics. The **parent function** is the most basic function in a family. Functions in the same family are *transformations* of their parent function.

Family	Constant	Linear	Absolute Value	Quadratic
Rule	$f(x) = 1$	$f(x) = x$	$f(x) = \|x\|$	$f(x) = x^2$
Graph	(horizontal line)	(diagonal line)		
Domain	$(-\infty, \infty)$	$(-\infty, \infty)$	$(-\infty, \infty)$	$(-\infty, \infty)$
Range	$y = 1$	$(-\infty, \infty)$	$[0, \infty)$	$[0, \infty)$

EXAMPLE 1 Identifying a Function Family

Identify the function family to which f belongs. Compare the graph of f to the graph of its parent function.

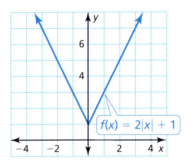

$f(x) = 2|x| + 1$

▶ The graph of f is V-shaped, so f is an absolute value function. The graph is shifted up and is narrower than the graph of the parent function. The domain of each function is all real numbers, but the range of f is $y \geq 1$ and the range of the parent absolute value function is $y \geq 0$.

In-Class Practice
Self-Assessment

Identify the function family to which g belongs. Compare the graph of g to the graph of its parent function.

1.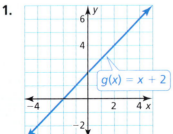
   $g(x) = x + 2$

2.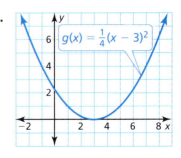
   $g(x) = \frac{1}{4}(x - 3)^2$

1 I don't understand yet. **2** I can do it with help. **3** I can do it on my own. **4** I can teach someone.

Describing Transformations

A **transformation** changes the size, shape, position, or orientation of a graph. A **translation** is a transformation that shifts a graph horizontally and/or vertically but does not change its size, shape, or orientation.

EXAMPLE 2 Graphing and Describing Translations

Graph $g(x) = x - 4$ and its parent function. Describe the transformation.

g is a linear function with a slope of 1 and a y-intercept of -4. So, draw a line through the point $(0, -4)$ with a slope of 1.

The graph of g is 4 units below the graph of the parent linear function f.

▶ So, the graph of g is a vertical translation 4 units down of the graph of the parent linear function.

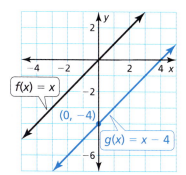

A **reflection** is a transformation that flips a graph over a line called the *line of reflection*. A reflected point is the same distance from the line of reflection as the original point but on the opposite side of the line.

EXAMPLE 3 Graphing and Describing Reflections

Graph $p(x) = -x^2$ and its parent function. Describe the transformation.

p is a quadratic function. Use a table to graph each function.

x	y = x²	y = -x²
-2	4	-4
-1	1	-1
0	0	0
1	1	-1
2	4	-4

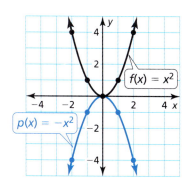

The graph of p is the graph of the parent function flipped over the x-axis.

▶ So, the graph of p is a reflection in the x-axis of the graph of the parent quadratic function.

In-Class Practice

Self-Assessment

Graph the function and its parent function. Describe the transformation.

3. $g(x) = x + 3$
4. $h(x) = (x - 2)^2$
5. $n(x) = -|x|$

1 I don't understand yet. **2** I can do it with help. **3** I can do it on my own. **4** I can teach someone.

You can transform the graph of a function by multiplying all the y-coordinates by the same positive factor k. If $k > 1$, the transformation is a **vertical stretch**. If $0 < k < 1$, it is a **vertical shrink**.

EXAMPLE 4 Graphing and Describing Stretches and Shrinks

a. **Graph $g(x) = 2|x|$ and its parent function. Describe the transformation.**

g is an absolute value function. Use a table to graph the functions.

x	$y = |x|$	$y = 2|x|$
-2	2	4
-1	1	2
0	0	0
1	1	2
2	2	4

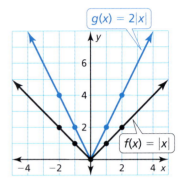

The y-coordinate of each point on g is two times the y-coordinate of the corresponding point on the parent function.

▶ So, the graph of g is a vertical stretch of the graph of the parent absolute value function by a factor of 2.

b. **Graph $h(x) = \frac{1}{2}x^2$ and its parent function. Describe the transformation.**

h is a quadratic function. Use a table to graph the functions.

x	$y = x^2$	$y = \frac{1}{2}x^2$
-2	4	2
-1	1	$\frac{1}{2}$
0	0	0
1	1	$\frac{1}{2}$
2	4	2

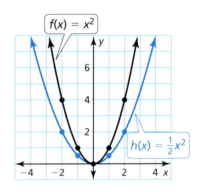

The y-coordinate of each point on h is one-half of the y-coordinate of the corresponding point on the parent function.

▶ So, the graph of h is a vertical shrink of the graph of the parent quadratic function by a factor of $\frac{1}{2}$.

In-Class Practice
Self-Assessment

6. Graph $h(x) = \frac{3}{2}x^2$ and its parent function. Describe the transformation.

1 I don't understand yet. **2** I can do it with help. **3** I can do it on my own. **4** I can teach someone.

Combinations of Transformations

EXAMPLE 5 Describing Combinations of Transformations

Use technology to graph $g(x) = -|x + 5| - 3$ and its parent function. Describe the transformations.

The function g is an absolute value function.

▶ The graph of $g(x) = -|x + 5| - 3$ is a reflection in the x-axis followed by a translation 5 units left and 3 units down of the graph of the parent absolute value function.

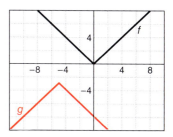

EXAMPLE 6 Estimating a Value from a Graph

STEM Video: Dirt Bike Trajectory

The table shows the height y of a dirt bike x seconds after jumping off a ramp. What type of function can you use to model the data? Estimate the height after 1.75 seconds.

Time (seconds), x	0	0.5	1	1.5	2
Height (feet), y	8	20	24	20	8

Create a scatter plot. The data appear to lie on a curve that resembles a quadratic function. Sketch the curve.

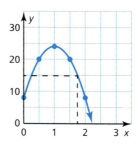

▶ So, you can model the data with a quadratic function. The graph shows that the height is about 15 feet after 1.75 seconds.

In-Class Practice

Self-Assessment

7. Use technology to graph $h(x) = -\frac{1}{4}x + 5$ and its parent function. Describe the transformations.

8. The table shows the distance remaining for a competitor in a snowshoeing race in the Arctic Winter Games. What type of function can you use to model the data? When will the competitor finish the race?

Time (minutes), x	0	10	20	30	40
Distance remaining (km), y	10	8	6	4	2

1 I don't understand yet. **2** I can do it with help. **3** I can do it on my own. **4** I can teach someone.

1.1 Practice

Identify the function family to which *f* belongs. Compare the graph of *f* to the graph of its parent function. (See Example 1.)

1.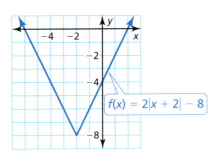

2.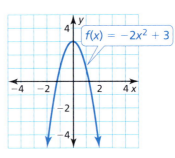

3.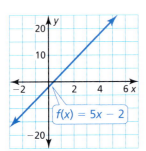

4.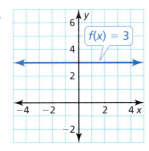

Graph the function and its parent function. Describe the transformation. (See Examples 2 and 3.)

5. $f(x) = x^2 - 1$

6. $g(x) = x + 4$

7. $h(x) = (x + 4)^2$

8. $f(x) = 4 + |x|$

9. $g(x) = -x$

10. $f(x) = -2$

11. **SMP.3 ERROR ANALYSIS** Describe and correct the error in graphing $g(x) = |x + 3|$ and its parent function.

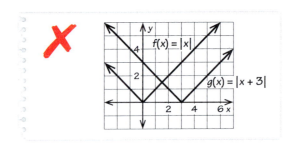

Graph the function and its parent function. Describe the transformation. (See Example 4.)

12. $f(x) = 2x^2$

13. $f(x) = \frac{1}{3}x$

14. $h(x) = \frac{1}{3}x^2$

15. $g(x) = \frac{4}{3}x$

16. $h(x) = 3|x|$

17. $f(x) = \frac{1}{2}|x|$

Use technology to graph the function and its parent function. Describe the transformations. (See Example 5.)

18. $h(x) = -3|x| - 1$

▶ **19.** $f(x) = 3x + 2$

20. $g(x) = \frac{1}{2}x^2 - 6$

21. $f(x) = -(x + 3)^2 + \frac{1}{4}$

CONNECT CONCEPTS Find the coordinates of the figure after the transformation.

22. Translate 2 units down.

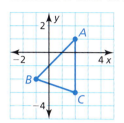

23. Reflect in the x-axis.

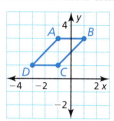

24. **ROBOTS** **BATTERY LIFE** The table shows the battery life of a robotic vacuum over time. What type of function can you use to model the data? Estimate the battery life after 45 minutes. (See Example 6.)

Time (minutes), x	30	90	120	180	240
Battery life remaining, y	75%	25%	0%	50%	100%

25. **CONNECTION TO REAL LIFE** The graph shows the balance of a savings account over time.

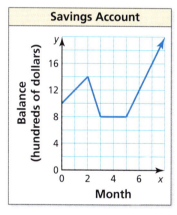

a. Write a function that represents the account balance for the domain shown. Identify the function type.

b. Can you use your function to predict the account balance after 1 year? Explain.

c. What is the initial balance? How would the graph change if the account had an initial balance of $2,000?

26. **SMP.2** The height (in feet) of a basketball t seconds after you take a shot is given by $f(t) = -16t^2 + 26t + 6.5$.

a. Without graphing, identify the type of function that models the height of the basketball.

b. How many feet above the ground is the ball when it is released from your hand? Explain.

27. **SMP.1** **DIG DEEPER** Use the values $-1, 0, 1,$ and 2 to complete each function so their graphs intersect the x-axis. Justify your answers.

a. $f(x) = 3x^{\boxed{}} + 1$

b. $f(x) = |2x - 6| - \boxed{}$

c. $f(x) = \boxed{} x^2 + 1$

d. $f(x) = \boxed{}$

Interpreting Data

DOUGLAS FIR TREES Lumber from Douglas fir trees is widely used by construction workers in the United States. The species also makes up almost half of the Christmas trees grown in the country. The scatter plot shows the heights and diameters of several Douglas fir trees.

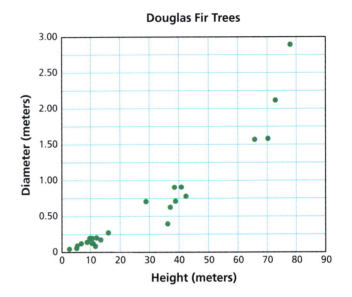

28. Describe the scatter plot. How is diameter related to height?

29. Explain which type of function best fits the data.

Review & Refresh

30. Tell whether (5, 2) is a solution of $y \leq x - 3$.

Find the x- and y-intercepts of the graph of the equation.

31. $y = x + 2$

32. $x - 2y = 8$

33. The sum of three-halves a number and eight is seventeen. What is the number?

34. Determine whether the graph represents a function.

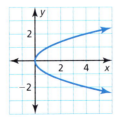

Find the volume of the solid.

35.
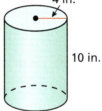

36.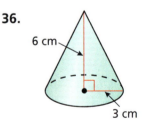

Factor the polynomial completely.

37. $x^2 - x - 30$

38. $3x^2 + 15x + 12$

39. Determine which of the lines, if any, are parallel or perpendicular.

   Line a: $2y + x = 12$
   Line b: $y = 2x - 3$
   Line c: $y + 2x = 1$

10   Chapter 1   Linear Functions

1.2 Transformations of Linear and Absolute Value Functions

Learning Target: Write functions that represent transformations of functions.

Success Criteria:
- I can write functions that represent transformations of linear functions.
- I can write functions that represent transformations of absolute value functions.

INVESTIGATE Transforming the Parent Absolute Value Function

Work with a partner. Graph the function for several values of k, h, or a. Then describe how the value of k, h, or a affects the graph.

1. $y = |x| + k$

2. $y = |x - h|$

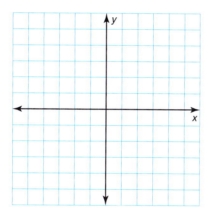
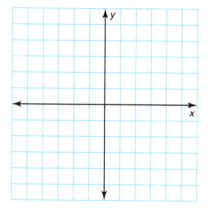

3. $y = a \cdot |x|$

4. $y = |a \cdot x|$

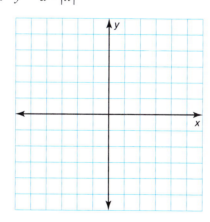
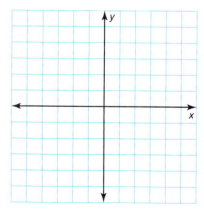

5. Let f be the parent absolute value function. How do the graphs compare to the graph of f?

   a. $y = f(x) + k$

   b. $y = f(x - h)$

   c. $y = a \cdot f(x)$

   d. $y = f(a \cdot x)$

Translations and Reflections

Horizontal Translations

The graph of $y = f(x - h)$ is a horizontal translation of the graph of $y = f(x)$, where $h \neq 0$.

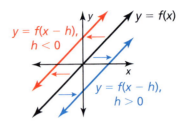

Vertical Translations

The graph of $y = f(x) + k$ is a vertical translation of the graph of $y = f(x)$, where $k \neq 0$.

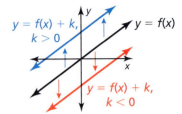

EXAMPLE 1 **Writing Translations of Functions**

Let $f(x) = 2x + 1$.

a. Write a function g whose graph is a translation 3 units down of the graph of f.

A translation 3 units down is a vertical translation that adds -3 to each output value.

$g(x) = f(x) + (-3)$ Add -3 to the output.
$= 2x + 1 + (-3)$ Substitute $2x + 1$ for $f(x)$.
$= 2x - 2$ Simplify.

▶ The translated function is $g(x) = 2x - 2$.

b. Write a function h whose graph is a translation 2 units left of the graph of f.

A translation 2 units left is a horizontal translation that subtracts -2 from each input value.

$h(x) = f(x - (-2))$ Subtract -2 from the input.
$= f(x + 2)$ Add the opposite.
$= 2(x + 2) + 1$ Replace x with $x + 2$ in $f(x)$.
$= 2x + 5$ Simplify.

▶ The translated function is $h(x) = 2x + 5$.

Check

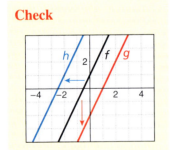

In-Class Practice

Self-Assessment

1. Write a function g whose graph represents a translation 5 units up of the graph of $f(x) = 3x$.

1 I don't understand yet. **2** I can do it with help. **3** I can do it on my own. **4** I can teach someone.

Reflections in the x-Axis

The graph of $y = -f(x)$ is a reflection in the x-axis of the graph of $y = f(x)$.

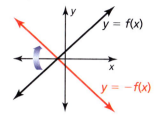

Reflections in the y-Axis

The graph of $y = f(-x)$ is a reflection in the y-axis of the graph of $y = f(x)$.

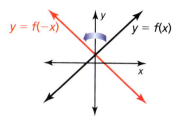

EXAMPLE 2 **Writing Reflections of Functions**

Let $f(x) = |x + 3| + 1$.

a. Write a function g whose graph is a reflection in the x-axis of the graph of f.

A reflection in the x-axis changes the sign of each output value.

$g(x) = -f(x)$ Multiply the output by -1.

$ = -(|x + 3| + 1)$ Substitute $|x + 3| + 1$ for $f(x)$.

$ = -|x + 3| - 1$ Distributive Property

▶ The reflected function is $g(x) = -|x + 3| - 1$.

b. Write a function h whose graph is a reflection in the y-axis of the graph of f.

A reflection in the y-axis changes the sign of each input value.

$h(x) = f(-x)$ Multiply the input by -1.

$ = |-x + 3| + 1$ Replace x with $-x$ in $f(x)$.

$ = |-(x - 3)| + 1$ Factor out -1.

$ = |-1| \cdot |x - 3| + 1$ Product Property of Absolute Value

$ = |x - 3| + 1$ Simplify.

▶ The reflected function is $h(x) = |x - 3| + 1$.

Check

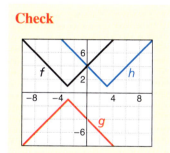

In-Class Practice

Self-Assessment

Write a function g whose graph represents the indicated transformation of the graph of f.

2. $f(x) = -|x + 2| - 1$; reflection in the x-axis

3. $f(x) = \frac{1}{2}x + 1$; reflection in the y-axis

 I don't understand yet.   I can do it with help.   I can do it on my own.   I can teach someone.

Stretches and Shrinks

Horizontal Stretches or Shrinks

The graph of $y = f(ax)$ is a horizontal stretch or shrink by a factor of $\frac{1}{a}$ of the graph of $y = f(x)$, where $a > 0$ and $a \neq 1$.

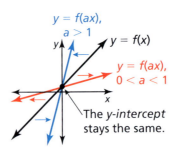

Vertical Stretches and Shrinks

The graph of $y = a \cdot f(x)$ is a vertical stretch or shrink by a factor of a of the graph of $y = f(x)$, where $a > 0$ and $a \neq 1$.

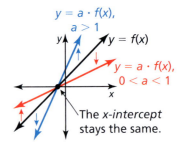

EXAMPLE 3 Writing Stretches and Shrinks of Functions

Let $f(x) = |x - 3| - 5$.

a. Write a function g whose graph is a horizontal shrink of the graph of f by a factor of $\frac{1}{3}$.

A horizontal shrink by a factor of $\frac{1}{3}$ multiplies each input value by 3.

$g(x) = f(3x)$ Multiply the input by 3.

$= |3x - 3| - 5$ Replace x with $3x$ in $f(x)$.

▶ The transformed function is $g(x) = |3x - 3| - 5$.

b. Write a function h whose graph is a vertical stretch of the graph of f by a factor of 2.

A vertical stretch by a factor of 2 multiplies each output value by 2.

$h(x) = 2 \cdot f(x)$ Multiply the output by 2.

$= 2 \cdot (|x - 3| - 5)$ Substitute $|x - 3| - 5$ for $f(x)$.

$= 2|x - 3| - 10$ Distributive Property

▶ The transformed function is $h(x) = 2|x - 3| - 10$.

Check

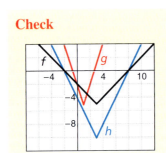

In-Class Practice

Self-Assessment

Write a function g whose graph represents the indicated transformation of the graph of f.

4. $f(x) = 4x + 2$; horizontal stretch by a factor of 2

5. $f(x) = |x| - 3$; vertical shrink by a factor of $\frac{1}{3}$

Combinations of Transformations

EXAMPLE 4 **Combining Transformations**

Let the graph of g be a vertical shrink by a factor of 0.25 followed by a translation 3 units up of the graph of $f(x) = x$. Write a rule for g.

Write a function h that represents the vertical shrink of f.

$h(x) = 0.25 \cdot f(x)$ Multiply the output by 0.25.

$ = 0.25x$ Substitute x for $f(x)$.

Write a function g that represents the translation of h.

$g(x) = h(x) + 3$ Add 3 to the output.

$ = 0.25x + 3$ Substitute $0.25x$ for $h(x)$.

▶ The transformed function is $g(x) = 0.25x + 3$.

EXAMPLE 5 **Using Combinations of Transfomations**

You open a food cart that sells kimbap, a popular Korean street food. Your revenue (in dollars) for x sales is given by $f(x) = 14x$ and your profit is $250 less than 90% of the revenue.

a. Write a function that represents your profit.

Write a function p that represents your profit.

profit = 90% · revenue − 250

$p(x) = \underbrace{0.9 \cdot f(x)}_{\text{Vertical shrink by a factor of 0.9}} \underbrace{- 250}_{\text{Translation 250 units down}}$

$ = 0.9 \cdot 14x - 250$ Substitute $14x$ for $f(x)$.

$ = 12.6x - 250$ Simplify.

▶ The function is $p(x) = 12.6x - 250$.

b. Find your profit for 100 sales.

To find the profit for 100 sales, evaluate p when $x = 100$.

$p(100) = 12.6(100) - 250 = 1{,}010$

▶ Your profit is $1,010 for 100 sales.

In-Class Practice

Self-Assessment

6. Let the graph of g be a translation 6 units down followed by a reflection in the x-axis of the graph of $f(x) = |x|$. Write a rule for g.

7. **WHAT IF?** In Example 5, your revenue function is $f(x) = 13x$. How does this affect your profit for 100 sales?

1.2 Practice

Write a function g whose graph represents the indicated transformation of the graph of f.
(See Example 1.)

1. $f(x) = x - 5$; translation 4 units left
2. $f(x) = x + 2$; translation 2 units right
3. $f(x) = |4x + 3| + 2$; translation 2 units down
4. $f(x) = 2|x| - 9$; translation 6 units up

5. Describe the translation from the graph of f to the graph of g in two different ways.

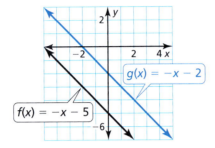

Write a function g whose graph represents the indicated transformation of the graph of f.
(See Example 2.)

6. $f(x) = \frac{1}{2}x - 3$; reflection in the x-axis
7. $f(x) = -5x + 2$; reflection in the x-axis
8. $f(x) = |6x| - 2$; reflection in the y-axis
9. $f(x) = -3 + |x - 11|$; reflection in the y-axis

Write a function g whose graph represents the indicated transformation of the graph of f.
(See Example 3.)

10. $f(x) = 2x + 6$; vertical shrink by a factor of $\frac{1}{2}$
11. $f(x) = x + 2$; vertical stretch by a factor of 5
12. $f(x) = |2x| + 4$; horizontal shrink by a factor of $\frac{1}{2}$
13. $f(x) = |x + 3|$; horizontal stretch by a factor of 4

MATCHING Match the graph of the transformation of f with the correct equation shown.

14.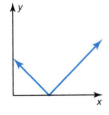
15.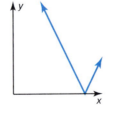
16.
17.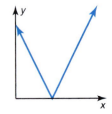

A. $y = 2f(x)$
B. $y = f(2x)$
C. $y = f(x + 2)$
D. $y = f(x) + 2$

16 Chapter 1 Linear Functions

Write a function g whose graph represents the indicated transformations of the graph of f.
(See Example 4.)

18. $f(x) = x$; vertical stretch by a factor of 2 followed by a translation 1 unit up

▶ 19. $f(x) = |x|$; translation 2 units right followed by a horizontal stretch by a factor of 2

20. $f(x) = x$; translation 3 units down followed by a vertical shrink by a factor of $\frac{1}{3}$

21. $f(x) = |x|$; reflection in the y-axis followed by a translation 3 units right

22. **SMP.3 ERROR ANALYSIS** Identify and correct the error in writing the function g whose graph represents the indicated transformations of the graph of f.

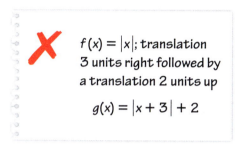

23. **CONNECTION TO REAL LIFE** The cost (in dollars) of a car ride from a ride sharing company during regular hours is modeled by $f(x) = 2.30x$, where x is the number of miles driven. The cost of a ride during high-demand hours, including a tip, is $5 more than 120% the cost during regular hours. What is the cost of a 6-mile ride during high-demand hours? (See Example 5.)

CONNECT CONCEPTS Describe the transformation of the graph of f to the graph of g. Then find the area of the shaded triangle.

24. $f(x) = |x - 3|$

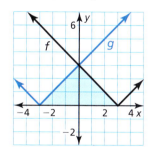

25. $f(x) = -x + 4$

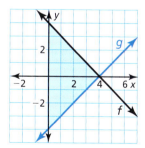

26. Consider the graph of $f(x) = mx + b$. Describe the effect each transformation has on the slope of the line and the intercepts of the graph.

    a. Reflect the graph of f in the y-axis.

    b. Shrink the graph of f vertically by a factor of $\frac{1}{3}$.

    c. Stretch the graph of f horizontally by a factor of 2.

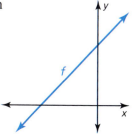

Interpreting Data

SEA TURTLES Olive ridley sea turtles are one of the smallest species of sea turtle. They lay about 100 eggs at a time and bury them in the sand. A marine biologist records information about the nest conditions of olive ridley sea turtles.

27. Describe the graph. What can you conclude about the relationship between nest temperature and incubation period?

28. The function $p(t) = 2.04t + 114.1$ can be used to model the data. Describe the transformations of the graph of the parent function to the graph of p.

Review & Refresh

29. Make a scatter plot of the data. Describe the relationship between the data.

x	8	10	11	12	15
f(x)	4	9	10	12	12

30. The function $f(x) = -1.5x + 50$ represents the amount (in pounds) of dog food in a bag after x days.

    a. Graph the function and find its domain and range.

    b. Interpret the slope and the intercepts of the graph.

31. Solve the system using any method.

    $3x - 2y = -15$
    $4x + 2y = 8$

32. Identify the function family to which g belongs. Compare the graph of the function to the graph of its parent function.

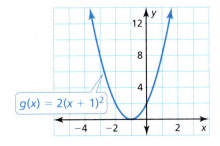

$g(x) = 2(x + 1)^2$

1.3 Modeling with Linear Functions

Learning Target: Use linear functions to model and analyze real-life situations.

Success Criteria:
- I can write equations of linear functions.
- I can compare linear equations to solve real-life problems.
- I can find a line of best fit.

INVESTIGATE Modeling with Linear Functions

Work with a partner.

1. **SMP.2** **INDUSTRIAL ROBOT VALUE** A company purchases an industrial robot for $87,000. The spreadsheet shows how the robot depreciates over an 8-year period.

	A	B
1	Year, t	Value, V
2	0	$87,000
3	1	$79,750
4	2	$72,500
5	3	$65,250
6	4	$58,000
7	5	$50,750
8	6	$43,500
9	7	$36,250
10	8	$29,000

   a. Write V as a function of t.

   b. Sketch a graph of the function. Explain why this type of depreciation is called *straight line depreciation*.

   c. Interpret the slope and intercepts of the graph in the context of the problem.

2. Describe a real-life situation that can be modeled by each graph.

   a.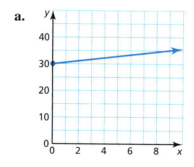

   b.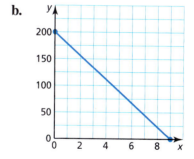

   c.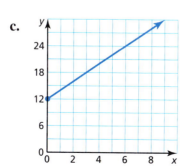

   d.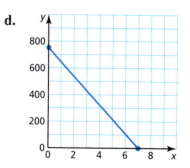

Vocabulary
line of fit
line of best fit
correlation coefficient

Writing Linear Equations

There are three basic ways to write an equation of a line.

Given slope m and y-intercept b:

Use slope-intercept form: $y = mx + b$

Given slope m and a point (x_1, y_1):

Use point-slope form: $y - y_1 = m(x - x_1)$

Given points (x_1, y_1) and (x_2, y_2):

Use the slope formula to find m. Then use point-slope form with either point.

EXAMPLE 1 Writing a Linear Equation from a Graph

The graph shows the distance Asteroid 2019 GC6 travels in x seconds.

a. Write an equation of the line and interpret the slope.

From the graph, you can see the slope is $m = \frac{21}{6} = 3.5$ and the y-intercept is $b = 0$. Use slope-intercept form to write an equation of the line.

$y = mx + b$ Slope-intercept form

$ = 3.5x + 0$ Substitute 3.5 for m and 0 for b.

▶ The equation is $y = 3.5x$. The slope indicates that the asteroid travels 3.5 miles per second.

b. The asteroid came within 136,000 miles of Earth in April, 2019. About how long does it take the asteroid to travel that distance?

Solve the equation in part (a) when $y = 136{,}000$.

$136{,}000 = 3.5x$ Substitute 136,000 for y.

$38{,}857 \approx x$ Divide each side by 3.5.

▶ Because there are 3,600 seconds in 1 hour and

$$38{,}857 \text{ sec} \div \frac{3{,}600 \text{ sec}}{1 \text{ h}} = 38{,}857 \text{ sec} \times \frac{1 \text{ h}}{3{,}600 \text{ sec}} \approx 11 \text{ h},$$

it takes the asteroid about 11 hours to travel 136,000 miles.

In-Class Practice

Self-Assessment

1. The graph shows the remaining balance y on a car loan after making x monthly payments.

   a. Write an equation of the line and interpret the slope and y-intercept.

   b. What is the remaining balance after 36 payments?

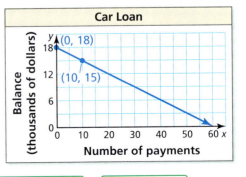

 I don't understand yet.
 I can do it with help.
 I can do it on my own.
 I can teach someone.

20   Chapter 1   Linear Functions

EXAMPLE 2 **Comparing Linear Equations**

Two prom venues charge a rental fee plus a fee per student. The table shows the total costs (in dollars) for different numbers of students at Lakeside Inn. The total cost y (in dollars) for x students at Sunview Resort is represented by the equation $y = 10x + 600$.

Lakeside Inn

Number of students, x	Total cost, y
100	$1,500
125	$1,800
150	$2,100
175	$2,400
200	$2,700

a. **Which venue charges less per student?**

Compare the slopes. The table shows a constant rate of change. Find the slope using any two points. Use $(x_1, y_1) = (100, 1{,}500)$ and $(x_2, y_2) = (125, 1{,}800)$.

$$m = \frac{y_2 - y_1}{x_2 - x_1} = \frac{1{,}800 - 1{,}500}{125 - 100} = \frac{300}{25} = 12$$

▶ Comparing the slopes, Sunview Resort charges $10 per student, which is less than the $12 per student that Lakeside Inn charges.

b. **How many students must attend for the total costs to be the same?**

Write an equation that represents the total cost at Lakeside Inn using the slope of 12 and a point from the table. Use $(x_1, y_1) = (100, 1{,}500)$.

$y - y_1 = m(x - x_1)$	Point-slope form
$y - 1{,}500 = 12(x - 100)$	Substitute for m, x_1, and y_1.
$y - 1{,}500 = 12x - 1{,}200$	Distributive Property
$y = 12x + 300$	Add 1,500 to each side.

Equate the cost expressions and solve.

$10x + 600 = 12x + 300$	Set cost expressions equal.
$300 = 2x$	Combine like terms.
$150 = x$	Divide each side by 2.

▶ The total costs are the same when 150 students attend the prom.

Check The total cost for 150 students at Lakeside Inn is $2,100. Verify that the total cost at Sunview Resort is also $2,100 for 150 students.

$y = 10(150) + 600$	Substitute 150 for x.
$= 2{,}100$ ✓	Simplify.

In-Class Practice

Self-Assessment

2. **WHAT IF?** Maple Ridge charges a rental fee plus a $10 fee per student. The total cost is $1,900 for 140 students. Describe the number of students that must attend for the total cost at Maple Ridge to be less than the total costs at the other two venues. Use a graph to justify your answer.

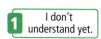

Finding Lines of Fit and Lines of Best Fit

When the data in a scatter plot do not show an *exact* linear relationship, you can model the data with a **line of fit**, as follows.

- Make a scatter plot of the data.
- Draw the line that most closely appears to follow the trend.
- Use two points on the line to write an equation.

EXAMPLE 3 **Finding a Line of Fit**

The table shows the femur lengths and heights of several people. Estimate the height of a person whose femur is 35 centimeters long.

Femur length (cm), x	Height (cm), y
40	170
45	183
32	151
50	195
37	162
41	174
30	141
34	151
47	185
45	182

Make a scatter plot. The data show a linear relationship, so you can draw a line of fit.

To find an equation of the line of fit, first find the slope. Use the points (40, 170) and (50, 195).

$$m = \frac{y_2 - y_1}{x_2 - x_1}$$

$$= \frac{195 - 170}{50 - 40}$$

$$= \frac{25}{10}, \text{ or } 2.5$$

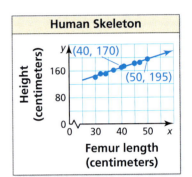

Use point-slope form to write an equation. Use $(x_1, y_1) = (40, 170)$.

$y - y_1 = m(x - x_1)$ Point-slope form

$y - 170 = 2.5(x - 40)$ Substitute for m, x_1, and y_1.

Use the equation to estimate the height of a person whose femur is 35 centimeters long.

$y - 170 = 2.5(35 - 40)$ Substitute 35 for x.

$y = 157.5$ Solve for y.

▶ The approximate height of a person whose femur is 35 centimeters long is 157.5 centimeters.

In-Class Practice

Self-Assessment

3. The data pairs (x, y) represent the humerus lengths x (in centimeters) and heights y (in centimeters) of several skeletons. Do the data show a linear relationship? If so, use an equation of a line of fit to estimate the height of a skeleton with a humerus length of 40 centimeters.

(33, 166), (25, 142), (22, 130), (30, 154), (28, 152), (32, 159), (26, 141), (27, 145)

   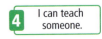

The **line of best fit** is the line that best models a set of data. Many technology tools have a *linear regression* feature that finds the line of best fit for a data set.

The **correlation coefficient**, denoted by r, is a number that ranges from -1 to 1. When r is near 1, there is a strong positive correlation. When r is near -1, there is a strong negative correlation. As r gets closer to 0, the correlation becomes weaker.

EXAMPLE 4 Finding a Line of Best Fit Using Technology

Use technology to find an equation of the line of best fit for the data in Example 3. Estimate the height of a person whose femur is 35 centimeters long. Compare this height to your estimate in Example 3.

Enter the data and use *linear regression*. The values in the equation can be rounded to obtain $y = 2.6x + 65$.

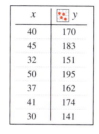

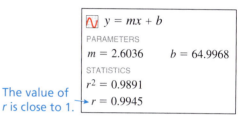

The value of r is close to 1.

Find the value of y when $x = 35$.

$y = 2.6x + 65$ Write the equation.

$ = 2.6(35) + 65$ Substitute 35 for x.

$ = 156$ Evaluate.

▶ The line of best fit is $y = 2.6x + 65$. The height of a person with a 35-centimeter femur is about 156 centimeters. This is less than the estimate of 157.5 centimeters found in Example 3.

Check Use technology to evaluate the equation when $x = 35$.

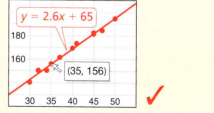

humerus

femur

In-Class Practice

Self-Assessment

4. Find an equation of the line of best fit for the data in Exercise 3. Compare the height using the line of best fit with the height from Exercise 3.

1 I don't understand yet.   **2** I can do it with help.   **3** I can do it on my own.   **4** I can teach someone.

1.3 Modeling with Linear Functions

1.3 Practice

Use the graph to write an equation of the line and interpret the slope. (See Example 1.)

1.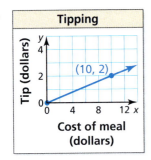

2.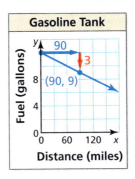

3.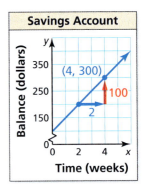

4. **SMP.3 ERROR ANALYSIS** Describe and correct the error in writing a linear equation that models the data in the table.

x	y
12	17
20	23
28	29
36	35
42	41

   $$m = \frac{20 - 12}{23 - 17} = \frac{8}{6} = \frac{4}{3}$$
   $$y - 17 = \tfrac{4}{3}(x - 12)$$
   $$y - 17 = \tfrac{4}{3}x - 16$$
   $$y = \tfrac{4}{3}x + 1$$

5. The table shows the total costs of a cell phone and service from Carrier A. The total cost y (in dollars) of the phone and x months of service from Carrier B is represented by $y = 55x + 300$. Which carrier charges less per month? After how many months of service are the total costs the same? (See Example 2.)

Months, x	3	6	9	12	15
Total cost, y	500	650	800	950	1,100

6. **SMP.4 CONNECTION TO REAL LIFE** Temperatures in Canada are reported in degrees Celsius. You know there is a linear relationship between degrees Fahrenheit and degrees Celsius, but you forget the formula. From science class, you remember the following:

   Freezing point of water: 0°C or 32°F

   Boiling point of water: 100°C or 212°F

   a. Write an equation that gives degrees Fahrenheit in terms of degrees Celsius.
   b. It is 15°C in Toronto. What is this temperature in degrees Fahrenheit?
   c. Rewrite the equation in part (a) to give degrees Celsius in terms of degrees Fahrenheit.
   d. It is 68°F in your city. What is this temperature in degrees Celsius?

24 Chapter 1 Linear Functions

7. The table shows the number of calories that a person burns by walking for x minutes. Do the data show a linear relationship? If so, write an equation of a line of fit and use it to estimate the number of calories the person burns by walking for 15 minutes. (See Example 3.)

Minutes walking, x	1	6	11	13	16
Calories burned, y	6	27	50	56	70

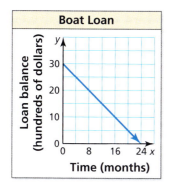

8. **SMP.2** You secure an interest-free loan to purchase a boat. You agree to make equal monthly payments for the next two years. The graph shows the amount of money you still owe.

   a. What is the slope of the line? What does the slope represent?

   b. What is the domain and range of the function? What does each represent?

   c. How much do you still owe after making payments for 12 months?

9. The data pairs (x, y) represent the average annual tuition, fees, room, and board y (in dollars) for 4-year colleges and universities in the United States x years after the 2009–2010 academic year. Find an equation of the line of best fit. Use the equation to estimate the average cost in the 2024–2025 academic year. (See Example 4.)

   (0, 21,126), (1, 22,074), (2, 23,011), (3, 23,871), (4, 24,701), (5, 25,409),

   (6, 26,132), (7, 26,592), (8, 27,357), (9, 28,121), (10, 28,774), (11, 29,033)

10. **OPEN-ENDED** Give two real-life quantities that have (a) a positive correlation, (b) a negative correlation, and (c) approximately no correlation.

11. **SMP.1 PERFORMANCE TASK** Your family wants to purchase a new vehicle that comes in either a gasoline model or an electric model.

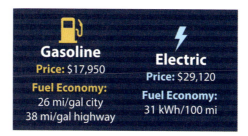

   a. Using the information shown, the approximate number of miles your family drives per year, and gas and electricity prices in your area, determine which vehicle is a better buy. Use linear equations to support your answer.

   b. Research other factors that impact the cost of vehicle ownership. Explain how these factors might support or change your answer.

Interpreting Data

SUPPLY AND DEMAND Economists study supply and demand. When the supply of an item exceeds the demand, the price tends to increase. When the demand exceeds the supply, the price tends to decrease. The scatter plot shows the sales of avocados at several stores compared to the price.

12. Write a linear equation that describes the situation.

13. Use supply and demand to give a possible explanation for why the average price was $1.70 at one location, but only $0.60 at another location.

Review & Refresh

14. What number is 34% of 50?

Solve the system using any method.

15. $4x - 6y = 2$
    $2x - 3y = 1$

16. $y = x - 4$
    $y = -4x + 6$

17. Write a system of inequalities represented by the graph.

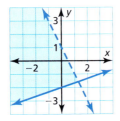

18. Solve the equation $z = 4y + 2x + 8$ for x.

19. What percent of 25 is 14?

Find the sum or difference.

20. $(x^2 + 2x + 16) + (4x^2 - 7x - 18)$

21. $(-5n^3 + n^2 - 12n) - (6n^2 + 4n - 13)$

Write a function g whose graph represents the indicated transformation of the graph of f.

22. $f(x) = 2x + 1$; translation 3 units up

23. $f(x) = -3|x - 4|$; vertical shrink by a factor of $\frac{1}{2}$

1.4 Solving Linear Systems

Learning Target: Solve linear systems in three variables.

Success Criteria:
- I can visualize solutions of linear systems in three variables.
- I can solve linear systems in three variables algebraically.
- I can solve real-life problems using systems of equations in three variables.

INVESTIGATE Solving Three-Variable Systems

Work with a partner.

1. Consider the system shown.

   $y = 4x$ Equation 1
   $x + 2y - z = 7$ Equation 2
   $3x - 4y + 2z = -9$ Equation 3

   a. How is this linear system different from linear systems you have solved in previous courses?

   b. Explain a method you can use to solve the system. Solve the system and show how you can represent the solution.

   c. The graph of each equation in the system is a plane in three-dimensional space. A three-dimensional coordinate system is shown below. How can the solution of this system be represented in the graph?

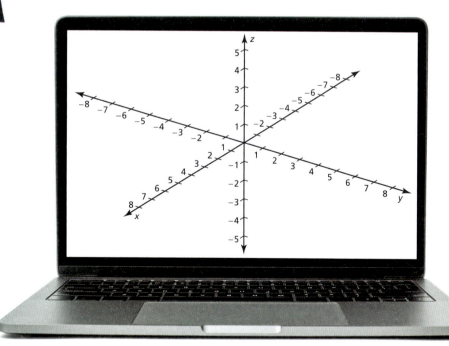

2. Can a linear system in three variables have no solution? infinitely many solutions? If so, sketch an example of what each type of solution might look like in three-dimensional space. Explain your reasoning.

> **Vocabulary**
> linear equation in three variables
> system of three linear equations
> solution of a system of three linear equations
> ordered triple

Visualizing Solutions of Systems

A **linear equation in three variables** x, y, and z is an equation of the form $ax + by + cz = d$, where a, b, and c are not all zero.

Here is an example of a **system of three linear equations** in three variables.

$3x + 4y - 8z = -3$ Equation 1
$x + y + 5z = -12$ Equation 2
$4x - 2y + z = 10$ Equation 3

A **solution** of such a system is an **ordered triple** (x, y, z) whose coordinates make each equation true.

The graph of a linear equation in three variables is a plane in three-dimensional space. A system of three linear equations in three variables can have no solution, one solution, or infinitely many solutions.

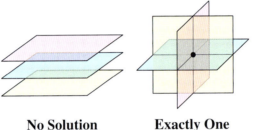

No Solution   Exactly One Solution   Infinitely Many Solutions

EXAMPLE 1 Interpreting Representations of Systems

Identify the number of solutions of a system represented by the diagram.

Any two planes intersect in a line. However, there is no point that is common to all three planes.

▶ So, the system has no solution.

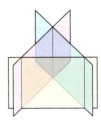

In-Class Practice

Self-Assessment

Identify the number of solutions of a system represented by the diagram.

1.

2.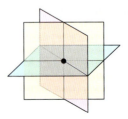

1 I don't understand yet.   **2** I can do it with help.   **3** I can do it on my own.   **4** I can teach someone.

Solving Systems of Equations Algebraically

You can solve linear systems in three variables similarly to how you solved linear systems in two variables.

- Rewrite the linear system in three variables as a linear system in two variables by using the substitution or elimination method.
- Solve the new linear system for both of its variables.
- Substitute the values found in Step 2 into one of the original equations and solve for the remaining variable.

When you obtain a false equation, the system has *no solution*. When you obtain an identity, the system has *infinitely many solutions*.

EXAMPLE 2   Solving a Three-Variable System (One Solution)

Solve the system.

$4x + 2y + 3z = 12$ Equation 1
$2x - 3y + 2z = -13$ Equation 2
$6x - y + 4z = -3$ Equation 3

Rewrite the system as a linear system in *two* variables.

$4x + 2y + 3z = 12$
$\underline{12x - 2y + 8z = -6}$ Add 2 times Equation 3 to Equation 1 (to eliminate y).
$16x + 11z = 6$ New Equation 1

$2x - 3y + 2z = -13$
$\underline{-18x + 3y - 12z = 9}$ Add -3 times Equation 3 to Equation 2 (to eliminate y).
$-16x - 10z = -4$ New Equation 2

Solve the new linear system for both of its variables.

$16x + 11z = 6$
$\underline{-16x - 10z = -4}$ Add new Equation 1 and new Equation 2.
$z = 2$
$x = -1$ Substitute into new Equation 1 or 2 to find x.

Substitute $x = -1$ and $z = 2$ into an original equation and solve for y.

$6(-1) - y + 4(2) = -3$ Substitute in original Equation 3.
$y = 5$ Solve for y.

▶ The solution is $x = -1$, $y = 5$, and $z = 2$, or the ordered triple $(-1, 5, 2)$.

In-Class Practice

Self-Assessment

3. Solve the system.

$x - 2y + z = -11$
$3x + 2y - z = 7$
$-x + 2y + 4z = -9$

1 I don't understand yet.   **2** I can do it with help.   **3** I can do it on my own.   **4** I can teach someone.

EXAMPLE 3 **Solving a Three-Variable System (No Solution)**

Solve the system.
$x + y + z = 2$ Equation 1
$5x + 5y + 5z = 3$ Equation 2
$4x + y - 3z = -6$ Equation 3

Rewrite the system as a linear system in *two* variables.

$$\begin{array}{l} -5x - 5y - 5z = -10 \\ \underline{5x + 5y + 5z = 3} \\ 0 = -7 \end{array}$$

Add -5 times Equation 1 to Equation 2.

▶ Because you obtain a false equation, the original system has no solution.

EXAMPLE 4 **Solving a Three-Variable System (Many Solutions)**

Solve the system.
$x - y + z = -3$ Equation 1
$x - y - z = -3$ Equation 2
$5x - 5y + z = -15$ Equation 3

Rewrite the system as a linear system in *two* variables.

$$\begin{array}{l} x - y + z = -3 \\ \underline{x - y - z = -3} \\ 2x - 2y = -6 \end{array}$$

Add Equation 1 to Equation 2 (to eliminate z).
New Equation 2

$$\begin{array}{l} x - y - z = -3 \\ \underline{5x - 5y + z = -15} \\ 6x - 6y = -18 \end{array}$$

Add Equation 2 to Equation 3 (to eliminate z).
New Equation 3

Solve the new linear system for both of its variables.

$$\begin{array}{l} -6x + 6y = 18 \\ \underline{6x - 6y = -18} \\ 0 = 0 \end{array}$$

Add -3 times new Equation 2 to new Equation 3.

Because you obtain an identity, the system has infinitely many solutions. You can write the solutions with an ordered triple.

Solving New Equation 2 for y gives $y = x + 3$. Substitute $x + 3$ for y in original Equation 1 gives $z = 0$.

▶ So, any ordered triple of the form $(x, x + 3, 0)$ is a solution.

In-Class Practice

Self-Assessment

Solve the system.

4. $x + y - z = -1$
   $4x + 4y - 4z = -2$
   $3x + 2y + z = 0$

5. $x + y + z = 8$
   $x - y + z = 8$
   $2x + y + 2z = 16$

 I don't understand yet.   I can do it with help.   I can do it on my own.   I can teach someone.

Connections to Real Life

EXAMPLE 5   **Writing and Solving a Linear System**

An amphitheater charges $75 for each seat in Section A, $55 for each seat in Section B, and $30 for each lawn seat. There are three times as many seats in Section B as in Section A. The revenue from selling all 23,000 seats is $870,000. How many seats are in each section of the amphitheater?

Write verbal models for the situation.

Seats in B, y = 3 · Seats in A, x

Seats in A, x + Seats in B, y + Lawn Seats, z = Total seats

75 · Seats in A, x + 55 · Seats in B, y + 30 · Lawn seats, z = Revenue

Write a system of equations.

$y = 3x$	Equation 1
$x + y + z = 23{,}000$	Equation 2
$75x + 55y + 30z = 870{,}000$	Equation 3

Use substitution to rewrite the system as a linear system in *two* variables.

$x + 3x + z = 23{,}000$	Substitute $3x$ for y in Equation 2.
$4x + z = 23{,}000$	New Equation 2
$75x + 55(3x) + 30z = 870{,}000$	Substitute $3x$ for y in Equation 3.
$240x + 30z = 870{,}000$	New Equation 3

Solve the new linear system for both of its variables.

$-120x - 30z = -690{,}000$	Add -30 times new Equation 2
$\underline{240x + 30z = 870{,}000}$	to new Equation 3.
$120x = 180{,}000$	
$x = 1{,}500$	Solve for x.
$y = 4{,}500$	Substitute into Equation 1 to find y.
$z = 17{,}000$	Substitute into Equation 2 to find z.

▶ The solution is (1,500, 4,500, 17,000). So, there are 1,500 seats in Section A, 4,500 seats in Section B, and 17,000 lawn seats.

In-Class Practice

Self-Assessment

6. WHAT IF? For another concert, 7,640 tickets are sold for $284,300, and twice as many tickets are sold for Section B as for Section A. How many tickets are sold for each section?

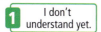

1.4 Practice

Identify the number of solutions of a system represented by the diagram. (See Example 1.)

1.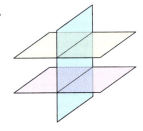

2.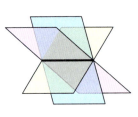

3.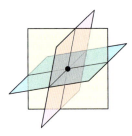

Solve the system. (See Examples 2, 3, and 4.)

4. $x + 4y - 6z = -1$
   $2x - y + 2z = -7$
   $-x + 2y - 4z = 5$

5. $x + y - 2z = 5$
   $-x + 2y + z = 2$
   $2x + 3y - z = 9$

6. $5x + y - z = 6$
   $x + y + z = 2$
   $12x + 4y = 10$

7. $3x - y + 2z = 4$
   $6x - 2y + 4z = -8$
   $2x - y + 3z = 10$

8. $x + 2y - z = 3$
   $-2x - y + z = -1$
   $6x - 3y - z = -7$

9. $x + 3y - z = 2$
   $x + y - z = 0$
   $3x + 2y - 3z = -1$

10. $2x + 2y + 5z = 6$
    $2x - y + z = 2$
    $2x + 4y - 3z = 14$

11. $-2x - 3y + z = -6$
    $x + y - z = 5$
    $7x + 8y - 6z = 31$

12. $x + 2y + 3z = 4$
    $-3x + 2y - z = 12$
    $-2x - 2y - 4z = -14$

13. **SMP.3 ERROR ANALYSIS** Describe and correct the error in the first step of solving the linear system.

    $4x - y + 2z = -18$ Equation 1
    $-x + 2y + z = 11$ Equation 2
    $3x + 3y - 4z = 44$ Equation 3

    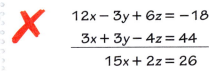

14. **CONNECTION TO REAL LIFE** Three orders at a coffee shop are shown. How much does each item cost? (See Example 5.)

    $11: 2 coffees, 1 latte, 1 bagel

    $15: 1 coffee, 1 latte, 3 bagels

    $16: 3 coffees, 1 latte, 2 bagels

Solve the system of linear equations using the substitution method.

15. $y = 2x - 6z + 1$
    $3x + 2y + 5z = 16$
    $7x + 3y - 4z = 11$

16. $x + y + z = 4$
    $5x + 5y + 5z = 12$
    $x - 4y + z = 9$

17. $4x + y + 5z = 5$
    $8x + 2y + 10z = 10$
    $x - y - 2z = -2$

32   Chapter 1   Linear Functions

18. The results of a track meet are described in the article below. How many athletes from Lawrence High finished in each place?

Local News

Lawrence High prevailed in Saturday's track meet with the help of 20 individual-event placers earning a combined 68 points. A first-place finish earns 5 points, a second-place finish earns 3 points, and a third-place finish earns 1 point. Lawrence had a strong second-place showing, with as many second place finishers as first- and third-place finishers combined.

CONNECT CONCEPTS Write and use a linear system to answer the question.

19. The triangle has a perimeter of 65 feet. What are the lengths of sides ℓ, m, and n?

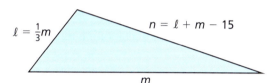

$\ell = \frac{1}{3}m$ $n = \ell + m - 15$

20. What are the measures of angles A, B, and C?

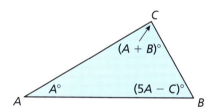

21. **OPEN-ENDED** Consider the system of linear equations shown. Choose nonzero values for a, b, and c so the system satisfies each condition.

$x + y + z = 2$
$ax + by + cz = 10$
$x - 2y + z = 4$

a. The system has no solution.
b. The system has exactly one solution.
c. The system has infinitely many solutions.

22. **SMP.1 DIG DEEPER** Solve the system. Explain your method.

$-\dfrac{1}{x} - \dfrac{1}{y} + \dfrac{6}{z} = -3$ Equation 1

$\dfrac{6}{x} + \dfrac{5}{y} - \dfrac{12}{z} = 11$ Equation 2

$\dfrac{3}{x} + \dfrac{2}{y} - \dfrac{2}{z} = 4$ Equation 3

23. **SMP.1 DIG DEEPER** The scales shown are used to compare the weights of apples, tangerines, grapefruits, and bananas. How many tangerines will balance one apple? Justify your answer using a linear system.

Interpreting Data

24. **SMP.2 FREE-FALLING OBJECT** The acceleration due to gravity on Earth is about -9.8 meters per second squared. The height h (in meters) of a launched or thrown object after t seconds is given by

$$h = at^2 + bt + c.$$

A construction worker tosses an object and it falls to the ground. The table shows the height of the object over time.

Time (sec), t	0	1	2
Height (m), h	18	15.1	2.4

a. Use the table and the height equation to write three linear equations in a, b, and c.

b. Solve the system in part (a).

c. How is the value of a related to acceleration due to gravity?

Review & Refresh

Write a function g described by the given transformation of $f(x) = |x| - 5$.

25. translation 2 units to the left

26. vertical stretch by a factor of 3

Find the product.

27. $(x - 2)^2$ 28. $(3m + 1)^2$

29. Find the value of x.

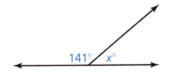

Solve the inequality. Graph the solution.

30. $6 + w > -15$

31. $2(x - 4) > 6x - 16$

32. $|2h + 3| - 3 < -1$

33. $4t + 21 < -7$ or $-\frac{1}{2}t \le 2$

34. The table shows the total distance a new car travels each month after it is purchased. What type of function can you use to model the data? Estimate the mileage after 1 year.

Time (months), x	Distance (miles), y
0	0
2	2,300
5	5,750
6	6,900
9	10,350

35. Solve $\dfrac{4}{x} = \dfrac{16}{10}$.

36. Create a nonnumerical data set that has more than one mode.

Simplify the expression. Write your answer using only positive exponents.

37. $b^{-12} \cdot b^9$ 38. $(2c)^6$

1 Chapter Review

Rate your understanding of each section.

1 — I don't understand yet. 2 — I can do it with help. 3 — I can do it on my own. 4 — I can teach someone.

1.1 Parent Functions and Transformations (pp. 3–10)

Learning Target: Graph and describe transformations of functions.

Vocabulary
parent function
transformation
translation
reflection
vertical stretch
vertical shrink

Graph the function and its parent function. Then describe the transformation.

1. $h(x) = 4$
2. $f(x) = x + 3$
3. $g(x) = |x| - 1$
4. $h(x) = \frac{1}{2}x^2$

5. A function g is a translation 4 units right and 6 units down, followed by a reflection in the y-axis of the graph of $f(x) = -\frac{1}{2}(x+1)^2$. Graph f and g.

6. The graphs of of f and g are shown. Describe a transformation from the graph of f to the graph of g.

7. The table shows the total distance traveled by a space probe after x seconds. What type of function can you use to model the data? Estimate the distance traveled by the space probe after 1 minute.

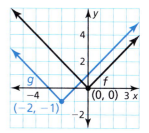

Time (seconds), x	0	8	20	36	50
Distance (miles), y	0	76	190	342	475

1.2 Transformations of Linear and Absolute Value Functions (pp. 11–18)

Learning Target: Write functions that represent transformations of functions.

Write a function g whose graph represents the indicated transformations of the graph of f.

8. $f(x) = x$; horizontal shrink by a factor of $\frac{1}{3}$

9. $f(x) = |x|$; reflection in the x-axis followed by a translation 4 units left

10. $f(x) = -3x + 4$; translation 3 units down and a reflection in the y-axis

11. $f(x) = |x + 1| - 2$ vertical shrink by a factor of $\frac{1}{2}$ followed by a translation 2 units up

12. The total cost of an annual pass to a park plus camping for x days can be modeled by the function $f(x) = 20x + 80$. A senior citizen pays $20 less than half of this price for x days. What is the total cost for a senior citizen to go camping for three days in the park?

1.3 Modeling with Linear Functions (pp. 19–26)

⊙ **Learning Target:** Use linear functions to model and analyze real-life situations.

Vocabulary
line of fit
line of best fit
correlation coefficient

Use the graph to write an equation of the line and interpret the slope.

13.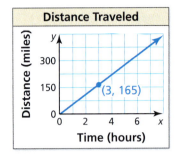

14.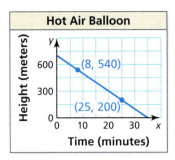

15. The table shows the costs to hire Babysitter A. The total cost y (in dollars) to hire Babysitter B for x hours is represented by $y = 18x + 14$. Which babysitter charges less per hour? For how many hours are the total costs the same?

Hours, x	2	4	6	8	10
Total cost, y	56	90	124	158	192

16. The table shows the numbers of ice cream cones sold for different outside temperatures (in degrees Fahrenheit). Do the data show a linear relationship? If so, write an equation of a line of fit and use it to estimate how many ice cream cones are sold when the temperature is 60°F.

Temperature, x	53	62	70	82	90
Number of cones, y	90	105	117	131	147

17. The table shows the total number y (in thousands) of tickets sold at a movie theater each year for x years. Use technology to find an equation of the line of best fit for the data. Then interpret the slope and y-intercept. Estimate the number of tickets sold in the 12th year.

Year, x	0	2	4	6	8	10
Tickets sold, y	224	226	239	247	249	257

18. A set of data pairs has a correlation coefficient of $r = 0.3$. Your friend says that because the correlation coefficient is positive, it is logical to use the line of best fit to make predictions. Explain whether your friend is correct.

1.4 Solving Linear Systems (pp. 27–34)

⊙ **Learning Target:** Solve linear systems in three variables.

Vocabulary
linear equation in three variables
system of three linear equations
solution of a system of three linear equations
ordered triple

Solve the system.

19. $x + y + z = 3$
    $-x + 3y + 2z = -8$
    $x = 4z$

20. $2x - 5y - z = 17$
    $x + y + 3z = 19$
    $-4x + 6y + z = -20$

21. $x + y + z = 2$
    $2x - 3y + z = 11$
    $-3x + 2y - 2z = -13$

22. $x + 4y - 2z = 3$
    $x + 3y + 7z = 1$
    $2x + 9y - 13z = 2$

23. $x - y + 3z = 6$
    $x - 2y = 5$
    $2x - 2y + 5z = 9$

24. $x + 2z = 4$
    $x + y + z = 6$
    $3x + 3y + 4z = 28$

25. A school band performs a spring concert for a crowd of 600 people. The revenue for the concert is $3,150. There are 150 more adults at the concert than students. How many of each type of ticket are sold?

26. Complete the equations so that the system has infinitely many solutions. Then write an ordered triple that represents the solutions of the system.

    $-2x + 2y - z = 4$
    $\boxed{}x + \boxed{}y + \boxed{}z = -2$
    $\boxed{}x + \boxed{}y + \boxed{}z = -8$

27. A total of 100 million people vote in a national election. The table shows the percentage of the total votes for each candidate that were cast in two regions. Find the total number of votes cast for each candidate.

Region	Party A candidate (%)	Party B candidate (%)	Other candidates (%)	Total voters (millions)
Northeast	20	15	20	18
South	30	35	25	31.5

28. A linear system in three variables has no solution. Your friend concludes that it is not possible for two of the three equations to have any points in common. Explain whether your friend is correct.

PERFORMANCE TASK 1
SMP.1 SMP.2

Flying Robot Design

Some of the smallest flying robots have masses as low as 175 milligrams and wing frequencies as high as 300 hertz.

Optical-flow sensors could potentially be used for stability and to navigate surroundings.

For a robot to fly, its mass (in grams) must be less than the lift force (in gram-forces) of its wings.

The frame houses actuators to transfer power to the wings.

hertz (Hz): cycles per second

gram-force (gf): the amount of force exerted by gravity on 1 gram of matter

Analyzing Data

Use the information on the previous page to complete the following exercises.

1. Explain what is shown in the display. What do you notice? What do you wonder?

2. An engineer wants to determine how much the mass of a flying robot differs from 15 grams. Write an absolute value function that represents the situation. Then graph the function and its parent function and describe the transformation.

CREATE A FLYING ROBOT

You are a member of a team that is creating a prototype for a flying robot. For each wing design, your team measures lift forces for various flapping frequencies. The tables show the results. Choose a wing design and a frame style for your robot and find the minimum flapping frequency needed for your robot to take flight.

Hint: Using the general form of a quadratic equation, $y = ax^2 + bx + c$, substitute three different pairs of x- and y-values from the table of your chosen design. Then solve the resulting linear system in three variables.

Wing A

Frequency (Hz), x	10	13	16	19
Lift Force (gf), y	3.2	7.1	11.8	16.9

Wing B

Frequency (Hz), x	11	14	17	20
Lift Force (gf), y	3.3	6.1	9.4	13.1

Wing C

Frequency (Hz), x	12	15	18	21
Lift Force (gf), y	4.6	8.0	11.9	16.4

Frame A
22 grams

Frame B
20 grams

Frame C
12 grams

2 Quadratic Functions

- 2.1 Transformations of Quadratic Functions
- 2.2 Characteristics of Quadratic Functions
- 2.3 Focus of a Parabola
- 2.4 Modeling with Quadratic Functions

NATIONAL GEOGRAPHIC EXPLORER
Jennifer Lopez DATA SCIENTIST

Jennifer Lopez is a technologist and data scientist with a mission to use citizen science to help unravel secrets of the cosmos. She is a founding member of NASA's Datanaut Corps, which inspires future engineers, data scientists, and entrepreneurs to engage with NASA in solving data challenges.

- What is a technologist? What is a data scientist?
- What is in-space manufacturing?
- Why is in-space manufacturing crucial to the success of long-term exploration missions in space?

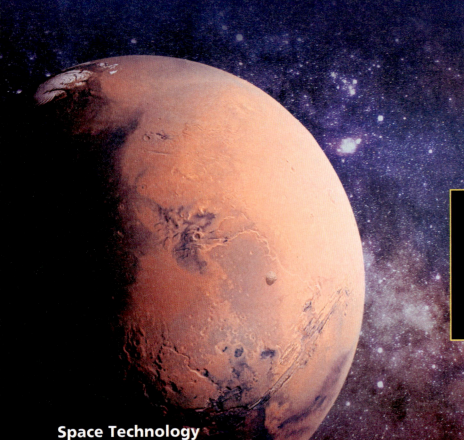

PERFORMANCE TASK
Radio telescopes can be used to study the compositions of stars, planets, and moons. In the Performance Task on pages 80 and 81, you will design a radio telescope and use a quadratic equation to describe its parabolic cross section.

Space Technology

Big Idea of the Chapter
Understand Quadratic Functions

A quadratic function can be written in the form $f(x) = ax^2 + bx + c$, where a, b, and c are real numbers. The graph of a quadratic function is a parabola. Parabolas are U-shaped and may open up, down, left, or right.

The Five-hundred-meter Aperture Spherical radio Telescope (FAST) is the largest radio telescope in the world, with a diameter of 500 meters. Its remote location in southwestern China helps protect it from radio-wave interference. The parabolic cross section of the telescope is shown.

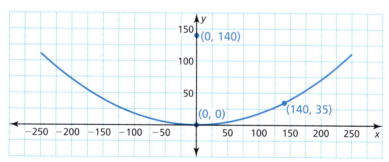

1. Write an equation that represents the cross section.

2. When a radio wave enters the dish, it is reflected at the same angle it strikes the dish. Sketch several radio waves as they enter and exit the telescope. What does the point (0, 140) represent?

3. Explain why the telescope was constructed in a parabolic shape.

Getting Ready for Chapter 2

Finding x-Intercepts

EXAMPLE 1 Find the x-intercept of the graph of the linear equation $y = 3x - 12$.

$y = 3x - 12$ Write the equation.

$0 = 3x - 12$ Substitute 0 for y.

$12 = 3x$ Add 12 to each side.

$4 = x$ Divide each side by 3.

▶ The x-intercept is 4.

Find the x-intercept of the graph of the linear equation.

1. $y = -10x - 36$
2. $y = 3(x - 5)$
3. $3x + 6y = 24$

Finding Distances in a Coordinate Plane

EXAMPLE 2 Find the distance between $(1, 4)$ and $(-3, 6)$.

Plot the points in a coordinate plane. Then draw a right triangle with a hypotenuse that represents the distance between the points.

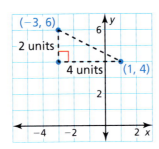

Use the Pythagorean Theorem to find the length of the hypotenuse.

$a^2 + b^2 = c^2$ Write the Pythagorean Theorem.

$2^2 + 4^2 = c^2$ Substitute 2 for a and 4 for b.

$4 + 16 = c^2$ Evaluate powers.

$20 = c^2$ Add.

$\sqrt{20} = c$ Take the positive square root of each side.

▶ The distance between $(1, 4)$ and $(-3, 6)$ is $\sqrt{20}$ units.

Find the distance between the points.

4. $(2, 5), (-4, 7)$
5. $(3, 10), (5, 9)$
6. $(4, -8), (4, 2)$

2.1 Transformations of Quadratic Functions

Learning Target: Describe and graph transformations of quadratic functions.

Success Criteria:
- I can describe transformations of quadratic functions.
- I can graph transformations of quadratic functions.
- I can write transformations of quadratic functions.

INVESTIGATE Identifying Graphs of Quadratic Functions

Work with a partner. Match each quadratic function with its graph. Explain your reasoning. Then use technology to check your answer.

1. $g(x) = -(x-2)^2$
2. $g(x) = (x-2)^2 + 2$
3. $g(x) = -(x+2)^2 - 2$
4. $g(x) = 0.5(x-2)^2 - 2$
5. $g(x) = 2(x-2)^2$
6. $g(x) = -(x+2)^2 + 2$

A.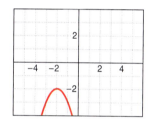

D.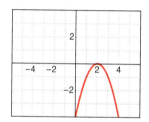

B.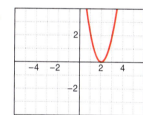

E.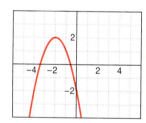

C.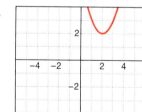

F.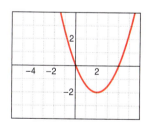

7. How do the constants a, h, and k affect the graph of the quadratic function $g(x) = a(x-h)^2 + k$?

8. Write the equation of the quadratic function whose graph is shown at the right. Explain your reasoning. Then use technology to check your answer.

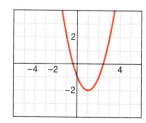

> **Vocabulary**
> quadratic function
> parabola
> vertex of a parabola
> vertex form

Describing Transformations of Quadratic Functions

A **quadratic function** is a function that can be written in the form $f(x) = a(x - h)^2 + k$, where $a \neq 0$. The U-shaped graph of a quadratic function is called a **parabola**.

In Section 1.1, you graphed quadratic functions using tables of values. You can also graph quadratic functions by applying transformations to the graph of the parent function $f(x) = x^2$.

Horizontal Translations
$f(x - h) = (x - h)^2$

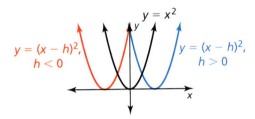

- shifts left when $h < 0$
- shifts right when $h > 0$

Vertical Translations
$f(x) + k = x^2 + k$

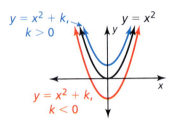

- shifts down when $k < 0$
- shifts up when $k > 0$

Reflections in the x-Axis
$-f(x) = -(x^2) = -x^2$

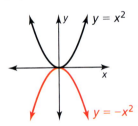

flips over the x-axis

Reflections in the y-Axis
$f(-x) = (-x)^2 = x^2$

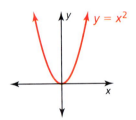

$y = x^2$ is its own reflection in the y-axis.

Horizontal Stretches and Shrinks
$f(ax) = (ax)^2$

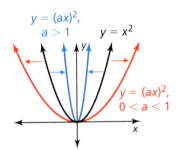

- horizontal stretch (away from y-axis) by a factor of $\frac{1}{a}$ when $0 < a < 1$
- horizontal shrink (toward y-axis) by a factor of $\frac{1}{a}$ when $a > 1$

Vertical Stretches and Shrinks
$a \cdot f(x) = ax^2$

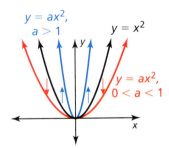

- vertical stretch (away from x-axis) by a factor of a when $a > 1$
- vertical shrink (toward x-axis) by a factor of a when $0 < a < 1$

EXAMPLE 1 Transformations of a Quadratic Function

Describe the transformation of $f(x) = x^2$ represented by $g(x) = (x + 4)^2 - 1$. Then graph each function.

Notice that the function is of the form $g(x) = (x - h)^2 + k$. Rewrite the function to identify h and k.

$$g(x) = (x - (-4))^2 + (-1)$$
$$\underset{h}{\uparrow}\underset{k}{\uparrow}$$

▶ Because $h = -4$ and $k = -1$, the graph of g is a translation 4 units left and 1 unit down of the graph of f.

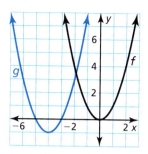

EXAMPLE 2 Transformations of Quadratic Functions

Describe the transformation of $f(x) = x^2$ represented by g. Then graph each function.

a. $g(x) = -\frac{1}{2}x^2$

Notice that the function is of the form $g(x) = -ax^2$, where $a = \frac{1}{2}$.

▶ So, the graph of g is a reflection in the x-axis and a vertical shrink by a factor of $\frac{1}{2}$ of the graph of f.

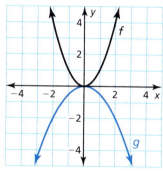

b. $g(x) = (2x)^2 + 1$

Notice that the function is of the form $g(x) = (ax)^2 + k$, where $a = 2$ and $k = 1$.

▶ So, the graph of g is a horizontal shrink by a factor of $\frac{1}{2}$, followed by a translation 1 unit up of the graph of f.

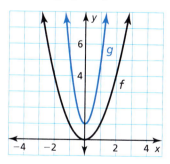

In-Class Practice

Self-Assessment

Describe the transformation of $f(x) = x^2$ represented by g. Then graph each function.

1. $g(x) = (x - 2)^2 - 2$
2. $g(x) = (x + 5)^2 + 1$
3. $g(x) = \left(\frac{1}{3}x\right)^2$
4. $g(x) = -(x + 3)^2 + 2$

1 I don't understand yet. **2** I can do it with help. **3** I can do it on my own. **4** I can teach someone.

2.1 Transformations of Quadratic Functions

Writing Transformations of Quadratic Functions

The lowest point on a parabola that opens up or the highest point on a parabola that opens down is the **vertex**. The **vertex form** of a quadratic function is $f(x) = a(x - h)^2 + k$, where $a \neq 0$ and the vertex is (h, k).

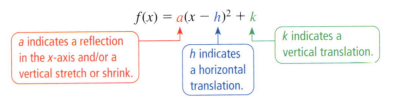

EXAMPLE 3 Writing a Transformed Quadratic Function

Let the graph of g be a vertical stretch by a factor of 2 and a reflection in the x-axis, followed by a translation 3 units down of the graph of $f(x) = x^2$. Write a rule for g and identify the vertex.

Identify how the transformations affect the constants in the vertex form.

$\left.\begin{array}{l}\text{reflection in } x\text{-axis} \\ \text{vertical stretch by 2}\end{array}\right\} a = -2$

translation 3 units down} $k = -3$

Write the transformed function.

$g(x) = a(x - h)^2 + k$ Vertex form of a quadratic function

$\quad\quad = -2(x - 0)^2 + (-3)$ Substitute -2 for a, 0 for h, and -3 for k.

$\quad\quad = -2x^2 - 3$ Simplify.

▶ The transformed function is $g(x) = -2x^2 - 3$. The vertex is $(0, -3)$.

Check

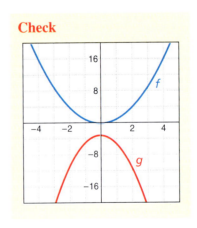

In-Class Practice
Self-Assessment

5. Let the graph of g be a vertical shrink by a factor of $\frac{1}{2}$, followed by a translation 2 units up of the graph of $f(x) = x^2$. Write a rule for g and identify the vertex.

Connections to Real Life

EXAMPLE 4 Using a Transformed Quadratic Function

The height (in feet) of water spraying from a fire hose can be modeled by

$$h(x) = -0.03x^2 + x + 25$$

where x is the horizontal distance (in feet) from the fire truck. The crew raises the aerial ladder so that the water hits the ground 10 feet farther from the fire truck. Write a function that models the new path of the water.

Use technology to graph the original function.

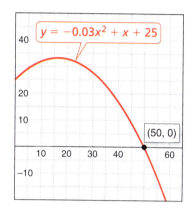

Because $h(50) = 0$, the water originally hits the ground 50 feet from the fire truck. After raising the ladder, the water hits the ground 60 feet from the fire truck. So, by observing that $h(60) = -23$ before the crew raises the ladder, you can determine that a translation 23 feet up causes the water to travel 10 feet farther from the fire truck.

$g(x) = h(x) + 23$ Add 23 to the output.

$\quad\quad = -0.03x^2 + x + 48$ Substitute for $h(x)$ and simplify.

▶ The new path of the water can be modeled by $g(x) = -0.03x^2 + x + 48$.

Check Verify that $g(60) = 0$.

$$g(60) = -0.03(60)^2 + 60 + 48$$
$$= -108 + 60 + 48$$
$$= 0 \checkmark$$

In-Class Practice

Self-Assessment

6. WHAT IF? In Example 4, the water hits the ground 10 feet closer to the fire truck after lowering the ladder. Write a function that models the new path of the water.

2.1 Practice

Describe the transformation of $f(x) = x^2$ represented by g. Then graph each function.
(See Example 1.)

1. $g(x) = (x + 6)^2 - 2$
2. $g(x) = (x - 9)^2 + 5$
3. $g(x) = (x - 7)^2 + 1$
4. $g(x) = (x + 10)^2 - 3$

MATCHING Match the function with the correct transformation of the graph of f.

5. $y = f(x - 1)$
6. $y = f(x) + 1$
7. $y = f(x - 1) + 1$
8. $y = f(x + 1) - 1$

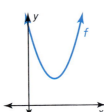

A. 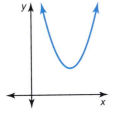 B. 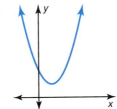 C. 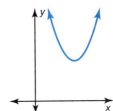 D.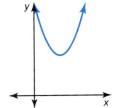

Describe the transformation of $f(x) = x^2$ represented by g. Then graph each function.
(See Example 2.)

9. $g(x) = 3x^2$
10. $g(x) = \frac{1}{3}x^2$
11. $g(x) = -(2x)^2$
12. $g(x) = \frac{1}{2}(x - 1)^2$

Write a rule for g described by the transformations of the graph of f. Then identify the vertex.
(See Example 3.)

13. $f(x) = x^2$; vertical stretch by a factor of 4 and a reflection in the x-axis, followed by a translation 2 units up

14. $f(x) = x^2$; vertical shrink by a factor of $\frac{1}{3}$ and a reflection in the y-axis, followed by a translation 3 units right

15. **CONNECTION TO REAL LIFE** The height (in feet) of a red kangaroo during a jump can be modeled by

$$h(x) = -0.03(x - 14)^2 + 6$$

where x is the horizontal distance traveled (in feet). When the kangaroo jumps from a higher location, it lands on the ground 5 feet farther away. Write a function that models the new path of the jump. (See Example 4.)

16. Describe the transformation of $f(x) = x^2$ represented by g.

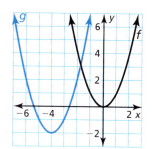

17. The functions shown model the heights (in feet) of an object t seconds after it is dropped on Earth and on the moon from a height of 10 feet. Describe the transformation of the graph of f to obtain g. From what height must the object be dropped on the moon so it hits the ground after the same number of seconds as on Earth?

$f(t) = -16t^2 + 10$ $g(t) = -\frac{8}{3}t^2 + 10$

Write a rule for g described by the transformations of the graph of f. Then identify the vertex.

18. $f(x) = (x + 6)^2 + 3$; horizontal shrink by a factor of $\frac{1}{2}$ and a translation 1 unit down, followed by a reflection in the x-axis

▶ 19. $f(x) = 8x^2 - 6$; horizontal stretch by a factor of 2 and a translation 2 units up, followed by a reflection in the y-axis

20. **SMP.2** Flying fish use their pectoral fins like airplane wings to glide through the air.

    a. Write an equation of the form $y = a(x - h)^2 + k$ with vertex $(33, 5)$ that models the flight path, assuming the fish leaves the water at $(0, 0)$.

    b. Find and interpret the domain and range of the function.

21. **CONNECT CONCEPTS** The area of a circle depends on the radius. A circular earring with a radius of r millimeters has a circular hole with a radius of $\frac{3r}{4}$ millimeters. Describe a transformation of the graph below that models the area of the black and white portion of the earring.

 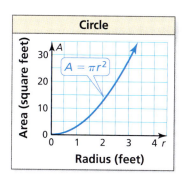

Interpreting Data

BEARS IN NORTH AMERICA There are 3 species of bears in North America: black bears, brown bears (including grizzly bears), and polar bears. The average heights of grizzly bears at Yellowstone National Park are shown.

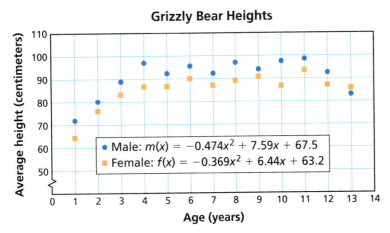

Male: $m(x) = -0.474x^2 + 7.59x + 67.5$
Female: $f(x) = -0.369x^2 + 6.44x + 63.2$

22. Describe the relationship between age and height of grizzly bears at Yellowstone.

23. According to the models, the maximum height of a male grizzly bear is about 98 centimeters and the maximum height of a female grizzly bear is about 91 centimeters. Is the graph of m a translation 7 units up of the graph of f?

24. How do you think this data was obtained?

Review & Refresh

25. Solve the system.

    $2x - y - 2z = -5$
    $-x + 4y + 5z = -7$
    $3x + y - 4z = 5$

26. Write an inequality that represents the graph.

    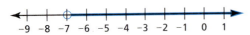

27. Factor $8x^4 - 40x^3$.

28. Write the next three terms of the arithmetic sequence.

    $21, 9, -3, -15, \ldots$

29. Display the data in a histogram. Describe the shape of the distribution.

Age	1–3	4–6	7–9	10–12	13–15
Frequency	8	12	5	3	2

30. The cost (in dollars) of x pairs of jeans at a store's regular price is modeled by the function $f(x) = 40x$. The cost of x pairs of jeans during a sale is $5 less than 85% of the cost at regular price. What is the cost of three pairs of jeans during the sale?

31. Simplify $\dfrac{5}{\sqrt{7}}$.

2.2 Characteristics of Quadratic Functions

Learning Target: Graph and describe quadratic functions.

Success Criteria:
- I can use properties of parabolas to graph quadratic functions.
- I can identify characteristics of quadratic functions and their graphs.
- I can use quadratic functions to solve real-life problems.

INVESTIGATE Parabolas and Symmetry

Work with a partner.

1. Use a piece of graph paper.

   a. Sketch the graph of
   $$f(x) = \tfrac{1}{2}x^2 - 2x - 2.$$
   Make sure you plot points on each side of the vertex.

   b. Find a vertical line on your graph paper so that when you fold the paper, the left portion of the graph coincides with the right portion of the graph. What is the equation of this line? How does it relate to the vertex?

   c. Show that the vertex form
   $$f(x) = \tfrac{1}{2}(x - 2)^2 - 4$$
   is equivalent to the function given in part (a).

   d. Repeat parts (a)–(c) for the function given by
   $$f(x) = -\tfrac{1}{3}x^2 + 2x + 3$$
   $$= -\tfrac{1}{3}(x - 3)^2 + 6.$$

2. Consider the graph of $f(x) = a(x - h)^2 + k$.
   - How can you describe the symmetry of the graph?
   - Explain how to tell whether the graph opens up or down.
   - What is the y-intercept?
   - What is the least or greatest value of the function?

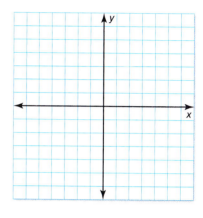

> **Vocabulary**
> axis of symmetry
> standard form
> minimum value
> maximum value
> intercept form

Exploring Properties of Parabolas

An **axis of symmetry** is a line that divides a parabola into mirror images and passes through the vertex. Because the vertex of $f(x) = a(x - h)^2 + k$ is (h, k), the axis of symmetry is the vertical line $x = h$.

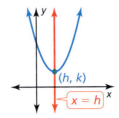

Previously, you used transformations to graph quadratic functions in vertex form. You can also use the axis of symmetry and the vertex to graph quadratic functions written in vertex form.

EXAMPLE 1 Using Symmetry to Graph a Quadratic Function

Graph $f(x) = -2(x + 3)^2 + 4$. Label the vertex and axis of symmetry.

Identify h and k.

$$f(x) = -2[x - (-3)]^2 + 4$$
$$hk$$

Plot the vertex $(h, k) = (-3, 4)$ and draw the axis of symmetry $x = -3$.

Evaluate the function for two values of x, such as $x = -2$ and $x = -1$.

$$f(-2) = -2(-2 + 3)^2 + 4$$
$$= 2$$
$$f(-1) = -2(-1 + 3)^2 + 4$$
$$= -4$$

Plot the points $(-2, 2)$, $(-1, -4)$, and their reflections in the axis of symmetry. Then draw a parabola through the plotted points.

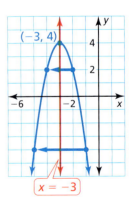

In-Class Practice

Self-Assessment

Graph the function. Label the vertex and axis of symmetry.

1. $g(x) = 2(x - 2)^2 + 5$
2. $f(x) = -(x + 4)^2 - 3$

3. A parabola passes through the points $(-1, 4)$ and $(4, 4)$. Find the axis of symmetry.

1 I don't understand yet. **2** I can do it with help. **3** I can do it on my own. **4** I can teach someone.

Quadratic functions can also be written in **standard form**, $f(x) = ax^2 + bx + c$, where $a \neq 0$.

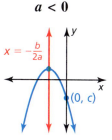

- The parabola opens up when $a > 0$ and opens down when $a < 0$.
- The graph is narrower than the graph of $f(x) = x^2$ when $|a| > 1$ and wider when $|a| < 1$.
- The axis of symmetry is $x = -\dfrac{b}{2a}$, and the vertex is $\left(-\dfrac{b}{2a}, f\left(-\dfrac{b}{2a}\right)\right)$.
- The y-intercept is c. So, the point $(0, c)$ is on the parabola.

EXAMPLE 2 Graphing a Quadratic Function in Standard Form

Graph $f(x) = 3x^2 - 6x + 1$. Label the vertex and axis of symmetry.

The coefficients are $a = 3$, $b = -6$, and $c = 1$.

Use the values of a and b to find the x-coordinate of the vertex. Then use the x-coordinate to find the y-coordinate.

x-coordinate: $x = -\dfrac{b}{2a} = -\dfrac{-6}{2(3)} = 1$

y-coordinate: $f(1) = 3(1)^2 - 6(1) + 1 = -2$

Plot the vertex $(1, -2)$ and draw the axis of symmetry $x = 1$.

The y-intercept is $c = 1$. So, the point $(0, 1)$ is on the parabola. Evaluate the function for another value of x, such as $x = 3$.

$f(3) = 3(3)^2 - 6(3) + 1$
$ = 10$

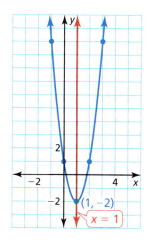

Plot the points $(0, 1)$, $(3, 10)$, and their reflections in the axis of symmetry. Then draw a parabola through the plotted points.

In-Class Practice

Self-Assessment

Graph the function. Label the vertex and axis of symmetry.

4. $h(x) = x^2 + 2x - 1$

5. $g(x) = -2x^2 - 8x + 1$

1 I don't understand yet.   **2** I can do it with help.   **3** I can do it on my own.   **4** I can teach someone.

Maximum and Minimum Values

For the quadratic function $f(x) = ax^2 + bx + c$, the y-coordinate of the vertex is the **minimum value** of the function when $a > 0$ and the **maximum value** when $a < 0$. These values can be used to describe other properties of the function, as shown below.

$a > 0$

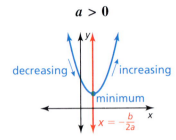

$a < 0$

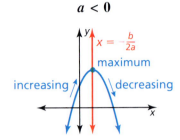

- Minimum value: $f\left(-\frac{b}{2a}\right)$
- Range: $y \geq f\left(-\frac{b}{2a}\right)$
- Decreasing when $x < -\frac{b}{2a}$
- Increasing when $x > -\frac{b}{2a}$

- Maximum value: $f\left(-\frac{b}{2a}\right)$
- Range: $y \leq f\left(-\frac{b}{2a}\right)$
- Increasing when $x < -\frac{b}{2a}$
- Decreasing when $x > -\frac{b}{2a}$

EXAMPLE 3 Finding a Minimum or a Maximum Value

Find the minimum or maximum value of $f(x) = \frac{1}{2}x^2 - 2x - 1$. Find the domain and range, and when the function is increasing and decreasing.

The coefficients are $a = \frac{1}{2}$, $b = -2$, and $c = -1$.

Because $a > 0$, the parabola opens up and the function has a minimum value. To find the minimum value, calculate the coordinates of the vertex.

$$x = -\frac{b}{2a} = -\frac{-2}{2\left(\frac{1}{2}\right)} = 2$$

$$f(2) = \tfrac{1}{2}(2)^2 - 2(2) - 1 = -3$$

▶ The minimum value is -3. So, the domain is all real numbers, and the range is $y \geq -3$. The function is decreasing when $x < 2$ and increasing when $x > 2$.

Check

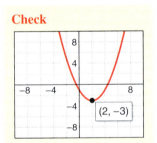

In-Class Practice

Self-Assessment

6. Find the minimum or maximum value of (a) $f(x) = 4x^2 + 16x - 3$ and (b) $h(x) = -x^2 + 5x + 9$. Find the domain and range of each function, and when each function is increasing and decreasing.

1 I don't understand yet. 2 I can do it with help. 3 I can do it on my own. 4 I can teach someone.

Graphing Quadratic Functions Using x-Intercepts

When the graph of a quadratic function has at least one x-intercept, the function can be written in **intercept form**, $f(x) = a(x - p)(x - q)$, where $a \neq 0$.

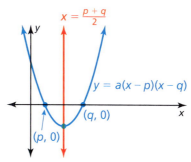

- Because $f(p) = 0$ and $f(q) = 0$, p and q are the x-intercepts of the graph of the function.
- The axis of symmetry is halfway between $(p, 0)$ and $(q, 0)$. So, the axis of symmetry is $x = \dfrac{p + q}{2}$.
- The parabola opens up when $a > 0$ and opens down when $a < 0$.

EXAMPLE 4 Graphing a Quadratic Function in Intercept Form

Graph $f(x) = -2(x + 3)(x - 1)$. Label the x-intercepts, vertex, and axis of symmetry.

Identify p and q.

$$f(x) = -2[x - (-3)](x - 1)$$
$$\quad\quad\quad\quad\quad\quad\ \uparrow\quad\quad\ \ \uparrow$$
$$\quad\quad\quad\quad\quad\quad\ p\quad\quad\ \ q$$

The x-intercepts are $p = -3$ and $q = 1$, so the parabola passes through the points $(-3, 0)$ and $(1, 0)$.

Find the coordinates of the vertex.

$$x = \frac{p + q}{2} = \frac{-3 + 1}{2} = -1$$
$$f(-1) = -2(-1 + 3)(-1 - 1) = 8$$

So, the axis of symmetry is $x = -1$, and the vertex is $(-1, 8)$.

Draw a parabola through the vertex and the points where the x-intercepts occur.

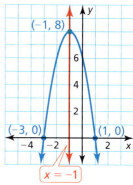

In-Class Practice

Self-Assessment

Graph the function. Label the x-intercepts, vertex, and axis of symmetry.

7. $f(x) = -(x + 1)(x + 5)$

8. $g(x) = \frac{1}{4}(x - 6)(x - 2)$

2.2 Characteristics of Quadratic Functions

Connections to Real Life

EXAMPLE 5 **Comparing Functions in Different Forms**

The parabola below shows the path of your first golf shot, where x is the horizontal distance (in yards) and y is the height (in yards). The path of your second shot is modeled by $f(x) = -0.02x(x - 80)$. Which shot travels farther before hitting the ground? Which travels higher?

First shot: The graph shows that the x-intercepts are 0 and 100. So, your first shot travels 100 yards before hitting the ground.

The axis of symmetry is halfway between (0, 0) and (100, 0). So, the axis of symmetry is $x = 50$ and the vertex is (50, 25). This means the maximum height of your first shot is 25 yards.

Second shot: Rewrite the function in intercept form as

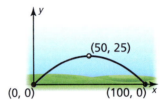

The x-intercepts are $p = 0$ and $q = 80$. So, your second shot travels 80 yards before hitting the ground.

To find the maximum height, find the coordinates of the vertex.

$$x = \frac{p + q}{2} = \frac{0 + 80}{2} = 40$$

$$f(40) = -0.02(40)(40 - 80) = 32$$

The maximum height of your second shot is 32 yards.

▶ Because 100 yards > 80 yards, your first shot travels farther.
Because 32 yards > 25 yards, your second shot travels higher.

In-Class Practice

Self-Assessment

9. **WHAT IF?** The graph of your third shot is a parabola through the origin that reaches a maximum height of 28 yards when $x = 45$. Compare the distance it travels before it hits the ground with the distances of the first two shots.

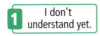

2.2 Practice

Graph the function. Label the vertex and axis of symmetry. (See Example 1.)

▶ 1. $g(x) = (x + 3)^2 + 5$

2. $y = (x - 7)^2 - 1$

3. $f(x) = -2(x - 1)^2 - 5$

4. $y = -\frac{1}{4}(x + 2)^2 + 1$

MATCHING Use the axis of symmetry to match the equation with its graph.

5. $y = 2(x - 3)^2 + 1$

6. $y = (x + 4)^2 - 2$

7. $y = \frac{1}{2}(x + 1)^2 + 3$

8. $y = (x - 2)^2 - 1$

A.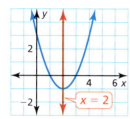

C.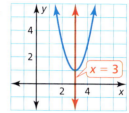

B.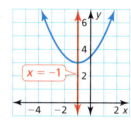

D.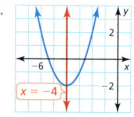

Graph the function. Label the vertex and axis of symmetry. (See Example 2.)

9. $y = x^2 + 2x + 1$

10. $y = 3x^2 - 6x + 4$

▶ 11. $y = -4x^2 + 8x + 2$

12. $f(x) = 0.5x^2 + x - 3$

13. **ERROR ANALYSIS** Describe and correct the error in analyzing the graph of $y = 4x^2 + 24x - 7$.

> ✗ The x-coordinate of the vertex is
> $x = \frac{b}{2a} = \frac{24}{2(4)} = 3.$

Find the minimum or maximum value, the domain and range, and when the function is increasing and decreasing. (See Example 3.)

14. $y = 6x^2 - 1$

▶ 15. $y = -x^2 - 4x - 2$

16. $f(x) = -2x^2 + 8x + 7$

17. $h(x) = 2x^2 - 12x$

2.2 Characteristics of Quadratic Functions 57

18. **SMP.7** A quadratic function is increasing when $x < 2$ and decreasing when $x > 2$. Explain whether the vertex is the highest or lowest point on the parabola.

19. The engine torque y (in foot-pounds) of one model of car is given by

    $y = -3.75x^2 + 23.2x + 38.8$

    where x is the speed (in thousands of revolutions per minute) of the engine.

    a. Find the engine speed that maximizes torque. What is the maximum torque?

    b. Explain what happens to the engine torque as the speed of the engine increases.

Graph the function. Label the x-intercept(s), vertex, and axis of symmetry. (See Example 4.)

20. $y = (x + 1)(x - 3)$

▶ 21. $y = 3(x + 2)(x + 6)$

22. $y = -4x(x + 7)$

23. $f(x) = -2(x - 3)^2$

24. **CONNECTION TO REAL LIFE** The height (in feet) of a flare above the water is given by $f(t) = -16t(t - 8)$, where t is the time (in seconds) since the flare was shot. The height of a second flare is modeled in the graph. Which flare travels higher? Which remains in the air longer? (See Example 5.)

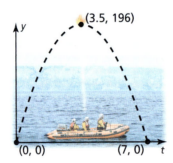

CONNECT CONCEPTS Write an equation for the area of the figure. Then determine the maximum possible area.

25.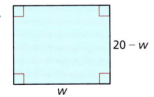

26.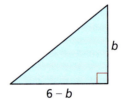

27. **SMP.7** The points $(2, 3)$ and $(-4, 2)$ lie on the graph of a quadratic function. Explain whether you can use these points to find the axis of symmetry.

28. **OPEN-ENDED** Write two different quadratic functions in intercept form whose graphs have the axis of symmetry $x = 3$.

29. Some football fields have parabola-shaped cross sections so that rain runs off to both sides. The cross section of a field can be modeled by $y = -0.000234x(x - 160)$, where x and y are measured in feet. What is the width of the field? What is the maximum height of the surface of the field?

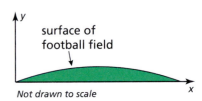

Not drawn to scale

58   Chapter 2   Quadratic Functions

30. An online music store sells about 4,000 songs each day when it charges $1 per song. For each $0.05 increase in price, about 80 fewer songs per day are sold. Use the model to determine how much the store should charge per song to maximize daily revenue.

Revenue (dollars)	=	Price (dollars/song)	·	Sales (songs)
$R(x)$	=	$(1 + 0.05x)$	·	$(4{,}000 - 80x)$

31. A hop of a woodland jumping mouse is given by

    $y = -0.2x^2 + 1.3x$

    where x is the horizontal distance (in feet) and y is the height (in feet). Can the mouse jump over a fence that is 3 feet tall?

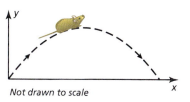

Not drawn to scale

32. **SMP.2** The arch of the Gateshead Millennium Bridge in England can be modeled by a parabola. The arch reaches a maximum height of 50 meters at a point roughly 63 meters across the river.

   a. Graph the curve of the arch.

   b. What are the domain and range? What do they represent in this situation?

33. Find the y-intercept in terms of a, p, and q for the quadratic function

    $f(x) = a(x - p)(x - q)$.

34. A function is written in intercept form with $a > 0$. What happens to the vertex of the graph as a increases? as a approaches 0?

35. **SMP.1 DIG DEEPER** A road worker has n feet of caution tape to mark a rectangular work site. What is the maximum area of the work site in terms of n? Use a quadratic equation to justify your answer.

36. **SMP.7** Consider the vertex form and the standard form of a quadratic function.

    Vertex Form: $f(x) = a(x - h)^2 + k$

    Standard Form: $f(x) = ax^2 + bx + c$

    Expand the function in vertex form. Use the result to explain the equation for the axis of symmetry, $x = -\dfrac{b}{2a}$.

Interpreting Data

FREE THROWS The graph shows the trajectory of three free throws in a basketball game.

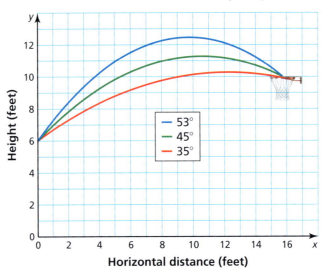

Basketball Free Throw Trajectory

37. Estimate the maximum height of the ball when shot at an angle of 35°.

38. Estimate the equation of the trajectory when the ball is shot at an angle of 45°.

39. What do you think is the best angle for shooting a free throw? Explain.

Review & Refresh

Solve the equation.

40. $2\sqrt{x-4} - 2 = 2$

41. $\sqrt{5x} + 5 = 0$

42. Describe the transformation of $f(x) = x^2$ represented by g.

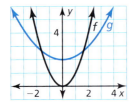

43. Solve the system.
$$2x - 5y - z = 3$$
$$-x + 3y + 2z = 10$$
$$4x - 2y - 3z = -16$$

44. Solve $|3x + 5| = 2|x - 10|$.

45. Find the volume of the pyramid.

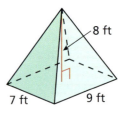

46. Does $y = 12(0.86)^t$ represent *exponential growth* or *exponential decay*? What is the percent rate of change?

47. Solve $-7 < \frac{1}{2}(3n - 8) \leq 11$. Graph the solution.

2.3 Focus of a Parabola

Learning Target: Graph and write equations of parabolas.

Success Criteria:
- I can explain the relationships among the focus, the directrix, and the graph of a parabola.
- I can graph parabolas using characteristics.
- I can write equations of parabolas using characteristics.

INVESTIGATE Analyzing Graphs of Parabolas

Work with a partner.

1. Use dashes along the bottom of a piece of lined paper to mark and number equidistant points from −5 to 5 as shown. These dashes represent the units along the x-axis. Plot a point $F(0, 2)$, using the same scale, that is two units above 0. Draw a line through F to represent the y-axis.

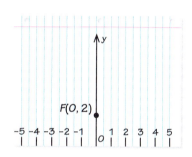

2. Fold the paper so the origin is on top of point F. Unfold the paper and describe the line represented by the fold you made.

3. Repeat the process in Exercise 1 with the points $(1, 0)$, $(-1, 0)$, $(2, 0)$, and $(-2, 0)$, and so on. The diagrams below show the fold for $(1, 0)$. After you are done, examine the folds. What do you notice?

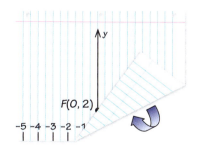 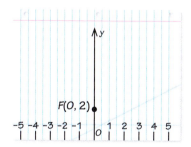

4. For each fold, use the Pythagorean Theorem to find and label a point (x, y) that is equidistant from F and the x-axis. Then find an equation that represents the curve that passes through these points.

> **Vocabulary**
> focus
> directrix

Exploring the Focus and Directrix

A parabola can be defined as the set of all points (x, y) in a plane that are equidistant from a fixed point called the **focus** and a fixed line called the **directrix**.

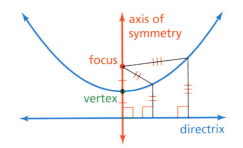

- The focus is in the interior of the parabola and lies on the axis of symmetry.

- The vertex lies halfway between the focus and the directrix.

- The directrix is perpendicular to the axis of symmetry.

EXAMPLE 1   Deriving an Equation

Write an equation of the parabola with focus $F(0, 2)$ and directrix $y = -2$.

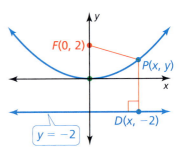

The vertex is halfway between the focus and the directrix, at $(0, 0)$. Notice the line segments drawn from point F to point P and from point P to point D. By the definition of a parabola, these line segments, PD and PF, must be congruent.

$PD = PF$	Definition of a parabola
$\|y - (-2)\| = \sqrt{x^2 + (2-y)^2}$	Write expressions for the lengths of the line segments.
$(y + 2)^2 = x^2 + (2 - y)^2$	Square each side.
$y^2 + 4y + 4 = x^2 + 4 - 4y + y^2$	Expand.
$8y = x^2$	Combine like terms.
$y = \frac{1}{8}x^2$	Divide each side by 8.

▶ So, an equation of the parabola is $y = \frac{1}{8}x^2$.

In-Class Practice

Self-Assessment

1. Write an equation of the parabola with focus $F(0, -3)$ and directrix $y = 3$.

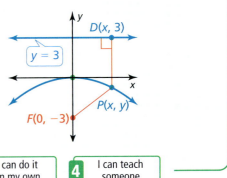

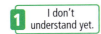 I don't understand yet.   I can do it with help.   I can do it on my own.   I can teach someone.

Key Concept

Standard Equations of a Parabola with Vertex at the Origin

Vertical axis of symmetry ($x = 0$)

Equation: $y = \dfrac{1}{4p}x^2$

Focus: $(0, p)$

Directrix: $y = -p$

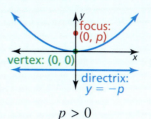
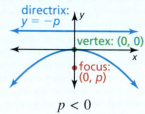

$p > 0 \qquad\qquad p < 0$

Horizontal axis of symmetry ($y = 0$)

Equation: $x = \dfrac{1}{4p}y^2$

Focus: $(p, 0)$

Directrix: $x = -p$

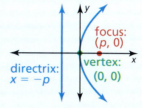
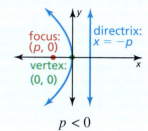

$p > 0 \qquad\qquad p < 0$

EXAMPLE 2 Writing and Graphing an Equation of a Parabola

Write an equation of the parabola with vertex (0, 0) and directrix $x = 1$. Then graph the parabola.

Notice that the directrix is a vertical line and $p = -1$.

$x = \dfrac{1}{4p}y^2$ Write the equation of a parabola.

$x = \dfrac{1}{4(-1)}y^2$ Substitute -1 for p.

$x = -\dfrac{1}{4}y^2$ Simplify.

y	x
±1	−0.25
±2	−1
±3	−2.25
±4	−4

Use a table of values to graph the parabola. Notice that opposite y-values result in the same x-value.

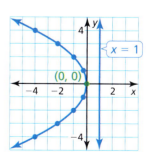

In-Class Practice

Self-Assessment

2. Write an equation of the parabola with vertex $(0, 0)$ and focus $F\left(0, \dfrac{1}{2}\right)$. Then graph the parabola.

| **1** I don't understand yet. | **2** I can do it with help. | **3** I can do it on my own. | **4** I can teach someone. |

> **Key Concept**

Standard Equations of a Parabola with Vertex at (h, k)

Vertical axis of symmetry (x = h)

Equation: $y = \dfrac{1}{4p}(x - h)^2 + k$

Focus: $(h, k + p)$

Directrix: $y = k - p$

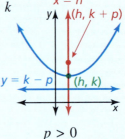
$p > 0$

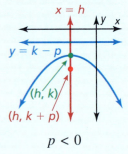
$p < 0$

Horizontal axis of symmetry (y = k)

Equation: $x = \dfrac{1}{4p}(y - k)^2 + h$

Focus: $(h + p, k)$

Directrix: $x = h - p$

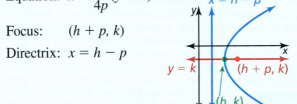
$p > 0$ $p < 0$

EXAMPLE 3   Writing and Graphing the Equation of a Translated Parabola

Write an equation of the parabola with vertex (6, 2) and focus $F(10, 2)$. Then graph the parabola.

Notice that the vertex and the focus lie on the same horizontal line.

y	x
6	7
4	6.25
2	6
0	6.25
−2	7

$x = \dfrac{1}{4p}(y - k)^2 + h$ Write the equation of a parabola.

$x = \dfrac{1}{4(4)}(y - 2)^2 + 6$ Substitute 6 for h, 2 for k, and 4 for p.

$x = \dfrac{1}{16}(y - 2)^2 + 6$ Simplify.

Use a table of values to graph the parabola.

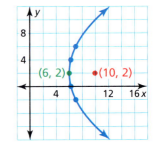

> **In-Class Practice**

Self-Assessment

3. Write an equation of a parabola with vertex $(-1, 4)$ and directrix $y = 6$. Then graph the parabola.

Connections to Real Life

Parabolic reflectors have parabolic cross sections that can reflect sound, light, or other energy. Waves that hit a parabolic reflector parallel to the axis of symmetry are directed to the focus. Waves that come from the focus and then hit the parabolic reflector are directed parallel to the axis of symmetry.

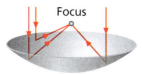

EXAMPLE 4 Using the Equation of a Parabola

An electricity-generating dish uses a parabolic reflector to concentrate sunlight onto a high-frequency engine located at the focus of the reflector. The sunlight heats helium to 650°C to power the engine. Write an equation that represents the cross section of the dish shown with its vertex at (0, 0). What is the depth of the dish?

STEM Video: Solar Energy using a Parabolic Mirror

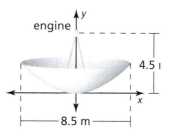

Because the vertex is at the origin, and the axis of symmetry is vertical, the equation has the form $y = \frac{1}{4p}x^2$. The engine is at the focus, which is 4.5 meters above the vertex. So, $p = 4.5$. Substitute 4.5 for p to write the equation.

$$y = \frac{1}{4(4.5)}x^2 = \frac{1}{18}x^2$$

The depth of the dish is the y-value at the dish's outside edge. The dish extends $\frac{8.5}{2} = 4.25$ meters to either side of the vertex (0, 0), so find y when $x = 4.25$.

$$y = \frac{1}{18}(4.25)^2 \approx 1$$

▶ The depth of the dish is about 1 meter.

In-Class Practice

Self-Assessment

4. A parabolic microwave antenna is 16 feet in diameter. Write an equation that represents the cross section of the antenna with its vertex at (0, 0) and its focus 10 feet to the right of the vertex. What is the depth of the antenna?

2.3 Practice

Write an equation of the parabola. (See Example 1.)

1.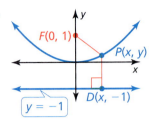

2.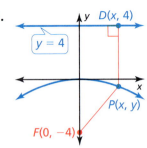

Write an equation of the parabola with the given characteristics. Then graph the parabola. (See Example 2.)

3. focus: $(-7, 0)$
   directrix: $x = 7$

4. focus: $\left(\frac{2}{3}, 0\right)$
   vertex: $(0, 0)$

5. directrix: $y = \frac{8}{3}$
   vertex: $(0, 0)$

6. focus: $\left(0, \frac{6}{7}\right)$
   vertex: $(0, 0)$

Write an equation of the parabola with the given characteristics. Then graph the parabola. (See Example 3.)

7. directrix: $y = 12$
   vertex: $(2, 3)$

8. directrix: $x = 4$
   vertex: $(-7, -5)$

9. focus: $\left(\frac{5}{4}, -1\right)$
   directrix: $x = \frac{3}{4}$

10. focus: $\left(-3, \frac{11}{2}\right)$
    directrix: $y = -\frac{3}{2}$

11. Identify the vertex, focus, directrix, and axis of symmetry of $g(x) = \frac{1}{8}(x - 3)^2 + 2$. Then describe the transformations of the graph of $f(x) = \frac{1}{4}x^2$ to the graph of g.

12. **CONNECTION TO REAL LIFE** A device simulates the clicking sound of a bottlenose dolphin and emits it from the focus of a parabolic reflector used to study echolocation. Write an equation that represents the cross section of the reflector shown, with its vertex at $(0, 0)$. What is the depth of the reflector? (See Example 4.)

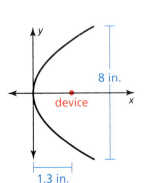

Write an equation of the parabola.

13.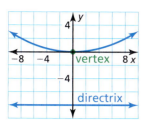

14.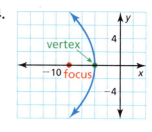

15. **SMP.2** **SOLAR ENERGY** Solar energy can be concentrated using a long trough that has a parabolic cross section, as shown in the figure. Write an equation that represents the cross section of the trough with its vertex at (0, 0). What are the domain and range in this situation? What do they represent?

16. Explain how the width of the graph of the equation $y = \dfrac{1}{4p}x^2$ changes as $|p|$ increases.

17. The graph shows the path of a volleyball served from an initial height of 6 feet as it travels over a net.

    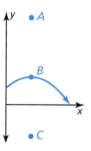

    a. Which point represents the vertex? focus? a point on the directrix?

    b. An underhand serve follows the same parabolic path but is hit from a height of 3 feet. How does this affect the focus? the directrix?

18. **SMP.1** **SMP.8** Derive the equation of a parabola that opens to the right with vertex (0, 0), focus $(p, 0)$, and directrix $x = -p$. Explain whether you can use the same method to derive the equation for a similar parabola that opens left, up, or down.

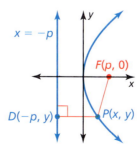

19. **SMP.5** **PERFORMANCE TASK** You can make a solar hot dog cooker by shaping foil-lined poster board into a trough that has a parabolic cross section and passing a wire through each end piece. Design and construct your own hot dog cooker. Explain your process.

Interpreting Data

SUSPENSION BRIDGES Civil engineers design suspension bridge cables in a parabolic shape to lessen tension on the supporting towers. The dimensions of the Golden Gate Bridge, which was once the largest suspension bridge in the world, are shown. Let (0, 0) represent the position of the center of the main cable.

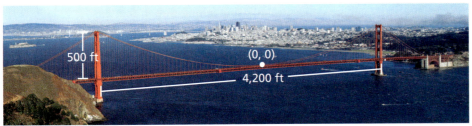

20. Write an equation of the parabola that represents the main cable of the Golden Gate Bridge.

21. Describe the location of the focus of the parabola.

22. How far above the roadway is the cable when it is 150 feet from the center of the bridge?

Review & Refresh

23. Write an equation of the line that passes through the points (−3, 12) and (0, 6).

24. The graph of square root function g is shown. Compare the average rate of change of g to the average rate of change of $h(x) = \sqrt[3]{\frac{3}{2}x}$ over the interval $0 \le x \le 3$.

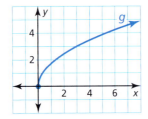

25. A quadratic function has a minimum value at $x = -3$. When is the function increasing? decreasing?

26. Determine whether the table represents a *linear* or *nonlinear* function.

x	−1	1	3	5	7
y	6	3	−2	−9	−18

27. Solve $3(2x - 4) = 3x + 9$.

28. You make a total of 11 one-point free throws, two-point shots, and three-point shots in a basketball game and score a total of 22 points. You make two more two-point shots than three-point shots. How many of each type of shot do you make?

29. Graph $y \le -2.5$ in a coordinate plane.

2.4 Modeling with Quadratic Functions

Learning Target: Write equations of quadratic functions using given characteristics.

Success Criteria:
- I can write equations of quadratic functions using vertices, points, and *x*-intercepts.
- I can write quadratic equations to model data sets.
- I can use technology to find a quadratic model for a set of data.

INVESTIGATE Modeling with Quadratic Functions

CELESTIAL OBJECTS DISTANCE Work with a partner.

1. **SMP.2** Consider the graph shown.

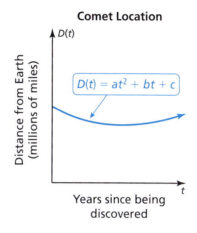

Comet Location

$D(t) = at^2 + bt + c$

Distance from Earth (millions of miles) vs. Years since being discovered

a. Explain what the graph represents.

b. What do you know about the value of a? How does the graph change if a is increased? decreased? What does this mean in this context?

c. Write an expression that gives the year when the comet is closest to Earth.

d. The comet is the same distance from Earth in 2016 and 2024. When is the comet closest to Earth?

e. What does c represent in this context? How does the graph change if c is increased? decreased?

2. **SMP.5** The table shows the distances y (in millions of miles) from Earth for a celestial object m months after being discovered.

Months, m	0	1	2	3	4	5	6	7	8	9
Distance (millions of miles), y	50	57	65	75	86	101	115	130	156	175

a. Use a tool to find a quadratic model for the data. Explain your method.

b. Explain how you know that your model in part (a) fits the data. Explain whether this is the only type of function you can use.

Writing Quadratic Equations

> **Key Concept**
>
> **Writing Quadratic Equations**
>
> **Given a point and the vertex (h, k)**
>
> Use vertex form: $y = a(x - h)^2 + k$
>
> **Given a point and the x-intercepts p and q**
>
> Use intercept form: $y = a(x - p)(x - q)$
>
> **Given three points**
>
> Write and solve a system of three equations in three variables.

EXAMPLE 1 **Writing an Equation Using the Vertex and a Point**

The parabolic path of a performer shot out of a cannon is shown. The performer lands in a net 90 feet away. What is the height of the net?

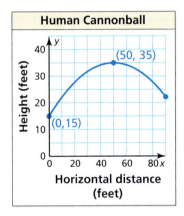

The vertex (h, k) is $(50, 35)$, and the parabola passes through $(0, 15)$. Use the points to solve for a in vertex form. Then write an equation of the parabola.

$y = a(x - h)^2 + k$	Vertex form
$15 = a(0 - 50)^2 + 35$	Substitute for h, k, x, and y.
$-0.008 = a$	Solve for a.

The path is given by $y = -0.008(x - 50)^2 + 35$, where $0 \le x \le 90$. Find the height when $x = 90$.

$y = -0.008(90 - 50)^2 + 35$	Substitute 90 for x.
$= 22.2$	Simplify.

▶ So, the height of the net is about 22 feet.

In-Class Practice

Self-Assessment

1. **WHAT IF?** The vertex of the parabola is $(50, 37.5)$. What is the height of the net?

EXAMPLE 2 **Writing an Equation Using a Point and *x*-Intercepts**

A meteorologist creates a parabola to predict the temperature tomorrow, where *x* is the number of hours after midnight and *y* is the temperature (in degrees Celsius). Write a function *f* that models the temperature over time. What is the coldest temperature?

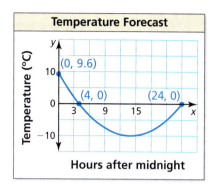

The *x*-intercepts are 4 and 24, and the parabola passes through (0, 9.6). Use the *x*-intercepts and the point to solve for *a* in intercept form. Then write an equation of the parabola.

$y = a(x - p)(x - q)$	Intercept form
$9.6 = a(0 - 4)(0 - 24)$	Substitute for *p*, *q*, *x*, and *y*.
$0.1 = a$	Simplify.

Because $a = 0.1$, $p = 4$, and $q = 24$, the temperature over time can be modeled by $f(x) = 0.1(x - 4)(x - 24)$, where $0 \leq x \leq 24$.

The coldest temperature is the minimum value. Find $f(x)$ when $x = \dfrac{4 + 24}{2} = 14$.

$f(14) = 0.1(14 - 4)(14 - 24)$	Substitute 14 for *x*.
$= -10$	Simplify.

▶ So, the coldest temperature is −10°C.

In-Class Practice

Self-Assessment

2. **WHAT IF?** In Example 2, suppose the *y*-intercept is 4.8. What is the coldest temperature?

3. Write an equation of the parabola shown. What is the maximum height of the jump?

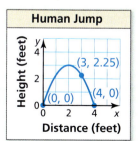

1. I don't understand yet.   2. I can do it with help.   3. I can do it on my own.   4. I can teach someone.

2.4 Modeling with Quadratic Functions 71

Writing Equations to Model Data

When function data have equally-spaced inputs, you can analyze patterns in the differences of the outputs to determine what type of function can be used to model the data. Linear data have constant *first differences*. Quadratic data have constant *second differences*.

EXAMPLE 3 Writing a Quadratic Equation Using Three Points

Time, t (seconds)	Height, $h(t)$ (feet)
10	26,900
15	29,025
20	30,600
25	31,625
30	32,100
35	32,025
40	31,400

A company creates a weightless environment for customers by flying a plane in parabolic paths. The table shows the heights of a plane t seconds after starting the flight path. After about 20.8 seconds, passengers begin to experience weightlessness. Write and evaluate a function to approximate the height at which this occurs.

The input values are equally spaced. So, analyze the differences in the outputs to determine what type of function you can use to model the data.

$h(10)$ $h(15)$ $h(20)$ $h(25)$ $h(30)$ $h(35)$ $h(40)$
26,900 29,025 30,600 31,625 32,100 32,025 31,400

  2,125   1,575   1,025   475   −75   −625   first differences

   −550   −550   −550   −550   −550   second differences

Because the second differences are constant, you can model the data with a quadratic function.

Write a function of the form $h(t) = at^2 + bt + c$ that models the data. Use any three points $(t, h(t))$ from the table to write a system.

Use (10, 26,900): $100a + 10b + c = 26{,}900$ Equation 1
Use (20, 30,600): $400a + 20b + c = 30{,}600$ Equation 2
Use (30, 32,100): $900a + 30b + c = 32{,}100$ Equation 3

Solving this system yields $a = -11$, $b = 700$, and $c = 21{,}000$.
So, $h(t) = -11t^2 + 700t + 21{,}000$. Evaluate h when $t = 20.8$.

$h(20.8) = -11(20.8)^2 + 700(20.8) + 21{,}000$

$\quad\quad\quad\; = 30{,}800.96$

▶ Passengers begin to experience weightlessness at about 30,800 feet.

In-Class Practice
Self-Assessment

4. The table shows the estimated profits y (in dollars) for a concert when the charge is x dollars per ticket. Write and evaluate a function to determine the maximum profit.

Ticket price, x	2	5	8	11	14	17
Profit, y	2,600	6,500	8,600	8,900	7,400	4,100

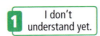 I don't understand yet.
 I can do it with help.
 I can do it on my own.
 I can teach someone.

Many technology tools have a *quadratic regression* feature that you can use to find a quadratic function that best models a set of data.

EXAMPLE 4 Using Quadratic Regression

The table shows fuel efficiencies of a vehicle at different speeds. Write a function that models the data. Then approximate the best gas mileage.

Miles per hour, x	Miles per gallon, y
20	14.5
24	17.5
30	21.2
36	23.7
40	25.2
45	25.8
50	25.8
56	25.1
60	24.0
70	19.5

The x-values are not equally spaced. So, you cannot analyze the differences in the outputs. Use technology to find a function that models the data.

Create a scatter plot. The data show a quadratic relationship.

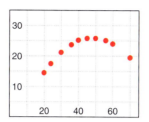

Use quadratic regression to find an equation. The values in the equation can be rounded to obtain

$$y = -0.014x^2 + 1.37x - 7.1.$$

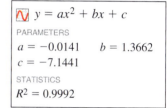

$y = ax^2 + bx + c$

PARAMETERS
$a = -0.0141$ $b = 1.3662$
$c = -7.1441$

STATISTICS
$R^2 = 0.9992$

Graph the regression equation with the scatter plot. The best gas mileage is the maximum value. Using technology, you can see that the maximum value is about 26.4.

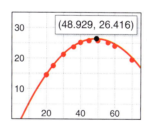

(48.929, 26.416)

▶ So, the best gas mileage is about 26.4 miles per gallon.

In-Class Practice

Self-Assessment

5. The table shows the results of an experiment testing the maximum weights y (in tons) supported by ice x inches thick. Write a function that models the data. How much weight can be supported by ice that is 22 inches thick?

Ice thickness, x	12	14	15	18	20	24	27
Maximum weight, y	3.4	7.6	10.0	18.3	25.0	40.6	54.3

 I don't understand yet.   I can do it with help.   I can do it on my own.   I can teach someone.

2.4 Modeling with Quadratic Functions

2.4 Practice

Write an equation of the parabola in vertex form. (See Example 1.)

1.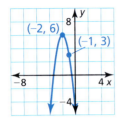

2.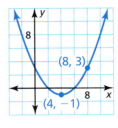

3. passes through (13, 8); vertex (3, 2)

4. passes through (−7, −15); vertex (−5, 9)

Write an equation of the parabola in intercept form. (See Example 2.)

5.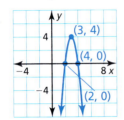

6.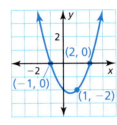

7. x-intercepts: 12 and −6; passes through (14, 4)

8. x-intercepts: 9 and 1; passes through (0, −18)

9. **ERROR ANALYSIS** Describe and correct the error in writing an equation of the parabola.

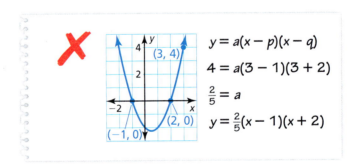

10. **CONNECT CONCEPTS** The area of a rectangle is modeled by the graph, where y is the area (in square meters) and x is the width (in meters). Write an equation of the parabola. What dimensions result in the maximum area?

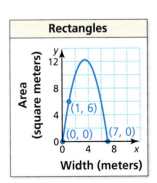

11. The table shows the safe working loads S (in pounds) for ropes with circumferences C (in inches). Write and evaluate a function to find the safe working load for a rope with a circumference of 10 inches. (See Example 3.)

Circumference, C	0	1	2	3
Safe working load, S	0	180	720	1,620

74 Chapter 2 Quadratic Functions

12. A baseball is thrown up in the air. The table shows the heights y (in feet) of the baseball after x seconds. Write and evaluate a function to find the height of the baseball after 1.7 seconds.

Time, x	0.5	1	1.5	2
Baseball height, y	18	24	22	12

▶ 13. The table shows the numbers y (in thousands) of people in a city who use sharable electric scooters x weeks after the scooters are introduced. Write a function that models the data. Then predict the number of users after 32 weeks. (See Example 4.)

Time, x	Number of users, y
1	1.5
4	2.2
6	2.4
10	3.9
12	5.5
15	6.8
20	12.3
24	16.4
25	17.6

14. The table shows the distances y a motorcyclist is from home after x hours.

Time (hours), x	0	1	2	3
Distance (miles), y	0	45	90	135

   a. Explain what type of function you can use to model the data.
   b. Write and evaluate a function to determine the distance the motorcyclist is from home after 6 hours.

15. **SMP.8** Consider the number of tiles in each figure. Verify that the relationship is quadratic. Then find the number of tiles in the 12th figure.

Figure 1   Figure 2   Figure 3   Figure 4

16. **SMP.1 DIG DEEPER** The table shows the temperatures y (in degrees Fahrenheit) of a cup of Moroccan mint tea after x minutes. Use an equation to predict the temperature of the tea after 20 minutes. Explain your choice of equation.

Time, x	0	2	4	6	8	10
Temperature, y	190	164	146	131	120	111

2.4   Modeling with Quadratic Functions

Interpreting Data

PHOTOSYNTHESIS Photosynthesis is the process by which plants convert light energy into chemical energy. The efficiency of photosynthesis is the percentage of the light energy that is converted to chemical energy. The scatter plot shows the percent efficiency for Antarctic hair grass at various temperatures.

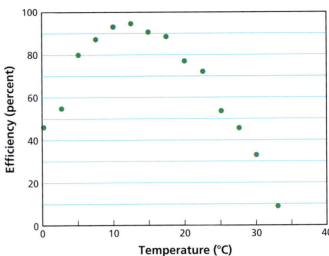

Antarctic hair grass, is one of two flowering plants native to Antarctica. The other is Antarctic pearlwort.

17. Describe the data in the scatter plot.

18. Find a quadratic model for the data.

19. At what temperature is photosynthesis most efficient for this species of grass?

Review & Refresh

20. Determine whether the graph represents a function.

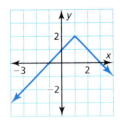

21. Graph $h(x) = 3x^2 + 6x - 2$. Label the vertex and axis of symmetry.

Solve the inequality. Graph the solution.

22. $m + 9 \geq 13$

23. $15 - n < -6$

24. $5p > 10$

25. $-\dfrac{q}{4} \leq 3$

26. Factor $3x^2 - 15x + 12$.

Identify the focus, directrix, and axis of symmetry of the parabola. Graph the equation.

27. $x = -\dfrac{1}{12}y^2$

28. $16y = x^2$

29. Determine whether the table represents a *linear* or an *exponential* function.

x	−1	0	1	2	3
y	$\dfrac{1}{8}$	$\dfrac{1}{2}$	2	8	32

30. Write an equation in slope-intercept form of the line that passes through the points $(-3, -2)$ and $(1, 4)$.

Chapter 2   Quadratic Functions

2 Chapter Review

Rate your understanding of each section.
1 — I don't understand yet.
2 — I can do it with help.
3 — I can do it on my own.
4 — I can teach someone.

2.1 Transformations of Quadratic Functions (pp. 43–50)

⊙ **Learning Target:** Describe and graph transformations of quadratic functions.

Vocabulary
quadratic function
parabola
vertex of a parabola
vertex form

Describe the transformation of $f(x) = x^2$ represented by g. Then graph each function.

1. $g(x) = (x + 4)^2$
2. $g(x) = -\frac{1}{5}x^2$
3. $g(x) = (x - 7)^2 + 2$
4. $g(x) = -3(x + 2)^2 - 1$

5. For each graph, determine whether h and k are *positive*, *negative*, or *zero*.

a.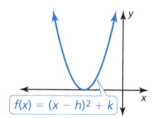
$f(x) = (x - h)^2 + k$

b.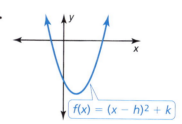
$f(x) = (x - h)^2 + k$

c.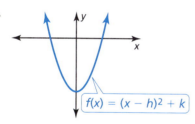
$f(x) = (x - h)^2 + k$

d.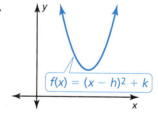
$f(x) = (x - h)^2 + k$

6. The graph represents the path of a football kicked by a player, where x is the horizontal distance (in yards) and y is the height (in yards). The player kicks the ball a second time so that it travels the same horizontal distance, but reaches a maximum height that is 6 yards greater than the maximum height of the first kick. Write a function that models the path of the second kick.

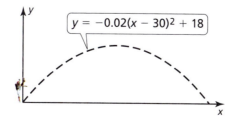
$y = -0.02(x - 30)^2 + 18$

2.2 Characteristics of Quadratic Functions (pp. 51–60)

⊙ **Learning Target:** Graph and describe quadratic functions.

Vocabulary
axis of symmetry
standard form
minimum value
maximum value
intercept form

Graph the function. Label the vertex and axis of symmetry. Find the minimum value or maximum value of the function. Find when the function is increasing and decreasing.

7. $g(x) = (x + 5)^2 - 8$

8. $f(x) = 3(x - 1)^2 - 4$

9. $g(x) = -2x^2 + 16x + 3$

10. $h(x) = (x - 3)(x + 7)$

11. Find the vertex of the quadratic function represented by the table.

x	−5	−2	1	4	7
g(x)	−68	−23	4	13	4

12. Write a quadratic function in standard form with axis of symmetry $x = -5$ and y-intercept 3.

13. You kick a kickball. The path of the ball is given by $y = x(0.6 - 0.02x)$, where x is the horizontal distance (in feet) and y is the corresponding height (in feet). Your second kick reaches a maximum height of 7 feet, 12 feet away from you. Which kick travels farther before hitting the ground? Which kick travels higher?

2.3 Focus of a Parabola (pp. 61–68)

⊙ **Learning Target:** Graph and write equations of parabolas.

Vocabulary
focus
directrix

Write an equation of the parabola with the given characteristics.

14. vertex: (0, 0)
    directrix: $x = 2$

15. focus: (2, 2)
    vertex: (2, 6)

Identify the focus, directrix, and axis of symmetry of the parabola. Graph the equation.

16. $36y = x^2$

17. $64x + 8y^2 = 0$

18. Write an equation of the parabola.

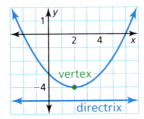

19. Parabolic microphones use a microphone at the focal point of a parabolic dish to amplify and record sound. One such device has a diameter of 20 inches and a depth of 6 inches. Describe the location of the microphone.

2.4 Modeling with Quadratic Functions (pp. 69–76)

Learning Target: Write equations of quadratic functions using given characteristics.

Write an equation of the parabola with the given characteristics.

20. passes through (1, 12) and has vertex (10, −4)

21. passes through (4, 3) and has *x*-intercepts −1 and 5

22. passes through (−2, 7), (1, 10), and (2, 27)

23. The graph shows the parabolic path of a stunt motorcyclist jumping off a ramp, where *y* is the height (in feet) and *x* is the horizontal distance traveled (in feet).

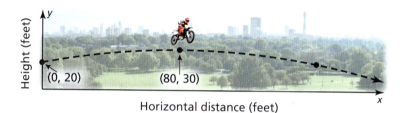

a. Write an equation of the parabola.

b. The motorcyclist lands on another ramp 160 feet from the first ramp. What is the height of the second ramp?

24. The table shows the heights *y* of a dropped object after *x* seconds. Verify that the data show a quadratic relationship. Then write a function that models the data. How long is the object in the air?

Time (seconds), x	0	0.5	1	1.5	2	2.5
Height (feet), y	150	146	134	114	86	50

25. The table shows the average total stopping distances of a vehicle on dry pavement at different speeds.

Speed (miles per hour), x	Total stopping distance (feet), y
20	63
30	119
40	164
55	265
65	344
70	387

a. Use technology to write a function that models the data.

b. Estimate the total stopping distance of a vehicle traveling 45 miles per hour.

PERFORMANCE TASK 2
SMP.4

Stargazing

DISTANT RADIO SOURCE

PARABOLIC DISH

RADIO WAVES

FOCAL POINT

Applications Of Radio Telescopes
- search for extraterrestrial life
- study stars, black holes, and other celestial objects
- transmit radio waves through our solar system
- detect ice on other planets
- track space probes

shorter wavelengths

Cosmic rays
Gamma rays
X-rays
Ultraviolet
Visible Light
Infrared
Microwaves
Radar
Radio
Broadcast band

longer wavelengths

Similar to how optical telescopes collect visible light waves, radio telescopes collect radio light waves.

The *focal ratio* of a telescope is the ratio of the *focal length* (the distance from the vertex to the focus) to the *aperture* (the width of the dish).

For example, a focal ratio of f/6.25 means

$$\frac{\text{focal length}}{\text{aperture}} = 6.25.$$

Analyzing Data

Use the information on the previous page to complete the following exercises.

1 Explain what is shown in the display. What do you notice? What do you wonder?

2 A radio telescope has a width of 25 meters and a focal ratio of f/0.35. Write an equation that could represent the shape of the parabolic dish.

TELESCOPE DESIGN

Design a parabolic radio telescope. Research existing telescopes to help you choose reasonable dimensions for your design. Write and graph an equation that represents the parabolic cross section of your telescope.

Radio telescopes are often arranged in an *array*. Describe the benefits of this kind of arrangement. Then determine whether you want your telescope to function independently or as part of an array.

3 Quadratic Equations and Complex Numbers

- **3.1** Solving Quadratic Equations
- **3.2** Complex Numbers
- **3.3** Completing the Square
- **3.4** Using the Quadratic Formula
- **3.5** Solving Nonlinear Systems of Equations
- **3.6** Quadratic Inequalities

NATIONAL GEOGRAPHIC EXPLORER
Leslie Dewan — NUCLEAR ENGINEER

Dr. Leslie Dewan believes that nuclear energy is a powerful tool to combat climate change. She has updated the design of the molten-salt reactor to keep its safety features and lower the cost of generating electricity. She hopes that this design can be used to generate electricity that is both carbon-free and cheaper than electricity generated from coal.

- What methods are used to generate electricity in the United States? Of these, which are classified as *renewable*?
- What percent of the electricity in the United States is generated from renewable energy sources?
- Is the Sun's heat a form of nuclear energy?

PERFORMANCE TASK

Nuclear fission has been used to generate electricity since the early 1950s. In the Performance Task on pages 144 and 145, you will investigate how the number of operable nuclear reactors has changed over time.

RESOURCES

Nuclear Engineering

Big Idea of the Chapter
Relate Quadratic Equations and Complex Numbers

You have solved quadratic equations with one, two, or no real solutions. However, quadratic equations with no real solutions have 2 imaginary solutions, meaning the solutions are complex numbers.

According to the U.S. Energy Information Administration, most of the United States' electricity is generated using coal, natural gas, and petroleum. Other prevalent types of energy include nuclear and renewable. The display shows how 5 categories of energy production have changed over 70 years in the U.S.

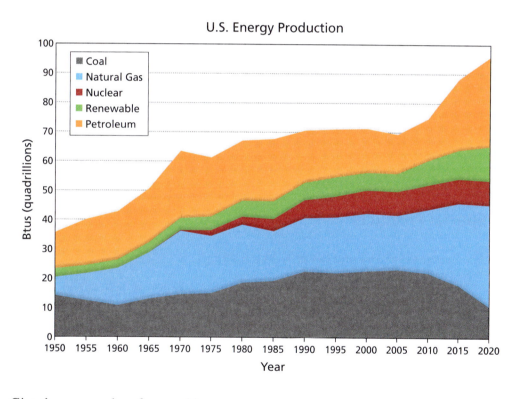

1. Give three examples of renewable energy.

2. The amount R of renewable energy (in quadrillions of btus) produced can be modeled by $R = 0.00013x^2 + 0.02x + 2.9753$, where x is the number of years after 1950. Determine the number of real solutions of the equation when $R = 0$. Interpret your answer.

RESOURCES

Getting Ready for Chapter 3

Simplifying Square Roots

EXAMPLE 1 Simplify $\sqrt{8}$.

$\sqrt{8} = \sqrt{4 \cdot 2}$ Factor using the greatest perfect square factor.

$= \sqrt{4} \cdot \sqrt{2}$ Product Property of Square Roots

$= 2\sqrt{2}$ Simplify.

EXAMPLE 2 Simplify $\sqrt{\dfrac{7}{36}}$.

$\sqrt{\dfrac{7}{36}} = \dfrac{\sqrt{7}}{\sqrt{36}}$ Quotient Property of Square Roots

$= \dfrac{\sqrt{7}}{6}$ Simplify.

Simplify the expression.

1. $\sqrt{27}$
2. $-\sqrt{112}$
3. $\sqrt{\dfrac{11}{64}}$
4. $\sqrt{\dfrac{18}{49}}$
5. $-\sqrt{\dfrac{65}{121}}$
6. $-\sqrt{80}$

Factoring Special Products

EXAMPLE 3 Factor (a) $x^2 - 4$ and (b) $x^2 - 14x + 49$.

a. $x^2 - 4 = x^2 - 2^2$ Write as $a^2 - b^2$.

$ = (x + 2)(x - 2)$ Difference of two squares pattern

▶ So, $x^2 - 4 = (x + 2)(x - 2)$.

b. $x^2 - 14x + 49 = x^2 - 2(x)(7) + 7^2$ Write as $a^2 - 2ab + b^2$.

$ = (x - 7)^2$ Perfect square trinomial pattern

▶ So, $x^2 - 14x + 49 = (x - 7)^2$.

Factor the polynomial.

7. $x^2 - 36$
8. $x^2 - 9$
9. $4x^2 - 25$
10. $x^2 - 22x + 121$
11. $x^2 + 28x + 196$
12. $49x^2 + 210x + 225$

3.1 Solving Quadratic Equations

Learning Target: Solve quadratic equations graphically and algebraically.

Success Criteria:
- I can solve quadratic equations by graphing.
- I can solve quadratic equations algebraically.
- I can use quadratic equations to solve real-life problems.

INVESTIGATE Solving Quadratic Equations

Work with a partner.

1. Match each quadratic equation with the graph of its related function. Then use the graph to find the real solutions (if any) of each equation.

   a. $x^2 - 2x = 0$ b. $x^2 - 2x + 1 = 0$

   c. $x^2 - 2x + 2 = 0$ d. $-x^2 + 2x = 0$

   e. $-x^2 + 2x - 1 = 0$ f. $-x^2 + 2x - 2 = 0$

   A.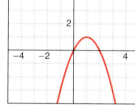

   D.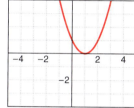

   B.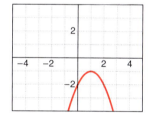

   E.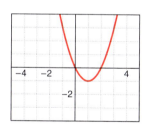

   C.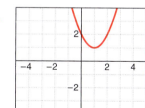

   F.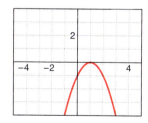

2. How can you use a graph to determine the number of real solutions of a quadratic equation?

3. What algebraic methods can you use to solve the equations in Exercise 1? Solve each equation using an algebraic method.

> **Vocabulary**
> quadratic equation in one variable
> root of an equation
> zero of a function

Solving Quadratic Equations by Graphing

A **quadratic equation in one variable** is an equation that can be written in the standard form $ax^2 + bx + c = 0$, where a, b, and c are real numbers and $a \neq 0$. A **root of an equation** is a solution of the equation. You can use various methods to solve quadratic equations.

By graphing	Find the x-intercepts of the graph of the related function $y = ax^2 + bx + c$.
Using square roots	Write the equation in the form $u^2 = d$, where u is an algebraic expression, and solve by taking the square root of each side.
By factoring	Write the quadratic equation $ax^2 + bx + c = 0$ in factored form and solve using the Zero-Product Property.

EXAMPLE 1 Solving Quadratic Equations by Graphing

Solve each equation by graphing.

a. $x^2 - x - 6 = 0$

The equation is in standard form. Graph the related function $y = x^2 - x - 6$.

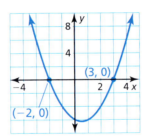

The x-intercepts are -2 and 3.

▶ The solutions, or roots, are $x = -2$ and $x = 3$.

b. $-2x^2 - 2 = 4x$

Add $-4x$ to each side to obtain $-2x^2 - 4x - 2 = 0$. Graph the related function $y = -2x^2 - 4x - 2$.

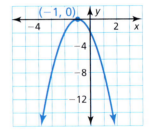

The x-intercept is -1.

▶ The solution, or root, is $x = -1$.

Check

$$x^2 - x - 6 = 0$$
$$(-2)^2 - (-2) - 6 \stackrel{?}{=} 0$$
$$0 = 0 \checkmark$$

$$x^2 - x - 6 = 0$$
$$3^2 - 3 - 6 \stackrel{?}{=} 0$$
$$0 = 0 \checkmark$$

In-Class Practice

Self-Assessment

Solve the equation by graphing.

1. $x^2 - 8x + 12 = 0$

2. $-\frac{1}{2}x^2 = 20 - 6x$

| **1** I don't understand yet. | **2** I can do it with help. | **3** I can do it on my own. | **4** I can teach someone. |

Chapter 3 Quadratic Equations and Complex Numbers

Solving Quadratic Equations Algebraically

EXAMPLE 2 Solving Quadratic Equations Using Square Roots

Solve each equation using square roots.

a. $4x^2 - 31 = 49$

$4x^2 - 31 = 49$	Write the equation.
$4x^2 = 80$	Add 31 to each side.
$x^2 = 20$	Divide each side by 4.
$x = \pm\sqrt{20}$	Take square root of each side.
$x = \pm 2\sqrt{5}$	Simplify.

▶ The solutions are $x = 2\sqrt{5}$ and $x = -2\sqrt{5}$.

b. $3x^2 + 9 = 0$

$3x^2 + 9 = 0$	Write the equation.
$3x^2 = -9$	Subtract 9 from each side.
$x^2 = -3$	Divide each side by 3.

▶ The square of a real number cannot be negative. So, the equation has no real solution.

c. $\frac{2}{5}(x + 3)^2 = 5$

$\frac{2}{5}(x + 3)^2 = 5$	Write the equation.
$(x + 3)^2 = \frac{25}{2}$	Multiply each side by $\frac{5}{2}$.
$x + 3 = \pm\sqrt{\frac{25}{2}}$	Take square root of each side.
$x = -3 \pm \sqrt{\frac{25}{2}}$	Subtract 3 from each side.
$x = -3 \pm \frac{\sqrt{25}}{\sqrt{2}}$	Quotient Property of Square Roots
$x = -3 \pm \frac{\sqrt{25}}{\sqrt{2}} \cdot \frac{\sqrt{2}}{\sqrt{2}}$	Multiply by $\frac{\sqrt{2}}{\sqrt{2}}$.
$x = -3 \pm \frac{5\sqrt{2}}{2}$	Simplify.

▶ The solutions are $x = -3 + \frac{5\sqrt{2}}{2}$ and $x = -3 - \frac{5\sqrt{2}}{2}$.

In-Class Practice

Self-Assessment

3. Solve $-2x^2 + 1 = -6$ using square roots.

1 I don't understand yet. **2** I can do it with help. **3** I can do it on my own. **4** I can teach someone.

Key Concept

Zero-Product Property

Words If the product of two expressions is zero, then one or both of the expressions equal zero.

Algebra If A and B are expressions and $AB = 0$, then $A = 0$ or $B = 0$.

EXAMPLE 3 Solving a Quadratic Equation by Factoring

Solve $x^2 - 4x = 45$ by factoring.

$x^2 - 4x = 45$	Write the equation.
$x^2 - 4x - 45 = 0$	Write in standard form.
$(x - 9)(x + 5) = 0$	Factor the polynomial.
$x - 9 = 0$ or $x + 5 = 0$	Zero-Product Property
$x = 9$ or $x = -5$	Solve for x.

▶ The solutions are $x = -5$ and $x = 9$.

You know the x-intercepts of the graph of $f(x) = a(x - p)(x - q)$ are p and q. Because the value of the function is zero when $x = p$ and when $x = q$, the numbers p and q are also called *zeros* of the function. A **zero of a function** f is an x-value for which $f(x) = 0$.

EXAMPLE 4 Finding the Zeros of a Quadratic Function

Find the zeros of $f(x) = 2x^2 - 11x + 12$.

To find the zeros of the function, find the x-values for which $f(x) = 0$.

$2x^2 - 11x + 12 = 0$	Set $f(x)$ equal to 0.
$(2x - 3)(x - 4) = 0$	Factor the polynomial.
$2x - 3 = 0$ or $x - 4 = 0$	Zero-Product Property
$x = 1.5$ or $x = 4$	Solve for x.

▶ The zeros of the function are $x = 1.5$ and $x = 4$.

In-Class Practice

Self-Assessment

Solve the equation by factoring.

4. $x^2 + 12x + 35 = 0$

5. $3x^2 - 5x = 2$

Find the zero(s) of the function.

6. $f(x) = x^2 - 8x$

7. $f(x) = 4x^2 + 28x + 49$

Connections to Real Life

EXAMPLE 5 Writing and Solving a Quadratic Equation

A streaming service charges $6 per month and has 15 million subscribers. For each $1 increase in price, the service loses 1.5 million subscribers. How much should the service charge to maximize monthly revenue? What is the maximum monthly revenue?

Let x represent the price increase and $R(x)$ represent the monthly revenue. Write a verbal model. Then write a quadratic function.

Monthly revenue (millions of dollars)	=	Number of subscribers (millions of people)	•	Subscription price (dollars/person)
$R(x)$	=	$(15 - 1.5x)$	•	$(6 + x)$

Rewrite the function in intercept form.

$R(x) = (15 - 1.5x)(6 + x)$ **Write the equation.**

$R(x) = (-1.5x + 15)(x + 6)$ **Rewrite**

$R(x) = -1.5(x - 10)(x + 6)$ **Write in intercept form.**

The maximum value of the function occurs at the average of the zeros of the function. Identify the zeros and find their average. Then find how much each subscription should cost to maximize monthly revenue.

- The zeros of the revenue function are 10 and -6.
- The average of the zeros is $\dfrac{10 + (-6)}{2} = 2$.
- To maximize revenue, each subscription should cost $6 + $2 = $8.

Find the maximum monthly revenue.

$R(2) = -1.5(2 - 10)(2 + 6) = 96$

▶ So, the service should charge $8 per subscription to maximize monthly revenue. The maximum monthly revenue is $96 million.

In-Class Practice
Self-Assessment

8. WHAT IF? The service charges $8 per month and has 15 million subscribers. How much should the service charge to maximize monthly revenue? What is the maximum monthly revenue?

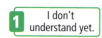 I don't understand yet.   I can do it with help.   I can do it on my own.   I can teach someone.

When an object is dropped, its height (in feet) above the ground after t seconds can be modeled by the function

$$h(t) = -16t^2 + s_0$$

where s_0 is the initial height (in feet) of the object. The graph of $h(t) = -16t^2 + 200$, representing the height of an object dropped from an initial height of 200 feet, is shown below.

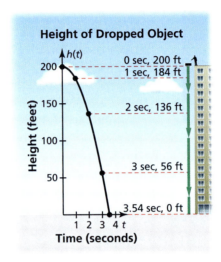

EXAMPLE 6 Using a Quadratic Equation

For a science competition, students must design a container that prevents an egg from breaking when dropped from a height of 50 feet. Write a function h that gives the height (in feet) of the container after t seconds. How long does the container take to hit the ground?

The initial height is 50, so the model is $h(t) = -16t^2 + 50$. Find the zeros of the function.

$h(t) = -16t^2 + 50$	Write the function.
$0 = -16t^2 + 50$	Substitute 0 for $h(t)$.
$-50 = -16t^2$	Subtract 50 from each side.
$\dfrac{-50}{-16} = t^2$	Divide each side by -16.
$\pm\sqrt{\dfrac{50}{16}} = t$	Take square root of each side.
$\pm 1.8 \approx t$	Use technology.

▶ Reject the negative solution, -1.8, because the time it takes the container to hit the ground after it is dropped must be positive. The container will fall for about 1.8 seconds before it hits the ground.

In-Class Practice

Self-Assessment

9. WHAT IF? The egg container is dropped from a height of 80 feet. How does this change your answer to Example 6?

3.1 Practice

Solve the equation by graphing. (See Example 1.)

1. $x^2 + 3x + 2 = 0$
2. $-x^2 + 2x + 3 = 0$
3. $3x^2 = 6x - 3$
4. $\frac{1}{5}x^2 + 6 = 2x$

Solve the equation using square roots. (See Example 2.)

5. $(z - 6)^2 = 25$
6. $(p - 4)^2 = 49$
7. $2(x + 2)^2 - 5 = 8$
8. $\frac{1}{2}r^2 - 10 = \frac{3}{2}r^2$

9. **SMP.3 ERROR ANALYSIS** Describe and correct the error in solving the equation.

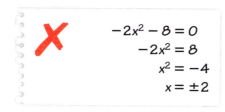

Solve the equation by factoring. (See Example 3.)

10. $x^2 - 11x = -30$
11. $x^2 - 8x = -12$
12. $n^2 - 6n = 0$
13. $3p^2 + 11p = 4$

Solve the equation using any method.

14. $u^2 = -9u$
15. $-(x + 9)^2 = 64$
16. $x^2 + 3x + \frac{5}{4} = 0$
17. $x^2 - 1.75 = 0.5$

Find the zero(s) of the function. (See Example 4.)

18. $f(x) = x^2 - 8x + 16$
19. $g(x) = x^2 + 6x + 8$
20. $g(x) = x^2 + 11x$
21. $h(x) = x^2 + 19x + 84$
22. $f(x) = 4x^2 - 12x + 9$
23. $q(x) = 10x^2 - 3x - 4$

24. **OPEN-ENDED** Write a quadratic function in the form $f(x) = x^2 + bx + c$ that has zeros 8 and 11.

25. **CONNECTION TO REAL LIFE** A restaurant sells 330 sandwiches each day. For each $0.25 decrease in price, the restaurant sells 15 more sandwiches. How much should the restaurant charge to maximize daily revenue? What is the maximum daily revenue? (See Example 5.)

26. **CONNECTION TO REAL LIFE** You drop a seashell into the ocean from a height of 40 feet above the water. Write a function h that gives the height (in feet) of the seashell above the water after t seconds. Interpret each term. How long does the seashell take to hit the water? (See Example 6.)

27. According to legend, in 1589, the Italian scientist Galileo Galilei dropped rocks of different weights from the top of the Leaning Tower of Pisa to prove his conjecture that the rocks would hit the ground at the same time.

    a. The original height of the tower was about 196 feet. Write a function h that gives the height (in feet) of a rock dropped from the top of the original tower after t seconds. Interpret each term. How long does the rock take to hit the ground?

    b. Find and interpret $h(1.25) - h(2.5)$.

CONNECT CONCEPTS Find the value of x.

28. Area of circle $= 25\pi$

29. Area of triangle $= 42$

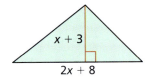

30. **OPEN-ENDED** Write a quadratic equation that has (a) one real solution and (b) no real solution.

31. An artist is painting a mural and drops a paintbrush. The graph represents the height h (in feet) of the paintbrush after t seconds.

    a. What is the initial height of the paintbrush?

    b. How long does the paintbrush take to hit the ground?

32. The equation $h = 0.019s^2$ models the height h (in feet) of the largest ocean waves when the wind speed is s knots. Compare the wind speeds required to generate 5-foot waves and 20-foot waves.

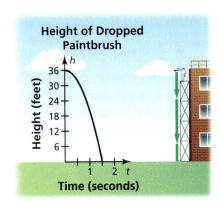

33. You make a rectangular quilt that is 5 feet by 4 feet. You use the remaining 10 square feet of fabric to add a border of uniform width to the quilt. What is the width of the border?

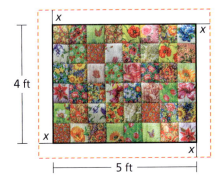

92   Chapter 3   Quadratic Equations and Complex Numbers

34. When an object is dropped on *any* planet, its height (in feet) after t seconds can be modeled by the function

$$h(t) = -\frac{g}{2}t^2 + s_0$$

where s_0 is the object's initial height and g is the planet's acceleration due to gravity. Two rocks are dropped from the same initial height on Earth and Mars. Which rock will hit the ground first?

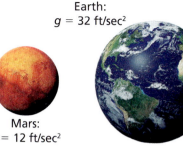

Earth: $g = 32$ ft/sec²

Mars: $g = 12$ ft/sec²

35. **SMP.2** A flea can jump very long distances relative to its size. The path of the jump of a flea can be modeled by the graph of the function $y = -0.189x^2 + 2.462x$, where x is the horizontal distance (in inches) and y is the vertical distance (in inches). Graph the function. Identify the vertex and zeros and interpret their meanings in this situation.

36. **SMP.6** Describe the relationship among zeros, x-intercepts, and roots.

37. A café has an outdoor, rectangular patio. The owner wants to add 329 square feet to the area of the patio by expanding the existing patio as shown. By what distance x should the patio be extended?

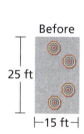
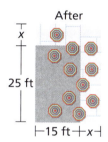

38. **SMP.7** Use an equation to find two consecutive odd integers whose product is 143.

39. An equation of the form $ax^2 + bx + c = 0$ has no real solution and a graph of the related function has a vertex that lies in the second quadrant.

   a. Is the value of a positive or negative?

   b. The graph is translated so the vertex is in the fourth quadrant. Does the graph have any x-intercepts?

40. The equation $x^2 - 2kx - 75 = 0$ has the solutions $x = k - 10$ and $x = k + 10$, where k is an integer. Find the possible values of k.

41. Write an equation of the form $ax^4 + bx^2 + c = 0$, where a, b, and c are real numbers, that can be solved by factoring and that has four real solutions. Explain how to solve your equation.

42. **SMP.1 DIG DEEPER** The first three figures of a pattern are shown. Explain whether the pattern has a figure with 480 dots. If so, which figure is it?

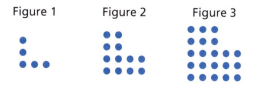

Interpreting Data

PARABOLOIDS A parabola that is rotated around its axis of symmetry creates a 3-D figure called a paraboloid, as shown at the right.

43. Consider the graph of the quadratic equation $y = x^2 + 2x - 8$. In what line can you rotate the graph to create a paraboloid?

44. The nose of a submarine is designed in the shape of a paraboloid. Why do you think this is?

45. Identify 2 other objects that are shaped like paraboloids.

Review & Refresh

46. Find the difference.

    $(-3x^3 + x^2 - 12x) - (3x - 6x^2 - 9)$

47. Write an equation of the parabola in vertex form.

    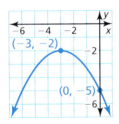

48. Find the product.

    $11x(-4x^2 + 3x + 8)$

49. Write the sentence as an absolute value inequality. Then solve the inequality.

    A number is more than 9 units from 3.

50. The table shows the donations made by 12 people on a fundraising site.

Donations (dollars)			
25	20	25	10
50	15	100	25
50	30	25	75

    a. Make a box-and-whisker plot that represents the data. Describe the shape of the distribution.

    b. Does the data set contain any outliers?

51. Find the minimum or maximum value of the function. Find the domain and range of the function, and when the function is increasing and decreasing.

    $y = -x^2 - 4x + 6$

3.2 Complex Numbers

Learning Target: Understand the imaginary unit *i* and perform operations with complex numbers.

Success Criteria:
- I can define the imaginary unit *i* and use it to rewrite the square root of a negative number.
- I can add, subtract, and multiply complex numbers.
- I can find complex solutions of quadratic equations.

INVESTIGATE Using Complex Numbers

Work with a partner.

1. A student solves the equations below as shown. Justify each solution step.

   a.
$x^2 = 36$	Original equation
$x = \pm\sqrt{36}$	_____
$x = \pm 6$	_____

   b.
$x^2 = -9$	Original equation
$x = \pm\sqrt{-9}$	_____
$x = \pm\sqrt{9}\sqrt{-1}$	_____
$x = \pm 3\sqrt{-1}$	_____

2. Describe the solutions of $x^2 = c$ when $c > 0$, when $c = 0$, and when $c < 0$.

3. The solutions of $x^2 = -9$ are *imaginary numbers*, and are written as $3i$ and $-3i$. Explain what *i* represents. What is the value of i^2?

4. In this lesson, the system of numbers is expanded to include imaginary numbers. The real numbers and imaginary numbers compose the set of *complex numbers*. Complete the diagram of the relationships among number systems.

   Integers
   Natural Numbers
   Rational Numbers
   Whole Numbers
   Real Numbers
   Complex Numbers
   Irrational Numbers
   Imaginary Numbers

5. Determine which subsets of numbers in Exercise 4 contain each number.

   a. $\sqrt{9}$ b. $\sqrt{0}$ c. $-\sqrt{4}$ d. $\sqrt{\dfrac{4}{9}}$ e. $\sqrt{2}$ f. $\sqrt{-1}$

Vocabulary
imaginary unit i
complex number
imaginary number
pure imaginary number
complex conjugates

The Imaginary Unit i

Not all quadratic equations have real-number solutions. For example, $x^2 = -3$ has no real-number solutions because the square of any real number is never a negative number.

To overcome this problem, mathematicians created an expanded system of numbers using the **imaginary unit i**, defined as $i = \sqrt{-1}$. Note that $i^2 = -1$. The imaginary unit i can be used to write the square root of *any* negative number.

Key Concept

The Square Root of a Negative Number

Property

1. If r is a positive real number, then $\sqrt{-r} = \sqrt{-1}\sqrt{r} = i\sqrt{r}$.

2. By the first property, it follows that $(i\sqrt{r})^2 = i^2 \cdot r = -r$.

Example

$\sqrt{-3} = \sqrt{-1}\sqrt{3} = i\sqrt{3}$

$(i\sqrt{3})^2 = i^2 \cdot 3 = -1 \cdot 3 = -3$

EXAMPLE 1 Finding Square Roots of Negative Numbers

a. Find $\sqrt{-25}$.

$\sqrt{-25} = \sqrt{25} \cdot \sqrt{-1} = 5i$

b. Find $\sqrt{-72}$.

$\sqrt{-72} = \sqrt{72} \cdot \sqrt{-1} = \sqrt{36} \cdot \sqrt{2} \cdot i = 6\sqrt{2}\,i = 6i\sqrt{2}$

c. Find $-5\sqrt{-9}$.

$-5\sqrt{-9} = -5\sqrt{9} \cdot \sqrt{-1} = -5 \cdot 3 \cdot i = -15i$

A **complex number** written in *standard form* is a number $a + bi$, where a and b are real numbers.

(real part) → $a + bi$ ← (imaginary part)

If $b \neq 0$, then $a + bi$ is an **imaginary number**. If $a = 0$ and $b \neq 0$, then $a + bi$ is a **pure imaginary number**.

In-Class Practice

Self-Assessment

Find the square root of the number.

1. $\sqrt{-4}$
2. $\sqrt{-12}$
3. $2\sqrt{-54}$

 I don't understand yet.
 I can do it with help.
 I can do it on my own.
 I can teach someone.

Operations with Complex Numbers

Two complex numbers $a + bi$ and $c + di$ are equal if and only if $a = c$ and $b = d$.

EXAMPLE 2 **Equating Two Complex Numbers**

Find the values of x and y that satisfy the equation $2x - 7i = 10 + yi$.

Set the real parts equal to each other and the imaginary parts equal to each other.

| $2x = 10$ | Equate the real parts. | $-7i = yi$ | Equate the imaginary parts. |
| $x = 5$ | Solve for x. | $-7 = y$ | Solve for y. |

▶ So, $x = 5$ and $y = -7$.

Key Concept

Sums and Differences of Complex Numbers

To add (or subtract) two complex numbers, add (or subtract) their real parts and their imaginary parts separately.

Sum of complex numbers:
$(a + bi) + (c + di) = (a + c) + (b + d)i$

Difference of complex numbers:
$(a + bi) - (c + di) = (a - c) + (b - d)i$

EXAMPLE 3 **Adding and Subtracting Complex Numbers**

a. Add $(8 - i) + (5 + 4i)$.

$(8 - i) + (5 + 4i) = (8 + 5) + (-1 + 4)i$ Definition of complex addition

$= 13 + 3i$ Write in standard form.

b. Subtract $(7 - 6i) - (3 - 6i)$.

$(7 - 6i) - (3 - 6i) = (7 - 3) + (-6 + 6)i$ Definition of complex subtraction

$= 4 + 0i$ Simplify.

$= 4$ Write in standard form.

In-Class Practice

Self-Assessment

4. Find the values of x and y that satisfy the equation $x + 3i = 9 - yi$.

Add or subtract.

5. $(9 - i) + (-6 + 7i)$

6. $(3 + 7i) - (8 - 2i)$

 I don't understand yet. I can do it with help. I can do it on my own. I can teach someone.

3.2 Complex Numbers

EXAMPLE 4 Multiplying Complex Numbers

a. Multiply $4i(-6 + i)$.

$$4i(-6 + i) = -24i + 4i^2 \qquad \text{Distributive Property}$$
$$= -24i + 4(-1) \qquad \text{Use } i^2 = -1.$$
$$= -4 - 24i \qquad \text{Write in standard form.}$$

b. Multiply $(9 - 2i)(-4 + 7i)$.

$$(9 - 2i)(-4 + 7i) = -36 + 63i + 8i - 14i^2 \qquad \text{Multiply using FOIL.}$$
$$= -36 + 71i - 14(-1) \qquad \text{Simplify and use } i^2 = -1.$$
$$= -36 + 71i + 14 \qquad \text{Simplify.}$$
$$= -22 + 71i \qquad \text{Write in standard form.}$$

Pairs of complex numbers of the forms $a + bi$ and $a - bi$, where $b \neq 0$, are **complex conjugates**. Consider the product of complex conjugates below.

$$(a + bi)(a - bi) = a^2 - (ab)i + (ab)i - b^2 i^2 \qquad \text{Multiply using FOIL.}$$
$$= a^2 - b^2(-1) \qquad \text{Simplify and use } i^2 = -1.$$
$$= a^2 + b^2 \qquad \text{Simplify.}$$

Because a and b are real numbers, $a^2 + b^2$ is a real number. So, the product of complex conjugates is a real number.

EXAMPLE 5 Multiplying Complex Conjugates

Multiply $5 + 2i$ by its complex conjugate.

The complex conjugate of $5 + 2i$ is $5 - 2i$. Use the pattern shown above, $(a + bi)(a - bi) = a^2 + b^2$ where $a = 5$ and $b = 2$.

$$(5 + 2i)(5 - 2i) = 5^2 + 2^2 \qquad a = 5, b = 2$$
$$= 25 + 4 \qquad \text{Evaluate exponents.}$$
$$= 29 \qquad \text{Add.}$$

In-Class Practice

Self-Assessment

Multiply.

7. $(-3i)(10i)$
8. $i(8 - i)$
9. $(3 + i)(5 - i)$

10. Multiply $-3 - 2i$ by its complex conjugate.

Connections to Real Life

Electrical circuit components, such as resistors, inductors, and capacitors, all oppose the flow of current. This opposition is called *resistance* for resistors and *reactance* for inductors and capacitors. Each of these quantities is measured in ohms. The symbol used for ohms is Ω, the uppercase Greek letter omega.

EXAMPLE 6 Finding the Impedance of a Series Circuit

STEM Video: Planning Electrical Circuits

The table shows the relationship between a component's resistance or reactance and its contribution to *impedance*. A *series circuit* is also shown with the resistance or reactance of each component labeled. The impedance for a series circuit is the sum of the impedances for the individual components. Find the impedance of the series circuit.

Component and symbol	Resistor —/\/\/—	Inductor —⦂⦂⦂—	Capacitor —⊦⊢—
Resistance or reactance (in ohms)	R	L	C
Impedance (in ohms)	R	Li	$-Ci$

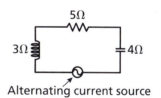

Alternating current source

- The resistor has a resistance of 5 ohms, so its impedance is 5 ohms.
- The inductor has a reactance of 3 ohms, so its impedance is $3i$ ohms.
- The capacitor has a reactance of 4 ohms, so its impedance is $-4i$ ohms.

$$\text{Impedance of circuit} = 5 + 3i + (-4i)$$
$$= 5 - i$$

▶ The impedance of the circuit is $(5 - i)$ ohms.

In-Class Practice

Self-Assessment

11. **WHAT IF?** In Example 6, what is the impedance of the circuit when the capacitor is replaced with one having a reactance of 7 ohms?

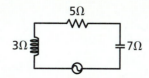

1 I don't understand yet. **2** I can do it with help. **3** I can do it on my own. **4** I can teach someone.

3.2 Complex Numbers

Complex Solutions and Zeros

EXAMPLE 7 Solving Quadratic Equations

a. Solve $x^2 + 4 = 0$.

$x^2 + 4 = 0$	Write original equation.
$x^2 = -4$	Subtract 4 from each side.
$x = \pm\sqrt{-4}$	Take square root of each side.
$x = \pm 2i$	Write in terms of i.

▶ The solutions are $2i$ and $-2i$.

b. Solve $2x^2 - 11 = -47$.

$2x^2 - 11 = -47$	Write original equation.
$2x^2 = -36$	Add 11 to each side.
$x^2 = -18$	Divide each side by 2.
$x = \pm\sqrt{-18}$	Take square root of each side.
$x = \pm i\sqrt{18}$	Write in terms of i.
$x = \pm 3i\sqrt{2}$	Simplify radical.

▶ The solutions are $3i\sqrt{2}$ and $-3i\sqrt{2}$.

EXAMPLE 8 Finding Zeros of a Quadratic Function

Find all complex zeros of the function.

$4x^2 + 20 = 0$	Set $f(x)$ equal to 0.
$4x^2 = -20$	Subtract 20 from each side.
$x^2 = -5$	Divide each side by 4.
$x = \pm\sqrt{-5}$	Take square root of each side.
$x = \pm i\sqrt{5}$	Write in terms of i.

▶ So, the zeros of f are $i\sqrt{5}$ and $-i\sqrt{5}$.

In-Class Practice

Self-Assessment

Solve the equation.

12. $x^2 = -13$
13. $x^2 - 8 = -36$
14. $5x^2 + 33 = 3$

Find all complex zeros of the function.

15. $f(x) = x^2 + 7$
16. $f(x) = -x^2 - 4$
17. $f(x) = 9x^2 + 1$

1 I don't understand yet.   **2** I can do it with help.   **3** I can do it on my own.   **4** I can teach someone.

3.2 Practice

Find the square root of the number. (See Example 1.)

1. $\sqrt{-18}$
2. $2\sqrt{-16}$
3. $-3\sqrt{-49}$
4. $-4\sqrt{-32}$

Find the values of x and y that satisfy the equation. (See Example 2.)

5. $-10x + 12i = 20 + 3yi$
6. $3x + 6i = 27 + yi$
7. $9x - 18i = -36 + 6yi$
8. $15 - 3yi = \frac{1}{2}x + 2i$

Add or subtract. (See Example 3.)

9. $(12 + 4i) - (3 - 7i)$
10. $(9 + 5i) + (11 + 2i)$
11. $(2 - 15i) - (4 + 5i)$
12. $-10 + (6 - 5i) - 9i$

13. Write each expression as a complex number in standard form.

    a. $\sqrt{-9} + \sqrt{-4} - \sqrt{16}$
    b. $\sqrt{-16} + \sqrt{8} + \sqrt{-36}$

14. The additive inverse of a complex number z is a complex number z_a such that $z + z_a = 0$. Find the additive inverse of each complex number.

    a. $z = 1 + i$
    b. $z = 3 - i$
    c. $z = -2 + 8i$

Multiply. (See Example 4.)

15. $(3 - 2i)(4 + i)$
16. $(7 + 5i)(8 - 6i)$
17. $(3 - 6i)^2$
18. $(8 + 3i)^2$

19. **SMP.3 ERROR ANALYSIS** Describe and correct the error in multiplying and writing the answer in standard form.

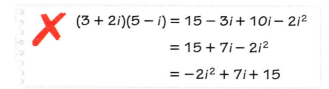

Multiply the complex number by its complex conjugate. (See Example 5.)

20. $5 - 6i$
21. $4 + 2i$
22. $-2 + 2i$
23. $-1 - 9i$

SMP.7 **Use the given numbers to complete the equation.**

24. (____ − ____i) − (____ − ____i) = $2 - 4i$

7   4   3   6

25. ____i(____ + ____i) = $-18 - 10i$

−5   9   2

CONNECTION TO REAL LIFE **Find the impedance of the series circuit.** (See Example 6.)

26.
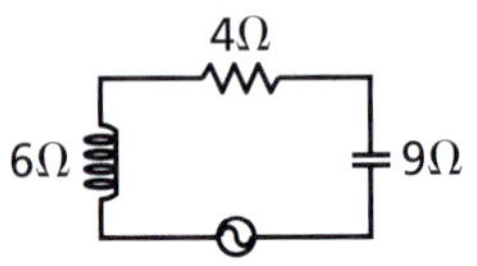

▶27.
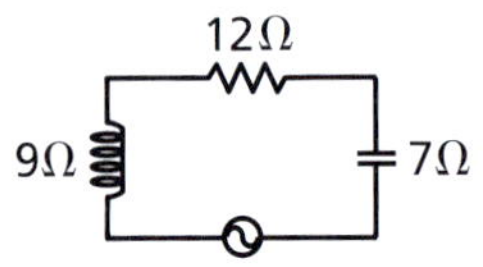

28.
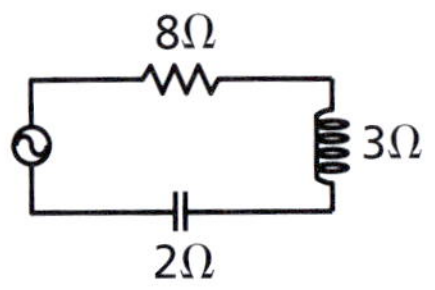

29.
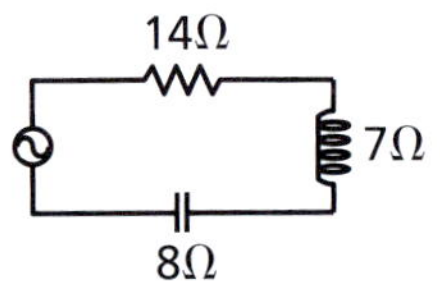

Solve the equation. (See Example 7.)

30. $x^2 + 49 = 0$

▶31. $x^2 - 4 = -11$

32. $2x^2 + 6 = -34$

33. $x^2 + 7 = -47$

Find all complex zeros of the function. (See Example 8.)

34. $k(x) = -5x^2 - 125$

▶35. $h(x) = 2x^2 + 72$

36. $p(x) = x^2 + 98$

37. $r(x) = -\frac{1}{2}x^2 - 24$

38. **CONNECT CONCEPTS** The coordinate system shown below is called the *complex plane*. In the complex plane, the point that corresponds to the complex number $a + bi$ is (a, b). Match each complex number with its corresponding point.

a. 2

b. $2i$

c. $4 - 2i$

d. $3 + 3i$

e. $-2 + 4i$

f. $-3 - 3i$

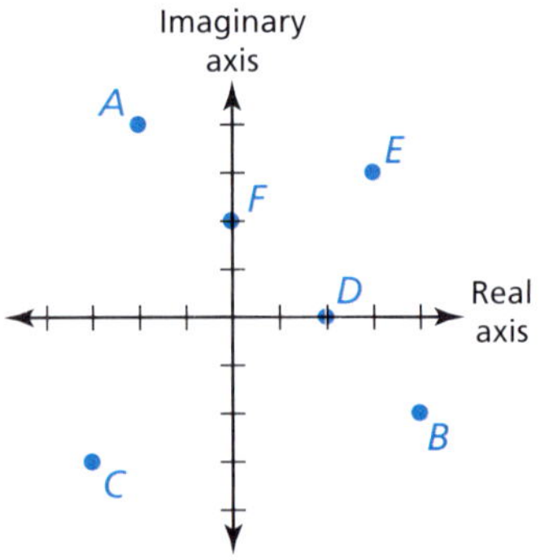

39. **SMP.6** Describe the methods shown for writing the complex expression in standard form. Explain which method you prefer.

Method 1
$$4i(2 - 3i) + 4i(1 - 2i) = 8i - 12i^2 + 4i - 8i^2$$
$$= 8i - 12(-1) + 4i - 8(-1)$$
$$= 20 + 12i$$

Method 2
$$4i(2 - 3i) + 4i(1 - 2i) = 4i[(2 - 3i) + (1 - 2i)]$$
$$= 4i[3 - 5i]$$
$$= 12i - 20i^2$$
$$= 12i - 20(-1)$$
$$= 20 + 12i$$

40. **SMP.8** Make a table that shows the powers of i from i^1 to i^8 in the first row and the simplified forms of these powers in the second row. Describe the pattern. Use the pattern to evaluate i^{25}, i^{50}, i^{75}, and i^{100}.

41. The graphs of three functions are shown. Explain which function(s) have real zeros and which function(s) have imaginary zeros.

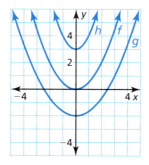

42. Justify each step in the simplification of i^2.

Algebraic Step	Justification
$i^2 = (\sqrt{-1})^2$	
$= -1$	

43. **SMP.3** Your friend claims that the conclusion in Exercise 42 is incorrect because $i^2 = i \cdot i = \sqrt{-1} \cdot \sqrt{-1} = \sqrt{-1(-1)} = \sqrt{1} = 1$. Explain whether your friend is correct.

44. Rewrite each expression with a real denominator.

a. $\dfrac{1 + 3i}{2i}$

b. $\dfrac{4 - 2i}{1 + i}$

45. **SMP.1** **DIG DEEPER** Write $\sqrt{i}$ as a complex number in standard form. Explain your method. (*Hint:* Use the equation $\sqrt{i} = a + bi$ to write a system of equations in terms of a and b.)

Interpreting Data

HISTORY OF COMPLEX NUMBERS Gerolamo Cardano (1501–1576) is considered to be the discoverer of complex numbers. However, the symbol *i*, denoting the imaginary unit, was first introduced by Leonhard Euler (1707–1783). The diagram shows how different types of complex numbers are related.

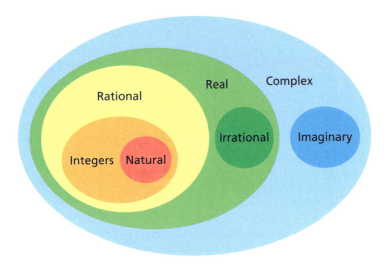

46. Give an example of an integer that is not a natural number.

47. Give an example of a real number that is not a rational number.

48. Give an example of a complex number that is not an imaginary number.

Review & Refresh

Graph the function and its parent function. Then describe the transformation.

49. $f(x) = \frac{1}{4}x^2 + 1$

50. $f(x) = -\frac{1}{2}x - 4$

Write an equation of the parabola with the given characteristics.

51. focus: $(0, -2)$; directrix: $y = 2$

52. vertex: $(5, -4)$; directrix: $x = 2$

53. Graph the system. Identify a solution. $y > x - 1$
$y \leq -4$

Write an inequality that represents the graph.

54.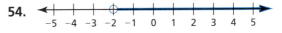

55.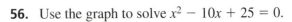

56. Use the graph to solve $x^2 - 10x + 25 = 0$.

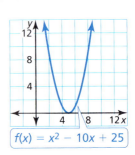

3.3 Completing the Square

Learning Target: Solve quadratic equations and rewrite quadratic functions by completing the square.

Success Criteria:
- I can solve quadratic equations by completing the square.
- I can apply completing the square to write quadratic functions in vertex form.

INVESTIGATE Using Algebra Tiles to Complete the Square

Work with a partner.

1. Write the expression modeled by the algebra tiles. How can you *complete the square*?

   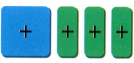

2. Use the model to find the value of c so that

   $$x^2 + 6x + c$$

   is a perfect square trinomial. Then write the expression as the square of a binomial.

3. Use the method outlined in Exercises 1 and 2 to complete the table.

Expression	Value of c needed to complete the square	Expression written as a binomial squared
$x^2 + 2x + c$		
$x^2 + 4x + c$		
$x^2 + 8x + c$		
$x^2 + 10x + c$		

4. Look for patterns in the table in Exercise 3. Consider the general statement $x^2 + bx + c = (x + d)^2$. In each case,

   - how are b and d related?
   - how are c and d related?
   - how are b and c related?

5. How can you complete the square for the expression $x^2 + bx$?

6. Solve $x^2 + 8x + 16 = 9$ by taking the square root of each side. Can you use this method to solve the equivalent equation $x^2 + 8x = -7$? What does this imply about solving quadratic equations?

Vocabulary
completing the square

Solving Quadratic Equations by Completing the Square

The expression $x^2 - 16x + 64$ is an example of a perfect square trinomial because it can be written as $(x - 8)^2$. In some situations, you will need to add a constant to an expression of the form $x^2 + bx$ to make it a perfect square trinomial. This process is called **completing the square**.

Key Concept

Completing the Square

Words To complete the square for the expression $x^2 + bx$, add $\left(\dfrac{b}{2}\right)^2$.

Diagrams In each diagram, the combined area of the shaded regions is $x^2 + bx$.

Adding $\left(\dfrac{b}{2}\right)^2$ completes the square in the second diagram.

Algebra $x^2 + bx + \left(\dfrac{b}{2}\right)^2 = \left(x + \dfrac{b}{2}\right)\left(x + \dfrac{b}{2}\right) = \left(x + \dfrac{b}{2}\right)^2$

EXAMPLE 1 Completing the Square

Complete the square for $x^2 + 14x$. Then factor the trinomial.

In this binomial, $b = 14$. Find $\left(\dfrac{b}{2}\right)^2$.

$$\left(\dfrac{b}{2}\right)^2 = \left(\dfrac{14}{2}\right)^2 = 7^2 = 49$$

Add the result to $x^2 + bx$.

$x^2 + 14x + 49$

▶ $x^2 + 14x + 49 = (x + 7)(x + 7) = (x + 7)^2$

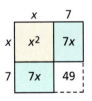

In-Class Practice

Self-Assessment

Complete the square for the expression. Then factor the trinomial.

1. $x^2 + 8x$
2. $x^2 - 2x$
3. $x^2 - 9x$

1 I don't understand yet. **2** I can do it with help. **3** I can do it on my own. **4** I can teach someone.

Completing the square can be used to solve any quadratic equation. First, write the equation in the form $x^2 + bx = d$. Then, when you complete the square, you must add the same number to *both* sides of the equation.

EXAMPLE 2 Solving $ax^2 + bx + c = 0$ when $a = 1$

Solve $x^2 - 10x + 7 = 0$ by completing the square.

$x^2 - 10x + 7 = 0$	Write the equation.
$x^2 - 10x = -7$	Write left side in the form $x^2 + bx$.
$x^2 - 10x + 25 = -7 + 25$	Add $\left(\dfrac{b}{2}\right)^2 = \left(\dfrac{-10}{2}\right)^2 = 25$ to each side.
$(x - 5)^2 = 18$	Write left side as a binomial squared.
$x - 5 = \pm\sqrt{18}$	Take square root of each side.
$x = 5 \pm \sqrt{18}$	Add 5 to each side.
$x = 5 \pm 3\sqrt{2}$	Simplify radical.

▶ The solutions are $x = 5 + 3\sqrt{2}$ and $x = 5 - 3\sqrt{2}$.

EXAMPLE 3 Solving $ax^2 + bx + c = 0$ when $a \neq 1$

Solve $3x^2 + 12x + 15 = 0$ by completing the square.

The coefficient a is not 1, so you must first divide each side of the equation by a.

$3x^2 + 12x + 15 = 0$	Write the equation.
$x^2 + 4x + 5 = 0$	Divide each side by 3.
$x^2 + 4x = -5$	Write left side in the form $x^2 + bx$.
$x^2 + 4x + 4 = -5 + 4$	Add $\left(\dfrac{b}{2}\right)^2 = \left(\dfrac{4}{2}\right)^2 = 4$ to each side.
$(x + 2)^2 = -1$	Write left side as a binomial squared.
$x + 2 = \pm\sqrt{-1}$	Take square root of each side.
$x = -2 \pm \sqrt{-1}$	Subtract 2 from each side.
$x = -2 \pm i$	Write in terms of i.

▶ The solutions are $x = -2 + i$ and $x = -2 - i$.

In-Class Practice

Self-Assessment

Solve the equation by completing the square.

4. $x^2 - 4x + 8 = 0$
5. $-3x^2 - 18x - 6 = 0$
6. $6x(x + 2) = -42$

Writing Quadratic Functions in Vertex Form

You can write a quadratic function in vertex form, $y = a(x - h)^2 + k$, by completing the square.

EXAMPLE 4 Writing a Quadratic Function in Vertex Form

a. Write $y = x^2 - 12x + 18$ in vertex form. Then identify the vertex.

$y = x^2 - 12x + 18$	Write the function.
$y + ? = (x^2 - 12x + ?) + 18$	Prepare to complete the square.
$y + 36 = (x^2 - 12x + 36) + 18$	Add $\left(\dfrac{b}{2}\right)^2 = \left(\dfrac{-12}{2}\right)^2 = 36$ to each side.
$y + 36 = (x - 6)^2 + 18$	Write $x^2 - 12x + 36$ as a binomial squared.
$y = (x - 6)^2 - 18$	Solve for y.

▶ The vertex form of the function is $y = (x - 6)^2 - 18$. The vertex is $(6, -18)$.

b. Write $y = \dfrac{1}{2}x^2 + 4x + 3$ in vertex form. Then identify the vertex.

$y = \dfrac{1}{2}x^2 + 4x + 3$	Write the function.
$y = \dfrac{1}{2}(x^2 + 8x) + 3$	Factor $\dfrac{1}{2}$ from first two terms.
$y + ? = \dfrac{1}{2}(x^2 + 8x + ?) + 3$	Prepare to complete the square.
$y + 8 = \dfrac{1}{2}(x^2 + 8x + 16) + 3$	Add $\left(\dfrac{1}{2}\right)\left(\dfrac{b}{2}\right)^2 = \left(\dfrac{1}{2}\right)(16)$ to each side.
$y + 8 = \dfrac{1}{2}(x + 4)^2 + 3$	Write $x^2 + 8x + 16$ as a binomial squared.
$y = \dfrac{1}{2}(x + 4)^2 - 5$	Solve for y.

▶ The vertex form of the function is $y = \dfrac{1}{2}(x + 4)^2 - 5$. The vertex is $(-4, -5)$.

Check

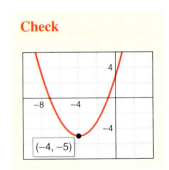

In-Class Practice

Self-Assessment

Write the quadratic function in vertex form. Then identify the vertex.

7. $y = x^2 - 8x + 18$

8. $y = 3x^2 + 18x + 22$

1 I don't understand yet. **2** I can do it with help. **3** I can do it on my own. **4** I can teach someone.

Classifying Graphs of Equations

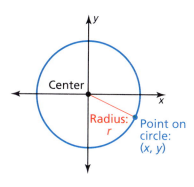

An equation of the form $(x - h)^2 + (y - k)^2 = r^2$ is the standard equation of a circle with center (h, k) and radius r. You can use completing the square to write equations of circles and parabolas in standard form.

Circle: $(x - h)^2 + (y - k)^2 = r^2$

Parabola (vertical axis of symmetry): $y = \dfrac{1}{4p}(x - h)^2 + k$

Parabola (horizontal axis of symmetry): $x = \dfrac{1}{4p}(y - k)^2 + h$

EXAMPLE 5 Writing Equations in Standard Form

Write the equation in standard form and tell whether it represents a circle or a parabola. Then graph the equation.

a. $x^2 + y^2 - 4y - 5 = 0$

Complete the square in y.

$x^2 + y^2 - 4y - 5 = 0$	Write the equation.
$x^2 + y^2 - 4y = 5$	Add 5 to each side.
$x^2 + (y^2 - 4y + \ ?\ ) = 5 + \ ?$	Prepare to complete the square.
$x^2 + (y^2 - 4y + 4) = 5 + 4$	Add $\left(\dfrac{b}{2}\right)^2 = \left(\dfrac{-4}{2}\right)^2 = 4$ to each side.
$x^2 + (y - 2)^2 = 9$	Simplify.

▶ The standard form is $x^2 + (y - 2)^2 = 9$. So, the equation represents a circle.

b. $2y^2 - 12y + 23 = x$

Complete the square in y.

$2y^2 - 12y + 23 = x$	Write the equation.
$2(y^2 - 6y + \ ?\ ) + 23 = x + \ ?$	Prepare to complete the square.
$2(y^2 - 6y + 9) + 23 = x + 18$	Add $2\left(\dfrac{b}{2}\right)^2 = 2\left(\dfrac{-6}{2}\right)^2 = 18$ to each side.
$2(y - 3)^2 + 5 = x$	Simplify.

▶ The standard form is $x = 2(y - 3)^2 + 5$. So, the equation represents a parabola.

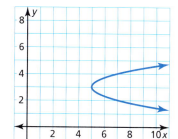

In-Class Practice
Self-Assessment

Write the equation in standard form and tell whether it represents a circle or a parabola. Then graph the equation.

9. $2x^2 - 4x + y - 12 = 0$

10. $x^2 + y^2 - 2x - 8y = 8$

Connections to Real Life

EXAMPLE 6 Using a Quadratic Equation in Vertex Form

The height y (in feet) of a baseball t seconds after it is hit can be modeled by $y = -16t^2 + 96t + 3$. Find the maximum height of the baseball. How long does the ball take to hit the ground?

Write the function in vertex form to identify the maximum height. Then find and interpret the zeros to determine how long the ball takes to hit the ground.

$y = -16t^2 + 96t + 3$	Write the function.
$y = -16(t^2 - 6t) + 3$	Factor -16 from first two terms.
$y + ? = -16(t^2 - 6t + ?) + 3$	Prepare to complete the square.
$y + (-16)(9) = -16(t^2 - 6t + 9) + 3$	Add $(-16)(9)$ to each side.
$y - 144 = -16(t - 3)^2 + 3$	Write $t^2 - 6t + 9$ as a binomial squared.
$y = -16(t - 3)^2 + 147$	Solve for y.

The vertex is $(3, 147)$. Find the zeros of the function.

$0 = -16(t - 3)^2 + 147$	Substitute 0 for y.
$-147 = -16(t - 3)^2$	Subtract 147 from each side.
$9.1875 = (t - 3)^2$	Divide each side by -16.
$\pm\sqrt{9.1875} = t - 3$	Take square root of each side.
$3 \pm \sqrt{9.1875} = t$	Add 3 to each side.

Reject the negative solution, $3 - \sqrt{9.1875} \approx -0.03$, because the time it takes the ball to hit the ground must be positive.

▶ So, the maximum height of the ball is 147 feet, and it takes $3 + \sqrt{9.1875} \approx 6$ seconds for the ball to hit the ground.

Check The vertex indicates that the maximum height of 147 feet occurs when $t = 3$. This makes sense because the graph of the function is parabolic with zeros near $t = 0$ and $t = 6$. You can use a graph to check the maximum height.

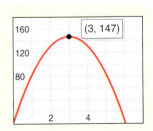

In-Class Practice

Self-Assessment

11. WHAT IF? The height of the baseball is given by $y = -16t^2 + 80t + 2$. Find the maximum height of the baseball. How long does the ball take to hit the ground?

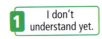

3.3 Practice

Complete the square for the expression. Then factor the trinomial. (See Example 1.)

1. $x^2 + 10x$
2. $y^2 - 12y$
3. $x^2 + 9x$
4. $s^2 - 17s$

5. **ERROR ANALYSIS** Describe and correct the error in completing the square for $x^2 + 30x$.

Find the value of c. Then write an expression represented by the diagram.

6.

7.

Solve the equation by completing the square. (See Examples 2 and 3.)

8. $t^2 - 8t - 5 = 0$
9. $x^2 + 6x + 3 = 0$
10. $7t^2 + 28t + 56 = 0$
11. $6r^2 + 6r + 12 = 0$
12. $4w(w - 3) = 24$
13. $3s^2 + 8s = 2s - 9$

Write the quadratic function in vertex form. Then identify the vertex. (See Example 4.)

14. $g(x) = x^2 + 12x + 37$
15. $y = x^2 - 8x + 19$
16. $y = -x^2 - 2x - 9$
17. $f(x) = 2x^2 - 8x - 13$

18. **ERROR ANALYSIS** Describe and correct the error in writing $y = 4x^2 + 24x - 11$ in vertex form.

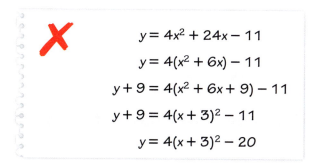

3.3 Completing the Square 111

Write the equation in standard form and tell whether it represents a circle or a parabola. Then graph the equation. (See Example 5.)

▶ **19.** $x^2 + 2x - 8y + 73 = 0$

20. $x^2 + y^2 - 2x + 4y = 0$

21. $y^2 + 10y + 20x - 15 = 0$

22. $0 = -4x^2 - 8x - y - 6$

23. $19 = x^2 + y^2 + 18x$

24. $2x - 6y = y^2 - 15$

25. CONNECTION TO REAL LIFE The height h (in feet) of a rugby ball t seconds after it is kicked can be modeled by $h = -16t^2 + 32t + 1$. (See Example 6.)

   a. Find the maximum height of the ball.

   b. How long does the ball take to hit the ground?

CONNECT CONCEPTS Find the value of x.

26. Area of rectangle = 50

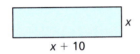

27. Area of parallelogram = 48

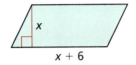

28. Area of triangle = 40

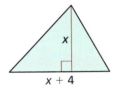

29. Area of trapezoid = 20

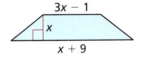

30. An online skateboard shop charges $70 per skateboard and sells 50 skateboards per week. For each $1 decrease in price, one additional skateboard per week is sold. The shop's revenue can be modeled by

$y = (70 - x)(50 + x)$.

   a. Find the maximum weekly revenue by using the intercept form of the function and by writing the function in vertex form.

   b. Which method do you prefer? Explain.

31. **SMP.7** The diagram represents completing the square for an expression. What is the expression? Complete the diagram and write the resulting perfect square trinomial.

32. **SMP.3** Your friend says the equation $x^2 + 10x = -20$ can be solved by either completing the square or factoring. Explain whether your friend is correct.

33. **OPEN-ENDED** Consider the function $f(x) = 2x^2 + 8x + 2$.

    a. Without solving, write a function g whose graph has the same x-intercepts as the graph of f. Explain your reasoning.

    b. Find the zeros of f and g by completing the square. Then graph each function.

34. A farmer is building a rectangular pen along the side of a barn for animals. The barn will serve as one side of the pen. The farmer has 120 feet of fence to enclose an area of 1,512 square feet and wants each side of the pen to be at least 20 feet long. What are the dimensions of the pen?

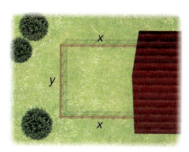

35. Solve $x^2 + bx + c = 0$ by completing the square. Your answer will be an expression for x in terms of b and c. What does your result represent?

36. **DIG DEEPER** In pottery class, you are given a lump of clay with a volume of 200 cubic centimeters to make a cylindrical pencil holder. The pencil holder should be 9 centimeters tall and have an inner radius of 3 centimeters. What thickness x does the pencil holder have when you use all of the clay?

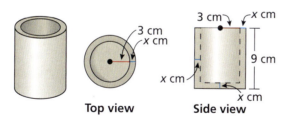

Top view   Side view

37. **SMP.1 SMP.4 PERFORMANCE TASK** A company wants to design a new smartphone. The ratio of the screen's height to its width should be 18 : 9. The total area of the screen and the border should be about 120 square centimeters.

    a. Decide what the thickness of the border will be on each side. Then find the dimensions of the screen. Justify your answer using a quadratic equation.

    b. Make a sketch of your design. Be sure to label the appropriate dimensions.

3.3 Completing the Square

Interpreting Data

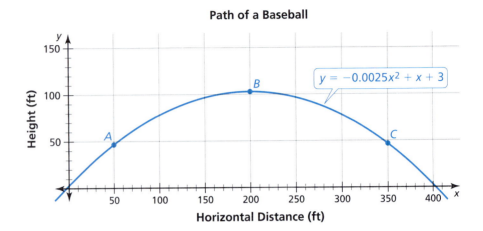

EFFECT OF AIR RESISTANCE The graph shows the path of a baseball hit from a height of 3 feet with a launch angle of 45°. The graph does not account for air resistance.

38. Write an equation in vertex form of the graph shown.

39. Air resistance always pushes in the opposite direction that an object travels. Sketch the graph. Draw arrows that represent the direction of air resistance at each point A, B, and C. Explain your reasoning.

40. Sketch a graph that could represent the path of a baseball when accounting for air resistance. Explain.

Review & Refresh

Solve the inequality. Graph the solution.

41. $2x - 3 < 5$

42. $4 - 8y \geq 12$

43. $\dfrac{n}{3} + 6 > 1$

44. $-\dfrac{2s}{5} \leq 8$

45. Identify the function family to which g belongs. Compare the graph of the function to the graph of its parent function.

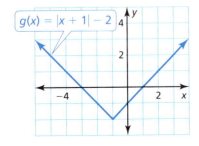

Perform the operation. Write the answer in standard form.

46. $(2 + 5i) + (-4 + 3i)$

47. $(3 + 9i) - (1 - 7i)$

48. $(2 + 4i)(-3 - 5i)$

49. For what value of m are the graphs of $-2y = 3x - 8$ and $y = mx - 6$ parallel? perpendicular?

50. Write a function that models the data.

x	1	2	3	4	5
y	9	22	45	78	121

114   Chapter 3   Quadratic Equations and Complex Numbers

3.4 Using the Quadratic Formula

Learning Target: Solve and analyze quadratic equations using the Quadratic Formula.

Success Criteria:
- I can solve quadratic equations using the Quadratic Formula.
- I can find and interpret the discriminant of an equation.
- I can write quadratic equations with different numbers of solutions using the discriminant.

INVESTIGATE Analyzing the Quadratic Formula

Work with a partner. Recall the *Quadratic Formula*, which can be used to find the solutions of any quadratic equation of the form $ax^2 + bx + c = 0$, where $a, b,$ and c are real numbers and $a \neq 0$.

$$x = \frac{-b \pm \sqrt{b^2 - 4ac}}{2a} \quad \text{Quadratic Formula}$$

1. Show how to derive this formula by completing the square for $ax^2 + bx + c = 0$. The first step has been done for you.

Step	Justification
$ax^2 + bx + c = 0$	General equation
$ax^2 + bx = -c$	Subtract c from each side.

2. What part of the Quadratic Formula tells whether a quadratic equation has real solutions or imaginary solutions? When does the formula produce real solutions for a quadratic equation? When does it produce imaginary solutions?

3. Can the Quadratic Formula produce one real solution and one imaginary solution?

4. Without solving, use your answer to Exercise 2 to determine whether each equation has real solutions or imaginary solutions. What does this tell you about the graph of each equation?

   a. $x^2 - 4x + 3 = 0$
   b. $x^2 + 4x + 6 = 0$
   c. $x^2 + 4x + 4 = 0$

5. Solve the quadratic equation in as many ways as you can.

   a. $x^2 + 2x - 3 = 0$
   b. $x^2 - 2x + 2 = 0$

6. Summarize the following methods you have learned for solving quadratic equations: graphing, using square roots, factoring, completing the square, and using the Quadratic Formula. Include when you would use each method.

Vocabulary
Quadratic Formula
discriminant

Solving Equations Using the Quadratic Formula

You have already learned how to solve quadratic equations by graphing, using square roots, factoring, and completing the square. In the Investigate, you derived the **Quadratic Formula** by completing the square. You can use the Quadratic Formula to find the solutions of any quadratic equation in standard form.

The solutions of the quadratic equation $ax^2 + bx + c = 0$ are

$$x = \frac{-b \pm \sqrt{b^2 - 4ac}}{2a}$$ Quadratic Formula

where a, b, and c are real numbers and $a \neq 0$.

EXAMPLE 1   Solving an Equation with Two Real Solutions

Solve $x^2 + 3x = 5$ using the Quadratic Formula.

Be sure to write the quadratic equation in standard form before applying the Quadratic Formula.

$x^2 + 3x = 5$	Write original equation.
$x^2 + 3x - 5 = 0$	Write in standard form.
$x = \dfrac{-b \pm \sqrt{b^2 - 4ac}}{2a}$	Quadratic Formula
$x = \dfrac{-3 \pm \sqrt{3^2 - 4(1)(-5)}}{2(1)}$	Substitute 1 for a, 3 for b, and -5 for c.
$x = \dfrac{-3 \pm \sqrt{29}}{2}$	Simplify.

▶ So, the solutions are $x = \dfrac{-3 + \sqrt{29}}{2}$ and $x = \dfrac{-3 - \sqrt{29}}{2}$.

Check

You can check your solutions by graphing $y = x^2 + 3x - 5$.

$-4.193 \approx \dfrac{-3 - \sqrt{29}}{2}$

$1.193 \approx \dfrac{-3 + \sqrt{29}}{2}$

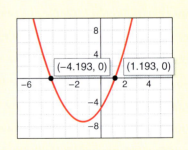

In-Class Practice

Self-Assessment

Solve the equation using the Quadratic Formula.

1. $x^2 - 6x + 4 = 0$
2. $2x^2 + 4 = -7x$

EXAMPLE 2 Solving an Equation with One Real Solution

Solve $25x^2 - 8x = 12x - 4$ using the Quadratic Formula.

$$25x^2 - 8x = 12x - 4 \quad \text{Write original equation.}$$
$$25x^2 - 20x + 4 = 0 \quad \text{Write in standard form.}$$
$$x = \frac{-(-20) \pm \sqrt{(-20)^2 - 4(25)(4)}}{2(25)} \quad a = 25, b = -20, c = 4$$
$$x = \frac{20 \pm \sqrt{0}}{50} \quad \text{Simplify.}$$
$$x = \frac{2}{5} \quad \text{Simplify.}$$

▶ So, the solution is $x = \frac{2}{5}$.

Check
Graph $y = 25x^2 - 20x + 4$.
The only x-intercept is $\frac{2}{5}$.

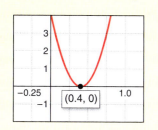

EXAMPLE 3 Solving an Equation with Imaginary Solutions

Solve $-x^2 + 4x = 13$ using the Quadratic Formula.

$$-x^2 + 4x = 13 \quad \text{Write original equation.}$$
$$-x^2 + 4x - 13 = 0 \quad \text{Write in standard form.}$$
$$x = \frac{-4 \pm \sqrt{4^2 - 4(-1)(-13)}}{2(-1)} \quad a = -1, b = 4, c = -13$$
$$x = \frac{-4 \pm \sqrt{-36}}{-2} \quad \text{Simplify.}$$
$$x = \frac{-4 \pm 6i}{-2} \quad \text{Write in terms of } i.$$
$$x = 2 \pm 3i \quad \text{Simplify.}$$

▶ The solutions are $x = 2 + 3i$ and $x = 2 - 3i$.

Check Graph $y = -x^2 + 4x - 13$. There are no x-intercepts. So, the original equation has no real solutions. An algebraic check for one of the imaginary solutions is shown.

$$-(2 + 3i)^2 + 4(2 + 3i) \stackrel{?}{=} 13$$
$$-(4 + 12i - 9) + 8 + 12i \stackrel{?}{=} 13$$
$$5 - 12i + 8 + 12i \stackrel{?}{=} 13$$
$$13 = 13 \checkmark$$

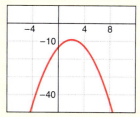

In-Class Practice
Self-Assessment

Solve the equation using the Quadratic Formula.

3. $x^2 + 41 = -8x$

4. $-9x^2 = 30x + 25$

| 1 I don't understand yet. | 2 I can do it with help. | 3 I can do it on my own. | 4 I can teach someone. |

3.4 Using the Quadratic Formula

Analyzing the Discriminant

In the Quadratic Formula, the expression $b^2 - 4ac$ is called the **discriminant** of the associated equation $ax^2 + bx + c = 0$.

$$x = \frac{-b \pm \sqrt{b^2 - 4ac}}{2a} \quad \leftarrow \text{discriminant}$$

You can analyze the discriminant of a quadratic equation to determine the number and type of solutions of the equation.

Value of discriminant	$b^2 - 4ac > 0$	$b^2 - 4ac = 0$	$b^2 - 4ac < 0$
Number and type of solutions	Two real solutions	One real solution	Two imaginary solutions
Graph of $y = ax^2 + bx + c$	Two x-intercepts	One x-intercept	No x-intercept

EXAMPLE 4 Analyzing the Discriminant

Find the discriminant of the quadratic equation and describe the number and type of solutions of the equation.

a. $x^2 - 6x + 10 = 0$

b. $x^2 - 6x + 9 = 0$

c. $x^2 - 6x + 8 = 0$

Equation	Discriminant	Solution(s)
$ax^2 + bx + c = 0$	$b^2 - 4ac$	$x = \dfrac{-b \pm \sqrt{b^2 - 4ac}}{2a}$
a. $x^2 - 6x + 10 = 0$	$(-6)^2 - 4(1)(10) = -4$	Two imaginary: $3 \pm i$
b. $x^2 - 6x + 9 = 0$	$(-6)^2 - 4(1)(9) = 0$	One real: 3
c. $x^2 - 6x + 8 = 0$	$(-6)^2 - 4(1)(8) = 4$	Two real: $2, 4$

In-Class Practice

Self-Assessment

Find the discriminant of the quadratic equation and describe the number and type of solutions of the equation.

5. $4x^2 + 8x + 4 = 0$

6. $\frac{1}{2}x^2 + x - 1 = 0$

7. $7x^2 - 3x = 6$

8. $4x^2 + 6x = -9$

1 I don't understand yet.   **2** I can do it with help.   **3** I can do it on my own.   **4** I can teach someone.

EXAMPLE 5 **Writing Quadratic Equations**

Find a possible pair of integer values for a and c so that the equation $ax^2 - 4x + c = 0$ has the given number and type of solution(s). Then write the equation.

a. one real solution

For the equation to have one real solution, the discriminant must equal 0.

$b^2 - 4ac = 0$	Write the discriminant.
$(-4)^2 - 4ac = 0$	Substitute -4 for b.
$16 - 4ac = 0$	Evaluate the power.
$-4ac = -16$	Subtract 16 from each side.
$ac = 4$	Divide each side by -4.

Because $ac = 4$, choose two integers whose product is 4, such as $a = 1$ and $c = 4$.

▶ So, one possible equation is $x^2 - 4x + 4 = 0$.

b. two imaginary solutions

For the equation to have two imaginary solutions, the discriminant must be less than zero.

$b^2 - 4ac < 0$	Write the discriminant.
$(-4)^2 - 4ac < 0$	Substitute -4 for b.
$16 - 4ac < 0$	Evaluate the power.
$-4ac < -16$	Subtract 16 from each side.
$ac > 4$	Divide each side by -4. Reverse inequality symbol.

Because $ac > 4$, choose two integers whose product is greater than 4, such as $a = 2$ and $c = 3$.

▶ So, one possible equation is $2x^2 - 4x + 3 = 0$.

Check
The graph of $y = 2x^2 - 4x + 3$ does not have any x-intercepts. ✓

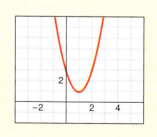

In-Class Practice

Self-Assessment

9. Find a possible pair of integer values for a and c so that the equation $ax^2 + 8x + c = 0$ has two real solutions. Then write the equation.

1 I don't understand yet. **2** I can do it with help. **3** I can do it on my own. **4** I can teach someone.

Connections to Real Life

The function $h = -16t^2 + s_0$ is used to model the height of a *dropped* object, where h is the height (in feet), t is the time in motion (in seconds), and s_0 is the initial height (in feet). For an object that is *launched* or *thrown*, an extra term $v_0 t$ must be added to the model to account for the object's initial vertical velocity v_0 (in feet per second).

$h = -16t^2 + s_0$ Object is dropped.

$h = -16t^2 + v_0 t + s_0$ Object is launched or thrown.

The value of v_0 can be positive, negative, or zero depending on whether the object is launched upward, downward, or parallel to the ground.

EXAMPLE 6 Interpreting the Discriminant

A juggler tosses a ball into the air. The ball leaves the juggler's hand 4 feet above the ground and has an initial vertical velocity of 30 feet per second. Does the ball reach a height of 10 feet? 25 feet?

Because the ball is *thrown*, use the model $h = -16t^2 + v_0 t + s_0$.

$h = -16t^2 + v_0 t + s_0$ Write the height model.

$h = -16t^2 + 30t + 4$ Substitute 30 for v_0 and 4 for s_0.

To determine whether the ball reaches each height, substitute each height for h to create two equations. Then solve each equation.

$10 = -16t^2 + 30t + 4$ $\quad\quad$ $25 = -16t^2 + 30t + 4$

$0 = -16t^2 + 30t - 6$ $\quad\quad$ $0 = -16t^2 + 30t - 21$

$t = \dfrac{-30 \pm \sqrt{30^2 - 4(-16)(-6)}}{2(-16)}$ $\quad$ $t = \dfrac{-30 \pm \sqrt{30^2 - 4(-16)(-21)}}{2(-16)}$

$t = \dfrac{-30 \pm \sqrt{516}}{-32}$ $\quad\quad$ $t = \dfrac{-30 \pm \sqrt{-444}}{-32}$

When $h = 10$, the equation has two real solutions, $t \approx 0.23$ and $t \approx 1.65$. When $h = 25$, the equation has two imaginary solutions because the discriminant is negative.

▶ So, the ball reaches a height of 10 feet, but it does not reach a height of 25 feet.

In-Class Practice

Self-Assessment

10. **WHAT IF?** The ball leaves the juggler's hand with an initial vertical velocity of 40 feet per second. Does the ball reach a height of 20 feet? 30 feet?

3.4 Practice

Solve the equation using the Quadratic Formula. (See Examples 1, 2, and 3.)

▶ 1. $x^2 - 4x + 3 = 0$
2. $x^2 + 6x + 15 = 0$
▶ 3. $x^2 - 14x = -49$

4. $-10x = -25 - x^2$
▶ 5. $3x^2 + 5 = -2x$
6. $2x^2 + 4x = 30$

7. $-4x^2 + 3x = -5$
8. $x^2 + 121 = -22x$
9. $-7w + 6 = -4w^2$

Find the discriminant of the quadratic equation and describe the number and type of solutions of the equation. (See Example 4.)

10. $x^2 - x + 6 = 0$
▶ 11. $x^2 + 12x + 36 = 0$
12. $4n^2 - 4n - 24 = 0$

13. $4x^2 = 5x - 10$
14. $-18p = p^2 + 81$
15. $-2x^2 - 6 = x$

MATCHING Use the discriminant to match each equation with the graph of its related function.

16. $x^2 - 6x + 25 = 0$
17. $2x^2 - 20x + 50 = 0$

18. $3x^2 + 6x - 9 = 0$
19. $-5x^2 + 10x + 35 = 0$

A.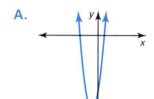
B.
C.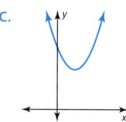
D.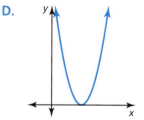

20. **SMP.3 ERROR ANALYSIS** Describe and correct the error in solving the equation.

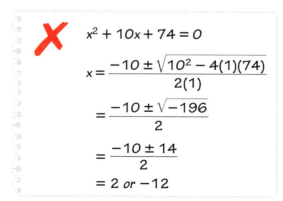

OPEN-ENDED Find a possible pair of integer values for a and c so that the quadratic equation has the given number and type of solution(s). Then write the equation. (See Example 5.)

21. $ax^2 + 4x + c = 0$; two imaginary solutions
22. $ax^2 + 6x + c = 0$; two real solutions

▶ 23. $ax^2 - 8x + c = 0$; two real solutions
24. $ax^2 - 6x + c = 0$; one real solution

25. **CONNECTION TO REAL LIFE** A lacrosse player throws a ball in the air from an initial height of 7 feet. The ball has an initial vertical velocity of 35 feet per second. Does the ball reach a height of 26 feet? 30 feet? (See Example 6.)

26. **CONNECTION TO REAL LIFE** A rocketry club is launching model rockets. The launching pad is 30 feet above the ground. Your model rocket has an initial vertical velocity of 105 feet per second. Your friend's model rocket has an initial vertical velocity of 100 feet per second.

    a. Does your rocket reach a height of 200 feet? Does your friend's rocket?

    b. Which rocket is in the air longer? How much longer?

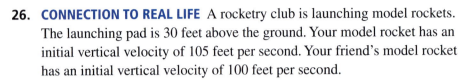

SMP.7 Use the Quadratic Formula to write a quadratic equation that has the given solutions.

27. $x = \dfrac{-8 \pm \sqrt{-176}}{-10}$

28. $x = \dfrac{-4 \pm 2}{6}$

Solve the quadratic equation using the Quadratic Formula. Then solve the equation using another method. Which method do you prefer?

29. $3x^2 - 21 = 3$

30. $2x^2 - 54 = 12x$

31. $8x^2 + 4x + 5 = 0$

32. $5x^2 - 50x = -135$

CONNECT CONCEPTS Find the value of x.

33. Area = 24 m²

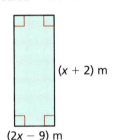

(x + 2) m

(2x − 9) m

34. Area = 8 ft²

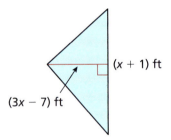

(x + 1) ft

(3x − 7) ft

OPEN-ENDED Find a possible pair of real number values for a and c so that the quadratic equation has one real solution. Then write the equation.

35. $ax^2 - 13x + c = 0$

36. $ax^2 - \sqrt{2}x + c = 0$

37. A gannet is a bird that feeds on fish by diving into the water. A gannet spots a fish on the surface of the water and flies down 100 feet to catch it. The bird plunges toward the water with an initial vertical velocity of −88 feet per second.

    a. How much time does the fish have to swim away?

    b. Another gannet spots the fish at the same time, but it is only 84 feet above the water. It has an initial vertical velocity of −70 feet per second. Which bird will reach the water first?

38. The graphs of three quadratic functions are shown. For each graph, determine whether the discriminant of the associated equation is *positive*, *negative*, or *zero*. Then state the number and type of solution(s) of the associated equation.

a.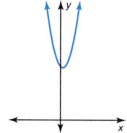
b.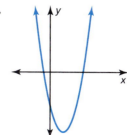
c.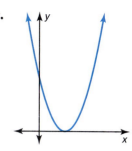

39. **NUCLEAR ENGINEERING** NUCLEAR ENERGY The amount A of nuclear energy (in billions of kilowatt hours) generated for consumer use in the United States can be modeled by the function

$$A = -0.6t^2 + 36.5t + 246$$

where t represents the number of years after 1980.

a. In what year did the amount of nuclear energy generated reach 800 billion kilowatt hours?

b. Find the average rate of change from 2005 to 2020 and interpret the meaning in the context of the situation.

c. Explain whether you think this model will be accurate in 2040.

40. **SMP.2** OPEN-ENDED Describe a real-life situation that can be modeled by $h = -16t^2 + v_0 t + s_0$. Write the height model for your situation and determine how long your object is in the air.

41. For a quadratic equation $ax^2 + bx + c = 0$ with two real solutions, show that the mean of the solutions is $-\dfrac{b}{2a}$. How is this fact related to the symmetry of the graph of $y = ax^2 + bx + c$?

42. The Stratosphere Tower in Las Vegas is 921 feet tall and has a "needle" at its top that extends even higher into the air. A thrill ride called Big Shot catapults riders 160 feet up the needle and then lets them fall back to the launching pad.

a. The height h (in feet) of a rider on the Big Shot can be modeled by $h = -16t^2 + v_0 t + 921$, where t is the elapsed time (in seconds) after launch and v_0 is the initial vertical velocity (in feet per second). Find v_0 using the fact that the maximum value of h is $921 + 160 = 1{,}081$ feet.

b. A brochure for the Big Shot states that the ride up the needle takes 2 seconds. Compare this time to the time given by the model $h = -16t^2 + v_0 t + 921$, where v_0 is the value you found in part (a). Discuss the accuracy of the model.

43. **SMP.7** Can you use the Quadratic Formula to find the solutions of $4x^4 + 35x^2 - 9 = 0$? If so, find the solutions. If not, explain why not.

Interpreting Data

CATENARIES Not all U-shaped graphs are parabolas. A catenary is one example of a U-shaped curve that cannot be modeled by a quadratic function.

44. Upon inspection, does a chain hanging between two poles appear to be a parabola or a catenary? Research whether your answer is correct.

45. Find two other real-life examples of catenaries.

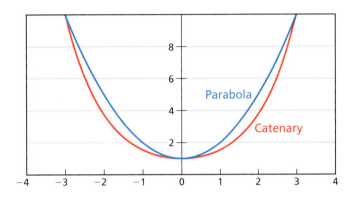

Review & Refresh

46. Solve the equation by completing the square.
$$9x^2 + 36x + 72 = 0$$

47. Solve the system using any method.
$$-x + 2y = 6$$
$$x + 4y = 24$$

48. Use the graph to solve $x^2 = -2x + 8$.

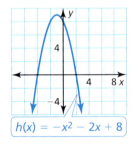

49. Find the values of x and y that satisfy the equation.
$$7x - 6i = 14 + yi$$

50. Write an inequality that represents the graph.

51. Solve $|4 - x| = |3x - 8|$.

52. The bar graph shows the results of a survey that asks a group of students their favorite movie genre. What percent of the students surveyed chose comedy?

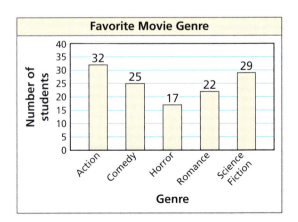

3.5 Solving Nonlinear Systems of Equations

Learning Target: Solve nonlinear systems graphically and algebraically.

Success Criteria:
- I can describe what a nonlinear system of equations is.
- I can solve systems using graphing, substitution, or elimination.
- I can solve quadratic equations by graphing each side of the equation.

INVESTIGATE Solving Systems of Equations

Work with a partner.

1. Graph the equation $x^2 + y^2 = 4$. Describe the graph.

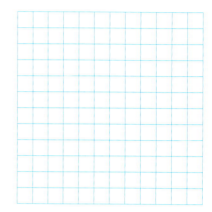

2. How many intersection points can the graphs of a line and a circle have? Use graphs to support your answers. What do the intersection points represent?

3. Consider the system below.

   $$x^2 + y^2 = 4$$
   $$y = -\tfrac{1}{2}x + 1$$

   a. Explain whether you can use a graph to solve the system.

   b. **SMP.5** Find the points of intersection of the graphs. Explain your method.

4. Write the equation of a line that intersects the graph of $x^2 + y^2 = 4$ at only one point. Explain how you found your answer.

5. Think of all the ways that a line can intersect the graph of a *parabola*. How many points of intersection are possible? Use graphs to support your answers.

6. Repeat Exercise 5 for the points of intersection of a parabola and a circle.

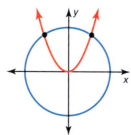

Vocabulary
system of nonlinear equations

Solutions of Nonlinear Systems

You can use graphing, substitution, and elimination to solve systems of *nonlinear* equations. A **system of nonlinear equations** is one in which at least one equation is nonlinear.

$y = x^2 + 2x - 4$ Equation 1 is nonlinear.
$y = 2x + 5$ Equation 2 is linear.

When a nonlinear system consists of a linear equation and a quadratic equation, the graphs can intersect in zero, one, or two points. So, the system can have zero, one, or two real solutions.

No real solution   One real solution   Two real solutions

When a nonlinear system consists of two parabolas that open up or open down, the graphs can intersect in zero, one, or two points. So, the system can have zero, one, or two real solutions.

No real solution   One real solution   Two real solutions

EXAMPLE 1   Solving a Nonlinear System by Graphing

Solve the system by graphing. $y = x^2 - 2x - 1$ Equation 1
   $y = -2x - 1$ Equation 2

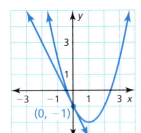

Graph each equation and estimate the point of intersection. The parabola and the line appear to intersect at the point $(0, -1)$.

Check that $(0, -1)$ is a solution of each equation.

Equation 1 $y = x^2 - 2x - 1$ Equation 2 $y = -2x - 1$
   $-1 \stackrel{?}{=} (0)^2 - 2(0) - 1$ $-1 \stackrel{?}{=} -2(0) - 1$
   $-1 = -1$ ✓ $-1 = -1$ ✓

▶ The solution is $(0, -1)$.

In-Class Practice

Self-Assessment

Solve the system by graphing.

1. $y = x^2 - 4x - 2$
   $y = x - 2$

2. $y = \frac{1}{2}x^2 - 2x + 4$
   $x + y = 3$

126   Chapter 3   Quadratic Equations and Complex Numbers

EXAMPLE 2 **Solving a Nonlinear System by Substitution**

Solve the system by substitution.
$x^2 + x - y = -1$ Equation 1
$x + y = 4$ Equation 2

Solving for y in Equation 2 gives $y = -x + 4$.

Substitute $-x + 4$ for y in Equation 1 and solve for x.

$x^2 + x - y = -1$	Equation 1
$x^2 + x - (-x + 4) = -1$	Substitute $-x + 4$ for y.
$x^2 + 2x - 4 = -1$	Simplify.
$x^2 + 2x - 3 = 0$	Write in standard form.
$(x + 3)(x - 1) = 0$	Factor.
$x + 3 = 0$ or $x - 1 = 0$	Zero-Product Property
$x = -3$ or $x = 1$	Solve for x.

Substitute -3 and 1 for x in $y = -x + 4$ and solve for y.

$y = -x + 4 = -(-3) + 4 = 7$ Substitute -3 for x.
$y = -x + 4 = -1 + 4 = 3$ Substitute 1 for x.

▶ So, the solutions are $(-3, 7)$ and $(1, 3)$.

Check

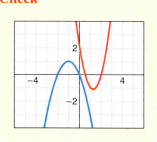

EXAMPLE 3 **Solving a Nonlinear System by Elimination**

Solve the system by elimination.
$2x^2 - 5x - y = -2$ Equation 1
$x^2 + 2x + y = 0$ Equation 2

Add the equations to eliminate the y-terms and obtain an equation in x.

$$2x^2 - 5x - y = -2$$
$$\underline{x^2 + 2x + y = 0}$$
$$3x^2 - 3x = -2$$ Add the equations.
$$3x^2 - 3x + 2 = 0$$ Write in standard form.
$$x = \frac{3 \pm \sqrt{-15}}{6}$$ Use the Quadratic Formula.

▶ Because the discriminant is negative, the equation $3x^2 - 3x + 2 = 0$ has no real solution. So, the original system has no real solution.

Check

In-Class Practice

Self-Assessment

Solve the system using any method.

3. $y = -x^2 + 4$
   $y = -4x + 8$

4. $x^2 + 3x + y = 0$
   $2x + y = 5$

3.5 Solving Nonlinear Systems of Equations

When a nonlinear system consists of the equation of a circle and a linear equation, the graphs can intersect in zero, one, or two points. So, the system can have zero, one, or two real solutions, as shown.

No real solution

One real solution

Two real solutions

EXAMPLE 4 Solving a Nonlinear System Involving a Circle

Solve the system by substitution. $x^2 + y^2 = 10$ Equation 1

$y = -3x + 10$ Equation 2

Equation 2 is already solved for y. So, substitute $-3x + 10$ for y in Equation 1 and solve for x.

$x^2 + y^2 = 10$	Equation 1
$x^2 + (-3x + 10)^2 = 10$	Substitute $-3x + 10$ for y.
$x^2 + 9x^2 - 60x + 100 = 10$	Expand the power.
$10x^2 - 60x + 90 = 0$	Write in standard form.
$x^2 - 6x + 9 = 0$	Divide each side by 10.
$(x - 3)^2 = 0$	Perfect square trinomial pattern
$x = 3$	Zero-Product Property

Find the y-coordinate of the solution by substituting $x = 3$ in Equation 2.

$y = -3(3) + 10 = 1$

▶ So, the solution is $(3, 1)$.

Check Use technology to check your answer.

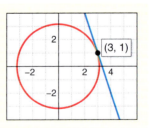

In-Class Practice

Self-Assessment

Solve the system.

5. $x^2 + y^2 = 4$
   $y = x + 4$

6. $x^2 + y^2 = 1$
   $y = \frac{1}{2}x + \frac{1}{2}$

 I don't understand yet.
 I can do it with help.
 I can do it on my own.
 I can teach someone.

Solving Equations by Graphing

One way to solve the equation $f(x) = g(x)$ is to graph the two functions $y = f(x)$ and $y = g(x)$. The x-value of an intersection point of the graphs is a solution of the equation $f(x) = g(x)$.

EXAMPLE 5 **Solving Quadratic Equations by Graphing**

a. **Solve $3x^2 + 5x - 1 = -x^2 + 2x + 1$ by graphing.**

   Write functions to represent each side of the original equation.

   $y = 3x^2 + 5x - 1$ and $y = -x^2 + 2x + 1$

   Use technology to graph the functions and find the x-coordinates of the intersection points of the graphs.

   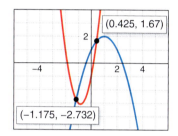

   ▶ The points of intersection are about $(-1.175, -2.732)$ and $(0.425, 1.67)$. So, the solutions are $x \approx -1.175$ and $x \approx 0.425$.

b. **Solve $-(x - 1.5)^2 + 2.25 = 2x(x + 1.5)$ by graphing.**

   Write functions to represent each side of the original equation.

   $y = -(x - 1.5)^2 + 2.25$ and $y = 2x(x + 1.5)$

   Use technology to graph the functions and find the x-coordinate of the intersection point of the graphs.

   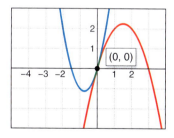

   ▶ The graphs intersect at $(0, 0)$. So, the solution is $x = 0$.

In-Class Practice

Self-Assessment

Solve the equation by graphing.

7. $x^2 - 6x + 15 = -(x - 3)^2 + 6$

8. $(x + 4)(x - 1) = -x^2 + 3x + 4$

3.5 Solving Nonlinear Systems of Equations

3.5 Practice

Solve the system by graphing. (See Example 1.)

1. $y = x + 2$
   $y = 0.5(x + 2)^2$

2. $y = (x - 3)^2 + 5$
   $y = 5$

3. $y = \frac{1}{3}x + 2$
   $y = -3x^2 - 5x - 4$

Solve the system by substitution. (See Examples 2 and 4.)

4. $y = x + 5$
   $y = x^2 - x + 2$

5. $2x^2 + 4x - y = -3$
   $-2x + y = -4$

6. $y = -2x - 5$
   $-3x^2 + 4x - y = 8$

7. $x^2 + y^2 = 20$
   $y = 2x - 10$

8. $x^2 + y^2 = 7$
   $x + 3y = 21$

9. $x^2 + y^2 = 5$
   $-x + y = -1$

Solve the system by elimination. (See Example 3.)

10. $2x^2 - 3x - y = -5$
    $-x + y = 5$

11. $-3x^2 + y = -18x + 29$
    $-3x^2 - y = 18x - 25$

12. $-10x^2 + y = -80x + 155$
    $5x^2 + y = 40x - 85$

13. **SMP.3 ERROR ANALYSIS** Describe and correct the error in using elimination to solve for one of the variables in the system.

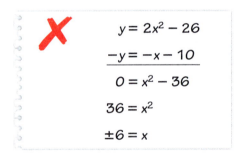

14. The table shows the inputs and outputs of two quadratic functions. Identify the solution(s) of the system. Explain your reasoning.

x	−3	−1	1	3	7	11
y_1	29	9	−3	−7	9	57
y_2	−11	9	21	25	9	−39

Solve the equation by graphing. (See Example 5.)

15. $x^2 + 2x = -\frac{1}{2}x^2 + 2x$

16. $(x + 2)(x - 2) = -x^2 + 6x - 7$

17. $-2x^2 - 16x - 25 = 6x^2 + 48x + 95$

18. $(-x + 4)(x + 8) - 42 = (x + 3)(x + 1) - 1$

19. **SMP.6** Explain why the x-coordinates of the points where the graphs of $y = f(x)$ and $y = g(x)$ intersect are the solutions of the equation $f(x) = g(x)$.

130   Chapter 3   Quadratic Equations and Complex Numbers

20. The equations shown model the range (in miles) of a broadcast signal from a radio tower and the path of a straight highway. For what length of the highway are cars able to receive the broadcast signal?

    $x^2 + y^2 = 1{,}620$ Broadcast signal
    $y = -\frac{1}{3}x + 30$ Highway

21. **SMP.7 OPEN-ENDED** Find a value for m so the system has (a) no real solution, (b) one real solution, and (c) two real solutions. Justify each answer using a graph.

    $3y = -x^2 + 8x - 7$
    $y = mx + 3$

22. **CONNECT CONCEPTS** The graph of a nonlinear system is shown. Estimate the solution(s). Then describe a transformation of the graph of the linear function that results in a system with no real solution.

    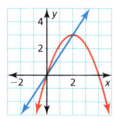

23. Each system shown includes the equation of a circle with center $(0, 0)$ and radius 1 and an equation of a line with a y-intercept of -1.

System A	**System B**	**System C**
$x^2 + y^2 = 1$	$x^2 + y^2 = 1$	$x^2 + y^2 = 1$
$y = 3x - 1$	$y = 4x - 1$	$y = 5x - 1$

    a. Without solving, find one solution that all three systems have in common. Explain your reasoning.

    b. Find the other solution of each system. What do you notice about the numerators and denominator of each solution?

24. Solve the system shown.

    $x^2 + y^2 = 4$
    $2y = x^2 - 2x + 4$
    $y = -x + 2$

25. **SMP.1 DIG DEEPER** To be eligible for a parking pass on a college campus, a student must live at least 1 mile from the campus center. For what length of Oak Lane are students *not* eligible for a parking pass? Justify your answer.

    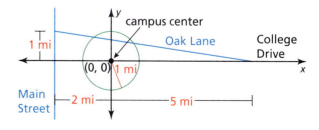

Interpreting Data

BREAK-EVEN POINT Entrepreneurs need to know the *break-even point* for a product. The total production cost has two components: the initial cost and the cost per unit. When enough units have been sold so that the total revenue equals the total cost, the sales are said to have reached the break-even point.

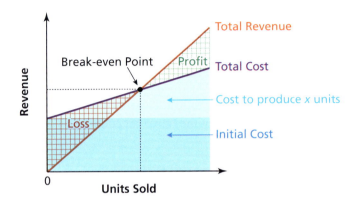

26. Explain whether the profit of a business can be negative.

27. **SMP.2** The cost C (in dollars) and revenue R (in dollars) for selling x units of a certain product are shown below. How much does it cost to produce each unit? What is the selling price per unit?

    $C = 14.5x + 100{,}000$ and $R = 22x$

28. In Exercise 27, how many units must be sold to reach the break-even point?

Review & Refresh

Write an inequality that represents the graph.

29.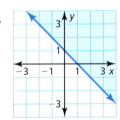

30.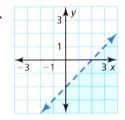

31. Graph $y = \begin{cases} -\frac{1}{2}x + 6, & \text{if } x \leq 2 \\ 3x - 5, & \text{if } x > 2 \end{cases}$.

32. You kick a soccer ball from an initial height of 2 feet. The ball has an initial vertical velocity of 45 feet per second. Does the ball reach a height of 35 feet?

Describe the transformation of $f(x) = x^2$ represented by g. Then graph each function.

33. $g(x) = (x - 5)^2 - 3$

34. $g(x) = \frac{1}{4}(x + 2)^2$

35. For what values of b can you complete the square for $x^2 + bx$ by adding 81?

36. Use technology to find an equation of the line of best fit for the data. Identify and interpret the correlation coefficient.

x	0	5	10	12	16
y	18	15	9	7	2

132   Chapter 3   Quadratic Equations and Complex Numbers

3.6 Quadratic Inequalities

Learning Target: Graph and solve quadratic inequalities.

Success Criteria:
- I can describe the graph of a quadratic inequality.
- I can graph quadratic inequalities.
- I can graph systems of quadratic inequalities.
- I can solve quadratic inequalities algebraically and graphically.

INVESTIGATE Solving Quadratic Inequalities

Work with a partner. The figure shows the graph of $f(x) = x^2 + 2x - 3$.

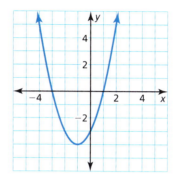

1. Explain how you can use the graph to solve the inequality $0 > x^2 + 2x - 3$. Then graph the solutions of the inequality.

2. Explain how the inequality $y > x^2 + 2x - 3$ is different from the inequality in Exercise 1.

3. Explain how you can use the graph above to represent the solutions of $y > x^2 + 2x - 3$. Then graph the inequality.

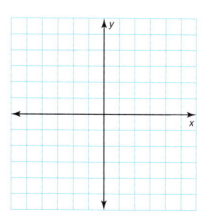

4. Repeat Exercises 1–3 by replacing $>$ with $\leq$.

5. Compare the graphs of the solutions of quadratic inequalities in one variable to the graphs of the solutions of quadratic inequalities in two variables.

3.6 Quadratic Inequalities 133

Vocabulary
quadratic inequality in two variables
system of quadratic inequalities
quadratic inequality in one variable

Graphing Quadratic Inequalities in Two Variables

A **quadratic inequality in two variables**, x and y, can be written in one of the following forms, where a, b, and c are real numbers and $a \neq 0$.

$$y < ax^2 + bx + c \qquad y > ax^2 + bx + c$$
$$y \leq ax^2 + bx + c \qquad y \geq ax^2 + bx + c$$

The graph of any such inequality consists of all solutions (x, y) of the inequality. You can use the procedure below to graph quadratic inequalities in two variables.

- Graph the parabola with the equation $y = ax^2 + bx + c$. Make the parabola *dashed* for inequalities with $<$ or $>$ and *solid* for inequalities with $\leq$ or $\geq$.

- Test a point (x, y) that does not lie on the parabola to determine whether the point is a solution of the inequality.

- When the test point is a solution, shade the region of the plane that contains the point. When the test point is not a solution, shade the region that does not contain the point.

EXAMPLE 1 Graphing a Quadratic Inequality in Two Variables

Graph $y < -x^2 - 2x - 1$.

Graph $y = -x^2 - 2x - 1$. Because the inequality symbol is $<$, make the parabola dashed.

Test a point that does not lie on the parabola, such as $(0, -3)$.

$y < -x^2 - 2x - 1$	Write the inequality.
$-3 \overset{?}{<} -0^2 - 2(0) - 1$	Substitute.
$-3 < -1$ ✓	Simplify.

Because $(0, -3)$ is a solution, shade the region inside the parabola that contains $(0, -3)$.

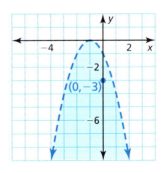

In-Class Practice

Self-Assessment

Graph the inequality.

1. $y \geq x^2 + 2x - 8$
2. $y > -x^2 + 2x + 4$

Graphing Systems of Quadratic Inequalities

A **system of quadratic inequalities** is a set of two or more quadratic inequalities in the same variables. Graphing a system of quadratic inequalities is similar to graphing a system of linear inequalities. First graph each inequality in the same coordinate plane. Then identify the region in the coordinate plane common to all of the graphs. This region is called *the graph of the system*.

EXAMPLE 2 Graphing a System of Quadratic Inequalities

Graph the system of quadratic inequalities.

$y < -x^2 + 3$ Inequality 1

$y \geq x^2 + 2x - 3$ Inequality 2

Graph $y < -x^2 + 3$. The graph is the red region inside (but not including) the parabola $y = -x^2 + 3$.

Graph $y \geq x^2 + 2x - 3$. The graph is the blue region inside and including the parabola $y = x^2 + 2x - 3$.

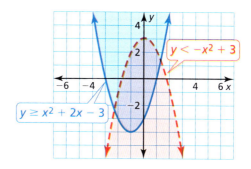

▶ Identify the purple region where the two graphs overlap. This region is the graph of the system.

> **Check**
>
> Check that a point in the solution region, such as (0, 0), is a solution of the system.
>
> $y < -x^2 + 3$ $y \geq x^2 + 2x - 3$
>
> $0 \stackrel{?}{<} -0^2 + 3$ $0 \stackrel{?}{\geq} 0^2 + 2(0) - 3$
>
> $0 < 3$ ✓ $0 \geq -3$ ✓

In-Class Practice

Self-Assessment

Graph the system of quadratic inequalities.

3. $y \geq x^2 + 2x - 1$
$y \geq 2x^2 + 4x - 1$

4. $y > x^2 + 1$
$y < -x^2 + x - 1$

 I don't understand yet.
 I can do it with help.
 I can do it on my own.
 I can teach someone.

Solving Quadratic Inequalities in One Variable

A **quadratic inequality in one variable**, x, can be written in one of the following forms, where a, b, and c are real numbers and $a \neq 0$.

$$ax^2 + bx + c < 0 \qquad ax^2 + bx + c > 0$$
$$ax^2 + bx + c \leq 0 \qquad ax^2 + bx + c \geq 0$$

You can solve quadratic inequalities using algebraic methods or graphs.

EXAMPLE 3 Solving a Quadratic Inequality Algebraically

Solve $x^2 - 3x - 4 < 0$ algebraically.

First, write and solve the equation obtained by replacing $<$ with $=$.

$x^2 - 3x - 4 = 0$	Write the related equation.
$(x - 4)(x + 1) = 0$	Factor.
$x = 4 \quad \text{or} \quad x = -1$	Zero-Product Property

The numbers -1 and 4 are the *critical values* of the original inequality. Plot -1 and 4 on a number line, using open dots because the values do not satisfy the inequality. The critical values partition the number line into three intervals. Test an x-value in each interval to determine whether it satisfies the inequality.

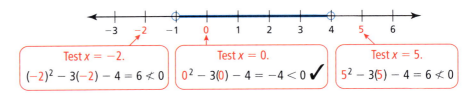

▶ So, the solution is $-1 < x < 4$.

Check
Graph the related equation $y = x^2 - 3x - 4$. Identify the x-values for which the graph lies below the x-axis.

$-1 < x < 4$

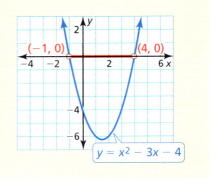

In-Class Practice

Self-Assessment

Solve the inequality algebraically.

5. $3x^2 - x - 5 \geq 0$

6. $2x^2 + 3x \leq 2$

Connections to Real Life

EXAMPLE 4 Writing and Solving a Quadratic Inequality

An archaeologist is roping off a rectangular region of land to dig for artifacts. The region must have a perimeter of 440 feet and an area of at least 8,000 square feet. Describe the possible lengths of the archaeological region.

Let ℓ represent the length (in feet) and let w represent the width (in feet) of the region.

$$\text{Perimeter} = 440 \qquad \text{Area} \geq 8,000$$
$$2\ell + 2w = 440 \qquad \ell w \geq 8,000$$

Solve the perimeter equation for w to obtain $w = 220 - \ell$. Substitute this into the area inequality to obtain a quadratic inequality in one variable.

$\ell w \geq 8,000$	Write the area inequality.
$\ell(220 - \ell) \geq 8,000$	Substitute $220 - \ell$ for w.
$220\ell - \ell^2 \geq 8,000$	Distributive Property
$-\ell^2 + 220\ell - 8,000 \geq 0$	Write in standard form.

Use technology to find the ℓ-intercepts of $y = -\ell^2 + 220\ell - 8,000$.

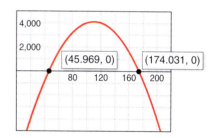

The ℓ-intercepts are $\ell \approx 45.969$ and $\ell \approx 174.031$. The solution consists of the ℓ-values for which the graph lies on or above the ℓ-axis. The graph lies on or above the ℓ-axis when $45.969 \leq \ell \leq 174.031$.

▶ So, the approximate lengths of the region are at least 46 feet and at most 174 feet.

Check Choose a length in the solution region, such as $\ell = 100$, and find the width. Then check that the dimensions satisfy the original area inequality.

$$2\ell + 2w = 440 \qquad\qquad \ell w \geq 8,000$$
$$2(100) + 2w = 440 \qquad\quad 100(120) \stackrel{?}{\geq} 8,000$$
$$w = 120 \qquad\qquad\qquad 12,000 \geq 8,000 \checkmark$$

In-Class Practice
Self-Assessment

7. **WHAT IF?** In Example 4, the area must be at least 8,500 square feet. Describe the possible lengths of the region.

3.6 Practice

Graph the inequality. (See Example 1.)

1. $y > x^2 - 9$
2. $y < -x^2$
3. $y \geq -2x^2 + 9x - 4$
4. $y \leq \left(x - \frac{1}{2}\right)^2 + \frac{5}{2}$

5. **SMP.3 ERROR ANALYSIS** Describe and correct the error in graphing $y \geq x^2 + 2$.

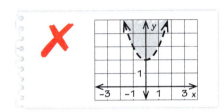

Graph the system of quadratic inequalities. (See Example 2.)

6. $y \geq x^2 - 3x - 6$
   $y \geq x^2 + 7x + 6$

7. $y \leq -x^2 + 4x - 4$
   $y < x^2 + 2x - 8$

8. $x^2 + y < 3x^2 + 2$
   $y < -x^2 + 5x + 10$

9. $3x^2 + y \leq -x - 3$
   $\frac{1}{2}x^2 + 2x \geq y - 2$

Solve the inequality algebraically. (See Example 3.)

10. $x^2 + 10x + 9 < 0$
11. $x^2 - 11x \geq -28$
12. $2x^2 - 5x - 3 \leq 0$
13. $\frac{1}{2}x^2 - x > 4$

14. A wire rope can safely support a weight W (in pounds) provided $W \leq 8{,}000d^2$, where d is the diameter (in inches) of the rope. Graph the inequality and interpret the solution.

Solve the inequality by graphing.

15. $x^2 - 3x + 1 < 0$
16. $\frac{3}{4}x^2 + 4x \geq 3$

17. **CONNECTION TO REAL LIFE** A rectangular fountain display has a perimeter of 400 feet and an area of at least 9,100 square feet. Describe the possible widths of the fountain. (See Example 4.)

18. **SMP.2** The number of teams that have participated in an engineering competition for high-school students over a recent period of time x (in years) can be modeled by $T(x) = 17.155x^2 + 193.68x + 235.81$, $0 \leq x \leq 6$. After how many years is the number of teams greater than 1,000?

19. **SMP.7** Consider the graph of the function $f(x) = ax^2 + bx + c$.

    a. What are the solutions of $ax^2 + bx + c < 0$? of $ax^2 + bx + c > 0$?

    b. The graph of g represents a reflection in the x-axis of the graph of f. For which values of x is $g(x)$ positive?

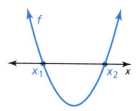

20. The length (in millimeters) of the larvae of a black porgy fish can be modeled by

    $$L(x) = 0.0058x^2 + 0.201x + 2.59, \ 0 \leq x \leq 44$$

    where x is the age (in days) of the larvae. At what ages is a larva's length typically greater than 10 millimeters? Explain how the given domain affects the solution.

21. **CONNECT CONCEPTS** The area A of the region bounded by a parabola and a horizontal line can be modeled by $A = \frac{2}{3}bh$, where b and h are as defined in the diagram. Find the area of the region determined by each pair of inequalities.

    a. $y \leq -x^2 + 4x$
       $y \geq 0$

    b. $y \geq x^2 - 4x - 5$
       $y \leq 7$

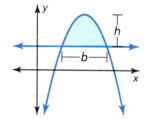

22. The arch of a bridge can be modeled by $y = -0.0625x^2 + 1.25x + 5.75$, where x and y are measured in feet.

    a. What is the maximum width that a truck 11 feet tall can have and still make it under the arch?

    b. What is the maximum height that a truck 7 feet wide can have and still make it under the arch?

23. The graph shows a system of quadratic inequalities.

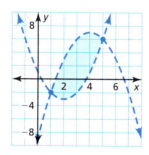

    a. Identify two solutions of the system.

    b. Are the points $(1, -2)$ and $(5, 6)$ solutions of the system?

    c. Explain whether it is possible to change the inequality symbol(s) so that one, but not both, of the points in part (b) is a solution of the system.

24. Consider the system of inequalities below, where a, b, c, and d are real numbers, $a < b$, and $c < d$. Write the solutions of the system, if any, as an inequality.

    $$y \leq -ax^2 + c$$
    $$y < -bx^2 + d$$

Interpreting Data

PARABOLAS IN ARCHITECTURE L'Oceanogràfic is an oceanarium in Valencia, Spain. It is home to 500 different species of animals and features a unique architectural design.

25. Trace the outline of the entrance shown using graph paper. Explain whether the outline appears to be a parabola.

26. Research why an architect might choose to use a parabolic design. Then find two other pieces of architecture that include parabolic elements.

Review & Refresh

27. Solve the system of nonlinear equations using the graph.

    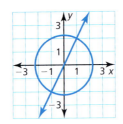

28. Solve the system.
    $$3x - y + 2z = 16$$
    $$-2x + 4y + 3z = -2$$
    $$6x + y - z = 0$$

29. Write an equation of the line that passes through $(2, -2)$ and is perpendicular to $y = \frac{1}{3}x - 6$.

30. Write an equation for the nth term of the geometric sequence. Then find a_8.

n	1	2	3	4
a_n	6	18	54	162

31. The linear function $y = 50 + 30x$ represents the cost y (in dollars) of renting a picnic pavilion for x hours. The pavilion can be rented for at most 24 hours.

    a. Interpret the terms and coefficient in the equation.

    b. Find the domain of the function. Is the domain discrete or continuous?

3 Chapter Review

Rate your understanding of each section.

1. I don't understand yet.
2. I can do it with help.
3. I can do it on my own.
4. I can teach someone.

3.1 Solving Quadratic Equations (pp. 85–94)

⊙ **Learning Target:** Solve quadratic equations graphically and algebraically.

Vocabulary
quadratic equation in one variable
root of an equation
zero of a function

Solve the equation using any method.

1. $6x^2 = 150$
2. $3x^2 - 4 = 8$
3. $x^2 + 6x - 16 = 0$
4. $2x^2 - 17x = -30$

5. Write a function that represents the height h (in feet) of a ball t seconds after it is dropped from an initial height of 3 feet. How long is the ball in the air?

6. For each case, determine whether it is possible for $ax^2 + bx + c = 0$ to have no solutions.

    a. $a > 0, c > 0$
    b. $a > 0, c < 0$
    c. $a < 0, c > 0$
    d. $a < 0, c < 0$

7. A rectangular enclosure at a zoo is 35 feet long by 18 feet wide. The zoo doubles the area of the enclosure by adding the same distance to the length and width. What are the new dimensions of the enclosure?

3.2 Complex Numbers (pp. 95–104)

⊙ **Learning Target:** Understand the imaginary unit i and perform operations with complex numbers.

Vocabulary
imaginary unit i
complex number
imaginary number
pure imaginary number
complex conjugates

8. Find the values of x and y that satisfy the equation $36 - yi = 4x + 3i$.

Perform the operation. Write the answer in standard form.

9. $(-2 + 3i) + (7 - 6i)$
10. $(9 + 3i) - (-2 - 7i)$
11. $(5 + 6i)(-4 + 7i)$
12. $(8 + 2i)(8 - 2i)$

13. Find the impedance of the series circuit.

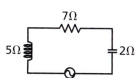

14. Solve $7x^2 + 21 = 0$.

15. Find all complex zeros of $f(x) = 2x^2 + 32$.

3.3 Completing the Square (pp. 105–114)

Learning Target: Solve quadratic equations and rewrite quadratic functions by completing the square.

Vocabulary
completing the square

Solve the equation by completing the square.

16. $x^2 + 16x + 17 = 0$

17. $9x(x - 6) = 81$

Write the equation in standard form and tell whether it represents a circle or a parabola. Then graph the equation.

18. $y^2 - x + 12y + 40 = 0$

19. $x^2 + y^2 - 2x + 8y = 64$

20. Write $y = x^2 - 2x + 20$ in vertex form. Then identify the vertex.

21. The path of a T-shirt launched from a T-shirt cannon is modeled by the function shown, where x is the horizontal distance (in feet) and y is the vertical distance (in feet). Find the maximum height of the T-shirt.

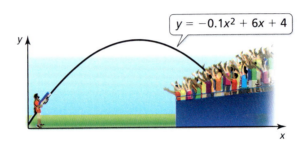

$y = -0.1x^2 + 6x + 4$

3.4 Using the Quadratic Formula (pp. 115–124)

Learning Target: Solve and analyze quadratic equations using the Quadratic Formula.

Vocabulary
Quadratic Formula
discriminant

Solve the equation using the Quadratic Formula.

22. $-x^2 + 5x = 2$

23. $2x^2 + 5x = 3$

24. $-x^2 + 3x = 2.25$

25. $3x^2 - 12x + 13 = 0$

Find the discriminant of the quadratic equation and describe the number and type of solutions of the equation.

26. $-x^2 - 6x - 9 = 0$

27. $x^2 - 2x - 9 = 0$

28. Find integer values for a and c so that the equation $ax^2 + 12x = -c$ has exactly one real solution.

29. A researcher studies the *generality* of plant and ant species on Mount Wilhelm in Papua New Guinea. Generality is the number of plant species per ant species. The generality can be modeled by the function $g(x) = 0.000004x^2 - 0.0119x + 10.605$, where x is the elevation (in meters). At what elevation(s) do you expect to find a generality of 3 plant species per ant species?

3.5 Solving Nonlinear Systems of Equations (pp. 125–132)

Learning Target: Solve nonlinear systems graphically and algebraically.

Vocabulary
system of nonlinear equations

Use the graph to solve the system.

30. $y = -3x^2 - 24x - 47$
    $y = 4(x + 4)^2 + 1$

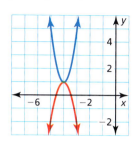

31. $y = -0.25(x - 5)^2 + 8$
    $y = 0.5x^2 - 5x + 8.5$

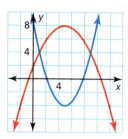

Solve the system by any method.

32. $2x^2 - 2 = y$
    $-2x + 2 = y$

33. $x^2 - 6x + 13 = y$
    $-y = -2x + 3$

34. Solve $-3x^2 + 5x - 1 = 5x^2 - 8x - 3$ by graphing.

35. The graph of quadratic function f has a vertex at $(2, 5)$ and a y-intercept of 1. The graph of linear function g has a slope of $-\frac{1}{2}$ and passes through the point $(8, -3)$. Solve $f(x) = g(x)$.

3.6 Quadratic Inequalities (pp. 133–140)

Learning Target: Graph and solve quadratic inequalities.

Vocabulary
quadratic inequality in two variables
system of quadratic inequalities
quadratic inequality in one variable

Graph the inequality.

36. $y > x^2 + 8x + 16$

37. $x^2 + y \leq 7x - 12$

Graph the system of quadratic inequalities.

38. $x^2 - 4x + 8 > y$
    $-x^2 + 4x + 2 \leq y$

39. $2x^2 - x \leq y + 5$
    $0.5x^2 > y - 2x - 1$

Solve the inequality.

40. $3x^2 + 3x - 60 \geq 0$

41. $3x^2 + 2 \leq 5x$

42. For each point, complete the inequality with $<, \leq, \geq,$ or $>$ so that the point is a solution of the inequality. Justify your answers.

$4x^2 - 3x \;\square\; y + 6$

a. $(-1, -1)$
b. $(1, -4)$
c. $(2, 4)$

3 PERFORMANCE TASK
SMP.2

RADIOACTIVE!

- When a uranium atom absorbs an extra neutron inside a reactor, the atom becomes unstable and splits in a process called *nuclear fission*.
- Nuclear fission releases energy in the form of radiation and heat, which is used to produce steam.
- The steam turns large turbines that drive generators to make electricity.
- Some of the steam is turned back into liquid water in a cooling tower and recycled back into the system.

Number of Operable Nuclear Reactors Worldwide

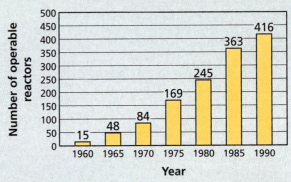

Electricity Generation in a Nuclear Power Plant

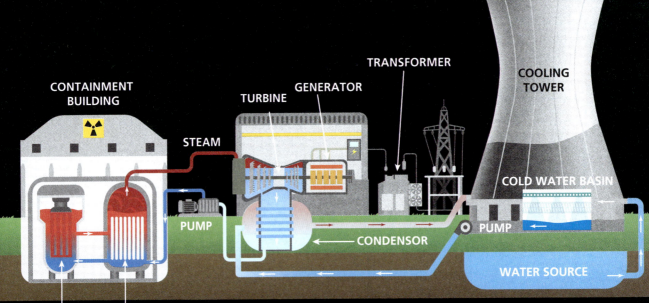

Analyzing Data

Use the information on the previous page to complete the following exercises.

1 Explain what is shown in the display. What do you notice? What do you wonder?

2 Use a model to estimate when there were 300 operable nuclear reactors worldwide.

NUCLEAR GROWTH

Use your model above to approximate when there are 500 operable reactors worldwide. Then use the Internet to compare your estimates with actual data. Describe any significant differences. Explain what factors may have contributed to those differences.

Use the actual data to write a quadratic model for the number of reactors from 1960 to 2020. Explain whether you expect the model to be reliable for years after 2020.

Connecting Big Ideas

For use after Chapter 3.
SMP.7

INFLATION!

The consumer price index (CPI) describes *inflation*, or the increase in prices over time. One way to report the CPI is to compare current prices to average prices from 1982 to 1984. For example, a CPI of 132 means that prices have increased 32% from the original averages.

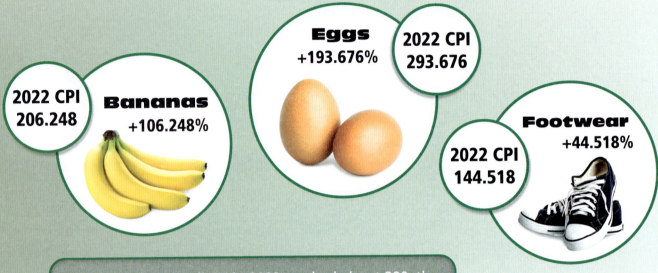

- Bananas: 2022 CPI 206.248, +106.248%
- Eggs: 2022 CPI 293.676, +193.676%
- Footwear: 2022 CPI 144.518, +44.518%

Although the overall CPI in 2022 reached about 290, the CPI for college tuition and fees skyrocketed to over 900.

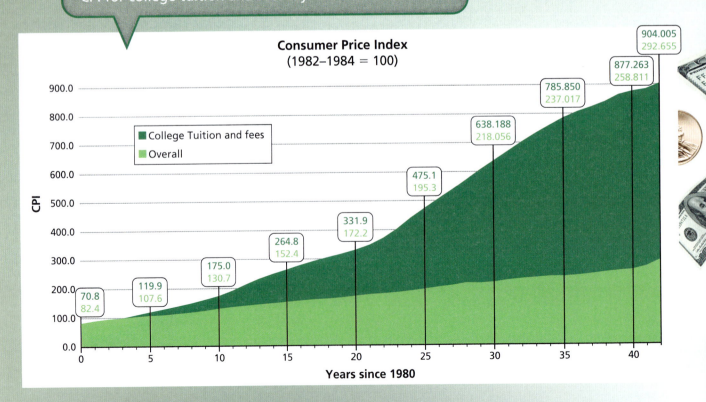

Consumer Price Index (1982–1984 = 100)

- College Tuition and fees
- Overall

Years since 1980	College Tuition	Overall
0	70.8	82.4
5	119.9	107.6
10	175.0	130.7
15	264.8	152.4
20	331.9	172.2
25	475.1	195.3
30	638.188	218.056
35	785.850	237.017
40	877.263	258.811
~42	904.005	292.655

146 Connecting Big Ideas

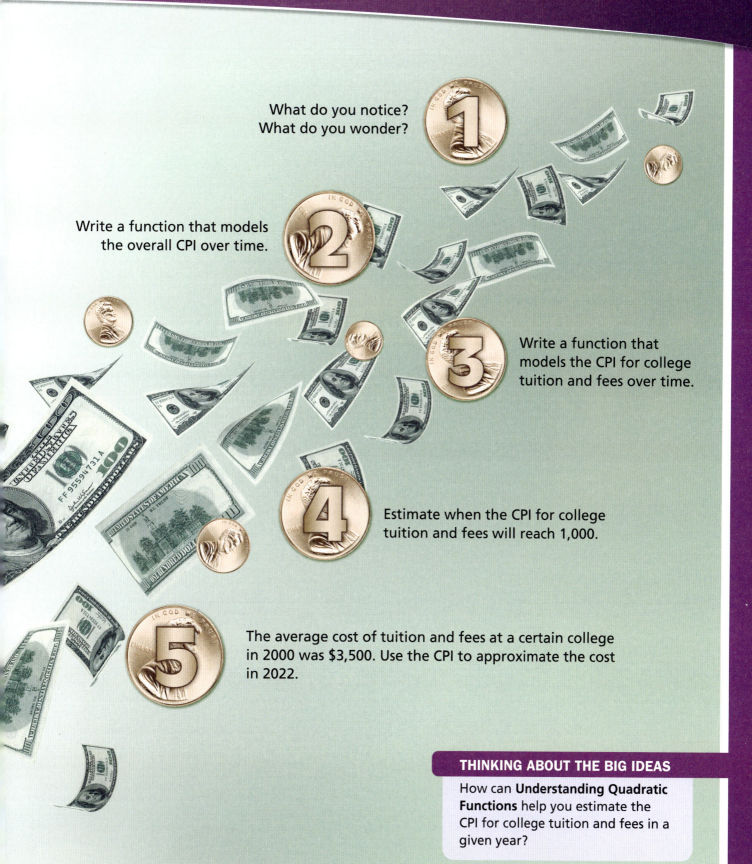

1 What do you notice? What do you wonder?

2 Write a function that models the overall CPI over time.

3 Write a function that models the CPI for college tuition and fees over time.

4 Estimate when the CPI for college tuition and fees will reach 1,000.

5 The average cost of tuition and fees at a certain college in 2000 was $3,500. Use the CPI to approximate the cost in 2022.

THINKING ABOUT THE BIG IDEAS

How can **Understanding Quadratic Functions** help you estimate the CPI for college tuition and fees in a given year?

Connecting Big Ideas

4 Polynomial Functions

- 4.1 Graphing Polynomial Functions
- 4.2 Adding, Subtracting, and Multiplying Polynomials
- 4.3 Dividing Polynomials
- 4.4 Factoring Polynomials
- 4.5 Solving Polynomial Equations
- 4.6 The Fundamental Theorem of Algebra
- 4.7 Transformations of Polynomial Functions
- 4.8 Analyzing Graphs of Polynomial Functions
- 4.9 Modeling with Polynomial Functions

NATIONAL GEOGRAPHIC EXPLORER
Robert Lonsinger WILDLIFE ECOLOGIST

Dr. Robert Lonsinger specializes in the conservation of endangered carnivore species. Dr. Lonsinger combines traditional approaches for monitoring wildlife populations with innovative conservation genetic techniques, noninvasive monitoring, and modeling platforms. He focuses on carnivores and their prey within desert and grassland communities.

- What are some examples of carnivorous mammals that live in deserts in the United States? in grasslands in the United States? Give examples of prey for each of these carnivore species.
- What is noninvasive monitoring of a species?

PERFORMANCE TASK
In 1995, wolves were reintroduced to Yellowstone National Park. In the Performance Task on pages 224 and 225, you will study the effects wolves have on the elk population in Yellowstone.

Wildlife Conservation

Big Idea of the Chapter
Understand Polynomial Functions

A polynomial function is a monomial or sum of monomials. Common types of polynomial functions include constant, linear, quadratic, and cubic functions. Polynomial functions can be used to model data, but are not always an exact fit.

The Florida manatee is a subspecies of the West Indian manatee. The main threats to manatees are boat accidents and lack of warm water habitats. Florida manatees were first listed as an endangered species in 1973. Due to conservation efforts, Florida manatees were removed from the endangered species list in 2017 and are now considered threatened. The graph shows the approximate Florida manatee population over several years.

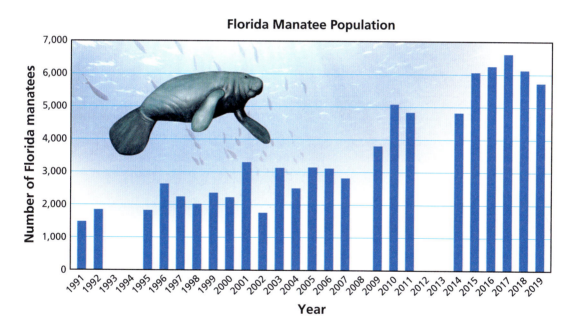

1. Describe the Florida manatee population from 1991 to 2019.

2. Write a linear function that can be used to model the Florida manatee population from 1991 to 2019.

3. Use your model to approximate the Florida manatee populations for the missing years in the graph. Then predict the Florida manatee population in 2030.

Getting Ready for Chapter 4

Adding and Subtracting Algebraic Expressions

EXAMPLE 1 Find $2(x + 4) + 3(6 - x)$.

$$2(x + 4) + 3(6 - x) = 2(x) + 2(4) + 3(6) + 3(-x) \qquad \text{Distributive Property}$$
$$= 2x + 8 + 18 - 3x \qquad \text{Multiply.}$$
$$= (2x - 3x) + (8 + 18) \qquad \text{Group like terms.}$$
$$= -x + 26 \qquad \text{Simplify.}$$

EXAMPLE 2 Find $(9x^2 + 4x) - (3x^2 - 6x + 3)$.

$$(9x^2 + 4x) - (3x^2 - 6x + 3) = 9x^2 + 4x - 3x^2 + 6x - 3 \qquad \text{Distributive Property}$$
$$= (9x^2 - 3x^2) + (4x + 6x) - 3 \qquad \text{Group like terms.}$$
$$= 6x^2 + 10x - 3 \qquad \text{Simplify.}$$

Find the sum or difference.

1. $9x - 4(2x - 1)$
2. $-(z + 2) - 2(1 - z)$
3. $-x^2 + 5x + x^2$
4. $(6x^2 - x + 9) + (5x - 4)$

Finding Volume

EXAMPLE 3 Find the volume of a rectangular prism with a length of 10 centimeters, a width of 4 centimeters, and a height of 5 centimeters.

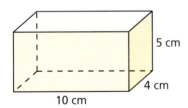

$$\text{Volume} = \ell w h \qquad \text{Write the volume formula.}$$
$$= (10)(4)(5) \qquad \text{Substitute 10 for } \ell, \text{ 4 for } w, \text{ and 5 for } h.$$
$$= 200 \qquad \text{Multiply.}$$

▶ The volume is 200 cubic centimeters.

Find the volume of the solid.

5. cube with edge length 4 inches

6. sphere with radius 2 feet

7. rectangular prism with length 4 feet, width 2 feet, and height 6 feet

8. cylinder with radius 3 centimeters and height 5 centimeters

4.1 Graphing Polynomial Functions

Learning Target: Graph and describe polynomial functions.

Success Criteria:
- I can identify and evaluate polynomial functions.
- I can graph polynomial functions.
- I can describe end behavior of polynomial functions.

INVESTIGATE Graphing Polynomial Functions

Work with a partner.

1. Determine whether $f(x)$ is a polynomial. If so, graph the function, describe the end behavior, and identify the degree of the polynomial.

   a. $f(x) = -x^2 - 1$ **b.** $f(x) = 2^x$ **c.** $f(x) = x^3 + 1$

   d. $f(x) = -\frac{1}{4}x^4 - x^3$ **e.** $f(x) = \sqrt{x}$ **f.** $f(x) = \dfrac{1}{x}$

   g. $f(x) = -4x^3$ **h.** $f(x) = 2x^4 - x$ **i.** $f(x) = x^3 + x^2$

2. Graph $y = x^3$ and $y = x^4$. Compare the graphs. One of these graphs is *cubic* and the other is *quartic*. Which do you think is which? Explain.

3. **MATCHING** Identify each function as *cubic* or *quartic*. Then explain your reasoning in matching each function with its graph.

   a. $f(x) = x^3 - x$ **b.** $f(x) = -x^3 + x$

   c. $f(x) = -x^4 + 1$ **d.** $f(x) = x^4 - x^2$

   A.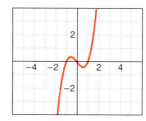

   C.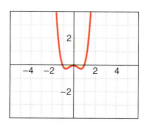

   B.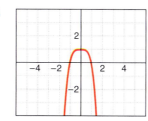

   D.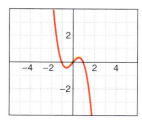

4. What are some characteristics of the graphs of cubic polynomial functions? quartic polynomial functions?

Vocabulary
polynomial
polynomial function
end behavior

Polynomial Functions

A monomial is a number, a variable, or the product of a number and one or more variables with whole number exponents. A **polynomial** is a monomial or a sum of monomials. A **polynomial function** is a function of the form

$$f(x) = a_n x^n + a_{n-1} x^{n-1} + \cdots + a_1 x + a_0$$

where $a_n \neq 0$, the exponents are all whole numbers, and the coefficients are all real numbers. For this function, a_n is the leading coefficient, n is the degree, and a_0 is the constant term. A polynomial function is in *standard form* when its terms are written in descending order of exponents from left to right.

Degree	Type	Standard Form
0	Constant	$f(x) = a_0$
1	Linear	$f(x) = a_1 x + a_0$
2	Quadratic	$f(x) = a_2 x^2 + a_1 x + a_0$
3	Cubic	$f(x) = a_3 x^3 + a_2 x^2 + a_1 x + a_0$
4	Quartic	$f(x) = a_4 x^4 + a_3 x^3 + a_2 x^2 + a_1 x + a_0$

EXAMPLE 1   Identifying Polynomial Functions

Determine whether each function is a polynomial function. If so, write it in standard form and state its degree, type, and leading coefficient.

a. $f(x) = -2x^3 + 5x + 8$

The function is a polynomial function that is already written in standard form. It has degree 3 (cubic) and leading coefficient -2.

b. $g(x) = -0.8x^3 + \sqrt{2}x^4 - 12$

The function is a polynomial function written as $g(x) = \sqrt{2}x^4 - 0.8x^3 - 12$ in standard form. It has degree 4 (quartic) and leading coefficient $\sqrt{2}$.

c. $h(x) = -x^2 + 7x^{-1} + 4x$

The function is not a polynomial function because the term $7x^{-1}$ has an exponent that is not a whole number.

d. $k(x) = x^2 + 3^x$

The function is not a polynomial function because the term 3^x does not have a variable base and an exponent that is a whole number.

In-Class Practice

Self-Assessment

Determine whether the function is a polynomial function. If so, write it in standard form and state its degree, type, and leading coefficient.

1. $f(x) = 7 - 1.6x^2 - 5x$
2. $p(x) = x + 2x^{-2} + 9.5$

EXAMPLE 2 Evaluating a Polynomial Function

Evaluate $f(x) = 2x^4 - 8x^2 + 5x - 7$ when $x = 3$.

$f(x) = 2x^4 - 8x^2 + 5x - 7$ Write the function.

$f(3) = 2(3)^4 - 8(3)^2 + 5(3) - 7$ Substitute 3 for x.

$= 162 - 72 + 15 - 7$ Evaluate powers and multiply.

$= 98$ Simplify.

▶ So, $f(3) = 98$.

The **end behavior** of a function is the behavior of the graph as x approaches positive infinity ($+\infty$) or negative infinity ($-\infty$). For a polynomial function, the end behavior is determined by its degree and the sign of its leading coefficient.

Degree: odd
Leading coefficient: positive

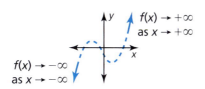

Degree: odd
Leading coefficient: negative

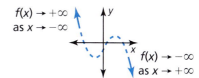

Degree: even
Leading coefficient: positive

Degree: even
Leading coefficient: negative

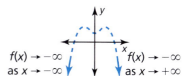

EXAMPLE 3 Describing End Behavior

Describe the end behavior of $f(x) = -0.5x^4 + 2.5x^2 + x - 1$.

The function has degree 4 and leading coefficient -0.5.

▶ Because the degree is even and the leading coefficient is negative, $f(x) \to -\infty$ as $x \to -\infty$ and $f(x) \to -\infty$ as $x \to +\infty$.

Check

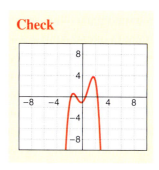

In-Class Practice

Self-Assessment

Evaluate the function for the given value of x.

3. $f(x) = -x^3 + 3x^2 + 9;\ x = 4$

4. $f(x) = 3x^5 - x^4 - 6x + 10;\ x = -2$

5. Describe the end behavior of $f(x) = 0.25x^3 - x^2 - 1$.

1 I don't understand yet.   **2** I can do it with help.   **3** I can do it on my own.   **4** I can teach someone.

Graphing Polynomial Functions

To graph a polynomial function, plot points to determine the shape of the graph's middle portion. Then use end behavior to sketch the graph.

EXAMPLE 4 **Graphing Polynomial Functions**

Graph $f(x) = -x^3 + x^2 + 3x - 3$.

To graph the function, make a table of values and plot the corresponding points. Use the end behavior and connect the points with a smooth curve.

x	−2	−1	0	1	2
f(x)	3	−4	−3	0	−1

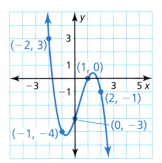

The degree is odd and the leading coefficient is negative. So, $f(x) \to +\infty$ as $x \to -\infty$ and $f(x) \to -\infty$ as $x \to +\infty$.

EXAMPLE 5 **Sketching a Graph**

Sketch a graph of the polynomial function f with the given characteristics. Then use the graph to describe the degree and leading coefficient of f.

- f is increasing when $x < 0$ and $x > 4$; f is decreasing when $0 < x < 4$.
- $f(x) > 0$ when $-2 < x < 3$ and $x > 5$; $f(x) < 0$ when $x < -2$ and $3 < x < 5$.

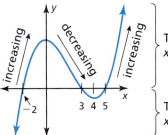

The graph is above the x-axis when $f(x) > 0$.

The graph is below the x-axis when $f(x) < 0$.

▶ From the graph, $f(x) \to -\infty$ as $x \to -\infty$ and $f(x) \to +\infty$ as $x \to +\infty$. So, the degree is odd and the leading coefficient is positive.

In-Class Practice

Self-Assessment

6. Graph $f(x) = x^4 + x^2 - 3$.

7. Sketch a graph of the polynomial function f with the given characteristics. Then use the graph to describe the degree and leading coefficient of f.

- f is decreasing when $x < -1.5$ and $x > 2.5$; f is increasing when $-1.5 < x < 2.5$.
- $f(x) > 0$ when $x < -3$ and $1 < x < 4$; $f(x) < 0$ when $-3 < x < 1$ and $x > 4$.

Connections to Real Life

EXAMPLE 6   Using a Polynomial Model

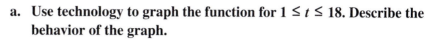 **ANIMAL POPULATION**   **AFRICAN WILD DOGS**   The African wild dog is one of the most endangered carnivores on Earth. A researcher estimates the population of African wild dogs under human care over an 18-year period. The population in year t can be modeled by the function

$$P(t) = 0.368t^3 - 11.45t^2 + 109.5t + 286.$$

a. Use technology to graph the function for $1 \leq t \leq 18$. Describe the behavior of the graph.

Using technology and the domain $1 \leq t \leq 18$, you obtain the graph shown.

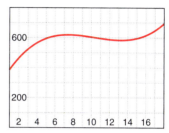

▶ The number of dogs increases from Year 1 to Year 7, decreases slightly from Year 7 to Year 13, and increases from Year 13 to Year 18.

b. What is the average rate of change in the number of dogs from Year 1 to Year 18?

Find the average rate of change over the interval $1 \leq t \leq 18$.

$$\frac{P(18) - P(1)}{18 - 1} = \frac{693.376 - 384.418}{17} = 18.174$$

▶ The average rate of change from Year 1 to Year 18 is about 18 dogs per year.

c. Explain whether you think this model can be used after Year 18.

Because the degree is odd and the leading coefficient is positive, $P(t) \to -\infty$ as $t \to -\infty$ and $P(t) \to +\infty$ as $t \to +\infty$. The end behavior indicates that the model has unlimited growth as t increases. While the model may be valid for a few years after Year 18, over time, unlimited growth is not reasonable.

In-Class Practice

Self-Assessment

8. **WHAT IF?** Repeat Example 6 using the following model for the African wild dog population.

$$P(t) = 0.0012t^4 + 0.321t^3 - 10.86t^2 + 106.8t + 289$$

4.1   Graphing Polynomial Functions   155

4.1 Practice

Determine whether the function is a polynomial function. If so, write it in standard form and state its degree, type, and leading coefficient. (See Example 1.)

▶ 1. $f(x) = -3x + 5x^3 - 6x^2 + 2$

2. $p(x) = \frac{1}{2}x^2 + 3x - 4x^3 + 6x^4 - 1$

3. $f(x) = 9x^4 + 8x^3 - 6x^{-2} + 2x$

4. $h(x) = \frac{5}{3}x^2 - \sqrt{7}x^4 + 8x^3 - \frac{1}{2} + x$

Evaluate the function for the given value of x. (See Example 2.)

5. $f(x) = 2x^3 - 5x^2 + 16;\ x = -4$

6. $p(x) = -x^5 + 11x^3 + 7;\ x = 3$

▶ 7. $h(x) = -3x^4 + 2x^3 - 12x - 6;\ x = -2$

8. $p(x) = 2x^3 + 4x^2 + 6x + 7;\ x = \frac{1}{2}$

9. **SMP.3 ERROR ANALYSIS** Describe and correct the error in analyzing f.

$f(x) = 8x^3 + 7x^5 - 9x - 3x^2 + 11$
- f is a polynomial function.
- The degree is 5.
- The leading coefficient is 8.
- $f(x) \to -\infty$ as $x \to -\infty$.
- $f(x) \to +\infty$ as $x \to +\infty$.

Describe the end behavior of the function. (See Example 3.)

10. $h(x) = -5x^4 + 7x^3 - 6x^2 + 9x + 2$

▶ 11. $f(x) = -2x^4 + 12x^8 + 17 + 15x^2$

12. $g(x) = 7x^7 + 12x^5 - 6x^3 - 2x - 18$

13. $f(x) = 11 - 18x^2 - 5x^5 - 12x^4 - 2x$

Graph the polynomial function. (See Example 4.)

14. $g(x) = x^3 + x + 3$

▶ 15. $p(x) = 3 - x^4$

16. $f(x) = 4x - 9 - x^3$

17. $h(x) = 5 + 3x^2 - x^4$

Describe the x-values for which (a) f is increasing, (b) f is decreasing, (c) $f(x) > 0$, and (d) $f(x) < 0$.

18.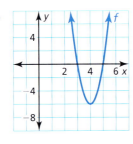

19.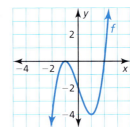

Sketch a graph of the polynomial function f **with the given characteristics. Use the graph to describe the degree and leading coefficient of the function** f. (See Example 5.)

20.
- f is increasing when $x < -1$ and $x > 1$;
  f is decreasing when $-1 < x < 1$.
- $f(x) > 0$ when $-1.5 < x < 0$ and $x > 1.5$;
  $f(x) < 0$ when $x < -1.5$ and $0 < x < 1.5$.

▶ 21.
- f is increasing when $-2 < x < 0$ and $x > 2$;
  f is decreasing when $x < -2$ and $0 < x < 2$.
- $f(x) > 0$ when $x < -3$, $-1 < x < 1$, and $x > 3$;
  $f(x) < 0$ when $-3 < x < -1$ and $1 < x < 3$.

22. **SMP.7 CONNECT CONCEPTS** The end behavior of a polynomial function f is described below. Describe the end behavior of (a) $g(x) = -f(x)$ and (b) $h(x) = f(-x)$.

- $f(x) \to +\infty$ as $x \to -\infty$
- $f(x) \to -\infty$ as $x \to +\infty$

▶ 23. **CONNECTION TO REAL LIFE** A researcher estimates the population of Sumatran tigers over an 18-year period. The function

$$P(t) = -0.077t^3 + 2.11t^2 - 7.1t + 166$$

models the population in year t. (See Example 6.)

a. Use technology to graph the function for $1 \leq t \leq 18$. Describe the behavior of the graph.

b. What is the average rate of change in the number of tigers from Year 1 to Year 18?

c. Explain whether you think this model can be used after Year 18.

24. **SMP.8** A graph is symmetric about the y-axis if for each point (a, b) on the graph, $(-a, b)$ is also a point on the graph. A graph is symmetric about the origin if for each point (a, b) on the graph, $(-a, -b)$ is also a point on the graph.

a. Use technology to graph $y = x^n$ when $n = 0, 1, 2, 3, 4, 5,$ and 6. In each case, identify the symmetry of the graph.

b. Describe the symmetry of the graphs of $y = x^{2n}$ and $y = x^{2n+1}$, for $n \geq 0$. Explain your reasoning.

25. **SMP.1 DIG DEEPER** A cubic polynomial function f has a leading coefficient of 2 and a constant term of -5. Explain your reasoning in completing the table.

x	−5	1	2
f(x)	?	0	3

4.1 Graphing Polynomial Functions

Interpreting Data

THREATENED SPECIES **SEA OTTERS** Sea otters are listed as a threatened species under the Endangered Species Act. Conservationists recorded the number of *stranded* sea otters along the California coast each year from 1985 to 2022. This data helps inform how to best care for the species.

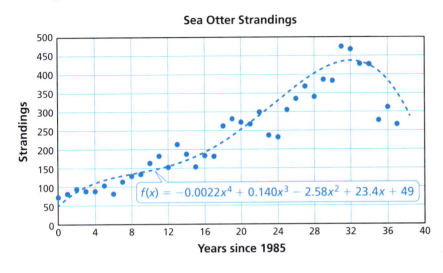

26. Describe the number of sea otter strandings from 1985 to 2022.

27. Do you think this model can be used for years after 2022?

28. What types of things do conservationists do to protect threatened or endangered species?

Review & Refresh

29. Simplify the expression.
    $$-wk + 3kz - 2kw + 9zk - kw$$

30. Write a function g whose graph represents the indicated transformation of the graph of $f(x) = -|x - 1| + 3$.

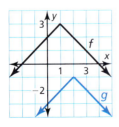

Solve the inequality.

31. $2x^2 - 7x - 4 \leq 0$ 32. $5x + 1 > 3x^2$

Describe the transformation of $f(x) = x^2$ represented by g. Then graph each function.

33. $g(x) = (x + 5)^2$

34. $g(x) = -\frac{3}{2}x^2$

35. You toss a penny into a park fountain. The penny leaves your hand 4 feet above the ground and has an initial vertical velocity of 25 feet per second. Does the penny reach a height of 10 feet?

36. Write an inequality that represents the graph.

158   Chapter 4   Polynomial Functions

4.2 Adding, Subtracting, and Multiplying Polynomials

Learning Target: Add, subtract, and multiply polynomials.

Success Criteria:
- I can add and subtract polynomials.
- I can multiply polynomials and use special product patterns.
- I can use Pascal's Triangle to expand binomials.

INVESTIGATE Expanding Binomials

Work with a partner.

1. Copy the diagram. Find the value of each expression. Write one digit of the value in each box.

   11^0
   11^1
   11^2
   11^3
   11^4

   What pattern(s) do you notice?

2. Find each product. Explain your steps.

   $(x + 1)^2$ $\qquad$ $(x + 1)^3$

   What pattern do you notice between the values of 11^n and the terms of $(x + 1)^n$ for $0 \leq n \leq 3$? Does this pattern continue for $(x + 1)^4$? Explain your reasoning.

3. Find each product. Explain your steps.

   $(a + b)^3$ $\qquad$ $(a - b)^3$

   What other pattern(s) do you notice when cubing these binomials?

4. Explain how you can use Pascal's Triangle to find each product. Then find the product.

   a. $(x + 2)^3$
   b. $(2x - 3)^3$

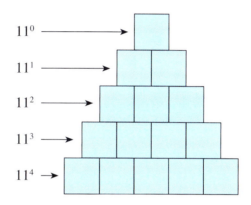

Pascal's Triangle

RESOURCES

4.2 Adding, Subtracting, and Multiplying Polynomials 159

Vocabulary
Pascal's Triangle
Binomial Theorem

Adding and Subtracting Polynomials

To add or subtract polynomials, add or subtract the coefficients of like terms. Note that the set of polynomials is closed under addition and subtraction.

EXAMPLE 1 Adding Polynomials Vertically and Horizontally

a. Add $3x^3 + 2x^2 - x - 7$ and $x^3 - 10x^2 + 8$ in a vertical format.

Align like terms vertically and add.

$$\begin{array}{r} 3x^3 + 2x^2 - x - 7 \\ + \ x^3 - 10x^2 + 8 \\ \hline 4x^3 - 8x^2 - x + 1 \end{array}$$

▶ The sum is $4x^3 - 8x^2 - x + 1$.

b. Add $9y^3 + 3y^2 - 2y + 1$ and $-5y^2 + y - 4$ in a horizontal format.

Group like terms and simplify.

$(9y^3 + 3y^2 - 2y + 1) + (-5y^2 + y - 4) = 9y^3 + 3y^2 - 5y^2 - 2y + y + 1 - 4$
$= 9y^3 - 2y^2 - y - 3$

▶ The sum is $9y^3 - 2y^2 - y - 3$.

EXAMPLE 2 Subtracting Polynomials Vertically and Horizontally

a. Subtract $2x^3 + 6x^2 - x + 1$ from $8x^3 - 3x^2 - 2x + 9$ in a vertical format.

Align like terms vertically, then add the opposite of the subtracted polynomial.

$$\begin{array}{r} 8x^3 - 3x^2 - 2x + 9 \\ - (2x^3 + 6x^2 - x + 1) \\ \hline \end{array} \quad \Rightarrow \quad \begin{array}{r} 8x^3 - 3x^2 - 2x + 9 \\ + -2x^3 - 6x^2 + x - 1 \\ \hline 6x^3 - 9x^2 - x + 8 \end{array}$$

▶ The difference is $6x^3 - 9x^2 - x + 8$.

b. Subtract $3z^2 + z - 4$ from $2z^2 + 3z$ in a horizontal format.

Write the opposite of the subtracted polynomial, then add like terms.

$(2z^2 + 3z) - (3z^2 + z - 4) = 2z^2 + 3z - 3z^2 - z + 4$
$= -z^2 + 2z + 4$

▶ The difference is $-z^2 + 2z + 4$.

In-Class Practice

Self-Assessment

Find the sum or difference.

1. $(2x^2 - 6x + 5) + (7x^2 - x - 9)$

2. $(3t^3 + 8t^2 - t - 4) - (5t^3 - t^2 + 17)$

[1] I don't understand yet. [2] I can do it with help. [3] I can do it on my own. [4] I can teach someone.

Multiplying Polynomials

To multiply two polynomials, multiply each term of the first polynomial by each term of the second polynomial. As with addition and subtraction, the set of polynomials is closed under multiplication.

EXAMPLE 3 **Multiplying a Binomial by a Monomial**

Multiply $x + 7$ and $-2x^2$.

$$(x + 7)(-2x^2) = (x)(-2x^2) + (7)(-2x^2)$$
$$= -2x^3 - 14x^2$$

▶ The product is $-2x^3 - 14x^2$.

EXAMPLE 4 **Multiplying Polynomials**

a. Multiply $-x^2 + 2x + 4$ and $x - 3$.

$$(x - 3)(-x^2 + 2x + 4) = (x - 3)(-x^2) + (x - 3)2x + (x - 3)4$$
$$= -x^3 + 3x^2 + 2x^2 - 6x + 4x - 12$$
$$= -x^3 + 5x^2 - 2x - 12$$

▶ The product is $-x^3 + 5x^2 - 2x - 12$.

b. Multiply $y + 5$ and $3y^2 - 2y + 2$.

$$(y + 5)(3y^2 - 2y + 2) = (y + 5)3y^2 - (y + 5)2y + (y + 5)2$$
$$= 3y^3 + 15y^2 - 2y^2 - 10y + 2y + 10$$
$$= 3y^3 + 13y^2 - 8y + 10$$

▶ The product is $3y^3 + 13y^2 - 8y + 10$.

EXAMPLE 5 **Multiplying Three Binomials**

Multiply $x - 1$, $x + 4$, and $x + 5$.

$$(x - 1)(x + 4)(x + 5) = (x^2 + 3x - 4)(x + 5)$$
$$= (x^2 + 3x - 4)x + (x^2 + 3x - 4)5$$
$$= x^3 + 3x^2 - 4x + 5x^2 + 15x - 20$$
$$= x^3 + 8x^2 + 11x - 20$$

▶ The product is $x^3 + 8x^2 + 11x - 20$.

In-Class Practice

Self-Assessment

Find the product.

3. $(4x^2 + x - 5)(2x)$

4. $(y - 2)(5y^2 + 3y - 1)$

5. Multiply $m - 2$, $m - 1$, and $m + 3$.

1 I don't understand yet. **2** I can do it with help. **3** I can do it on my own. **4** I can teach someone.

4.2 Adding, Subtracting, and Multiplying Polynomials

Special Product Patterns

You can use a model to develop a formula for the square of a binomial. This and several other special patterns are shown below.

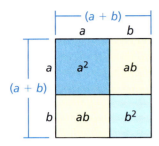

Sum and Difference
$(a + b)(a - b) = a^2 - b^2$

Example
$(x + 3)(x - 3) = x^2 - 9$

Square of a Binomial
$(a + b)^2 = a^2 + 2ab + b^2$
$(a - b)^2 = a^2 - 2ab + b^2$

Example
$(y + 4)^2 = y^2 + 8y + 16$
$(2t - 5)^2 = 4t^2 - 20t + 25$

Cube of a Binomial
$(a + b)^3 = a^3 + 3a^2b + 3ab^2 + b^3$
$(a - b)^3 = a^3 - 3a^2b + 3ab^2 - b^3$

Example
$(z + 3)^3 = z^3 + 9z^2 + 27z + 27$
$(m - 2)^3 = m^3 - 6m^2 + 12m - 8$

EXAMPLE 6 Proving a Polynomial Identity

Prove the polynomial identity for the cube of a binomial representing a sum: $(a + b)^3 = a^3 + 3a^2b + 3ab^2 + b^3$.

Expand and simplify the expression on the left side of the equation.

$$(a + b)^3 = (a + b)(a + b)(a + b)$$
$$= (a^2 + 2ab + b^2)(a + b)$$
$$= (a^2 + 2ab + b^2)a + (a^2 + 2ab + b^2)b$$
$$= a^3 + 2a^2b + ab^2 + a^2b + 2ab^2 + b^3$$
$$= a^3 + 3a^2b + 3ab^2 + b^3 \checkmark$$

▶ The simplified left side equals the right side of the original identity. So, the identity $(a + b)^3 = a^3 + 3a^2b + 3ab^2 + b^3$ is true.

EXAMPLE 7 Using Special Product Patterns

a. Find $(4n + 5)(4n - 5)$.

$(4n + 5)(4n - 5) = (4n)^2 - 5^2$ Sum and difference pattern
$\qquad\qquad\qquad\quad = 16n^2 - 25$ Simplify.

b. Find $(9y - 2)^2$.

$(9y - 2)^2 = (9y)^2 - 2(9y)(2) + 2^2$ Square of a binomial pattern
$\qquad\qquad = 81y^2 - 36y + 4$ Simplify.

In-Class Practice
Self-Assessment

6. Find (a) $(5a + 2)^2$ and (b) $(xy - 3)^3$.

7. Prove the polynomial identity for the cube of a binomial representing a difference: $(a - b)^3 = a^3 - 3a^2b + 3ab^2 - b^3$.

1 I don't understand yet. **2** I can do it with help. **3** I can do it on my own. **4** I can teach someone.

Pascal's Triangle and the Bionomial Theorem

Consider the expansion of the binomial $(a + b)^n$ for whole number values of n. When you arrange the coefficients of the variables in the expansion of $(a + b)^n$, you obtain a special pattern called **Pascal's Triangle**, named after French mathematician Blaise Pascal (1623–1662). In Pascal's Triangle, every number other than 1 is the sum of the closest two numbers in the row directly above it.

Row n	$(a+b)^n$	Binomial Expansion	Pascal's Triangle
0	$(a+b)^0 =$	1	1
1	$(a+b)^1 =$	$1a + 1b$	1　1
2	$(a+b)^2 =$	$1a^2 + 2ab + 1b^2$	1　2　1
3	$(a+b)^3 =$	$1a^3 + 3a^2b + 3ab^2 + 1b^3$	1　3　3　1
4	$(a+b)^4 =$	$1a^4 + 4a^3b + 6a^2b^2 + 4ab^3 + 1b^4$	1　4　6　4　1
5	$(a+b)^5 =$	$1a^5 + 5a^4b + 10a^3b^2 + 10a^2b^3 + 5ab^4 + 1b^5$	1　5　10　10　5　1

The **Binomial Theorem** states that for any positive integer n, the binomial expansion of $(a + b)^n$ is

$$(a + b)^n = C_0 a^n b^0 + C_1 a^{n-1} b^1 + C_2 a^{n-2} b^2 + \ldots + C_n a^0 b^n$$

where $C_0, C_1, C_2, \ldots, C_{n-1}$, and C_n are the values in the nth row of Pascal's Triangle. Note the following properties of the expansion of $(a + b)^n$.

- There are $n + 1$ terms and the sum of the exponents of a and b in each term is n.
- The exponent of a in the first term is n, and decreases by 1 in each successive term.
- The exponent of b in the first term is 0, and increases by 1 in each successive term.

EXAMPLE 8　Using the Binomial Theorem to Expand Binomials

Use the Binomial Theorem to expand $(x - 2)^5$.

Substitute $n = 5$, $a = x$, $b = -2$, and the coefficients from the fifth row of Pascal's Triangle (1, 5, 10, 10, 5, and 1) into the Bionomial Theorem.

$(x - 2)^5 = 1x^5 + 5x^4(-2) + 10x^3(-2)^2 + 10x^2(-2)^3 + 5x(-2)^4 + 1(-2)^5$

$= x^5 - 10x^4 + 40x^3 - 80x^2 + 80x - 32$

▶ The expansion of $(x - 2)^5$ is $x^5 - 10x^4 + 40x^3 - 80x^2 + 80x - 32$.

STUDY TIP

The calculator function nCr gives the rth value in row n of Pascal's Triangle.

In-Class Practice

Self-Assessment

Use the Binomial Theorem to expand the binomial.

8. $(z + 3)^4$

9. $(2t - 1)^5$

| 1 | I don't understand yet. | 2 | I can do it with help. | 3 | I can do it on my own. | 4 | I can teach someone. |

4.2 Practice

Find the sum. (See Example 1.)

1. $(3x^2 + 4x - 1) + (-2x^2 - 3x + 2)$

2. $(-5x^2 + 4x - 2) + (-8x^2 + 2x + 1)$

▶ 3. $(12x^5 - 3x^4 + 2x - 5) + (8x^4 - 3x^3 + 4x + 1)$

4. $(2x^5 + 7x^6 - 3x^2 + 9x) + (5x^5 + 8x^3 - 6x^2 + 2x - 5)$

Find the difference. (See Example 2.)

▶ 5. $(3x^3 - 2x^2 + 4x - 8) - (5x^3 + 12x^2 - 3x - 4)$

6. $(7x^4 - 9x^3 - 4x^2 + 5x + 6) - (2x^4 + 3x^3 - x^2 + x - 4)$

7. $(4x^5 - 7x^3 - 9x^2 + 18) - (14x^5 - 8x^4 + 11x^2 + x)$

8. $(3x - 9x^2 + 11x^4 + 11) - (2x^4 + 6x^3 + 2x - 9)$

9. **SMP.3 ERROR ANALYSIS** Describe and correct the error in finding the difference.

$$\begin{align}(x^2 - 3x + 4) - (x^3 + 7x - 2) \\ = x^2 - 3x + 4 - x^3 + 7x - 2 \\ = -x^3 + x^2 + 4x + 2\end{align}$$

Find the product. (See Examples 3 and 4.)

10. $7x^3(5x^2 + 3x + 1)$

▶ 11. $-4x^5(11x^3 + 2x^2 + 9x + 1)$

12. $(5x^2 - 4x + 6)(-2x + 3)$

▶ 13. $(x^2 - 2x - 4)(x^2 - 3x - 5)$

14. $(3x^2 + x - 2)(-4x^2 - 2x - 1)$

15. $(4x^2 - 8x - 2)(x^4 + 3x^2 + 4x)$

Find the product of the binomials. (See Example 5.)

16. $(x - 3)(x + 2)(x + 4)$

▶ 17. $(x - 2)(3x + 1)(4x - 3)$

18. $(2x + 5)(x - 2)(3x + 4)$

19. $(4 - 5x)(1 - 2x)(3x + 2)$

20. Your Spanish club wants to order 29 hooded sweatshirts that cost $31 each. Explain how you can use the polynomial identity $(a + b)(a - b) = a^2 - b^2$ and mental math to find the total cost of the hooded sweatshirts.

▶ 21. Prove the polynomial identity for a sum and difference: $(a + b)(a - b) = a^2 - b^2$. (See Example 6.)

22. Explain how to use a cube of a binomial identity to calculate 11^3.

Find the product. (See Example 7.)

23. $(x - 9)(x + 9)$ **24.** $(2y - 5)(2y + 5)$ **25.** $(2k + 6)^3$

26. $(3c - 5)^2$ **27.** $(pq - 2)^3$ **28.** $(wz + 8)^3$

Use the Binomial Theorem to expand the binomial. (See Example 8.)

29. $(6m + 2)^2$ **30.** $(2t + 4)^3$ **31.** $(2q - 3)^4$

32. $(g + 2)^5$ **33.** $(yz + 1)^5$ **34.** $(np - 1)^4$

CONNECT CONCEPTS Write an expression for the volume of the figure as a polynomial in standard form.

35.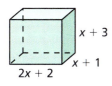

36.

37. **SMP.2 CONNECTION TO REAL LIFE** Two people make three deposits into their bank accounts. The accounts earn interest at the same rate r at the end of each year.

Person A		
Date	Transaction	Amount
01/01/2022	Deposit	$2,000.00
01/01/2023	Deposit	$3,000.00
01/01/2024	Deposit	$1,000.00

Person B		
Date	Transaction	Amount
01/01/2022	Deposit	$5,000.00
01/01/2023	Deposit	$1,000.00
01/01/2024	Deposit	$4,000.00

On January 1, 2025, Person A's account is worth $2{,}000(1 + r)^3 + 3{,}000(1 + r)^2 + 1{,}000(1 + r)$.

a. Write a polynomial for the value of Person B's account on January 1, 2025.

b. Write the total value of the two accounts as a polynomial in standard form. Then interpret the coefficients of the polynomial.

38. **SMP.8** The first four square numbers are represented below.

1   4   9   16

a. Find the differences between consecutive square numbers. What do you notice?

b. Show how the polynomial identity $(n + 1)^2 - n^2 = 2n + 1$ models the differences between consecutive square numbers. Then prove the identity.

39. A Pythagorean triple is a set of positive integers a, b, and c such that $a^2 + b^2 = c^2$. You can use the polynomial identity $(x^2 - y^2)^2 + (2xy)^2 = (x^2 + y^2)^2$ to generate Pythagorean triples.

a. Prove the polynomial identity.

b. Use the identity to generate the Pythagorean triple when $x = 6$ and $y = 5$. Then verify that your answer satisfies $a^2 + b^2 = c^2$.

Interpreting Data

SPECIAL PRODUCTS Models can be a useful tool to understand mathematical concepts. Use the model shown below and what you know about special product patterns to answer each question.

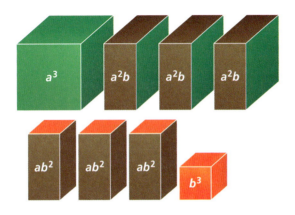

40. The blocks can be arranged to form a single solid figure. What is the figure?

41. Which special product pattern does the model represent?

42. Write the special product pattern for the expansion of $(a + b)^4$.

Review & Refresh

43. Write an equation of the parabola.

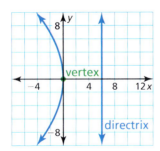

44. Describe the end behavior of the function.
$$f(x) = -2x^5 + 4x^3 - x^2 - 8$$

45. Evaluate $y = 2(0.5)^x$ when $x = 3$.

46. Graph the system of quadratic inequalities.
$$y > x^2 + 4x + 5$$
$$y \leq x^2 - 1$$

47. Multiply $(4 + i)(2 - i)$.

48. A contractor is hired to build an apartment complex. Each unit has a bedroom, kitchen, and bathroom. The bedroom will have the same area as the kitchen. The owner orders 980 square feet of tile to completely cover the floors of two kitchens and two bathrooms. Determine how many square feet of carpet is needed for each bedroom.

166 Chapter 4 Polynomial Functions

4.3 Dividing Polynomials

Learning Target: Divide polynomials and use the Remainder Theorem.

Success Criteria:
- I can use long division to divide polynomials by other polynomials.
- I can divide polynomials by binomials of the form $x - k$ using synthetic division.
- I can explain the Remainder Theorem.

INVESTIGATE Dividing Polynomials

Work with a partner.

1. Consider the polynomial $x^3 + 2x^2 - x - 2$. Use technology to explore the graph of the polynomial divided by the binomial $x + a$ for the given values of a. What do you notice? What can you conclude?

   a. $a = 1$
   b. $a = 2$
   c. $a = 3$
   d. $a = -1$
   e. $a = -2$
   f. $a = 4$

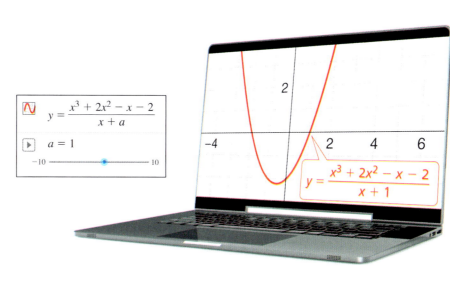

2. Repeat Exercise 1 for the polynomial $x^3 - 3x^2 - 10x + 24$ and the given values of a. What do you notice? What can you conclude?

   a. $a = -1$
   b. $a = 2$
   c. $a = -2$
   d. $a = 3$
   e. $a = -3$
   f. $a = 4$

3. Use technology to explore the graph of the polynomial $x^4 + 7x^3 + 9x^2 - 7x - 10$ divided by the binomial $x + a$ for several values of a. Make several observations about the graphs.

Vocabulary
polynomial long division
synthetic division

Long Division of Polynomials

When you divide a polynomial $f(x)$ by a nonzero polynomial divisor $d(x)$, you get a quotient polynomial $q(x)$ and a remainder polynomial $r(x)$.

$$\frac{f(x)}{d(x)} = q(x) + \frac{r(x)}{d(x)}$$

In this course, the degree of the divisor $d(x)$ is less than or equal to the degree of the dividend $f(x)$. Also, the degree of the remainder $r(x)$ must be less than the degree of the divisor. When the remainder is 0, the divisor *divides evenly* into the dividend. One way to divide polynomials is called **polynomial long division**.

EXAMPLE 1 Using Polynomial Long Division

Divide $2x^4 + 3x^3 + 5x - 1$ by $x^2 + 3x + 2$.

Write polynomial division in the same format you use when dividing numbers. Include a "0" as the coefficient of x^2 in the dividend. At each step, divide the term with the highest power in what is left of the dividend by the first term of the divisor. This gives the next term of the quotient.

$$\begin{array}{r}
2x^2 - 3x + 5 \\
x^2 + 3x + 2 \overline{\smash{)}\, 2x^4 + 3x^3 + 0x^2 + 5x - 1} \\
\underline{2x^4 + 6x^3 + 4x^2} \\
-3x^3 - 4x^2 + 5x \\
\underline{-3x^3 - 9x^2 - 6x} \\
5x^2 + 11x - 1 \\
\underline{5x^2 + 15x + 10} \\
-4x - 11
\end{array}$$

← quotient

Multiply divisor by $\frac{2x^4}{x^2} = 2x^2$.

Subtract. Bring down next term.

Multiply divisor by $\frac{-3x^3}{x^2} = -3x$.

Subtract. Bring down next term.

Multiply divisor by $\frac{5x^2}{x^2} = 5$.

← remainder

▶ $\dfrac{2x^4 + 3x^3 + 5x - 1}{x^2 + 3x + 2} = 2x^2 - 3x + 5 + \dfrac{-4x - 11}{x^2 + 3x + 2}$

Check Multiply the quotient by the divisor and add the remainder. The result should be the dividend.

$(2x^2 - 3x + 5)(x^2 + 3x + 2) + (-4x - 11)$

$= (2x^2)(x^2 + 3x + 2) - (3x)(x^2 + 3x + 2) + (5)(x^2 + 3x + 2) - 4x - 11$

$= 2x^4 + 3x^3 + 5x - 1$ ✓

In-Class Practice

Self-Assessment

Divide using polynomial long division.

1. $(2x^2 - 5x - 3) \div (x - 3)$

2. $(x^4 + 2x^2 - x + 5) \div (x^2 - x + 1)$

Synthetic Division

Synthetic division is a shortcut for dividing polynomials by binomials of the form $x - k$.

EXAMPLE 2 **Using Synthetic Division**

a. Divide $-x^3 + 4x^2 + 9$ by $x - 3$.

Write the coefficients of the dividend in order of descending exponents. Include a "0" for the missing x-term. Because the divisor is $x - 3$, $k = 3$. Write the k-value to the left of the vertical bar.

k-value → $3 \mid -1 \quad 4 \quad 0 \quad 9$ ← coefficients of $-x^3 + 4x^2 + 9$

Bring down the leading coefficient. Multiply the leading coefficient by k. Write the product under the second coefficient. Add.

$$3 \mid -1 \quad 4 \quad 0 \quad 9$$
$$ \quad -3$$
$$ -1 \quad 1$$

Multiply the previous sum by k. Write the product under the third coefficient. Add. Repeat this process for the remaining coefficient. The first three numbers in the bottom row are the coefficients of the quotient, and the last number is the remainder.

$$3 \mid -1 \quad 4 \quad 0 \quad 9$$
$$ \quad -3 \quad 3 \quad 9$$

coefficients of quotient → $-1 \quad 1 \quad 3 \quad 18$ ← remainder

▶ $\dfrac{-x^3 + 4x^2 + 9}{x - 3} = -x^2 + x + 3 + \dfrac{18}{x - 3}$

b. Divide $3x^3 - 2x^2 + 2x - 5$ by $x + 1$.

Use synthetic division. Because the divisor is $x + 1 = x - (-1)$, $k = -1$.

$$-1 \mid 3 \quad -2 \quad 2 \quad -5$$
$$ \quad -3 \quad 5 \quad -7$$
$$ 3 \quad -5 \quad 7 \quad -12$$

▶ $\dfrac{3x^3 - 2x^2 + 2x - 5}{x + 1} = 3x^2 - 5x + 7 - \dfrac{12}{x + 1}$

In-Class Practice

Self-Assessment

3. Divide (a) $(x^3 - 3x^2 - 7x + 6) \div (x - 2)$ and (b) $(2x^3 - x - 7) \div (x + 3)$ using synthetic division.

The Remainder Theorem

When you divide a polynomial $f(x)$ by $x - k$, the result is

$$\frac{f(x)}{x - k} = q(x) + \frac{r(x)}{x - k} \qquad \text{Substitute } x - k \text{ for } d(x).$$

$$f(x) = (x - k)q(x) + r(x). \qquad \text{Multiply both sides by } x - k.$$

Because either $r(x) = 0$ or the degree of $r(x)$ is less than the degree of $x - k$, you know that $r(x)$ is a constant function. So, let $r(x) = r$, where r is a real number, and evaluate $f(x)$ when $x = k$.

$$f(k) = (k - k)q(k) + r \qquad \text{Substitute } k \text{ for } x \text{ and } r \text{ for } r(x).$$

$$f(k) = r \qquad \text{Simplify.}$$

This result is stated in the *Remainder Theorem*.

Key Concept

The Remainder Theorem

If a polynomial $f(x)$ is divided by $x - k$, then the remainder is $r = f(k)$.

The Remainder Theorem tells you that synthetic division can be used to evaluate a polynomial function. So, to evaluate $f(x)$ when $x = k$, divide $f(x)$ by $x - k$. The remainder will be $f(k)$.

EXAMPLE 3 Evaluating a Polynomial

Use synthetic division to evaluate $f(x) = 5x^3 - x^2 + 13x + 29$ when $x = -4$.

```
-4 | 5   -1    13     29
   |     -20   84   -388
     5   -21   97   -359
```

▶ The remainder is -359. So, you can conclude from the Remainder Theorem that $f(-4) = -359$.

Check Check this by substituting $x = -4$ in the original function.

$$f(-4) = 5(-4)^3 - (-4)^2 + 13(-4) + 29$$
$$= -320 - 16 - 52 + 29$$
$$= -359 \checkmark$$

In-Class Practice

Self-Assessment

4. Use synthetic division to evaluate $f(x) = 5x^4 + 2x^3 - 20x - 6$ when $x = 2$.

1 I don't understand yet. **2** I can do it with help. **3** I can do it on my own. **4** I can teach someone.

4.3 Practice

Divide using polynomial long division. (See Example 1.)

1. $(x^3 + x^2 + x + 2) \div (x^2 - 1)$
2. $(3x^2 - 14x - 5) \div (x - 5)$
3. $(8x^3 - 3x + 1) \div (4x^3 + x^2 - 2x - 3)$
4. $(5x^4 - 2x^3 - 7x^2 - 39) \div (x^2 + 2x - 4)$

Divide using synthetic division. (See Example 2.)

5. $(x^3 - 4x + 6) \div (x + 3)$
6. $(x^2 + 8x + 1) \div (x - 4)$
7. $(3x^3 - 5x^2 - 2) \div (x - 1)$
8. $(x^4 + 4x^3 + 16x - 35) \div (x + 5)$

9. **SMP.3 ERROR ANALYSIS** Describe and correct the error in using synthetic division to divide $x^3 - 5x + 3$ by $x - 2$.

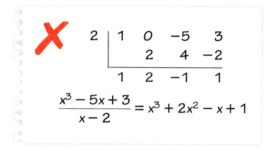

Use synthetic division to evaluate the function for the indicated value of x. (See Example 3.)

10. $f(x) = -x^2 - 8x + 30; x = -1$
11. $f(x) = x^3 - 2x^2 + 4x + 3; x = 2$
12. $f(x) = x^3 + x^2 - 3x + 9; x = -4$
13. $f(x) = -x^4 - x^3 - 2; x = 5$

14. **CONNECTION TO REAL LIFE** The profit P (in millions of dollars) earned by a company x years after 2019 can be modeled by $P = 0.1x^3 - x^2 + 2.5x + 1.7$, where $0 < x < 6$. Use synthetic division to show that the company earned a profit of $2.3 million in 2025.

15. You use synthetic division to divide $f(x)$ by $x - a$ and find that the remainder is 25. Your friend concludes that $f(25) = a$. Explain whether your friend is correct.

16. The graph represents the polynomial function $f(x) = x^3 + 3x^2 - x - 3$.

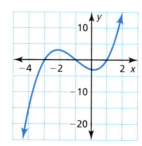

   a. When $f(x)$ is divided by $x - k$, the remainder is -15. What is the value of k?
   b. Use the graph to determine the remainders of $(x^3 + 3x^2 - x - 3) \div (x + 3)$ and $(x^3 + 3x^2 - x - 3) \div (x + 1)$.

Interpreting Data

CALIFORNIA CONDOR The California condor is the largest land bird in North America. In 1982, only 23 known California condors existed in the wild. Due to conservation efforts, the California condor population, both in the wild and in captivity, has steadily increased.

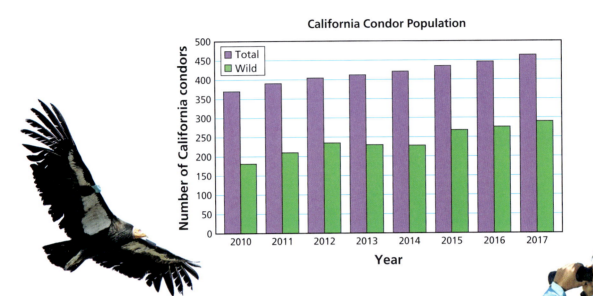

17. The total California condor population P and the wild California condor population W can be modeled by

    $P = 12.3x + 362$ and $W = 0.525x^3 - 7.19x^2 + 42.1x + 149$

    where x is the number of years after 2010. Find the number of California condors that exist in captivity. Write your answer in terms of x.

18. Use synthetic division to predict the total population of *wild* California condors in 2030.

Review & Refresh

19. Simplify $\sqrt{300x^3}$.

20. Write an equation of the parabola in vertex form.

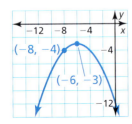

21. Find $(4k + 3)^3$.

22. Graph the function.

    $f(x) = x^3 - 3x + 1$

23. Find the zeros of the function.

    $g(x) = x^2 + 14x + 45$

24. City officials want to build a rectangular flower bed in a downtown park. The flower bed must have a perimeter of 50 feet and an area of at least 100 square feet. Describe the possible lengths of the flower bed.

4.4 Factoring Polynomials

Learning Target: Factor polynomials and use the Factor Theorem.

Success Criteria:
- I can find common monomial factors of polynomials.
- I can factor polynomials.
- I can use the Factor Theorem.

INVESTIGATE Factoring Polynomials

Work with a partner.

1. When sketching the graph of the function $f(x) = x^3 + 7x^2 + 7x - 15$, you notice that the sum of the coefficients of the terms is zero.

   $$1 + 7 + 7 + (-15) = 0$$

   a. What does this tell you about $f(1)$?

   b. Use the result of part (a) to algebraically find all the zeros of f. Use the zeros to sketch the graph.

2. **MATCHING** Use technology to match each polynomial function with its graph. Then write each polynomial function in factored form.

   a. $f(x) = x^2 + 5x + 4$
   b. $f(x) = x^3 - 2x^2 - x + 2$
   c. $f(x) = x^3 + x^2 - 2x$
   d. $f(x) = x^3 - x$
   e. $f(x) = x^4 - 5x^2 + 4$
   f. $f(x) = x^4 - 2x^3 - x^2 + 2x$

   A.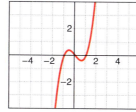

   B.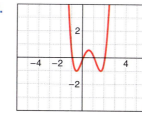

   C.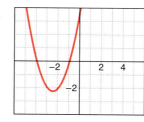

   D.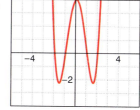

   E.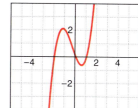

   F.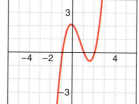

3. What information can you obtain from the factored form of a polynomial function?

Vocabulary
factored completely
factor by grouping
quadratic form

Factoring Polynomials

A polynomial with integer coefficients is **factored completely** when it is written as a product of unfactorable polynomials with integer coefficients.

EXAMPLE 1 Finding a Common Monomial Factor

a. Factor $x^3 - 4x^2 - 5x$ completely.

$$x^3 - 4x^2 - 5x = x(x^2 - 4x - 5)$$ Factor common monomial.
$$= x(x - 5)(x + 1)$$ Factor trinomial.

b. Factor $3y^5 - 48y^3$ completely.

$$3y^5 - 48y^3 = 3y^3(y^2 - 16)$$ Factor common monomial.
$$= 3y^3(y - 4)(y + 4)$$ Difference of two squares pattern

Example 1(b) uses the difference of two squares pattern. There are also patterns that you can use to factor the sum or difference of two *cubes*.

Sum of Two Cubes

$$a^3 + b^3 = (a + b)(a^2 - ab + b^2)$$

Difference of Two Cubes

$$a^3 - b^3 = (a - b)(a^2 + ab + b^2)$$

EXAMPLE 2 Factoring the Sum or Difference of Two Cubes

a. Factor $x^3 - 125$ completely.

$$x^3 - 125 = x^3 - 5^3$$ Write as $a^3 - b^3$.
$$= (x - 5)(x^2 + 5x + 25)$$ Difference of two cubes pattern

b. Factor $16s^5 + 54s^2$ completely.

$$16s^5 + 54s^2 = 2s^2(8s^3 + 27)$$ Factor common monomial.
$$= 2s^2[(2s)^3 + 3^3]$$ Write $8s^3 + 27$ as $a^3 + b^3$.
$$= 2s^2(2s + 3)(4s^2 - 6s + 9)$$ Sum of two cubes pattern

In-Class Practice

Self-Assessment

Factor the polynomial completely.

1. $x^3 - 7x^2 + 10x$
2. $8m^5 - 16m^4 + 8m^3$
3. $a^3 + 27$
4. $6z^5 - 750z^2$

 I don't understand yet.
 I can do it with help.
 I can do it on my own.
4 I can teach someone.

For some polynomials, you can **factor by grouping** pairs of terms that have a common monomial factor. The pattern for factoring by grouping is shown below.

$$ra + rb + sa + sb = r(a + b) + s(a + b)$$
$$= (r + s)(a + b)$$

EXAMPLE 3 **Factoring by Grouping**

a. Factor $z^3 + 5z^2 - 4z - 20$ completely.

$z^3 + 5z^2 - 4z - 20 = z^2(z + 5) - 4(z + 5)$	Factor by grouping.
$= (z^2 - 4)(z + 5)$	Distributive Property
$= (z - 2)(z + 2)(z + 5)$	Difference of two squares pattern

b. Factor $4y^3 + 8y^2 - 9y - 18$ completely.

$4y^3 + 8y^2 - 9y - 18 = 4y^2(y + 2) - 9(y + 2)$	Factor by grouping.
$= (4y^2 - 9)(y + 2)$	Distributive Property
$= (2y - 3)(2y + 3)(y + 2)$	Difference of two squares pattern

An expression of the form $au^2 + bu + c$, where u is an algebraic expression, is said to be in **quadratic form**. The factoring techniques you have studied can sometimes be used to factor such expressions.

EXAMPLE 4 **Factoring Polynomials in Quadratic Form**

a. Factor $16x^4 - 81$ completely.

$16x^4 - 81 = (4x^2)^2 - 9^2$	Write as $a^2 - b^2$.
$= (4x^2 + 9)(4x^2 - 9)$	Difference of two squares pattern
$= (4x^2 + 9)(2x - 3)(2x + 3)$	Difference of two squares pattern

STUDY TIP
The expression $16x^4 - 81$ is in quadratic form because it can be written as $u^2 - 81$ where $u = 4x^2$.

b. Factor $3p^8 + 15p^5 + 18p^2$ completely.

$3p^8 + 15p^5 + 18p^2 = 3p^2(p^6 + 5p^3 + 6)$	Factor common monomial.
$= 3p^2(p^3 + 3)(p^3 + 2)$	Factor trinomial in quadratic form.

In-Class Practice
Self-Assessment

Factor the polynomial completely.

5. $x^3 + 4x^2 - x - 4$

6. $3y^3 + y^2 + 9y + 3$

7. $-16n^4 + 625$

8. $5w^6 - 25w^4 + 30w^2$

4.4 Factoring Polynomials

The Factor Theorem

The *Factor Theorem* is a special case of the Remainder Theorem from the previous section.

> ### Key Concept
>
> **The Factor Theorem**
>
> A polynomial $f(x)$ has a factor $x - k$ if and only if $f(k) = 0$.

EXAMPLE 5 Determining Whether a Linear Binomial is a Factor

Determine whether (a) $x - 2$ is a factor of $f(x) = x^2 + 2x - 4$ and (b) $x + 5$ is a factor of $f(x) = 3x^4 + 15x^3 - x^2 + 25$.

a. Find $f(2)$ by direct substitution.

$$f(2) = 2^2 + 2(2) - 4$$
$$= 4 + 4 - 4$$
$$= 4$$

▶ Because $f(2) \neq 0$, the binomial $x - 2$ is not a factor of $f(x) = x^2 + 2x - 4$.

b. Find $f(-5)$ by synthetic division.

$$\begin{array}{r|rrrrr} -5 & 3 & 15 & -1 & 0 & 25 \\ & & -15 & 0 & 5 & -25 \\ \hline & 3 & 0 & -1 & 5 & 0 \end{array}$$

▶ Because $f(-5) = 0$, the binomial $x + 5$ is a factor of $f(x) = 3x^4 + 15x^3 - x^2 + 25$.

EXAMPLE 6 Factoring a Polynomial

Show that $x + 3$ is a factor of $f(x) = x^4 + 3x^3 - x - 3$. Then factor $f(x)$ completely.

Show that $f(-3) = 0$ by synthetic division.

$$\begin{array}{r|rrrrr} -3 & 1 & 3 & 0 & -1 & -3 \\ & & -3 & 0 & 0 & 3 \\ \hline & 1 & 0 & 0 & -1 & 0 \end{array}$$

Because $f(-3) = 0$, you can conclude that $x + 3$ is a factor of $f(x)$ by the Factor Theorem. Use the result to factor completely.

$f(x) = x^4 + 3x^3 - x - 3$	Write original polynomial.
$= (x + 3)(x^3 - 1)$	Write as a product of two factors.
$= (x + 3)(x - 1)(x^2 + x + 1)$	Difference of two cubes pattern

In-Class Practice
Self-Assessment

9. Determine whether $x - 4$ is a factor of $f(x) = 2x^2 + 5x - 12$.

10. Show that $x - 6$ is a factor of $f(x) = x^3 - 5x^2 - 6x$. Then factor $f(x)$ completely.

Connections to Real Life

EXAMPLE 7   **Factoring to Solve a Real-Life Problem**

A roller coaster starts at a height of 34 feet and then goes through an underground tunnel. The function shown gives the coaster's height h (in feet) after t seconds over the domain $\{t \mid 0 \leq t \leq 5\}$. How long is the coaster in the tunnel?

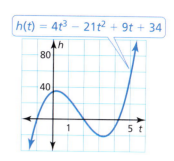

From the graph, two of the zeros appear to be -1 and 2. The third zero is between 4 and 5. Determine whether -1 is a zero using synthetic division.

$$\begin{array}{r|rrrr} -1 & 4 & -21 & 9 & 34 \\ & & -4 & 25 & -34 \\ \hline & 4 & -25 & 34 & 0 \end{array}$$

Because $h(-1) = 0$, you know that -1 is a zero of h and $t + 1$ is a factor of $h(t)$. Use the resulting quotient polynomial $4x^2 - 25x + 34$ to determine whether 2 is also a zero.

$$\begin{array}{r|rrr} 2 & 4 & -25 & 34 \\ & & 8 & -34 \\ \hline & 4 & -17 & 0 \end{array}$$

Because the remainder is 0, you know that 2 is a zero of h and $t - 2$ is a factor of $h(t)$. So, $h(t) = (t + 1)(t - 2)(4t - 17)$. Solve $4t - 17 = 0$ to find the remaining zero of the function.

$4t - 17 = 0$	Write the equation.
$4t = 17$	Add 17 to each side.
$t = \frac{17}{4}$, or 4.25	Divide each side by 4.

▶ The zeros are -1, 2, and 4.25. Only $t = 2$ and $t = 4.25$ are in the given domain. The graph shows that the roller coaster is in the underground tunnel for $4.25 - 2 = 2.25$ seconds.

In-Class Practice

Self-Assessment

11. In Example 7, does your answer change when you first determine whether 2 is a zero and then whether -1 is a zero? Justify your answer.

 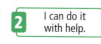

4.4 Practice

Factor the polynomial completely. (See Examples 1 and 2.)

1. $x^3 - 2x^2 - 24x$
2. $4k^5 - 100k^3$
3. $2q^4 + 9q^3 - 18q^2$
4. $10w^{10} - 19w^9 + 6w^8$
5. $x^3 + 64$
6. $y^3 + 512$
7. $4h^9 - 256h^6$
8. $16t^7 + 250t^4$

SMP.3 ERROR ANALYSIS Describe and correct the error in factoring the polynomial completely.

9.
$$3x^3 + 27x = 3x(x^2 + 9)$$
$$= 3x(x+3)(x-3)$$

10.
$$x^9 + 8x^3 = (x^3)^3 + (2x)^3$$
$$= (x^3 + 2x)[(x^3)^2 - (x^3)(2x) + (2x)^2]$$
$$= (x^3 + 2x)(x^6 - 2x^4 + 4x^2)$$

Factor the polynomial completely. (See Examples 3 and 4.)

11. $y^3 - 5y^2 + 6y - 30$
12. $3a^3 + 18a^2 + 8a + 48$
13. $x^3 - 8x^2 - 4x + 32$
14. $16n^3 + 32n^2 - n - 2$
15. $c^4 + 9c^2 + 20$
16. $49k^4 - 9$
17. $16z^4 - 625$
18. $3r^8 + 3r^5 - 60r^2$

Determine whether the binomial is a factor of the polynomial. (See Example 5.)

19. $f(x) = 2x^3 + 5x^2 - 37x - 60;\ x - 4$
20. $g(x) = 3x^3 - 28x^2 + 29x + 140;\ x + 7$
21. $h(x) = 6x^5 - 15x^4 - 9x^3;\ x + 3$
22. $t(x) = 48x^4 + 36x^3 - 138x^2 - 36x;\ x + 2$

Show that the binomial is a factor of the polynomial. Then factor the polynomial completely. (See Example 6.)

23. $g(x) = x^3 - x^2 - 20x;\ x + 4$
24. $t(x) = x^3 - 5x^2 - 9x + 45;\ x - 5$
25. $f(x) = x^4 - 6x^3 - 8x + 48;\ x - 6$
26. $h(x) = x^3 - x^2 - 24x - 36;\ x + 2$

178 Chapter 4 Polynomial Functions

27. **MATCHING** Match each function with its graph.

   a. $f(x) = (x - 2)(x - 3)(x + 1)$ **b.** $g(x) = x(x + 2)(x + 1)(x - 2)$

   c. $h(x) = (x + 2)(x + 3)(x - 1)$ **d.** $k(x) = x(x - 2)(x - 1)(x + 2)$

A.
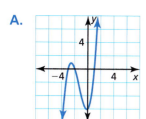

C.
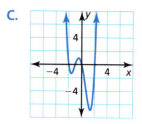

B.
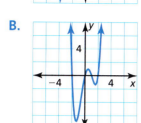

D.
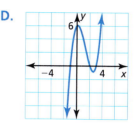

28. **CONNECTION TO REAL LIFE** The expected profit P (in millions of dollars) for a smart speaker manufacturer can be modeled by

$$P = -21x^3 + 46x$$

where x is the number (in millions) of speakers produced. The company expects a profit of $25 million when 1 million speakers are produced. What lesser number of speakers could the company produce and still expect the same profit? *(See Example 7.)*

Factor the polynomial completely.

29. $7ac^2 + bc^2 - 7ad^2 - bd^2$

30. $x^{2n} - 2x^n + 1$

31. $a^5b^2 - a^2b^4 + 2a^4b - 2ab^3 + a^3 - b^2$

32. **DIG DEEPER** Justify each step in finding the value of k such that $x - 7$ is a factor of $h(x) = 2x^3 - 13x^2 - kx + 105$.

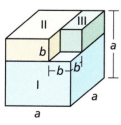

33. Consider the diagram shown.

   a. Explain why $a^3 - b^3$ is equal to the sum of the volumes of the solids I, II, and III.

   b. Write an algebraic expression for the volume of each of the three solids. Leave your expressions in factored form.

   c. Use the results from parts (a) and (b) to derive the difference of two cubes pattern.

34. **DIG DEEPER** Consider the equation $\dfrac{a^3 - b^3}{(a - b)^3} = \dfrac{31}{3}$, where a and b are real numbers and $a > b > 0$. Justify each step in finding $\dfrac{b}{a}$.

4.4   Factoring Polynomials

Interpreting Data

SMP.2 STOCK VOLATILITY Volatility is the rate at which the price of a stock changes over a particular period. Higher volatility often means higher risk. The graph shows the price of a stock each week in a year and a polynomial function f that represents the data.

Stock Price

35. How did the price of the stock change during the year?

36. Describe the possible degrees and leading coefficients of f.

37. Consider the function $g(x) = f(x) - 20.30$. Describe two methods that you could use to determine whether $(x - 25)$ is a factor of g. What do factors of g indicate in this context?

Review & Refresh

38. Divide $-x^3 + x^2 - 2x - 16$ by $x + 2$.

39. Write an expression for the area and perimeter of the figure shown.

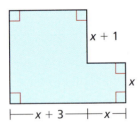

40. Determine whether the function is a polynomial function. If so, write it in standard form and state its degree, type, and leading coefficient.

$$f(x) = 5 + 2x^2 - 3x^4 - 2x - x^3$$

41. Determine whether the table represents an *exponential growth function*, an *exponential decay function*, or *neither*.

x	−1	0	1	2
y	80	20	5	1.25

Graph the function. Label the vertex and axis of symmetry.

42. $f(x) = -(x - 4)^2 + 3$

43. $g(x) = x^2 - 10x + 11$

44. $h(x) = -2(x - 7)(x + 3)$

45. Write the sentence as an inequality.
A number n plus 8.5 is no more than 17.

4.5 Solving Polynomial Equations

Learning Target: Solve polynomial equations and find zeros of polynomial functions.

Success Criteria:
- I can solve polynomial equations.
- I can write a polynomial function when given information about its zeros.

INVESTIGATE   Solving Polynomial Equations with Repeated Solutions

Work with a partner. Polynomial equations can have distinct solutions or *repeated solutions*.

1. Solve the equation algebraically. Then use the graph to describe the behavior of the related function near any repeated zeros. What do you notice?

    a. $x^3 - 6x^2 + 12x - 8 = 0$

    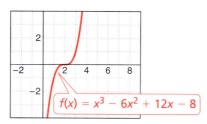

    b. $x^3 + 3x^2 + 3x + 1 = 0$

    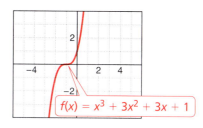

    c. $x^3 - 3x + 2 = 0$

    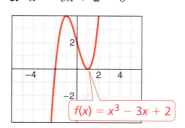

    d. $x^3 + x^2 - 2x = 0$

    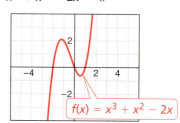

    e. $x^3 - 3x - 2 = 0$

    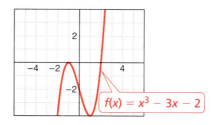

    f. $x^3 - 3x^2 + 2x = 0$

    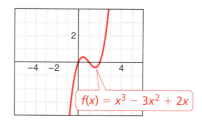

2. Graph the related function for each quartic equation and describe the behavior of the function near its zeros.

    a. $x^4 - 4x^3 + 5x^2 - 2x = 0$

    b. $x^4 - 2x^3 - x^2 + 2x = 0$

    c. $x^4 - 4x^3 + 4x^2 = 0$

    d. $x^4 + 3x^3 = 0$

3. Describe what it means when a polynomial equation has a repeated solution. How can you determine whether a polynomial equation has a repeated solution?

Vocabulary
repeated solution

Finding Solutions and Zeros

When a factor appears more than once in a polynomial equation $f(x) = 0$, it creates a **repeated solution**. You can use the Zero-Product Property and factoring to solve some higher-degree polynomial equations.

EXAMPLE 1 Solving a Polynomial Equation by Factoring

Solve $2x^3 - 12x^2 + 18x = 0$.

$2x^3 - 12x^2 + 18x = 0$	Write the equation.
$2x(x^2 - 6x + 9) = 0$	Factor common monomial.
$2x(x - 3)^2 = 0$	Perfect square trinomial pattern.
$2x = 0$ or $(x - 3)^2 = 0$	Zero-Product Property
$x = 0$ or $x = 3$	Solve for x.

▶ The solutions, or roots, are $x = 0$ and $x = 3$.

Check

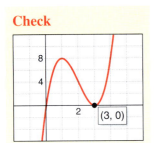

- When a factor $x - k$ of a polynomial is raised to an odd power, the graph of the related function crosses the x-axis at $x = k$.

- When a factor $x - k$ of a polynomial is raised to an even power, the graph of the related function touches (but does not cross) the x-axis at $x = k$.

EXAMPLE 2 Finding Zeros of a Polynomial Function

Find the zeros of $f(x) = -2x^4 + 16x^2 - 32$. Then sketch a graph of f.

$0 = -2x^4 + 16x^2 - 32$	Set $f(x)$ equal to 0.
$0 = -2(x^4 - 8x^2 + 16)$	Factor out -2.
$0 = -2(x^2 - 4)(x^2 - 4)$	Factor trinomial in quadratic form.
$0 = -2(x + 2)(x - 2)(x + 2)(x - 2)$	Difference of two squares pattern
$0 = -2(x + 2)^2(x - 2)^2$	Rewrite using exponents.

Both $x + 2$ and $x - 2$ are raised to an even power. So, the graph of f touches the x-axis at $x = -2$ and $x = 2$.

Use the original function to find the y-intercept and the end behavior. Use these characteristics to sketch a graph of f.

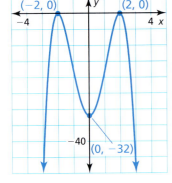

In-Class Practice

Self-Assessment

1. Solve $4x^4 - 40x^2 + 36 = 0$.

2. Find all the zeros of $f(x) = 3x^4 - 6x^2 + 3$. Then sketch a graph of f.

1 I don't understand yet. **2** I can do it with help. **3** I can do it on my own. **4** I can teach someone.

The Rational Root Theorem

> **Key Concept**
>
> **The Rational Root Theorem**
> If $f(x) = a_n x^n + \ldots + a_1 x + a_0$ has *integer* coefficients, then every rational solution of $f(x) = 0$ has the following form.
>
> $$\frac{p}{q} = \frac{\text{factor of constant term } a_0}{\text{factor of leading coefficient } a_n}$$

The Rational Root Theorem can be a starting point for finding solutions of polynomial equations. However, the theorem lists only *possible* solutions. To find the *actual* solutions, you must test values from the possible solutions.

EXAMPLE 3 **Using the Rational Root Theorem**

Find all the real solutions of $x^3 - 8x^2 + 11x + 20 = 0$.

The polynomial that defines the function $f(x) = x^3 - 8x^2 + 11x + 20$ is not easily factorable. Begin by using the Rational Root Theorem.

The leading coefficient of $f(x)$ is 1 and the constant term is 20. So, the possible rational solutions of $f(x) = 0$ are

$$x = \pm\frac{1}{1}, \pm\frac{2}{1}, \pm\frac{4}{1}, \pm\frac{5}{1}, \pm\frac{10}{1}, \pm\frac{20}{1}.$$

Test possible solutions using synthetic division until a solution is found.

Test $x = 1$:

```
1 | 1   -8   11   20
  |      1   -7    4
  |_____
    1   -7    4   24
```

$f(1) \neq 0$, so $x - 1$ is not a factor of $f(x)$.

Test $x = -1$:

```
-1 | 1   -8   11   20
   |     -1    9  -20
   |_____
     1   -9   20    0
```

$f(-1) = 0$, so $x + 1$ is a factor of $f(x)$.

Factor completely using the result of the synthetic division.

$(x + 1)(x^2 - 9x + 20) = 0$ Write as a product of factors.

$(x + 1)(x - 4)(x - 5) = 0$ Factor the trinomial.

▶ So, the solutions are $x = -1$, $x = 4$, and $x = 5$.

In-Class Practice

Self-Assessment

3. Find all the real solutions of $x^3 + 2x^2 - 13x + 10 = 0$.

1 I don't understand yet.   **2** I can do it with help.   **3** I can do it on my own.   **4** I can teach someone.

When the list of possible rational solutions or zeros is large, the search can be shortened by using a graph.

EXAMPLE 4 Finding Zeros of a Polynomial Function

Find all the real zeros of $f(x) = 10x^4 - 11x^3 - 42x^2 + 7x + 12$.

List the possible rational zeros of f: $\pm\frac{1}{1}, \pm\frac{2}{1}, \pm\frac{3}{1}, \pm\frac{4}{1}, \pm\frac{6}{1}, \pm\frac{12}{1}, \pm\frac{1}{2}, \pm\frac{3}{2}, \pm\frac{1}{5}, \pm\frac{2}{5}, \pm\frac{3}{5}, \pm\frac{4}{5}, \pm\frac{6}{5}, \pm\frac{12}{5}, \pm\frac{1}{10}, \pm\frac{3}{10}$.

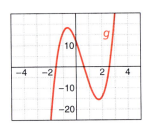

Use the graph of f to choose reasonable values from the list.

The values $x = -\frac{3}{2}$, $x = -\frac{1}{2}$, $x = \frac{3}{5}$, and $x = \frac{12}{5}$ appear to be reasonable.

$$-\frac{3}{2} \begin{array}{|ccccc} 10 & -11 & -42 & 7 & 12 \\ & -15 & 39 & \frac{9}{2} & -\frac{69}{4} \\ \hline 10 & -26 & -3 & \frac{23}{2} & -\frac{21}{4} \end{array}$$

$-\frac{3}{2}$ is *not* a zero.

$$-\frac{1}{2} \begin{array}{|ccccc} 10 & -11 & -42 & 7 & 12 \\ & -5 & 8 & 17 & -12 \\ \hline 10 & -16 & -34 & 24 & 0 \end{array}$$

$-\frac{1}{2}$ is a zero.

Factor out a binomial using the result of the synthetic division.

$f(x) = \left(x + \frac{1}{2}\right)(10x^3 - 16x^2 - 34x + 24)$ Write as a product of factors.

$ = \left(x + \frac{1}{2}\right)(2)(5x^3 - 8x^2 - 17x + 12)$ Factor 2 out of the second factor.

$ = (2x + 1)(5x^3 - 8x^2 - 17x + 12)$ Multiply the first factor by 2.

Any other zeros of f will also be zeros of $g(x) = 5x^3 - 8x^2 - 17x + 12$. Use g to continue testing reasonable values. Synthetic division shows that $\frac{3}{5}$ is a zero and $g(x) = \left(x - \frac{3}{5}\right)(5x^2 - 5x - 20) = (5x - 3)(x^2 - x - 4)$.

It follows that $f(x) = (2x + 1)(5x - 3)(x^2 - x - 4)$. Solve $x^2 - x - 4 = 0$.

$x = \dfrac{-(-1) \pm \sqrt{(-1)^2 - 4(1)(-4)}}{2(1)}$ Substitute 1 for a, -1 for b, and -4 for c in the Quadratic Formula.

$x = \dfrac{1 \pm \sqrt{17}}{2}$ Simplify.

▶ The real zeros of f are $-\dfrac{1}{2}, \dfrac{3}{5}, \dfrac{1 + \sqrt{17}}{2}$, and $\dfrac{1 - \sqrt{17}}{2}$.

In-Class Practice

Self-Assessment

4. Find all the real zeros of $f(x) = 3x^4 - 2x^3 - 37x^2 + 24x + 12$

1 I don't understand yet.   **2** I can do it with help.   **3** I can do it on my own.   **4** I can teach someone.

The Irrational Conjugates Theorem

> **Key Concept**
>
> **The Irrational Conjugates Theorem**
>
> Let f be a polynomial function with rational coefficients, and let a and b be rational numbers such that $\sqrt{b}$ is irrational. If $a + \sqrt{b}$ is a zero of f, then its *conjugate*, $a - \sqrt{b}$, is also a zero of f.

EXAMPLE 5 Using Zeros to Write a Polynomial Function

Write a polynomial function f of least degree that has rational coefficients, a leading coefficient of 1, and the zeros 3 and $2 + \sqrt{5}$.

Because the coefficients are rational and $2 + \sqrt{5}$ is a zero, $2 - \sqrt{5}$ must also be a zero by the Irrational Conjugates Theorem. Use the three zeros and the Factor Theorem to write $f(x)$ as a product of three factors.

$$\begin{aligned}
f(x) &= (x-3)\left[x - (2+\sqrt{5})\right]\left[x - (2-\sqrt{5})\right] &&\text{Write } f(x) \text{ in factored form.}\\
&= (x-3)\left[(x-2) - \sqrt{5}\right]\left[(x-2) + \sqrt{5}\right] &&\text{Regroup terms.}\\
&= (x-3)\left[(x-2)^2 - 5\right] &&\text{Multiply.}\\
&= (x-3)\left[(x^2 - 4x + 4) - 5\right] &&\text{Expand binomial.}\\
&= (x-3)(x^2 - 4x - 1) &&\text{Simplify.}\\
&= x^3 - 4x^2 - x - 3x^2 + 12x + 3 &&\text{Multiply.}\\
&= x^3 - 7x^2 + 11x + 3 &&\text{Combine like terms.}
\end{aligned}$$

Check You can check this result by evaluating f at each of the given zeros.

$$f(3) = 3^3 - 7(3)^2 + 11(3) + 3 = 27 - 63 + 33 + 3 = 0 \checkmark$$

$$\begin{aligned}
f(2+\sqrt{5}) &= (2+\sqrt{5})^3 - 7(2+\sqrt{5})(2+\sqrt{5}) + 3\\
&= 38 + 17\sqrt{5} - 63 - 28\sqrt{5} + 22 + 11\sqrt{5} + 3\\
&= 0 \checkmark
\end{aligned}$$

Because $f(2+\sqrt{5}) = 0$, by the Irrational Conjugates Theorem $f(2-\sqrt{5}) = 0$. $\checkmark$

In-Class Practice

Self-Assessment

Write a polynomial function f of least degree that has rational coefficients, a leading coefficient of 1, and the given zero(s).

5. $3 + \sqrt{2}$

6. $4, 1 - \sqrt{5}$

4.5 Solving Polynomial Equations

4.5 Practice

Solve the equation. (See Example 1.)

1. $z^3 - z^2 - 12z = 0$

2. $a^3 - 4a^2 + 4a = 0$

3. $v^3 - 2v^2 - 16v = -32$

4. $9m^5 = 27m^3$

5. $2c^4 - 6c^3 = 12c^2 - 36c$

6. $y^3 - 27 = 9y^2 - 27y$

Find the zeros of the function. Then sketch a graph of the function. (See Example 2.)

7. $h(x) = x^4 + x^3 - 6x^2$

8. $g(x) = -4x^4 + 8x^3 + 60x^2$

9. $h(x) = -x^3 - 2x^2 + 15x$

10. $p(x) = x^3 - 5x^2 - 4x + 20$

Explain whether $f(x) = 0$ has any repeated real solutions.

11.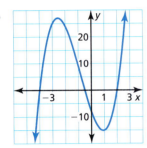

12.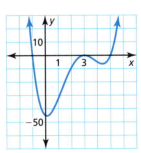

Find all the real solutions of the equation. (See Example 3.)

13. $x^3 + x^2 - 17x + 15 = 0$

14. $x^3 - 2x^2 - 5x + 6 = 0$

15. $x^3 - 10x^2 + 19x + 30 = 0$

16. $3x^3 + x^2 - 38x + 24 = 0$

Find all the real zeros of the function. (See Example 4.)

17. $f(x) = x^3 - 3x - 2$

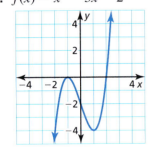

18. $f(x) = x^3 - 28x - 48$

19. $p(x) = 2x^3 - x^2 - 27x + 36$

20. $g(x) = 3x^3 - 25x^2 + 58x - 40$

21. $f(x) = 4x^3 - 20x + 16$

22. $f(x) = 4x^3 - 49x - 60$

23. $h(x) = 64x^4 + 32x^3 - 44x^2 - 12x + 9$

24. $f(x) = 3x^4 - 2x^3 - 25x^2 - 20x - 4$

25. **SMP.3 ERROR ANALYSIS** Describe and correct the error in listing the possible rational zeros of the function.

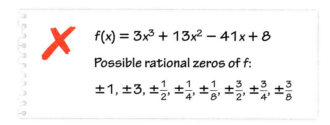

$f(x) = 3x^3 + 13x^2 - 41x + 8$

Possible rational zeros of f:

$\pm 1, \pm 3, \pm \frac{1}{2}, \pm \frac{1}{4}, \pm \frac{1}{8}, \pm \frac{3}{2}, \pm \frac{3}{4}, \pm \frac{3}{8}$

Write a polynomial function f of least degree that has rational coefficients, a leading coefficient of 1, and the given zero(s). (See Example 5.)

26. $-2, 3, 6$

27. $-2, 1 + \sqrt{7}$

28. $-2 + \sqrt{5}$

29. $0, 5, -5 + \sqrt{8}$

30. Archaeologists discovered several huge concrete blocks at the ruins of Caesarea. One of the blocks has a volume of 180 cubic meters and the dimensions shown. Find the value of x.

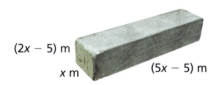

$(2x - 5)$ m

x m

$(5x - 5)$ m

31. You design a marble basin to hold a fountain for a city park. The sides and bottom of the basin are 1 foot thick. Its outer length is twice its outer width and outer height. What are the outer dimensions of the basin if it holds 36 cubic feet of water?

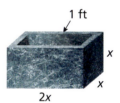

32. **SMP.1 DIG DEEPER** All the possible rational solutions and actual rational solutions of the equation below are shown. Complete the equation. Justify your answer.

Possible: $x = \pm 1, \pm 2, \pm 4, \pm 8, \pm 16$

Actual: $x = -1, 2$

$\left(x + \boxed{}\right)\left(x + \boxed{}\right)\left(x^2 + \boxed{}\right) = 0$

Find the value of k so that the given x-value is a solution of the equation.

33. $x^3 - 6x^2 - 7x + k = 0; x = 4$

34. $2x^3 + 7x^2 - kx - 18 = 0; x = -6$

35. $kx^3 - 35x^2 + 19x + 30 = 0; x = 5$

36. **SMP.7 DIG DEEPER** Let a_n be the leading coefficient of a polynomial function f and a_0 be the constant term. If a_n has r factors and a_0 has s factors, what is the greatest number of possible rational zeros of f that can be generated by the Rational Root Theorem?

Interpreting Data

ONLINE SHOPPING To start an online store, entrepreneurs choose a product, a domain name, an e-commerce platform, and a marketing strategy. The scatter plot shows the sales of an online business over time.

Sales of an Online Business

(Scatter plot: Sales in thousands of dollars vs. Months after opening)

37. The function $f(x) = 0.0002x^3 - 0.001x^2 + 0.079x - 0.03$ models the data in the graph. Use the model to project the sales after 3 years.

38. If you started an online store, what kinds of things would you do to promote your website?

Review & Refresh

Find the product or quotient.

39. $(2b + 3)(2b - 3)$

40. $(5x + 8)^2$

41. $(x^4 + 4x^3 - 10x^2 - 28x - 15) \div (x - 3)$

42. Write a function to model the data.

x	−1	0	1	2	3
y	4.5	8	10.5	12	12.5

43. Write the function $f(x) = x^2 + 7x + 13$ in vertex form. Then identify the vertex.

Solve the equation.

44. $-5 = 3x^2 + 7$

45. $9 = \frac{1}{2}(x - 4)^2 - 6$

46. The profit P (in millions of dollars) for a manufacturer of cell phone grips can be modeled by $P = -\frac{1}{4}(x^3 - 49x)$, where x is the number (in tens of millions) of grips produced. The company produces 50 million grips and makes a profit of $30 million. What lesser number of grips could the company produce and still make the same profit?

47. Write an equation of the parabola.

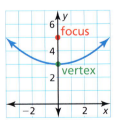

48. Write a function g whose graph represents a reflection in the y-axis of $f(x) = \frac{2}{3}x - 9$.

188   Chapter 4   Polynomial Functions

4.6 The Fundamental Theorem of Algebra

Learning Target: Use the Fundamental Theorem of Algebra to find all complex roots of polynomial equations.

Success Criteria:
- I can explain the Fundamental Theorem of Algebra.
- I can find all the zeros of a polynomial function.

INVESTIGATE Finding Zeros of Functions

Work with a partner.

1. Use technology to explore each function for several values of a, b, c, and d.

   $f(x) = (x + a)(x + b)$

   $g(x) = (x + a)(x + b)(x + c)$

   $h(x) = (x + a)(x + b)(x + c)(x + d)$

   How does the graph change when you change the values of a, b, c, and d? Does the number of real zeros change?

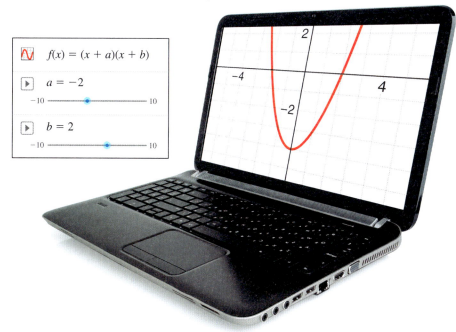

2. Repeat Exercise 1 for the following functions.

   $m(x) = ax^2 + bx + c$

   $n(x) = ax^3 + bx^2 + cx + d$

   $p(x) = ax^4 + bx^3 + cx^2 + dx + e$

3. Make a conjecture about the number of real zeros of $y = f(x)$ when the degree of $f(x)$ is a positive number n.

The Fundamental Theorem of Algebra

Several polynomial equations and their solutions are shown, including repeated solutions. Note the relationship between the degree of the polynomial $f(x)$ and the number of solutions of $f(x) = 0$.

Equation	Degree	Solution(s)	Number of solutions
$2x - 1 = 0$	1	$\frac{1}{2}$	1
$x^2 - 2 = 0$	2	$\pm\sqrt{2}$	2
$x^3 - 8 = 0$	3	$2, -1 \pm i\sqrt{3}$	3
$x^3 + x^2 - x - 1 = 0$	3	$-1, -1, 1$	3

Key Concept

The Fundamental Theorem of Algebra

Theorem If $f(x)$ is a polynomial of degree n where $n > 0$, then the equation $f(x) = 0$ has at least one solution in the set of complex numbers.

Corollary If $f(x)$ is a polynomial of degree n where $n > 0$, then the equation $f(x) = 0$ has exactly n solutions counting all repeated solutions. This means that an nth-degree polynomial function f has exactly n zeros.

EXAMPLE 1 Finding Solutions of a Polynomial Equation

How many solutions does $x^4 + x^3 + 8x + 8 = 0$ have? Find the solutions.

Because $x^4 + x^3 + 8x + 8 = 0$ is a polynomial equation of degree 4, it has four solutions. Notice that you can factor by grouping to begin solving the equation.

$(x^4 + x^3) + (8x + 8) = 0$	Group terms with common factors.
$x^3(x + 1) + 8(x + 1) = 0$	Factor out GCF of each pair of terms.
$(x + 1)(x^3 + 8) = 0$	Distributive Property
$(x + 1)(x + 2)(x^2 - 2x + 4) = 0$	Sum of two cubes pattern

The linear factors indicate that -2 and -1 are solutions. To find the remaining two solutions, solve $x^2 - 2x + 4 = 0$ by using the Quadratic Formula.

$$x = \frac{-(-2) \pm \sqrt{(-2)^2 - 4(1)(4)}}{2(1)} = 1 \pm i\sqrt{3}$$

▶ The solutions are $-2, -1, 1 - i\sqrt{3}$, and $1 + i\sqrt{3}$.

In-Class Practice
Self-Assessment

1. How many solutions does $x^5 - 4x^3 - x^2 + 4 = 0$ have? Find the solutions.

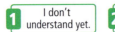   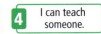

EXAMPLE 2 Finding the Zeros of a Polynomial Function

a. Find all the zeros of $g(x) = x^4 - 9x^2 - 4x + 12$.

Find the rational zeros of g. Because g is a polynomial function of degree 4, it has four zeros. The possible rational zeros are ± 1, ± 2, ± 3, ± 4, ± 6, and ± 12.

Using synthetic division, you can determine that -2 is a zero repeated twice and 1 and 3 are also zeros.

▶ The zeros of g are -2, -2, 1, and 3.

b. Find all the zeros of $f(x) = x^5 + x^3 - 2x^2 - 12x - 8$.

Find the rational zeros of f. Because f is a polynomial function of degree 5, it has five zeros. The possible rational zeros are ± 1, ± 2, ± 4, and ± 8.

Using synthetic division, you can determine that -1 is a zero repeated twice and 2 is also a zero.

Write $f(x)$ in factored form. Dividing $f(x)$ by its known factors $x + 1$, $x + 1$, and $x - 2$ gives a quotient of $x^2 + 4$. So,

$$f(x) = (x + 1)^2(x - 2)(x^2 + 4).$$

Find the imaginary zeros of f. Solving $x^2 + 4 = 0$, you get $x = \pm 2i$. This means $x^2 + 4 = (x + 2i)(x - 2i)$.

$$f(x) = (x + 1)^2(x - 2)(x + 2i)(x - 2i)$$

▶ From the factorization, the zeros of f are -1, -1, 2, $-2i$, and $2i$.

Check

The graph of f and the real zeros are shown.

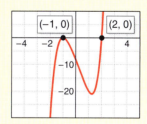

Notice that only the *real* zeros appear as x-intercepts. Also, the graph of f touches the x-axis at the repeated zero $x = -1$ and crosses the x-axis at $x = 2$. ✓

In-Class Practice

Self-Assessment

Find all the zeros of the polynomial function.

2. $f(x) = x^3 + 7x^2 + 16x + 12$

3. $f(x) = x^5 - 3x^4 + 5x^3 - x^2 - 6x + 4$

| 1 I don't understand yet. | 2 I can do it with help. | 3 I can do it on my own. | 4 I can teach someone. |

Complex Conjugates

Pairs of complex numbers of the forms $a + bi$ and $a - bi$, where $b \neq 0$, are called *complex conjugates*. In Example 2, notice that the zeros $2i$ and $-2i$ are complex conjugates.

> ### Key Concept
>
> **The Complex Conjugates Theorem**
>
> If f is a polynomial function with real coefficients and $a + bi$ is an imaginary zero of f, then $a - bi$ is also a zero of f.

EXAMPLE 3 Using Zeros to Write a Polynomial Function

Write a polynomial function f of least degree that has rational coefficients, a leading coefficient of 1, and the zeros 2 and $3 + i$.

Because the coefficients are rational and $3 + i$ is a zero, $3 - i$ must also be a zero by the Complex Conjugates Theorem. Use the three zeros and the Factor Theorem to write $f(x)$ as a product of three factors.

$$\begin{aligned}
f(x) &= (x - 2)[x - (3 + i)][x - (3 - i)] && \text{Write } f(x) \text{ in factored form.} \\
&= (x - 2)[(x - 3) - i][(x - 3) + i] && \text{Regroup terms.} \\
&= (x - 2)[(x - 3)^2 - i^2] && \text{Multiply.} \\
&= (x - 2)[(x^2 - 6x + 9) - (-1)] && \text{Expand binomial and use } i^2 = -1. \\
&= (x - 2)(x^2 - 6x + 10) && \text{Simplify.} \\
&= x^3 - 6x^2 + 10x - 2x^2 + 12x - 20 && \text{Multiply.} \\
&= x^3 - 8x^2 + 22x - 20 && \text{Combine like terms.}
\end{aligned}$$

▶ The polynomial is $f(x) = x^3 - 8x^2 + 22x - 20$.

Check

You can check this result by evaluating f at each of the given zeros.

$f(2) = 2^3 - 8(2)^2 + 22(2) - 20 = 8 - 32 + 44 - 20 = 0$ ✓

$f(3 + i) = (3 + i)^3 - 8(3 + i)^2 + 22(3 + i) - 20 = 0$ ✓

Because $f(3 + i) = 0$, by the Complex Conjugates Theorem $f(3 - i) = 0$. ✓

In-Class Practice

Self-Assessment

Write a polynomial function f of least degree that has rational coefficients, a leading coefficient of 1, and the given zeros.

4. $-1, 4i$

5. $2, 2i, 4 - \sqrt{6}$

Descartes's Rule of Signs

French mathematician René Descartes (1596−1650) found the following relationship between the coefficients of a polynomial function and the number of positive and negative zeros of the function.

> ### Key Concept
>
> **Descartes's Rule of Signs**
>
> Let $f(x) = a_n x^n + a_{n-1} x^{n-1} + \cdots + a_2 x^2 + a_1 x + a_0$ be a polynomial function with real coefficients.
>
> - The number of *positive real zeros* of f is equal to the number of changes in sign of the coefficients of $f(x)$ or is less than this by an even number.
> - The number of *negative real zeros* of f is equal to the number of changes in sign of the coefficients of $f(-x)$ or is less than this by an even number.

EXAMPLE 4 Using Descartes's Rule of Signs

Determine the possible numbers of positive real zeros, negative real zeros, and imaginary zeros for $f(x) = x^6 - 2x^5 + 3x^4 - 10x^3 - 6x^2 - 8x - 8$.

$$f(x) = x^6 - 2x^5 + 3x^4 - 10x^3 - 6x^2 - 8x - 8$$

The coefficients in $f(x)$ have 3 sign changes, so f has 3 or 1 positive real zero(s).

$$f(-x) = (-x)^6 - 2(-x)^5 + 3(-x)^4 - 10(-x)^3 - 6(-x)^2 - 8(-x) - 8$$
$$= x^6 + 2x^5 + 3x^4 + 10x^3 - 6x^2 + 8x - 8$$

The coefficients in $f(-x)$ have 3 sign changes, so f has 3 or 1 negative real zero(s).

▶ The possible numbers of zeros for f are summarized in the table below.

Positive real zeros	Negative real zeros	Imaginary zeros	Total zeros
3	3	0	6
3	1	2	6
1	3	2	6
1	1	4	6

In-Class Practice

Self-Assessment

Determine the possible numbers of positive real zeros, negative real zeros, and imaginary zeros for the function.

6. $f(x) = x^3 + 9x - 25$

7. $f(x) = 3x^4 - 7x^3 + x^2 - 13x + 8$

 I don't understand yet.
 I can do it with help.
 I can do it on my own.
 I can teach someone.

Connections to Real Life

EXAMPLE 5 Interpreting the Zeros of a Function

A tachometer measures the speed (in revolutions per minute, or RPMs) at which an engine shaft rotates. For a certain boat, the speed x (in hundreds of RPMs) of the engine shaft and the speed s (in miles per hour) of the boat are modeled by

$$s(x) = 0.00547x^3 - 0.225x^2 + 3.62x - 11.0.$$

What is the tachometer reading when the boat travels 15 miles per hour?

Substitute 15 for $s(x)$ in the function. You can rewrite the resulting equation as

$$0 = 0.00547x^3 - 0.225x^2 + 3.62x - 26.0.$$

The related function is

$$f(x) = 0.00547x^3 - 0.225x^2 + 3.62x - 26.0.$$

By Descartes's Rule of Signs, you know f has 3 or 1 positive real zero(s). In the context of speed, negative real zeros and imaginary zeros do not make sense, so you do not need to check for them. To approximate the positive real zeros of f, use technology.

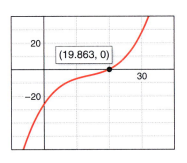

From the graph, there is 1 real zero, $x \approx 19.9$.

▶ The tachometer reading is about 1,990 RPMs.

In-Class Practice
Self-Assessment

8. For the 12 years that a grocery store has been open, its annual revenue R (in millions of dollars) can be modeled by the function

$$R = 0.0001(-t^4 + 12t^3 - 77t^2 + 600t + 13{,}650)$$

where t is the number of years since the store opened. In which year(s) was the revenue $1.5 million?

 I don't understand yet. I can do it with help. I can do it on my own. I can teach someone.

4.6 Practice

Identify the number of solutions of the polynomial equation. Then find the solutions. (See Example 1.)

1. $x^3 + 4x^2 - 11x - 30 = 0$
2. $z^3 + 10z^2 + 28z + 24 = 0$
3. $4x^5 - 8x^4 + 6x^3 = 0$
4. $-2x^6 - 8x^5 - x^4 = 0$
5. $t^4 - 2t^3 + t = 2$
6. $y^4 + 5y^3 - 125y = 625$

Find all the zeros of the polynomial function. (See Example 2.)

7. $f(x) = x^4 - 6x^3 + 7x^2 + 6x - 8$
8. $f(x) = x^4 + 5x^3 - 7x^2 - 29x + 30$
9. $h(x) = x^3 + 5x^2 - 4x - 20$
10. $h(x) = x^4 - x^3 + 7x^2 - 9x - 18$
11. $g(x) = x^5 + 3x^4 - 4x^3 - 2x^2 - 12x - 16$
12. $f(x) = x^5 - 20x^3 + 20x^2 - 21x + 20$

Determine the number of imaginary zeros for the function with the given degree and graph.

13. Degree: 4

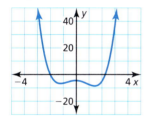

14. Degree: 5

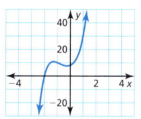

15. Degree: 2

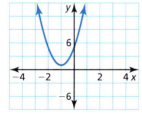

16. Degree: 3

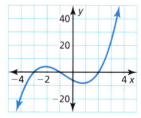

Write a polynomial function f of least degree that has rational coefficients, a leading coefficient of 1, and the given zeros. (See Example 3.)

17. $-5, -1, 2$
18. $-2, 1, 3$
19. $3, 4 + i$
20. $4, -\sqrt{5}$
21. $2, 1 + i, 2 - \sqrt{3}$
22. $3, 4 + 2i, 1 + \sqrt{7}$

23. **OPEN-ENDED** Write a polynomial function of degree 6 with zeros 1, 2, and $-i$.

24. Show why the Fundamental Theorem of Algebra is true for all quadratic functions.

SMP.3 ERROR ANALYSIS Describe and correct the error in writing a polynomial function with rational coefficients and the given zero(s).

25. Zeros: $2, 1 + i$

✗ $f(x) = (x - 2)[x - (1 + i)]$
$= x(x - 1 - i) - 2(x - 1 - i)$
$= x^2 - x - ix - 2x + 2 + 2i$
$= x^2 - (3 + i)x + (2 + 2i)$

26. Zero: $2 + i$

✗ $f(x) = [x - (2 + i)][x + (2 + i)]$
$= (x - 2 - i)(x + 2 + i)$
$= x^2 + 2x + ix - 2x - 4$
$\quad - 2i - ix - 2i - i^2$
$= x^2 - 4i - 3$

Determine the possible numbers of positive real zeros, negative real zeros, and imaginary zeros for the function. (See Example 4.)

27. $g(x) = x^4 - x^2 - 6$

28. $g(x) = -x^3 + 5x^2 + 12$

29. $g(x) = x^3 - 4x^2 + 8x + 7$

30. $g(x) = x^5 - 3x^3 + 8x - 10$

31. $g(x) = x^7 + 4x^4 - 10x + 25$

32. $g(x) = x^6 + x^5 - 3x^4 + x^3 + 5x^2 + 9x - 18$

33. CONNECTION TO REAL LIFE A state maintains a list of the bodies of water infested by zebra mussels. The number N of bodies of water on the list in a given year t can be modeled by

$$N = 0.0004t^4 + 0.042t^3 + 0.35t^2 - 1.0t + 14$$

where $0 \le t \le 18$. Since what year have 25 bodies of water been infested by zebra mussels? (See Example 5.)

34. SMP.7 What is the least number of possible terms of an nth-degree polynomial function with root $4i$?

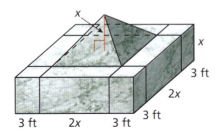

35. CONNECT CONCEPTS A solid monument with the dimensions shown is to be built using 1,000 cubic feet of marble. What is the value of x?

36. Two zeros of $f(x) = x^3 - 6x^2 - 16x + 96$ are 4 and -4. Use Descartes's rule of signs to explain whether the third zero is *real* or *imaginary*.

37. The graph of the constant polynomial function $f(x) = 2$ is a line that does not have any *x*-intercepts. Explain whether the function contradicts the Fundamental Theorem of Algebra.

38. The graph represents a polynomial function of degree 6.

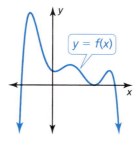

  a. How many positive real zeros does the function have? negative real zeros? imaginary zeros?

  b. Use Descartes's Rule of Signs and your answers in part (a) to describe the possible sign changes in the coefficients of $f(x)$.

39. Find the zeros of several polynomial functions with leading coefficients of 1. For functions of this form, make a conjecture about the relationship between (a) the sum of the zeros and the coefficients, and (b) the product of the zeros and the coefficients.

40. **SMP.5** Use a tool to graph f for $n = 2, 3, 4, 5, 6,$ and 7.

  $f(x) = (x + 3)^n$

  a. Compare the graphs when n is even and n is odd.

  b. Describe the behavior of the graph near $x = -3$ as n increases.

  c. Use your results from parts (a) and (b) to describe the behavior of the graph of $g(x) = (x - 4)^{20}$ near $x = 4$.

41. At the end of each summer, you deposit $1,000 earned from summer jobs into your bank account. The table shows the values of your deposits over a four-year period (g is the growth factor $1 + r$ where r is the annual interest rate expressed as a decimal).

Deposit	Year 1	Year 2	Year 3	Year 4
1st Deposit	1,000	$1,000g$	$1,000g^2$	$1,000g^3$
2nd Deposit	—	1,000		
3rd Deposit	—	—	1,000	
4th Deposit	—	—	—	1,000

  a. Copy and complete the table.

  b. What annual interest rate do you need in order to have $4,300 after the four years?

Interpreting Data

MOTOR VEHICLES IN THE U.S. The United States is the second largest automobile market in the world. Vehicle registrations have generally increased over the last 30 years.

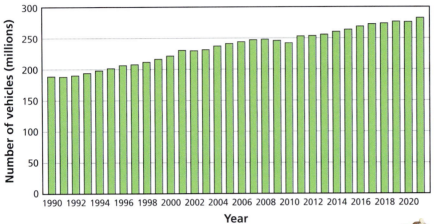

42. The number of registered motor vehicles V (in millions) can be modeled by the function

    $$V = 0.001x^3 - 0.077x^2 + 4.62x + 179$$

    where x is the number of years after 1990. In which year(s) was the number of registered motor vehicles about 262 million?

43. Research the population of the U.S. in 1990 and 2020. Then compare the number of registered motor vehicles per person in 1990 and 2020.

Review & Refresh

44. The graph of which function is shown?

    $f(x) = x(x - 3)(x + 1)$
    $g(x) = x(x + 3)(x - 1)$

    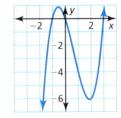

45. Solution A is 10% acid and Solution B is 35% acid. How much of each solution should a chemist mix to make 2 cups of a solution that is 15% acid?

46. Write a function g whose graph represents a reflection in the x-axis, followed by a translation 2 units right and 7 units up of the graph of $f(x) = x^2$.

47. The volume V of the rectangular prism is given by

    $$V = 2x^3 + 17x^2 + 46x + 40.$$

    Find an expression for the missing dimension.

    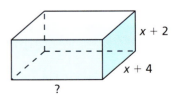

198 Chapter 4 Polynomial Functions

4.7 Transformations of Polynomial Functions

Learning Target: Describe and graph transformations of polynomial functions.

Success Criteria:
- I can describe transformations of polynomial functions.
- I can graph transformations of polynomial functions.
- I can write transformed polynomial functions.

INVESTIGATE Transforming Graphs of Cubic and Quartic Functions

Work with a partner. The graphs of the parent cubic function $f(x) = x^3$ and the parent quartic function $g(x) = x^4$ are shown.

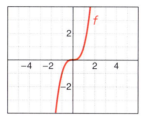
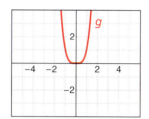

Use technology to explore the given function for several values of k, h, and a. How does the graph change when you change the values of k, h, and a?

1. $y = f(x) + k$
2. $y = f(x - h)$
3. $y = a \cdot f(x)$
4. $y = f(ax)$
5. $y = g(x) + k$
6. $y = g(x - h)$
7. $y = a \cdot g(x)$
8. $y = g(ax)$

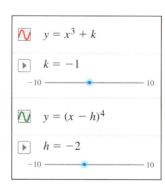
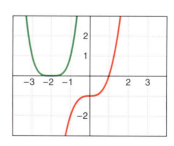

4.7 Transformations of Polynomial Functions

Transformations of Polynomial Functions

Transformation	Examples	
Horizontal Translation: $f(x - h)$ Graph shifts left or right.	$g(x) = (x - 5)^4$ $g(x) = (x + 2)^4$	5 units right 2 units left
Vertical Translation: $f(x) + k$ Graph shifts up or down.	$g(x) = x^4 + 1$ $g(x) = x^4 - 4$	1 unit up 4 units down
Reflection: $f(-x)$ or $-f(x)$ Graph flips over a line.	$g(x) = (-x)^4 = x^4$ $g(x) = -x^4$	in the y-axis in the x-axis
Horizontal Stretch or Shrink: $f(ax)$ Graph stretches away from or shrinks toward y-axis by a factor of $\frac{1}{a}$.	$g(x) = (2x)^4$ $g(x) = \left(\frac{1}{2}x\right)^4$	shrink by a factor of $\frac{1}{2}$ stretch by a factor of 2
Vertical Stretch or Shrink: $a \cdot f(x)$ Graph stretches away from or shrinks toward x-axis by a factor of a.	$g(x) = 8x^4$ $g(x) = \frac{1}{4}x^4$	stretch by a factor of 8 shrink by a factor of $\frac{1}{4}$

EXAMPLE 1   Translating a Polynomial Function

Describe the transformation of $f(x) = x^3$ represented by $g(x) = (x + 5)^3 + 2$. Then graph each function.

Notice that the function is of the form $g(x) = (x - h)^3 + k$. Rewrite the function to identify h and k.

$$g(x) = (x - (-5))^3 + 2$$
$$\quad\quad\quad\quad\;\; \uparrow \quad\quad\; \uparrow$$
$$\quad\quad\quad\quad\;\; h \quad\quad\; k$$

▶ Because $h = -5$ and $k = 2$, the graph of g is a translation 5 units left and 2 units up of the graph of f.

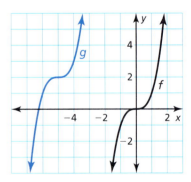

In-Class Practice

Self-Assessment

Describe the transformation of f represented by g. Then graph each function.

1. $f(x) = x^3$, $g(x) = x^3 - 2$
2. $f(x) = x^4$, $g(x) = (x - 3)^4 - 1$

1 I don't understand yet.   **2** I can do it with help.   **3** I can do it on my own.   **4** I can teach someone.

EXAMPLE 2 Transforming Polynomial Functions

Describe the transformation of f represented by g. Then graph each function.

a. $f(x) = x^4, g(x) = -\frac{1}{4}x^4$

Notice that the function is of the form $g(x) = -ax^4$, where $a = \frac{1}{4}$.

▶ So, the graph of g is a reflection in the x-axis and a vertical shrink by a factor of $\frac{1}{4}$ of the graph of f.

b. $f(x) = x^5, g(x) = (2x)^5 - 3$

Notice that the function is of the form $g(x) = (ax)^5 + k$, where $a = 2$ and $k = -3$.

▶ So, the graph of g is a horizontal shrink by a factor of $\frac{1}{2}$ and a translation 3 units down of the graph of f.

EXAMPLE 3 Writing Transformed Polynomial Functions

Let $f(x) = x^3 + x^2 + 1$. Write a rule for g and then graph each function. Describe the graph of g as a transformation of the graph of f.

a. $g(x) = f(-x)$

$g(x) = f(-x) = (-x)^3 + (-x)^2 + 1$
$\quad = -x^3 + x^2 + 1$

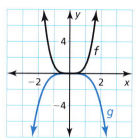

▶ The graph of g is a reflection in the y-axis of the graph of f.

b. $g(x) = 3f(x)$

$g(x) = 3f(x) = 3(x^3 + x^2 + 1)$
$\quad = 3x^3 + 3x^2 + 3$

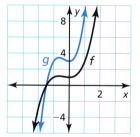

▶ The graph of g is a vertical stretch by a factor of 3 of the graph of f.

In-Class Practice

Self-Assessment

3. Describe the transformation of $f(x) = x^3$ represented by $g(x) = 4(x + 2)^3$. Then graph each function.

4. Let $f(x) = x^5 - 4x + 6$ and $g(x) = -f(x)$. Write a rule for g and then graph each function. Describe the graph of g as a transformation of the graph of f.

| 1 I don't understand yet. | 2 I can do it with help. | 3 I can do it on my own. | 4 I can teach someone. |

EXAMPLE 4 Writing a Transformed Polynomial Function

Let the graph of g be a vertical stretch by a factor of 2, followed by a translation 3 units up of the graph of $f(x) = x^4 - 2x^2$. Write a rule for g.

First write a function h that represents the vertical stretch of f.

$h(x) = 2 \cdot f(x)$ Multiply the output by 2.

$ = 2(x^4 - 2x^2)$ Substitute $x^4 - 2x^2$ for $f(x)$.

$ = 2x^4 - 4x^2$ Distributive Property

Then write a function g that represents the translation of h.

$g(x) = h(x) + 3$ Add 3 to the output.

$ = 2x^4 - 4x^2 + 3$ Substitute $2x^4 - 4x^2$ for $h(x)$.

▶ The transformed function is $g(x) = 2x^4 - 4x^2 + 3$.

EXAMPLE 5 Writing a Polynomial Model

The function $V(x) = \frac{1}{3}x^3 - x^2$ represents the volume (in cubic feet) of the square pyramid shown. The function $W(x) = V(3x)$ represents the volume (in cubic feet) when x is measured in yards. Write a rule for W. Find and interpret $W(10)$.

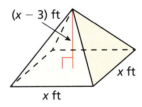

$W(x) = V(3x)$

$ = \frac{1}{3}(3x)^3 - (3x)^2$ Replace x with $3x$ in $V(x)$.

$ = 9x^3 - 9x^2$ Simplify.

Next, find $W(10)$.

$W(10) = 9(10)^3 - 9(10)^2$ Substitute 10 for x.

$ = 8{,}100$ Simplify.

▶ So, $W(x) = 9x^3 - 9x^2$, and when x is 10 yards, the volume is 8,100 cubic feet.

In-Class Practice

Self-Assessment

5. Let the graph of g be a horizontal stretch by a factor of 2, followed by a translation 3 units right of the graph of $f(x) = 8x^3 + 3$. Write a rule for g.

6. **WHAT IF?** In Example 5, the height of the pyramid is $6x$ feet, and the volume (in cubic feet) is represented by $V(x) = 2x^3$. Write a rule for W. Find and interpret $W(7)$.

4.7 Practice

Describe the transformation of f represented by g. Then graph each function.
(See Examples 1 and 2.)

1. $f(x) = x^4$, $g(x) = x^4 + 3$

2. $f(x) = x^6$, $g(x) = (x + 1)^6 - 4$

▶ 3. $f(x) = x^5$, $g(x) = (x - 2)^5 - 1$

4. $f(x) = x^6$, $g(x) = -\frac{1}{4}x^6$

▶ 5. $f(x) = x^3$, $g(x) = 5x^3 + 1$

6. $f(x) = x^4$, $g(x) = (3x)^4 - 2$

Write a rule for g and then graph each function. Describe the graph of g as a transformation of the graph of f. (See Example 3.)

▶ 7. $f(x) = x^4 + 1$, $g(x) = f(x + 2)$

8. $f(x) = x^5 - 2x + 3$, $g(x) = 3f(x)$

9. $f(x) = 2x^3 - 2x^2 + 6$, $g(x) = -\frac{1}{2}f(x)$

10. $f(x) = x^4 + x^3 - 1$, $g(x) = f(-x) - 5$

11. **SMP.3 ERROR ANALYSIS** Describe and correct the error in graphing the transformation of $f(x) = x^4$ represented by $g(x) = (x + 2)^4 - 6$.

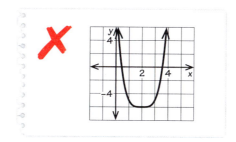

Write a rule for g that represents the indicated transformations of the graph of f.
(See Example 4.)

12. $f(x) = x^3 + 2x^2 - 9$; horizontal shrink by a factor of $\frac{1}{3}$ and a translation 2 units up, followed by a reflection in the x-axis

▶ 13. $f(x) = x^3 - 6$; translation 3 units left, followed by a reflection in the y-axis

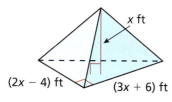

14. **CONNECT CONCEPTS** The function $V(x) = x^3 - 4x$ represents the volume (in cubic feet) of the pyramid. The function $W(x) = V(3x)$ represents the volume (in cubic feet) of the pyramid when x is measured in yards. Write a rule for W. Find and interpret $W(5)$. (See Example 5.)

15. **SMP.6 OPEN-ENDED** Describe two transformations of $f(x) = x^5$ where the order in which the transformations are performed is important. Then describe two transformations where the order is *not* important. Explain your reasoning.

16. **DIG DEEPER** Write a function g that has a y-intercept of -2 and is a transformation of $f(x) = -\frac{1}{4}(2x^2 - 3)(x + 2)^2$.

Interpreting Data

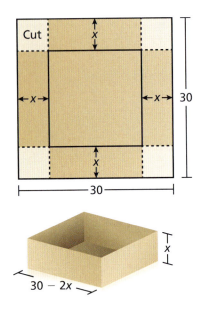

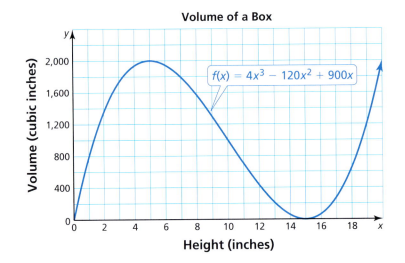

OPTIMIZATION A common problem in calculus is finding the minimum or maximum value of a function. The function shown represents the volume (in cubic inches) of the cardboard box shown, when the height is x inches.

17. Describe how to cut the cardboard shown so that the volume of the folded box is maximized.

18. Find and interpret $g(x) = 2f(x)$ in this situation. Describe the graph of g as a transformation of the graph of f.

19. Describe another real-life situation involving optimization.

Review & Refresh

Find the minimum value or maximum value of f. Find the domain and range, and when f is increasing and decreasing.

20. $f(x) = (x + 5)^2 - 7$

21. $f(x) = -2x^2 + 4x - 1$

22. Write an inequality that is represented by the graph.

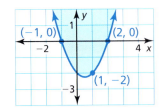

Graph the function and its parent function. Then describe the transformation.

23. $g(x) = |x + 3|$

24. $h(x) = \frac{3}{2}x^2$

25. How many solutions does $x^4 + 8x^2 - 9 = 0$ have? Find all the solutions.

Perform the operation.

26. $(12 - 4i) + (1 - i)$

27. $(3 + 8i) - (-6 + 2i)$

28. $7i(5 - 3i)$

29. $(9 - 11i)(-2 + 4i)$

4.8 Analyzing Graphs of Polynomial Functions

Learning Target: Analyze graphs of polynomial functions.

Success Criteria:
- I can identify a turning point of a polynomial function.
- I can analyze real zeros and turning points numerically.
- I can explain the relationship among the degree of a polynomial function, real zeros, and turning points.

INVESTIGATE Approximating Turning Points

Work with a partner.

1. The graph of the function at the left has two *turning points*. What is meant by a turning point?

2. Use technology to approximate the coordinates of the turning points of the graph of each function.

   a.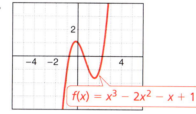
      $f(x) = x^3 - 2x^2 - x + 1$

   b.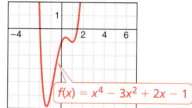
      $f(x) = x^4 - 3x^2 + 2x - 1$

   c.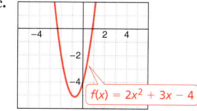
      $f(x) = 2x^2 + 3x - 4$

   d.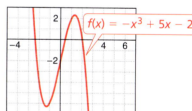
      $f(x) = -x^3 + 5x - 2$

   e.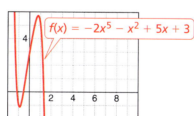
      $f(x) = -2x^5 - x^2 + 5x + 3$

   f.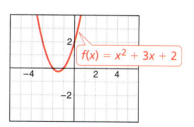
      $f(x) = x^2 + 3x + 2$

   g.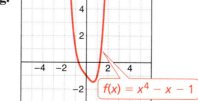
      $f(x) = x^4 - x - 1$

   h.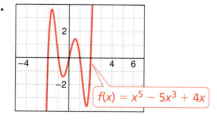
      $f(x) = x^5 - 5x^3 + 4x$

3. Make a conjecture about the number of turning points of the graph of a polynomial function of degree n.

Vocabulary
local maximum
local minimum
even function
odd function

Graphing Polynomial Functions

In this chapter, you have learned that zeros, factors, solutions, and x-intercepts are closely related concepts. Here is a summary of these relationships.

Let $f(x) = a_n x^n + a_{n-1} x^{n-1} + \cdots + a_1 x + a_0$ be a polynomial function. The following statements are equivalent.

Zero: k is a zero of the polynomial function f.

Factor: $x - k$ is a factor of the polynomial $f(x)$.

Solution: k is a solution (or root) of the polynomial equation $f(x) = 0$.

x-Intercept: If k is a real number, then k is an x-intercept of the graph of the polynomial function f. The graph of f passes through $(k, 0)$.

EXAMPLE 1 Using x-intercepts to Graph a Polynomial Function

Graph $f(x) = \frac{1}{6}(x + 3)(x - 2)^2$.

Find points corresponding to the x-intercepts. Because -3 and 2 are zeros of f, the points are $(-3, 0)$ and $(2, 0)$. Find points between and beyond these points.

x	−3	−2	−1	0	1	2	3
y	0	$\frac{8}{3}$	3	2	$\frac{2}{3}$	0	1

Determine the end behavior. Because $f(x)$ has three factors of the form $x - k$ and a constant factor of $\frac{1}{6}$, f is a cubic function with a positive leading coefficient. So, $f(x) \to -\infty$ as $x \to -\infty$ and $f(x) \to +\infty$ as $x \to +\infty$.

Plot the points. Draw the graph so that it passes through the plotted points and has the appropriate end behavior.

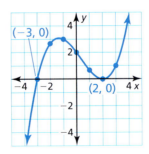

In-Class Practice

Self-Assessment

Graph the function.

1. $f(x) = \frac{1}{2}(x + 1)(x - 4)^2$

2. $f(x) = -\frac{1}{4}(x + 2)(x - 1)(x - 3)$

 I don't understand yet.
 I can do it with help.
 I can do it on my own.
 I can teach someone.

The Location Principle

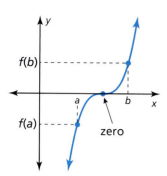

Key Concept

The Location Principle

If f is a polynomial function, and a and b are two real numbers such that $f(a) < 0$ and $f(b) > 0$, then f has at least one real zero between a and b.

You can use this principle to find real zeros of polynomial functions by finding a value a at which the polynomial function is negative and another value b at which the function is positive. You can conclude that the function has *at least* one real zero between a and b.

EXAMPLE 2 Finding Real Zeros of a Polynomial Function

Find all the real zeros of $f(x) = 6x^3 + 5x^2 - 17x - 6$.

x	$f(x)$
0	−6
1	−12
2	28
3	150
4	390
5	784
6	1,368

Use technology to make a table.

Use the Location Principle. From the table shown, you can see that $f(1) < 0$ and $f(2) > 0$. So, by the Location Principle, f has at least one real zero between 1 and 2. Because f is a polynomial function of degree 3, it has three zeros. By the Rational Root Theorem, the only possible *rational* zero between 1 and 2 is $\frac{3}{2}$. Use synthetic division to confirm that $\frac{3}{2}$ is a zero.

$$\begin{array}{r|rrrr} \frac{3}{2} & 6 & 5 & -17 & -6 \\ & & 9 & 21 & 6 \\ \hline & 6 & 14 & 4 & 0 \end{array}$$

The remainder is 0, so $x - \frac{3}{2}$ is a factor of $f(x)$.

Write $f(x)$ in factored form using its known factor $x - \frac{3}{2}$ and the quotient polynomial $6x^2 + 14x + 4$.

$$f(x) = \left(x - \tfrac{3}{2}\right)(6x^2 + 14x + 4)$$
$$= 2\left(x - \tfrac{3}{2}\right)(3x^2 + 7x + 2)$$
$$= 2\left(x - \tfrac{3}{2}\right)(3x + 1)(x + 2)$$

▶ From the factorization, there are three zeros. The zeros of f are $\frac{3}{2}$, $-\frac{1}{3}$, and -2.

Check

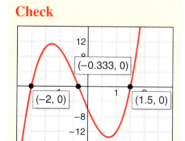

In-Class Practice

Self-Assessment

Find all the real zeros of the function.

3. $f(x) = 18x^3 + 21x^2 - 13x - 6$

4. $f(x) = 2x^4 + x^3 - 9x^2 - 13x - 5$

1 I don't understand yet. **2** I can do it with help. **3** I can do it on my own. **4** I can teach someone.

4.8 Analyzing Graphs of Polynomial Functions

Turning Points

A turning point of a graph of a function is a point at which the function changes from increasing to decreasing, or decreasing to increasing.

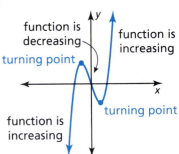

- The y-coordinate of a turning point is a **local maximum** of the function when the point is higher than all nearby points.

- The y-coordinate of a turning point is a **local minimum** of the function when the point is lower than all nearby points.

Key Concept

Turning Points of Polynomial Functions

1. The graph of every polynomial function of degree n has *at most* $n - 1$ turning points.

2. If a polynomial function of degree n has n distinct real zeros, then its graph has *exactly* $n - 1$ turning points.

EXAMPLE 3 Finding Turning Points

Graph $g(x) = x^4 - 6x^3 + 3x^2 + 10x - 3$. Identify the x-intercepts and the points where the local maximums and local minimums occur. Determine the intervals for which each function is increasing or decreasing.

Use technology to graph the function.

The graph of g has four x-intercepts and three turning points. Approximate the x-intercepts and the turning points.

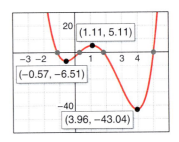

▶ x-intercepts: $x \approx -1.14$, $x \approx 0.29$, $x \approx 1.82$, and $x \approx 5.03$
local maximum: $(1.11, 5.11)$
local minimums: $(-0.57, -6.51)$ and $(3.96, -43.04)$
increasing when $-0.57 < x < 1.11$ and $x > 3.96$
decreasing when $x < -0.57$ and $1.11 < x < 3.96$

In-Class Practice

Self-Assessment

5. Graph $f(x) = 0.5x^3 + x^2 - x + 2$. Identify the x-intercepts and the points where the local maximums and local minimums occur. Determine the intervals for which the function is increasing or decreasing.

Even and Odd Functions

A function f is an **even function** when $f(-x) = f(x)$ for all x in its domain. The graph of an even function is *symmetric about the y-axis*.

A function f is an **odd function** when $f(-x) = -f(x)$ for all x in its domain. The graph of an odd function is *symmetric about the origin*. One way to recognize a graph as symmetric about the origin is that it looks the same after a 180° rotation about the origin.

Even Function

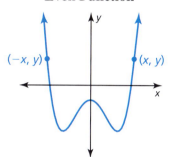

Odd Function

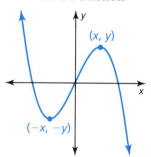

For an even function, if (x, y) is on the graph, then $(-x, y)$ is also on the graph.

For an odd function, if (x, y) is on the graph, then $(-x, -y)$ is also on the graph.

EXAMPLE 4 — Identifying Even and Odd Functions

a. Determine whether $f(x) = x^3 - 7x$ is *even*, *odd*, or *neither*.

Replace x with $-x$ in the equation for f, and then simplify.

$$f(-x) = (-x)^3 - 7(-x) = -x^3 + 7x = -(x^3 - 7x) = -f(x)$$

▶ Because $f(-x) = -f(x)$, the function is odd.

b. Determine whether $g(x) = x^4 + x^2 - 1$ is *even*, *odd*, or *neither*.

Replace x with $-x$ in the equation for g, and then simplify.

$$g(-x) = (-x)^4 + (-x)^2 - 1 = x^4 + x^2 - 1 = g(x)$$

▶ Because $g(-x) = g(x)$, the function is even.

c. Determine whether $h(x) = x^3 + 2$ is *even*, *odd*, or *neither*.

Replacing x with $-x$ in the equation for h produces

$$h(-x) = (-x)^3 + 2 = -x^3 + 2.$$

▶ Because $h(-x) \neq h(x)$ and $h(-x) \neq -h(x)$, the function is neither even nor odd.

In-Class Practice

Self-Assessment

Determine whether the function is *even*, *odd*, or *neither*.

6. $f(x) = x^4 - 5x^3$

7. $f(x) = 2x^5$

8. $f(x) = |2x^3|$

4.8 Practice

Graph the function. (See Example 1.)

1. $f(x) = (x + 2)^2(x + 4)^2$
2. $g(x) = 4(x + 1)(x + 2)(x - 1)$
3. $h(x) = (x + 1)^2(x - 1)(x - 3)$
4. $f(x) = (x - 4)(2x^2 - 2x + 1)$

5. **SMP.3 ERROR ANALYSIS** Describe and correct the error in using factors to graph $f(x) = x^2(x - 3)^3$.

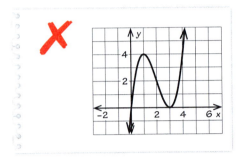

Find all the real zeros of the function. (See Example 2.)

6. $f(x) = x^3 - 4x^2 - x + 4$
7. $h(x) = 2x^3 + 7x^2 - 5x - 4$
8. $h(x) = 4x^3 - 2x^2 - 24x - 18$
9. $m(x) = 24x^4 - 14x^3 - 37x^2 + 4x + 3$

Graph the function. Identify the x-intercepts and the points where the local maximums and local minimums occur. Determine the intervals for which the function is increasing or decreasing. (See Example 3.)

10. $h(x) = x^4 - 3x^2 + x$
11. $g(x) = 2x^3 + 8x^2 - 3$
12. $f(x) = x^5 - 4x^3 + x^2 + 2$
13. $f(x) = 0.7x^4 - 3x^3 + 5x$

Determine the least possible degree of f.

14.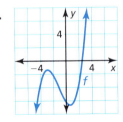

15.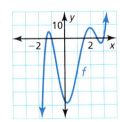

16. Sketch a graph of a polynomial function f having the given characteristics.
    - The graph of f has x-intercepts of -3, 1, and 5.
    - f has a local maximum when $x = 1$.
    - f has a local minimum when $x = -2$ and when $x = 4$.

17. Explain whether it is possible to sketch the graph of a cubic polynomial function that has *no* turning points.

Determine whether the function is *even*, *odd*, or *neither*. (See Example 4.)

18. $h(x) = 4x^7$

▶ **19.** $f(x) = x^4 + 3x^2 - 2$

20. $f(x) = x^5 + 3x^3 - x$

21. $g(x) = x^2 + 5x + 1$

22. $f(x) = -x^3 + 2x - 9$

23. $f(x) = x^4 - 12x^2$

24. **SMP.2** **CONNECTION TO REAL LIFE** When a swimmer does the breaststroke, the function

$$S = -241t^7 + 1{,}060t^6 - 1{,}870t^5 + 1{,}650t^4 - 737t^3 + 144t^2 - 2.43t$$

models the speed S (in meters per second) of the swimmer during one complete stroke, where t is the number of seconds since the start of the stroke and $0 \leq t \leq 1.22$. Use technology to graph the function. At what time during the stroke is the swimmer traveling the fastest?

25. The graph of a polynomial function is shown.

  a. Approximate the real zeros of the function and the points where the local maximum and local minimum occur.

  b. Compare the x-intercepts of the graphs of $y = f(x)$ and $y = -f(x)$.

  c. Compare the local maximums and local minimums of the functions $y = f(x)$ and $y = -f(x)$.

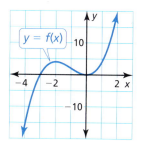

26. **SMP.7** Write and graph a polynomial function that has one real zero in each of the intervals $-2 < x < -1$, $0 < x < 1$, and $4 < x < 5$. Is there a maximum degree that such a polynomial function can have?

27. **SMP.6** Explain whether the product of two odd functions is an odd function.

28. Quonset huts are temporary, all-purpose structures shaped like half cylinders. You have 1,100 square feet of material to build a quonset hut.

  a. Write an equation that gives the surface area S of the hut. Then write an expression for ℓ in terms of r.

  b. Write an equation that gives the volume V of a quonset hut as a function of r only. Then find the value of r that maximizes the volume of the hut.

STEM Video: Quonset Huts

Interpreting Data

CARBON DIOXIDE LEVELS The carbon dioxide level of the atmosphere is monitored at Mauna Loa Observatory in Hawaii. The graph shows the carbon dioxide levels at this observatory each month in 2021.

29. Describe the change in the carbon dioxide level throughout 2021.

30. How many turning points occur on the trendline shown? During which month(s) did these turning points occur?

31. Why is it important to monitor carbon dioxide levels in the atmosphere?

Review & Refresh

32. Find $(3z + 4)(3z - 4)$.

33. Find all the zeros of f.
$$f(x) = x^5 + 3x^4 + 9x^3 + 23x^2 - 36$$

34. Describe the transformation of f represented by g. Then graph each function.
$$f(x) = x^3$$
$$g(x) = (x + 2)^3 - 5$$

35. Determine whether the data are *linear*, *quadratic*, or *neither*.

Time (seconds), x	0	1	2	3
Height (feet), y	300	284	236	156

36. Solve $n^3 + n^2 - 6n = 0$.

37. Use the graph to solve $2x^2 + 16 = 12x$.

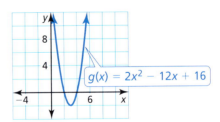

38. During a game of "Spud," a kickball is thrown straight up into the air. The height h (in feet) of the ball t seconds after it is thrown can be modeled by $h = -16t^2 + 24t + 5$.

   a. Find the maximum height of the ball.

   b. A player catches the ball when it is 5 feet above the ground. How long is the ball in the air?

4.9 Modeling with Polynomial Functions

Learning Target: Write polynomial functions.

Success Criteria:
- I can write a polynomial function given a graph or a set of points.
- I can write a polynomial function using finite differences.
- I can use technology to find a polynomial model for a set of data.

INVESTIGATE Modeling Real-Life Data

Work with a partner.

1. The data show the prices per share y (in dollars) for a stock after t years.

t	0	1	2	3	4	5	6
y	81.50	15.81	10.93	19.19	52.76	44.95	47.47

t	7	8	9	10	11	12	13
y	38.68	95.35	51.35	136.25	181.37	175.89	256.08

t	14	15	16	17	18	19
y	398.80	312.48	656.29	757.92	1,172.00	1,465.20

a. Use technology to make a scatter plot of the data. Describe the scatter plot.

b. Use technology to find a linear model and a quadratic model to represent the data. Is either model a good fit? How can you tell?

c. Is there another type of model you can use that better represents the data in the table? Use technology to find the model and explain why it is a better fit. Compare your results with your classmates.

d. Explain whether you can use the model you found in part (c) to make predictions about the share prices for the stock in future years.

2. How can you tell when a model fits a set of data *exactly*?

Vocabulary
finite differences

Writing a Polynomial Function for a Set of Points

You know that two points determine a line and three points not on a line determine a parabola. In Example 1, you will see that four points not on a line or a parabola determine the graph of a cubic function.

EXAMPLE 1 Writing a Cubic Function

Write the cubic function whose graph is shown.

a.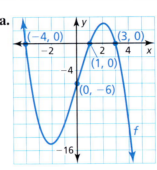

Use the three x-intercepts to write the function in intercept form.

$$f(x) = a(x+4)(x-1)(x-3)$$

Find the value of a by substituting the coordinates of the point $(0, -6)$.

$$-6 = a(0+4)(0-1)(0-3)$$
$$-6 = 12a$$
$$-\tfrac{1}{2} = a$$

▶ The function is $f(x) = -\tfrac{1}{2}(x+4)(x-1)(x-3)$.

b.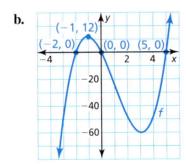

Use the three x-intercepts to write the function in intercept form.

$$f(x) = ax(x+2)(x-5)$$

Find the value of a by substituting the coordinates of the point $(-1, 12)$.

$$12 = a(-1)(-1+2)(-1-5)$$
$$12 = 6a$$
$$2 = a$$

▶ The function is $f(x) = 2x(x+2)(x-5)$.

Check

Check the end behavior of f. The degree of f is odd and $a > 0$. So, $f(x) \to -\infty$ as $x \to -\infty$ and $f(x) \to +\infty$ as $x \to +\infty$, which matches the graph. ✓

In-Class Practice
Self-Assessment

Write a cubic function whose graph passes through the given points.

1. $(-4, 0), (0, 10), (2, 0), (5, 0)$
2. $(-1, 0), (0, -12), (2, 0), (3, 0)$

1 I don't understand yet. **2** I can do it with help. **3** I can do it on my own. **4** I can teach someone.

Finite Differences

When *x*-values are equally spaced, the differences of consecutive *y*-values are called **finite differences**. The first and second differences of $y = x^2$ are:

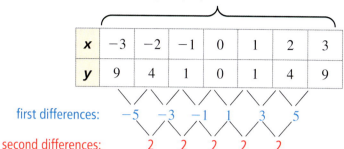

This illustrates the following properties of finite differences:

- If a polynomial function $y = f(x)$ has degree n, then the nth differences of function values for equally-spaced *x*-values are nonzero and constant.

- If the nth differences of equally-spaced data are nonzero and constant, then the data can be represented by a polynomial function of degree n.

EXAMPLE 2 Writing a Function Using Finite Differences

Use finite differences to determine the degree of the polynomial function that fits the data. Then use technology to find the polynomial function.

x	1	2	3	4	5	6	7
y	1	4	10	20	35	56	84

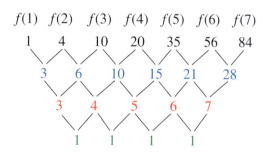

$y = ax^3 + bx^2 + cx + d$

PARAMETERS
$a = 0.166667 \quad b = 0.5$
$c = 0.333333 \quad d = 0$

STATISTICS
$R^2 = 1$

The third differences are nonzero and constant, so a cubic function *exactly* models the data. Use *cubic regression* to find a polynomial function.

▶ Write the coefficients as fractions to obtain $f(x) = \frac{1}{6}x^3 + \frac{1}{2}x^2 + \frac{1}{3}x$.

In-Class Practice

Self-Assessment

3. Use finite differences to determine the degree of the polynomial function that fits the data. Then use technology to find the polynomial function.

x	−3	−2	−1	0	1	2
y	6	15	22	21	6	−29

1 I don't understand yet. **2** I can do it with help. **3** I can do it on my own. **4** I can teach someone.

4.9 Modeling with Polynomial Functions

Connections to Real Life

EXAMPLE 3 Using Polynomial Regression

The table shows the numbers of visitors to a national park over time. Use a model to estimate the number of visitors in 2019.

Years since 2000	Visitors, y (thousands)
0	374.9
2	388.1
4	379.7
6	388.7
8	377.4
10	384.6
12	407.7
14	433.0
16	536.1
18	499.4
20	542.3

Make a scatter plot of the data.

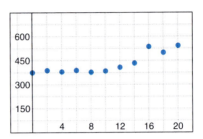

The data suggest some type of polynomial model such as a cubic or quartic function. Using *cubic* and *quartic regression*, the coefficients can be rounded to obtain:

$$y = -0.013t^3 + 1.06t^2 - 8.0t + 388 \qquad \text{Cubic model}$$

$$y = -0.0126t^4 + 0.490t^3 - 5.22t^2 + 17.2t + 373 \qquad \text{Quartic model}$$

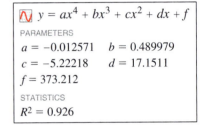

Graph the equations with the data and compare the models. The graph of the quartic model appears to be closer to the data points than the graph of the cubic model.

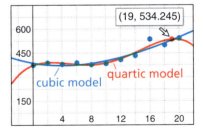

So, a model is $y = -0.0126t^4 + 0.490t^3 - 5.22t^2 + 17.2t + 373$.

Using the model, you can determine that $y \approx 534$ when $t = 19$.

▶ Using the model, the number of visitors in 2019 was about 534,000.

In-Class Practice

Self-Assessment

4. Use a model to estimate the value of y when $x = 5.5$.

x	1	2	5	7	8	11	14	15	17
y	8	7	10	17	20	21	14	9	3

1 I don't understand yet.   **2** I can do it with help.   **3** I can do it on my own.   **4** I can teach someone.

4.9 Practice

Write a cubic function whose graph is shown. (See Example 1.)

1.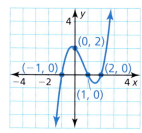

2.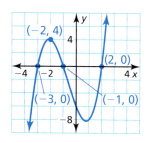

Use finite differences to determine the degree of the polynomial function that fits the data. Then use technology to find the polynomial function. (See Example 2.)

3.
x	−6	−3	0	3	6	9
y	−2	15	−4	49	282	803

4. $(-4, -317), (-3, -37), (-2, 21), (-1, 7), (0, -1), (1, 3), (2, -47), (3, -289), (4, -933)$

5. **SMP.4 CONNECTION TO REAL LIFE** The table shows the number of passengers who board urban rail systems in a city for several years. Use a model to approximate the number of passengers in Year 5. (See Example 3.)

Year, t	1	2	3	4	6	7	9	10
Passengers, y (millions)	220	216	234	244	250	235	220	228

6. The graph shows typical speeds y (in feet per second) of a space shuttle x seconds after it is launched.

   a. Explain whether the data appear to be best represented by a *linear*, *quadratic*, or *cubic* function.

   b. Explain which *n*th differences should be constant for the function in part (a).

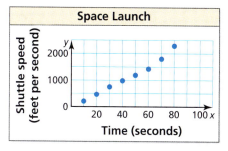

7. **SMP.1 DIG DEEPER** Write a polynomial function that has constant fourth differences of −2. Justify your answer.

8. **SMP.8** The *n*th pentagonal number is equal to the number of dots in the *n*th figure of the pattern shown. Determine the degree of the polynomial function that fits the data. Then find the 10th pentagonal number.

4.9 Modeling with Polynomial Functions 217

Interpreting Data

HIGH SCHOOL SENIORS In 1980, about 71% of American high school seniors had smoked a cigarette at some point in their lives. The graph shows how this percentage has changed from 1980 to 2020.

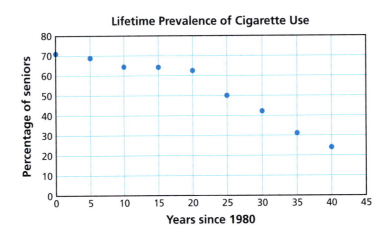

9. Write a polynomial function that models the data.

10. Compare the average rate of change from 1980 to 2000 to the average rate of change from 2000 to 2020.

11. Why do you think the percentage of smokers has declined?

Review & Refresh

Use the graph to describe the degree and leading coefficient of f.

12.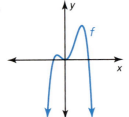

13.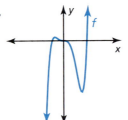

Solve the system using any method.

14. $y = -2x + 5$
    $x^2 + y^2 = 5$

15. $x^2 - 3x - y = -3$
    $3x^2 - 8x - y = -5$

16. Identify the focus and the directrix of $y = ax^2 + c$ in terms of a and c.

17. Determine the possible numbers of positive real zeros, negative real zeros, and imaginary zeros for $g(x) = -x^5 - 2x^4 + 7x^2 - 3x + 8$.

18. Write an expression for the volume of the rectangular prism as a polynomial in standard form.

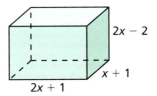

19. Graph $f(x) = -x^4 + 4x^3 - 8x$. Identify the x-intercepts and the points where the local maximums and local minimums occur. Determine the intervals for which the function is increasing or decreasing.

4 Chapter Review

Rate your understanding of each section.

1. I don't understand yet.
2. I can do it with help.
3. I can do it on my own.
4. I can teach someone.

4.1 Graphing Polynomial Functions (pp. 151–158)

◉ **Learning Target:** Graph and describe polynomial functions.

Vocabulary
polynomial
polynomial function
end behavior

Graph the polynomial function.

1. $h(x) = x^2 + 6x^5 - 5$
2. $p(x) = 2x^3 - 4x + 6$
3. $f(x) = 3x^4 - 5x^2 + 1$
4. $g(x) = -x^4 + x + 2$

5. The life expectancy (in years) at birth of a person in the United States can be modeled by the function

$$f(t) = -0.0013t^3 + 0.023t^2 + 0.09t + 76.8$$

where t is the number of years after 2000.

a. Use technology to graph the function for $0 \le t \le 16$. Describe the behavior of the graph on this interval.

b. What was the average rate of change in life expectancy at birth from 2000 to 2016?

c. Explain whether you think this model can be used for years after 2016.

4.2 Adding, Subtracting, and Multiplying Polynomials (pp. 159–166)

◉ **Learning Target:** Add, subtract, and multiply polynomials.

Vocabulary
Pascal's Triangle
Binomial Theorem

Find the sum or difference.

6. $(4x^3 - 12x^2 - 5) - (-8x^2 + 4x + 3)$

7. $(x^4 + 3x^3 - x^2 + 6) + (2x^4 - 3x + 9)$

8. $(3x^2 + 9x + 13) - (x^2 - 2x + 12)$

Find the product.

9. $(2y^2 + 4y - 7)(y + 3)$
10. $(2m + n)^3$
11. $(s + 2)(s + 4)(s - 3)$

Use the Binomial Theorem to expand the binomial.

12. $(m + 4)^4$
13. $(3s + 2)^5$
14. $(z + 1)^6$

RESOURCES

4.3 Dividing Polynomials (pp. 167–172)

Learning Target: Divide polynomials and use the Remainder Theorem.

Vocabulary
polynomial long division
synthetic division

Divide using polynomial long division or synthetic division.

15. $(x^3 + x^2 + 3x - 4) \div (x^2 + 2x + 1)$

16. $(x^4 + 3x^3 - 4x^2 + 5x + 3) \div (x^2 + x + 4)$

17. $(-2x^3 + 3x - 5) \div (x - 2)$

Use synthetic division to evaluate the function for the indicated value of x.

18. $f(x) = 4x^3 + 2x^2 - 4;\ x = 5$

19. $f(x) = -x^4 - 3x^3 + 6x;\ x = -3$

20. Find the missing values. Then write the dividend, divisor, and quotient represented by the synthetic division.

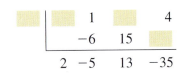

21. The total numbers N (in thousands) of overnight stays at Zion National Park x years after 2000 can be modeled by

$$N = -0.029x^3 + 0.61x^2 + 3.2x + 246$$

where $0 \leq x \leq 22$. Use synthetic division to find the total number of overnight stays in 2022.

4.4 Factoring Polynomials (pp. 173–180)

Learning Target: Factor polynomials and use the Factor Theorem.

Vocabulary
factored completely
factor by grouping
quadratic form

Factor the polynomial completely.

22. $64x^3 - 8$

23. $8y^3 + 125y^6$

24. $2z^5 - 12z^3 + 10z$

25. $2a^3 - 7a^2 - 8a + 28$

26. Show that $x + 2$ is a factor of $f(x) = x^4 + 2x^3 - 27x - 54$. Then factor $f(x)$ completely.

27. A rectangular prism has a volume of $x^3 + 13x^2 + 34x - 48$ cubic inches. Give one possible set of dimensions for the prism in terms of x.

28. The profit P (in millions of dollars) for a game company can be modeled by $P = -x^3 + 3x^2 + 3$, where x is the number (in millions) of copies of a new game produced. The company now produces 1 million copies of the new game and makes a profit of $5 million, but it would like to increase production. What greater number of copies could the company produce and still make the same profit?

4.5 Solving Polynomial Equations (pp. 181–188)

⦿ **Learning Target:** Solve polynomial equations and find zeros of polynomial functions.

Vocabulary
repeated solution

Find all the real solutions of the equation.

29. $x^3 + 3x^2 - 10x - 24 = 0$

30. $x^3 + 5x^2 - 2x - 24 = 0$

Find the zeros of the function. Then sketch a graph of the function.

31. $f(x) = -3x^3 - 6x^2$

32. $f(x) = -x^4 + 18x^2 - 81$

Write a polynomial function f of least degree that has rational coefficients, a leading coefficient of 1, and the given zeros.

33. $1, 2 - \sqrt{3}$

34. $-2, 5, 3 + \sqrt{6}$

35. The Willis Tower in Chicago is composed of nine rectangular prisms with square bases and varying heights. A model of one of the two tallest prisms is shown.

  a. The volume of the prism in the model is 522 cubic inches. What are the dimensions?

  b. The height of the actual prism is about 1,450 feet. Use the model to approximate the volume of the actual prism.

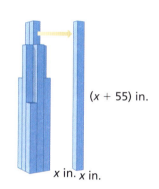
$(x + 55)$ in.
x in. x in.

4.6 The Fundamental Theorem of Algebra (pp. 189–198)

⦿ **Learning Target:** Use the Fundamental Theorem of Algebra to find all complex roots of polynomial equations.

36. Find all the zeros of $f(x) = x^5 + 5x^4 + 8x^3 + 8x^2 + 7x + 3$.

Write a polynomial function f of least degree that has rational coefficients, a leading coefficient of 1, and the given zeros.

37. $-1, 2, 4i$

38. $-5, -4, 1 - i\sqrt{3}$

Determine the possible numbers of positive real zeros, negative real zeros, and imaginary zeros for the function.

39. $f(x) = x^4 - 10x + 8$

40. $f(x) = -6x^4 - x^3 + 3x^2 + 2x + 18$

41. The average monthly low temperature (in degrees Celsius) in Fargo, North Dakota, can be modeled by

$$f(t) = 0.0226t^4 - 0.645t^3 + 5.15t^2 - 8.0t - 14$$

where $t = 1$ represents January. For what month(s) is the average low temperature about 8 degrees Celsius?

4.7 Transformations of Polynomial Functions (pp. 199–204)

⊙ **Learning Target:** Describe and graph transformations of polynomial functions.

Describe the transformation of f represented by g. Then graph each function.

42. $f(x) = x^3$, $g(x) = (-x)^3 + 2$

43. $f(x) = x^4$, $g(x) = -(x+9)^4$

Write a rule for g.

44. Let the graph of g be a horizontal stretch by a factor of 4, followed by a translation 3 units right and 5 units down of the graph of $f(x) = x^5 + 3x$.

45. Let the graph of g be a translation 5 units up, followed by a reflection in the y-axis of the graph of $f(x) = x^4 - 2x^3 - 12$.

Match the function with the correct transformation of the graph of f shown below.

46. $y = f(2x)$

47. $y = -2f(x)$

48. $y = f(-2x)$

49. $y = 2f(-x)$

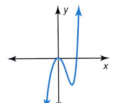

A.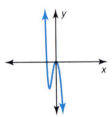

C.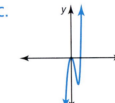

B.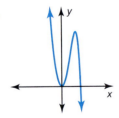

D.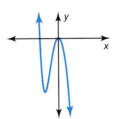

50. Write a function V for the volume (in cubic yards) of the right circular cone shown. Then write a function W that represents the volume (in cubic yards) of the cone when x is measured in feet. Find and interpret $W(3)$.

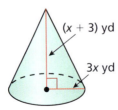

4.8 Analyzing Graphs of Polynomial Functions (pp. 205–212)

○ **Learning Target:** Analyze graphs of polynomial functions.

Vocabulary
local maximum
local minimum
even function
odd function

Graph the function. Identify the x-intercepts and the points where the local maximums and local minimums occur. Determine the intervals for which the function is increasing or decreasing.

51. $f(x) = -2x^3 - 3x^2 - 1$

52. $f(x) = x^4 + 3x^3 - x^2 - 8x + 2$

Determine whether the function is *even*, *odd*, or *neither*.

53. $f(x) = 2x^3 + 3x$

54. $g(x) = 3x^2 - 7$

55. $h(x) = x^6 + 3x^5$

56. Compare the domains and ranges of odd-degree polynomial functions with the domains and ranges of even-degree polynomial functions.

4.9 Modeling with Polynomial Functions (pp. 213–218)

○ **Learning Target:** Write polynomial functions.

Vocabulary
finite differences

Write a cubic function whose graph is shown.

57.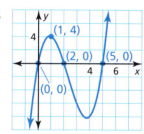

58.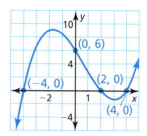

Use finite differences to determine the degree of the polynomial function that fits the data. Then use technology to find the polynomial function.

59.

x	1	2	3	4	5	6	7
f(x)	−11	−24	−27	−8	45	144	301

60.

x	−4	−2	0	2	4	6	8
f(x)	−60	10	4	−6	4	10	−60

61. The table shows the numbers y of moose on Isle Royale in Michigan in the year t, where t = 0 corresponds to 2010. Find a model for the data. Use the model to predict the number of moose on Isle Royale in 2020.

t	0	1	2	3	4	5	6	7	8	9
y	510	515	750	975	1,050	1,250	1,300	1,600	1,500	2,060

4 PERFORMANCE TASK
SMP.1 SMP.2

Thrown to the Wolves

BEFORE ← **1995** The gray wolf is reintroduced to Yellowstone National Park. → **AFTER**

Elk feed heavily along rivers and streams, drastically reducing vegetation.

Elk spend less time feeding in exposed areas along rivers and streams, allowing vegetation to flourish.

With reduced vegetation, riverbanks are exposed and erode easily.

Willows and other plants stabilize the soil along rivers and streams, preventing erosion.

The population of beavers decreases and dams cease to be constructed.

Vegetation attracts beavers, who return to the area and build dams, increasing water quality.

Scavengers such as ravens, eagles, and coyotes must hunt for their own food supplies.

Wolves leave a leftover food supply for scavengers.

Coyotes multiply, and dominate the food supply.

The number of coyotes decreases, increasing the amount of prey available to other animals.

Chapter 4 Polynomial Functions

Analyzing Data

Use the information on the previous page to complete the following exercises.

1 Explain what is shown in the display. What do you notice? What do you wonder?

2 The number of wolves in Yellowstone x years after 1995 can be modeled by the function shown.

$$w(x) = 0.001x^4 + 0.019x^3 - 2.24x^2 + 32.9x + 9$$

Use technology to graph the function for $0 \leq x \leq 25$. Describe how the wolf population in Yellowstone has changed over this period.

YELLOWSTONE WOLF REINTRODUCTION

As a researcher, you want to understand how the number of wolves in Yellowstone impacts the population of the northern Yellowstone elk herd. You conduct 10 surveys of the populations over several years. The results are shown in the table.

Explore several different models that relate the populations. Then decide which model best represents the situation. Explain how you chose the best model. Then summarize how the number of wolves impacts the elk herd population.

Wolves	Northern Yellowstone elk herd
132	13,400
148	11,950
174	9,100
171	8,400
118	9,600
171	6,900
96	7,100
97	6,050
98	4,800
83	4,150

5 Rational Exponents and Radical Functions

- **5.1** *n*th Roots and Rational Exponents
- **5.2** Properties of Rational Exponents and Radicals
- **5.3** Graphing Radical Functions
- **5.4** Solving Radical Equations and Inequalities
- **5.5** Performing Function Operations
- **5.6** Composition of Functions
- **5.7** Inverse of a Function

NATIONAL GEOGRAPHIC EXPLORER
Ben Mirin | ACOUSTIC BIOLOGIST

Ben Mirin is an acoustic biologist, sound artist, and science communicator. He is the creator and host of the digital series WILD BEATS. Ben travels the world recording animal sounds and samples them to create music that connects people to nature. He leads expeditions to record and catalog acoustic data from many of the planet's most endangered ecosystems.

- What are some animal species that sing?
- Why do you think animals sing? Use the Internet or another resource to find at least two reasons.
- Give examples of animal sounds you can hear where you live. Do you have a favorite animal sound?

PERFORMANCE TASK

Have you ever heard of a song being played in a certain *octave*? In the Performance Task on pages 284 and 285, you will compare the sounds of notes in different octaves. Then you will explain properties of the sound waves that produce those notes.

Sound Art

Big Idea of the Chapter
Understand Rational Exponents and Radical Functions

A radical function has a radical expression with the independent variable in the radicand. Radical functions where the radical is a square root, such as $y = \sqrt{x}$, are called square root functions.

Humans can typically hear frequencies between 20 and 20,000 hertz (Hz). Frequencies below 20 Hz are called infrasonic and frequencies above 20,000 Hz are called ultrasonic. However, some animals can hear these frequencies. The display shows the results of a study that tested the range of frequencies heard by several animals.

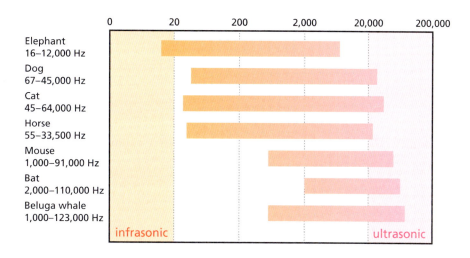

Elephant 16–12,000 Hz
Dog 67–45,000 Hz
Cat 45–64,000 Hz
Horse 55–33,500 Hz
Mouse 1,000–91,000 Hz
Bat 2,000–110,000 Hz
Beluga whale 1,000–123,000 Hz

1. The frequency f (in hertz) of the nth key of a piano is given by the function below.

   $$f(n) = 440 \times \left(\sqrt[12]{2}\right)^{n-49}$$

   What is the frequency of the note played by the 80th key? the 49th key?

2. Your friend guesses that a piano has 120 keys. Explain whether your friend's guess makes sense.

3. Which animals shown in the display can hear the note played by the 11th key on a piano?

Getting Ready for Chapter 5

Properties of Integer Exponents

EXAMPLE 1 Simplify the expression $\dfrac{x^5 \cdot x^2}{x^3}$.

$$\dfrac{x^5 \cdot x^2}{x^3} = \dfrac{x^{5+2}}{x^3} \qquad \text{Product of Powers Property}$$

$$= \dfrac{x^7}{x^3} \qquad \text{Simplify.}$$

$$= x^{7-3} \qquad \text{Quotient of Powers Property}$$

$$= x^4 \qquad \text{Simplify.}$$

EXAMPLE 2 Simplify the expression $\left(\dfrac{2s^3}{t}\right)^2$.

$$\left(\dfrac{2s^3}{t}\right)^2 = \dfrac{(2s^3)^2}{t^2} \qquad \text{Power of a Quotient Property}$$

$$= \dfrac{2^2 \cdot (s^3)^2}{t^2} \qquad \text{Power of a Product Property}$$

$$= \dfrac{4s^6}{t^2} \qquad \text{Power of a Power Property}$$

Simplify. Write the expression using only positive exponents.

1. $y^6 \cdot y$
2. $\dfrac{n^4}{n^3}$
3. $\dfrac{x^5}{x^6 \cdot x^2}$
4. $\dfrac{x^6}{x^5} \cdot 3x^2$
5. $\left(\dfrac{4w^3}{2z^2}\right)^3$
6. $\left(\dfrac{m^7 \cdot m}{z^2 \cdot m^3}\right)^2$

Rewriting Literal Equations

EXAMPLE 3 Solve the literal equation $-5y - 2x = 10$ for y.

$$-5y - 2x = 10 \qquad \text{Write the equation.}$$

$$-5y - 2x + 2x = 10 + 2x \qquad \text{Add } 2x \text{ to each side.}$$

$$-5y = 10 + 2x \qquad \text{Simplify.}$$

$$\dfrac{-5y}{-5} = \dfrac{10 + 2x}{-5} \qquad \text{Divide each side by } -5.$$

$$y = -2 - \dfrac{2}{5}x \qquad \text{Simplify.}$$

Solve the literal equation for y.

7. $4x + y = 2$
8. $x - \tfrac{1}{3}y = -1$
9. $8x - 4xy = 3$

5.1 nth Roots and Rational Exponents

> **Learning Target:** Evaluate expressions and solve equations using nth roots.
>
> **Success Criteria:**
> - I can explain the meaning of a rational exponent.
> - I can evaluate expressions with rational exponents.
> - I can solve equations using nth roots.

Previously, you learned that the nth root of a is

$$\sqrt[n]{a} = a^{1/n} \qquad \text{Definition of rational exponent}$$

for any real number a and integer n greater than 1.

INVESTIGATE Writing Expressions in Different Forms

Work with a partner.

1. Use the definition of a rational exponent and the properties of exponents to write each expression as a base with a single rational exponent or as a radical raised to an exponent.

	Radical raised to an exponent	Base with a single rational exponent
a.	$(\sqrt{5})^3$	
b.	$(\sqrt[4]{4})^2$	
c.	$(\sqrt[3]{9})^2$	
d.	$(\sqrt[5]{10})^4$	
e.	$(\sqrt{15})^3$	
f.	$(\sqrt[3]{27})^4$	
g.		$8^{2/3}$
h.		$6^{5/2}$
i.		$12^{3/4}$
j.		$10^{3/2}$
k.		$16^{3/2}$
l.		$20^{6/5}$

2. Use technology to evaluate each expression in Exercise 1. Round your answer to two decimal places, if necessary.

3. Simplify $\sqrt[n]{a^n}$. What does this imply about the relationship between raising an expression to the nth power and taking the nth root? How can you use this result to solve the equation $x^4 = 6$?

Vocabulary
nth root of a
index of a radical

Finding nth Roots

For an integer n greater than 1, if $b^n = a$, then b is an **nth root of a**. An nth root of a is written as $\sqrt[n]{a}$, where n is the **index of the radical**.

You can also write an nth root of a as a power of a.

$(a^{1/2})^2 = a^{(1/2) \cdot 2} = a^1 = a$

$(a^{1/3})^3 = a^{(1/3) \cdot 3} = a^1 = a$

$(a^{1/4})^4 = a^{(1/4) \cdot 4} = a^1 = a$

Because the square of $a^{1/2}$ is a, you can write $\sqrt{a} = a^{1/2}$. Similarly, $\sqrt[3]{a} = a^{1/3}$ and $\sqrt[4]{a} = a^{1/4}$. In general, $\sqrt[n]{a} = a^{1/n}$ for any integer n greater than 1.

Key Concept

Real nth Roots of a

Let n be an integer greater than 1 and let a be a real number.

n is an even integer:	$a < 0$	No real nth roots
	$a = 0$	One real nth root: $\sqrt[n]{0} = 0$
	$a > 0$	Two real nth roots: $\pm\sqrt[n]{a} = \pm a^{1/n}$
n is an odd integer:	$a < 0$	One real nth root: $\sqrt[n]{a} = a^{1/n}$
	$a = 0$	One real nth root: $\sqrt[n]{0} = 0$
	$a > 0$	One real nth root: $\sqrt[n]{a} = a^{1/n}$

EXAMPLE 1 Finding nth Roots

Find the indicated real nth root(s) of a.

a. $n = 3, a = -216$

Because $n = 3$ is odd and $a = -216 < 0$, -216 has one real cube root.

You can determine that $(-6)^3 = -216$.

▶ So, you can write $\sqrt[3]{-216} = -6$ or $(-216)^{1/3} = -6$.

b. $n = 4, a = 81$

Because $n = 4$ is even and $a = 81 > 0$, 81 has two real fourth roots.

You can determine that $3^4 = 81$ and $(-3)^4 = 81$.

▶ So, you can write $\pm\sqrt[4]{81} = \pm 3$ or $\pm 81^{1/4} = \pm 3$.

In-Class Practice

Self-Assessment

Find the indicated real nth root(s) of a.

1. $n = 4, a = 16$
2. $n = 3, a = -125$

Rational Exponents

Key Concept

Rational Exponents

Let $a^{1/n}$ be an nth root of a, and let m be a positive integer.

$$a^{m/n} = (a^{1/n})^m = (\sqrt[n]{a})^m \quad \text{or} \quad a^{m/n} = (a^m)^{1/n} = \sqrt[n]{a^m}$$

$$a^{-m/n} = \frac{1}{(a^{1/n})^m} = \frac{1}{(\sqrt[n]{a})^m}, a \neq 0 \quad \text{or} \quad a^{-m/n} = \frac{1}{(a^m)^{1/n}} = \frac{1}{\sqrt[n]{a^m}}, a \neq 0$$

EXAMPLE 2 — Evaluating Expressions with Rational Exponents

a. Evaluate $16^{3/2}$.

Rational Exponent Form: $16^{3/2} = (16^{1/2})^3 = 4^3 = 64$

Radical Form: $16^{3/2} = (\sqrt{16})^3 = 4^3 = 64$

b. Evaluate $32^{-3/5}$.

Rational Exponent Form: $32^{-3/5} = \dfrac{1}{32^{3/5}} = \dfrac{1}{(32^{1/5})^3} = \dfrac{1}{2^3} = \dfrac{1}{8}$

Radical Form: $32^{-3/5} = \dfrac{1}{32^{3/5}} = \dfrac{1}{(\sqrt[5]{32})^3} = \dfrac{1}{2^3} = \dfrac{1}{8}$

EXAMPLE 3 — Approximating Expressions with Rational Exponents

Evaluate each expression using technology. Round your answer to two decimal places.

a. $9^{1/5}$

$$9^{\frac{1}{5}} = 1.55184557392$$

▶ So, $9^{1/5} \approx 1.55$.

b. $(\sqrt[4]{7})^3$

Rewrite the expression as $7^{3/4}$.

$$7^{\frac{3}{4}} = 4.30351707066$$

▶ So, $(\sqrt[4]{7})^3 = 7^{3/4} \approx 4.30$.

In-Class Practice

Self-Assessment

Evaluate the expression without using technology.

3. $4^{5/2}$
4. $9^{-1/2}$
5. $81^{3/4}$

Evaluate the expression using technology. Round your answer to two decimal places.

6. $6^{2/5}$
7. $64^{-2/3}$
8. $(\sqrt[3]{-30})^2$

 I don't understand yet. I can do it with help. I can do it on my own. I can teach someone.

5.1 nth Roots and Rational Exponents

Solving Equations Using *n*th Roots

Raising to the *n*th power and taking the *n*th root are inverse operations.

$$\sqrt[n]{a^n} = (a^n)^{1/n} = a^{n \cdot 1/n} = a^1 = a$$

So, you can solve an equation of the form $u^n = d$, where u is an algebraic expression and d is a real number, by taking the *n*th root of each side.

EXAMPLE 4 Solving Equations Using *n*th Roots

Solve $(x - 3)^4 = 21$. Round your answer(s) to two decimal places.

$(x - 3)^4 = 21$	Write original equation.
$x - 3 = \pm\sqrt[4]{21}$	Take fourth root of each side.
$x = 3 \pm \sqrt[4]{21}$	Add 3 to each side.

▶ The solutions are $x = 3 + \sqrt[4]{21} \approx 5.14$ and $x = 3 - \sqrt[4]{21} \approx 0.86$.

EXAMPLE 5 Using a Formula

A university uses the formula $S = C(1 - r)^n$ to find the *salvage value* S (in dollars) of a seismograph, where C is the original cost (in dollars), r is the annual depreciation rate (in decimal form), and n is time (in years). What is the annual depreciation rate for a seismograph that depreciates from \$50,000 to \$8,000 over 10 years?

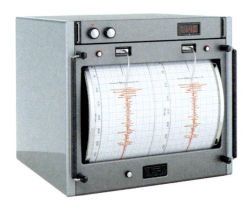

$S = C(1 - r)^n$	Write the depreciation formula.
$8{,}000 = 50{,}000(1 - r)^{10}$	Substitute for S, C, and n.
$\dfrac{4}{25} = (1 - r)^{10}$	Divide each side by 50,000 and simplify.
$\sqrt[10]{\dfrac{4}{25}} = 1 - r$	Take tenth root of each side.
$1 - \sqrt[10]{\dfrac{4}{25}} = r$	Solve for r.

▶ The annual depreciation rate is $1 - \sqrt[10]{\dfrac{4}{25}} \approx 0.167$, or about 16.7%.

In-Class Practice

Self-Assessment

Solve the equation. Round your answer(s) to two decimal places.

9. $8x^3 = 64$

10. $(x + 5)^4 = 16$

11. **WHAT IF?** In Example 5, what is the annual depreciation rate when the salvage value is \$6,000?

1 I don't understand yet. **2** I can do it with help. **3** I can do it on my own. **4** I can teach someone.

5.1 Practice

Find the indicated real nth root(s) of a. (See Example 1.)

1. $n = 3, a = 8$
2. $n = 5, a = -1$
3. $n = 4, a = 256$
4. $n = 6, a = -729$

Evaluate the expression without using technology. (See Example 2.)

5. $64^{1/6}$
6. $(-243)^{1/5}$
7. $25^{3/2}$
8. $16^{-7/4}$

SMP.3 ERROR ANALYSIS Describe and correct the error in evaluating the expression.

9.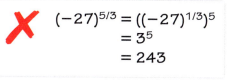
$$(-27)^{5/3} = ((-27)^{1/3})^5$$
$$= 3^5$$
$$= 243$$

10.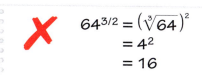
$$64^{3/2} = (\sqrt[3]{64})^2$$
$$= 4^2$$
$$= 16$$

Evaluate the expression using technology. Round your answer to two decimal places. (See Example 3.)

11. $25^{-1/3}$
12. $\sqrt[5]{32{,}768}$
13. $86^{-5/6}$
14. $(\sqrt[5]{-8})^8$

Solve the equation. Round your answer(s) to two decimal places. (See Example 4.)

15. $(x + 10)^5 = 70$
16. $5x^3 = 1{,}080$
17. $7x^4 = 56$
18. $\frac{1}{3}x^4 = 27$

19. When the average price of an item increases from p_1 to p_2 over a period of n years, the annual rate of inflation r (in decimal form) is given by $r = \left(\dfrac{p_2}{p_1}\right)^{1/n} - 1$. Find the rate of inflation for each item in the table. (See Example 5.)

Item	Price per pound in 2013	Price per pound in 2023
Potatoes	$0.611	$0.968
Oranges	$0.988	$1.509
Ground beef	$3.332	$4.813

20. **SMP.6** Between which two consecutive integers does $\sqrt[4]{125}$ lie? Explain your reasoning.

21. **SMP.1 DIG DEEPER** The mass of the particles that a river can transport is proportional to the sixth power of the speed of the river. A certain river normally flows at a speed of 1 meter per second. What must its speed be in order to transport particles that are twice as massive as usual? 10 times as massive? 100 times as massive? Justify your answers.

Interpreting Data

KEPLER'S LAWS OF PLANETARY MOTION Kepler's Laws describe the orbits of planets around the Sun. The third law can be given by $d^3 = t^2$, where d is the mean distance (in astronomical units) of a planet from the Sun and t is the time (in years) it takes the planet to orbit the Sun.

22. Rewrite the equation for the third law in the form $t = d^n$. Does the graph support your function?

23. The orbital period of Jupiter is 5.2 years. What is its mean distance from the Sun?

Review & Refresh

24. Use finite differences to determine the degree of the polynomial function that fits the data. Then use technology to find the polynomial function.

x	−2	−1	0	1	2	3
f(x)	1	9	1	1	9	1

25. Write an equation of the parabola in vertex form.

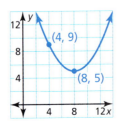

26. Graph $f(x) = (x + 1)(x - 2)(x - 4)$.

27. The table shows the distances run by an athlete on a treadmill over time. What type of function can you use to model the data? Predict the distance traveled by the runner after 30 minutes.

Time (minutes), x	Distance (miles), y
5	0.5
10	1.0
15	1.5
20	2.0
25	2.5

5.2 Properties of Rational Exponents and Radicals

Learning Target: Simplify radical expressions.

Success Criteria:
- I can simplify radical expressions with rational exponents.
- I can explain when radical expressions are in simplest form.
- I can simplify variable expressions containing rational exponents and radicals.

INVESTIGATE Reviewing Properties of Radicals

Work with a partner.

1. The Product Property of Square Roots states that the square root of a product equals the product of the square roots of the factors.

$$\sqrt{64x^2} = \sqrt{64} \cdot \sqrt{x^2} \quad \text{Product Property of Square Roots}$$
$$= 8x \quad \text{Simplify.}$$

   Describe the behavior of the graphs of $y = \sqrt{64x^2}$ and $y = 8x$. What do you notice? Use technology to check your graphs and explain the results.

2. You can extend the Product Property of Square Roots to other radicals, such as cube roots.

$$\sqrt[3]{64x^3} = \sqrt[3]{64} \cdot \sqrt[3]{x^3} \quad \text{Product Property of Cube Roots}$$
$$= 4x \quad \text{Simplify.}$$

   Describe the behavior of the graphs of $y = \sqrt[3]{64x^3}$ and $y = 4x$. What do you notice? Use technology to check your graphs and explain the results.

3. Explain how you can change the function $y = 8x$ so that it coincides with the graph of $y = \sqrt{64x^2}$ for all values of x.

4. Determine the values of n for which $\sqrt[n]{x^n} = x$ and $\sqrt[n]{x^n} = |x|$.

5. **SMP.5** Explain how you can use a tool to help you determine the values of n in Exercise 4.

Vocabulary
simplest form of a radical
like radicals

Properties of Rational Exponents

The properties of integer exponents can also be applied to rational exponents.

Let a and b be real numbers and let m and n be rational numbers, such that the quantities in each property are real numbers.

Property Name	Definition	Example
Product of Powers	$a^m \cdot a^n = a^{m+n}$	$5^{1/2} \cdot 5^{3/2} = 5^{(1/2 + 3/2)} = 5^2 = 25$
Power of a Power	$(a^m)^n = a^{mn}$	$(3^{5/2})^2 = 3^{(5/2 \cdot 2)} = 3^5 = 243$
Power of a Product	$(ab)^m = a^m b^m$	$(16 \cdot 9)^{1/2} = 16^{1/2} \cdot 9^{1/2} = 4 \cdot 3 = 12$
Negative Exponent	$a^{-m} = \dfrac{1}{a^m},\ a \neq 0$	$36^{-1/2} = \dfrac{1}{36^{1/2}} = \dfrac{1}{6}$
Zero Exponent	$a^0 = 1,\ a \neq 0$	$213^0 = 1$
Quotient of Powers	$\dfrac{a^m}{a^n} = a^{m-n},\ a \neq 0$	$\dfrac{4^{5/2}}{4^{1/2}} = 4^{(5/2 - 1/2)} = 4^2 = 16$
Power of a Quotient	$\left(\dfrac{a}{b}\right)^m = \dfrac{a^m}{b^m},\ b \neq 0$	$\left(\dfrac{27}{64}\right)^{1/3} = \dfrac{27^{1/3}}{64^{1/3}} = \dfrac{3}{4}$

EXAMPLE 1 Using Properties of Exponents

Use the properties of rational exponents to simplify each expression.

a. $7^{1/4} \cdot 7^{1/2} = 7^{(1/4 + 1/2)} = 7^{3/4}$ Product of Powers Property

b. $(4^5 \cdot 3^5)^{-1/5} = [(4 \cdot 3)^5]^{-1/5}$ Power of a Product Property

$\qquad = (12^5)^{-1/5}$ Multiply.

$\qquad = 12^{[5 \cdot (-1/5)]}$ Power of a Power Property

$\qquad = 12^{-1}$ Simplify.

$\qquad = \dfrac{1}{12}$ Definition of negative exponent

c. $\dfrac{5}{5^{1/3}} = \dfrac{5^1}{5^{1/3}} = 5^{(1 - 1/3)} = 5^{2/3}$ Quotient of Powers Property

d. $\left(\dfrac{42^{1/3}}{6^{1/3}}\right)^2 = \left[\left(\dfrac{42}{6}\right)^{1/3}\right]^2$ Power of a Quotient Property

$\qquad = (7^{1/3})^2$ Divide.

$\qquad = 7^{2/3}$ Power of a Power Property

In-Class Practice

Self-Assessment

Simplify the expression.

1. $2^{3/4} \cdot 2^{1/2}$

2. $\dfrac{3}{3^{1/4}}$

3. $(5^{1/3} \cdot 7^{1/4})^3$

 I don't understand yet.   I can do it with help.   I can do it on my own.   I can teach someone.

Simplifying Radical Expressions

Key Concept

Properties of Radicals

Let a and b be real numbers such that the indicated roots are real numbers, and let n be an integer greater than 1.

Property Name	Definition	Example
Product Property	$\sqrt[n]{a \cdot b} = \sqrt[n]{a} \cdot \sqrt[n]{b}$	$\sqrt[3]{4} \cdot \sqrt[3]{2} = \sqrt[3]{8} = 2$
Quotient Property	$\sqrt[n]{\dfrac{a}{b}} = \dfrac{\sqrt[n]{a}}{\sqrt[n]{b}}, b \neq 0$	$\dfrac{\sqrt[4]{162}}{\sqrt[4]{2}} = \sqrt[4]{\dfrac{162}{2}} = \sqrt[4]{81} = 3$

EXAMPLE 2   Using Properties of Radicals

Use the properties of radicals to simplify each expression.

a. $\sqrt[3]{12} \cdot \sqrt[3]{18} = \sqrt[3]{12 \cdot 18} = \sqrt[3]{216} = 6$ **Product Property of Radicals**

b. $\dfrac{\sqrt[4]{80}}{\sqrt[4]{5}} = \sqrt[4]{\dfrac{80}{5}} = \sqrt[4]{16} = 2$ **Quotient Property of Radicals**

An expression involving a radical with index n is in **simplest form** when these three conditions are met.

- No radicands have perfect nth powers as factors other than 1.
- No radicands contain fractions.
- No radicals appear in the denominator of a fraction.

EXAMPLE 3   Writing Radicals in Simplest Form

Write each expression in simplest form.

a. $\sqrt[3]{135} = \sqrt[3]{27 \cdot 5}$ **Factor out perfect cube.**

$\phantom{\sqrt[3]{135}} = \sqrt[3]{27} \cdot \sqrt[3]{5} = 3\sqrt[3]{5}$ **Product Property of Radicals**

b. $\dfrac{\sqrt[5]{7}}{\sqrt[5]{8}} = \dfrac{\sqrt[5]{7}}{\sqrt[5]{8}} \cdot \dfrac{\sqrt[5]{4}}{\sqrt[5]{4}}$ **Make the radicand in the denominator a perfect fifth power.**

$\phantom{\dfrac{\sqrt[5]{7}}{\sqrt[5]{8}}} = \dfrac{\sqrt[5]{28}}{\sqrt[5]{32}} = \dfrac{\sqrt[5]{28}}{2}$ **Product Property of Radicals**

In-Class Practice

Self-Assessment

4. Simplify (a) $\sqrt[4]{27} \cdot \sqrt[4]{3}$ and (b) $\dfrac{\sqrt[3]{250}}{\sqrt[3]{2}}$.

1 I don't understand yet.   **2** I can do it with help.   **3** I can do it on my own.   **4** I can teach someone.

For a denominator that is a sum or difference involving square roots, multiply both the numerator and denominator by the *conjugate* of the denominator. The expressions $a\sqrt{b} + c\sqrt{d}$ and $a\sqrt{b} - c\sqrt{d}$ are conjugates of each other, where a, b, c, and d are rational numbers.

EXAMPLE 4 Writing a Radical Expression in Simplest Form

Write each expression in simplest form.

a. $\dfrac{1}{5 + \sqrt{3}} = \dfrac{1}{5 + \sqrt{3}} \cdot \dfrac{5 - \sqrt{3}}{5 - \sqrt{3}}$ The conjugate is $5 - \sqrt{3}$.

$= \dfrac{1(5 - \sqrt{3})}{5^2 - (\sqrt{3})^2}$ Sum and Difference Pattern

$= \dfrac{5 - \sqrt{3}}{22}$ Simplify.

b. $\dfrac{\sqrt{7}}{\sqrt{10} - \sqrt{2}} = \dfrac{\sqrt{7}}{\sqrt{10} - \sqrt{2}} \cdot \dfrac{\sqrt{10} + \sqrt{2}}{\sqrt{10} + \sqrt{2}}$ The conjugate is $\sqrt{10} + \sqrt{2}$.

$= \dfrac{\sqrt{7}(\sqrt{10} + \sqrt{2})}{(\sqrt{10})^2 - (\sqrt{2})^2}$ Sum and Difference Pattern

$= \dfrac{\sqrt{70} + \sqrt{14}}{8}$ Simplify.

Radical expressions with the same index and radicand are **like radicals**. To add or subtract like radicals, use the Distributive Property.

EXAMPLE 5 Adding and Subtracting Like Radicals and Roots

Simplify each expression.

a. $\sqrt[4]{10} + 7\sqrt[4]{10} = (1 + 7)\sqrt[4]{10} = 8\sqrt[4]{10}$ Distributive Property

b. $2(8^{1/5}) + 10(8^{1/5}) = (2 + 10)(8^{1/5}) = 12(8^{1/5})$ Distributive Property

c. $\sqrt[3]{54} - \sqrt[3]{2} = \sqrt[3]{27} \cdot \sqrt[3]{2} - \sqrt[3]{2}$ Product Property of Radicals

$= 3\sqrt[3]{2} - \sqrt[3]{2}$ Simplify.

$= (3 - 1)\sqrt[3]{2} = 2\sqrt[3]{2}$ Distributive Property

In-Class Practice

Self-Assessment

Simplify the expression.

5. $\dfrac{3}{6 - \sqrt{2}}$

6. $7\sqrt[5]{12} - \sqrt[5]{12}$

7. $4(9^{2/3}) + 8(9^{2/3})$

Simplifying Variable Expressions

The properties of rational exponents and radicals can also be applied to expressions involving variables. Because a variable can be positive, negative, or zero, sometimes absolute value is needed when simplifying a variable expression.

	Rule	Example
When n is odd	$\sqrt[n]{x^n} = x$	$\sqrt[7]{5^7} = 5$ and $\sqrt[7]{(-5)^7} = -5$
When n is even	$\sqrt[n]{x^n} = |x|$	$\sqrt[4]{3^4} = 3$ and $\sqrt[4]{(-3)^4} = 3$

Absolute value is not needed when all variables are assumed to be positive.

EXAMPLE 6 Simplifying Variable Expressions

Simplify each expression.

a. $\sqrt[3]{64y^6} = \sqrt[3]{4^3(y^2)^3} = \sqrt[3]{4^3} \cdot \sqrt[3]{(y^2)^3} = 4y^2$

b. $\sqrt[4]{\dfrac{x^4}{y^8}} = \dfrac{\sqrt[4]{x^4}}{\sqrt[4]{y^8}} = \dfrac{\sqrt[4]{x^4}}{\sqrt[4]{(y^2)^4}} = \dfrac{|x|}{y^2}$

EXAMPLE 7 Writing Variable Expressions in Simplest Form

Write each expression in simplest form. Assume all variables are positive.

a. $\sqrt[4]{16a^7b^{11}c^4} = \sqrt[4]{16a^4a^3b^8b^3c^4}$ Factor out perfect fourth powers.

  $= \sqrt[4]{16a^4b^8c^4} \cdot \sqrt[4]{a^3b^3}$ Product Property of Radicals

  $= 2ab^2c\sqrt[4]{a^3b^3}$ Simplify.

b. $\dfrac{14xy^{1/3}}{2x^{3/4}z^{-6}} = 7x^{(1-3/4)}y^{1/3}z^{-(-6)} = 7x^{1/4}y^{1/3}z^6$

c. $5\sqrt{y} + 6\sqrt{y} = (5+6)\sqrt{y} = 11\sqrt{y}$

d. $12\sqrt[3]{2z^5} - z\sqrt[3]{54z^2} = 12z\sqrt[3]{2z^2} - 3z\sqrt[3]{2z^2} = (12z - 3z)\sqrt[3]{2z^2} = 9z\sqrt[3]{2z^2}$

In-Class Practice

Self-Assessment

Simplify the expression.

8. $\sqrt[3]{27q^3}$

9. $\sqrt[4]{81y^8}$

10. $\sqrt[4]{\dfrac{a^8}{256b^4}}$

Simplify the expression. Assume all variables are positive.

11. $\sqrt[6]{36p^6q^8r^{10}}$

12. $\dfrac{6xy^{3/4}}{3x^{1/2}y^{1/2}}$

13. $\sqrt{9w^5} - w\sqrt{w^3}$

1 I don't understand yet. **2** I can do it with help. **3** I can do it on my own. **4** I can teach someone.

5.2 Practice

Use the properties of rational exponents to simplify the expression. (See Example 1.)

1. $(9^2)^{1/3}$

2. $\dfrac{6}{6^{1/4}}$

3. $\left(\dfrac{8^4}{10^4}\right)^{-1/4}$

4. $(3^{-2/3} \cdot 3^{1/3})^{-1}$

5. $\dfrac{2^{2/3} \cdot 16^{2/3}}{4^{2/3}}$

6. $\dfrac{49^{3/8} \cdot 49^{7/8}}{7^{5/4}}$

Use the properties of radicals to simplify the expression. (See Example 2.)

7. $\sqrt{2} \cdot \sqrt{72}$

8. $\sqrt[4]{5} \cdot \sqrt[4]{125}$

9. $\dfrac{\sqrt[5]{486}}{\sqrt[5]{2}}$

10. $\dfrac{\sqrt{2}}{\sqrt{32}}$

11. $\dfrac{\sqrt[3]{6} \cdot \sqrt[3]{72}}{\sqrt[3]{2}}$

12. $\dfrac{\sqrt[3]{3} \cdot \sqrt[3]{18}}{\sqrt[6]{2} \cdot \sqrt[6]{2}}$

Write the expression in simplest form. (See Example 3.)

13. $\sqrt[4]{567}$

14. $\sqrt[5]{288}$

15. $\dfrac{\sqrt[3]{5}}{\sqrt[3]{4}}$

16. $\sqrt{\dfrac{3}{8}}$

17. $\sqrt[3]{\dfrac{7}{4}}$

18. $\sqrt[4]{\dfrac{1{,}296}{25}}$

19. **ERROR ANALYSIS** Describe and correct the error in simplifying the expression.

$$\sqrt[3]{104} = \sqrt[3]{26 \cdot 4} = 2\sqrt[3]{26}$$

Write the expression in simplest form. (See Example 4.)

20. $\dfrac{1}{1+\sqrt{3}}$

21. $\dfrac{5}{3-\sqrt{2}}$

22. $\dfrac{11}{9-\sqrt{6}}$

23. $\dfrac{9}{\sqrt{3}+\sqrt{7}}$

24. $\dfrac{2}{\sqrt{8}+\sqrt{7}}$

25. $\dfrac{\sqrt{6}}{\sqrt{3}-\sqrt{5}}$

Simplify the expression. (See Example 5.)

26. $8\sqrt[6]{5} - 12\sqrt[6]{5}$

27. $9\sqrt[3]{11} + 3\sqrt[3]{11}$

28. $3(14^{1/4}) + 9(14^{1/4})$

29. $\sqrt[5]{224} + 3\sqrt[5]{7}$

30. $5\sqrt{12} - 19\sqrt{3}$

31. $5(24^{1/3}) - 4(3^{1/3})$

32. **ERROR ANALYSIS** Describe and correct the error in simplifying the expression.

$$\sqrt[6]{\dfrac{64}{w^6}} = \dfrac{\sqrt[6]{64}}{\sqrt[6]{w^6}} = \dfrac{\sqrt[6]{2^6}}{\sqrt[6]{w^6}} = \dfrac{2}{w}$$

240 Chapter 5 Rational Exponents and Radical Functions

Simplify the expression. (See Example 6.)

33. $\sqrt[4]{81y^8}$

34. $\sqrt[3]{64r^3t^6}$

35. $\sqrt[5]{\dfrac{m^{10}}{n^5}}$

36. $\sqrt[4]{\dfrac{k^{16}}{16z^4}}$

▶ 37. $\sqrt[6]{\dfrac{g^6 h}{h^7}}$

38. $\sqrt[8]{\dfrac{n^2 p^{-1}}{n^{18} p^7}}$

39. **OPEN-ENDED** Write two variable expressions involving radicals, one that needs absolute value when simplifying and one that does not need absolute value.

Write the expression in simplest form. Assume all variables are positive. (See Example 7.)

40. $\sqrt{81 a^7 b^{12} c^9}$

▶ 41. $\sqrt[5]{\dfrac{160 m^6}{n^7}}$

42. $\dfrac{w^7}{\sqrt[5]{z^{13}}}$

▶ 43. $12\sqrt[3]{y} + 9\sqrt[3]{y}$

44. $\dfrac{18 w^{1/3} v^{5/4}}{27 w^{4/3} v^{1/2}}$

45. $\sqrt[4]{16 w^{10}} + 2w\sqrt[4]{w^6}$

CONNECT CONCEPTS Find simplified expressions for the perimeter and area of the figure.

46.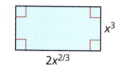

47.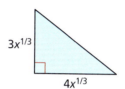

48. **CONNECTION TO REAL LIFE** The apparent magnitude of a star is a number that indicates how faint the star is in relation to other stars. The expression $\dfrac{2.512^{m_1}}{2.512^{m_2}}$ tells how many times fainter a star with apparent magnitude m_1 is than a star with apparent magnitude m_2.

Star	Apparent magnitude
Vega	0.03
Altair	0.77
Deneb	1.25

a. How many times fainter is Altair than Vega?

b. How many times fainter is Deneb than Altair?

c. How many times fainter is Deneb than Vega?

49. **CONNECTION TO REAL LIFE** You fill two round balloons with water. One balloon contains twice as much water as the other balloon.

a. Solve the formula for the volume of a sphere, $V = \frac{4}{3}\pi r^3$, for r.

b. Use your result from part (a) and the formula for the surface area of a sphere, $S = 4\pi r^2$, to show that $S = (4\pi)^{1/3}(3V)^{2/3}$.

c. Compare the surface areas of the two water balloons using the formula in part (b).

50. **SMP.7** Explain whether the expressions $(x^2)^{1/6}$ and $(x^{1/6})^2$ are equivalent for all values of x.

Interpreting Data

RADICAL FUNCTIONS The graphs of the functions $y = \sqrt{x}$, $y = \sqrt[3]{x}$, $y = \sqrt[4]{x}$, and $y = \sqrt[5]{x}$ are shown.

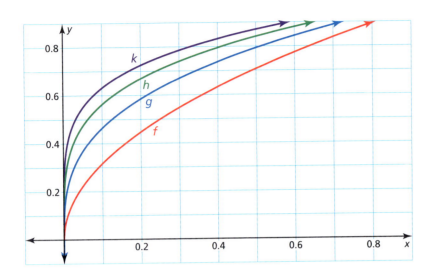

51. Match each graph with its function.

52. Do any of the graphs of the functions share a common point? Which point?

53. Which of the graphs extend into the third quadrant?

Review & Refresh

54. Evaluate $125^{2/3}$ without using technology.

55. Identify the focus, directrix, and axis of symmetry of the parabola. Then graph the equation.

$$y = 2x^2$$

56. Write the cubic function whose graph is shown.

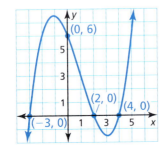

57. Write a rule for g. Describe the graph of g as a transformation of the graph of f.

$$f(x) = x^4 + 2x^3 - 4x^2$$
$$g(x) = f(2x)$$

58. While standing on an apartment balcony, you drop a pair of sunglasses from a height of 25 feet.

a. Write a function h that gives the height (in feet) of the pair of sunglasses after t seconds. How long do the sunglasses take to hit the ground?

b. Find and interpret $h(0.25) - h(1)$.

59. Determine whether $g(x) = x^5 + 2x - 3$ is *even*, *odd*, or *neither*.

5.3 Graphing Radical Functions

Learning Target: Describe and graph transformations of radical functions.

Success Criteria:
- I can graph radical functions.
- I can describe transformations of radical functions.
- I can write functions that represent transformations of radical functions.

INVESTIGATE Graphing Radical Functions

Work with a partner.

1. In your own words, define a *radical* function. Give several examples.

2. Graph each function. How are the graphs alike? How are they different?

   a. $f(x) = \sqrt{x}$
   b. $f(x) = \sqrt[3]{x}$
   c. $f(x) = \sqrt[4]{x}$
   d. $f(x) = \sqrt[5]{x}$

3. Match each function with its graph. Then describe g as a transformation of its parent function f.

   a. $g(x) = \sqrt{x+2}$
   b. $g(x) = \sqrt{x}-2$
   c. $g(x) = \sqrt[3]{x}+2$
   d. $g(x) = \sqrt[4]{x}-2$
   e. $g(x) = \sqrt[3]{x+2}-2$
   f. $g(x) = -\sqrt[5]{x+2}$

   A.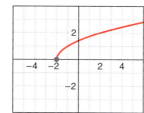
   D.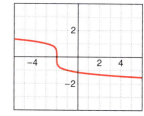
   B.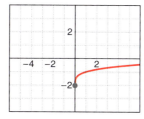
   E.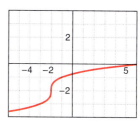
   C.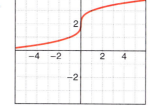
   F.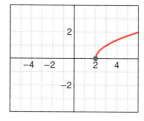

4. Describe the transformation of $f(x) = \sqrt{x}$ represented by $g(x) = -\sqrt{x+1}$. Then graph each function.

Vocabulary

radical function

Graphing Radical Functions

A **radical function** contains a radical expression with the independent variable in the radicand. When the radical is a square root, the function is a *square root function*. When the radical is a cube root, the function is a *cube root function*.

The parent function for the family of square root functions is $f(x) = \sqrt{x}$.

The parent function for the family of cube root functions is $f(x) = \sqrt[3]{x}$.

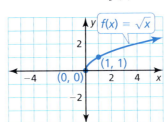
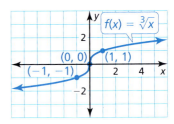

Domain: $x \geq 0$, Range: $y \geq 0$

Domain and range: All real numbers

EXAMPLE 1 Graphing Radical Functions

a. Graph $f(x) = \sqrt{\frac{1}{4}x}$. Find the domain and range.

Make a table of values and sketch the graph.

x	0	4	8	12	16
y	0	1	1.41	1.73	2

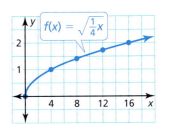

▶ The radicand of a square root must be nonnegative. So, the domain is $\{x \mid x \geq 0\}$. The range is $\{y \mid y \geq 0\}$.

b. Graph $g(x) = -3\sqrt[3]{x}$. Find the domain and range.

Make a table of values and sketch the graph.

x	−2	−1	0	1	2
y	3.78	3	0	−3	−3.78

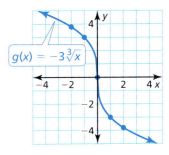

▶ The radicand of a cube root can be any real number. So, the domain and range are all real numbers.

In-Class Practice

Self-Assessment

Graph the function. Find the domain and range.

1. $g(x) = \sqrt{x+1}$

2. $f(x) = \sqrt[3]{2x}$

 I don't understand yet.

 I can do it with help.

 I can do it on my own.

4 I can teach someone.

Graphing Transformations of Radical Functions

Transformation	Examples	
Horizontal Translation: $f(x-h)$	$g(x) = \sqrt{x-2}$	2 units right
	$g(x) = \sqrt{x+3}$	3 units left
Vertical Translation: $f(x)+k$	$g(x) = \sqrt{x}+7$	7 units up
	$g(x) = \sqrt{x}-1$	1 unit down
Reflection: $f(-x)$ or $-f(x)$	$g(x) = \sqrt{-x}$	in the y-axis
	$g(x) = -\sqrt{x}$	in the x-axis
Horizontal Stretch or Shrink: $f(ax)$	$g(x) = \sqrt{3x}$	shrink by a factor of $\frac{1}{3}$
	$g(x) = \sqrt{\frac{1}{2}x}$	stretch by a factor of 2
Vertical Stretch or Shrink: $a \cdot f(x)$	$g(x) = 4\sqrt{x}$	stretch by a factor of 4
	$g(x) = \frac{1}{5}\sqrt{x}$	shrink by a factor of $\frac{1}{5}$

EXAMPLE 2 — Transforming Radical Functions

Describe the transformation of f represented by g. Then graph each function.

a. $f(x) = \sqrt{x}, g(x) = \sqrt{x-3}+4$

The function is of the form $g(x) = \sqrt{x-h}+k$, where $h = 3$ and $k = 4$.

▶ So, the graph of g is a translation 3 units right and 4 units up of the graph of f.

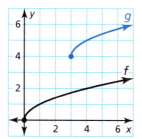

b. $f(x) = \sqrt[3]{x}, g(x) = \sqrt[3]{-8x}$

The function is of the form $g(x) = \sqrt[3]{ax}$, where $a = -8$.

▶ So, the graph of g is a horizontal shrink by a factor of $\frac{1}{8}$ and a reflection in the y-axis of the graph of f.

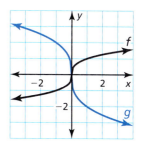

In-Class Practice

Self-Assessment

3. Describe the transformation of $f(x) = \sqrt[3]{x}$ represented by $g(x) = -\sqrt[3]{x} - 2$. Then graph each function.

Writing Transformations of Radical Functions

EXAMPLE 3 **Using a Transformed Radical Function**

The function $E(d) = 0.25\sqrt{d}$ approximates the number of seconds it takes a dropped object to fall d feet on Earth. The function $M(d) = 1.6 \cdot E(d)$ approximates the number of seconds it takes a dropped object to fall d feet on Mars. How long does it take a dropped object to fall 64 feet on Mars?

Write a rule for M. Then find $M(64)$.

$M(d) = 1.6 \cdot E(d)$

$ = 1.6 \cdot 0.25\sqrt{d}$ Substitute $0.25\sqrt{d}$ for $E(d)$.

$ = 0.4\sqrt{d}$ Simplify.

$M(64) = 0.4\sqrt{64} = 0.4(8) = 3.2$

▶ It takes a dropped object about 3.2 seconds to fall 64 feet on Mars.

EXAMPLE 4 **Writing a Transformed Radical Function**

Let the graph of g be a horizontal shrink by a factor of $\frac{1}{6}$, followed by a translation 3 units left of the graph of $f(x) = \sqrt[3]{x}$. Write a rule for g.

First write a function h that represents the horizontal shrink of f.

$h(x) = f(6x)$ Multiply the input by $1 \div \frac{1}{6} = 6$.

$ = \sqrt[3]{6x}$ Replace x with $6x$ in $f(x)$.

Then write a function g that represents the translation of h.

$g(x) = h(x + 3)$ Subtract -3, or add 3, to the input.

$ = \sqrt[3]{6(x + 3)}$ Replace x with $x + 3$ in $h(x)$.

$ = \sqrt[3]{6x + 18}$ Distributive Property

▶ The transformed function is $g(x) = \sqrt[3]{6x + 18}$.

In-Class Practice

Self-Assessment

4. **WHAT IF?** In Example 3, the function $N(d) = 2.4 \cdot E(d)$ approximates the number of seconds it takes a dropped object to fall d feet on the Moon. How long does it take a dropped object to fall 25 feet on the Moon?

5. In Example 4, is the transformed function the same when you perform the translation followed by the horizontal shrink? Explain your reasoning.

Graphing Parabolas and Circles

EXAMPLE 5   **Graphing a Parabola (Horizontal Axis of Symmetry)**

Use radical functions to graph $\frac{1}{2}y^2 = x$. Identify the vertex and the direction that the parabola opens.

Solve for y.

$\frac{1}{2}y^2 = x$ Write the original equation.

$y^2 = 2x$ Multiply each side by 2.

$y = \pm\sqrt{2x}$ Take square root of each side.

Graph both radical functions.

$y_1 = \sqrt{2x}$

$y_2 = -\sqrt{2x}$

▶ The vertex is $(0, 0)$ and the parabola opens right.

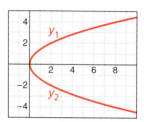

EXAMPLE 6   **Graphing a Circle (Center at the Origin)**

Use radical functions to graph $x^2 + y^2 = 16$. Identify the radius and the intercepts.

Solve for y.

$x^2 + y^2 = 16$ Write the original equation.

$y^2 = 16 - x^2$ Subtract x^2 from each side.

$y = \pm\sqrt{16 - x^2}$ Take square root of each side.

Graph both radical functions.

$y_1 = \sqrt{16 - x^2}$

$y_2 = -\sqrt{16 - x^2}$

▶ The radius is 4 units. The x-intercepts are ± 4. The y-intercepts are also ± 4.

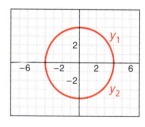

In-Class Practice

Self-Assessment

6. Use radical functions to graph $-4y^2 = x + 1$. Identify the vertex and the direction that the parabola opens.

7. Use radical functions to graph $y^2 = 49 - x^2$. Identify the radius and the intercepts of the circle.

1 I don't understand yet.   **2** I can do it with help.   **3** I can do it on my own.   **4** I can teach someone.

5.3 Practice

Graph the function. Find the domain and range. (See Example 1.)

1. $g(x) = \frac{1}{5}\sqrt{x-3}$

2. $f(x) = \sqrt[3]{-5x}$

3. $g(x) = -3(x+1)^{1/3}$

4. $h(x) = -\sqrt[4]{x}$

Describe the transformation of f represented by g. Then graph each function. (See Example 2.)

5. $f(x) = \sqrt[3]{x}$, $g(x) = -\sqrt[3]{x} - 1$

6. $f(x) = \sqrt{x}$, $g(x) = 2\sqrt{x-1}$

7. $f(x) = x^{1/2}$, $g(x) = \frac{1}{4}(-x)^{1/2}$

8. $f(x) = \sqrt[4]{x}$, $g(x) = 2\sqrt[4]{x+5} - 4$

9. The functions approximate the velocity (in feet per second) of an object dropped from a height of x feet right before it hits the ground on Earth and on Mars.

   Earth: $E(x) = 8\sqrt{x}$

   Mars: $M(x) = 0.6 \cdot E(x)$

   What is the velocity of an object dropped from a height of 25 feet right before it hits the ground on Mars? (See Example 3.)

10. **SMP.3 ERROR ANALYSIS** Describe and correct the error in graphing $f(x) = \sqrt{x-2} - 2$.

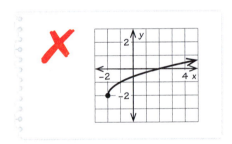

Write a rule for g described by the transformations of the graph of f. (See Example 4.)

11. Let g be a vertical stretch by a factor of 2, followed by a translation 2 units up of the graph of $f(x) = \sqrt{x} + 3$.

12. Let g be a translation 1 unit down and 5 units right, followed by a reflection in the x-axis of the graph of $f(x) = -\frac{1}{2}\sqrt[4]{x} + \frac{3}{2}$.

Write a rule for g.

13.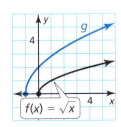

14.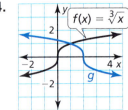

Write a rule for g that represents the indicated transformation of the graph of f.

15. $f(x) = \frac{1}{3}\sqrt{x-1}$, $g(x) = -f(x) + 9$

16. $f(x) = \sqrt[3]{x^2 + 10x}$, $g(x) = \frac{1}{4}f(-x) + 6$

Use radical functions to graph the equation of the parabola. Identify the vertex and the direction that the parabola opens. (See Example 5.)

17. $\frac{1}{4}y^2 = x$

18. $3y^2 = x$

▶ **19.** $-8y^2 + 2 = x$

20. $\frac{1}{2}x = y^2 - 4$

Use radical functions to graph the equation of the circle. Identify the radius and the intercepts. (See Example 6.)

21. $x^2 + y^2 = 9$

22. $x^2 + y^2 = 4$

▶ **23.** $1 - y^2 = x^2$

24. $-y^2 = x^2 - 36$

SMP.6 Complete the statement with *sometimes*, *always*, or *never*.

25. The domain of the function $y = a\sqrt{x}$ is _____ $x \geq 0$.

26. The range of the function $y = a\sqrt{x}$ is _____ $y \geq 0$.

27. The domain and range of the function $y = \sqrt[3]{x - h} + k$ are _____ all real numbers.

28. The domain of the function $y = a\sqrt{-x} + k$ is _____ $x \geq 0$.

29. The *period* of a pendulum is the time the pendulum takes to complete one back-and-forth swing. The period T (in seconds) can be modeled by the function $T = 1.11\sqrt{\ell}$, where ℓ is the length (in feet) of the pendulum. Estimate the length of a pendulum with a period of 2 seconds.

30. CONNECT CONCEPTS The surface area S of a right circular cone with a slant height of 1 unit is given by $S = \pi r + \pi r^2$, where r is the radius of the cone.

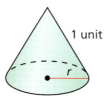

a. Use completing the square to show that $r = \frac{1}{\sqrt{\pi}}\sqrt{S + \frac{\pi}{4}} - \frac{1}{2}$.

b. Use technology to graph the equation in part (a). Then find the radius of a right circular cone with a slant height of 1 unit and a surface area of $\frac{3\pi}{4}$ square units.

31. SMP.1 DIG DEEPER The graph of a radical function f passes through $(3, 1)$ and $(4, 0)$. Explain your reasoning in writing two different functions that can represent $f(x + 2) + 1$.

Interpreting Data

INCLINED PLANE In one of Galileo's experiments, he placed an inclined plane on a table, and a shelf at the end of the plane. He released a metal ball that traveled down the plane, across the shelf, and fell to the floor. The initial heights H (in points) above the table and the horizontal distances traveled D (in points) from the end of the shelf are shown.

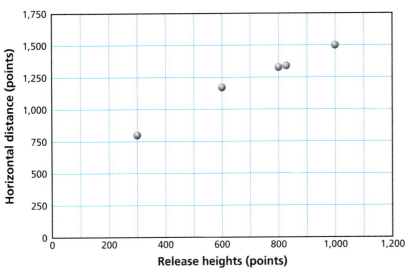

32. Describe the shape of the data.

33. Graph the function $D = 47.086\sqrt{H}$. Does the function appear to be a good fit for the data?

Review & Refresh

Write the expression in simplest form. Assume all variables are positive.

34. $\sqrt[3]{216p^9}$

35. $\dfrac{\sqrt[5]{32}}{\sqrt[5]{m^3}}$

36. $\sqrt[4]{n^4 q} + 7n\sqrt[4]{q}$

37. $\dfrac{21ab^{3/2}}{3a^{1/3}b^{1/2}c^{-1/4}}$

38. Use finite differences to determine the degree of the polynomial function that fits the data. Then use technology to find the polynomial function.

x	−3	−2	−1	0	1	2
f(x)	−7	−3	−2	−1	3	13

39. Evaluate $10^{2/3}$ using technology. Round your answer to two decimal places.

Solve the equation.

40. $|3x + 2| = 5$

41. $|x + 8| = |2x + 2|$

42. Write a piecewise function represented by the graph.

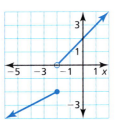

43. Solve the system.

$3x + 2y - z = -11$
$2x + y + 2z = 3$
$4x - 5y + z = -13$

5.4 Solving Radical Equations and Inequalities

Learning Target: Solve equations and inequalities containing radicals.

Success Criteria:
- I can solve radical equations and inequalities.
- I can identify extraneous solutions of radical equations.
- I can solve real-life problems involving radical equations.

INVESTIGATE Solving Radical Equations

Work with a partner.

1. Two students solve the equation $x + 2 = \sqrt{5x + 16}$ as shown. Justify each solution step in the first student's solution. Then describe each student's method. Are the methods valid? Explain.

Student 1

$x + 2 = \sqrt{5x + 16}$ Write the equation.

$(x + 2)^2 = \left(\sqrt{5x + 16}\right)^2$ _____

$x^2 + 4x + 4 = 5x + 16$ _____

$x^2 - x - 12 = 0$ _____

$(x - 4)(x + 3) = 0$ _____

$x - 4 = 0$ or $x + 3 = 0$ _____

$x = 4$ or $x = -3$ _____

Student 2

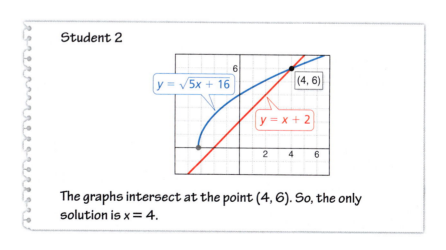

The graphs intersect at the point (4, 6). So, the only solution is $x = 4$.

2. Which student is correct? Explain why the other student's solution is incorrect and how the student arrived at an incorrect answer.

3. Explain how you might solve the equation $(9n)^{3/2} - 7 = 20$.

Vocabulary
radical equation
extraneous solution

Solving Equations

A **radical equation** contains radicals that have variables in the radicands. An example of a radical equation is $2\sqrt{x+1} = 4$. You can solve a radical equation using the following steps.

- Isolate the radical on one side of the equation, if necessary.
- Raise each side of the equation to the same exponent to eliminate the radical and obtain a linear, quadratic, or other polynomial equation.
- Solve the resulting equation using techniques you learned in previous chapters. Check your solution.

EXAMPLE 1 Solving Radical Equations

a. Solve $2\sqrt{x+1} = 4$.

$2\sqrt{x+1} = 4$	Write the equation.
$\sqrt{x+1} = 2$	Divide each side by 2.
$(\sqrt{x+1})^2 = 2^2$	Square each side to eliminate the radical.
$x + 1 = 4$	Simplify.
$x = 3$	Subtract 1 from each side.

▶ The solution is $x = 3$.

Check

b. Solve $\sqrt[3]{2x-9} - 1 = 2$.

$\sqrt[3]{2x-9} - 1 = 2$	Write the equation.
$\sqrt[3]{2x-9} = 3$	Add 1 to each side.
$(\sqrt[3]{2x-9})^3 = 3^3$	Cube each side to eliminate the radical.
$2x - 9 = 27$	Simplify.
$2x = 36$	Add 9 to each side.
$x = 18$	Divide each side by 2.

▶ The solution is $x = 18$.

Check
$\sqrt[3]{2(18)-9} - 1 \stackrel{?}{=} 2$
$\sqrt[3]{27} - 1 \stackrel{?}{=} 2$
$2 = 2$ ✓

In-Class Practice

Self-Assessment

Solve the equation.

1. $\sqrt{x+25} = 2$

2. $2\sqrt[3]{x-3} = 4$

 I don't understand yet.   I can do it with help.   I can do it on my own.   I can teach someone.

> **EXAMPLE 2** Using a Radical Equation
>
> The mean sustained wind velocity (in meters per second) of a hurricane is modeled by $v(p) = 6.3\sqrt{1{,}013 - p}$, where p is the air pressure (in millibars) at the center of the hurricane. Estimate the air pressure at the center of the hurricane when the mean sustained wind velocity is 54.5 meters per second.
>
> | | |
> |---|---|
> | $v(p) = 6.3\sqrt{1{,}013 - p}$ | Write the function. |
> | $54.5 = 6.3\sqrt{1{,}013 - p}$ | Substitute 54.5 for $v(p)$. |
> | $8.65 \approx \sqrt{1{,}013 - p}$ | Divide each side by 6.3. |
> | $8.65^2 \approx \left(\sqrt{1{,}013 - p}\right)^2$ | Square each side. |
> | $74.8 \approx 1{,}013 - p$ | Simplify. |
> | $938.2 \approx p$ | Solve for p. |
>
> ▶ The air pressure at the center of the hurricane is about 938 millibars.

Raising each side of an equation to the same exponent may introduce solutions that are *not* solutions of the original equation. These solutions are called **extraneous solutions**. When you use this procedure, you should always check each apparent solution in the *original* equation.

> **EXAMPLE 3** Solving an Equation with an Extraneous Solution
>
> Solve $x + 1 = \sqrt{7x + 15}$.
>
> | | |
> |---|---|
> | $x + 1 = \sqrt{7x + 15}$ | Write the equation. |
> | $(x + 1)^2 = \left(\sqrt{7x + 15}\right)^2$ | Square each side. |
> | $x^2 + 2x + 1 = 7x + 15$ | Expand left side and simplify right side. |
> | $x^2 - 5x - 14 = 0$ | Write in standard form. |
> | $(x - 7)(x + 2) = 0$ | Factor. |
> | $x = 7$ or $x = -2$ | Solve for x. |
>
> **Check**
>
> $7 + 1 \stackrel{?}{=} \sqrt{7(7) + 15}$ $-2 + 1 \stackrel{?}{=} \sqrt{7(-2) + 15}$
>
> $8 = 8$ ✓ $-1 \neq 1$ ✓
>
> ▶ $x = -2$ is an extraneous solution. So, the only solution is $x = 7$.

In-Class Practice

Self-Assessment

3. WHAT IF? In Example 2, estimate the air pressure at the center of the hurricane when the mean sustained wind velocity is 48.3 meters per second.

4. Solve $\sqrt{10x + 9} = x + 3$.

5.4   Solving Radical Equations and Inequalities

EXAMPLE 4 Solving an Equation with Two Radicals

Solve $\sqrt{x+2} + 1 = \sqrt{3-x}$.

$$\sqrt{x+2} + 1 = \sqrt{3-x} \quad \text{Write the equation.}$$
$$(\sqrt{x+2} + 1)^2 = (\sqrt{3-x})^2 \quad \text{Square each side.}$$
$$x + 2 + 2\sqrt{x+2} + 1 = 3 - x \quad \text{Expand left side and simplify right side.}$$
$$\sqrt{x+2} = -x \quad \text{Isolate the radical.}$$
$$(\sqrt{x+2})^2 = (-x)^2 \quad \text{Square each side.}$$
$$x + 2 = x^2 \quad \text{Simplify.}$$
$$0 = x^2 - x - 2 \quad \text{Write in standard form.}$$
$$0 = (x - 2)(x + 1) \quad \text{Factor.}$$
$$x = 2 \quad \text{or} \quad x = -1 \quad \text{Solve for } x.$$

Check

$$\sqrt{2+2} + 1 \stackrel{?}{=} \sqrt{3-2} \qquad \sqrt{-1+2} + 1 \stackrel{?}{=} \sqrt{3-(-1)}$$
$$3 \neq 1 \; \text{✗} \qquad\qquad 2 = 2 \; \checkmark$$

▶ $x = 2$ is an extraneous solution. So, the only solution is $x = -1$.

When an equation contains a power with a rational exponent, isolate the power and then raise each side of the equation to the reciprocal of the rational exponent.

EXAMPLE 5 Solving an Equation with a Rational Exponent

Solve $(x + 30)^{1/2} = x$.

$$(x + 30)^{1/2} = x \quad \text{Write the equation.}$$
$$[(x + 30)^{1/2}]^2 = x^2 \quad \text{Square each side.}$$
$$x + 30 = x^2 \quad \text{Simplify.}$$
$$0 = x^2 - x - 30 \quad \text{Write in standard form.}$$
$$0 = (x - 6)(x + 5) \quad \text{Factor.}$$
$$x = 6 \quad \text{or} \quad x = -5 \quad \text{Solve for } x.$$

Check

$(6 + 30)^{1/2} \stackrel{?}{=} 6$

$6 = 6 \; \checkmark$

$(-5 + 30)^{1/2} \stackrel{?}{=} -5$

$5 \neq -5 \; \text{✗}$

▶ $x = -5$ is an extraneous solution. So, the only solution is $x = 6$.

In-Class Practice

Self-Assessment

Solve the equation.

5. $\sqrt{x+6} - 2 = \sqrt{x-2}$

6. $(x + 2)^{3/4} = 8$

Solving Radical Inequalities

To solve a simple radical inequality of the form $\sqrt[n]{u} < d$, where u is an algebraic expression and d is a nonnegative number, raise each side to the exponent n. This procedure also works for $>$, $\leq$, and $\geq$. Be sure to consider the possible values of the radicand.

EXAMPLE 6 **Solving a Radical Inequality**

a. Solve $3\sqrt{x-1} \leq 12$.

Solve for x.

$3\sqrt{x-1} \leq 12$	Write the inequality.
$\sqrt{x-1} \leq 4$	Divide each side by 3.
$x - 1 \leq 16$	Square each side.
$x \leq 17$	Add 1 to each side.

Consider the radicand.

$x - 1 \geq 0$	The radicand cannot be negative.
$x \geq 1$	Add 1 to each side.

▶ So, the solution is $1 \leq x \leq 17$.

Check

The graph of $y = 3\sqrt{x-1}$ is on or below the graph of $y = 12$ when $1 \leq x \leq 17$.

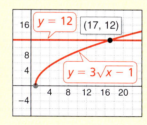

b. Solve $\sqrt[3]{x-5} \geq 3$.

$\sqrt[3]{x-5} \geq 3$	Write the inequality.
$x - 5 \geq 27$	Cube each side.
$x \geq 32$	Add 4 to each side.

▶ So, the solution is $x \geq 32$.

In-Class Practice

Self-Assessment

Solve the inequality.

7. $2\sqrt{x} - 3 \geq 3$

8. $4\sqrt[3]{x+1} < 8$

5.4 Practice

Solve the equation. (See Example 1.)

1. $\sqrt{5x+1} = 6$
2. $\sqrt{3x+10} = 8$
3. $\frac{1}{5}\sqrt[3]{3x} + 10 = 8$
4. $\sqrt[4]{4x} - 13 = -15$

5. **SMP.3 ERROR ANALYSIS** Describe and correct the error in solving the equation.

$$\sqrt[3]{3x-8} = 4$$
$$\left(\sqrt[3]{3x-8}\right)^3 = 4$$
$$3x - 8 = 4$$
$$3x = 12$$
$$x = 4$$

6. **CONNECTION TO REAL LIFE** The maximum speed v (in meters per second) of a trapeze artist is represented by $v = \sqrt{2gh}$, where g is the acceleration due to gravity ($g \approx 9.8$ m/sec^2) and h is the height (in meters) of the swing path. Find the height of the swing path for a performer whose maximum speed is 7 meters per second. (See Example 2.)

Solve the equation. (See Examples 3 and 4.)

7. $x - 6 = \sqrt{3x}$
8. $\sqrt{44 - 2x} = x - 10$
9. $\sqrt[3]{3 - 8x^2} = 2x$
10. $\sqrt{3x - 3} = \sqrt{x + 12}$
11. $\sqrt{4x+1} = \sqrt{x+10}$
12. $\sqrt[3]{x+5} - 2\sqrt[3]{2x+6} = 0$

Solve the equation. (See Example 5.)

13. $2x^{2/3} = 8$
14. $x^{1/4} + 3 = 0$
15. $(x+6)^{1/2} = x$
16. $(5-x)^{1/2} - 2x = 0$

17. **SMP.3 ERROR ANALYSIS** Describe and correct the error in solving the equation.

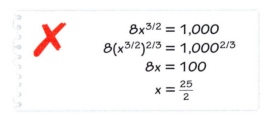

Solve the inequality. (See Example 6.)

18. $\sqrt[3]{x-4} \leq 5$
19. $4\sqrt{x} - 2 > 18$
20. $-2\sqrt[3]{x+4} < 12$
21. $-0.25\sqrt{x} - 6 \leq -3$

22. **SOUND ART** **FREQUENCY** The least possible frequency of a string is its *fundamental frequency*. The fundamental frequency n (in hertz) of a certain string on a violin is represented by

$$n = \sqrt{\frac{T}{0.0054}}$$

where T is the tension (in newtons). The fundamental frequency of the string is 196 hertz. What is the tension of the string?

23. Use the graph to find the solution of the equation $2\sqrt{x-4} = -\sqrt{x-1} + 4$.

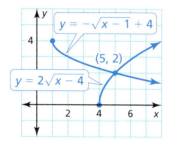

24. **SMP.7** Explain whether it is possible for a radical equation to have two extraneous solutions.

25. **CONNECTION TO REAL LIFE** The speed s (in miles per hour) of a car is given by $s = \sqrt{30fd}$, where f is the coefficient of friction and d is the stopping distance (in feet). The table shows the coefficient of friction for different surfaces.

Surface	Coefficient of friction, f
dry asphalt	0.75
wet asphalt	0.60
snow	0.30
ice	0.15

a. Compare the stopping distances of a car traveling 45 miles per hour on the surfaces given in the table.

b. You are driving 35 miles per hour on an icy road when a deer jumps in front of your car. How far away must you begin to brake to avoid hitting the deer?

26. Bowling Ball Beach is known for its stone spheres scattered along the sand. A formula for the radius of a sphere is

$$r = \frac{1}{2}\sqrt{\frac{S}{\pi}}$$

where S is the surface area of the sphere. Find the surface area of a stone on Bowling Ball Beach with a radius of 1.25 feet.

Interpreting Data

ASIAN ELEPHANTS Asian elephants are an endangered species that can be found in South and Southeastern Asia. The display shows the ages and weights of several male Asian elephants.

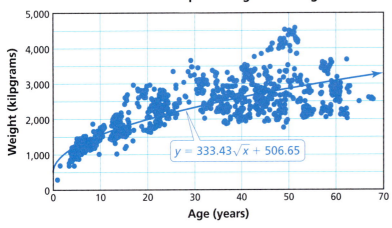

27. Describe the shape of the scatter plot.

28. Predict the weight of a male Asian elephant that is 55 years old. Then predict the age of a male Asian elephant that weighs 1,500 kilograms.

Review & Refresh

29. Find the product $(x^3 + 2x^2 + 1)(x^2 + 5)$.

30. Simplify $\sqrt[4]{81m^4n^8}$.

31. Write rule for g.

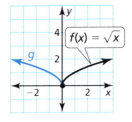

32. Solve the system using any method.

$$3x - y + 4z = 14$$
$$-x - 2y + 3z = 25$$
$$-5x + 3y - 2z = 24$$

33. A Fujita rating is used to describe the strength of tornados. The rating can be found using the equation $y = \left(\dfrac{w}{14.1}\right)^{2/3} - 2$, where w is the wind speed (in miles per hour). What is the rating for a tornado with wind speeds of 200 miles per hour?

y	Rating
$y < 1$	F0
$1 \leq y < 2$	F1
$2 \leq y < 3$	F2
$3 \leq y < 4$	F3
$4 \leq y < 5$	F4
$5 \leq y$	F5

5.5 Performing Function Operations

Learning Target: Perform arithmetic operations on two functions.

Success Criteria:
- I can find arithmetic combinations of two functions.
- I can find the domain of an arithmetic combination of two functions.
- I can evaluate an arithmetic combination of two functions.

Just as two real numbers can be combined by the operations of addition, subtraction, multiplication, and division to form other real numbers, two functions can be combined to form other functions.

INVESTIGATE   Graphing Arithmetic Combinations of Two Functions

Work with a partner. Consider the graphs of f and g.

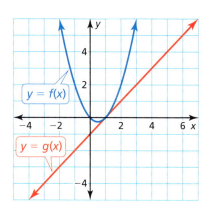

1. Describe what it means to add two functions. Then describe what it means to subtract one function from another function.

2. **MATCHING** Match each function with its graph.

   a. $m(x) = f(x) + g(x)$
   b. $n(x) = f(x) - g(x)$
   c. $p(x) = f(x) \cdot g(x)$
   d. $q(x) = f(x) \div g(x)$

   A.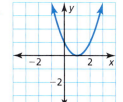

   B.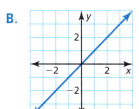

   C.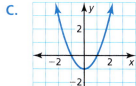

   D.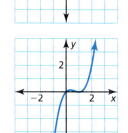

3. What is the domain of each function in Exercise 2? How do you know?

4. Check your answers in Exercise 2 by writing function rules for f and g, performing each arithmetic combination, and graphing the results.

Operations on Functions

You have learned how to add, subtract, multiply, and divide polynomial expressions. These operations are also defined for functions.

Let f and g be any two functions. A new function can be defined by performing any of the four basic operations on f and g.

Operation	Definition	Example: $f(x) = 5x$, $g(x) = x + 2$
Addition	$(f + g)(x) = f(x) + g(x)$	$(f + g)(x) = 5x + (x + 2) = 6x + 2$
Subtraction	$(f - g)(x) = f(x) - g(x)$	$(f - g)(x) = 5x - (x + 2) = 4x - 2$
Multiplication	$(fg)(x) = f(x) \cdot g(x)$	$(fg)(x) = 5x(x + 2) = 5x^2 + 10x$
Division	$\left(\dfrac{f}{g}\right)(x) = \dfrac{f(x)}{g(x)}$	$\left(\dfrac{f}{g}\right)(x) = \dfrac{5x}{x + 2}$

The domains of the sum, difference, product, and quotient functions consist of the x-values that are in the domains of both f and g. Additionally, the domain of the quotient does not include x-values for which $g(x) = 0$.

EXAMPLE 1 Adding Two Functions

Let $f(x) = 3\sqrt{x}$ and $g(x) = -10\sqrt{x}$. Find $(f + g)(x)$ and state the domain. Then evaluate $(f + g)(4)$.

$(f + g)(x) = f(x) + g(x)$ — Definition of function addition

$ = 3\sqrt{x} + (-10\sqrt{x})$ — Write sum of $f(x)$ and $g(x)$.

$ = (3 - 10)\sqrt{x}$ — Distributive Property

$ = -7\sqrt{x}$ — Subtract.

The functions f and g each have the same domain: all nonnegative real numbers. So, the domain of $f + g$ also consists of all nonnegative real numbers. To evaluate $f + g$ when $x = 4$, you can use several methods. Here are two:

Use an algebraic approach.

$(f + g)(4) = -7\sqrt{4} = -14$

Use a graphical approach.

Use technology to graph the sum of the functions. The graph shows that $(f + g)(4) = -14$.

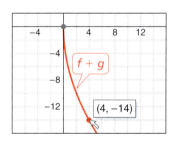

In-Class Practice

Self-Assessment

1. Let $f(x) = -2x^{2/3}$ and $g(x) = 7x^{2/3}$. Find $(f + g)(x)$ and state the domain. Then evaluate $(f + g)(8)$.

1 I don't understand yet. **2** I can do it with help. **3** I can do it on my own. **4** I can teach someone.

EXAMPLE 2 **Subtracting Two Functions**

Let $f(x) = 3x^3 - 2x^2 + 5$ and $g(x) = x^3 - 3x^2 + 4x - 2$. Find $(f - g)(x)$ and state the domain. Then evaluate $(f - g)(-2)$.

$$(f - g)(x) = f(x) - g(x)$$
$$= 3x^3 - 2x^2 + 5 - (x^3 - 3x^2 + 4x - 2)$$
$$= 2x^3 + x^2 - 4x + 7$$

The functions f and g each have the same domain: all real numbers. So, the domain of $f - g$ also consists of all real numbers.

$$(f - g)(-2) = 2(-2)^3 + (-2)^2 - 4(-2) + 7 = 3$$

EXAMPLE 3 **Multiplying Two Functions**

Let $f(x) = x^2$ and $g(x) = \sqrt{x}$. Find $(fg)(x)$ and state the domain. Then evaluate $(fg)(9)$.

$$(fg)(x) = f(x) \cdot g(x) = x^2(\sqrt{x}) = x^2(x^{1/2}) = x^{(2 + 1/2)} = x^{5/2}$$

The domain of f consists of all real numbers, and the domain of g consists of all nonnegative real numbers. So, the domain of fg consists of all nonnegative real numbers.

$$(fg)(9) = 9^{5/2} = (9^{1/2})^5 = 3^5 = 243$$

EXAMPLE 4 **Dividing Two Functions**

Let $f(x) = 6x$ and $g(x) = x^{3/4}$. Find $\left(\dfrac{f}{g}\right)(x)$ and state the domain. Then evaluate $\left(\dfrac{f}{g}\right)(16)$.

$$\left(\frac{f}{g}\right)(x) = \frac{f(x)}{g(x)} = \frac{6x}{x^{3/4}} = 6x^{(1 - 3/4)} = 6x^{1/4}$$

The domain of f consists of all real numbers, the domain of g consists of all nonnegative real numbers, and $g(0) = 0$. So, the domain of $\dfrac{f}{g}$ is restricted to all *positive* real numbers.

$$\left(\frac{f}{g}\right)(16) = 6(16)^{1/4} = 6(2^4)^{1/4} = 12$$

In-Class Practice

Self-Assessment

2. Let $f(x) = \sqrt[4]{3x}$ and $g(x) = -3\sqrt[4]{3x}$. Find $(f - g)(x)$ and state the domain. Then evaluate $(f - g)(27)$.

3. Let $f(x) = 3x$ and $g(x) = x^{1/5}$. Find $(fg)(x)$ and $\left(\dfrac{f}{g}\right)(x)$ and state the domain of each. Then evaluate $(fg)(32)$ and $\left(\dfrac{f}{g}\right)(32)$.

1 I don't understand yet. **2** I can do it with help. **3** I can do it on my own. **4** I can teach someone.

Connections to Real Life

EXAMPLE 5 **Using Function Operations**

For a white rhino, heart rate (in beats per minute) and life span (in minutes) are related to body mass m (in kilograms) by the following functions.

Heart rate: $r(m) = 241m^{-0.25}$

Life span: $s(m) = (6 \times 10^6)m^{0.2}$

STEM Video:
The Heartbeat Hypothesis

a. Find $(rs)(m)$ and explain what it represents.

$(rs)(m) = r(m) \cdot s(m)$	Definition of function multiplication
$= 241m^{-0.25}[(6 \times 10^6)m^{0.2}]$	Write product of $r(m)$ and $s(m)$.
$= 241(6 \times 10^6)m^{-0.25 + 0.2}$	Product of Powers Property
$= (1{,}446 \times 10^6)m^{-0.05}$	Simplify.
$= (1.446 \times 10^9)m^{-0.05}$	Use scientific notation.

▶ So, $(rs)(m) = (1.446 \times 10^9)m^{-0.05}$. Multiplying heart rate by life span gives the total number of heartbeats over the lifetime of a white rhino with body mass m.

b. Use technology to evaluate $(rs)(1.9 \times 10^5)$.

Enter r and s. From the screen, you can see that $(rs)(1.9 \times 10^5) \approx 7.875 \times 10^8$.

> $r(m) = 241m^{-0.25}$
>
> $s(m) = (6 \times 10^6)m^{0.2}$
>
> $(rs)(1.9 \times 10^5)$
> $= 787{,}463{,}826.6$

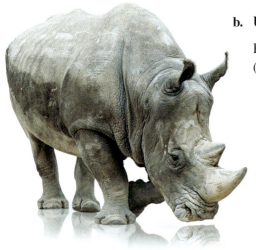

In-Class Practice

Self-Assessment

4. Use the answer in Example 5 to find the total number of heartbeats over the lifetime of a white rhino when its body mass is 1.7×10^5 kilograms.

5. The cost (in dollars) to rent a scooter for x minutes in City A is represented by $A(x) = 0.15x + 1$. The cost (in dollars) in City B is represented by $B(x) = 0.29x + 1$. Find $(B - A)(x)$ and explain what it represents.

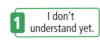 I don't understand yet. I can do it with help. I can do it on my own. 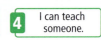 I can teach someone.

5.5 Practice

Find $(f + g)(x)$ and $(f - g)(x)$ and state the domain of each. Then evaluate $f + g$ and $f - g$ for the given value of x. (See Examples 1 and 2.)

1. $f(x) = -5\sqrt[4]{x}$, $g(x) = 19\sqrt[4]{x}$; $x = 16$

2. $f(x) = \sqrt[3]{2x}$, $g(x) = -11\sqrt[3]{2x}$; $x = -4$

▶ 3. $f(x) = 6x - 4x^2 - 7x^3$, $g(x) = 9x^2 - 5x$; $x = -1$

4. $f(x) = 11x + 2x^2$, $g(x) = -7x - 3x^2 + 4$; $x = 2$

Find $(fg)(x)$ and $\left(\dfrac{f}{g}\right)(x)$ and state the domain of each. Then evaluate fg and $\dfrac{f}{g}$ for the given value of x. (See Examples 3 and 4.)

▶ 5. $f(x) = 2x^3$, $g(x) = \sqrt[3]{x}$; $x = -27$

6. $f(x) = x^4$, $g(x) = 3\sqrt{x}$; $x = 4$

7. $f(x) = 4x$, $g(x) = 9x^{1/2}$; $x = 9$

8. $f(x) = 7x^{3/2}$, $g(x) = -14x^{1/3}$; $x = 64$

9. **SMP.3 ERROR ANALYSIS** Describe and correct the error in stating the domain.

> $f(x) = x^{1/2}$ and $g(x) = x^{3/2}$
> The domain of $(fg)(x) = x^2$ is all real numbers.

10. **CONNECTION TO REAL LIFE** Over a period of 12 years, the numbers (in millions) of full-time and part-time employees in the United States can be modeled by the functions

    $F(t) = -0.0074t^3 + 0.046t^2 + 2.07t + 110.9$ and $P(t) = 0.0035t^3 - 0.094t^2 + 0.48t + 27.1$

    where t is the number of years since 2010. Find $(F + P)(t)$ and explain what it represents. Then use technology to evaluate $(F + P)(8)$. (See Example 5.)

Use technology to evaluate $(f + g)(x)$, $(f - g)(x)$, $(fg)(x)$, and $\left(\dfrac{f}{g}\right)(x)$ when $x = 5$.

11. $f(x) = 4x^4$; $g(x) = 24x^{1/3}$

12. $f(x) = -2x^{1/3}$; $g(x) = 5x^{1/2}$

13. Use the table to find each value.

    a. $(f + g)(3)$
    b. $(f - g)(1)$
    c. $(fg)(2)$
    d. $\left(\dfrac{f}{g}\right)(0)$

x	0	1	2	3	4
f(x)	−2	−4	0	10	26
g(x)	−1	−3	−13	−31	−57

14. Explain whether the addition of functions and the multiplication of functions are commutative.

5.5 Performing Function Operations 263

Interpreting Data

PREDATOR AND PREY The snowshoe hare is a common prey of the lynx. The number of snowshoe hare pelts and the number of lynx pelts purchased by the Hudson Bay Company of Canada were recorded for 90 years. A 10-year period of this data is shown.

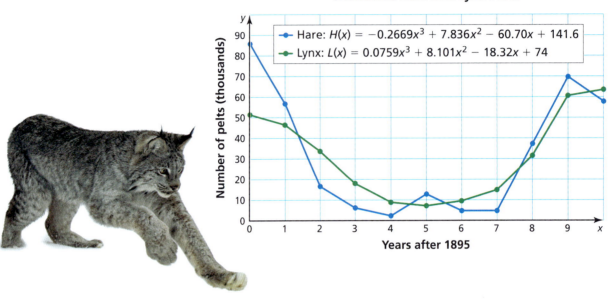

Snowshoe Hare and Lynx Pelts

Hare: $H(x) = -0.2669x^3 + 7.836x^2 - 60.70x + 141.6$
Lynx: $L(x) = 0.0759x^3 + 8.101x^2 - 18.32x + 74$

Years after 1895

15. Use the models shown to find $(H + L)(x)$ and explain what it represents. Then find and interpret $(H + L)(8)$.

16. Explain why an increase or decrease in prey may lead to an increase or decrease in predators.

Review & Refresh

17. Describe the transformation of f represented by g. Then graph each function.

    $f(x) = \sqrt{x}$
    $g(x) = -\sqrt{x + 2}$

18. Determine whether the table represents a *linear* or *nonlinear* function.

x	12	9	6	3
y	−1	0	1	2

19. Simplify $6\sqrt[3]{9} - 10\sqrt[3]{9}$.

20. Solve $\sqrt{-x - 3} = x + 5$.

21. The number A of commercial drones sold (in thousands) can be modeled by the function $A = 19t^2 + 30t + 110$, where t represents the number of years after 2016.

    a. In what year did commercial drone sales reach 200,000?

    b. Find and interpret the average rate of change from 2016 to 2018.

    c. Do you think this model will be accurate after 20 years?

5.6 Composition of Functions

Learning Target: Evaluate and find compositions of functions.

Success Criteria:
- I can evaluate a composition of functions.
- I can find a composition of functions.
- I can state the domain of a composition of functions.

INVESTIGATE Finding a Composition of Functions

Work with a partner. The formulas below represent the temperature F (in degrees Fahrenheit) when the temperature is C degrees Celsius, and the temperature C when the temperature is K (Kelvin).

$$F = \tfrac{9}{5}C + 32 \qquad C = K - 273$$

1. Write an expression for F in terms of K.

2. Given that

$$f(x) = \tfrac{9}{5}x + 32$$

and

$$g(x) = x - 273$$

write an expression for $f(g(x))$. What does $f(g(x))$ represent in this situation?

3. Water freezes at about 273 Kelvin. Find $f(g(273))$. Does your answer make sense? Explain your reasoning.

4. Interpret the point shown in the graph.

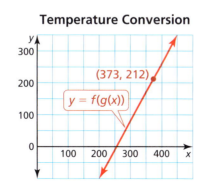

Temperature Conversion
(373, 212)
$y = f(g(x))$

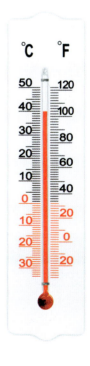

Vocabulary
composition

Evaluating Compositions of Functions

You have combined functions by finding sums, differences, products, and quotients. Another way of combining two functions is by *composition*.

Key Concept

Composition of Functions

The **composition** of a function g with a function f is

$$h(x) = g(f(x)).$$

The domain of h is the set of all x-values such that x is in the domain of f and $f(x)$ is in the domain of g.

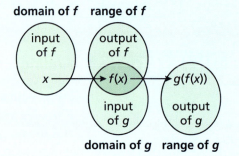

EXAMPLE 1 Evaluating Compositions of Functions

Let $f(x) = \sqrt{2x + 1}$ and $g(x) = x^2 - 4$.

a. **Find $g(f(4))$.**

Find $f(4)$. Use the result to find $g(f(4))$.

$$f(4) = \sqrt{2(4) + 1} = \sqrt{8 + 1} = \sqrt{9} = 3$$
$$g(f(4)) = g(3) = 3^2 - 4 = 9 - 4 = 5$$

▶ So, $g(f(4))$ is 5.

b. **Find $f(g(2))$.**

Find $g(2)$. Use the result to find $f(g(2))$.

$$g(2) = 2^2 - 4 = 4 - 4 = 0$$
$$f(g(2)) = f(0) = \sqrt{2(0) + 1} = \sqrt{0 + 1} = \sqrt{1} = 1$$

▶ So, $f(g(2))$ is 1.

c. **Find $g(g(-2))$.**

Find $g(-2)$. Use the result to find $g(g(-2))$.

$$g(-2) = (-2)^2 - 4 = 4 - 4 = 0$$
$$g(g(-2)) = g(0) = 0^2 - 4 = 0 - 4 = -4$$

▶ So, $g(g(-2))$ is -4.

In-Class Practice

Self-Assessment

1. Use $f(x) = x - 2$ and $g(x) = x^2$ to find $f(g(-1))$.

1 I don't understand yet.   **2** I can do it with help.   **3** I can do it on my own.   **4** I can teach someone.

Chapter 5 Rational Exponents and Radical Functions

Finding Compositions of Functions

EXAMPLE 2 Finding Compositions of Functions

Let $f(x) = 5x^{-1}$ and $g(x) = 3x - 3$.

a. Find $f(g(x))$ and state the domain.

$f(g(x)) = f(3x - 3)$	Substitute $3x - 3$ for $g(x)$.
$= 5(3x - 3)^{-1}$	Replace x with $3x - 3$ in $f(x)$.
$= \dfrac{5}{3x - 3}$	Definition of negative exponents

▶ The domain of $y = f(g(x))$ is $\{x \mid x \neq 1\}$, because $g(1) = 0$ is not in the domain of f.

b. Find $g(f(x))$ and state the domain.

$g(f(x)) = g(5x^{-1})$	Substitute $5x^{-1}$ for $f(x)$.
$= 3(5x^{-1}) - 3$	Replace x with $5x^{-1}$ in $g(x)$.
$= 15x^{-1} - 3$	Multiply.
$= \dfrac{15}{x} - 3$	Definition of negative exponents

▶ The domain of $y = g(f(x))$ is $\{x \mid x \neq 0\}$, because 0 is not in the domain of f.

c. Find $f(f(x))$ and state the domain.

$f(f(x)) = f(5x^{-1})$	Substitute $5x^{-1}$ for $f(x)$.
$= 5(5x^{-1})^{-1}$	Replace x with $5x^{-1}$ in $f(x)$.
$= 5(5^{-1}x^{1})$	Use properties of exponents.
$= 5\left(\dfrac{1}{5}x\right)$	Definition of negative exponents
$= x$	Multiply.

▶ The domain of $y = f(f(x))$ is $\{x \mid x \neq 0\}$, because 0 is not in the domain of f.

In-Class Practice

Self-Assessment

Let $f(x) = 2x^{-1}$, $g(x) = 4x - 3$, and $h(x) = 0.5x + 2$. Perform the indicated composition and state the domain.

2. $f(g(x))$

3. $g(f(x))$

4. $f(f(x))$

5. $h(h(x))$

 I don't understand yet.
 I can do it with help.
 I can do it on my own.
 I can teach someone.

Connections to Real Life

EXAMPLE 3 Using a Composition of Functions

The function $C(m) = 15 - 10.5m$ approximates the temperature (in degrees Celsius) at an altitude of m miles. The diagram shows the altitude (in miles) of an airplane t minutes after taking off, where $0 \leq t \leq 30$. Find $C(m(t))$. Evaluate $C(m(30))$ and explain what it represents.

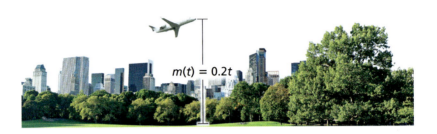

$m(t) = 0.2t$

The composition $C(m(t))$ represents the temperature at the airplane's altitude t minutes after taking off. Find $C(m(t))$.

$C(m(t)) = C(0.2t)$ Substitute 0.2t for m(t).

$ = 15 - 10.5(0.2t)$ Replace m with 0.2t in C(m).

$ = 15 - 2.1t$ Multiply.

Evaluate $C(m(30))$.

$C(m(30)) = 15 - 2.1(30)$ Substitute 30 for t.

$ = 15 - 63$ Multiply.

$ = -48$ Subtract.

▶ So, $C(m(30)) = -48$ indicates that after 30 minutes, the airplane is at an altitude that has a temperature of about $-48°C$.

In-Class Practice

Self-Assessment

6. **SMP.2** The function $C(x) = 50x + 100$ represents the cost (in dollars) of producing x bee hive boxes. The number of bee hive boxes produced in t hours is represented by $x(t) = 6t$.

   a. Find $C(x(t))$.

   b. Evaluate $C(x(8))$ and explain what it represents.

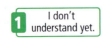 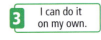

5.6 Practice

Let $f(x) = \sqrt{x+1}$, $g(x) = 2x - 5$, and $h(x) = 3x^2 - 3$. Find the indicated value. (See Example 1.)

1. $f(g(4))$

2. $g(h(-2))$

3. $h(f(10))$

4. $g(g(-2.5))$

Find (a) $f(g(x))$, (b) $g(f(x))$, and (c) $f(f(x))$. State the domain of each composition. (See Example 2.)

5. $f(x) = x - 9$, $g(x) = |x + 2|$

6. $f(x) = x^2 + 7$, $g(x) = 2x + 5$

7. $f(x) = 3x - 7$, $g(x) = \sqrt{x + 7}$

8. $f(x) = 10x^{-1}$, $g(x) = x^2 - 9$

9. SMP.2 CONNECTION TO REAL LIFE The function $p(d) = 0.03d + 1$ models the pressure (in atmospheres) d feet below sea level. The function $d(t) = 60t$ gives the depth (in feet) of a diver t minutes after beginning a descent from sea level, where $0 \le t \le 2$. Find $p(d(t))$. Evaluate $p(d(1.5))$ and explain what it represents. (See Example 3.)

10. Use the table to find each value.

a. $f(g(-1))$
b. $g(f(2))$
c. $f(f(0))$
d. $g(g(-2))$

x	−2	−1	0	1	2	3
f(x)	7	5	3	2	0	−2
g(x)	1	−2	−1	5	2	0

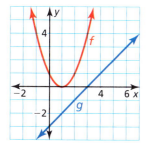

11. Use the graphs of f and g to find each value.

a. $f(g(6))$
b. $g(f(-1))$
c. $f(f(2))$
d. $g(g(3))$

12. SMP.7 CONNECT CONCEPTS Complete the table using the following information.

- f and g are linear functions.
- $f(g(1)) = 6.5$
- $g(f(2)) = -5$

x	1	2	4	7
f(x)				6.5
g(x)			−5	

13. SMP.1 DIG DEEPER Show that the function $f(x) = \frac{1}{3}\sqrt{x - 2} + 3$ is a composition, in some order, of functions g, h, p, and q.

$g(x) = \frac{1}{3}x$ $h(x) = x - 2$ $p(x) = x + 9$ $q(x) = \sqrt{x}$

Interpreting Data

SLEEP NEEDED When sleeping, the human body works to support healthy brain function and maintain physical health. Over time, inadequate sleep increases the risk of chronic health problems.

14. Describe the relationship between age and the amount of sleep needed.

15. The amount of time (in hours) spent in REM (rapid eye movement) sleep for someone who sleeps s hours can be approximated by $r(s) = 0.25s$. Evaluate $r(s(16))$ and explain what it represents.

Review & Refresh

16. Describe the x-values for which (a) f is increasing or decreasing, (b) $f(x) > 0$, and (c) $f(x) < 0$.

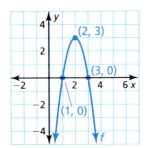

Solve the system using any method.

17. $2x^2 + 4x - y = -5$
    $2x + y = 1$

18. $x^2 - 3x - y = 4$
    $-x^2 + 7x + y = 10$

Solve the inequality.

19. $5\sqrt{x} - 3 < 17$

20. $\sqrt[3]{x+1} + 4 \geq -2$

21. Find the volume of the cone.

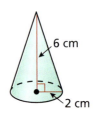

22. Let $f(x) = 8x^3$ and $g(x) = -2x^{3/2}$. Find $(fg)(x)$ and $\left(\dfrac{f}{g}\right)(x)$ and state the domain of each. Then evaluate fg and $\dfrac{f}{g}$ when $x = 4$.

5.7 Inverse of a Function

Learning Target: Understand the relationship between inverse functions.

Success Criteria:
- I can explain what inverse functions are.
- I can find inverses of linear and nonlinear functions.

INVESTIGATE Describing Functions and Their Inverses

Work with a partner.

1. Each pair of functions are *inverses* of each other. For each pair f and g, create an input-output table of values for each function. Use the outputs of f as the inputs of g. What do you notice?

   a. $f(x) = 4x + 3$
      $g(x) = \dfrac{x-3}{4}$

   b. $f(x) = x^3 + 1$
      $g(x) = \sqrt[3]{x-1}$

   c. $f(x) = \sqrt{x-3}$
      $g(x) = x^2 + 3,\ x \geq 0$

2. What do you notice about the graphs of each pair of functions in Exercise 1?

3. For each pair of functions in Exercise 1, find $f(g(x))$ and $g(f(x))$. What do you notice?

4. The functions h and j are inverses of each other. Use the graph of h to find the given value. Explain how you found your answers.

   a. $j(-6)$

   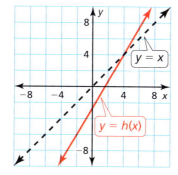

   b. $j(4)$

   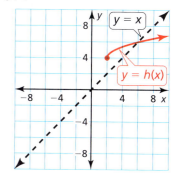

   c. $j(-6)$

   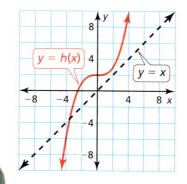

   d. $j(2)$

   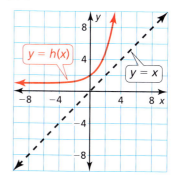

Vocabulary
inverse functions

Exploring Inverses of Functions

You can solve equations of the form $y = f(x)$ for x to obtain an equation that gives the input for a specific output of f.

EXAMPLE 1 Writing a Formula for the Input of a Function

Let $f(x) = 2x + 3$. Solve $y = f(x)$ for x. Then find the input when the output is -7.

$y = 2x + 3$ Set y equal to $f(x)$.

$y - 3 = 2x$ Subtract 3 from each side.

$\dfrac{y - 3}{2} = x$ Divide each side by 2.

Find the input when $y = -7$.

$x = \dfrac{-7 - 3}{2}$ Substitute -7 for y.

$= \dfrac{-10}{2}$ Subtract.

$= -5$ Divide.

▶ So, the input is -5 when the output is -7.

Check
$f(-5) = 2(-5) + 3$
$= -10 + 3$
$= -7$ ✓

In Example 1, notice the operations in the equations $y = 2x + 3$ and $x = \dfrac{y - 3}{2}$.

$y = 2x + 3$ $x = \dfrac{y - 3}{2}$

Multiply by 2.   Subtract 3.
Add 3.   inverse operations   Divide by 2.
       in the reverse order

These operations *undo* each other. **Inverse functions** are functions that undo each other. In Example 1, use the equation solved for x to write the inverse of f by switching x and y.

$x = \dfrac{y - 3}{2}$ switch x and y $y = \dfrac{x - 3}{2}$

In-Class Practice

Self-Assessment

Solve $y = f(x)$ for x. Then find the input(s) when the output is 2.

1. $f(x) = x - 2$

2. $f(x) = -x^3 + 3$

An inverse function can be denoted by f^{-1}, read as "f inverse." Because an inverse function switches the input and output values of the original function, the domain and range are also switched.

Original function: $f(x) = 2x + 3$ **Inverse function:** $f^{-1}(x) = \dfrac{x-3}{2}$

x	−2	−1	0	1	2
y	−1	1	3	5	7

x	−1	1	3	5	7
y	−2	−1	0	1	2

The graph of f^{-1} is a *reflection* of the graph of f. The *line of reflection* is $y = x$. This is true for all inverses.

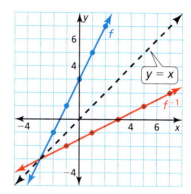

EXAMPLE 2   Finding the Inverse of a Linear Function

Find the inverse of $f(x) = 3x - 1$.

Method 1 Use inverse operations in the reverse order.

$f(x) = 3x - 1$ Multiply the input x by 3 and then subtract 1.

To find the inverse, apply inverse operations in the reverse order.

$f^{-1}(x) = \dfrac{x+1}{3}$ Add 1 to the input x and then divide by 3.

▶ The inverse of f is $f^{-1}(x) = \dfrac{x+1}{3}$.

Method 2 Set y equal to $f(x)$. Switch the roles of x and y and solve for y.

$y = 3x - 1$ Set y equal to $f(x)$.

$x = 3y - 1$ Switch x and y.

$x + 1 = 3y$ Add 1 to each side.

$\dfrac{x+1}{3} = y$ Divide each side by 3.

▶ The inverse of f is $f^{-1}(x) = \dfrac{x+1}{3}$.

Check
The graph of f^{-1} appears to be a reflection of the graph of f in the line $y = x$. ✓

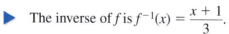

In-Class Practice

Self-Assessment

3. Find the inverse of $f(x) = \tfrac{1}{3}x - 2$. Then graph the function and its inverse.

1 I don't understand yet.   **2** I can do it with help.   **3** I can do it on my own.   **4** I can teach someone.

Inverses of Nonlinear Functions

In the previous examples, the inverses of the linear functions were also functions. However, inverses of functions are *not* always functions. The graphs of $f(x) = x^2$ and $f(x) = x^3$ are shown along with their reflections in the line $y = x$. Notice that the inverse of $f(x) = x^3$ is a function, but the inverse of $f(x) = x^2$ is *not* a function.

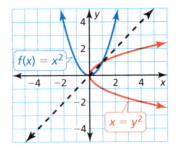
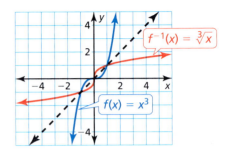

When the domain of $f(x) = x^2$ is *restricted* to only nonnegative real numbers, the inverse of f is a function, as shown in the next example.

EXAMPLE 3 Finding the Inverse of a Quadratic Function

Find the inverse of $f(x) = x^2$, $x \geq 0$. Then graph the function and its inverse.

$f(x) = x^2$	Write the original function.
$y = x^2$	Set *y* equal to *f(x)*.
$x = y^2$	Switch *x* and *y*.
$\pm\sqrt{x} = y$	Take square root of each side.

The domain of f is restricted to nonnegative values of x. So, the range of the inverse must also be restricted to nonnegative values.

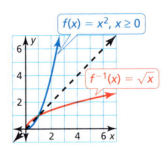

▶ So, the inverse of f is $f^{-1}(x) = \sqrt{x}$.

In-Class Practice

Self-Assessment

Find the inverse of the function. Then graph the function and its inverse.

4. $f(x) = -x^2$, $x \leq 0$

5. $f(x) = (x+4)^2$, $x \geq -4$

1 I don't understand yet.   **2** I can do it with help.   **3** I can do it on my own.   **4** I can teach someone.

274   Chapter 5   Rational Exponents and Radical Functions

Recall the *Horizontal Line Test*, which states that the inverse of a function f is also a function if and only if no horizontal line intersects the graph of f more than once.

EXAMPLE 4   Finding the Inverse of a Cubic Function

Consider the function $f(x) = 2x^3 + 1$. Determine whether the inverse of f is a function. Then find the inverse.

Graph the function f. Notice that no horizontal line intersects the graph more than once. So, the inverse of f is a function. Find the inverse.

$y = 2x^3 + 1$	Set y equal to $f(x)$.
$x = 2y^3 + 1$	Switch x and y.
$x - 1 = 2y^3$	Subtract 1 from each side.
$\dfrac{x-1}{2} = y^3$	Divide each side by 2.
$\sqrt[3]{\dfrac{x-1}{2}} = y$	Take cube root of each side.

▶ So, the inverse of f is $f^{-1}(x) = \sqrt[3]{\dfrac{x-1}{2}}$.

EXAMPLE 5   Finding the Inverse of a Radical Function

Consider the function $f(x) = 2\sqrt{x - 3}$. Determine whether the inverse of f is a function. Then find the inverse.

Graph the function f. Notice that no horizontal line intersects the graph more than once. So, the inverse of f is a function. Find the inverse.

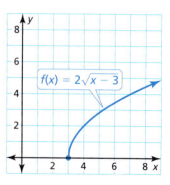

$y = 2\sqrt{x-3}$	Set y equal to $f(x)$.
$x = 2\sqrt{y-3}$	Switch x and y.
$x^2 = \left(2\sqrt{y-3}\right)^2$	Square each side.
$x^2 = 4(y - 3)$	Simplify.
$\tfrac{1}{4}x^2 = y - 3$	Divide each side by 4.
$\tfrac{1}{4}x^2 + 3 = y$	Add 3 to each side.

Because the range of f is $y \geq 0$, the domain of the inverse is restricted to $x \geq 0$.

▶ So, the inverse of f is $f^{-1}(x) = \tfrac{1}{4}x^2 + 3$, $x \geq 0$.

In-Class Practice

Self-Assessment

Determine whether the inverse of f is a function. Then find the inverse.

6. $f(x) = -x^3 + 4$

7. $f(x) = \sqrt{x + 2}$

1 I don't understand yet.   **2** I can do it with help.   **3** I can do it on my own.   **4** I can teach someone.

Connections to Real Life

EXAMPLE 6 Interpreting the Inverse of a Function

SOUND ART **SPEED OF SOUND** The speed of sound (in meters per second) through air is approximated by the function

$$f(x) = 20\sqrt{x + 273}$$

where x is the temperature in degrees Celsius. Find and interpret $f^{-1}(340)$.

Graph the function f.

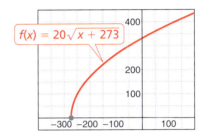

Notice that no horizontal line intersects the graph more than once. So, the inverse of f is a function. Find the inverse.

$y = 20\sqrt{x + 273}$	Set y equal to $f(x)$.
$x = 20\sqrt{y + 273}$	Switch x and y.
$x^2 = \left(20\sqrt{y + 273}\right)^2$	Square each side.
$x^2 = 400(y + 273)$	Simplify.
$\frac{1}{400}x^2 = y + 273$	Divide each side by 400.
$\frac{1}{400}x^2 - 273 = y$	Subtract 273 from each side.

Because the range of f is $y \geq 0$, the domain of the inverse is restricted to $x \geq 0$. The inverse of f is $f^{-1}(x) = \frac{1}{400}x^2 - 273$, $x \geq 0$.

▶ Using $f^{-1}(x)$, you obtain $f^{-1}(340) = 16$. This represents that the temperature is 16 degrees Celsius when the speed of sound through air is 340 meters per second.

In-Class Practice

Self-Assessment

8. **WHAT IF?** In Example 6, find and interpret $f^{-1}(350)$.

5.7 Practice

Solve $y = f(x)$ for x. Then find the input(s) when the output is -3. (See Example 1.)

1. $f(x) = 3x + 5$
2. $f(x) = -\frac{2}{3}x + 1$
3. $f(x) = 3x^3$
4. $f(x) = (x - 2)^2 - 7$

Find the inverse of the function. Then graph the function and its inverse. (See Example 2.)

5. $f(x) = 6x$
6. $f(x) = 6x - 3$
7. $f(x) = -2x + 5$
8. $f(x) = \frac{2}{3}x - \frac{1}{3}$

9. **SMP.3 ERROR ANALYSIS** Describe and correct the error in finding the inverse of the function.

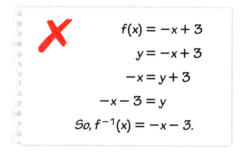

Determine whether functions f and g are inverses.

10.
x	-2	-1	0	1	2
f(x)	-2	1	4	7	10

x	-2	1	4	7	10
g(x)	-2	-1	0	1	2

11.
x	2	3	4	5	6
f(x)	8	6	4	2	0

x	2	3	4	5	6
g(x)	-8	-6	-4	-2	0

Find the inverse of the function. Then graph the function and its inverse. (See Example 3.)

12. $f(x) = 4x^2,\ x \leq 0$
13. $f(x) = (x - 3)^2,\ x \geq 3$
14. $f(x) = -(x - 1)^2 + 6,\ x \geq 1$
15. $f(x) = 2(x + 5)^2 - 2,\ x \leq -5$

16. **SMP.3 ERROR ANALYSIS** Describe and correct the error in finding the inverse of the function.

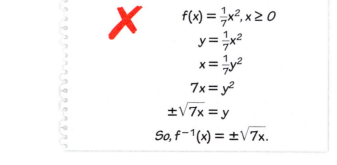

Use the graph to determine whether the inverse of f is a function.

17.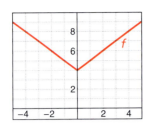

18.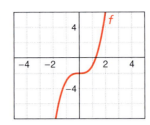

Determine whether the inverse of f is a function. Then find the inverse. (See Examples 4 and 5.)

19. $f(x) = x^3 - 1$

20. $f(x) = 2x^3 - 5$

21. $f(x) = \sqrt{x + 4}$

22. $f(x) = 3\sqrt[3]{x + 1}$

23. $f(x) = -\frac{2}{5}(x - 2)^3 - 4$

24. $f(x) = -\sqrt[3]{\dfrac{2x + 4}{3}}$

25. **CONNECTION TO REAL LIFE** The maximum hull speed (in knots) of a boat with a displacement hull can be approximated by $f(x) = 1.34\sqrt{x}$, where x is the waterline length (in feet) of the boat. Find and interpret $f^{-1}(7.5)$. (See Example 6.)

26. **CONNECTION TO REAL LIFE** Elastic bands can be used for exercising to provide a range of resistance. The resistance (in pounds) of a band can be modeled by $r(x) = \frac{3}{8}x - 5$, where x is the total length (in inches) of the stretched band. Find and interpret $r^{-1}(19)$.

Use the table or graph to find $f^{-1}(-2)$.

27.

x	−2	−1	0	1	2	3
f(x)	−1	−2	1	4	7	10

28.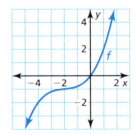

29. The graph of a function passes through the points $(-2, 5)$, $(0, 1)$, $(3, -6)$, and $(7, n)$. For what values of n could the inverse be a function?

30. **SMP.7** Explain whether every quadratic function whose domain is restricted to nonnegative values has an inverse function.

If for functions f and g, $f(g(x)) = x$ and $g(f(x)) = x$, then f and g are inverse functions. Use this property to determine whether the functions are inverse functions.

31. $f(x) = 2x - 9,\ g(x) = \dfrac{x}{2} + 9$

32. $f(x) = \dfrac{x - 1}{5},\ g(x) = 5x + 1$

33. $f(x) = \sqrt[5]{\dfrac{x + 9}{5}},\ g(x) = 5x^5 - 9$

34. $f(x) = 7x^{3/2} - 4,\ g(x) = \left(\dfrac{x + 4}{7}\right)^{3/2}$

MATCHING Match the function with the graph of its inverse.

35. $f(x) = \sqrt[3]{x} - 4$

36. $f(x) = \sqrt[3]{x} + 4$

37. $f(x) = \sqrt{x+1} - 3$

38. $f(x) = \sqrt{x-1} + 3$

A.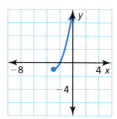

B.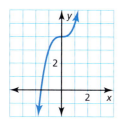

C.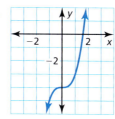

D.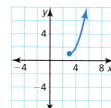

39. CONNECTION TO REAL LIFE At the start of a dog sled race in Anchorage, Alaska, the temperature was 5°C. By the end of the race, the temperature was −10°C. The temperature in degrees Celsius is represented by $C(x) = \frac{5}{9}(x - 32)$, where x is the temperature in degrees Fahrenheit.

   a. Find the inverse function. Describe what it represents.

   b. Find the Fahrenheit temperatures at the start and end of the race.

40. The graph of the function f is shown. Name three points that lie on the graph of the inverse of f.

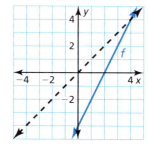

41. PERFORMANCE TASK When using a secret code, the sender and the receiver of a message each use the same *key*. The sender uses the key to encode the message, and the receiver uses the key to decipher the message. This process is called *cryptography*. Work with a partner to write a function that can be used as the key for a secret code. Each of you encode a message and then decipher your partner's message. Explain how inverse functions are used in this process.

42. **SMP.6** Explain whether each statement is *true* or *false*.

   a. If $f(x) = x^n$ and n is a positive even integer, then the inverse of f is a function.

   b. If $f(x) = x^n$ and n is a positive odd integer, then the inverse of f is a function.

Interpreting Data

BODY MASS INDEX Body Mass Index (BMI) is a tool used to calculate body composition. The projected body fat percentage for several people given their BMI is shown.

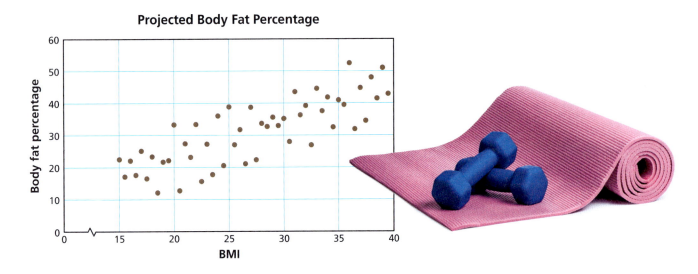

43. Describe the relationship between BMI and body fat percentage.

44. The body fat percentage of a person can be modeled by $f(x) = 1.116x + 0.71$, where x is the person's BMI. Find and interpret $f^{-1}(32)$.

Review & Refresh

45. Describe the x-values for which the function is increasing, decreasing, positive, and negative.

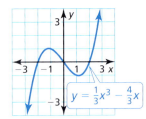

46. Find the values of x and y that satisfy the equation $7yi + 3 = 18x + 14i$.

47. Find $(f + g)(x)$ and $(f - g)(x)$ and state the domain of each. Then evaluate $f + g$ and $f - g$ for the given value of x.

$f(x) = 2x^2 - 3 + 7x$

$g(x) = 11 + 4x^2$; $x = 3$

48. Write an expression for the volume of the figure as a polynomial in standard form.

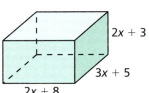

49. Write an equation of the parabola.

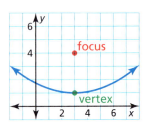

50. Let $f(x) = 6x - 2$ and $g(x) = 2x^{-1}$. Find $f(g(x))$ and state the domain.

5 Chapter Review

Rate your understanding of each section.

1 I don't understand yet. | 2 I can do it with help. | 3 I can do it on my own. | 4 I can teach someone.

5.1 nth Roots and Rational Exponents (pp. 229–234)

Learning Target: Evaluate expressions and solve equations using nth roots.

Vocabulary
nth root of a
index of a radical

Find the indicated nth root(s) of a.

1. $n = 4, a = 1{,}296$
2. $n = 5, a = -1{,}024$

Evaluate the expression without using technology.

3. $9^{5/2}$
4. $(-27)^{-2/3}$

Find the real solution(s) of the equation.

5. $7x^3 = 189$
6. $(x + 8)^4 = 16$

7. Without using technology, show that $3^{1.45}$ must be less than 6.

8. A diamond has eight equilateral triangles as faces. The formula $V = 0.47s^3$ approximates the volume V (in cubic millimeters) of the diamond, where s is the side length (in millimeters) of each edge. Approximate the length of each edge.

$V = 161$ mm^3

5.2 Properties of Rational Exponents and Radicals (pp. 235–242)

Learning Target: Simplify radical expressions.

Vocabulary
simplest form of a radical
like radicals

Simplify the expression.

9. $\left(\dfrac{6^{2/5}}{6^{1/5}}\right)^3$
10. $\dfrac{1}{2 - \sqrt{7}}$
11. $2\sqrt{48} - \sqrt{3}$
12. $(5^{2/3} \cdot 2^{3/2})^{1/2}$

Simplify the expression. Assume all variables are positive.

13. $\dfrac{2^{1/4} z^{5/4}}{6z}$
14. $\sqrt{10z^5} - z^2\sqrt{40z}$

5.3 Graphing Radical Functions (pp. 243–250)

Learning Target: Describe and graph transformations of radical functions.

Vocabulary
radical function

Describe the transformation of f represented by g. Then graph each function.

15. $f(x) = \sqrt{x}$, $g(x) = -2\sqrt{x}$

16. $f(x) = \sqrt[3]{x}$, $g(x) = \sqrt[3]{-x} - 6$

17. Use radical functions to graph $2y^2 = x - 8$. Identify the vertex and the direction the parabola opens.

18. Use radical functions to graph $x^2 + y^2 = 81$. Identify the radius and the intercepts.

19. An investigator uses the model $s = 4\sqrt{d}$ to estimate the speed s (in miles per hour) of a car just prior to an accident, where d is the length (in feet) of the skid marks. Graph the model. The skid marks are 90 feet long. Was the car traveling at the posted speed limit prior to the accident?

5.4 Solving Radical Equations and Inequalities (pp. 251–258)

Learning Target: Solve equations and inequalities containing radicals.

Vocabulary
radical equation
extraneous solution

Solve the equation.

20. $\sqrt{4x - 4} = \sqrt{5x - 1} - 1$

21. $(6x)^{2/3} = 36$

Solve the inequality.

22. $2\sqrt{x - 8} < 24$

23. $7\sqrt[3]{x - 3} \geq 21$

24. In a tsunami, the wave speeds (in meters per second) can be modeled by $s(d) = \sqrt{9.8d}$, where d is the depth (in meters) of the water. Estimate the depth of the water when the wave speed is 200 meters per second.

5.5 Performing Function Operations (pp. 259–264)

Learning Target: Perform arithmetic operations on two functions.

25. Let $f(x) = 2\sqrt{3 - x}$ and $g(x) = 4\sqrt[3]{3 - x}$. Find $(fg)(x)$ and $\left(\dfrac{f}{g}\right)(x)$ and state the domain of each. Then evaluate $(fg)(2)$ and $\left(\dfrac{f}{g}\right)(2)$.

26. Let $f(x) = 3x^2 + 1$ and $g(x) = x + 4$. Find $(f + g)(x)$ and $(f - g)(x)$ and state the domain of each. Then evaluate $(f + g)(-5)$ and $(f - g)(-5)$.

Determine whether the statement is *always*, *sometimes*, or *never* true.

27. For two quadratic functions f and g, $f + g$ is also a quadratic function.

28. For two functions f and g, when $f(a) = 3$ and $g(a) = 4$, $(fg)(a) = 12$.

5.6 Composition of Functions (pp. 265–270)

Learning Target: Evaluate and find compositions of functions.

Vocabulary
composition

Let $f(x) = x + 3$, $g(x) = 4x^2$, and $h(x) = \sqrt{x - 7}$. Find the indicated value.

29. $f(h(11))$

30. $g(f(-8))$

31. $h(g(2))$

32. $f(f(3))$

Let $f(x) = 2x - 5$, $g(x) = x^{-2}$, and $h(x) = 3x + 4$. Perform the indicated composition and state the domain.

33. $f(g(x))$

34. $h(f(x))$

35. $g(h(x))$

36. $g(g(x))$

37. Let f be a radical function and let g be a linear function with a nonzero slope. What type of function results when you compose f and g?

38. You have the coupons shown to use for a purchase at an online store. Use a composition of functions to determine which coupon you should apply first.

5.7 Inverse of a Function (pp. 271–280)

Learning Target: Understand the relationship between inverse functions.

Vocabulary
inverse functions

Find the inverse of the function. Then graph the function and its inverse.

39. $f(x) = -\frac{1}{2}x + 10$

40. $f(x) = x^2 + 8$, $x \geq 0$

41. $f(x) = -x^3 - 9$

42. $f(x) = 3\sqrt{x} + 5$

Determine whether the functions are inverse functions.

43. $f(x) = 4(x - 11)^2$, $g(x) = \frac{1}{4}(x + 11)^2$

44. $f(x) = -2x + 6$, $g(x) = -\frac{1}{2}x + 3$

45. On a certain day, the function that gives U.S. dollars in terms of British pounds is $d(p) = 1.247p$, where p represents British pounds. Find and interpret $d^{-1}(100)$.

5 PERFORMANCE TASK
SMP.1 SMP.2

THE SOUNDS OF MUSIC

Sound is transmitted in waves.
Each sound wave has a frequency, in hertz (Hz), that determines its pitch.

High-frequency sound waves produce high-pitched sounds. →

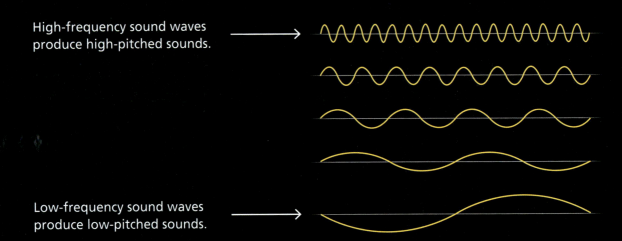

Low-frequency sound waves produce low-pitched sounds. →

Each white key and each black key on a piano represents a distinct musical note. The frequency of a sound wave produced by each note is $2^{1/12}$ times the frequency of a sound wave produced by the previous note.

27.5 Hz — 4,186 Hz

1st octave 2nd octave 3rd octave 4th octave 5th octave 6th octave 7th octave

Musical tones are separated into groups called *octaves*. On a piano, 7 white keys and 5 black keys make up each octave.

284 Chapter 5 Rational Exponents and Radical Functions

Analyzing Data

Use the information on the previous page to complete the following exercises.

1 Explain what is shown in the display. What do you notice? What do you wonder?

2 The display shows that the frequency of A_0 is 27.5 hertz. What is the frequency of the next note, $A_0^\#$?

3 Without calculating, determine which note in the first octave has a frequency of $27.5 \cdot \left(\sqrt[3]{2}\right)^2$ hertz. Explain your reasoning.

COMPARING OCTAVES

Use an instrument or the Internet to listen to the same tone in different octaves. Compare and contrast their sounds. How do the frequencies of the sound waves in the second octave on a piano compare to the frequencies of the sound waves in the first and third octaves? Justify your answers.

Which key on a piano is known as *middle C*? Show how you can use the information above to quickly find the frequency of a sound wave produced by middle C. Then find the frequencies of every note in the same octave as middle C.

6 Exponential and Logarithmic Functions

6.1 Exponential Growth and Decay Functions
6.2 The Natural Base e
6.3 Logarithms and Logarithmic Functions
6.4 Transformations of Exponential and Logarithmic Functions
6.5 Properties of Logarithms
6.6 Solving Exponential and Logarithmic Equations
6.7 Modeling with Exponential and Logarithmic Functions

NATIONAL GEOGRAPHIC EXPLORER
Matthew Piscitelli — ARCHAEOLOGIST

Dr. Matthew Piscitelli is an archaeologist, educator, and researcher. His archaeological fieldwork has taken him to locations in Peru, Bolivia, and Greece. He specializes in prehistoric archaeology, geographic information systems, and public archaeology.

- What is archaeology?
- Why is archaeology an important tool for understanding human history?
- What kinds of archaeological discoveries have been made in Peru? in Bolivia? in Greece?

PERFORMANCE TASK
When archaeologists discover organic matter, they can use carbon dating to approximate when the organic matter died. In the Performance Task on pages 346 and 347, you will use carbon dating to approximate the age of an ancient manuscript made from a plant called papyrus.

Archaeology

Big Idea of the Chapter
Relate Exponential and Logarithmic Functions

Functions with values that are raised to variable powers are called exponential functions. The inverse of an exponential function is a logarithmic function.

Radiocarbon dating can be used to approximate the ages of organisms that died up to about 60,000 years ago. Radiocarbon dating is based on the fact that all living organisms absorb carbon-14 into their tissue. When the organism dies, it stops absorbing carbon-14, a radioactive substance. By determining how much of the carbon-14 remains, scientists can approximate when the organism died.

Radioactive Decay of Carbon-14

1. A human bone contains 25% of the normal amount of carbon-14. Approximate when the human died.

2. Approximate the percent of the original amount of carbon-14 that remains in the bones of a person who died 5,000 years ago.

3. Why do you think radiocarbon dating only works for organisms that died less than 60,000 years ago?

Getting Ready for Chapter 6

Using Properties of Exponents

EXAMPLE 1 Simplify $\left(\dfrac{4p}{3}\right)^3$.

$\left(\dfrac{4p}{3}\right)^3 = \dfrac{(4p)^3}{3^3}$ Power of a Quotient Property

$= \dfrac{4^3 p^3}{3^3}$ Power of a Product Property

$= \dfrac{64p^3}{27}$ Simplify.

Simplify the expression. Write your answer using only positive exponents.

1. $6b^0$
2. $(-2n)^5$
3. $\left(\dfrac{3w}{2x}\right)^4$
4. $\dfrac{3g}{4^{-2}}$

Finding the Domain and Range of a Function

EXAMPLE 2 Find the domain and range of the function represented by the graph.

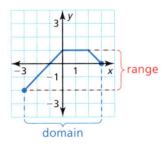

▶ The domain is $-3 \leq x \leq 3$.

The range is $-2 \leq y \leq 1$.

Find the domain and range of the function represented by the graph.

5.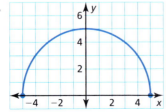
6.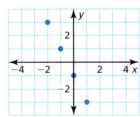

6.1 Exponential Growth and Decay Functions

Learning Target: Write and graph exponential growth and decay functions.

Success Criteria:
- I can identify and graph exponential growth and decay functions.
- I can write exponential growth and decay functions.
- I can solve real-life problems using exponential growth and decay functions.

INVESTIGATE Describing Exponential Growth

Work with a partner. You are studying bacteria growth in a laboratory.

1. **SMP.8** The study starts with a population of 100 bacteria. You notice that the population doubles every hour.

   a. Complete the table.

Time (hours), t	0	1	2	3	4	5
Population, P						

   b. Write a model that represents the population P of the bacteria after t hours.

   c. Use the model in part (b) to complete the table. By what factor does the population increase every half hour? Explain your reasoning.

Time (hours), t	0	$\frac{1}{2}$	1	$\frac{3}{2}$	2	$\frac{5}{2}$	3
Population, P							

   d. Use the model in part (b) to complete the table. By what factor does the population increase every 20 minutes? Explain your reasoning.

Time (hours), t	0	$\frac{1}{3}$	$\frac{2}{3}$	1	$\frac{4}{3}$	$\frac{5}{3}$	2
Population, P							

   e. Create a graph that shows the population P after t hours. Would you expect the actual bacteria population to closely follow this model as t increases? Explain your reasoning.

2. The population P of a different type of bacteria after t hours is given by

   $P = 10(3)^t$.

   How does the growth pattern of this bacteria compare with the growth rate of the bacteria in Exercise 1?

Vocabulary
exponential function
exponential growth function
growth factor
asymptote
exponential decay function
decay factor

Exponential Growth and Decay Functions

An **exponential function** has the form $y = ab^x$, where $a \neq 0$ and the base b is a positive real number other than 1. If $a > 0$ and $b > 1$, then $y = ab^x$ is an **exponential growth function**, and b is called the **growth factor**. The simplest type of exponential growth function has the form $y = b^x$.

Key Concept

Parent Function for Exponential Growth Functions

The function $f(x) = b^x$, where $b > 1$, is the parent function for the family of exponential growth functions with base b. The graph shows the general shape of an exponential growth function.

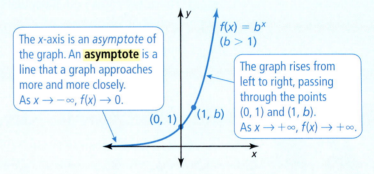

The x-axis is an *asymptote* of the graph. An **asymptote** is a line that a graph approaches more and more closely. As $x \to -\infty$, $f(x) \to 0$.

The graph rises from left to right, passing through the points $(0, 1)$ and $(1, b)$. As $x \to +\infty$, $f(x) \to +\infty$.

The domain of $f(x) = b^x$ is all real numbers. The range is $y > 0$.

EXAMPLE 1 Graphing an Exponential Growth Function

Graph $y = 2^x$.

Make a table of values.

x	−2	−1	0	1	2	3
y	$\frac{1}{4}$	$\frac{1}{2}$	1	2	4	8

Plot the points from the table. Then draw, from *left to right*, a smooth curve that begins just above the x-axis, passes through the plotted points, and moves up to the right.

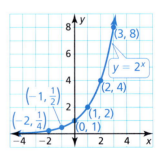

In-Class Practice

Self-Assessment

Graph the function.

1. $y = 4^x$
2. $f(x) = (1.5)^x$

 I don't understand yet.
 I can do it with help.
 I can do it on my own.
 I can teach someone.

If $a > 0$ and $0 < b < 1$, then $y = ab^x$ is an **exponential decay function**, and b is called the **decay factor**.

> ### Key Concept
>
> **Parent Function for Exponential Decay Functions**
>
> The function $f(x) = b^x$, where $0 < b < 1$, is the parent function for the family of exponential decay functions with base b. The graph shows the general shape of an exponential decay function.
>
>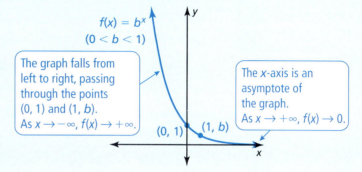
>
> The graph falls from left to right, passing through the points $(0, 1)$ and $(1, b)$. As $x \to -\infty$, $f(x) \to +\infty$.
>
> The x-axis is an asymptote of the graph. As $x \to +\infty$, $f(x) \to 0$.
>
> The domain of $f(x) = b^x$ is all real numbers. The range is $y > 0$.

EXAMPLE 2 Graphing an Exponential Decay Function

Graph $y = \left(\frac{1}{2}\right)^x$.

Make a table of values.

x	−3	−2	−1	0	1	2
y	8	4	2	1	$\frac{1}{2}$	$\frac{1}{4}$

Plot the points from the table. Then draw, from *right to left*, a smooth curve that begins just above the x-axis, passes through the plotted points, and moves up to the left.

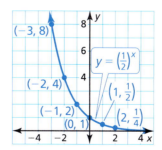

In-Class Practice

Self-Assessment

Graph the function.

3. $y = \left(\frac{2}{3}\right)^x$

4. $f(x) = (0.25)^x$

Exponential Models

Some real-life quantities increase or decrease by a fixed percent each year (or some other time period). The amount y of such a quantity after t years can be modeled by one of these equations:

Exponential Growth Model
$$y = a(1 + r)^t$$

Exponential Decay Model
$$y = a(1 - r)^t$$

The initial amount is a, the percent increase or decrease (in decimal form) is r, the growth factor is $1 + r$, and the decay factor is $1 - r$.

EXAMPLE 3 Identifying Exponential Growth and Decay Functions

The value of a car y (in thousands of dollars) is modeled by $y = 25(0.85)^t$, where t is the number of years since the car was purchased.

a. Determine whether the model represents *exponential growth* or *exponential decay*.

The base, 0.85, is greater than 0 and less than 1, so the model represents exponential decay.

b. Identify the annual percent increase or decrease in the value of the car.

Because t is given in years and the decay factor $0.85 = 1 - 0.15$, the annual percent decrease is 0.15, or 15%.

EXAMPLE 4 Rewriting an Exponential Function

The amount y (in grams) of the radioactive isotope chromium-51 remaining after t days is $y = a(0.5)^{t/28}$, where a is the initial amount (in grams). What percent of the chromium-51 decays each day?

$y = a(0.5)^{t/28}$ Write original function.

$= a[(0.5)^{1/28}]^t$ Power of a Power Property

$\approx a(0.9755)^t$ Evaluate power.

$= a(1 - 0.0245)^t$ Rewrite in form $y = a(1 - r)t$.

▶ The daily decay rate is about 0.0245, or 2.45%.

In-Class Practice

Self-Assessment

5. **WHAT IF?** In Example 3, the value of the car is modeled by $y = 25(0.9)^t$. Identify the annual percent decrease in the value of the car.

6. The amount y (in grams) of the radioactive isotope iodine-123 remaining after t hours is $y = a(0.5)^{t/13}$, where a is the initial amount (in grams). What percent of the iodine-123 decays each hour?

  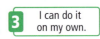

Key Concept

Compound Interest

Consider an initial principal P deposited in an account that pays interest at an annual rate r (expressed as a decimal), compounded n times per year. The amount A in the account after t years is given by

$$A = P\left(1 + \frac{r}{n}\right)^{nt}.$$

EXAMPLE 5 Finding the Balance in an Account

You deposit $9,000 in an account that pays 1.46% annual interest. Find the balance after 3 years when the interest is compounded as described.

a. compounded quarterly

$A = P\left(1 + \frac{r}{n}\right)^{nt}$ Write compound interest formula.

$= 9{,}000\left(1 + \dfrac{0.0146}{4}\right)^{4 \cdot 3}$ $P = 9{,}000, r = 0.0146, n = 4, t = 3$ (compounded quarterly)

$\approx 9{,}402.21$ Use technology.

▶ The balance after 3 years is $9,402.21.

b. compounded monthly

$A = P\left(1 + \frac{r}{n}\right)^{nt}$ Write compound interest formula.

$= 9{,}000\left(1 + \dfrac{0.0146}{12}\right)^{12 \cdot 3}$ $P = 9{,}000, r = 0.0146, n = 12, t = 3$ (compounded monthly)

$\approx 9{,}402.71$ Use technology.

▶ The balance after 3 years is $9,402.71.

c. compounded daily

$A = P\left(1 + \frac{r}{n}\right)^{nt}$ Write compound interest formula.

$= 9{,}000\left(1 + \dfrac{0.0146}{365}\right)^{365 \cdot 3}$ $P = 9{,}000, r = 0.0146, n = 365, t = 3$ (compounded daily)

$\approx 9{,}402.95$ Use technology.

▶ The balance after 3 years is $9,402.95.

In-Class Practice

Self-Assessment

7. You deposit $500 in an account that pays 2.5% annual interest. Find the balance after 2 years when the interest is compounded daily.

1 I don't understand yet.   **2** I can do it with help.   **3** I can do it on my own.   **4** I can teach someone.

6.1 Exponential Growth and Decay Functions

6.1 Practice

Graph the function. (See Examples 1 and 2.)

1. $y = 6^x$
2. $f(x) = \left(\frac{1}{6}\right)^x$
3. $y = \left(\frac{4}{3}\right)^x$
4. $y = \left(\frac{2}{5}\right)^x$
5. $f(x) = (0.75)^x$
6. $f(x) = (1.2)^x$

Use the graph of $f(x) = b^x$ to identify the value of the base b.

7.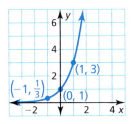
8.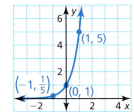

9. The value of a mountain bike y (in dollars) can be approximated by the model $y = 200(0.65)^t$, where t is the number of years since the bike was purchased. (See Example 3.)

    a. Determine whether the model represents *exponential growth* or *exponential decay*.

    b. Identify the annual percent increase or decrease in the value of the bike.

10. In 2018, a county's population was about 90.8 thousand. During the next 4 years, the population increased by about 0.51% each year.

    a. Write an exponential model that represents the population y (in thousands) t years after 2018.

    b. Estimate the population in 2022.

11. The amount y (in grams) of carbon-14 in the body of an organism t years after the organism dies is $y = a(0.5)^{t/5{,}730}$, where a is the initial amount (in grams). What percent of the carbon-14 decays each year? (See Example 4.)

Rewrite the function in the form $y = a(1 + r)^t$ or $y = a(1 - r)^t$. State the growth or decay rate, and describe the end behavior of the function.

12. $y = a(0.5)^{t/12}$
13. $y = a(2)^{t/3}$
14. $y = a\left(\frac{5}{4}\right)^{t/22}$

15. You deposit $5,000 in an account that pays 2.25% annual interest. Find the balance after 5 years when the interest is compounded quarterly. (See Example 5.)

16. **SMP.3 ERROR ANALYSIS** You deposit $250 in an account that pays 1.25% annual interest. Describe and correct the error in finding the balance after 3 years when the interest is compounded quarterly.

$$A = 250\left(1 + \frac{1.25}{4}\right)^{4 \cdot 3}$$
$$= \$6,533.29$$

Use the given information to find the balance in the account earning compound interest after 6 years when the principal is $3,500.

17. $r = 2.16\%$, compounded quarterly

18. $r = 2.29\%$, compounded monthly

19. $r = 1.26\%$, compounded monthly

20. $r = 1.83\%$, compounded daily

21. **SMP.2 SMP.7** In the compound interest formula for interest compounded yearly, $A = P(1 + r)^t$, what does P represent? What does $(1 + r)^t$ represent? Does P depend on $(1 + r)^t$? Does $(1 + r)^t$ depend on P?

22. Compare the graph of $f(x) = 2(1.5)^x$ to the graph of g. Which graph has a greater y-intercept? Explain which graph is increasing at a faster rate.

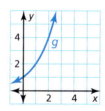

23. The population p of a small town after x years can be modeled by the function $p = 6,850(1.03)^x$. What is the average rate of change in the population over the first 6 years?

24. **SMP.7** Consider the exponential function $f(x) = ab^x$.

    a. Show that $\dfrac{f(x + 1)}{f(x)} = b$.

    b. Use the equation in part (a) to explain why there is no exponential function of the form $f(x) = ab^x$ whose graph passes through the points in the table.

x	0	1	2	3	4
y	4	4	8	24	72

25. **DIG DEEPER** You buy a new laptop for $1,300 and sell it 4 years later for $275. Assume that the resale value of the laptop decays exponentially with time. Write an equation that represents the resale value V (in dollars) of the laptop as a function of the time t (in years) since it was purchased.

Interpreting Data

SPREAD OF A VIRUS Virologists study how viruses are transmitted. The transmission rate at an event is the ratio of the number of people who become infected to the total number of people at the event. The graph shows the transmission rates and the numbers of people at several different events.

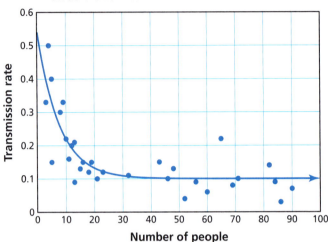

Virus Transmission at Close-Contact Events

26. Describe the relationship between the transmission rate and the number of people at the event.

27. Explain whether the relationship is an example of *exponential growth* or *exponential decay*.

Review & Refresh

Simplify the expression.

28. $x^9 \cdot x^2$

29. $(2x \cdot 3x^5)^3$

30. $\left(\dfrac{4x^8}{2x^6}\right)^4$

31. $\dfrac{12x}{4x} + 5x$

Determine whether the functions are inverse functions.

32. $f(x) = -\dfrac{1}{2}x + 5,\ g(x) = -2x + 10$

33. $f(x) = \sqrt[3]{4x},\ g(x) = \dfrac{x^3}{64}$

Let $f(x) = x^2 - 6$, $g(x) = -\dfrac{1}{2}x + 5$, and $h(x) = 4x^{-1}$. **Perform the indicated composition and state the domain.**

34. $f(g(x))$

35. $h(f(x))$

36. Let $f(x) = -x^3$ and $g(x) = 4\sqrt{x}$. Find $(fg)(x)$ and $\left(\dfrac{f}{g}\right)(x)$ and state the domain of each. Then evaluate $(fg)(4)$ and $\left(\dfrac{f}{g}\right)(4)$.

37. Describe the x-values for which (a) f is increasing, (b) f is decreasing, (c) $f(x) > 0$, and (d) $f(x) < 0$.

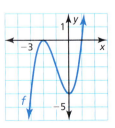

38. Solve $4|x - 3| \geq 20$.

6.2 The Natural Base e

Learning Target: Use the natural base e and graph natural base functions.

Success Criteria:
- I can simplify natural base expressions.
- I can graph natural base functions.
- I can solve real-life problems using exponential growth and decay functions.

INVESTIGATE Approximating the Natural Base e

Work with a partner. So far in your study of mathematics, you have worked with special numbers such as π and i. Another special number is called the *natural base* and is denoted by e.

1. One way to approximate the natural base e is to approximate the sum

$$1 + \frac{1}{1} + \frac{1}{1 \cdot 2} + \frac{1}{1 \cdot 2 \cdot 3} + \frac{1}{1 \cdot 2 \cdot 3 \cdot 4} + \cdots.$$

Approximate this sum and explain your method. Then compare your result with those of your classmates.

2. Another way to approximate the natural base e is to use the expression

$$\left(1 + \frac{1}{x}\right)^x.$$

Complete the table. What do you notice as x increases?

x	10^1	10^2	10^3	10^4	10^5	10^6
$\left(1 + \frac{1}{x}\right)^x$						

Use your results to approximate e. Compare this approximation to the one in Exercise 1.

3. Explain what you think the graph of the *natural base exponential function* $y = e^x$ looks like.

4. Use your result in Exercise 1 or Exercise 2 to complete the table. Then graph $y = e^x$. Find the domain and range. Make several observations about the graph.

x	-2	-1	0	1	2
$y = e^x$					

5. Repeat Exercise 4 for the natural base exponential function $y = e^{-x}$. Compare the graphs of $y = e^x$ and $y = e^{-x}$.

Vocabulary
natural base e

The Natural Base e

The history of mathematics is marked by the discovery of special numbers, such as π and i. Another special number is denoted by the letter e. The number is called the **natural base e**. The expression

$$\left(1 + \frac{1}{x}\right)^x$$

approaches e as x increases, as shown in the graph and table.

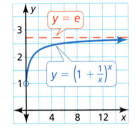

x	10^1	10^2	10^3	10^4	10^5	10^6
$\left(1 + \frac{1}{x}\right)^x$	2.59374	2.70481	2.71692	2.71815	2.71827	2.71828

Key Concept

The Natural Base e

The natural base e is irrational. It is defined as follows:

As x approaches $+\infty$, $\left(1 + \frac{1}{x}\right)^x$ approaches $e \approx 2.71828182846$.

EXAMPLE 1 Simplifying Natural Base Expressions

a. Simplify $e^3 \cdot e^6$.

$e^3 \cdot e^6 = e^{3+6}$
$= e^9$

b. Simplify $\dfrac{16e^5}{4e^4}$.

$\dfrac{16e^5}{4e^4} = 4e^{5-4}$
$= 4e$

c. Simplify $(3e^{-4x})^2$.

$(3e^{-4x})^2 = 3^2(e^{-4x})^2$
$= 9e^{-8x}$
$= \dfrac{9}{e^{8x}}$

d. Simplify $\sqrt{4e^{2x}}$.

$\sqrt{4e^{2x}} = \sqrt{4} \cdot \sqrt{e^{2x}}$
$= 2 \cdot (e^{2x})^{1/2}$
$= 2e^x$

In-Class Practice

Self-Assessment

Simplify the expression.

1. $e^7 \cdot e^4$

2. $\dfrac{24e^8}{8e^5}$

3. $(10e^{-3x})^3$

4. $\sqrt{\dfrac{1}{9}e^{8x}}$

1. I don't understand yet.
2. I can do it with help.
3. I can do it on my own.
4. I can teach someone.

Graphing Natural Base Functions

A function of the form $y = ae^{rx}$ is called a *natural base exponential function*.

- When $a > 0$ and $r > 0$, the function is an exponential growth function.
- When $a > 0$ and $r < 0$, the function is an exponential decay function.

The graphs of the basic functions $y = e^x$ and $y = e^{-x}$ are shown.

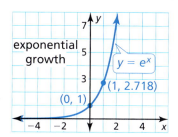
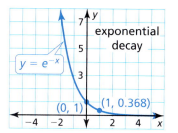

EXAMPLE 2 Graphing Natural Base Functions

Determine whether each function represents *exponential growth* or *exponential decay*. Then graph the function.

a. $y = 3e^x$

b. $f(x) = e^{-0.5x}$

Because $a = 3$ is positive and $r = 1$ is positive, the function is an exponential growth function. Use a table to graph the function.

Because $a = 1$ is positive and $r = -0.5$ is negative, the function is an exponential decay function. Use a table to graph the function.

x	−2	−1	0	1
y	0.41	1.10	3	8.15

x	−4	−2	0	2
f(x)	7.39	2.72	1	0.37

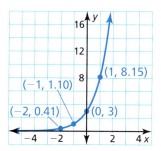
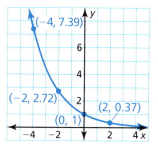

In-Class Practice

Self-Assessment

Determine whether the function represents *exponential growth* or *exponential decay*. Then graph the function.

5. $y = \frac{1}{2}e^x$

6. $y = 4e^{-x}$

7. $g(x) = \frac{1}{3}e^{-4x}$

8. $f(x) = 2e^{2x}$

1 I don't understand yet. **2** I can do it with help. **3** I can do it on my own. **4** I can teach someone.

Connections to Real Life

You have learned that the balance of an account earning compound interest is given by $A = P\left(1 + \dfrac{r}{n}\right)^{nt}$. As the frequency n of compounding approaches positive infinity, the compound interest formula approximates the following formula.

> ### Key Concept
>
> **Continuously Compounded Interest**
>
> When interest is compounded *continuously*, the amount A in an account after t years is given by the formula
>
> $$A = Pe^{rt}$$
>
> where P is the principal and r is the annual interest rate expressed as a decimal.

EXAMPLE 3 Using Continuously Compounded Interest

You and your friend each have accounts that earn annual interest compounded continuously. The balance A (in dollars) of your account after t years can be modeled by $A = 4{,}500e^{0.04t}$. The graph shows the balance of your friend's account over time. Which account has a greater principal? Which has a greater balance after 10 years?

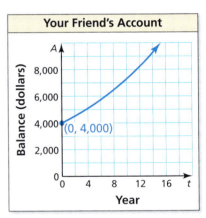

The equation $A = 4{,}500e^{0.04t}$ is of the form $A = Pe^{rt}$, where $P = 4{,}500$. So, your principal is \$4,500. Your balance A when $t = 10$ is

$$A = 4{,}500e^{0.04(10)} = \$6{,}713.21.$$

Because the graph passes through $(0, 4{,}000)$, your friend's principal is \$4,000. The graph also shows that the balance is about \$7,250 when $t = 10$.

▶ So, your account has a greater principal, but your friend's account has a greater balance after 10 years.

In-Class Practice

Self-Assessment

9. You deposit \$4,250 in an account that earns 5% annual interest compounded continuously. How much more money does this account earn after 10 years with interest compounded continuously than with interest compounding monthly? yearly?

  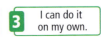

Chapter 6 Exponential and Logarithmic Functions

6.2 Practice

Simplify the expression. (See Example 1.)

1. $e^3 \cdot e^5$
2. $\dfrac{11e^9}{22e^{10}}$
3. $(4e^{-2x})^3$
4. $\sqrt{9e^{6x}}$
5. $\sqrt[3]{8e^{12x}}$
6. $e^x \cdot e^{-6x} \cdot e^8$

Determine whether the function represents *exponential growth* or *exponential decay*. Then graph the function. (See Example 2.)

7. $y = e^{3x}$
8. $y = 2e^{-x}$
9. $y = 3e^{2x}$
10. $y = \frac{1}{4}e^{-3x}$
11. $y = 0.4e^{-0.25x}$
12. $y = 0.6e^{0.5x}$

SMP.7 Use the properties of exponents to rewrite the function in the form $y = a(1 + r)^t$ or $y = a(1 - r)^t$. Then find the percent rate of change.

13. $y = e^{-0.75t}$
14. $y = 2e^{0.4t}$
15. $y = 0.5e^{0.8t}$

16. **CONNECTION TO REAL LIFE** Investment accounts for a house and education earn annual interest compounded continuously. The balance A (in dollars) of the house account after t years can be modeled by $A = 3{,}224e^{0.05t}$. The graph shows the balance of the education account over time. Which account has a greater principal? Which account has a greater balance after 12 years? (See Example 3.)

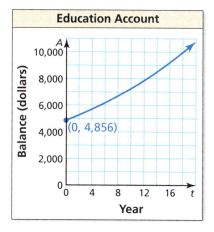

17. The number of *Mycobacterium tuberculosis* bacteria after t hours can be modeled by the function $N(t) = ae^{0.166t}$, where a is the number of bacteria at 12:00 P.M. At 1:00 P.M., there are 30 *M. tuberculosis* bacteria in a sample. Find the number of bacteria in the sample at 3:45 P.M.

18. Use the graph to complete each statement.

    a. $f(x)$ approaches _____ as x approaches $+\infty$.
    b. $f(x)$ approaches _____ as x approaches $-\infty$.

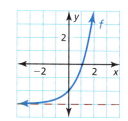

6.2 The Natural Base e **301**

Interpreting Data

LOGISTIC GROWTH Exponential growth occurs when there is no environmental restriction, meaning the function can continue to increase forever. *Logistic growth* occurs when there is such a restriction, meaning the function will reach a maximum. The graph below shows an example for a population over time.

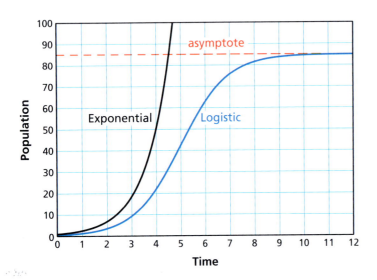

19. Use technology to graph the functions below.

    $$f(x) = \frac{1}{1 + e^{-x}} \qquad g(x) = \frac{1}{e^{-x}}$$

    Which function represents exponential growth? logistic growth?

20. Describe a real-life example of logistic growth.

Review & Refresh

21. Write the cubic function whose graph is shown.

    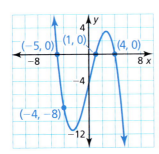

22. Find the inverse of the function. Then graph the function and its inverse.

    $$y = \sqrt{x} + 6$$

23. Determine whether *the function* represents *exponential growth* or *exponential decay*. Then graph the function.

    $$f(x) = (4.25)^x$$

24. The function $f(t) = 9.75t$ represents your earnings (in dollars) for working t hours. The function $t(x) = 15x$ represents the total number of hours you work after x weeks.

    a. Find $f(t(x))$. Interpret the coefficient.

    b. Evaluate $f(t(12))$ and explain what it represents.

6.3 Logarithms and Logarithmic Functions

> **Learning Target:** Understand logarithms and graph logarithmic functions.
>
> **Success Criteria:**
> - I can explain the meaning of a logarithm with base b.
> - I can evaluate logarithmic expressions.
> - I can graph logarithmic functions.

INVESTIGATE Understanding Logarithmic Functions

Work with a partner.

1. Look for a pattern and complete each statement.

   $\log_2 8 = 3$ $\log_3 27 = \underline{}$

   $\log_5 25 = 2$ $\log_2 32 = \underline{}$

   $\log_{10} 1{,}000 = 3$ $\log_4 64 = \underline{}$

   $\log_7 49 = \underline{}$ $\log_2 \frac{1}{2} = \underline{}$

2. Use your results in Exercise 1 to describe the relationship among the values of b, x, and y in the equation shown.

   $\log_b y = x$

3. Use your results in Exercise 2 to complete the table of values.

x		$\frac{1}{10}$					1,000
$\log_{10} x$	-2	-1	0	1	2	3	

4. Plot the points $(x, \log_{10} x)$ from Exercise 3. Draw a smooth curve through the points. Make several observations about the graph.

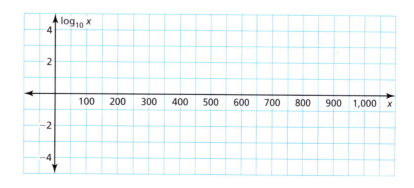

Vocabulary
logarithm of y with base b
common logarithm
natural logarithm

Logarithms

You know that $2^2 = 4$ and $2^3 = 8$. However, for what value of x does $2^x = 6$? Mathematicians define this x-value using a *logarithm* and write $x = \log_2 6$. The definition of a logarithm can be generalized as follows.

Key Concept

Definition of Logarithm with Base b

Let b and y be positive real numbers with $b \neq 1$. The **logarithm of y with base b** is denoted by $\log_b y$ and is defined as

$$\log_b y = x \quad \text{if and only if} \quad b^x = y.$$

The expression $\log_b y$ is read as "log base b of y." This definition tells you that the equations $\log_b y = x$ and $b^x = y$ are equivalent. The first is in *logarithmic form*, and the second is in *exponential form*.

EXAMPLE 1 Rewriting Logarithmic Equations

a. Write $\log_2 16 = 4$ in exponential form.

$\log_2 16 = 4 \longrightarrow 2^4 = 16$ $b = 2, x = 4, \text{ and } y = 16$

▶ The exponential form is $2^4 = 16$.

b. Write $\log_{1/4} 4 = -1$ in exponential form.

$\log_{1/4} 4 = -1 \longrightarrow \left(\frac{1}{4}\right)^{-1} = 4$ $b = \frac{1}{4}, x = -1, \text{ and } y = 4$

▶ The exponential form is $\left(\frac{1}{4}\right)^{-1} = 4$.

EXAMPLE 2 Rewriting Exponential Equations

a. Write $5^2 = 25$ in logarithmic form.

$5^2 = 25 \longrightarrow \log_5 25 = 2$ $b = 5, x = 2, \text{ and } y = 25$

▶ The logarithmic form is $\log_5 25 = 2$.

b. Write $8^{2/3} = 4$ in logarithmic form.

$8^{2/3} = 4 \longrightarrow \log_8 4 = \frac{2}{3}$ $b = 8, x = \frac{2}{3}, \text{ and } y = 4$

▶ The logarithmic form is $\log_8 4 = \frac{2}{3}$.

In-Class Practice

Self-Assessment

1. Write $\log_{1/2} 32 = -5$ in exponential form.

2. Write $7^2 = 49$ in logarithmic form.

Let b be a positive real number such that $b \neq 1$.

Logarithm of 1

$\log_b 1 = 0$ because $b^0 = 1$.

Logarithm of b with Base b

$\log_b b = 1$ because $b^1 = b$.

EXAMPLE 3 **Evaluating Logarithmic Expressions**

a. Evaluate $\log_4 64$.

▶ $4^3 = 64$, so $\log_4 64 = 3$.

b. Evaluate $\log_5 0.2$.

▶ $5^{-1} = 0.2$, so $\log_5 0.2 = -1$.

c. Evaluate $\log_{1/5} 125$.

▶ $\left(\frac{1}{5}\right)^{-3} = 125$, so $\log_{1/5} 125 = -3$.

d. Evaluate $\log_{36} 6$.

▶ $36^{1/2} = 6$, so $\log_{36} 6 = \frac{1}{2}$.

STUDY TIP
To help you find the value of $\log_b y$, ask yourself, "What power of b gives you y?"

A **common logarithm** is a logarithm with base 10. It is denoted by $\log_{10}$ or simply by log. A **natural logarithm** is a logarithm with base e. It can be denoted by $\log_e$ but is usually denoted by ln.

Common Logarithm

$\log_{10} x = \log x$

Natural Logarithm

$\log_e x = \ln x$

EXAMPLE 4 **Evaluating Common and Natural Logarithms**

Use technology to evaluate each logarithm. Round your answer to three decimal places.

a. log 8

log 8 = 0.903089987

▶ So, log 8 ≈ 0.903.

b. ln 0.3

ln 0.3 = −1.203972804

▶ So, ln 0.3 ≈ −1.204.

In-Class Practice

Self-Assessment

Evaluate the logarithm. If necessary, use technology and round your answer to three decimal places.

3. $\log_2 32$

4. $\log_{27} 3$

5. $\log 12$

6. $\ln 0.75$

Using Inverse Properties

By the definition of logarithm, it follows that the logarithmic function $g(x) = \log_b x$ is the inverse of the exponential function $f(x) = b^x$.

$$g(f(x)) = \log_b b^x = x \quad \text{and} \quad f(g(x)) = b^{\log_b x} = x$$

In other words, exponential functions and logarithmic functions "undo" each other.

EXAMPLE 5 Using Inverse Properties

a. Simplify $10^{\log 4}$.

$\quad 10^{\log 4} = 4 \qquad\qquad b^{\log_b x} = x$

b. Simplify $\log_5 25^x$.

$\quad \log_5 25^x = \log_5 (5^2)^x \qquad$ Express 25 as a power with base 5.

$\qquad\qquad\; = \log_5 5^{2x} \qquad$ Power of a Power Property

$\qquad\qquad\; = 2x \qquad\qquad\;\; \log_b b^x = x$

EXAMPLE 6 Finding Inverse Functions

a. Find the inverse of $f(x) = 6^x$.

From the definition of logarithm, the inverse of $f(x) = 6^x$ is $f^{-1}(x) = \log_6 x$.

b. Find the inverse of $f(x) = \ln(x + 3)$.

Set y equal to $f(x)$. Switch the roles of x and y and solve for y.

$\qquad y = \ln(x + 3) \qquad$ Set y equal to $f(x)$.

$\qquad x = \ln(y + 3) \qquad$ Switch x and y.

$\qquad e^x = y + 3 \qquad\;\;$ Write in exponential form.

$\qquad e^x - 3 = y \qquad\;\;$ Subtract 3 from each side.

▶ The inverse of f is $f^{-1}(x) = e^x - 3$.

In-Class Practice

Self-Assessment

Simplify the expression.

7. $8^{\log_8 x}$

8. $\log_7 7^{-3x}$

Find the inverse of the function.

9. $f(x) = 4^x$

10. $f(x) = \ln(x - 5)$

Graphing Logarithmic Functions

The graph of $f(x) = \log_b x$ is shown below for $b > 1$ and for $0 < b < 1$. Because $f(x) = \log_b x$ and $g(x) = b^x$ are inverse functions, you can graph f by reversing coordinates of points on the graph of g. The graph of f is the reflection of the graph of g in the line $y = x$.

Graph of $f(x) = \log_b x$ for $b > 1$

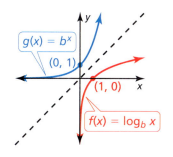

Graph of $f(x) = \log_b x$ for $0 < b < 1$

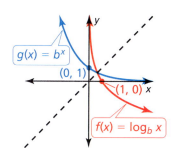

Note that the y-axis is a vertical asymptote of the graph of $f(x) = \log_b x$. The domain of $f(x) = \log_b x$ is $x > 0$, and the range is all real numbers.

EXAMPLE 7 — Graphing a Logarithmic Function

Graph $f(x) = \log_3 x$.

Find the inverse of f. From the definition of logarithm, the inverse of $f(x) = \log_3 x$ is $f^{-1}(x) = 3^x$.

Make a table of values for f^{-1}. Use the result to make a table of values for f.

x	−2	−1	0	1	2
$f^{-1}(x)$	$\frac{1}{9}$	$\frac{1}{3}$	1	3	9

x	$\frac{1}{9}$	$\frac{1}{3}$	1	3	9
$f(x)$	−2	−1	0	1	2

Plot the points from each table. Connect each set of points with a smooth curve.

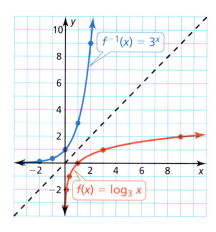

In-Class Practice

Self-Assessment

Graph the function.

11. $y = \log_2 x$ **12.** $f(x) = \log_5 x$ **13.** $y = \log_{1/2} x$

1 I don't understand yet. **2** I can do it with help. **3** I can do it on my own. **4** I can teach someone.

6.3 Practice

Rewrite the equation in exponential form. (See Example 1.)

1. $\log_3 9 = 2$
2. $\log_6 1 = 0$
3. $\log_{1/2} 16 = -4$

Rewrite the equation in logarithmic form. (See Example 2.)

4. $6^2 = 36$
5. $16^{-1} = \frac{1}{16}$
6. $125^{2/3} = 25$

Evaluate the logarithm. (See Example 3.)

7. $\log_3 81$
8. $\log_5 \frac{1}{625}$
9. $\log_{10} 0.001$

10. **SMP.6 SMP.7** How many times greater is the value of $\log_{10} 10^{20}$ than the value of $\log_{10} 10^5$? Explain.

Use technology to evaluate the logarithm. Round your answer to three decimal places. (See Example 4.)

11. $\ln \frac{1}{3}$
12. $\log 6$
13. $3 \ln 0.5$

14. Skydivers use an *altimeter* to track their altitudes as they fall. The altimeter determines altitude by measuring air pressure. The altitude h (in meters) above sea level is related to the air pressure P (in pascals) by the function shown in the diagram. What is the altitude above sea level when the air pressure is 57,000 pascals?

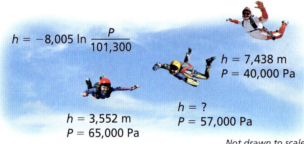

$h = -8{,}005 \ln \dfrac{P}{101{,}300}$

$h = 7{,}438$ m
$P = 40{,}000$ Pa

$h = 3{,}552$ m
$P = 65{,}000$ Pa

$h = ?$
$P = 57{,}000$ Pa

Not drawn to scale

Simplify the expression. (See Example 5.)

15. $7^{\log_7 x}$
16. $e^{\ln 4}$
17. $\log_3 3^{2x}$
18. $10^{\log 15}$
19. $\log_2 8^{3x}$
20. $\ln e^{4 + 5x}$

21. **SMP.3 ERROR ANALYSIS** Describe and correct the error in rewriting $4^{-3} = \frac{1}{64}$ in logarithmic form.

$\log_4 (-3) = \dfrac{1}{64}$ ✗

Find the inverse of the function. (See Example 6.)

22. $f(x) = 0.3^x$
23. $y = \log_2 x$
24. $y = \ln(x - 1)$
25. $f(x) = e^{3x}$
26. $y = 5^x - 9$
27. $y = 13 + \log x$

308   Chapter 6   Exponential and Logarithmic Functions

28. **SMP.2** The *moment magnitude* of an earthquake can be modeled by $f(x) = \frac{2}{3}\log x - 9.1$, where x is the *seismic moment* (in dyne-centimeters).

   a. In 2022, an earthquake in Papua New Guinea had a seismic moment of 1.12×10^{25} dyne-centimeters. What was the moment magnitude of the earthquake?

   b. Find and interpret $f^{-1}(x)$.

Graph the function. (See Example 7.)

29. $y = \log_{1/3} x$

30. $f(x) = \log_4 x$

31. $y = \log_2 x - 1$

32. $f(x) = \log_3(x + 2)$

Use technology to graph the function. Determine the domain, range, and asymptote of the function.

33. $y = \log(x + 2)$

34. $y = -\ln x$

35. $y = \ln(-x)$

36. $y = 3 - \log x$

37. Order the functions from the least average rate of change to the greatest average rate of change when $1 \le x \le 10$.

   a. $y = \log_6 x$

   b. $y = \log_{3/5} x$

   c.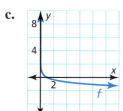

   d.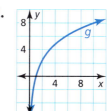

38. **SMP.4** Biologists have found that the length ℓ (in inches) of an alligator and its weight w (in pounds) are related by the function $\ell = 27.1 \ln w - 32.8$.

   a. Use technology to graph the function.

   b. Use your graph to estimate the weight of an alligator that is 10 feet long.

   c. Does the *x*-intercept of the graph of the function make sense in this situation? Explain.

39. Explain why a base of 1 is excluded from the definition of logarithm.

40. **SMP.1** **DIG DEEPER** Evaluate each logarithm without using technology. Explain your method.

   a. $\log_{125} 25$

   b. $\log_8 32$

   c. $\log_{27} 81$

   d. $\log_4 128$

41. **OPEN-ENDED** Write a logarithmic function f that satisfies both characteristics. Then graph the function.

$$f(0) = -3; \text{ end behavior: as } x \to +\infty, f(x) \to +\infty$$

Interpreting Data

BLOOD ALCOHOL CONCENTRATION Data from 2,871 vehicle accidents were used to compare a driver's blood alcohol concentration and the relative risk of being involved in a vehicle accident. A relative risk of y indicates that the risk of being in an accident is y times the risk of an individual with a blood alcohol concentration of 0 being in an accident.

Blood Alcohol and Risk of an Accident

$y = 0.48e^{25.15x}$

Relative risk vs. Blood alcohol concentration (mg of alcohol per 100mL of blood)

42. About how much more likely is a driver with a 0.09 blood alcohol level to have an accident than a driver who hasn't been drinking?

43. Complete the equation below for someone with a blood alcohol concentration of 0.15. Then write the equation in logarithmic form.

$$\frac{y}{\boxed{}} = e^{\boxed{}}$$

Review & Refresh

Simplify the expression.

44. $-e^2 \cdot e^9$

45. $\dfrac{3e^2}{15e^4}$

46. $(2e^x)^4$

47. $\sqrt{4e^{8x}}$

Solve the equation.

48. $0 = x^2 + 12x + 11$

49. $n^2 - n = 0$

Determine whether the function represents *exponential growth* or *exponential decay*. Then graph the function.

50. $y = (0.8)^x$

51. $y = \left(\dfrac{6}{5}\right)^x$

Determine whether the inverse of f is a function. Then find the inverse.

52. $f(x) = 3x^3 + 2$

53. $f(x) = \sqrt{x+1}$

54. **ARCHAEOLOGY** **PYRAMIDS** The volume of the largest of the six pyramids constructed by the Norte Chico people in Caral, Peru is about 4,500,000 cubic feet. What is the height of the pyramid?

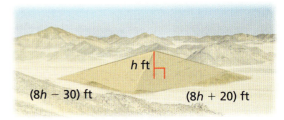

h ft, $(8h - 30)$ ft, $(8h + 20)$ ft

310   Chapter 6   Exponential and Logarithmic Functions

6.4 Transformations of Exponential and Logarithmic Functions

Learning Target: Graph transformations of exponential and logarithmic functions.

Success Criteria:
- I can describe transformations of exponential and logarithmic functions.
- I can graph transformations of exponential and logarithmic functions.
- I can write functions that represent transformations of exponential and logarithmic functions.

INVESTIGATE Identifying Transformations

Work with a partner. You can transform graphs of exponential and logarithmic functions in the same way you transformed graphs of functions previously.

1. Each graph shown is a transformation of the parent function

   $$f(x) = e^x \quad \text{or} \quad f(x) = \ln x.$$

   Match each graph with one of the functions in the list at the left. Explain your reasoning. Then describe the transformation of f represented by g.

   A. $g(x) = e^{x+2} - 3$
   B. $g(x) = -e^{x+2} + 1$
   C. $g(x) = -e^{x-2} + 3$
   D. $g(x) = e^{x-2} - 1$
   E. $g(x) = \ln(x + 2)$
   F. $g(x) = \ln(x - 2)$
   G. $g(x) = 2 + \ln x$
   H. $g(x) = 2 + \ln(-x)$

   a.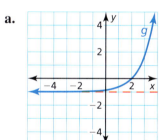
   b.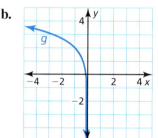
   c.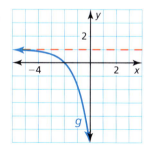
   d.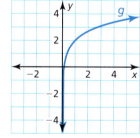
   e.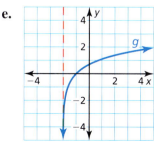
   f.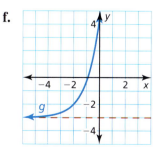

2. The graph of h is a translation 4 units right and 1 unit up of the graph of $f(x) = e^x$. Write a rule for h. Then graph each function.

6.4 Transformations of Exponential and Logarithmic Functions 311

Transforming Graphs of Exponential Functions

You can transform graphs of exponential and logarithmic functions in the same way you transformed graphs of functions in previous chapters. Examples of transformations of the graph of $f(x) = 4^x$ are shown below.

Transformation	Examples	
Horizontal Translation: $f(x - h)$ Graph shifts left or right.	$g(x) = 4^{x-3}$ $g(x) = 4^{x+2}$	3 units right 2 units left
Vertical Translation: $f(x) + k$ Graph shifts up or down.	$g(x) = 4^x + 5$ $g(x) = 4^x - 1$	5 units up 1 unit down
Reflection: $f(-x)$ or $-f(x)$ Graph flips over a line.	$g(x) = 4^{-x}$ $g(x) = -4^x$	in the y-axis in the x-axis
Horizontal Stretch or Shrink: $f(ax)$ Graph stretches away from or shrinks toward y-axis by a factor of $\frac{1}{a}$.	$g(x) = 4^{2x}$ $g(x) = 4^{x/2}$	shrink by a factor of $\frac{1}{2}$ stretch by a factor of 2
Vertical Stretch or Shrink: $a \cdot f(x)$ Graph stretches away from or shrinks toward x-axis by a factor of a.	$g(x) = 3(4^x)$ $g(x) = \frac{1}{4}(4^x)$	stretch by a factor of 3 shrink by a factor of $\frac{1}{4}$

EXAMPLE 1 Translating an Exponential Function

Describe the transformation of $f(x) = \left(\frac{1}{2}\right)^x$ represented by $g(x) = \left(\frac{1}{2}\right)^x - 4$. Then graph each function.

Notice that the function is of the form $g(x) = \left(\frac{1}{2}\right)^x + k$.

Rewrite the function to identify k.

$g(x) = \left(\frac{1}{2}\right)^x + (-4)$
$\phantom{g(x) = \left(\frac{1}{2}\right)^x + (}\uparrow$
$\phantom{g(x) = \left(\frac{1}{2}\right)^x + (}k$

▶ Because $k = -4$, the graph of g is a translation 4 units down of the graph of f.

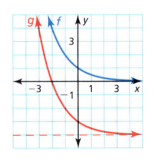

In-Class Practice

Describe the transformation of f represented by g. Then graph each function.

1. $f(x) = 3^x$, $g(x) = 3^x + 2$
2. $f(x) = 0.5^x$, $g(x) = 0.5^{x+1} - 6$

1 I don't understand yet.   **2** I can do it with help.   **3** I can do it on my own.   **4** I can teach someone.

EXAMPLE 2 **Translating a Natural Base Exponential Function**

Describe the transformation of $f(x) = e^x$ represented by $g(x) = e^{x+3} + 2$. Then graph each function.

Notice that the function is of the form $g(x) = e^{x-h} + k$.

Rewrite the function to identify h and k.

$$g(x) = e^{x-(-3)} + 2$$
$$\phantom{g(x) = e^{x-}}\uparrow\uparrow$$
$$\phantom{g(x) = e^{x-}}hk$$

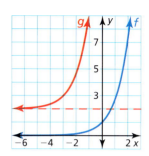

▶ Because $h = -3$ and $k = 2$, the graph of g is a translation 3 units left and 2 units up of the graph of f.

EXAMPLE 3 **Transforming Exponential Functions**

Describe the transformation of f represented by g. Then graph each function.

a. $f(x) = 3^x, g(x) = 3^{3x-5}$

Notice that the function is of the form $g(x) = 3^{ax-h}$, where $a = 3$ and $h = 5$.

▶ So, the graph of g is a translation 5 units right, followed by a horizontal shrink by a factor of $\frac{1}{3}$ of the graph of f.

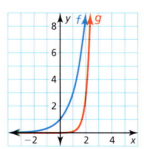

b. $f(x) = e^{-x}, g(x) = -\frac{1}{8}e^{-x}$

Notice that the function is of the form $g(x) = ae^{-x}$, where $a = -\frac{1}{8}$.

▶ So, the graph of g is a reflection in the x-axis and a vertical shrink by a factor of $\frac{1}{8}$ of the graph of f.

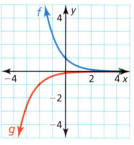

In-Class Practice

Self-Assessment

Describe the transformation of f represented by g. Then graph each function.

3. $f(x) = e^x, g(x) = e^{x-3}$

4. $f(x) = e^{-x}, g(x) = e^{-x} - 5$

5. $f(x) = 0.4^x, g(x) = 0.4^{-2x}$

6. $f(x) = e^x, g(x) = -e^{x+6}$

1 I don't understand yet.   **2** I can do it with help.   **3** I can do it on my own.   **4** I can teach someone.

6.4 Transformations of Exponential and Logarithmic Functions

Transforming Graphs of Logarithmic Functions

Examples of transformations of the graph of $f(x) = \log x$ are shown below.

Transformation	Examples	
Horizontal Translation: $f(x - h)$ Graph shifts left or right.	$g(x) = \log(x - 4)$ $g(x) = \log(x + 7)$	4 units right 7 units left
Vertical Translation: $f(x) + k$ Graph shifts up or down.	$g(x) = \log x + 3$ $g(x) = \log x - 1$	3 units up 1 unit down
Reflection: $f(-x)$ or $-f(x)$ Graph flips over a line.	$g(x) = \log(-x)$ $g(x) = -\log x$	in the y-axis in the x-axis
Horizontal Stretch or Shrink: $f(ax)$ Graph stretches away from or shrinks toward y-axis by a factor of $\frac{1}{a}$.	$g(x) = \log(4x)$ $g(x) = \log\left(\frac{1}{3}x\right)$	shrink by a factor of $\frac{1}{4}$ stretch by a factor of 3
Vertical Stretch or Shrink: $a \cdot f(x)$ Graph stretches away from or shrinks toward x-axis by a factor of a.	$g(x) = 5 \log x$ $g(x) = \frac{2}{3} \log x$	stretch by a factor of 5 shrink by a factor of $\frac{2}{3}$

EXAMPLE 4 Transforming Logarithmic Functions

Describe the transformation of $f(x) = \log_{1/2} x$ represented by $g(x) = 2 \log_{1/2}(x + 4)$. Then graph each function.

Notice that the function is of the form $g(x) = a \log_{1/2}(x - h)$, where $a = 2$ and $h = -4$.

▶ So, the graph of g is a horizontal translation 4 units left and a vertical stretch by a factor of 2 of the graph of f.

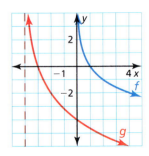

In-Class Practice

Self-Assessment

Describe the transformation of f represented by g. Then graph each function.

7. $f(x) = \log_2 x$, $g(x) = -3 \log_2 x$

8. $f(x) = \log_{1/4} x$, $g(x) = \log_{1/4}(4x) - 5$

| 1 | I don't understand yet. | 2 | I can do it with help. | 3 | I can do it on my own. | 4 | I can teach someone. |

Chapter 6 Exponential and Logarithmic Functions

Writing Transformations of Graphs of Functions

EXAMPLE 5 Writing Transformed Functions

a. **Let the graph of g be a reflection in the x-axis, followed by a translation 4 units right of the graph of $f(x) = 2^x$. Write a rule for g.**

First write a function h that represents the reflection of f.

$h(x) = -f(x)$ Multiply the output by -1.

$= -2^x$ Substitute 2^x for $f(x)$.

Then write a function g that represents the translation of h.

$g(x) = h(x - 4)$ Subtract 4 from the input.

$= -2^{x-4}$ Replace x with $x - 4$ in $h(x)$.

▶ The transformed function is $g(x) = -2^{x-4}$.

Check

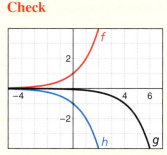

b. **Let the graph of g be a translation 2 units up, followed by a vertical stretch by a factor of 2 of the graph of $f(x) = \log_{1/3} x$. Write a rule for g.**

First write a function h that represents the translation of f.

$h(x) = f(x) + 2$ Add 2 to the output.

$= \log_{1/3} x + 2$ Substitute $\log_{1/3} x$ for $f(x)$.

Then write a function g that represents the vertical stretch of h.

$g(x) = 2 \cdot h(x)$ Multiply the output by 2.

$= 2 \cdot (\log_{1/3} x + 2)$ Substitute $\log_{1/3} x + 2$ for $h(x)$.

$= 2 \log_{1/3} x + 4$ Distributive Property

▶ The transformed function is $g(x) = 2 \log_{1/3} x + 4$.

Check

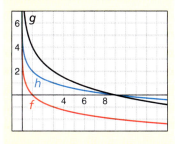

In-Class Practice

Self-Assessment

9. Let the graph of g be a horizontal stretch by a factor of 3, followed by a translation 2 units up of the graph of $f(x) = e^{-x}$. Write a rule for g.

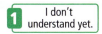

6.4   Transformations of Exponential and Logarithmic Functions   **315**

6.4 Practice

Describe the transformation of f represented by g. Then graph each function.
(See Examples 1 and 2.)

1. $f(x) = 2^x$, $g(x) = 2^{x-7}$

2. $f(x) = e^x$, $g(x) = e^x + 4$

3. $f(x) = e^{-x}$, $g(x) = e^{-x} + 6$

4. $f(x) = \left(\frac{1}{3}\right)^x$, $g(x) = \left(\frac{1}{3}\right)^{x+2} - \frac{2}{3}$

Describe the transformation of f represented by g. Then graph each function.
(See Example 3.)

5. $f(x) = e^x$, $g(x) = e^{2x}$

6. $f(x) = 2^x$, $g(x) = -2^{x-3}$

7. $f(x) = e^{-x}$, $g(x) = e^{-5x} + 2$

8. $f(x) = 0.5^x$, $g(x) = 6(0.5)^{x+5} - 2$

Describe the transformation of f represented by g. Then graph each function.
(See Example 4.)

9. $f(x) = \log_4 x$, $g(x) = 3\log_4 x - 5$

10. $f(x) = \log_{1/3} x$, $g(x) = \log_{1/3}(-x) + 6$

11. $f(x) = \log_{1/5} x$, $g(x) = -\log_{1/5}(x - 7)$

12. $f(x) = \log_2 x$, $g(x) = \log_2(x + 2) - 3$

13. **MATCHING** Match the transformation of f with its graph.

   a. $y = f(x - 2)$
   b. $y = f(x + 2)$
   c. $y = 2f(x)$
   d. $y = f(2x)$

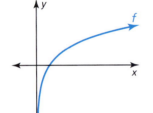

A.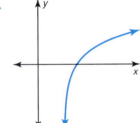

C.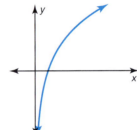

B.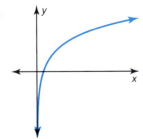

D.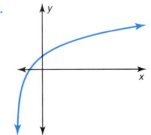

Write a rule for g that represents the indicated transformations of the graph of f.
(See Example 5.)

14. $f(x) = e^x$; horizontal shrink by a factor of $\frac{1}{2}$, followed by a translation 5 units up

15. $f(x) = 5^x$; translation 2 units down, followed by a reflection in the y-axis

16. $f(x) = \ln x$; translation 3 units right and 1 unit up, followed by a horizontal stretch by a factor of 8

17. $f(x) = \log_6 x$; vertical stretch by a factor of 6, followed by a translation 5 units down

CONNECT CONCEPTS Describe the transformation of the graph of f represented by the graph of g. Then give an equation of the asymptote.

18. $f(x) = 3^x$, $g(x) = 3^{x-9}$

19. $f(x) = \log_{1/5} x$, $g(x) = \log_{1/5} x + 13$

20. **SMP.2** The speed (in miles per hour) of a hoverboard can be modeled by the function $g(t) = 9 - 9e^{-at}$, where t is the number of seconds since activation and $0 < a < 1$.

   a. Describe how changing the value of a affects the graph of g. What does this mean in terms of the speed of the hoverboard?

   b. Explain why the advertisement below is misleading.

Up to 12 miles per hour

21. **SMP.3 SMP.7** Explain whether a horizontal stretch by a factor of 4 has the same result as a vertical shrink by a factor of $\frac{1}{4}$ for $f(x) = \log_4 x$.

22. The amount P (in grams) of 100 grams of plutonium-239 that remains after t years can be modeled by $P = 100(0.99997)^t$.

   a. How much plutonium-239 remains after 12,000 years?

   b. Describe the transformation of the function when the initial amount of plutonium-239 is 550 grams.

   c. Explain whether the transformation in part (b) affects the domain and range of the function.

23. **OPEN-ENDED** Write a function whose graph has a y-intercept of 5 and an asymptote of $y = 2$.

Interpreting Data

GEIGER COUNTER A *geiger counter* measures radiation levels by counting *ionizing events* over a period of time. A researcher measures the number of ionizing events detected near a sample of Indium-116 over time. The scatter plot shows the results.

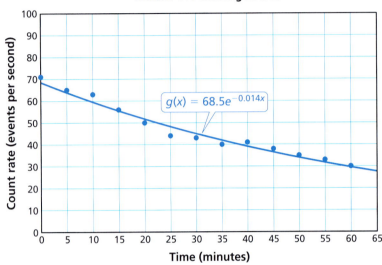

24. Describe the count rate over time. Why is the rate decreasing?

25. Describe the transformation of $f(x) = e^x$ represented by g.

Review & Refresh

Simplify the expression.

26. $9^{\log_9 x}$

27. $e^{\ln 9}$

28. $\log_2 2^{2x}$

29. $10^{\log(x-3)}$

30. The table shows the number of people who visit a community garden each month after it opens. Write an equation of a line of fit. Then predict the attendance in Month 16.

Months, x	3	6	9	12
People (thousands), y	2	2.1	2.2	2.3

31. Find the zeros of $h(x) = x^4 + x^3 - 12x^2$. Then sketch the graph of h.

32. Write an equation of the parabola.

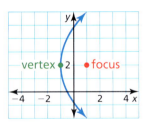

33. Solve $\sqrt{2x + 11} = 5$.

Rewrite the function in the form $y = a(1 + r)^t$ or $y = a(1 - r)^t$. State the growth or decay rate, and describe the end behavior of the function.

34. $y = a(2)^{t/4}$

35. $y = a\left(\dfrac{1}{3}\right)^{2t}$

318 Chapter 6 Exponential and Logarithmic Functions

6.5 Properties of Logarithms

Learning Target: Use properties of logarithms.

Success Criteria:
- I can evaluate logarithms.
- I can expand or condense logarithmic expressions.
- I can explain how to use the change-of-base formula.

INVESTIGATE Deriving Properties of Logarithms

Work with a partner. You can use properties of exponents to derive several properties of logarithms. Let $x = \log_b m$ and $y = \log_b n$. The corresponding exponential forms of these two equations are

$$b^x = m \quad \text{and} \quad b^y = n.$$

1. The diagram shows a way to derive the Product Property of Logarithms. Complete and explain the diagram.

   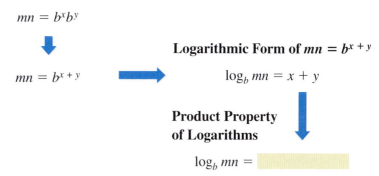

   Exponential Form of mn

   $mn = b^x b^y$

   $mn = b^{x+y}$

   Logarithmic Form of $mn = b^{x+y}$

   $\log_b mn = x + y$

   Product Property of Logarithms

   $\log_b mn = $ _____

2. Derive the Quotient Property of Logarithms shown below using a diagram similar to that in Exercise 1. Explain your reasoning.

   $$\log_b \frac{m}{n} = \log_b m - \log_b n \qquad \text{Quotient Property of Logarithms}$$

   Give some examples to show that the property works. Revise your work if needed.

3. Use the substitution $m = b^x$ to derive the Power Property of Logarithms shown below.

   $$\log_b m^n = n \log_b m \qquad \text{Power Property of Logarithms}$$

4. How are these three properties of logarithms similar to properties of exponents?

Properties of Logarithms

You know that the logarithmic function with base b is the inverse function of the exponential function with base b. Because of this relationship, it makes sense that logarithms have properties similar to properties of exponents.

Key Concept

Properties of Logarithms

Let b, m, and n be positive real numbers with $b \neq 1$.

Product Property $\qquad \log_b mn = \log_b m + \log_b n$

Quotient Property $\qquad \log_b \dfrac{m}{n} = \log_b m - \log_b n$

Power Property $\qquad \log_b m^n = n \log_b m$

EXAMPLE 1 Using Properties of Logarithms

Use $\log_2 3 \approx 1.585$ and $\log_2 7 \approx 2.807$ to evaluate each logarithm.

a. $\log_2 \dfrac{3}{7}$

$\log_2 \dfrac{3}{7} = \log_2 3 - \log_2 7$ — Quotient Property

$\qquad \approx 1.585 - 2.807$ — Use the given values of $\log_2 3$ and $\log_2 7$.

$\qquad = -1.222$ — Subtract.

b. $\log_2 21$

$\log_2 21 = \log_2 (3 \cdot 7)$ — Write 21 as $3 \cdot 7$.

$\qquad = \log_2 3 + \log_2 7$ — Product Property

$\qquad \approx 1.585 + 2.807$ — Use the given values of $\log_2 3$ and $\log_2 7$.

$\qquad = 4.392$ — Add.

c. $\log_2 49$

$\log_2 49 = \log_2 7^2$ — Write 49 as 7^2.

$\qquad = 2 \log_2 7$ — Power Property

$\qquad \approx 2(2.807)$ — Use the given value of $\log_2 7$.

$\qquad = 5.614$ — Multiply.

In-Class Practice

Self-Assessment

Use $\log_6 5 \approx 0.898$ and $\log_6 8 \approx 1.161$ to evaluate the logarithm.

1. $\log_6 \dfrac{5}{8}$
2. $\log_6 40$
3. $\log_6 125$

320   Chapter 6   Exponential and Logarithmic Functions

Expanding and Condensing Logarithmic Expressions

EXAMPLE 2 Expanding a Logarithmic Expression

a. Expand $\log_3 2x^4$.

$\log_3 2x^4 = \log_3 2 + \log_3 x^4$ — Product Property

$ = \log_3 2 + 4 \log_3 x$ — Power Property

b. Expand $\ln \dfrac{5x^7}{y}$.

$\ln \dfrac{5x^7}{y} = \ln 5x^7 - \ln y$ — Quotient Property

$\phantom{\ln \dfrac{5x^7}{y}} = \ln 5 + \ln x^7 - \ln y$ — Product Property

$\phantom{\ln \dfrac{5x^7}{y}} = \ln 5 + 7 \ln x - \ln y$ — Power Property

c. Expand $\log \sqrt{x}$.

$\log \sqrt{x} = \log x^{1/2}$ — Rewrite the expression.

$\phantom{\log \sqrt{x}} = \tfrac{1}{2} \log x$ — Power Property

EXAMPLE 3 Condensing a Logarithmic Expression

a. Condense $\ln 12 - \ln 4 - \ln x$.

$\ln 12 - \ln 4 - \ln x = \ln 12 - (\ln 4 + \ln x)$ — Distributive Property

$ = \ln 12 - \ln 4x$ — Product Property

$ = \ln \dfrac{12}{4x}$ — Quotient Property

$ = \ln \dfrac{3}{x}$ — Quotient Property

b. Condense $\log 9 + 3 \log 2 - \log 3$.

$\log 9 + 3 \log 2 - \log 3 = \log 9 + \log 2^3 - \log 3$ — Power Property

$ = \log(9 \cdot 2^3) - \log 3$ — Product Property

$ = \log \dfrac{9 \cdot 2^3}{3}$ — Quotient Property

$ = \log 24$ — Simplify.

In-Class Practice

Self-Assessment

Expand the logarithmic expression.

4. $\log_6 3x^4$
5. $\ln \dfrac{5}{12x}$
6. $\log_5 2\sqrt{x}$

Condense the logarithmic expression.

7. $\log x - \log 9$
8. $4 \ln x + 8 \ln y$
9. $\ln 4 + 3 \ln 3 - \ln 12$

1 I don't understand yet. **2** I can do it with help. **3** I can do it on my own. **4** I can teach someone.

6.5 Properties of Logarithms

Change-of-Base Formula

Logarithms with any base other than 10 or e can be written in terms of common or natural logarithms using the *change-of-base formula*. This allows you to evaluate any logarithm using a calculator.

Key Concept

Change-of-Base Formula

If a, b, and c are positive real numbers with $b \neq 1$ and $c \neq 1$, then

$$\log_c a = \frac{\log_b a}{\log_b c}.$$

In particular, $\log_c a = \dfrac{\log a}{\log c}$ and $\log_c a = \dfrac{\ln a}{\ln c}$.

EXAMPLE 4 Changing a Base Using Common Logarithms

a. Evaluate $\log_3 8$ using common logarithms.

$$\log_3 8 = \frac{\log 8}{\log 3} \qquad \log_c a = \frac{\log a}{\log c}$$

$$\approx 1.893 \qquad \text{Use technology.}$$

b. Evaluate $\log_7 15$ using common logarithms.

$$\log_8 15 = \frac{\log 15}{\log 8} \qquad \log_c a = \frac{\log a}{\log c}$$

$$\approx 1.302 \qquad \text{Use technology.}$$

EXAMPLE 5 Changing a Base Using Natural Logarithms

a. Evaluate $\log_6 24$ using natural logarithms.

$$\log_6 24 = \frac{\ln 24}{\ln 6} \qquad \log_c a = \frac{\ln a}{\ln c}$$

$$\approx 1.774 \qquad \text{Use technology.}$$

b. Evaluate $\log_{24} 6$ using natural logarithms.

$$\log_{24} 6 = \frac{\ln 6}{\ln 24} \qquad \log_c a = \frac{\ln a}{\ln c}$$

$$\approx 0.564 \qquad \text{Use technology.}$$

In-Class Practice

Self-Assessment

Use the change-of-base formula to evaluate the logarithm.

10. $\log_5 8$
11. $\log_8 14$
12. $\log_{26} 9$

Connections to Real Life

EXAMPLE 6 **Using a Logarithmic Function**

For a sound with intensity I (in watts per square meter), the loudness $L(I)$ of the sound (in decibels) is given by the function

$$L(I) = 10 \log \frac{I}{I_0}$$

where I_0 is the intensity of a barely audible sound (about 10^{-12} watt per square meter). An artist in a recording studio turns up the volume of a track so that the intensity of the sound doubles. By how many decibels does the loudness increase?

Let I be the original intensity, so that $2I$ is the doubled intensity.

increase in loudness $= L(2I) - L(I)$		Write an expression.
$= 10 \log \frac{2I}{I_0} - 10 \log \frac{I}{I_0}$		Substitute.
$= 10 \left(\log \frac{2I}{I_0} - \log \frac{I}{I_0} \right)$		Distributive Property
$= 10 \left(\log 2 + \log \frac{I}{I_0} - \log \frac{I}{I_0} \right)$		Product Property
$= 10 \log 2$		Simplify.

▶ The loudness increases by $10 \log 2$ decibels, or about 3 decibels.

In-Class Practice

Self-Assessment

13. WHAT IF? In Example 6, the artist turns up the volume so that the intensity of the sound triples. By how many decibels does the loudness increase?

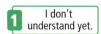

6.5 Practice

with Calc Chat and Calc View

MATCHING **Match the expression with the logarithm that has the same value.**

1. $\log_3 6 - \log_3 2$	**A.** $\log_3 64$
2. $2 \log_3 6$	**B.** $\log_3 3$
3. $6 \log_3 2$	**C.** $\log_3 12$
4. $\log_3 6 + \log_3 2$	**D.** $\log_3 36$

Use $\log_7 4 \approx 0.712$ and $\log_7 12 \approx 1.277$ to evaluate the logarithm. (See Example 1.)

▶**5.** $\log_7 3$

6. $\log_7 48$

7. $\log_7 16$

8. $\log_7 64$

9. $\log_7 \frac{1}{4}$

10. $\log_7 \frac{1}{3}$

Expand the logarithmic expression. (See Example 2.)

11. $\log_3 2x$

12. $\log_8 3x$

▶**13.** $\log 10x^5$

14. $\ln \dfrac{x}{3y}$

15. $\log_7 5\sqrt{x}$

16. $\log_5 \sqrt[3]{x^2y}$

17. SMP.3 **ERROR ANALYSIS** Describe and correct the error in expanding the logarithmic expression.

✗
$$\begin{aligned} \ln 7x^3 &= 3 \ln 7x \\ &= 3(\ln 7 + \ln x) \\ &= 3 \ln 7 + 3 \ln x \end{aligned}$$

Condense the logarithmic expression. (See Example 3.)

18. $\log_4 7 - \log_4 10$

▶**19.** $6 \ln x + 4 \ln y$

20. $2 \log x + \log 11$

21. $6 \ln 2 - 4 \ln y$

22. $5 \ln 2 + 7 \ln x + 4 \ln y$

23. $\log_3 4 + 2 \log_3 \frac{1}{2} + \log_3 x$

24. SMP.3 **ERROR ANALYSIS** Describe and correct the error in condensing the logarithmic expression.

✗
$$\begin{aligned} \log 2 - \log 5 - 2 \log 4 &= \log 2 - \log 5 - \log 4^2 \\ &= \log(2 \cdot 5) - \log 4^2 \\ &= \log(2 \cdot 5 \cdot 4^2) \\ &= \log(160) \end{aligned}$$

RESOURCES

Use the change-of-base formula to evaluate the logarithm. (See Examples 4 and 5.)

▶ 25. $\log_4 7$

26. $\log_5 13$

27. $\log_9 15$

28. $\log_8 22$

29. $\log_6 17$

30. $\log_2 28$

31. $\log_7 \frac{3}{16}$

32. $\log_3 \frac{9}{40}$

CONNECTION TO REAL LIFE Use the function $L(I) = 10 \log \frac{I}{I_0}$ given in Example 6.

33. The intensity of the sound of a television commercial is 10 times greater than the intensity of the television program it follows. By how many decibels does the loudness increase? (See Example 6.)

34. The blue whale can produce sound with an intensity that is 1 million times greater than the intensity of the loudest sound a human can make. Find the difference in the loudness of the sounds made by a blue whale and a human.

35. Under certain conditions, the wind speed (in knots) at an altitude of h meters above a grassy plain can be modeled by the function $s(h) = 2 \ln 100h$.

   a. By what amount does the wind speed increase when the altitude doubles?

   b. Show that the given function can be written in terms of common logarithms as $s(h) = \frac{2}{\log e}(\log h + 2)$.

36. Use the graph to determine the value of $\frac{\log 8}{\log 2}$.

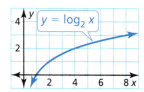

37. **SMP.7** Explain whether $\log_b(M + N) = \log_b M + \log_b N$ is true for all positive, real values of M, N, and b (with $b \neq 1$).

38. Use properties of exponents to prove the change-of-base formula.
   (*Hint:* Let $x = \log_b a$, $y = \log_b c$, and $z = \log_c a$.)

39. **SMP.1 DIG DEEPER** Explain three ways you can transform the graph of $f(x) = \log x$ to obtain the graph of $g(x) = \log 100x - 1$.

Interpreting Data

POPULATION BY ELEVATION The graph shows the result of a worldwide study that recorded the elevations at which the population lives. Each point on the graph represents the percentage y of the world's population that live below an elevation x.

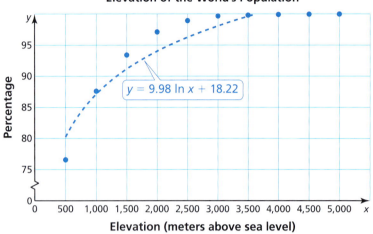

40. Describe the shape of the graph.

41. Use the given model to estimate the percentage of the world's population that live less than 1,000 meters above sea level.

42. Research the elevation where you live. Estimate the percentage of the world's population that lives at a higher elevation than you.

Review & Refresh

43. Write an equation of the parabola in vertex form.

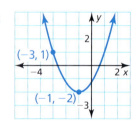

44. At a frozen yogurt stand, two small cones, one medium cone, and two large cones cost $14.60. One small cone, one medium cone, and one large cone cost $8.70. Three small cones, two medium cones, and one large cone cost $16.50. How much does each cone size cost?

45. Solve the equation by graphing.
$$4x^2 - 3x - 6 = -x^2 + 5x + 3$$

46. Simplify $\dfrac{e^{11} \cdot e^{-3}}{e^2}$.

47. The graph of g is a transformation of the graph of $f(x) = 3^x$. Write a rule for g.

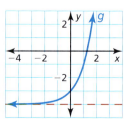

326 Chapter 6 Exponential and Logarithmic Functions

6.6 Solving Exponential and Logarithmic Equations

Learning Target: Solve exponential and logarithmic equations and inequalities.

Success Criteria:
- I can solve exponential equations.
- I can solve logarithmic equations.
- I can solve exponential and logarithmic inequalities.

INVESTIGATE Solving Exponential and Logarithmic Equations

Work with a partner.

1. Find the intersection point of the graphs. Explain how this point can be used to solve each equation.

    a. $4^x = 2$ b. $\log_4 x = 1$

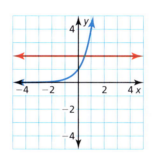 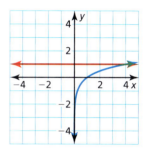

2. Solve each equation by graphing.

    a. $e^x = 2$

    b. $\ln x = -1$

    c. $2^x = 3^{-x}$

    d. $\log_5 x = \frac{1}{2}$

3. **SMP.5** Solve one of the equations in Exercise 2 using a *numerical approach*, such as using a table or a spreadsheet.

4. Solve one of the equations in Exercise 2 using an *analytical approach*, such as using properties of exponents and logarithms.

5. What are some of the advantages and disadvantages of the solution methods in Exercises 2–4?

Vocabulary
exponential equations
logarithmic equations

Solving Exponential Equations

Exponential equations are equations in which variable expressions occur as exponents.

Key Concept

Property of Equality for Exponential Equations

Algebra If b is a positive real number other than 1, then $b^x = b^y$ if and only if $x = y$.

Example If $3^x = 3^5$, then $x = 5$. If $x = 5$, then $3^x = 3^5$.

The property above is useful for solving an exponential equation when each side has the same base (or can be rewritten using the same base). You can also try to solve the equation by taking a logarithm of each side.

EXAMPLE 1 Solving Exponential Equations

a. Solve $100^x = \left(\frac{1}{10}\right)^{x-3}$.

$$100^x = \left(\frac{1}{10}\right)^{x-3}$$ Write original equation.

$$(10^2)^x = (10^{-1})^{x-3}$$ Rewrite 100 and $\frac{1}{10}$ as powers with base 10.

$$10^{2x} = 10^{-x+3}$$ Power of a Power Property

$$2x = -x + 3$$ Property of Equality for Exponential Equations

$$x = 1$$ Solve for x.

Check
$100^1 \stackrel{?}{=} \left(\frac{1}{10}\right)^{1-3}$
$100 \stackrel{?}{=} \left(\frac{1}{10}\right)^{-2}$
$100 = 100$ ✓

b. Solve $2^x = 7$.

$$2^x = 7$$ Write original equation.

$$\log_2 2^x = \log_2 7$$ Take $\log_2$ of each side.

$$x = \log_2 7$$ $\log_b b^x = x$

$$x \approx 2.807$$ Use technology.

Check
Use technology to graph $y = 2^x$ and $y = 7$. Then find the intersection point of the graphs.

The graphs intersect at about (2.807, 7). ✓

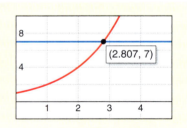

In-Class Practice

Self-Assessment

Solve the equation.

1. $8^{2x-1} = 2^{4x-4}$
2. $7^{9x} = 15$

 I don't understand yet.
 I can do it with help.
3 I can do it on my own.
 I can teach someone.

Solving Logarithmic Equations

Logarithmic equations are equations that involve one or more logarithms of variable expressions.

> ### Key Concept
>
> **Property of Equality for Logarithmic Equations**
>
> **Algebra** If b, x, and y are positive real numbers with $b \neq 1$, then $\log_b x = \log_b y$ if and only if $x = y$.
>
> **Example** If $\log_2 x = \log_2 7$, then $x = 7$. If $x = 7$, then $\log_2 x = \log_2 7$.

EXAMPLE 2 Solving Logarithmic Equations

Solve $\ln(4x - 7) = \ln(x + 5)$.

$\ln(4x - 7) = \ln(x + 5)$	Write original equation.
$4x - 7 = x + 5$	Property of Equality for Logarithmic Equations
$3x - 7 = 5$	Subtract x from each side.
$x = 4$	Solve for x.

Check
$\ln(4 \cdot 4 - 7) \stackrel{?}{=} \ln(4 + 5)$
$\ln 9 = \ln 9$ ✓

EXAMPLE 3 Solving an Equation with an Extraneous Solution

Solve $\log 2x + \log(x - 5) = 2$.

$\log 2x + \log(x - 5) = 2$	Write original equation.
$\log[2x(x - 5)] = 2$	Product Property of Logarithms
$10^{\log[2x(-5)]} = 10^2$	Exponentiate each side using base 10.
$2x(x - 5) = 100$	$b^{\log_b x} = x$
$2x^2 - 10x - 100 = 0$	Use Distributive Property and write in standard form.
$2(x - 10)(x + 5) = 0$	Factor.
$x = 10 \quad \text{or} \quad x = -5$	Zero-Product Property

Check
$\log(2 \cdot 10) + \log(10 - 5) \stackrel{?}{=} 2$ $\log[2 \cdot (-5)] + \log(-5 - 5) \stackrel{?}{=} 2$
$\log 20 + \log 5 \stackrel{?}{=} 2$ $\log(-10) + \log(-10) \stackrel{?}{=} 2$
$\log 100 \stackrel{?}{=} 2$ Because $\log(-10)$ is not defined,
$2 = 2$ ✓ -5 is not a solution.

In-Class Practice

Self-Assessment

Solve the equation.

3. $\log_7(4x - 1) = \log_7 23$ **4.** $\log_4(x + 12) + \log_4 x = 3$

Solving Exponential and Logarithmic Inequalities

To solve exponential and logarithmic inequalities, use the following properties. Note that the properties are also true for ≤ and ≥.

Exponential Property of Inequality: If b is a positive real number greater than 1, then $b^x > b^y$ if and only if $x > y$, and $b^x < b^y$ if and only if $x < y$.

Logarithmic Property of Inequality: If b, x, and y are positive real numbers with b greater than 1, then $\log_b x > \log_b y$ if and only if $x > y$, and $\log_b x < \log_b y$ if and only if $x < y$.

You can also solve an inequality by taking a logarithm of each side or by exponentiating each side.

EXAMPLE 4 Solving an Exponential Inequality

Solve $3^x < 81$.

$3^x < 81$	Write original inequality.
$3^x < 3^4$	Rewrite 81 using exponents.
$x < 4$	Exponential Property of Inequality

▶ The solution is $x < 4$.

EXAMPLE 5 Solving a Logarithmic Inequality

Solve $\log x \leq 2$.

Method 1 Use an algebraic approach.

$\log x \leq 2$	Write original inequality.
$10^{\log_{10} x} \leq 10^2$	Exponentiate each side using base 10.
$x \leq 100$	$b^{\log_b x} = x$

▶ Because $\log x$ is only defined when $x > 0$, the solution is $0 < x \leq 100$.

Method 2 Use a graphical approach.

Use technology to graph $y = \log x$ and $y = 2$. Then find the intersection point of the graphs. The graphs intersect at (100, 2). The graph of $y = \log x$ is on or below the graph of $y = 2$ when $0 < x \leq 100$.

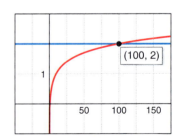

▶ The solution is $0 < x \leq 100$.

In-Class Practice

Self-Assessment

Solve the inequality.

5. $10^{2x-6} > 3$

6. $2 \ln x - 1 > 4$

 I don't understand yet.   I can do it with help.   I can do it on my own.   I can teach someone.

Connections to Real Life

An important application of exponential equations is *Newton's Law of Cooling*. This law states that for a cooling substance with initial temperature T_0, the temperature T after t minutes can be modeled by

$$T = (T_0 - T_R)e^{-rt} + T_R$$

where T_R is the surrounding temperature and r is the cooling rate of the substance.

EXAMPLE 6 Newton's Law of Cooling

You are cooking *aleecha*, an Ethiopian stew. When you take it off the stove, its temperature is 212°F. The room temperature is 70°F, and the cooling rate of the stew is $r = 0.046$. How long will it take to cool the stew to a serving temperature of 100°F?

STEM Video: Food Safety Regulations

Use Newton's Law of Cooling with $T = 100$, $T_0 = 212$, $T_R = 70$, and $r = 0.046$.

$T = (T_0 - T_R)e^{-rt} + T_R$	Newton's Law of Cooling
$100 = (212 - 70)e^{-0.046t} + 70$	Substitute for T, T_0, T_R, and r.
$30 = 142e^{-0.046t}$	Subtract 70 from each side.
$0.211 \approx e^{-0.046t}$	Divide each side by 142.
$\ln 0.211 \approx \ln e^{-0.046t}$	Take natural log of each side.
$-1.556 \approx -0.046t$	$\ln e^x = \log_e e^x = x$
$33.8 \approx t$	Divide each side by -0.046.

▶ You should wait about 34 minutes before serving the stew.

In-Class Practice

Self-Assessment

7. WHAT IF? Use the information in Example 6.

   a. How long will it take to cool the stew to 100°F when the room temperature is 75°F?

   b. How much sooner can your guests begin to eat when the serving temperature is 140°F instead of 100°F?

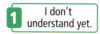

6.6 Practice

Solve the equation. (See Example 1.)

1. $2^{3x+5} = 2^{1-x}$

2. $3^x = 7$

3. $100^{5x+2} = \left(\frac{1}{10}\right)^{11-x}$

4. $3e^{4x} + 9 = 15$

5. **CONNECTION TO REAL LIFE** The length ℓ (in centimeters) of a scalloped hammerhead shark can be modeled by the function

   $\ell = 266 - 219e^{-0.05t}$

   where t is the age (in years) of the shark. How old is a shark that is 175 centimeters long?

Solve the equation. (See Example 2.)

6. $\ln(4x - 12) = \ln x$

7. $\log_2(3x - 4) = \log_2 5$

8. $\log_6(5x + 9) = \log_6 6x$

9. $\log_2(x^2 - x - 6) = 2$

Solve the equation. (See Example 3.)

10. $\ln x + \ln(x + 3) = 4$

11. $\log_2 x + \log_2(x - 2) = 3$

12. $\log_3 3x^2 + \log_3 3 = 2$

13. $\log_4(-x) + \log_4(x + 10) = 2$

14. **SMP.3 ERROR ANALYSIS** Describe and correct the error in solving the equation.

    $\log_3(5x - 1) = 4$
    $3^{\log_3(5x-1)} = 4^3$
    $5x - 1 = 64$
    $5x = 65$
    $x = 13$

15. **CONNECTION TO REAL LIFE** You deposit $100 in an account that pays 6% annual interest. How long will it take for the balance to reach $1,000 for quarterly compounding? continuous compounding?

16. The *apparent magnitude* of a star is a measure of the brightness of the star viewed from Earth. The apparent magnitude M of the dimmest star that can be seen with a telescope is

    $M = 5 \log D + 2$

    where D is the diameter (in millimeters) of the telescope's objective lens. What is the diameter of the objective lens of a telescope that can reveal stars with an apparent magnitude of 12?

332 Chapter 6 Exponential and Logarithmic Functions

Approximate the solution of the equation using the graph.

17. $1 - 5^{5-x} = -9$

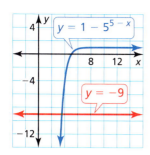

18. $\log_2 5x = 2$

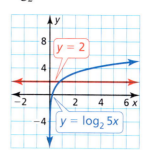

Solve the inequality. (See Examples 4 and 5.)

▶ 19. $2^x < 8$

20. $4^x \leq 36$

▶ 21. $\log(x - 1) > \log 2$

22. $\log_4 x < 4$

23. $\ln x \geq 3$

24. $e^{3x+4} > 11$

▶ 25. CONNECTION TO REAL LIFE You are driving on a hot day when your car overheats and stops running. The car overheats at 280°F and can be driven again at 230°F. When it is 80°F outside, the cooling rate of the car is $r = 0.0058$. How long do you have to wait until you can continue driving? (See Example 6.)

26. You buy an autographed jersey for $55. The value of the jersey is expected to increase by 8% each year. How long will it take the jersey to double in value?

Use a tool to solve the equation.

27. $\log x = 7^{-x}$

28. $\ln 2x = e^{x-3}$

29. A biologist estimates the age a (in years) of an African elephant by measuring the length ℓ (in centimeters) of its footprint and using the equation $\ell = 45 - 25.7e^{-0.09a}$. Find the ages of the elephants whose footprints are shown.

Solve the equation.

30. $2^{x+3} = 5^{3x-1}$

31. $\log_3(x - 6) = \log_9 2x$

32. $\log_4 x = \log_8 4x$

33. $2^{2x} - 7 \cdot 2^x + 6 = 0$

34. PERFORMANCE TASK You find reward apps to help you resist using your phone during school. Points from an app are redeemable for prizes. Research other aspects of reward apps. Then create a plan for an app to compete with the ones below, including a model for the number of points earned over time.

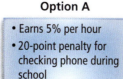

Interpreting Data

FORENSICS Forensic pathologists use Newton's Law of Cooling to determine times of death. A body will gradually change temperature to adjust to the temperature of the air. The graph shows the results of a pathologist measuring the temperature of a body in a 70°F room.

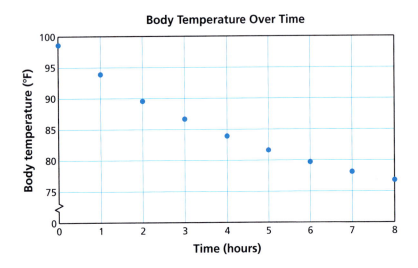

35. Describe the shape of the graph.

36. Use Newton's Law of Cooling to find the temperature of the body after 9.5 hours. Use an initial temperature of 98.6°F and a cooling rate of $r = 0.003$.

Review & Refresh

37. Use the graph to solve $3 = x^2 - 2x$.

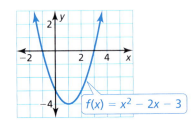

38. The intensity of the sound of a musical overture is 5 times greater than the intensity of a sensory friendly musical overture. Use the function $L(I) = 10 \log \dfrac{I}{I_0}$ to determine the loudness increase (in decibels).

39. Solve $x^2 + 3x - 11 = 0$.

40. Describe the transformation of $f(x) = x^3$ represented by $g(x) = 2(x + 1)^3$. Then graph each function.

41. Simplify $\sqrt[5]{\dfrac{m^{25}}{n^5}}$.

42. Use the table to find the product of $3x^2 - x + 1$ and $2x - 1$.

	$3x^2$	$-x$	1
$2x$		$-2x^2$	$2x$
-1	$-3x^2$		

43. Evaluate $\log_3 729$.

334 Chapter 6 Exponential and Logarithmic Functions

6.7 Modeling with Exponential and Logarithmic Functions

Learning Target: Write exponential and logarithmic functions to model sets of data.

Success Criteria:
- I can use a constant factor to determine whether data can be represented by an exponential function.
- I can write an exponential function using two points.
- I can use technology to find exponential and logarithmic models.

INVESTIGATE Writing Exponential Functions

Work with a partner.

1. Write an exponential function of the form $f(x) = ab^x$ that passes through the points shown. Explain your reasoning.

   a.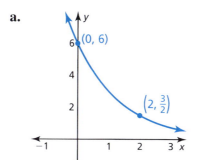

   b.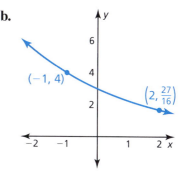

2. A function f is of the form $f(x) = ab^x$, where a is a real number and $b > 0$. Can you find the values of a and b so that f passes through the points $(0, 4)$ and $(2, -2)$? Explain your reasoning.

3. You perform an experiment where you measure the temperature T (in degrees Fahrenheit) of coffee m minutes after it is poured into a cup. The temperature of the coffee is initially 185°F. After 5 minutes, the temperature of the coffee is about 150°F. Can you use a model of the form $y = ab^x$ to model this situation? Explain. If not, sketch a graph that could model the temperature over time and make several observations about the graph.

Choosing Functions to Model Data

You have analyzed *finite differences* of data with equally-spaced inputs to determine what type of polynomial function can be used to model the data. To determine whether an exponential function can be used to model the data, the outputs must be multiplied by a constant factor. So, consecutive outputs form equivalent ratios.

EXAMPLE 1 Using Differences or Ratios to Identify Functions

Determine the type of function represented by each table.

a.

x	−2	−1	0	1	2	3	4
y	0.5	1	2	4	8	16	32

The inputs are equally spaced. Look for a pattern in the outputs.

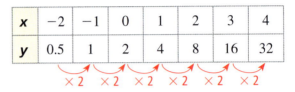

▶ As x increases by 1, y is multiplied by 2. So, the common ratio is 2, and the data represent an exponential function.

b.

x	−8	−6	−4	−2	0	2	4
y	−1	8	7	2	−1	4	23

The inputs are equally spaced. The outputs do not have a common ratio. So, analyze the finite differences.

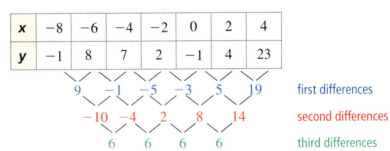

▶ The third differences are nonzero and constant. So, the data represent a cubic function.

In-Class Practice
Self-Assessment

Determine the type of function represented by the table.

1.

x	0	10	20	30
y	15	12	9	6

2.

x	0	2	4	6
y	27	9	3	1

Writing Exponential Functions

EXAMPLE 2 Writing an Exponential Function Using Two Points

Write an exponential function $y = ab^x$ whose graph passes through (1, 6) and (3, 54).

Substitute the coordinates of the two given points into $y = ab^x$.

$6 = ab^1$ Equation 1: Substitute 6 for y and 1 for x.
$54 = ab^3$ Equation 2: Substitute 54 for y and 3 for x.

Solve for a in Equation 1 to obtain $a = \dfrac{6}{b}$ and substitute this expression for a in Equation 2.

$54 = \left(\dfrac{6}{b}\right)b^3$ Substitute $\dfrac{6}{b}$ for a in Equation 2.

$54 = 6b^2$ Simplify.

$9 = b^2$ Divide each side by 6.

$3 = b$ Take the positive square root because $b > 0$.

Substitute 3 for b to determine that $a = \dfrac{6}{b} = \dfrac{6}{3} = 2$.

▶ So, the exponential function is $y = 2(3)^x$.

EXAMPLE 3 Finding an Exponential Model

The table shows the numbers y (in thousands) of visitors to Machu Picchu over a period of 28 years. Write a function that models the data.

Year, x	Number of visitors, y
0	150
4	210
8	360
12	470
16	700
20	700
24	1,150
28	1,580

Make a scatter plot of the data.

The data appear exponential. Substitute the coordinates of any two points, such as (0, 150) and (20, 700) into $y = ab^x$.

$150 = ab^0$
$700 = ab^{20}$

The first equation shows that $a = 150$. Substitute 150 for a in the second equation to obtain $b = \sqrt[20]{\dfrac{700}{150}} \approx 1.08$.

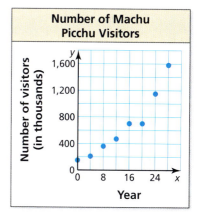

▶ So, an exponential function that models the data is $y = 150(1.08)^x$.

In-Class Practice

Self-Assessment

3. Write an exponential function $y = ab^x$ whose graph passes through (2, 12) and (3, 24).

4. Repeat Example 3 using the points (4, 210) and (24, 1,150).

A set of more than two points (x, y) fits an exponential pattern if and only if the set of transformed points $(x, \ln y)$ fits a linear pattern.

Graph of points (x, y)

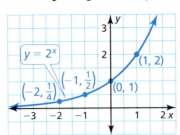

The graph is an exponential curve.

Graph of points $(x, \ln y)$

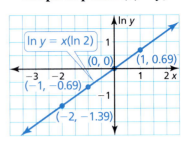

The graph is a line.

EXAMPLE 4 Writing a Model Using Transformed Points

Use the data in Example 3. Make a scatter plot of the data pairs $(x, \ln y)$ to show that an exponential model should be a good fit for the original data pairs (x, y). Then write an exponential model for the original data.

Create a table of data pairs $(x, \ln y)$.

x	0	4	8	12	16	20	24	28
ln y	5.01	5.35	5.89	6.15	6.55	6.55	7.05	7.37

Plot the transformed points as shown. The points lie close to a line, so an exponential model should be a good fit for the original data.

Find an exponential model $y = ab^x$ by choosing any two points on the line, such as $(0, 5.01)$ and $(20, 6.55)$. Use these points to write an equation of the line. Then solve for y.

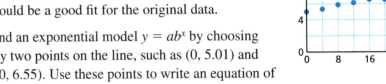

$\ln y - 5.01 = 0.08(x - 0)$	Equation of line
$\ln y = 0.08x + 5.01$	Simplify.
$y = e^{0.08x + 5.01}$	Exponentiate each side using base e.
$y = e^{0.08x}(e^{5.01})$	Use properties of exponents.
$y = 149.90(1.08)^x$	Simplify.

▶ So, an exponential function that models the data is $y = 149.90(1.08)^x$.

In-Class Practice

Self-Assessment

5. The table shows the numbers y of gaming laptops sold at a store during the xth month that the store has been open. Repeat Example 4 using these data.

Month, x	1	2	3	4	5	6	7
Number of gaming laptops, y	12	16	25	36	50	67	96

1 I don't understand yet. **2** I can do it with help. **3** I can do it on my own. **4** I can teach someone.

Connections to Real Life

EXAMPLE 5 **Finding an Exponential Model**

Use technology to find an exponential model for the data in Example 3. Then use this model and the models in Examples 3 and 4 to estimate the number of visitors in Year 25. Compare the estimates.

Use technology to enter the data and perform an exponential regression.

The model is $y = 163.73(1.08)^x$.

$y = ab^x$
PARAMETERS
$a = 163.729 \quad b = 1.08489$
STATISTICS
$r^2 = 0.9799$
$r = 0.9899$

Substitute $x = 25$ into each model.

Example 3: $y = 150(1.08)^{25} \approx 1{,}027$

Example 4: $y = 149.90(1.08)^{25} \approx 1{,}027$

Regression model: $y = 163.73(1.08)^{25} \approx 1{,}121$

▶ The estimates for the models in Examples 3 and 4 are the same. These estimates are less than the estimate for the regression model.

EXAMPLE 6 **Finding a Logarithmic Model**

The table shows the air pressures p (in atmospheres) at several altitudes h (in kilometers). Use technology to find a logarithmic model of the form $h = a + b \ln p$ for the data. Estimate the altitude when the air pressure is 0.75 atmosphere.

Air pressure, p	1	0.55	0.25	0.12	0.06	0.02
Altitude, h	0	5	10	15	20	25

Use technology to enter the data and perform a logarithmic regression.
The model is $h = 0.86 - 6.45 \ln p$.

$y = a + b \ln(x)$
PARAMETERS
$a = 0.862658 \quad b = -6.44738$
STATISTICS
$R^2 = 0.9926$

Substitute $p = 0.75$ into the model to obtain

$h = 0.86 - 6.45 \ln 0.75 \approx 2.7$.

▶ So, when the air pressure is 0.75 atmosphere, the altitude is about 2.7 kilometers.

In-Class Practice

Self-Assessment

6. Use technology to find an exponential model for the data in Exercise 5. Then use this model and the model you found in Exercise 5 to predict the number of gaming laptops sold during the eighth month. Compare the predictions.

7. Use technology to find a logarithmic model of the form $p = a + b \ln h$ for the data in Example 6. Explain the result.

6.7 Practice

Determine the type of function represented by the table. (See Example 1.)

1.
x	0	3	6	9	12	15
y	0.25	1	4	16	64	256

2.
x	−3	−1	1	3	5	7
y	61	5	5	13	−19	−139

ERROR ANALYSIS Describe and correct the error in determining the type of function represented by the table.

3.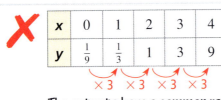

The outputs have a common ratio of 3, so the data represent a linear function.

4.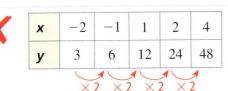

The outputs have a common ratio of 2, so the data represent an exponential function.

Write an exponential function $y = ab^x$ whose graph passes through the given points. (See Example 2.)

5. $(-1, 4), (1, 1)$

6. $(-2, 96), (1, 1.5)$

7.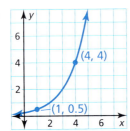

8.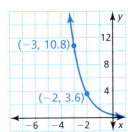

9. A store sells electric scooters. The table shows the numbers y of scooters sold during the xth year that the store has been open. Write a function that models the data. (See Example 3.)

x	1	2	3	4	5	6	7
y	9	14	19	25	37	53	71

Create a scatter plot of the points $(x, \ln y)$ to determine whether an exponential model fits the data. If so, find an exponential model for the data.

10.
x	1	2	3	4	5
y	18	36	72	144	288

▶ 11.
x	−13	−6	1	8	15
y	9.8	12.2	15.2	19	23.8

12. Your visual near point is the closest point at which your eyes can see an object distinctly. The diagram shows the near point y (in centimeters) at age x (in years). Make a scatter plot of the data pairs $(x, \ln y)$ to show that an exponential model should be a good fit for the original data pairs (x, y). Then write an exponential model for the original data. (See Example 4.)

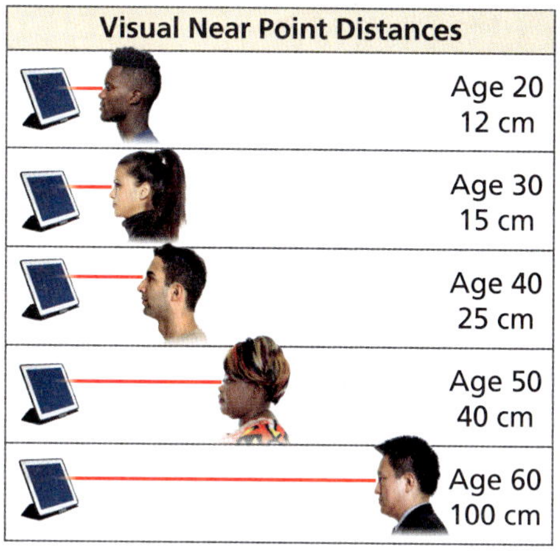

Visual Near Point Distances

Age 20 — 12 cm
Age 30 — 15 cm
Age 40 — 25 cm
Age 50 — 40 cm
Age 60 — 100 cm

▶ 13. **SMP.4 CONNECTION TO REAL LIFE** Use technology to find an exponential model for the data in Exercise 9. Then use the model to predict the number of electric scooters sold during the tenth year. (See Example 5.)

14. Is it possible to write y as an exponential function of x when p is positive? If so, write the function. If not, explain why not.

x	1	2	3	4	5
y	p	2p	4p	8p	16p

▶ 15. **SMP.4 CONNECTION TO REAL LIFE** The table shows the temperatures d (in degrees Celsius) of a clay pot at several times t (in hours) after it is removed from a kiln. Use technology to find a logarithmic model of the form $t = a + b \ln d$ that represents the data. Estimate how long it takes for the clay pot to cool to 50°C. (See Example 6.)

d	160	90	56	38	29	24
t	0	1	2	3	4	5

16. **SMP.2 DIG DEEPER** You plant a sunflower seedling. The height (in centimeters) of the sunflower after t weeks can be modeled by the *logistic function*

$$h(t) = \frac{256}{1 + 13e^{-0.65t}}.$$

a. Find the time it takes the sunflower to reach a height of 200 centimeters.

b. Use technology to graph the function. Interpret the meaning of the asymptote(s) in this situation.

Interpreting Data

17. EARTH'S POPULATION Demographers study how population changes over time. The graph shows the population y (in billions) of Earth x years since 1950.

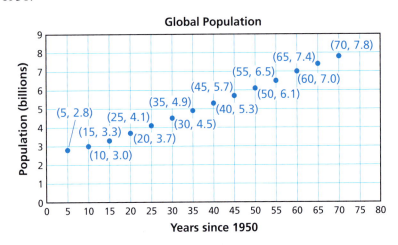

a. Describe the change in population since 1950.

b. Use technology to write an exponential model for the data.

c. Use your model in part (b) to predict the population in 2050. Do you expect your prediction to be accurate? Explain why or why not.

Review & Refresh

Tell whether x and y are in a proportional relationship.

18. $y = \dfrac{x}{2}$

19. $y = 3x - 12$

20. Determine whether functions f and g are inverses.

x	−2	−1	0	1	2
f(x)	15	11	7	3	−1

x	15	11	7	3	−1
g(x)	−2	−1	0	1	2

Use the change-of-base formula to evaluate the logarithm.

21. $\log_3 20$

22. $\log_4 \dfrac{5}{12}$

23. Identify the focus, directrix, and axis of symmetry of $x = \dfrac{1}{8}y^2$. Graph the equation.

24. The function g is a transformation of $f(x) = \log_3 x$. Write a rule for g.

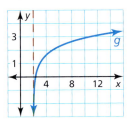

Solve the equation.

25. $e^{3x} = e^{5x-6}$

26. $\log_2(3x - 1) = 5$

27. Show that $x + 5$ is a factor of $f(x) = x^3 - 2x^2 - 23x + 60$. Then factor $f(x)$ completely.

28. Complete the square for $x^2 - 4x$. Then factor the trinomial.

6 Chapter Review

Rate your understanding of each section.

1 I don't understand yet. 2 I can do it with help. 3 I can do it on my own. 4 I can teach someone.

6.1 Exponential Growth and Decay Functions (pp. 289–296)

⊙ **Learning Target:** Write and graph exponential growth and decay functions.

Vocabulary
exponential function
exponential growth function
growth factor
asymptote
exponential decay function
decay factor

Graph the function.

1. $f(x) = \left(\frac{1}{3}\right)^x$
2. $y = 5^x$
3. $f(x) = (0.2)^x$

4. You deposit $1,500 in an account that pays 7% annual interest. Find the balance after 2 years when the interest is compounded daily.

5. Consider two exponential decay functions f and g. Determine whether each statement is *always*, *sometimes*, or *never* true.

    a. $(fg)(x)$ is an exponential decay function.

    b. $\left(\dfrac{f}{g}\right)(x)$ is an exponential decay function.

6. A substance decays 10% each year. Find the initial amount of the substance when there are about 5.8 grams remaining after 9 years.

6.2 The Natural Base e (pp. 297–302)

⊙ **Learning Target:** Use the natural base e and graph natural base functions.

Vocabulary
natural base e

Simplify the expression.

7. $e^4 \cdot e^{11}$
8. $\dfrac{20e^3}{10e^6}$
9. $(-3e^{-5x})^2$

Determine whether the function represents *exponential growth* or *exponential decay*. Then graph the function.

10. $f(x) = \frac{1}{3}e^x$
11. $y = 6e^{-x}$
12. $y = 3e^{-0.75x}$

13. An account earns 3% annual interest compounded continuously. Find the principal when the balance is $100 after 10 years.

14. In a sample of tritium, the amount y (in milligrams) remaining after t years is given by $y = 10e^{-0.0562t}$. The graph shows the amount of sodium-22 remaining in a sample over time. Which sample has a greater initial amount? Which sample has a greater amount remaining after 5 years?

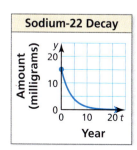

Sodium-22 Decay

6.3 Logarithms and Logarithmic Functions (pp. 303–310)

⊙ **Learning Target:** Understand logarithms and graph logarithmic functions.

Vocabulary
logarithm of y with base b
common logarithm
natural logarithm

Evaluate the logarithm.

15. $\log_2 8$

16. $\log_6 \frac{1}{36}$

Find the inverse of the function.

17. $f(x) = 8^x$

18. $y = \ln(x - 4)$

19. Graph $y = \log_{1/5} x$.

20. The Richter magnitude R of an earthquake is given by

$$R = 0.67 \ln E + 1.17$$

where E is the energy (in kilowatt-hours) released by the earthquake. To the nearest tenth, what is the Richter magnitude of an earthquake that releases 23,000 kilowatt-hours of energy?

6.4 Transformations of Exponential and Logarithmic Functions (pp. 311–318)

⊙ **Learning Target:** Graph transformations of exponential and logarithmic functions.

Describe the transformation of f represented by g. Then graph each function.

21. $f(x) = e^{-x}$, $g(x) = e^{-5x} - 8$

22. $f(x) = \log_4 x$, $g(x) = \frac{1}{2}\log_4(x + 5)$

Write a rule for g.

23. Let the graph of g be a vertical stretch by a factor of 3, followed by a translation 6 units left and 3 units up of the graph of $f(x) = e^x$.

24. Let the graph of g be a translation 2 units down, followed by a reflection in the y-axis of the graph of $f(x) = \log x$.

6.5 Properties of Logarithms (pp. 319–326)

⊙ **Learning Target:** Use properties of logarithms.

Expand or condense the logarithmic expression.

25. $\log 10x^3y$

26. $2 \ln x + 5 \ln 2 - \ln 8$

Use the change-of-base formula to evaluate the logarithm.

27. $\log_2 10$

28. $\log_7 9$

6.6 Solving Exponential and Logarithmic Equations (pp. 327–334)

⊙ **Learning Target:** Solve exponential and logarithmic equations and inequalities.

Vocabulary
exponential equations
logarithmic equations

Solve the equation.

29. $5^x = 8$

30. $\ln x + \ln(x + 2) = 3$

Solve the inequality.

31. $6^x > 12$

32. $\ln x \leq 9$

33. The the percent chance y (in decimal form) that a player on a football team successfully kicks x extra points in a row is represented by

$$y = 0.95^x.$$

For what number x does the percent chance fall to 25%?

34. A scientist studying memory determines that the percent y of new information that a certain individual remembers after x minutes can be modeled by

$$y = \frac{184}{(\log x)^{1.25} + 1.84}.$$

After how long does the person remember 50% of new information?

6.7 Modeling with Exponential and Logarithmic Functions (pp. 335–342)

⊙ **Learning Target:** Write exponential and logarithmic functions to model sets of data.

Write an exponential function $y = ab^x$ whose graph passes through the given points.

35. $(3, 8), (5, 2)$

36. $(1, 3), (4, 648)$

37. Create a scatter plot of the points $(x, \ln y)$ to determine whether an exponential model fits the data. If so, find an exponential model for the data.

x	1	4	7	10	13
y	3.3	10.1	30.6	92.7	280.9

38. The table shows the pairs of basketball shoes s that a store sells over time t (in weeks). Use technology to find a logarithmic model of the form $s = a + b \ln t$ that represents the data. Estimate the number of pairs of shoes sold after 6 weeks.

Week, t	1	3	5	7	9
Pairs sold, s	5	32	48	58	65

6 PERFORMANCE TASK
SMP.1 SMP.4

CARBON DATING

Carbon dating is a process that measures the amount of carbon-14 in an organism in order to approximate when it died.

Carbon-12
- 6 Protons
- 6 Neutrons
- 6 Electrons

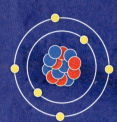
Carbon-13
- 6 Protons
- 7 Neutrons
- 6 Electrons

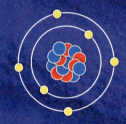
Carbon-14
- 6 Protons
- 8 Neutrons
- 6 Electrons

Non-radioactive (Carbon-12, Carbon-13)

Radioactive (Carbon-14)

Concentration: 1.2 parts per trillion
There are about 1.2 atoms of carbon-14 in the atmosphere for every 1 trillion atoms of non-radioactive carbon.

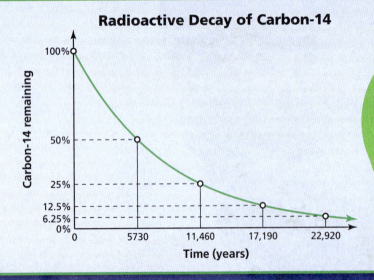

The concentration of carbon-14 in living organic matter is equal to the concentration found in the atmosphere.

Half-life of Carbon-14: 5,730 years
Due to radioactive decay, the amount of carbon-14 in a sample is halved every 5,730 years after an organism dies.

Analyzing Data

Use the information on the previous page to complete the following exercises.

Explain what is shown in the display. What do you notice? What do you wonder?

Write an equation that represents the radioactive decay of carbon-14 over time.

How long does it take for 75% of the original amount of carbon-14 to remain in a sample?

ANCIENT DISCOVERY

You discover an ancient manuscript at an archaeological site. The manuscript is written on an organic material made from a plant called papyrus. You determine that the concentration of carbon-14 in the papyrus is about 0.93 part per trillion. Use the model you found in Exercise 2 to approximate the number of years since the papyrus plant died. Explain your reasoning.

Use the Internet or another resource to research carbon dating. What are some of its limitations? What assumptions do scientists make when using this dating method?

Connecting Big Ideas

For use after Chapter 6.
SMP.2

Inventors can apply for patents. A patent gives an owner the legal right to prevent others from making, using, or selling an invention. Patents can be approved for physical objects such as machines and tools, or for processes and procedures. A patent is typically valid for 20 years, after which the owner must reapply. About 50% of patent applications in the United States are approved.

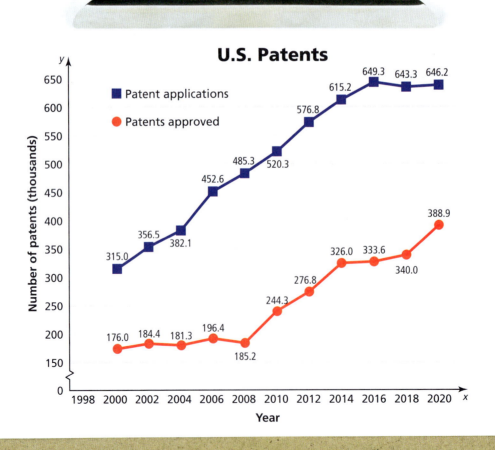

 What do you notice?
What do you wonder?

 Write a polynomial function f that models the number (in thousands) of patent applications over time.

 Write an exponential function g that models the number (in thousands) of patents approved over time.

 Find $(f - g)(x)$ and explain what it represents. Then find and interpret $(f - g)(20)$.

Find and interpret $g^{-1}(200)$.

THINKING ABOUT THE BIG IDEAS

How can **Understanding Polynomial Functions** help you estimate the number of patent applications in a given year?

7 Rational Functions

- **7.1** Inverse Variation
- **7.2** Graphing Rational Functions
- **7.3** Multiplying and Dividing Rational Expressions
- **7.4** Adding and Subtracting Rational Expressions
- **7.5** Solving Rational Equations

NATIONAL GEOGRAPHIC EXPLORER
Skylar Tibbits — COMPUTER SCIENTIST

Skylar Tibbits is the founder of the Self-Assembly Lab at the Massachusetts Institute of Technology's International Design Center. His invention of 4-D printing involves programmable materials that can sense and respond to internal or external stimuli. His research is the first to apply principles of self-assembly to construction and manufacturing: for example, a cell phone that can build itself or a chair that self-assembles.

- What is self-assembly?
- How are 3-D printing and 4-D printing similar? How are they different?
- What kinds of stimuli can be used to trigger a material to self-assemble?

PERFORMANCE TASK

As 3-D printing becomes more and more affordable, many people are starting their own 3-D printing business. In the Performance Task on pages 394 and 395, you will analyze the costs and profits of creating and selling your own 3-D-printed object.

3-D and 4-D Printing

Big Idea of the Chapter
Reason About Rational Functions

A rational number can be written as a ratio of two integers $\frac{a}{b}$, where $b \neq 0$. Similarly, a rational function can be written as a ratio of two polynomials $\frac{p(x)}{q(x)}$, where $q(x) \neq 0$.

Three-dimensional (3-D) printing is the process of making 3-D solid objects from a digital blueprint. The objects are created using layers of material that are laid down one on top of another. Each of these layers is a cross-section of the object. 3-D printing is the opposite of subtractive manufacturing, which is the process of removing material from a solid object. One of the benefits of 3-D printing is that it uses less material than many other manufacturing methods.

You manufacture and sell 3-D-printed cell phone cases. The 3-D printer costs $300, and materials for each case cost $1.50.

1. Complete the table using the cost of the printer and materials.

Number of cases	Average cost per case (dollars)
30	
60	
90	
120	

2. Let x be the number of cases produced and let y be the average cost per case. Write y as a function of x.

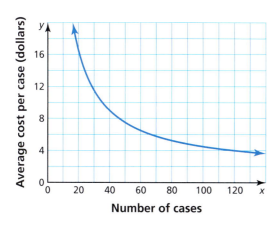

3. Use technology to explain what happens to the average cost per case as the number of cases approaches infinity.

Getting Ready for Chapter 7

Adding and Subtracting Rational Numbers

EXAMPLE 1 Find $-\dfrac{7}{4} + \dfrac{3}{4}$.

Because the signs are different and $\left|-\dfrac{7}{4}\right| > \left|\dfrac{3}{4}\right|$, subtract $\left|\dfrac{3}{4}\right|$ from $\left|-\dfrac{7}{4}\right|$.

$\left|-\dfrac{7}{4}\right| - \left|\dfrac{3}{4}\right| = \dfrac{7}{4} - \dfrac{3}{4}$ Find the absolute values.

$= \dfrac{7-3}{4}$ Write the difference of the numerators over the common denominator.

$= 1$ Simplify.

Because $\left|-\dfrac{7}{4}\right| > \left|\dfrac{3}{4}\right|$, use the sign of $-\dfrac{7}{4}$.

▶ So, $-\dfrac{7}{4} + \dfrac{3}{4} = -1$.

EXAMPLE 2 Find $-\dfrac{7}{8} - \dfrac{5}{16}$.

Rewrite the difference as a sum by adding the opposite.

$-\dfrac{7}{8} - \dfrac{5}{16} = -\dfrac{7}{8} + \left(-\dfrac{5}{16}\right)$

Because the signs are the same, add $\left|-\dfrac{7}{8}\right|$ and $\left|-\dfrac{5}{16}\right|$.

$\left|-\dfrac{7}{8}\right| + \left|-\dfrac{5}{16}\right| = \dfrac{7}{8} + \dfrac{5}{16}$ Find the absolute values.

$= \dfrac{14}{16} + \dfrac{5}{16}$ Rewrite $\dfrac{7}{8}$ as $\dfrac{14}{16}$.

$= \dfrac{14+5}{16}$ Write the sum of the numerators over the common denominator.

$= \dfrac{19}{16}$, or $1\dfrac{3}{16}$ Simplify.

Because $-\dfrac{7}{8}$ and $-\dfrac{5}{16}$ are both negative, use a negative sign in the difference.

▶ So, $-\dfrac{7}{8} - \dfrac{5}{16} = -1\dfrac{3}{16}$.

Find the sum or difference.

1. $\dfrac{7}{9} - \dfrac{4}{9}$

2. $\dfrac{3}{5} + \dfrac{2}{3}$

3. $-\dfrac{4}{7} + \dfrac{1}{6}$

4. $\dfrac{5}{12} - \left(-\dfrac{1}{2}\right)$

5. $\dfrac{2}{7} + \dfrac{1}{7} - \dfrac{6}{7}$

6. $\dfrac{3}{10} - \dfrac{3}{4} + \dfrac{2}{5}$

7.1 Inverse Variation

Learning Target: Understand inverse variation.

Success Criteria:
- I can identify equations and data sets that show direct variation.
- I can identify equations and data sets that show inverse variation.
- I can write inverse variation equations.
- I can solve real-life problems using inverse variation functions.

INVESTIGATE   Describing Types of Variation

Work with a partner.

1. Consider the side length s (in inches) and the perimeter P (in inches) of a square.

   a. Complete the table. Describe the relationship between s and P. Explain why the perimeter P is said to vary *directly* with the side length s.

s	1	2	3	4	5	6
P						

   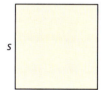

   b. Make a scatter plot of the data. What are some characteristics of the graph?

   c. Write an equation that represents P as a function of s.

2. Consider the length ℓ (in inches) and the width w (in inches) of a rectangle that has an area of 64 square inches.

   a. Complete the table. Describe the relationship between ℓ and w. Explain why the width w is said to vary *inversely* with the length ℓ.

ℓ	1	2	4	8	16	32	64
w							

   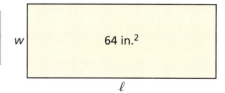

   b. Make a scatter plot of the data. Compare the characteristics of the graph with the graph in Exercise 1(b).

   c. Write an equation that represents w as a function of ℓ. Compare it with the equation in Exercise 1(c).

3. How can you recognize when two quantities vary directly or inversely?

Vocabulary
direct variation
constant of variation
inverse variation

Understanding Direct and Inverse Variation

Key Concept

Direct Variation

Variables x and y show **direct variation** when they are related as follows:

$y = ax, a \neq 0$ Direct variation

The constant a is the **constant of variation**, and y is said to *vary directly* with x.

Inverse Variation

Variables x and y show **inverse variation** when they are related as follows:

$y = \dfrac{a}{x}, a \neq 0$ Inverse variation

The constant a is the constant of variation, and y is said to *vary inversely* with x.

EXAMPLE 1   Classifying Equations

Tell whether x and y show *direct variation*, *inverse variation*, or *neither*.

a. $xy = 5$

$xy = 5$ Write the equation.

$y = \dfrac{5}{x}$ Solve for y.

▶ The equation is of the form $y = \dfrac{a}{x}$. So, x and y show inverse variation.

b. $y = x - 4$

▶ The equation is not of the form $y = ax$ or $y = \dfrac{a}{x}$. So, x and y show neither direct nor inverse variation.

c. $\dfrac{y}{2} = x$

$\dfrac{y}{2} = x$ Write the equation.

$y = 2x$ Solve for y.

▶ The equation is of the form $y = ax$. So, x and y show direct variation.

In-Class Practice

Self-Assessment

Tell whether x and y show *direct variation*, *inverse variation*, or *neither*.

1. $6x = y$
2. $xy = -0.25$
3. $y + x = 10$

1 I don't understand yet.   **2** I can do it with help.   **3** I can do it on my own.   **4** I can teach someone.

- A set of data pairs (x, y) shows direct variation when the ratios $\frac{y}{x}$ are constant.
- A set of data pairs (x, y) shows inverse variation when the products xy are constant.

EXAMPLE 2 Classifying Data

Tell whether x and y show *direct variation*, *inverse variation*, or *neither*.

x	2	4	6	8
y	−12	−6	−4	−3

Find the products xy and ratios $\frac{y}{x}$.

xy	−24	−24	−24	−24	The products are constant.
$\frac{y}{x}$	$\frac{-12}{2} = -6$	$\frac{-6}{4} = -\frac{3}{2}$	$\frac{-4}{6} = -\frac{2}{3}$	$-\frac{3}{8}$	The ratios are not constant.

▶ So, x and y show inverse variation.

EXAMPLE 3 Writing an Inverse Variation Equation

The variables x and y vary inversely, and $y = 4$ when $x = 3$. Write an equation that relates x and y. Then find y when $x = -2$.

$y = \dfrac{a}{x}$ Write general equation for inverse variation.

$4 = \dfrac{a}{3}$ Substitute 4 for y and 3 for x.

$12 = a$ Multiply each side by 3.

▶ The inverse variation equation is $y = \dfrac{12}{x}$. When $x = -2$, $y = \dfrac{12}{-2} = -6$.

In-Class Practice

Self-Assessment

Tell whether x and y show *direct variation*, *inverse variation*, or *neither*.

4.

x	−4	−3	−2	−1
y	20	15	10	5

5.

x	1	2	3	4
y	60	30	20	15

The variables x and y vary inversely. Use the given values to write an equation relating x and y. Then find y when $x = 2$.

6. $x = 6, y = -1$

7. $x = \frac{1}{2}, y = 16$

1 I don't understand yet.   **2** I can do it with help.   **3** I can do it on my own.   **4** I can teach someone.

7.1 Inverse Variation

Connections to Real Life

EXAMPLE 4 Using an Inverse Variation Equation

The time t (in hours) that it takes a group of volunteers to decorate a float for a Chinese New Year parade varies inversely with the number n of volunteers. It takes a group of 10 volunteers 8 hours to decorate the float.

a. Write an equation that relates n and t.

$t = \dfrac{a}{n}$ Write general equation for inverse variation.

$8 = \dfrac{a}{10}$ Substitute 8 for t and 10 for n.

$80 = a$ Multiply each side by 10.

▶ The inverse variation equation is $t = \dfrac{80}{n}$.

b. Make a table showing the times that it takes to decorate the float when the number of volunteers is 15, 20, 25, and 30. What happens to the time as the number of volunteers increases?

Use the inverse variation equation to make a table of values.

n	15	20	25	30
t	$\dfrac{80}{15}$ = 5 h 20 min	$\dfrac{80}{20}$ = 4 h	$\dfrac{80}{25}$ = 3 h 12 min	$\dfrac{80}{30}$ = 2 h 40 min

▶ As the number of volunteers increases, the time it takes to decorate the float decreases.

Check Because the time decreases as the number of volunteers increases, the time for 5 volunteers to decorate the float should be greater than 8 hours.

$t = \dfrac{80}{5} = 16$ hours ✓

In-Class Practice

Self-Assessment

8. **WHAT IF?** In Example 4, it takes a group of 10 volunteers 12 hours to decorate the float. How long does it take a group of 15 volunteers?

9. A company determines that the demand d for a keychain light varies inversely with the price p of the light. When the price is $8.25, the demand is 550 lights. When the price is doubled, is the demand halved? Justify your answer.

7.1 Practice

Tell whether x and y show *direct variation, inverse variation,* or *neither*.
(See Examples 1 and 2.)

▶ 1. $\dfrac{y}{x} = 8$

2. $xy = 12$

3. $xy = \dfrac{1}{5}$

4. $x + y = 6$

▶ 5.
x	12	18	23	29	34
y	132	198	253	319	374

6.
x	4	5	6.2	7	11
y	16	11	10	9	6

The variables x and y vary inversely. Use the given values to write an equation relating x and y. Then find y when x = 3. (See Example 3.)

▶ 7. $x = 5, y = -4$

8. $x = 1, y = 9$

9. $x = \dfrac{3}{4}, y = 28$

10. $x = -12, y = -\dfrac{1}{6}$

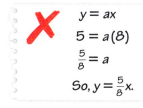

11. **SMP.3 ERROR ANALYSIS** The variables x and y vary inversely, and x = 8 when y = 5. Describe and correct the error in writing an equation relating x and y.

12. **CONNECTION TO REAL LIFE** The number y of apps that can be stored on a tablet varies inversely with the average size x of an app. A certain tablet can store 250 apps when the average size of an app is 64 megabytes (MB). (See Example 4.)

   a. Write an equation that relates x and y.

   b. Make a table showing the numbers of apps that will fit on the tablet when the average size of an app is 32 MB, 40 MB, 50 MB, and 80 MB. What happens to the number of apps as the average app size increases?

13. Complete the table. Explain your reasoning.

Variables	Type of Variation
x and y	inverse
y and z	inverse
x and z	?

14. **SMP.1 DIG DEEPER** To balance the board, the distances of the animals from the fulcrum must vary directly. The animals move 6 feet apart and the board remains balanced. How far is each animal from the fulcrum? Justify your answer.

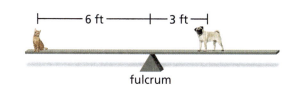

Interpreting Data

GAME SHOW WINNINGS Contestants on a show each play a game to win money. The graph shows the amount of money won per person for different numbers of winning contestants.

15. Describe the shape of the graph.

16. What type of function models the graph? Write the amount won as a function of the number of winning contestants.

17. A total of 4 contestants won the game. How much money does each winning contestant receive?

Review & Refresh

Solve the equation.

18. $64^x = \left(\frac{1}{4}\right)^{2x+15}$

19. $\log(x+6) = \log 7x$

20. Which properties of logarithms can you use to condense the expression $3 \ln 0.5x - \ln 6$?

21. Create a scatter plot of the points $(x, \ln y)$ to determine whether an exponential model fits the data. If so, find an exponential model for the data.

x	2	5	8	11	14
y	1.8	5.4	16.2	48.6	145.8

22. Divide $(x^2 + 2x - 99) \div (x + 11)$.

23. The table shows the heights of a snowboarder x seconds after jumping from a halfpipe. What type of function can you use to model the data? Estimate the height after 0.75 second.

Time (seconds), x	Height (feet), y
0	0
0.5	12
1.0	16
1.5	12
2.0	0

Simplify the expression.

24. $8^{3/2} \cdot 8^{1/4}$

25. $\dfrac{\sqrt[3]{54}}{\sqrt[3]{2}}$

358   Chapter 7   Rational Functions

7.2 Graphing Rational Functions

Learning Target: Describe and graph rational functions.

Success Criteria:
- I can graph rational functions.
- I can describe transformations of rational functions.
- I can explain how to find the asymptotes of a rational function from an equation.
- I can write rational functions in different forms.

INVESTIGATE Graphing Rational Functions

Work with a partner. The function $f(x) = \dfrac{1}{x}$ is a simple *rational* function.

1. What does the graph of f look like? How is the graph similar to other functions you have studied? How is it different?

2. Describe the end behavior of f. Then describe the behavior of the graph when x is between -1 and 1. Why is there an asymptote at the y-axis?

3. Use technology to explore the graph of $y = f(x - h)$ for several values of h. How does the graph change when you change the value of h?

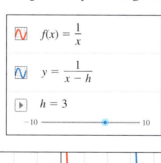

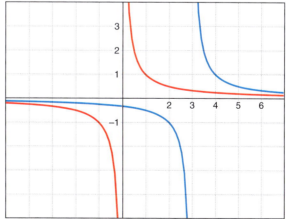

4. Use technology to explore the graph of $y = f(x) + k$ for several values of k. How does the graph change when you change the value of k?

Vocabulary
rational function

Graphing Simple Rational Functions

A **rational function** has the form $f(x) = \dfrac{p(x)}{q(x)}$, where $p(x)$ and $q(x)$ are polynomials and $q(x) \neq 0$. The inverse variation function $f(x) = \dfrac{a}{x}$ is a rational function.

The graph of the parent function $f(x) = \dfrac{1}{x}$ is a *hyperbola*, which consists of two symmetrical parts called branches. The domain and range are all nonzero real numbers.

Any function of the form $g(x) = \dfrac{a}{x}$ ($a \neq 0$) has the same asymptotes, domain, and range as the function $f(x) = \dfrac{1}{x}$.

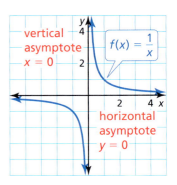

vertical asymptote $x = 0$

horizontal asymptote $y = 0$

$f(x) = \dfrac{1}{x}$

EXAMPLE 1 Graphing a Rational Function of the Form $y = \dfrac{a}{x}$

Graph $g(x) = \dfrac{4}{x}$. Compare the graph with the graph of $f(x) = \dfrac{1}{x}$.

The function is of the form $g(x) = \dfrac{a}{x}$, so the vertical asymptote is $x = 0$, and the horizontal asymptote is $y = 0$.

Make a table of values and plot the points. Include both positive and negative values of x.

x	−3	−2	−1	1	2	3
y	$-\dfrac{4}{3}$	−2	−4	4	2	$\dfrac{4}{3}$

Draw the two branches of the hyperbola so that they pass through the plotted points and approach the asymptotes.

▶ The graph of g lies farther from the axes than the graph of f. Both graphs lie in the first and third quadrants and have the same asymptotes, domain, and range.

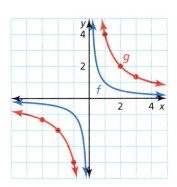

In-Class Practice

Self-Assessment

Graph the function. Compare the graph with the graph of $f(x) = \dfrac{1}{x}$.

1. $g(x) = \dfrac{2}{x}$

2. $g(x) = \dfrac{-6}{x}$

1 I don't understand yet. **2** I can do it with help. **3** I can do it on my own. **4** I can teach someone.

360 Chapter 7 Rational Functions

Translating Simple Rational Functions

To graph a rational function of the form $y = \dfrac{a}{x-h} + k$, follow these steps.

- Draw the asymptotes $x = h$ and $y = k$.
- Plot points to the left and to the right of the vertical asymptote.
- Draw the two branches of the hyperbola so that they pass through the plotted points and approach the asymptotes.

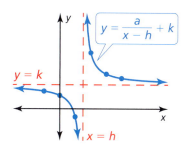

EXAMPLE 2 Graphing a Translation of a Rational Function

Graph $g(x) = \dfrac{-4}{x+2} - 1$. Find the domain and range.

Draw the asymptotes $x = -2$ and $y = -1$.

Make a table of values and plot the points. Include points to the left of the vertical asymptote and points to the right of the vertical asymptote.

x	−6	−4	−3	−1	0	2
y	0	1	3	−5	−3	−2

Draw the two branches of the hyperbola so that they pass through the plotted points and approach the asymptotes.

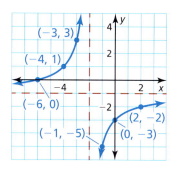

▶ The domain is all real numbers except $x = -2$, and the range is all real numbers except $y = -1$.

In-Class Practice

Self-Assessment

Graph the function. Find the domain and range.

3. $y = \dfrac{3}{x} - 2$

4. $y = \dfrac{1}{x-1} + 5$

1 I don't understand yet. 2 I can do it with help. 3 I can do it on my own. 4 I can teach someone.

Graphing Other Rational Functions

Rational functions of the form $y = \dfrac{ax + b}{cx + d}$ have graphs that are hyperbolas.

- The vertical asymptote of the graph is the line $x = -\dfrac{d}{c}$.
- The horizontal asymptote is the line $y = \dfrac{a}{c}$.

EXAMPLE 3 Graphing a Rational Function of the Form $y = \dfrac{ax + b}{cx + d}$

Graph $f(x) = \dfrac{2x + 1}{x - 3}$. Find the domain and range.

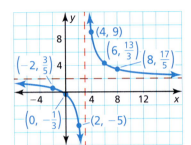

The vertical asymptote is $x = -\dfrac{d}{c} = -\left(-\dfrac{3}{1}\right) = 3$. The horizontal asymptote is $y = \dfrac{a}{c} = \dfrac{2}{1} = 2$. Draw the asymptotes.

Plot at least 3 points to the left of the vertical asymptote and 3 points to the right of the vertical asymptote.

Draw the two branches of the hyperbola so that they pass through the plotted points and approach the asymptotes.

▶ The domain is all real numbers except $x = 3$, and the range is all real numbers except $y = 2$.

Rewriting a rational function in the form $y = \dfrac{a}{x - h} + k$ shows a translation of $y = \dfrac{a}{x}$ with vertical asymptote $x = h$ and horizontal asymptote $y = k$.

EXAMPLE 4 Rewriting and Graphing a Rational Function

Rewrite $g(x) = \dfrac{3x + 5}{x + 1}$ in the form $g(x) = \dfrac{a}{x - h} + k$. Graph the function. Describe the graph of g as a transformation of the graph of $f(x) = \dfrac{a}{x}$.

Rewrite the function by using polynomial long division.

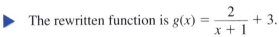

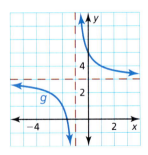

▶ The rewritten function is $g(x) = \dfrac{2}{x + 1} + 3$.

The graph of g is a translation 1 unit left and 3 units up of the graph of $f(x) = \dfrac{2}{x}$.

In-Class Practice
Self-Assessment

5. Graph $f(x) = \dfrac{2x + 1}{4x - 2}$. Find the domain and range.

6. Repeat Example 4 for the function $g(x) = \dfrac{2x + 3}{x + 1}$.

| **1** I don't understand yet. | **2** I can do it with help. | **3** I can do it on my own. | **4** I can teach someone. |

Connections to Real Life

EXAMPLE 5 Interpreting the Graph of a Rational Function

3-D PRINTING **MEDICAL RESEARCH** A 3-D printer builds objects by depositing material one layer at a time. The layers are bonded together, creating a solid object.

A medical researcher makes prosthetic hands using a 3-D printer. The printer costs $1,000 and the material for each hand costs $50.

- How many prosthetic hands must be printed for the average cost per hand to fall to $90?
- What happens to the average cost as more prosthetic hands are printed?

Let $c(x)$ be the average cost (in dollars) for printing x hands.

$$c(x) = \frac{(\text{Unit cost})(\text{Number printed}) + (\text{Cost of printer})}{\text{Number printed}} = \frac{50x + 1{,}000}{x}$$

Use technology to graph the function. Because the number of hands and average cost cannot be negative, graph the function in the first quadrant.

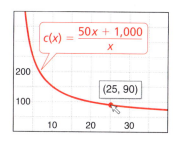

▶ The graph shows that the average cost falls to $90 per hand after 25 hands are printed. Because the horizontal asymptote is $c(x) = 50$, the average cost approaches $50 as more hands are printed.

In-Class Practice

Self-Assessment

7. To join a rock climbing gym, you must pay an initial fee of $100 and a monthly fee of $59.

   a. How many months must you have a membership for the average cost per month to fall to $69?

   b. What happens to the average cost as the number of months that you are a member increases?

7.2 Practice

Graph the function. Compare the graph with the graph of $f(x) = \dfrac{1}{x}$. (See Example 1.)

1. $g(x) = \dfrac{-5}{x}$
2. $g(x) = \dfrac{3}{x}$
3. $g(x) = \dfrac{15}{x}$
4. $g(x) = \dfrac{0.1}{x}$

Graph the function. Find the domain and range. (See Example 2.)

5. $h(x) = \dfrac{6}{x-1}$
6. $y = \dfrac{1}{x+2}$
7. $f(x) = \dfrac{-2}{x-7}$
8. $y = \dfrac{10}{x+7} - 5$

9. **SMP.3 ERROR ANALYSIS** Describe and correct the error in finding the vertical and horizontal asymptotes of the graph of $f(x) = \dfrac{3}{x+6} - 2$.

The vertical asymptote is $x = 6$.
The horizontal asymptote is $y = -2$.

Graph the function. Find the domain and range. (See Example 3.)

10. $f(x) = \dfrac{x+4}{x-3}$
11. $y = \dfrac{x+6}{4x-8}$
12. $f(x) = \dfrac{-5x+2}{4x+5}$
13. $h(x) = \dfrac{-5x}{-2x-3}$

Rewrite the function in the form $g(x) = \dfrac{a}{x-h} + k$. Graph the function. Describe the graph of g as a transformation of the graph of $f(x) = \dfrac{a}{x}$. (See Example 4.)

14. $g(x) = \dfrac{5x+6}{x+1}$
15. $g(x) = \dfrac{2x-4}{x-5}$
16. $g(x) = \dfrac{x+18}{x-6}$
17. $g(x) = \dfrac{9x-3}{x+7}$

18. **CONNECTION TO REAL LIFE** Your school purchases a math software application. The program has an initial cost of $500 plus $20 for each student who subscribes. (See Example 5.)

   a. How many students must subscribe for the average cost per student to fall to $30?

   b. What happens to the average cost as more students subscribe?

19. **SMP.5** The time t (in seconds) it takes for sound to travel 1 kilometer can be modeled by

$$t = \frac{1,000}{0.6T + 331}$$

where T is the air temperature (in degrees Celsius).

a. You are 1 kilometer from a lightning strike. You hear thunder 2.9 seconds later. Use a tool to find the approximate air temperature.

b. Find the average rate of change in the time it takes sound to travel 1 kilometer as the air temperature increases from 0°C to 10°C.

Use technology to graph the function. Then determine whether the function is *even*, *odd*, or *neither*.

20. $h(x) = \dfrac{6}{x^2 + 1}$

21. $y = \dfrac{x^3}{3x^2 + x^4}$

22. $f(x) = \dfrac{4x^2}{2x^3 - x}$

23. Internet service provider A charges a $50 installation fee and a monthly fee of $43. The table shows the average monthly costs y of provider B for x months of service. Which provider would you choose if you plan to stay with the provider for 12 months? 18 months? 24 months?

Months, x	Average monthly cost (dollars), y
12	$46.92
18	$45.94
24	$45.46

24. The graph of $f(x) = \dfrac{1}{x - h} + k$ is shown. Find the values of h and k. Then describe the end behavior of f.

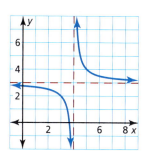

25. Sketch a graph of the rational function f with the given characteristics.
    - The domain of f is all real numbers except $x = 1$.
    - $f(x) \to -5$ as $x \to -\infty$ and as $x \to +\infty$.

26. A rational function f is of the form $f(x) = \dfrac{a}{x - h} + k$. The asymptotes of the graph of f intersect at $(3, 2)$. The point $(2, 1)$ is on the graph of f. Find three other points on the graph of f.

27. Describe the intervals where the graph of $y = \dfrac{a}{x}$ is increasing or decreasing when (a) $a > 0$ and (b) $a < 0$.

Interpreting Data

TETANUS CASES It is recommended that adults get a tetanus vaccine once every 10 years. Tetanus can be deadly, but it is unlikely that someone who receives the tetanus vaccine as recommended will contract tetanus.

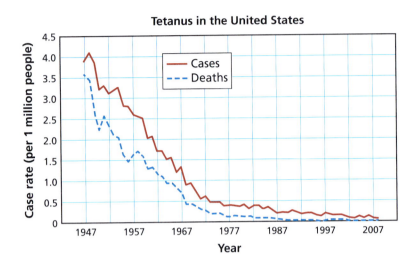

28. What type of function would you use to model the graph?

29. Does it appear from the graph that the number of deaths could be a transformation of the number of cases? If so, describe the type of transformation.

Review & Refresh

30. Factor the polynomial completely.
    $$2x^3 - 14x^2 + 5x - 35$$

31. The time t (in minutes) required to empty a tank varies inversely with the pumping rate r (in gallons per minute). The rate of a certain pump is 70 gallons per minute. It takes the pump 20 minutes to empty the tank. Complete the table for the times it takes the pump to empty a tank for the given pumping rates.

Pumping rate (gal/min)	Time (min)
50	
56	

32. Find the discriminant of the equation $4x^2 - 10x + 7 = 0$ and describe the number and type of solutions of the equation.

33. Solve the equation.
    $$\log_3(5x + 1) = 4$$

34. Determine the type of function represented by the table.

x	−3	−2	−1	0	1	2
y	128	32	8	2	$\frac{1}{2}$	$\frac{1}{8}$

35. Simplify the expression.
    $$2^{1/2} \cdot 2^{3/5}$$

7.3 Multiplying and Dividing Rational Expressions

Learning Target: Multiply and divide rational expressions.

Success Criteria:
- I can simplify rational expressions and identify any excluded values.
- I can multiply rational expressions.
- I can divide rational expressions.

INVESTIGATE Analyzing Rational Expressions

Work with a partner.

1. A student divides $2x^2 + 9x + 4$ by $x + 4$ as shown below.

   a. Justify each solution step and describe the method.

   $$\begin{array}{r} 2x + 1 \\ x + 4 \overline{\smash{)}2x^2 + 9x + 4} \\ \underline{2x^2 + 8x} \\ x + 4 \\ \underline{x + 4} \\ 0 \end{array}$$

   So, $(2x^2 + 9x + 4) \div (x + 4) = 2x + 1$.

   What other methods can you use to divide these polynomials?

   b. Create a table of values for $\dfrac{2x^2 + 9x + 4}{x + 4}$ and $2x + 1$. What happens when $x = -4$? Why does this happen? Explain how this affects your answer in part (a).

2. You can multiply and divide rational expressions in the same way that you multiply and divide fractions. Find each product or quotient. Determine whether you need to restrict the domains for any of the products or quotients.

   a. $\dfrac{x}{x+1} \cdot \dfrac{1}{x}$

   b. $\dfrac{1}{x-2} \cdot \dfrac{x-2}{x+1}$

   c. $\dfrac{1}{x} \div \dfrac{x}{x+1}$

   d. $\dfrac{x}{x+2} \div \dfrac{x}{x-1}$

3. Explain whether the set of rational expressions is closed under multiplication and division.

Vocabulary
rational expression
simplified form of a rational expression

Simplifying Rational Expressions

A **rational expression** is a fraction whose numerator and denominator are nonzero polynomials. The *domain* of a rational expression excludes values that make the denominator zero. A rational expression is in **simplified form** when its numerator and denominator have no common factors (other than ±1).

Key Concept

Simplifying Rational Expressions

Let a, b, and c be expressions with $b \neq 0$ and $c \neq 0$.

Property $\quad \dfrac{ac}{bc} = \dfrac{a}{b}$ $\qquad$ Divide out common factor c.

Examples $\quad \dfrac{15}{65} = \dfrac{3 \cdot 5}{13 \cdot 5} = \dfrac{3}{13}$ $\qquad$ Divide out common factor 5.

$\qquad \qquad \dfrac{4(x+3)}{(x+3)(x+3)} = \dfrac{4}{x+3}$ $\qquad$ Divide out common factor $x + 3$.

Simplifying a rational expression usually requires two steps. First, factor the numerator and denominator. Then divide out any factors that are common to both the numerator and denominator.

EXAMPLE 1 Simplifying a Rational Expression

Simplify $\dfrac{x^2 - 4x - 12}{x^2 - 4}$.

$\dfrac{x^2 - 4x - 12}{x^2 - 4} = \dfrac{(x+2)(x-6)}{(x+2)(x-2)}$ $\qquad$ Factor numerator and denominator.

$\qquad \qquad = \dfrac{(x+2)(x-6)}{(x+2)(x-2)}$ $\qquad$ Divide out common factor.

$\qquad \qquad = \dfrac{x-6}{x-2}, \; x \neq -2$ $\qquad$ Simplified form

The original expression is undefined when $x = -2$. To make the original and simplified expressions equivalent, restrict the domain of the simplified expression by excluding $x = -2$. Both expressions are undefined when $x = 2$, so it is not necessary to list it.

▶ So, the simplified expression is $\dfrac{x-6}{x-2}, \; x \neq -2$.

In-Class Practice

Self-Assessment

Simplify the rational expression, if possible.

1. $\dfrac{x+4}{x^2 - 16}$
2. $\dfrac{4}{x(x+2)}$
3. $\dfrac{x^2 - 2x - 3}{x^2 - x - 6}$

1 I don't understand yet. **2** I can do it with help. **3** I can do it on my own. **4** I can teach someone.

Multiplying Rational Expressions

> **Key Concept**
>
> **Multiplying Rational Expressions**
> Let a, b, c, and d be expressions with $b \neq 0$ and $d \neq 0$.
>
> **Property** $\quad \dfrac{a}{b} \cdot \dfrac{c}{d} = \dfrac{ac}{bd} \qquad$ Simplify $\dfrac{ac}{bd}$ if possible.

EXAMPLE 2 **Multiplying Rational Expressions**

Find the product $\dfrac{8x^3y}{2xy^2} \cdot \dfrac{7x^4y^3}{4y}$.

$\dfrac{8x^3y}{2xy^2} \cdot \dfrac{7x^4y^3}{4y} = \dfrac{56x^7y^4}{8xy^3} \qquad$ Multiply numerators and denominators.

$\qquad = \dfrac{8 \cdot 7 \cdot x \cdot x^6 \cdot y^3 \cdot y}{8 \cdot x \cdot y^3} \qquad$ Factor and divide out common factors.

$\qquad = 7x^6y, \quad x \neq 0, y \neq 0 \qquad$ Simplified form

▶ So, the product is $7x^6y$, $x \neq 0$, $y \neq 0$.

EXAMPLE 3 **Multiplying a Rational Expression by a Polynomial**

Find the product $\dfrac{x + 2}{x^3 - 27} \cdot (x^2 + 3x + 9)$.

$\dfrac{x + 2}{x^3 - 27} \cdot (x^2 + 3x + 9) = \dfrac{x + 2}{x^3 - 27} \cdot \dfrac{x^2 + 3x + 9}{1} \qquad$ Write polynomial as a rational expression.

$\qquad = \dfrac{(x + 2)(x^2 + 3x + 9)}{(x - 3)(x^2 + 3x + 9)} \qquad$ Multiply. Factor denominator.

$\qquad = \dfrac{(x + 2)\cancel{(x^2 + 3x + 9)}}{(x - 3)\cancel{(x^2 + 3x + 9)}} \qquad$ Divide out common factor.

$\qquad = \dfrac{x + 2}{x - 3} \qquad$ Simplified form

▶ So the product is $\dfrac{x + 2}{x - 3}$.

In-Class Practice

Self-Assessment

Find the product.

4. $\dfrac{3x^5y^2}{8xy} \cdot \dfrac{6xy^2}{9x^3y}$

5. $\dfrac{x + 5}{x^3 - 1} \cdot (x^2 + x + 1)$

1 I don't understand yet. **2** I can do it with help. **3** I can do it on my own. **4** I can teach someone.

7.3 Multiplying and Dividing Rational Expressions

Dividing Rational Expressions

> **Key Concept**
>
> **Dividing Rational Expressions**
>
> Let a, b, c, and d be expressions with $b \neq 0$, $c \neq 0$, and $d \neq 0$.
>
> **Property** $\quad \dfrac{a}{b} \div \dfrac{c}{d} = \dfrac{a}{b} \cdot \dfrac{d}{c} = \dfrac{ad}{bc} \qquad$ Simplify $\dfrac{ad}{bc}$ if possible.

EXAMPLE 4 — Dividing Rational Expressions

Find the quotient $\dfrac{7x}{2x-10} \div \dfrac{-x^2+6x}{x^2-11x+30}$.

$\dfrac{7x}{2x-10} \div \dfrac{-x^2+6x}{x^2-11x+30} = \dfrac{7x}{2x-10} \cdot \dfrac{x^2-11x+30}{-x^2+6x} \qquad$ Multiply by reciprocal.

$\qquad = \dfrac{7x}{2(x-5)} \cdot \dfrac{(x-5)(x-6)}{-1x(x-6)} \qquad$ Factor.

$\qquad = \dfrac{7x(x-5)(x-6)}{2(x-5)(-1x)(x-6)} \qquad$ Multiply. Divide out common factors.

$\qquad = -\dfrac{7}{2}, \quad x \neq 0,\, x \neq 5,\, x \neq 6 \qquad$ Simplified form

▶ So, the quotient is $-\dfrac{7}{2}$, $x \neq 0$, $x \neq 5$, $x \neq 6$.

EXAMPLE 5 — Dividing a Rational Expression by a Polynomial

Find the quotient $\dfrac{6x^2+x-15}{4x^2} \div (3x^2+5x)$.

$\dfrac{6x^2+x-15}{4x^2} \div (3x^2+5x) = \dfrac{6x^2+x-15}{4x^2} \cdot \dfrac{1}{3x^2+5x} \qquad$ Multiply by reciprocal.

$\qquad = \dfrac{(3x+5)(2x-3)}{4x^2} \cdot \dfrac{1}{x(3x+5)} \qquad$ Factor.

$\qquad = \dfrac{(3x+5)(2x-3)}{4x^2(x)(3x+5)} \qquad$ Multiply. Divide out common factor.

$\qquad = \dfrac{2x-3}{4x^3}, \quad x \neq -\dfrac{5}{3} \qquad$ Simplified form

▶ So, the quotient is $\dfrac{2x-3}{4x^3}$, $x \neq -\dfrac{5}{3}$.

In-Class Practice

Self-Assessment

6. Find (a) $\dfrac{4x}{5x-20} \div \dfrac{x^2-2x}{x^2-6x+8}$ and (b) $\dfrac{2x^2+3x-5}{6x} \div (2x^2+5x)$.

1 I don't understand yet.   **2** I can do it with help.   **3** I can do it on my own.   **4** I can teach someone.

Connections to Real Life

EXAMPLE 6 **Evaluating a Rational Expression**

The total amount E (in millions of dollars) of healthcare expenditures and the residential population P (in millions) of the United States can be modeled by

$$E = \frac{75{,}382t + 1{,}469{,}400}{1 - 0.013t} \quad \text{and} \quad P = 2.418t + 281.41$$

where t represents the number of years since 2000. Estimate the annual healthcare expenditures per resident in 2025.

Find a model M for the annual healthcare expenditures per resident by dividing the total amount E by the population P.

$M = \dfrac{75{,}382t + 1{,}469{,}400}{1 - 0.013t} \div (2.418t + 281.41)$ Divide E by P.

$= \dfrac{75{,}382t + 1{,}469{,}400}{1 - 0.013t} \cdot \dfrac{1}{2.418t + 281.41}$ Multiply by reciprocal.

$= \dfrac{75{,}382t + 1{,}469{,}400}{(1 - 0.013t)(2.418t + 281.41)}$ Multiply.

To estimate the annual healthcare expenditures per resident in 2025, let $t = 25$ in the model.

$M = \dfrac{75{,}382 \cdot 25 + 1{,}469{,}400}{(1 - 0.013 \cdot 25)(2.418 \cdot 25 + 281.41)}$ Substitute 25 for t.

$\approx 14{,}535$ Use technology.

▶ In 2025, the model predicts annual healthcare expenditures of about $14,535 per resident.

> **Check** Evaluate each equation. Then divide.
>
> $E = \dfrac{75{,}382 \cdot 25 + 1{,}469{,}400}{1 - 0.013 \cdot 25} \approx 4{,}968{,}815$
>
> $P = 2.418 \cdot 25 + 281.41 = 341.86$
>
> $\dfrac{4{,}968{,}815}{341.86} \approx 14{,}535$ ✓

In-Class Practice
Self-Assessment

7. WHAT IF? In Example 6, estimate the annual healthcare expenditures per resident in 2025 when $P = -0.029t^2 + 3.07t + 278.8$.

7.3 Multiplying and Dividing Rational Expressions

7.3 Practice

Simplify the expression, if possible. (See Example 1.)

1. $\dfrac{2x^2}{3x^2 - 4x}$

2. $\dfrac{x^2 - 3x - 18}{x^2 - 7x + 6}$

3. $\dfrac{x^2 + 13x + 36}{x^2 - 7x + 10}$

4. $\dfrac{x^2 + 11x + 18}{x^3 + 8}$

5. **SMP.3 ERROR ANALYSIS** Describe and correct the error in simplifying the rational expression.

$$\require{cancel}\dfrac{x^2 + \overset{2}{\cancel{16}}x + \overset{3}{\cancel{48}}}{x^2 + \underset{1}{\cancel{8}}x + \underset{1}{\cancel{16}}} = \dfrac{x^2 + 2x + 3}{x^2 + x + 1}$$

Find the product. (See Examples 2 and 3.)

6. $\dfrac{4xy^3}{x^2 y} \cdot \dfrac{y}{8x}$

7. $\dfrac{x^2 - 3x}{x - 2} \cdot \dfrac{x^2 + x - 6}{x}$

8. $\dfrac{x^2 - 4x}{x - 1} \cdot \dfrac{x^2 + 3x - 4}{2x}$

9. $\dfrac{x^2 + 3x - 4}{x^2 + 4x + 4} \cdot \dfrac{2x^2 + 4x}{x^2 - 4x + 3}$

10. $\dfrac{x^2 - x - 6}{4x^3} \cdot \dfrac{2x^2 + 2x}{x^2 + 5x + 6}$

11. $\dfrac{x^2 - x - 12}{x^2 - 16} \cdot (x^2 + 2x - 8)$

12. **SMP.3 ERROR ANALYSIS** Describe and correct the error in finding the product.

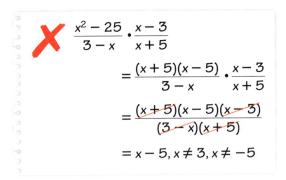

Find the quotient. (See Examples 4 and 5.)

13. $\dfrac{32x^3 y}{y^8} \div \dfrac{y^7}{8x^4}$

14. $\dfrac{2xyz}{x^3 z^3} \div \dfrac{6y^4}{2x^2 z^2}$

15. $\dfrac{x^2 - x - 6}{2x^4 - 6x^3} \div \dfrac{x + 2}{4x^3}$

16. $\dfrac{2x^2 - 12x}{x^2 - 7x + 6} \div \dfrac{2x}{3x - 3}$

17. $\dfrac{x^2 - 5x - 36}{x + 2} \div (x^2 - 18x + 81)$

18. $\dfrac{x^2 + 9x + 18}{x^2 + 6x + 8} \div \dfrac{x^2 - 3x - 18}{x^2 + 2x - 8}$

372 Chapter 7 Rational Functions

19. **CONNECTION TO REAL LIFE** The total amount S (in millions of dollars) of revenue and the number of users U (in millions) of a social media platform is modeled by

$$S = \frac{293t - 62}{1 - 0.16t} \quad \text{and} \quad U = 88.5t + 144$$

where t represents the number of years since January 1, 2018. Estimate the revenue per user after 5 years. (See Example 6.)

20. **SMP.2** Refer to the model for the number of users in Exercise 19.

    a. Interpret the meaning of the coefficient of t.
    b. Interpret the meaning of the constant term.

21. **SMP.7** Find the expression that makes the following statement true. Assume $x \neq -2$ and $x \neq 5$.

$$\frac{x - 5}{x^2 + 2x - 35} \div \frac{\boxed{}}{x^2 - 3x - 10} = \frac{x + 2}{x + 7}$$

22. **SMP.5** Complete the table for the function $y = \frac{x + 4}{x^2 - 16}$. Then use technology to explain the behavior of the function at $x = -4$.

x	−3.5	−3.8	−3.9	−4.1	−4.2
y					

23. Use the graphs of f and g to determine the excluded values of each function.

    a. $h(x) = (fg)(x)$

    b. $k(x) = \left(\dfrac{f}{g}\right)(x)$

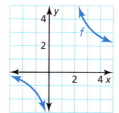
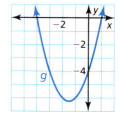

24. **SMP.1 DIG DEEPER** Is it possible to write two radical functions whose product represents a parabola and whose quotient represents a hyperbola? Justify your answer.

25. Find two rational functions f and g that have the stated product and quotient before considering domain restrictions.

$$(fg)(x) = x^2; \quad \left(\frac{f}{g}\right)(x) = \frac{(x-1)^2}{(x+2)^2}$$

26. **SMP.1 PERFORMANCE TASK** Animals can better conserve body heat as their surface area to volume ratios decrease.

    a. Explain which penguin shown is better equipped to live in a colder climate.
    b. Research other factors that influence the survival of penguins in cold climates. How do these factors support or change your answer?

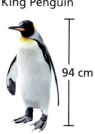

Galapagos Penguin — 53 cm, radius = 6 cm

King Penguin — 94 cm, radius = 11 cm

Not drawn to scale

Interpreting Data

BASKETBALL TOURNAMENT In a basketball tournament, 32 teams compete for a championship. After each round, only the winners move to the next round. Tournament organizers prepare for 100 people to attend each game in the first round, and for the number of people attending each game to vary inversely with the number of games played in a given round.

Tournament Bracket

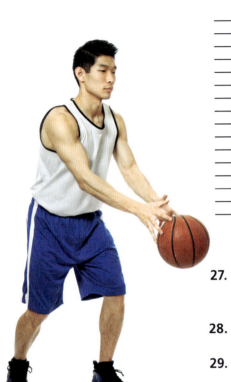

27. Let y be the anticipated attendance per game when n games are played in a round. Write y as a function of n.

28. Sketch the graph of the function $y = f(n)$. What type of function is f?

29. Explain the domain and range of f in this context.

Review & Refresh

30. The number N (in hundreds) of active cell phones of a particular model after t years can be modeled by

    $N = 0.622t^3 + 0.31t^2 - 1.1t + 20$

    where $0 \leq t \leq 12$. After how many years are there 10,000 active phones?

31. Determine the type of function represented by the data.

x	0	2	4	6	8
y	1	2	4	8	16

Graph the function. Find the domain and range.

32. $f(x) = \dfrac{x+1}{x-1}$

33. $y = \dfrac{-2x+5}{-x+10}$

34. Write an exponential growth function represented by the graph.

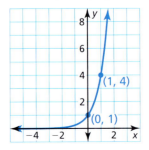

374 Chapter 7 Rational Functions

7.4 Adding and Subtracting Rational Expressions

Learning Target: Add and subtract rational expressions.

Success Criteria:
- I can add and subtract rational expressions with like denominators.
- I can explain how to find a common denominator for rational expressions.
- I can add and subtract rational expressions with unlike denominators.

INVESTIGATE Adding and Subtracting Rational Expressions

Work with a partner.

1. Explain how to find each sum or difference.

   a. $\frac{3}{8} + \frac{1}{8}$ **b.** $\frac{9}{10} - \frac{3}{10}$

   c. $\frac{1}{2} + \frac{3}{4}$ **d.** $\frac{5}{8} - \frac{7}{12}$

2. You can add and subtract rational expressions in the same way that you add and subtract fractions. Find each sum or difference. Explain your methods.

Expression	Sum or Difference
$\frac{3}{x} + \frac{1}{x}$	
$\frac{9}{x} - \frac{3}{x}$	
$\frac{1}{x} + \frac{3}{2x}$	
$\frac{5}{x+1} - \frac{7}{x+1}$	
$\frac{7}{x+2} + \frac{3}{x-4}$	
$\frac{4}{x+1} - \frac{3x-3}{x^2-1}$	

3. Explain whether it is necessary to restrict the domain for any of the sums or differences in Exercise 2.

4. Explain whether the set of rational expressions is closed under addition and subtraction.

> **Vocabulary**
> complex fraction

Adding or Subtracting Rational Expressions

The procedure to add or subtract rational expressions depends upon whether the expressions have like or unlike denominators.

Key Concept

Adding or Subtracting Rational Expressions

Let a, b, c, and d be expressions with $c \neq 0$ and $d \neq 0$.

Addition	Subtraction
$\dfrac{a}{c} + \dfrac{b}{c} = \dfrac{a + b}{c}$	$\dfrac{a}{c} - \dfrac{b}{c} = \dfrac{a - b}{c}$
$\dfrac{a}{c} + \dfrac{b}{d} = \dfrac{ad}{cd} + \dfrac{bc}{cd} = \dfrac{ad + bc}{cd}$	$\dfrac{a}{c} - \dfrac{b}{d} = \dfrac{ad}{cd} - \dfrac{bc}{cd} = \dfrac{ad - bc}{cd}$

You can always find a common denominator of rational expressions by multiplying the denominators. However, when you use the least common denominator (LCD), which is the least common multiple (LCM) of the denominators, simplifying your answer may take fewer steps.

EXAMPLE 1 Adding or Subtracting with Like Denominators

Find (a) the sum $\dfrac{7}{4x} + \dfrac{3}{4x}$ and (b) the difference $\dfrac{2x}{x+6} - \dfrac{5}{x+6}$.

a. $\dfrac{7}{4x} + \dfrac{3}{4x} = \dfrac{7+3}{4x} = \dfrac{10}{4x} = \dfrac{5}{2x}$ Add numerators and simplify.

b. $\dfrac{2x}{x+6} - \dfrac{5}{x+6} = \dfrac{2x-5}{x+6}$ Subtract numerators.

EXAMPLE 2 Finding a Least Common Multiple (LCM)

Find the least common multiple of $4x^2 - 16$ and $6x^2 - 24x + 24$.

Factor each polynomial. Write numerical factors as products of primes.

$$4x^2 - 16 = 4(x^2 - 4) = (2^2)(x+2)(x-2)$$
$$6x^2 - 24x + 24 = 6(x^2 - 4x + 4) = (2)(3)(x-2)^2$$

The LCM is the product of the highest power of each factor that appears in either polynomial.

$$\text{LCM} = (2^2)(3)(x+2)(x-2)^2 = 12(x+2)(x-2)^2$$

In-Class Practice

Self-Assessment

1. Find (a) the sum $\dfrac{2}{3x^2} + \dfrac{1}{3x^2}$ and (b) the difference $\dfrac{4x}{x-2} - \dfrac{x}{x-2}$.

2. Find the least common multiple of $5x$ and $5x - 10$.

EXAMPLE 3 Adding with Unlike Denominators

Find the sum $\dfrac{7}{9x^2} + \dfrac{x}{3x^2 + 3x}$.

Find the LCD by finding the LCM of the denominators, then add. Note that $9x^2 = 3^2 x^2$ and $3x^2 + 3x = 3x(x + 1)$, so the LCD is $(3^2)(x^2)(x + 1) = 9x^2(x + 1)$.

$$\dfrac{7}{9x^2} + \dfrac{x}{3x^2 + 3x} = \dfrac{7}{9x^2} + \dfrac{x}{3x(x + 1)}$$ Factor second denominator.

$$= \dfrac{7}{9x^2} \cdot \dfrac{x + 1}{x + 1} + \dfrac{x}{3x(x + 1)} \cdot \dfrac{3x}{3x}$$ LCD is $9x^2(x + 1)$.

$$= \dfrac{7x + 7}{9x^2(x + 1)} + \dfrac{3x^2}{9x^2(x + 1)}$$ Multiply.

$$= \dfrac{3x^2 + 7x + 7}{9x^2(x + 1)}$$ Add numerators.

EXAMPLE 4 Subtracting with Unlike Denominators

Find the difference $\dfrac{x + 2}{2x - 2} - \dfrac{-2x - 1}{x^2 - 4x + 3}$.

$$\dfrac{x + 2}{2x - 2} - \dfrac{-2x - 1}{x^2 - 4x + 3} = \dfrac{x + 2}{2(x - 1)} - \dfrac{-2x - 1}{(x - 1)(x - 3)}$$ Factor each denominator.

$$= \dfrac{x + 2}{2(x - 1)} \cdot \dfrac{x - 3}{x - 3} - \dfrac{-2x - 1}{(x - 1)(x - 3)} \cdot \dfrac{2}{2}$$ LCD is $2(x - 1)(x - 3)$.

$$= \dfrac{x^2 - x - 6}{2(x - 1)(x - 3)} - \dfrac{-4x - 2}{2(x - 1)(x - 3)}$$ Multiply.

$$= \dfrac{x^2 - x - 6 - (-4x - 2)}{2(x - 1)(x - 3)}$$ Subtract numerators.

$$= \dfrac{x^2 + 3x - 4}{2(x - 1)(x - 3)}$$ Simplify numerator.

$$= \dfrac{(x - 1)(x + 4)}{2(x - 1)(x - 3)}$$ Factor numerator.

$$= \dfrac{\cancel{(x - 1)}(x + 4)}{2\cancel{(x - 1)}(x - 3)}$$ Divide out common factor

$$= \dfrac{x + 4}{2(x - 3)}, \quad x \neq 1$$ Simplify.

In-Class Practice

Self-Assessment

Find the sum or difference.

3. $\dfrac{1}{3x^2} + \dfrac{x}{9x^2 - 12}$

4. $\dfrac{3}{4x} - \dfrac{1}{7}$

5. $\dfrac{9}{x - 3} + \dfrac{2x}{x + 1}$

6. $\dfrac{x^2 - 5}{x^2 + 5x - 14} - \dfrac{x + 3}{x + 7}$

 I don't understand yet.   I can do it with help.   I can do it on my own.   I can teach someone.

7.4   Adding and Subtracting Rational Expressions

Rewriting Rational Functions

Rewriting a rational function may reveal properties of the function and its graph. In Example 4 of Section 7.2, you used long division to rewrite a rational function. In the next example, you will use inspection.

EXAMPLE 5 Rewriting and Graphing a Rational Function

Rewrite $g(x) = \dfrac{3x + 5}{x + 1}$ in the form $g(x) = \dfrac{a}{x - h} + k$. Graph the function. Describe the graph of g as a transformation of the graph of $f(x) = \dfrac{a}{x}$.

Rewrite by inspection.

$\dfrac{3x + 5}{x + 1} = \dfrac{3x + 3 + 2}{x + 1}$ Rewrite numerator.

$= \dfrac{3(x + 1) + 2}{x + 1}$ Factor numerator.

$= \dfrac{3(x + 1)}{x + 1} + \dfrac{2}{x + 1}$ Rewrite as the sum of two fractions.

$= \dfrac{3(\cancel{x + 1})}{\cancel{x + 1}} + \dfrac{2}{x + 1}$ Divide out common factor.

$= 3 + \dfrac{2}{x + 1}$ Simplify.

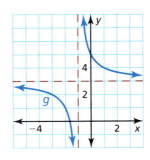

▶ The rewritten function is $g(x) = \dfrac{2}{x + 1} + 3$. The graph of g is a translation 1 unit left and 3 units up of the graph of $f(x) = \dfrac{2}{x}$.

In-Class Practice

Self-Assessment

Rewrite the function in the form $g(x) = \dfrac{a}{x - h} + k$. Graph the function. Describe the graph of g as a transformation of the graph of $f(x) = \dfrac{a}{x}$.

7. $g(x) = \dfrac{2x - 4}{x - 3}$

8. $g(x) = \dfrac{8x}{x + 13}$

Complex Fractions

A **complex fraction** is a fraction that contains a fraction in its numerator or denominator. A complex fraction can be simplified using either of the methods below.

Method 1 If necessary, simplify the numerator and denominator by writing each as a single fraction. Then divide by multiplying the numerator by the reciprocal of the denominator.

Method 2 Multiply the numerator and the denominator by the LCD of *every* fraction in the numerator and denominator. Then simplify.

EXAMPLE 6 Simplifying a Complex Fraction

Simplify $\dfrac{\dfrac{5}{x+4}}{\dfrac{1}{x+4} + \dfrac{2}{x}}$.

Method 1

$\dfrac{\dfrac{5}{x+4}}{\dfrac{1}{x+4} + \dfrac{2}{x}} = \dfrac{\dfrac{5}{x+4}}{\dfrac{3x+8}{x(x+4)}}$ Add fractions in denominator.

$= \dfrac{5}{x+4} \cdot \dfrac{x(x+4)}{3x+8}$ Multiply by reciprocal.

$= \dfrac{5x(x+4)}{(x+4)(3x+8)}$ Multiply. Divide out common factors.

$= \dfrac{5x}{3x+8}, \quad x \neq -4, x \neq 0$ Simplify.

Method 2 The LCD of the numerator and denominator is $x(x+4)$.

$\dfrac{\dfrac{5}{x+4}}{\dfrac{1}{x+4} + \dfrac{2}{x}} = \dfrac{\dfrac{5}{x+4}}{\dfrac{1}{x+4} + \dfrac{2}{x}} \cdot \dfrac{x(x+4)}{x(x+4)}$ Multiply numerator and denominator by the LCD.

$= \dfrac{\dfrac{5}{x+4} \cdot x(x+4)}{\dfrac{1}{x+4} \cdot x(x+4) + \dfrac{2}{x} \cdot x(x+4)}$ Multiply. Divide out common factors.

$= \dfrac{5x}{x + 2(x+4)}$ Simplify.

$= \dfrac{5x}{3x+8}, \quad x \neq -4, x \neq 0$ Simplify.

In-Class Practice

Self-Assessment

9. Simplify $\dfrac{\dfrac{x}{6} - \dfrac{x}{3}}{\dfrac{x}{5} - \dfrac{7}{10}}$.

7.4 Practice

Find the sum or difference. (See Example 1.)

1. $\dfrac{15}{4x} + \dfrac{5}{4x}$

2. $\dfrac{9}{16x^2} - \dfrac{4}{16x^2}$

3. $\dfrac{9}{x+1} - \dfrac{2x}{x+1}$

4. $\dfrac{3x^2}{x-8} + \dfrac{6x}{x-8}$

Find the least common multiple of the expressions. (See Example 2.)

5. $3x,\ 3(x-2)$

6. $2x,\ 2(x+6)$

7. $2x^2 - 18,\ x^2 + x - 12$

8. $x^2 + 3x - 40,\ x - 8$

Find the sum or difference. (See Examples 3 and 4.)

9. $\dfrac{12}{5x} - \dfrac{7}{6x}$

10. $\dfrac{8}{3x} + \dfrac{5}{4x}$

11. $\dfrac{3}{x+4} - \dfrac{1}{x+6}$

12. $\dfrac{12}{x^2 + 5x - 24} + \dfrac{3}{x-3}$

13. **ERROR ANALYSIS** Describe and correct the error in finding the sum.

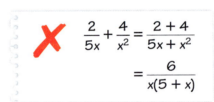

$$\cancel{}\ \dfrac{2}{5x} + \dfrac{4}{x^2} = \dfrac{2+4}{5x + x^2} = \dfrac{6}{x(5+x)}$$

Rewrite the function in the form $g(x) = \dfrac{a}{x-h} + k$. Graph the function. Describe the graph of g as a transformation of the graph of $f(x) = \dfrac{a}{x}$. (See Example 5.)

14. $g(x) = \dfrac{12x}{x-5}$

15. $g(x) = \dfrac{5x-7}{x-1}$

16. $g(x) = \dfrac{2x+3}{x}$

17. $g(x) = \dfrac{3x+11}{x-3}$

Simplify the complex fraction. (See Example 6.)

18. $\dfrac{\dfrac{16}{x-2}}{\dfrac{4}{x+1} + \dfrac{6}{x}}$

19. $\dfrac{\dfrac{x}{3} - 6}{10 + \dfrac{4}{x}}$

20. $\dfrac{\dfrac{1}{2x-5} - \dfrac{7}{8x-20}}{\dfrac{x}{2x-5}}$

21. $\dfrac{\dfrac{3}{x-2} - \dfrac{6}{x^2-4}}{\dfrac{3}{x+2} + \dfrac{1}{x-2}}$

22. **CONNECTION TO REAL LIFE** The total time T (in hours) needed to fly from New York to Los Angeles and back can be modeled by the equation below, where d is the distance (in miles) each way, a is the average airplane speed (in miles per hour), and j is the average speed (in miles per hour) of the jet stream. Simplify the equation. Then find the total time it takes to fly 2,468 miles when $a = 510$ and $j = 115$.

$$T = \frac{d}{a-j} + \frac{d}{a+j}$$

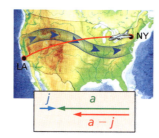
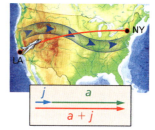

23. **SMP.6** Explain whether the statement is *always*, *sometimes*, or *never* true.

    a. The LCD of two rational expressions is the product of the denominators.

    b. The LCD of two rational expressions will have a degree greater than or equal to that of the denominator with the higher degree.

24. **3-D PRINTING** **MANUFACTURING** One 3-D printer creates 10% of a medical instrument in one minute. Another 3-D printer takes x minutes to create the same instrument. Write an expression for the number of instruments the two printers create in one full hour.

STEM Video: 3-D Printing

25. Is the result of adding or subtracting two rational expressions always a rational expression? Use two examples of each operation to justify your answer.

26. **SMP.8** Find the next two expressions in the pattern. Then evaluate all five expressions. What value do the expressions approach?

$$1 + \cfrac{1}{2 + \cfrac{1}{2}}, \ 1 + \cfrac{1}{2 + \cfrac{1}{2 + \cfrac{1}{2}}}, \ 1 + \cfrac{1}{2 + \cfrac{1}{2 + \cfrac{1}{2 + \cfrac{1}{2}}}}, \ \ldots$$

27. **SMP.1 DIG DEEPER** The amount A (in milligrams) of aspirin in a person's bloodstream is modeled by

$$A = \frac{391t^2 + 0.112}{0.218t^4 + 0.991t^2 + 1}$$

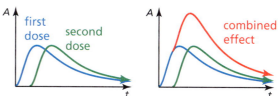

where t is the time (in hours) after one dose is taken. A second dose is taken 1 hour after the first dose. Write an equation for the total amount of aspirin in the bloodstream after the second dose is taken. Justify your answer.

Interpreting Data

PHYTOPLANKTON The Shannon index is a measurement of the species diversity in an ecosystem. A researcher studying phytoplankton took samples from a reservoir. The graph shows the phytoplankton abundance and the value of the Shannon index for each sample.

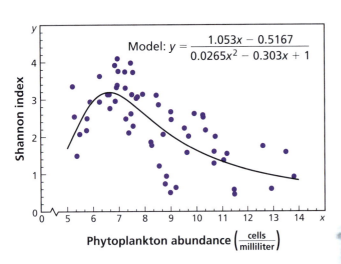

28. Write the model as the difference of two rational functions.

29. Research how global phytoplankton populations have changed over time. How does this affect the environment?

Review & Refresh

30. Tell whether x and y show *direct variation*, *inverse variation*, or *neither*.

x	6	8	10	12	14
y	15	20	25	30	35

31. Simplify the expression.

$$\frac{xy^3}{x^2} \div \frac{y^4}{x^3}$$

32. An app store sells 60 apps each day and charges $8.00 per download. For each $0.50 decrease in price, the store sells 10 more apps. How much should the store charge to maximize daily revenue?

33. Solve $\left|\dfrac{x}{3}\right| = 3$.

34. Write an equation of the parabola.

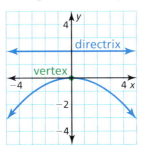

35. Graph the inequality.

$$y \geq 2x^2 - 5x - 3$$

7.5 Solving Rational Equations

Learning Target: Solve rational equations.

Success Criteria:
- I can solve rational equations by cross multiplying and by using least common denominators.
- I can identify extraneous solutions of rational equations.
- I can solve real-life problems using inverses of rational functions.

INVESTIGATE Solving Rational Equations

Work with a partner.

1. **MATCHING** Match each equation with its related graph. Then use the graph to approximate the solution(s) of the equation.

   a. $\dfrac{2}{x-1} = 1$
   b. $\dfrac{-x-1}{x-3} = x+1$

   c. $\dfrac{1}{x} = x^2$
   d. $\dfrac{1}{x} = \dfrac{-1}{x-2}$

   A.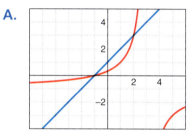

   C.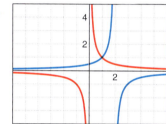

   B.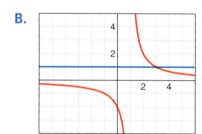

   D.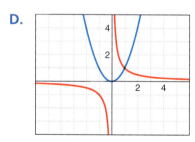

2. Solve $\dfrac{3}{4} = \dfrac{8}{x}$ algebraically. Then solve the rational equations in Exercise 1 using the same algebraic method. Compare your answers with your approximations in Exercise 1.

3. A student solves $\dfrac{5x}{x^2 - 4} = \dfrac{3}{x+2}$ as shown. Explain the student's method. Then explain whether the answer is correct.

   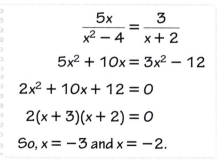

   $$\dfrac{5x}{x^2 - 4} = \dfrac{3}{x+2}$$
   $$5x^2 + 10x = 3x^2 - 12$$
   $$2x^2 + 10x + 12 = 0$$
   $$2(x+3)(x+2) = 0$$
   So, $x = -3$ and $x = -2$.

Solving by Cross Multiplying

EXAMPLE 1 Solving a Rational Equation by Cross Multiplying

Solve $\dfrac{3}{x+1} = \dfrac{9}{4x+5}$.

$\dfrac{3}{x+1} = \dfrac{9}{4x+5}$	Write original equation.
$3(4x+5) = 9(x+1)$	Cross multiply.
$12x + 15 = 9x + 9$	Distributive Property
$3x + 15 = 9$	Subtract $9x$ from each side.
$3x = -6$	Subtract 15 from each side.
$x = -2$	Divide each side by 3.

▶ The solution is $x = -2$. Check this in the original equation.

Check

$\dfrac{3}{-2+1} \stackrel{?}{=} \dfrac{9}{4(-2)+5}$

$\dfrac{3}{-1} \stackrel{?}{=} \dfrac{9}{-3}$

$-3 = -3$ ✓

EXAMPLE 2 Writing and Solving a Rational Equation

Sterling silver is an *alloy* composed of 92.5% silver and 7.5% copper by weight. You have 15 ounces of 800 grade silver, which is 80% silver and 20% copper by weight. How much pure silver should you mix with the 800 grade silver to make sterling silver?

percent of copper in mixture = $\dfrac{\text{weight of copper in mixture}}{\text{total weight of mixture}}$

$\dfrac{7.5}{100} = \dfrac{(0.2)(15)}{15 + x}$	x is the amount of silver added.
$7.5(15 + x) = 100(0.2)(15)$	Cross multiply.
$112.5 + 7.5x = 300$	Simplify.
$7.5x = 187.5$	Subtract 112.5 from each side.
$x = 25$	Divide each side by 7.5.

▶ You should mix 25 ounces of pure silver with the 15 ounces of 800 grade silver.

In-Class Practice

Self-Assessment

Solve the equation by cross multiplying.

1. $\dfrac{3}{5x} = \dfrac{2}{x-7}$

2. $\dfrac{1}{2x+5} = \dfrac{x}{11x+8}$

3. **WHAT IF?** You have 12 ounces of an alloy that is 90% silver and 10% copper by weight. How much pure silver should you mix with the alloy to make sterling silver?

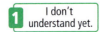 I don't understand yet.   I can do it with help.   I can do it on my own.   I can teach someone.

Solving by Using the Least Common Denominator

EXAMPLE 3 Solving Rational Equations by Using the LCD

a. Solve $\dfrac{5}{x} + \dfrac{7}{4} = -\dfrac{9}{x}$.

Check
$\dfrac{5}{-8} + \dfrac{7}{4} \stackrel{?}{=} -\dfrac{9}{-8}$
$-\dfrac{5}{8} + \dfrac{14}{8} \stackrel{?}{=} \dfrac{9}{8}$
$\dfrac{9}{8} = \dfrac{9}{8}$ ✓

$\dfrac{5}{x} + \dfrac{7}{4} = -\dfrac{9}{x}$	Write original equation.
$4x\left(\dfrac{5}{x} + \dfrac{7}{4}\right) = 4x\left(-\dfrac{9}{x}\right)$	Multiply each side by the LCD, $4x$.
$20 + 7x = -36$	Simplify.
$7x = -56$	Subtract 20 from each side.
$x = -8$	Divide each side by 7.

▶ The solution is $x = -8$. Check this in the original equation.

b. Solve $1 - \dfrac{8}{x-5} = \dfrac{3}{x}$.

$1 - \dfrac{8}{x-5} = \dfrac{3}{x}$	Write original equation.
$x(x-5)\left(1 - \dfrac{8}{x-5}\right) = x(x-5) \cdot \dfrac{3}{x}$	Multiply each side by the LCD, $x(x-5)$.
$x(x-5) - 8x = 3(x-5)$	Simplify.
$x^2 - 5x - 8x = 3x - 15$	Distributive Property
$x^2 - 16x + 15 = 0$	Write in standard form.
$(x-1)(x-15) = 0$	Factor.
$x = 1$ or $x = 15$	Zero-Product Property

▶ The solutions are $x = 1$ and $x = 15$. Check these in the original equation.

Check

$1 - \dfrac{8}{1-5} \stackrel{?}{=} \dfrac{3}{1}$ Substitute for x. $1 - \dfrac{8}{15-5} \stackrel{?}{=} \dfrac{3}{15}$

$1 + 2 \stackrel{?}{=} 3$ Simplify. $1 - \dfrac{4}{5} \stackrel{?}{=} \dfrac{1}{5}$

$3 = 3$ ✓ $\dfrac{1}{5} = \dfrac{1}{5}$ ✓

In-Class Practice

Self-Assessment

Solve the equation by using the LCD.

4. $\dfrac{15}{x} + \dfrac{4}{5} = \dfrac{7}{x}$

5. $\dfrac{3x}{x+1} - \dfrac{5}{2x} = \dfrac{3}{2x}$

 1 I don't understand yet.   2 I can do it with help.   3 I can do it on my own.   4 I can teach someone.

EXAMPLE 4 Solving an Equation with an Extraneous Solution

Solve $\dfrac{6}{x-3} = \dfrac{8x^2}{x^2-9} - \dfrac{4x}{x+3}$.

Write each denominator in factored form. The LCD is $(x+3)(x-3)$.

$$\dfrac{6}{x-3} = \dfrac{8x^2}{(x+3)(x-3)} - \dfrac{4x}{x+3}$$

$$(x+3)(x-3) \cdot \dfrac{6}{x-3} = (x+3)(x-3) \cdot \dfrac{8x^2}{(x+3)(x-3)} - (x+3)(x-3) \cdot \dfrac{4x}{x+3}$$

$$6(x+3) = 8x^2 - 4x(x-3)$$

$$6x + 18 = 8x^2 - 4x^2 + 12x$$

$$0 = 4x^2 + 6x - 18$$

$$0 = 2x^2 + 3x - 9$$

$$0 = (2x-3)(x+3)$$

$$2x - 3 = 0 \quad \text{or} \quad x + 3 = 0$$

$$x = \dfrac{3}{2} \quad \text{or} \quad x = -3$$

Check

Check $x = \dfrac{3}{2}$:

$$\dfrac{6}{\frac{3}{2} - 3} \stackrel{?}{=} \dfrac{8\left(\frac{3}{2}\right)^2}{\left(\frac{3}{2}\right)^2 - 9} - \dfrac{4\left(\frac{3}{2}\right)}{\frac{3}{2} + 3}$$

$$\dfrac{6}{-\frac{3}{2}} \stackrel{?}{=} \dfrac{18}{-\frac{27}{4}} - \dfrac{6}{\frac{9}{2}}$$

$$-4 \stackrel{?}{=} -\dfrac{8}{3} - \dfrac{4}{3}$$

$$-4 = -4 \checkmark$$

Check $x = -3$:

$$\dfrac{6}{-3 - 3} \stackrel{?}{=} \dfrac{8(-3)^2}{(-3)^2 - 9} - \dfrac{4(-3)}{-3 + 3}$$

$$\dfrac{6}{-6} \stackrel{?}{=} \dfrac{72}{0} - \dfrac{-12}{0} \quad ✗$$

Division by zero is undefined.

▶ The apparent solution $x = -3$ is extraneous. So, the only solution is $x = \dfrac{3}{2}$.

In-Class Practice

Self-Assessment

Solve the equation.

6. $\dfrac{3}{x-1} - 1 = \dfrac{6}{x^2 - 1}$

7. $\dfrac{9}{x-2} + \dfrac{6x}{x+2} = \dfrac{9x^2}{x^2 - 4}$

Using Inverses of Functions

EXAMPLE 5 **Finding the Inverse of a Rational Function**

Consider the function $f(x) = \dfrac{2}{x+3}$. Determine whether the inverse of f is a function. Then find the inverse.

Graph the function f. Notice that no horizontal line intersects the graph more than once. So, the inverse of f is a function. Find the inverse.

Check

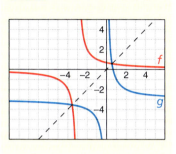

$$y = \dfrac{2}{x+3} \quad \text{Set } y \text{ equal to } f(x).$$

$$x = \dfrac{2}{y+3} \quad \text{Switch } x \text{ and } y.$$

$$x(y+3) = 2 \quad \text{Cross multiply.}$$

$$y + 3 = \dfrac{2}{x} \quad \text{Divide each side by } x.$$

$$y = \dfrac{2}{x} - 3 \quad \text{Subtract 3 from each side.}$$

▶ So, the inverse of f is $f^{-1}(x) = \dfrac{2}{x} - 3$.

EXAMPLE 6 **Using a Rational Function**

In Section 7.2 Example 5, you wrote the function $c(x) = \dfrac{50x + 1{,}000}{x}$ to represent the average cost (in dollars) of making x prosthetic hands using a 3-D printer. How many hands must be printed for the average cost per hand to fall to $90?

Method 1 Substitute 90 for $c(x)$ and solve.

$$90 = \dfrac{50x + 1{,}000}{x}$$

$$90x = 50x + 1{,}000$$

$$40x = 1{,}000$$

$$x = 25$$

Method 2 Find $c^{-1}(x)$. Then evaluate $c^{-1}(90)$.

$$y = \dfrac{50x + 1{,}000}{x} \quad \text{Set } y \text{ equal to } c(x).$$

$$x = \dfrac{50y + 1{,}000}{y} \quad \text{Switch } x \text{ and } y.$$

$$xy = 50y + 1{,}000 \quad \text{Cross multiply.}$$

$$y = \dfrac{1{,}000}{x - 50} \quad \text{Solve for } y.$$

The inverse of c is $c^{-1}(x) = \dfrac{1{,}000}{x - 50}$.

$$c^{-1}(90) = \dfrac{1{,}000}{90 - 50} = 25$$

▶ So, the average cost falls to $90 per hand after 25 hands are printed.

In-Class Practice

Self-Assessment

8. Determine whether the inverse of $f(x) = \dfrac{1}{x} - 2$ is a function. Then find the inverse.

9. **WHAT IF?** How does the answer in Example 6 change when $c(x) = \dfrac{50x + 800}{x}$?

| 1 I don't understand yet. | 2 I can do it with help. | 3 I can do it on my own. | 4 I can teach someone. |

7.5 Practice

Solve the equation by cross multiplying. (See Example 1.)

1. $\dfrac{4}{2x} = \dfrac{5}{x+6}$

2. $\dfrac{8}{3x-2} = \dfrac{2}{x-1}$

3. $\dfrac{x}{2x+7} = \dfrac{x-5}{x-1}$

4. $\dfrac{-1}{x-3} = \dfrac{x-4}{x^2-27}$

5. Brass is an alloy composed of 55% copper and 45% zinc by weight. You have 25 ounces of copper. How many ounces of zinc do you need to make brass? (See Example 2.)

6. You have 0.2 liter of an acid solution whose acid concentration is 16 moles per liter. You want to dilute the solution with water so that its acid concentration is only 12 moles per liter. Use the given model to determine how many liters of water you should add to the solution.

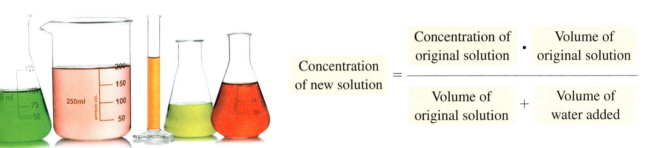

Solve the equation by using the LCD. (See Examples 3 and 4.)

7. $\dfrac{3}{2} + \dfrac{1}{x} = 2$

8. $\dfrac{2}{3x} + \dfrac{1}{6} = \dfrac{4}{3x}$

9. $\dfrac{8}{x-4} + \dfrac{4}{x} = \dfrac{2x}{x-4}$

10. $\dfrac{2}{x-3} + \dfrac{1}{x} = \dfrac{x-1}{x-3}$

11. $\dfrac{18}{x^2-3x} - \dfrac{6}{x-3} = \dfrac{5}{x}$

12. $\dfrac{x+1}{x+6} + \dfrac{1}{x} = \dfrac{2x+1}{x+6}$

13. $\dfrac{x+3}{x-3} + \dfrac{x}{x-5} = \dfrac{x+5}{x-5}$

14. $\dfrac{5}{x} - 2 = \dfrac{2}{x+3}$

15. **SMP.3 ERROR ANALYSIS** Describe and correct the error in the first step of solving the equation.

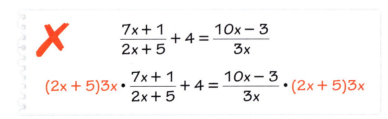

16. **OPEN-ENDED** Give an example of a rational equation that you would solve using cross multiplication and one that you would solve using the LCD. Explain your reasoning.

Determine whether the inverse of *f* is a function. Then find the inverse. (See Example 5.)

17. $f(x) = \dfrac{7}{x+6}$

18. $f(x) = \dfrac{5}{x} - 6$

▶ 19. $f(x) = \dfrac{3}{x} - 2$

20. $f(x) = \dfrac{8}{9+5x}$

21. $f(x) = \dfrac{1}{x^2} + 4$

22. $f(x) = \dfrac{1}{x^4} - 7$

▶ 23. The recommended percentage (in decimal form) of nitrogen (by volume) in the air that a diver breathes is given by

$$p(d) = \dfrac{105.07}{d+33}$$

where *d* is the depth (in feet) of the diver. Find the depth where the air is recommended to contain 47% nitrogen by (a) solving an equation and (b) using the inverse of the function. (See Example 6.)

24. **CONNECT CONCEPTS** In a *golden rectangle*, the ratio of the width *w* to the length ℓ is equal to the ratio of ℓ to $\ell + w$. The ratio of the length to the width for these rectangles is called the golden ratio. Find the value of the golden ratio using a rectangle with a width of 1 unit.

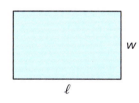

25. **SMP.3** Is it possible to write a rational equation that has the given number of solutions? Justify your answers.

   a. no solution
   b. exactly one solution
   c. exactly two solutions
   d. infinitely many solutions

26. **SMP.1 DIG DEEPER** A kayaker paddles upstream for 2 miles and downstream for 2 miles. The speed of the current is 1 mile per hour. The entire trip takes 2 hours and 40 minutes. Write and solve an equation to find the average speed at which the kayaker paddles.

SMP.7 Find the inverse of the function. (*Hint:* Try rewriting the function by using either inspection or long division.)

27. $f(x) = \dfrac{3x+1}{x-4}$

28. $f(x) = \dfrac{4x-7}{2x+3}$

29. Find the inverse of rational functions of the form

$$f(x) = \dfrac{ax+b}{cx+d}.$$

Verify your answer is correct by using it to find $f^{-1}(x)$ in Exercises 27 and 28.

Interpreting Data

OBLIQUE ASYMPTOTES An oblique asymptote occurs in a rational function when the degree of the denominator is one less than the degree of the numerator. For example, the rational function shown has a numerator of degree 2 and a denominator of degree 1.

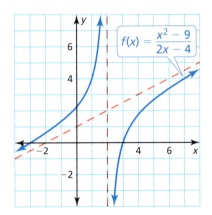

30. Solve $\dfrac{x^2 - 9}{2x - 4} = \dfrac{1}{2}x + 1$. Justify your answer.

31. Research a procedure for finding an equation of an oblique asymptote. Then show how to find an equation of the oblique asymptote for the graph above.

Review & Refresh

32. Let $f(x) = 3x^2 + 1$ and $g(x) = \sqrt{x - 4}$. Find $f(g(8))$ and $g(f(-2))$.

Evaluate the function for the given value of x.

33. $f(x) = x^3 - 2x + 7$; $x = -2$

34. $g(x) = -2x^4 + 7x^3 + x - 2$; $x = 3$

Perform the operation.

35. $\dfrac{x^2}{x + 2} - \dfrac{4}{x + 2}$

36. $\dfrac{x - 1}{-2x + 6} + \dfrac{2x + 3}{x^2 + 3x - 18}$

37. $\dfrac{x^2 + 5x - 14}{4x^3 + 28x^2} \div \dfrac{x - 2}{2x^3}$

38. $\dfrac{2x^2 + 4x}{x^2 - 3x - 10} \cdot \dfrac{x^2 - 8x + 15}{2x}$

Match the function with its graph.

39. $g(x) = \dfrac{-2}{x}$

40. $f(x) = \dfrac{3}{x} + 2$

41. $y = \dfrac{-2}{x + 3} - 2$

42. $h(x) = \dfrac{2x + 2}{3x + 1}$

A.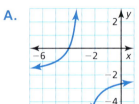

C.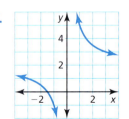

B.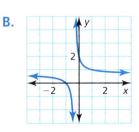

D.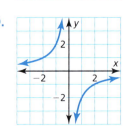

7 Chapter Review

Rate your understanding of each section.

1 I don't understand yet. **2** I can do it with help. **3** I can do it on my own. **4** I can teach someone.

7.1 Inverse Variation *(pp. 353–358)*

Learning Target: Understand inverse variation.

Vocabulary
direct variation
constant of variation
inverse variation

Tell whether x and y show *direct variation*, *inverse variation*, or *neither*.

1. $xy = 5$
2. $5y = 6x$
3. $15 = \dfrac{x}{y}$
4. $y - 3 = 2x$

5.
x	7	11	15	20
y	35	55	75	100

6.
x	5	8	10	20
y	6.4	4	3.2	1.6

The variables x and y vary inversely. Use the given values to write an equation relating x and y. Then find y when $x = -3$.

7. $x = 1, y = 5$
8. $x = -4, y = -6$
9. $x = \dfrac{5}{2}, y = 18$
10. $x = -12, y = \dfrac{2}{3}$

7.2 Graphing Rational Functions *(pp. 359–366)*

Learning Target: Describe and graph rational functions.

Vocabulary
rational function

Graph the function. State the domain and range.

11. $y = \dfrac{4}{x - 3}$
12. $y = \dfrac{1}{x + 5} + 2$
13. $f(x) = \dfrac{3x - 2}{x - 4}$
14. $y = -\dfrac{1}{x} - 1$

15. A teacher orders tablet stands. There is a delivery fee of $10 and each stand costs $2.

   a. How many stands must the teacher buy for the average cost per stand to fall to $2.50?

   b. What happens to the average cost as more stands are ordered?

7.3 Multiplying and Dividing Rational Expressions (pp. 367–374)

⊙ **Learning Target:** Multiply and divide rational expressions.

Vocabulary
rational expression
simplified form of a rational expression

Find the product or quotient.

16. $\dfrac{80x^4}{y^3} \cdot \dfrac{xy}{5x^2}$

17. $\dfrac{x-3}{2x-8} \cdot \dfrac{6x^2 - 96}{x^2 - 9}$

18. $\dfrac{16x^2 - 8x + 1}{x^3 - 7x^2 + 12x} \div \dfrac{20x^2 - 5x}{15x^3}$

19. $\dfrac{x^2 - 13x + 40}{x^2 - 2x - 15} \div (x^2 - 5x - 24)$

20. Find an expression that completes the equation below.

$$\dfrac{3-x}{x^2 + 3x - 18} \div \dfrac{\boxed{}}{x^2 + 7x + 6} = x + 1$$

21. What is the domain of $g(x) = \dfrac{2+x}{8 - 2x^2}$?

7.4 Adding and Subtracting Rational Expressions (pp. 375–382)

⊙ **Learning Target:** Add and subtract rational expressions.

Vocabulary
complex fraction

Find the sum or difference.

22. $\dfrac{5}{6(x+3)} + \dfrac{x+4}{2x}$

23. $\dfrac{5x}{x+8} + \dfrac{4x - 9}{x^2 + 5x - 24}$

24. $\dfrac{x+2}{x^2 + 4x + 3} - \dfrac{5x}{x^2 - 9}$

25. $\dfrac{1}{2} + \dfrac{x^2 + 4}{x - 2}$

Rewrite the function in the form $g(x) = \dfrac{a}{x - h} + k$. Graph the function. Describe the graph of g as a transformation of the graph of $f(x) = \dfrac{a}{x}$.

26. $g(x) = \dfrac{5x + 1}{x - 3}$

27. $g(x) = \dfrac{4x + 2}{x + 7}$

28. Simplify $\dfrac{\dfrac{3}{x+5}}{\dfrac{2}{x-3} + \dfrac{1}{x+5}}$.

29. Members of a student council prepare banners, balloons, and party bags for a celebration. The table shows the rates of completion for the requested materials. Write a model in simplified form for the total time (in minutes) it takes to prepare the materials.

	Number	Rate (objects per minute)
Banners	10	x
Balloons	50	$x - 10$
Party Bags	80	$x + 5$

7.5 Solving Rational Equations (pp. 383–390)

Learning Target: Solve rational equations.

Solve the equation.

30. $\dfrac{5}{x} = \dfrac{7}{x+2}$

31. $\dfrac{8(x-1)}{x^2-4} = \dfrac{4}{x+2}$

32. $\dfrac{2(x+7)}{x+4} - 2 = \dfrac{2x+20}{2x+8}$

33. $\dfrac{2}{x+1} = x - 1$

Determine whether the inverse of f is a function. Then find the inverse.

34. $f(x) = \dfrac{3}{x+6}$

35. $f(x) = \dfrac{10}{x-7}$

36. $f(x) = \dfrac{1}{x} + 8$

37. $f(x) = \dfrac{x}{1-x}$

38. Use the graph to identify the solution(s) of the rational equation $\dfrac{4(x-1)}{x-1} = \dfrac{2x-2}{x+1}$.

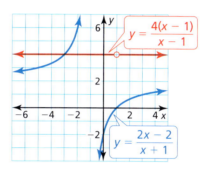

39. You play 30 levels of a video game and achieve an expert rating in 11 of those levels. Solve the equation

$$0.5 = \dfrac{11+x}{30+x}$$

to find the number of consecutive expert ratings you need to achieve so that you have achieved an expert rating on half of the levels you have played.

40. A nonprofit charges $50 to host a benefit walk at your school plus $20 for each participant. Determine how many people must participate for the average cost per person to fall to $25.

41. Find the extraneous solution of the equation

$$\dfrac{1}{x-6} + \dfrac{x}{x-2} = \dfrac{4}{x^2-8x+12}.$$

Explain why the solution is extraneous.

42. Use technology to solve the equation $\dfrac{2}{x} + 1 = x^2 + 1$.

7 PERFORMANCE TASK
SMP.2 SMP.4

3-D Printing

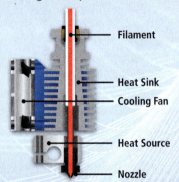

Print Head
Filament is heated and passes through the print head.
- Filament
- Heat Sink
- Cooling Fan
- Heat Source
- Nozzle

Print Bed
The print bed is the surface that objects are printed on.

Filament
Filaments used in 3-D printing include:
- plastics
- metals
- clay
- nylon
- wax
- and many others.

Axes
Unlike ink printers, which use two axes, a 3-D printer moves along three axes.

In 3-D printing, a blueprint is created using computer-aided design software. The blueprint data is then uploaded to the printer, and an object is built by depositing material one layer at a time.

Analyzing Data

Use the information on the previous page to complete the following exercises.

1. Explain what is shown in the display. What do you notice? What do you wonder?

2. The cost of one spool of nylon filament for a 3-D printer is $38, and the shipping fee is $22. How many spools must you buy for the average cost per spool to fall to $40?

3. In Exercise 2, the function $f(x) = \dfrac{38x + 22}{x}$ represents the average cost per spool when you order x spools. Graph the function. Find and interpret the domain and range.

STARTING A BUSINESS

You want to start a business selling 3-D printed items. Choose an object to print and then sketch a design. Research the costs associated with starting your business, including the cost of the printer and the estimated cost of materials to print each copy of your object. Finally, determine the selling price of each copy.

Write and graph several functions that represent the following relationships. Describe each relationship as the number of copies increases.

- the average cost per copy when n copies are printed
- the cost of printing n copies compared to your revenue after selling n copies
- your average profit or loss per copy after printing and selling n copies

8 Data Analysis and Statistics

- 8.1 Using Normal Distributions
- 8.2 Populations, Samples, and Hypotheses
- 8.3 Collecting Data
- 8.4 Experimental Design
- 8.5 Making Inferences from Sample Surveys
- 8.6 Making Inferences from Experiments

NATIONAL GEOGRAPHIC EXPLORER
Arianna Soldati VOLCANOLOGIST

Dr. Arianna Soldati is a volcanologist. She is especially interested in the interplay between the physical properties of lava, which can only be measured in the lab, and the appearance of lava in the field. Field observations are often the only data available to volcanologists, but it is physical properties that determine the distance and speed of a lava flow.

- What does a volcanologist do?
- The United States has over 150 active volcanoes. Name some of the volcanoes in the United States. Have you ever visited a volcano?
- What is the temperature of molten lava? What physical properties might influence the speed of lava flow?
- What is the difference between lava and magma?

PERFORMANCE TASK
Volcanologists record cases of new and ongoing volcanic activity around the world. In the Performance Task on pages 448 and 449, you will use data to write a report about worldwide volcanic activity.

Volcanology

Big Idea of the Chapter
Understand Data Analysis

Data analysis is the practice of organizing data to draw conclusions, which can be used to make informed decisions. Data is more readily available today than at any other time in history.

Volcanologists study the processes of volcanic eruptions to gather information about where and how volcanoes are likely to erupt. The Hawaiian Islands continue to be formed by volcanic eruptions. Molten lava flows from the volcanoes, cools in the ocean, and increases the land mass of the islands.

Three researchers each use a different survey to determine whether people in the United States favor more government funding to monitor volcanic activity. The table shows the results.

Survey Question	Sample	"Yes"	"No"	Conclusion
Should the government spend more to monitor volcanic activity?	1,000 randomly selected people living near a volcano	940	60	About 94% of people favor more funding.
Should the government spend more to monitor volcanic activity?	1,000 randomly selected people in Maryland	80	920	About 8% of people favor more funding.
Should the government spend more of our limited tax dollars to monitor volcanic activity?	1,000 randomly selected people in the United States	190	810	About 19% of people favor more funding.

1. Are you confident in any of the conclusions drawn by the researchers?

2. Write a survey question and describe a sample that the researchers can use to draw a valid conclusion. Explain your reasoning.

Getting Ready for Chapter 8

Comparing Measures of Center

EXAMPLE 1 Find the mean, median, and mode of the data set 4, 11, 16, 8, 9, 40, 4, 12, 13, 5, and 10. Then determine which measure of center best represents the data.

Mean $\bar{x} = \dfrac{4 + 11 + 16 + 8 + 9 + 40 + 4 + 12 + 13 + 5 + 10}{11} = 12$

Median 4, 4, 5, 8, 9, 10, 11, 12, 13, 16, 40   Order the data. The middle value is 10.

Mode 4, 4, 5, 8, 9, 10, 11, 12, 13, 16, 40   4 occurs most often.

▶ The mean is 12, the median is 10, and the mode is 4. The median best represents the data. The mode is less than most of the data, and the mean is greater than most of the data.

Find the mean, median, and mode of the data set. Then determine which measure of center best represents the data.

1. 36, 82, 94, 83, 86, 82

2. 1, 18, 12, 16, 11, 15, 17, 44, 44

Finding a Standard Deviation

EXAMPLE 2 Find and interpret the standard deviation of the data set 10, 2, 6, 8, 12, 15, 18, and 25. Use a table to organize your work.

x	$\bar{x}$	$x - \bar{x}$	$(x - \bar{x})^2$
10	12	−2	4
2	12	−10	100
6	12	−6	36
8	12	−4	16
12	12	0	0
15	12	3	9
18	12	6	36
25	12	13	169

Find the mean, $\bar{x}$.

$\bar{x} = \dfrac{96}{8} = 12$

Find the deviation of each data value, $x - \bar{x}$. Then square each deviation, $(x - \bar{x})^2$, as shown in the table.

Find the mean of the squared deviations.

$\dfrac{(x_1 - \bar{x})^2 + (x_2 - \bar{x})^2 + \cdots + (x_n - \bar{x})^2}{n}$

$= \dfrac{4 + 100 + \cdots + 169}{8} = \dfrac{370}{8} = 46.25$

Take the square root of the mean of the squared deviations.

$\sqrt{46.25} \approx 6.80$

▶ The standard deviation is about 6.80. This means that the typical data value differs from the mean by about 6.80 units.

Find and interpret the standard deviation of the data set.

3. 43, 48, 41, 51, 42

4. 28, 26, 21, 44, 29, 32

8.1 Using Normal Distributions

Learning Target: Understand normal distributions.

Success Criteria:
- I can find probabilities in normal distributions.
- I can interpret normal distributions.
- I can find probabilities in standard normal distributions.

The *standard deviation* σ of a numerical data set is a measure of how much a typical value in the data set differs from the mean μ. It is given by

$$\sigma = \sqrt{\frac{(x_1 - \mu)^2 + (x_2 - \mu)^2 + \cdots + (x_n - \mu)^2}{n}}$$

where n is the number of values in the data set.

INVESTIGATE Analyzing a Normal Distribution

Work with a partner. In many naturally occurring data sets, the histogram of the data is bell-shaped. In statistics, such data sets are said to have a *normal distribution*.

1. For the normal distribution shown below, estimate the percent of the data that lies within one, two, and three standard deviations of the mean.

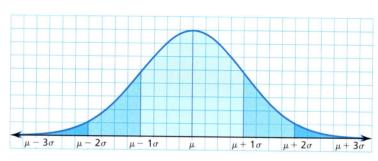

2. You randomly select a data value from a data set that has a normal distribution. Estimate the probability that the value you select is at least 1 standard deviation from the mean. Explain your reasoning.

3. A famous data set, collected in the mid-1800s, contains the chest sizes of 5,738 men in the Scottish Militia. The distribution is approximately normal. Approximate the number of men with chest sizes of at least 44 inches.

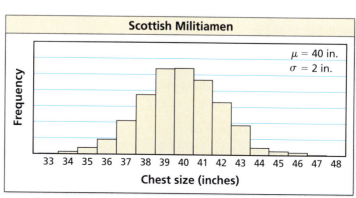

> **Vocabulary**
> normal distribution
> normal curve
> standard normal distribution
> z-score

Normal Distributions

You have studied probability distributions. One type of probability distribution is a *normal distribution*. The graph of a **normal distribution** is a bell-shaped curve called a **normal curve** that is symmetric about the mean.

A normal distribution with mean μ (the Greek letter *mu*) and standard deviation σ (the Greek letter *sigma*) has these properties.

- The total area under the related normal curve is 1.
- About 68% of the area lies within 1 standard deviation of the mean.
- About 95% of the area lies within 2 standard deviations of the mean.
- About 99.7% of the area lies within 3 standard deviations of the mean.

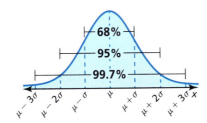
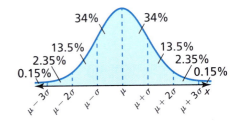

The areas under a normal curve can be interpreted as probabilities in a normal distribution. In a normal distribution, the probability that a randomly chosen x-value is between a and b is given by the area under the normal curve between a and b. Recall that the probability of an event A is written as $P(A)$.

EXAMPLE 1 Finding a Normal Probability

A normal distribution has mean μ and standard deviation σ. An x-value is randomly selected from the distribution. Find $P(\mu - 2\sigma \leq x \leq \mu)$.

The probability that a randomly selected x-value lies between $\mu - 2\sigma$ and μ is the shaded area under the normal curve shown.

$P(\mu - 2\sigma \leq x \leq \mu) = 0.135 + 0.34$
$= 0.475$

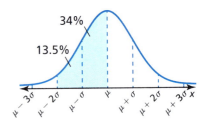

▶ The probability is about 47%.

In-Class Practice

Self-Assessment

A normal distribution has mean μ and standard deviation σ. Find the indicated probability for a randomly selected x-value from the distribution.

1. $P(x \geq \mu + \sigma)$
2. $P(\mu \leq x \leq \mu + 2\sigma)$

  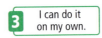

EXAMPLE 2 **Interpreting Normally Distributed Data**

The scores for a state's peace officer standards and training test are normally distributed with a mean of 55 and a standard deviation of 12. The test scores range from 0 to 100.

a. **About what percent of the people taking the test have scores between 43 and 67?**

Use the standard deviation to label the test scores on the axis. The scores of 43 and 67 represent one standard deviation on either side of the mean.

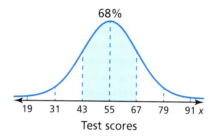

▶ So, about 68% of the people taking the test have scores between 43 and 67.

b. **An agency in the state will only hire applicants with test scores of 67 or greater. About what percent of the people have test scores that make them eligible to be hired by the agency?**

A score of 67 is one standard deviation to the right of the mean.

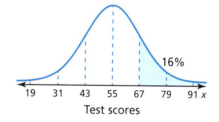

▶ So, the percent of the people who have test scores that make them eligible is about 13.5% + 2.35% + 0.15%, or 16%.

Check

You can use technology to find probabilities involving normal distributions.

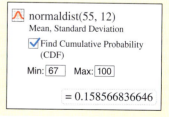

In-Class Practice

Self-Assessment

3. **WHAT IF?** In Example 2, about what percent of the people taking the test have scores between 43 and 79?

 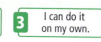

The Standard Normal Distribution

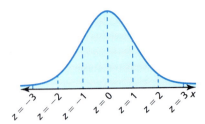

The **standard normal distribution** is the normal distribution with mean 0 and standard deviation 1. The formula below can be used to transform x-values from a normal distribution with mean μ and standard deviation σ into z-values having a standard normal distribution.

Formula $z = \dfrac{x - \mu}{\sigma}$ ← Subtract the mean from the given x-value, then divide by the standard deviation.

The z-value for a particular x-value is called the **z-score** for the x-value and is the number of standard deviations the x-value lies above or below the mean μ. For a randomly selected z-value from a standard normal distribution, you can use the standard normal table (available in the *Quick Reference*) to find the probability that z is less than or equal to a given value.

EXAMPLE 3 — Using a z-Score and the Standard Normal Table

A study finds that the masses of infants at birth are normally distributed with a mean of 3,270 grams and a standard deviation of 600 grams. An infant from the study is randomly chosen. What is the probability that the mass of the infant is 4,170 grams or less?

Find the z-score corresponding to an x-value of 4,170.

$$z = \dfrac{x - \mu}{\sigma} = \dfrac{4{,}170 - 3{,}270}{600} = 1.5$$

Find the value of $P(z \leq 1.5)$ by finding where the row representing 1 and the column representing .5 intersect in the table.

Standard Normal Table

z	.0	.1	.2	.3	.4	.5	.6	.7	.8	.9
−3	.0013	.0010	.0007	.0005	.0003	.0002	.0002	.0001	.0001	.0000+
−2	.0228	.0179	.0139	.0107	.0082	.0062	.0047	.0035	.0026	.0019
−1	.1587	.1357	.1151	.0968	.0808	.0668	.0548	.0446	.0359	.0287
−0	.5000	.4602	.4207	.3821	.3446	.3085	.2743	.2420	.2119	.1841
0	.5000	.5398	.5793	.6179	.6554	.6915	.7257	.7580	.7881	.8159
1	.8413	.8643	.8849	.9032	.9192	**.9332**	.9452	.9554	.9641	.9713

Check Use a spreadsheet to find the area.

	A	B
1	NORM.S.DIST(1.5, TRUE)	
2		0.9331928

▶ So, the probability that the mass of the infant is 4,170 grams or less is about 0.9332.

In-Class Practice

Self-Assessment

4. **WHAT IF?** In Example 3, what is the probability that the infant weighs 3,990 grams or less? 3,990 grams or more?

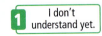

Not all distributions are normal. In the histograms below, the first has a normal distribution, the second is *skewed left*, and the third is *skewed right*.

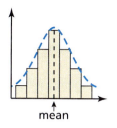
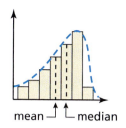
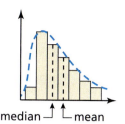

Bell-shaped and symmetric
- histogram has a normal distribution
- mean = median

Skewed left
- histogram does not have a normal distribution
- mean < median

Skewed right
- histogram does not have a normal distribution
- mean > median

EXAMPLE 4 Recognizing Normal Distributions

Determine whether each histogram has a normal distribution.

a.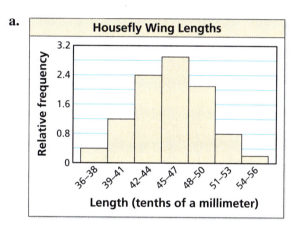

b.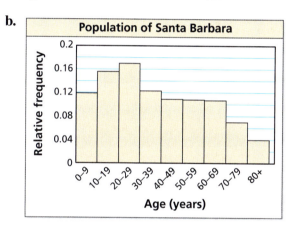

a. The histogram is bell-shaped and fairly symmetric. So, the histogram has an approximately normal distribution.

b. The histogram is skewed right. So, the histogram does not have a normal distribution, and you cannot use a normal distribution to interpret the histogram.

In-Class Practice

Self-Assessment

5. Determine whether the histogram has a normal distribution.

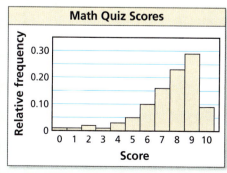

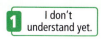 I don't understand yet.
 I can do it with help.
 I can do it on my own.
 I can teach someone.

8.1 Using Normal Distributions

8.1 Practice

Give the percent of the area under the normal curve represented by the shaded region(s).

1.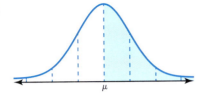

2.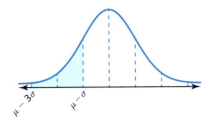

A normal distribution has mean μ and standard deviation σ. Find the indicated probability for a randomly selected x-value from the distribution. (See Example 1.)

3. $P(x \leq \mu - \sigma)$

4. $P(x \geq \mu + 2\sigma)$

5. $P(\mu - \sigma \leq x \leq \mu + \sigma)$

6. $P(\mu - 3\sigma \leq x \leq \mu)$

7. **CONNECTION TO REAL LIFE** The daily amounts of time Internet users spend on social networking platforms are normally distributed with a mean of 142 minutes and a standard deviation of 32 minutes. (See Example 2.)

   a. About what percent of Internet users spend between 78 minutes and 174 minutes on social networking platforms each day?

   b. About what percent of Internet users spend more than 238 minutes on social networking platforms each day?

8. **SMP.3 ERROR ANALYSIS** A normal distribution has a mean of 25 and a standard deviation of 2. Describe and correct the error in finding the probability that a randomly selected x-value is at least 21.

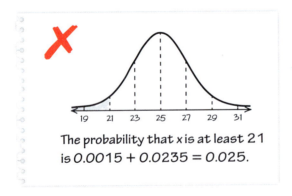

The probability that x is at least 21 is $0.0015 + 0.0235 = 0.025$.

9. The numbers of text messages U.S. teenagers send and receive daily are normally distributed with a mean of 67 messages and a standard deviation of 13 messages. What is the probability that a randomly chosen U.S. teenager sends and receives (a) at most 50 text messages and (b) between 75 and 100 text messages in a day? (See Example 3.)

Determine whether the histogram has a normal distribution. (See Example 4.)

10.
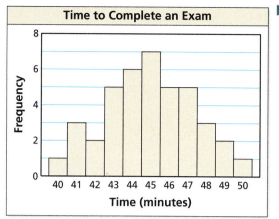

▶ 11.
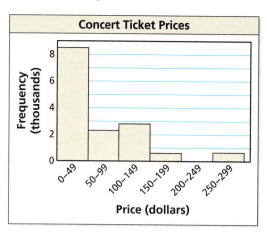

SMP.5 A normal distribution has a mean of 86 and a standard deviation of 9. Use a tool to find the indicated probability.

12. $P(x \leq 75)$

13. $P(x \geq 110)$

14. $P(90 \leq x \leq 100)$

15. $P(x \leq 70)$ or $P(x \geq 105)$

16. Boxes of cereal are filled by a machine. Tests show that the amount of cereal in each box varies. The weights are normally distributed with a mean of 20 ounces and a standard deviation of 0.25 ounce. Four boxes of cereal are randomly chosen.

   a. What is the probability that all four boxes contain no more than 19.4 ounces of cereal?

   b. Explain whether you think the machine is functioning properly when all four boxes have more than 19.4 ounces of cereal.

17. A data set has a median of 80 and a mean of 90. Your friend claims that the distribution of the data is skewed left. Explain whether your friend correct.

18. In the figure, the shaded region represents 47.5% of the area under a normal curve. What are the mean and standard deviation of the normal distribution?

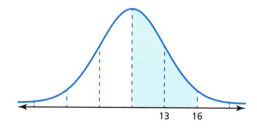

19. The scores on a history test are normally distributed with a mean of 75 and a standard deviation of 10. You randomly select a test score x. Find $P(|x - \mu| \geq 5)$.

20. When $n\%$ of normally distributed data are less than or equal to a certain value, that value is called the nth *percentile*. Describe the value that represents the 84th percentile of normally distributed data in terms of the mean and standard deviation.

Interpreting Data

SHOE SIZE Feet can change size or shape with age. It is estimated that about 3 in 5 people over the age of 60 are wearing the wrong shoe size, which can affect balance and posture.

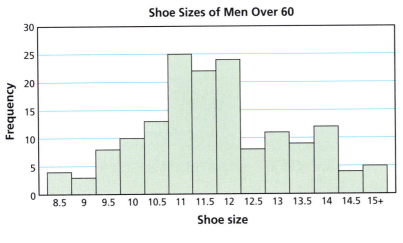

21. Describe the shape of the graph.

22. Estimate the standard deviation of the distribution.

23. A store wants to carry shoes that fit 90% of men over 60. Based on the data, what shoe sizes should the store carry?

Review & Refresh

24. Graph the function. Identify the x-intercepts and the points where the local maximums and local minimums occur. Determine the intervals for which the function is increasing or decreasing.

    $g(x) = \frac{1}{4}x^4 - 2x^2 - x - 3$

25. Solve the system using any method.

    $2x^2 - 3x + y = 8$
    $-x^2 + 5x - y = -12$

26. Tell whether x and y show *direct variation*, *inverse variation*, or *neither*.

x	1	3	6	9
y	5	15	30	45

27. Evaluate log 7 using technology.

28. Write the product $2i(i - 9)$ in standard form.

29. Write an equation of the parabola.

    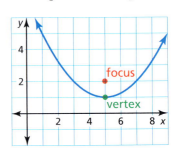

30. Solve the equation.

    $\frac{7}{x} - \frac{3}{5} = -\frac{2}{x}$

406 Chapter 8 Data Analysis and Statistics

8.2 Populations, Samples, and Hypotheses

Learning Target: Use random samples and simulations to make conclusions.

Success Criteria:
- I can distinguish between populations and samples.
- I can find a sample proportion.
- I can use a simulation to test a hypothesis.

INVESTIGATE

Using a Simulation

Work with a partner. For a study, 10 babies were shown the same puppet scene.

A panda puppet rolls a ball to a cat puppet, who rolls it back to the panda puppet. The panda puppet then rolls the ball to a wolf puppet, who picks it up and runs away with it.

When given the opportunity to reach toward the cat puppet or the wolf puppet, 8 babies reached toward the cat puppet.

1. If each of the 10 babies randomly selected a puppet, how many babies would you expect to select the cat puppet?

2. How can you use a coin to *simulate* one trial of a baby randomly selecting a puppet? How can you simulate multiple trials?

3. Perform the simulation in Exercise 2. Then extend the simulation to explain whether it is *unusual* for 8 out of 10 babies to randomly select the cat puppet.

4. Explain whether it is *possible* that the babies randomly selected a puppet. Explain whether it is *likely*.

5. Use the simulator available online to simulate 200 trials of flipping a coin 10 times. Do the results support your answer in Exercise 4?

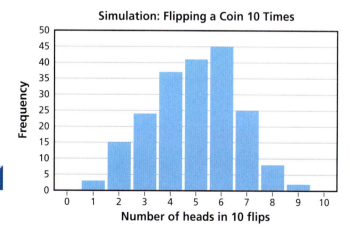

Vocabulary
population
sample
census
parameter
statistic
hypothesis

Populations and Samples

A **population** is a collection of all data, such as responses, measurements, or counts. A **sample** is a subset of a population.

A **census** consists of data from an entire population. But, unless a population is small, it is usually impractical to obtain all the data. In most studies, information is instead obtained from a *random sample*. It is important for a sample to be representative of a population so that sample data can be used to draw valid conclusions about the population.

EXAMPLE 1   Distinguishing Between Populations and Samples

Identify the population and the sample.

a. **In North Carolina, a survey of 1,648 adults found that 742 of them think hurricanes are a big problem in their part of the state.**

The population consists of all adults living in North Carolina, and the sample consists of the responses of the 1,648 adults in the survey.

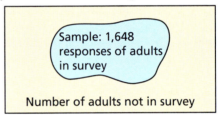

b. **To estimate the gas mileage of new vehicles sold in the United States, a consumer advocacy group tests 845 new vehicles and finds they have an average gas mileage of 25.4 miles per gallon.**

The population consists of the gas mileages of all new vehicles in the United States, and the sample consists of the gas mileages of the 845 new vehicles tested by the group.

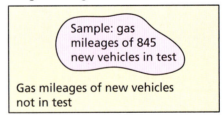

In-Class Practice

Self-Assessment

1. A survey of 2,013 adults in the United States found that 78% of them shopped or spent money over a recent Thanksgiving weekend. Identify the population and the sample.

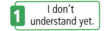

- A **parameter** is a numerical description of a population characteristic.
- A **statistic** is a numerical description of a sample characteristic.

Because some populations are too large to measure, a statistic is used to estimate the parameter.

EXAMPLE 2   **Distinguishing Between Parameters and Statistics**

a. **For all students taking the SAT in a recent year, the mean mathematics score was 521. Is the mean score a parameter or a statistic?**

The mean score of 521 is based on all students who took the SAT in a recent year.

▶ So, the mean score is a parameter.

b. **A survey of 536 retired people in the United States, found that the mean retirement age was 62.4 years. Is the mean retirement age a parameter or a statistic?**

Because there are more than 536 retired people in the United States, the survey is based on a subset of the population.

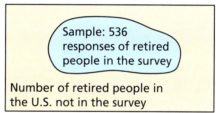

▶ So, the mean is a statistic.

c. **The standard deviation of the years that the states in the United States were admitted to the Union is about 47.8. Is the standard deviation of the years a parameter or a statistic?**

The standard deviation of 47.8 is based on all 50 states.

▶ So, the standard deviation of the years is a parameter.

In-Class Practice

Self-Assessment

2. A survey found that the median salary of 1,068 statisticians is about $95,570. Is the median salary a parameter or a statistic?

3. The median age of all Senators at the start of the 118th Congress was 65.3 years. Is the median age a parameter or a statistic?

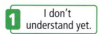 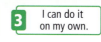

- A *population proportion* is the ratio of members of a population with a particular characteristic to the total members of the population.

- A *sample proportion* is the ratio of members of a sample of the population with a particular characteristic to the total members of the sample.

EXAMPLE 3 Finding a Sample Proportion

a. **Use technology to simulate rolling a die 50 times.**

You can simulate the rolling of a die 50 times by randomly generating 50 numbers from one through six and organizing the results in a bar graph.

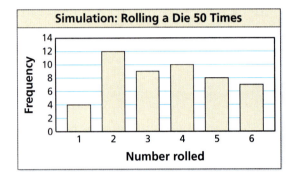

b. **What proportion of the 50 rolls result in an odd number?**

Use the graph to find the number of times that the odd numbers were rolled.

⚀ : 4 times   ⚂ : 9 times   ⚄ : 8 times

Getting $4 + 9 + 8 = 21$ odd numbers in 50 rolls corresponds to a proportion of $\frac{21}{50} = 0.42$.

▶ So, 42% of the rolls resulted in an odd number.

c. **What proportion of the 50 rolls result in a number no greater than 5?**

The only number greater than 5 is 6. Use the graph to find the number of times that a 6 was rolled.

 : 7 times

Getting $50 - 7 = 43$ numbers no greater than 5 in 50 rolls corresponds to a proportion of $\frac{43}{50} = 0.86$.

▶ So, 86% of the rolls resulted in a number no greater than 5.

In-Class Practice

Self-Assessment

4. Use technology to simulate rolling a die 100 times. What proportion of the 100 rolls result in a multiple of 3?

Analyzing Hypotheses

In statistics, a **hypothesis** is a claim about a characteristic of a population. One way to analyze a hypothesis is to perform a simulation. When the results occur rarely in the simulation, the hypothesis is probably false.

EXAMPLE 4 Analyzing a Hypothesis

You roll a six-sided die 5 times and do not get an even number. The probability of this happening is $\left(\frac{1}{2}\right)^5 = 0.03125$, so you suspect this die favors odd numbers. The die maker claims the die does not favor odd numbers or even numbers. What should you conclude when you roll the actual die 50 times and get 32 odd numbers?

The maker's claim, or hypothesis, is "the die does not favor odd numbers or even numbers." One way to test the hypothesis is to extend the simulation in Example 3 to 200 samples. For each sample, calculate the proportion of the 50 rolls that resulted in an odd number. Make a histogram of the distribution of the sample proportions.

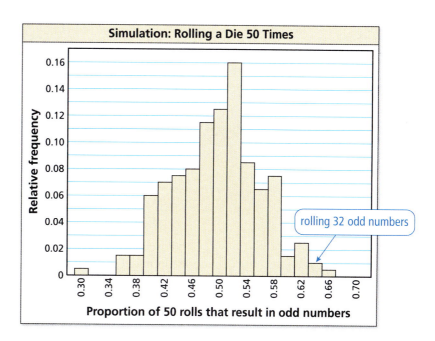

Getting 32 odd numbers in 50 rolls corresponds to a proportion of $\frac{32}{50} = 0.64$. In the simulation, this result had a relative frequency of 0.01. Because getting 32 odd numbers is highly unlikely to occur by chance, you can conclude that the maker's claim is most likely false.

In-Class Practice

Self-Assessment

5. WHAT IF? In Example 4, what should you conclude when you roll the actual die 50 times and get (a) 18 odd numbers and (b) 24 odd numbers?

8.2 Practice

Identify the population and the sample. (See Example 1.)

▶ 1. In the United States, a survey of 1,502 adults found that 60 of them do not own a cell phone.

2. In the United States, a survey of 743 teenagers ages 13–17 found that 201 of them never post selfies on social media.

Determine whether the numerical value is a parameter or a statistic. (See Example 2.)

▶ 3. The average cost of admission to some amusement parks in a state is $36.93.

4. **VOLCANOLOGIST ERUPTIONS** You create a database of all volcano eruptions in the United States and its territories. You determine that 1.2% of potentially active volcanoes in the U.S. had a significant eruption in a recent ten-year period.

▶ 5. You use technology to simulate flipping a coin 25 times. The results are shown. What proportion of the 25 flips resulted in tails? (See Example 3.)

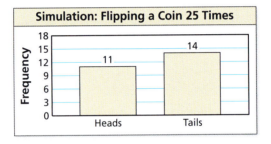

6. **SMP.6 OPEN-ENDED** Describe the difference between a parameter and a statistic. Give an example of each.

▶ 7. A coin maker claims that a coin does not favor heads or tails. You use technology to simulate 200 random samples of flipping a coin 50 times. The histogram shows the results. What should you conclude when you flip the actual coin 50 times and get (a) 27 heads and (b) 33 heads? (See Example 4.)

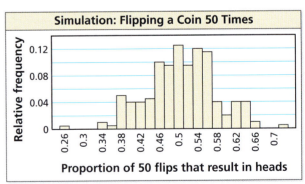

8. **SMP.3 ERROR ANALYSIS** A survey of 127 students at a high school found that 96 students felt added stress because of their workload. Describe and correct the error in identifying the population and the sample.

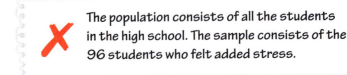

9. You perform two simulations of repeatedly drawing a card from a standard deck of cards with replacement.

   Simulation 1: 20 random samples of size 10

   Simulation 2: 400 random samples of size 10

   Explain which simulation you should use to accurately analyze a hypothesis.

10. **OPEN-ENDED** Find an article that describes a survey. Identify the population and sample. Describe the sample.

11. **SMP.4** You suspect that an eight-sided die favors the number four. The die maker claims that the die does not favor any number.

    a. Use technology to simulate 200 random samples of rolling the die 50 times to test the die maker's claim. Display the results in a histogram.

    b. What should you conclude when you roll the actual die 50 times and get 20 fours? 7 fours?

12. Conclusions made about a hypothesis may or may not be correct. Complete the table with *correct decision* or *incorrect decision*.

		Truth of Hypothesis	
		Hypothesis is true.	Hypothesis is false.
Decision	You decide that the hypothesis is true.		
	You decide that the hypothesis is false.		

13. You choose a random sample of 200 from a population of 2,000. Each person in the sample is asked how many hours of sleep they get each night. The mean of your sample is 5 hours. Explain whether it is possible that the mean of the entire population is 8 hours. Then explain whether it is likely.

14. **SMP.1 DIG DEEPER** Each of 20 students has a bag with blue marbles and green marbles. The contents of each bag are identical. Each student randomly selects a marble from the bag, records the result, and replaces the marble. The table shows the results after 25 rounds. Which is most likely to be the actual probability of selecting a blue marble: 0.5, 0.6, or 0.7? Use the simulator available online to justify your answer.

Number of students out of 20 with a blue marble	Frequency
9	2
10	3
11	5
12	6
13	3
14	2
15	3
16	1

Interpreting Data

AGE DISTRIBUTION IN THE UNITED STATES A demographer studies the ages of people in the United States from 2011 through 2021. The data display shows the age distribution.

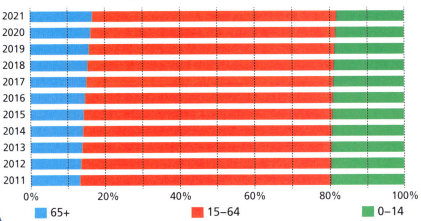

15. Describe the percent changes in the three age groups.

16. Do you think the percents shown are parameters or statistics? Explain your reasoning.

17. Why is the portion of the U.S. population that is 65+ increasing?

Review & Refresh

Solve the equation.

18. $x^2 - 10x = 4$

19. $n^2 + 2n + 2 = 0$

20. Determine whether the histogram has a normal distribution.

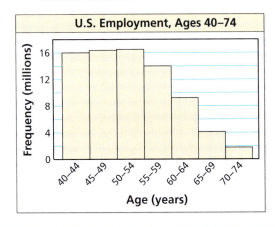

21. The number y of duckweed fronds in a pond after t days is $y = a(1{,}230.25)^{t/16}$, where a is the initial number of fronds. By what percent does the duckweed increase each day?

22. The table shows the inputs and outputs of two functions. Use the table to find each value.

x	−2	−1	0	1	2	3
f(x)	−5	−3	−1	1	3	5
g(x)	1	0	1	2	3	4

a. $f(g(-1))$

b. $g(f(2))$

23. Find the product $\dfrac{3xy^2}{x^3y} \cdot \dfrac{x}{9y}$.

8.3 Collecting Data

Learning Target: Describe sampling methods and recognize bias when collecting data.

Success Criteria:
- I can identify types of sampling methods in statistical studies.
- I can describe bias in sampling and in survey questions.

A conclusion that you draw using the results of a statistical study is only as reliable as the process used to obtain the data. If the process is flawed, then the resulting decision is questionable.

INVESTIGATE Conducting a Survey

Work with a partner. For a class project, your class will survey 20 students about the use of technology in your school.

1. Your class proposes the following methods for selecting individuals to participate in the survey.

   > Method 1: Select the first 20 students who volunteer to participate in the survey.

   > Method 2: Assign each student a unique number. Then use a random number generator to select 20 of the numbers.

   > Method 3: Randomly select 20 students in a computer programming class.

   a. Explain which method is most likely to result in a sample that will be representative of students in your school.

   b. Describe any disadvantages of the other two methods.

2. Explain how the wording can be improved in both of the proposed survey questions. Then write a new question for the survey.

   > Would you rather use older methods in education, or have the school provide a tablet for each student?

   > Should the school spend money to provide a tablet for each student instead of using the money for more urgent needs?

Vocabulary
random sample
self-selected sample
systematic sample
stratified sample
cluster sample
convenience sample
bias
unbiased sample
biased sample
experiment
observational study
survey
simulation
biased question

Identifying Sampling Methods in Statistical Studies

In a **random sample**, each member of a population has an equal chance of being selected. A random sample is most likely to be representative of a population. Here are other types of samples.

For a **self-selected sample**, members of a population can volunteer to be in the sample.

For a **systematic sample**, a rule is used to select members of a population. For instance, selecting every other person.

For a **stratified sample**, a population is divided into smaller groups that share a similar characteristic. A sample is then randomly selected from each group.

For a **cluster sample**, a population is divided into groups, called *clusters*. All the members in one or more of the clusters are selected.

For a **convenience sample**, only members of a population who are easy to reach are selected.

EXAMPLE 1 Identifying Types of Samples

You want to determine whether students in your school like the new design of the school's website. Identify the type of sample described.

a. **You list all the students alphabetically and choose every sixth student.**

   You are using a rule to select students. So, it is a *systematic* sample.

b. **You mail questionnaires and use only the ones that are returned.**

   The students can choose whether to respond. So, it is a *self-selected* sample.

c. **You ask all the students in your algebra class.**

   You are selecting students who are readily available. So, it is a *convenience* sample.

In-Class Practice
Self-Assessment

1. **WHAT IF?** In Example 1, you divide students according to their zip codes, then select all the students who live in one zip code. What type of sample are you using?

| 1 I don't understand yet. | 2 I can do it with help. | 3 I can do it on my own. | 4 I can teach someone. |

Recognizing Bias in Sampling

A **bias** is an error that results in a misrepresentation of a population. In order to obtain reliable information and draw accurate conclusions about a population, it is important to select an *unbiased sample*. An **unbiased sample** is representative of a population. A sample that overrepresents or under-represents part of a population is a **biased sample**. When a sample is biased, conclusions based on the data may be invalid. A random sample can help reduce the possibility of a biased sample.

EXAMPLE 2 Identifying Biased Samples

A news organization asks its viewers to participate in an online poll about bullying. Identify the type of sample and explain why the sample is biased.

The viewers can choose whether to participate in the poll. So, the sample is a *self-selected* sample. The sample is biased because people who go online and respond to the poll most likely have a strong opinion on the subject of bullying.

EXAMPLE 3 Selecting an Unbiased Sample

You want to poll members of the senior class to determine the theme of the school yearbook. There are 246 students in the senior class. Describe a method for selecting a random sample of 50 seniors to poll.

Make a list of all 246 seniors. Assign each senior a different integer from 1 to 246. Use technology to generate 50 unique random integers from 1 to 246.

	A	B
1	RANDBETWEEN(1,246)	207
2		101
3		109
4		81
5		173
6		7

Choose the 50 students who correspond to the 50 integers you generated.

In-Class Practice
Self-Assessment

2. The manager of a concert hall wants to know how often people in the community attend concerts. The manager asks 45 people standing in line for a rock concert how many concerts they attend per year. Identify the type of sample the manager is using and explain why the sample is biased.

3. In Example 3, what is another method you can use to generate a random sample of 50 students? Explain why your sampling method is random.

Analyzing Methods of Data Collection

There are several ways to collect data for a statistical study. The objective of the study often dictates the best method for collecting the data.

Key Concept

Methods of Collecting Data

An **experiment** imposes a treatment on individuals in order to collect data on their response to the treatment. The treatment may be a medical treatment, or it can be any action that might affect a variable in the experiment, such as adding methanol to gasoline and then measuring its effect on fuel efficiency.

An **observational study** observes individuals and measures variables without controlling the individuals or their environment. This type of study is used when it is difficult to control or isolate the variable being studied, or when it may be unethical to subject people to a certain treatment or to withhold it from them.

A **survey** is an investigation of one or more characteristics of a population. In a survey, every member of a sample is asked one or more questions.

A **simulation** uses a model to reproduce the conditions of a situation or process so that the simulated outcomes closely match the real-world outcomes. Simulations allow you to study situations that are impractical or dangerous to create in real life.

EXAMPLE 4 Identifying Methods of Data Collection

Identify the method of data collection.

a. **A researcher records whether people at a restaurant use hand sanitizer.**

   The researcher is gathering data without controlling the individuals or applying a treatment. So, this situation is an *observational study*.

b. **A landscaper fertilizes 20 lawns with a regular fertilizer mix and 20 lawns with an organic fertilizer. The landscaper then compares the lawns after 10 weeks and determines which fertilizer is more effective.**

   A treatment (organic fertilizer) is being applied to some of the individuals (lawns) in the study. So, this situation is an *experiment*.

In-Class Practice

Self-Assessment

4. A park ranger measures and records the heights of trees in a park as they grow. Identify the method of data collection.

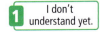 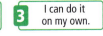

Recognizing Bias in Survey Questions

When designing a survey, it is important to word survey questions so they do not lead to biased results. Answers to poorly worded questions may not accurately reflect the opinions or actions of those being surveyed. Questions that are flawed in a way that leads to inaccurate results are called **biased questions**.

Avoid questions that:

- encourage a particular response
- are too sensitive to answer truthfully
- do not provide enough information to give an accurate opinion
- address more than one issue

EXAMPLE 5   Identifying and Correcting Bias in Survey Questions

Explain why each question may be biased or otherwise introduce bias into the survey. Then describe a way to correct the flaw.

a. A dentist asks patients,

   "Do you brush your teeth at least twice per day and floss every day?"

   Patients who brush less than twice per day or do not floss daily may be afraid to admit this because a dentist is asking the question.

   One improvement may be to have patients answer questions about dental hygiene on paper and then put the paper anonymously into a box.

b. A researcher studying daylight saving time asks,

   "Should the very beneficial daylight saving time by repealed?"

   By referring to daylight saving time as very beneficial, the question encourages a no response.

   One improvement is to reword the question as "Should daylight saving time be repealed?"

In-Class Practice

Self-Assessment

Explain why the survey question may be biased or otherwise introduce bias into the survey. Then describe a way to correct the flaw.

5. *"Should the school change its unhealthy cafeteria menu?"*

6. *"Should the latest bill being discussed in the United States Congress be passed into law?*

7. *"Was the customer service representative respectful and able to adequately address your situation?"*

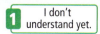 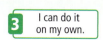

8.3 Practice

Identify the type of sample described. (See Example 1.)

1. A local politician wants to know how people will vote in an upcoming election. The politician conducts telephone surveys and uses only the results from the people who agree to participate.

2. A ride-sharing company wants to know if its customers are satisfied with the service. Drivers survey every tenth customer during the day.

▶ 3. Each employee in a company writes their name on a card and places it in a hat. The employees whose names are on the first two cards drawn each win a gift card.

4. The owner of a community pool wants to ask patrons if they think the water should be colder. Patrons are divided into four age groups, and a sample is randomly surveyed from each age group.

Identify the type of sample and explain why the sample is biased. (See Example 2.)

5. A town council wants to know whether residents support having an off-leash area for dogs in the town park. Eighty dog owners are surveyed at the park.

6. School officials want to gather feedback on teacher performance. They mail surveys to all parents and use the surveys that are returned.

▶ 7. You want to find out whether booth holders at a convention are pleased with their booth locations. You divide the convention center into six sections and survey every booth holder in the fifth section.

8. **SMP.3 ERROR ANALYSIS** Surveys are mailed to every other household in a neighborhood. Each survey that is returned is used. Describe and correct the error in identifying the type of sample that is used.

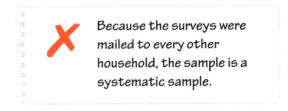

Because the surveys were mailed to every other household, the sample is a systematic sample.

9. The staff of a student newsletter wants to conduct a survey about students' favorite television shows. There are 1,225 students in the school. Describe a method for selecting a random sample of 250 students to survey. (See Example 3.)

Identify the method of data collection described in the situation. (See Example 4.)

10. An online seller asks 20 customers whether they are satisfied with their purchases.

11. **VOLCANOLOGIST DAMAGE** A researcher uses technology to estimate the damage that will be done if a volcano erupts.

STEM Video: Volcano Damage

12. A store manager records when customers choose to use the regular checkout or the self-checkout.

13. A researcher places two of the bacteria samples in two different climates. The researcher then measures the bacteria growth in each sample after 3 days.

Explain why the survey question may be biased or otherwise introduce bias into the survey. Then describe a way to correct the flaw. (See Example 5.)

14. "Would you rather watch the latest award-winning movie or just read some book?"

15. "Isn't it true that the budget of our city should be cut?"

16. A child asks, "Do you support the construction of a new children's hospital?"

17. "Are you satisfied with the selection of colors and the quality of the clothing?"

18. **OPEN-ENDED** You are in charge of designing a survey to assess the performance of a customer service team. Write three unbiased questions for the survey.

19. **SMP.1** A poll is conducted to predict the results of a statewide election in California before all the votes are counted. Fifty voters in each of the state's 58 counties are asked how they voted as they leave the polls.

   a. Identify the type of sample described.

   b. Explain how the diagram shows that the polling method could result in a biased sample.

Population by County (millions)
- Over 3.5
- 3–3.5
- 2.5–3
- 2–2.5
- 1.5–2
- 1–1.5
- 0.5–1
- Under 0.5

Interpreting Data

U.S. LANGUAGES Unlike many countries, the United States does not have an official language. English is the most common language spoken at home, but many other languages are also spoken.

Languages Spoken at Home in the United States

English only: 78.4%
Spanish: 13.2%
Other Indo-European Languages: 3.8%
Asian & Pacific Island Languages: 3.5%
Other: 1.2%

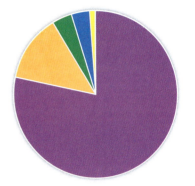

20. A person is randomly chosen from the U.S. population. What is the probability that the person speaks Spanish at home?

21. Five people are chosen from the U.S. population. All five of them speak German at home. Explain whether it is likely that this was a random sample.

22. Name 3 Indo-European languages other than Spanish. Name 3 Asian or Pacific Island languages.

Review & Refresh

23. The median number of years of experience for all teachers at a school is 8. Is the median number of years a parameter or a statistic?

Simplify the expression.

24. $(4^{3/2} \cdot 4^{1/4})^4$

25. $(6^{1/3} \cdot 3^{1/3})^{-2}$

26. $\sqrt[3]{4} \cdot \sqrt[3]{16}$

27. $\dfrac{\sqrt[4]{405}}{\sqrt[4]{5}}$

28. Graph $f(x) = \dfrac{5}{x} - 1$. Find the domain and range.

A normal distribution has a mean of 57 and a standard deviation of 3. Find the probability that a randomly selected x-value from the distribution is in the given interval.

29. at most 54

30. between 51 and 60

Expand the logarithmic expression.

31. $\log_2 \dfrac{4x}{y}$

32. $\ln xy^6$

Evaluate the expression without using technology.

33. $-64^{1/2}$

34. $27^{2/3}$

422 Chapter 8 Data Analysis and Statistics

8.4 Experimental Design

Learning Target: Describe and analyze experiments and their designs.

Success Criteria:
- I can assess the validity of an experiment's results.
- I can design an experiment or observational study.
- I can analyze experimental designs.

INVESTIGATE Designing Experiments

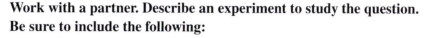

Work with a partner. Describe an experiment to study the question. Be sure to include the following:

- How should you select students?
- How many students should you select?
- Will your results be valid?

1. *Can students create and send text messages faster using their dominant hand or non-dominant hand?*

2. *Can students create and send text messages faster using a particular mobile device?*

3. *Can students create and send text messages faster typing or using a voice command feature?*

INVESTIGATE Analyzing Experiments

Work with a partner. A researcher is studying the following topic.

Does texting while driving result in more accidents?

To gather data, the researcher plans an experiment in which one group of drivers text every time they drive, and another group do not text at all while they drive. The number of accidents for each driver will be monitored over time and the results will be compared between the two groups.

4. What ethical problems might this type of experiment pose?

5. How else might the researcher study this topic?

6. The researcher asks a group of drivers how often they text while driving and the number of vehicular accidents they have had in the last several years. The results show that the drivers who admitted to texting while driving have been involved in more accidents than those who did not admit to texting while driving. The researcher concludes that texting while driving causes more accidents. Explain whether you think this conclusion valid.

Vocabulary
controlled experiment
treatment group
control group
placebo
randomization
randomized comparative experiment

Describing Experiments

In a **controlled experiment**, the group that is subjected to a treatment is the **treatment group** and the group that is not subjected to the treatment is the **control group**. Subjects in the control group are sometimes given a **placebo**, which is a harmless, "fake" treatment that is similar to the actual treatment.

Randomization randomly assigns subjects to different treatment groups. In a **randomized comparative experiment**, subjects are randomly assigned to the control group or the treatment group. Conclusions drawn from an experiment that is not a randomized comparative experiment may not be valid.

EXAMPLE 1 Evaluating Published Reports

Determine whether each study is a randomized comparative experiment. If it is, describe the treatment, the treatment group, and the control group. If it is not, explain why not and discuss whether the conclusions drawn from the study are valid.

a. A clinic determined that Vitamin C lowers cholesterol. The clinic let patients choose whether to take a daily vitamin C supplement. Fifty patients who took the supplement and fifty that did not were monitored for one year. Patients who took the supplement had 15% lower cholesterol levels than patients who did not.

▶ The study is not a randomized comparative experiment because the individuals are not randomly assigned to a control group and a treatment group. The conclusion that vitamin C lowers cholesterol may or may not be valid. There may be other reasons why patients who took the supplement had lower cholesterol levels.

b. A restaurant determined that a new touch-screen kiosk decreases wait times. The restaurant randomly selected and divided 186 customers into two groups. One group used the new touch-screen kiosks and the other group ordered at the counter. Users of the new kiosks received their food orders 25% faster.

▶ The study is a randomized comparative experiment. The treatment is the use of the new touch-screen kiosks. The treatment group is the individuals who use the new touch-screen kiosks. The control group is the individuals who order at the counter.

In-Class Practice

Self-Assessment

1. Repeat Example 1 for the study shown below.

   A recent study shows that adults who rise before 6:30 A.M. are better drivers than other adults. The study monitored the driving records of 140 drivers who always wake up before 6:30 A.M. and 140 drivers who never wake up before 6:30 A.M. The early risers had 12% fewer accidents.

Correlation in Experiments and Studies

A well designed experiment or observational study uses randomization to identify relationships between variables.

Randomized Comparative Experiment: By eliminating sources of variation other than the controlled variable, a randomized comparative experiment can make it possible to draw valid *cause-and-effect* conclusions.

Observational Study: An observational study can identify *correlation* between variables, but not *causality*. Variables other than what is being measured may affect the results.

EXAMPLE 2   Designing an Experiment or Observational Study

Determine whether the following research topic is best investigated through an experiment or an observational study. Then describe the design of the experiment or observational study.

Does practicing yoga result in fewer falls for older people?

The treatment, practicing yoga, may not be possible for those older people who are already unhealthy, so it is not ethical to assign individuals to a control or treatment group.

Use an observational study. Randomly choose one group of older people who already practice yoga. Then randomly choose one group of older people who do not practice yoga. Monitor the numbers of falls the individuals in both groups have at regular intervals. Note that because you are using an observational study, you may be able to identify a *correlation* between practicing yoga in older people and number of falls, but not *causality*.

In-Class Practice
Self-Assessment

2. Determine whether the following research topic is best investigated through an experiment or an observational study. Then describe the design of the experiment or observational study.

    You want to know if flowers sprayed twice per day with a mist of water stay fresh longer than flowers that are not sprayed.

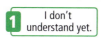 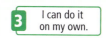

Analyzing Experimental Designs

The validity of an experiment is dependent on proper randomization and sufficiently large *sample sizes*.

EXAMPLE 3 **Analyzing Experimental Designs**

A company wants to test the effectiveness of a new chewing gum designed to help people lose weight. Identify a potential problem, if any, with each experimental design. Then describe how you can improve it.

a. The company randomly selects 10 people who are overweight, 5 of whom are randomly assigned to receive the gum and 5 of whom receive a placebo. After 3 months, it is determined that the 5 subjects who have been using the gum have lost weight.

▶ The sample size is not large enough to produce valid results. To improve the validity, the sample size must be larger.

b. The company randomly selects 10,000 people who are overweight and divides them into groups according to where they live. Subjects who live in a city receive the gum and subjects who live in rural areas receive the placebo. After 3 months, a significantly large number of the subjects who live in a city have lost weight.

▶ Because the subjects are divided into groups according to where they live, the groups are not similar. The gum may have different effects because of lifestyle. The subjects can be divided into groups according to where they live, but within each group, they must be randomly assigned to the treatment group or the control group.

c. The company randomly selects 10,000 people who are overweight, and divides them into groups according to age. Within each age group, subjects are randomly assigned to receive the gum or the placebo. After 3 months, a significantly large number of the subjects who received the gum have lost weight.

▶ The subjects are divided into groups according to a similar characteristic (age). Because subjects within each age group are randomly assigned to receive the gum or the placebo, the groups are similar. So, there appear to be no potential problems with the experimental design.

In-Class Practice
Self-Assessment

3. You design an experiment to test the effectiveness of a vaccine against a strain of influenza. In the experiment, 100,000 people under 40 years old are randomly assigned to receive the vaccine and another 100,000 people over 40 years old receive a placebo. Identify a potential problem with the experimental design. Then describe how you can improve it.

 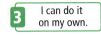

8.4 Practice with CalcChat and CalcView

Determine whether the study is a randomized comparative experiment. If it is, describe the treatment, the treatment group, and the control group. If it is not, explain why not and discuss whether the conclusions drawn from the study are valid. (See Example 1.)

▶ **1.**

A New Drug Improves Sleep

A pharmaceutical company randomly selected and divided 200 adults into two groups. One group received the drug and one group received a placebo. After one month, the adults who took the drug slept 18% longer, while those who took the placebo experienced no significant change.

2.

Milk Fights Cavities

Seventy-five students who chose milk during lunch were monitored for one year, as were seventy-five students who chose other beverages. At the end of the year, students in the "milk" group had 25% fewer cavities than students in the other group.

Determine whether the research topic is best investigated through an experiment or an observational study. Then describe the design of the experiment or observational study. (See Example 2.)

▶ **3.** A farmer wants to know if a new fertilizer affects the weight of the fruit produced by strawberry plants.

4. You want to know if homes that are close to parks or schools have higher property values.

▶ **5.** A company wants to test if a supplement has an effect on an athlete's heart rate while exercising. The company randomly selects 250 athletes. Half of the athletes are randomly assigned to receive the supplement and their heart rates are monitored while they run on a treadmill. The other half of the athletes receive a placebo and their heart rates are monitored while they lift weights. The heart rates of the athletes who took the supplement significantly increased while exercising. Identify a potential problem, if any, with the experimental design. Then describe how you can improve it. (See Example 3.)

6. A fitness company claims that its workout program will increase vertical jump heights in 6 weeks. To test the program, 10 athletes are divided into two groups. The double bar graph shows the results. Identify a potential problem with the experimental design. Then describe how you can improve it.

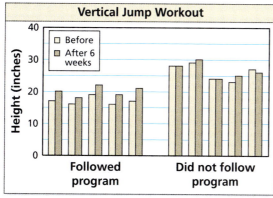

8.4 Experimental Design 427

Interpreting Data

POLIO VACCINE In 1954, field trials for a polio vaccine began. Involving 1.8 million children, the trials used a variety of methods, including the *double-blind method*, in which neither the patient nor the administrator knew if the vaccination was real or a placebo. The vaccine was found to be safe and effective after a year of trials.

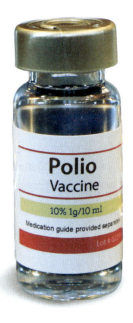

7. Describe the number of cases of polio from 1940 to 2019.

8. How might the sample for the study have been selected?

9. How does a field trial differ from other types of experiments? Why do you think the double-blind method is often used when conducting a field trial?

Review & Refresh

10. Explain why the survey question may be biased or otherwise introduce bias into the survey. Then describe a way to correct the flaw.

"Should the manufacturer update its outdated cell phone model?"

11. Display the data in a dot plot. Describe the shape of the distribution.

Ages			
17	15	18	15
16	17	16	16
15	14	17	16

12. A pitcher throws 16 strikes in the first 38 pitches. How many consecutive strikes must the pitcher throw to reach a strike percentage of 50%?

13. A normal distribution has a mean of 15. The probability that a randomly selected *x*-value is between 13 and 17 is 0.68. What is the standard deviation of the distribution?

14. Tell whether the function represents *exponential growth* or *exponential decay*. Then graph the function.

$$y = \left(\frac{1}{5}\right)^x$$

8.5 Making Inferences from Sample Surveys

Learning Target: Use sample surveys to make conclusions about populations.

Success Criteria:
- I can estimate population parameters.
- I can analyze the accuracy of a hypothesis using simulations.
- I can find margins of error for surveys.

INVESTIGATE

Observing Variability in Sample Surveys

Work with a partner. A poll says that 40% of dog owners let their dogs sleep on their beds. To test this, you survey 50 randomly chosen dog owners in your city and find that 16 of them let their dogs sleep on their beds.

Dog owners in your city

1. Based on your sample survey, what percent of dog owners let their dogs sleep on their beds?

2. Explain whether it is still possible that 40% of all dog owners let their dogs sleep on their beds.

3. You take a second random sample of 50 dog owners. Explain whether you should expect the sample proportion to be the same as the sample proportion in part (a).

4. Use the simulator online to simulate taking samples from the population of dog owners in your city. Assume that the population proportion is 40%. What do you notice as you adjust the number of samples and the sample size?

Vocabulary
descriptive statistics
inferential statistics
margin of error

Estimating Population Parameters

The study of statistics has two major branches: *descriptive statistics* and *inferential statistics*. **Descriptive statistics** involves the organization, summarization, and display of data. **Inferential statistics** involves using a sample to draw conclusions about a population. You can use inferential statistics to make reasonable predictions, or *inferences*, about an entire population when the sample is representative of that population.

EXAMPLE 1   Estimating a Population Mean

The numbers of liked songs for a random sample of 40 teen users of a music platform are shown. Estimate the population mean μ.

Number of Liked Songs

281	342	229	384	320
247	298	248	312	445
385	286	314	260	186
287	342	225	308	343
262	220	320	310	150
274	291	300	410	255
279	351	370	257	350
369	215	325	338	278

To estimate the unknown population mean μ, find the sample mean $\bar{x}$.

$$\bar{x} = \frac{x_1 + x_2 + x_3 + \ldots + x_{40}}{n} = \frac{11{,}966}{40} = 299.15$$

The probability that the population mean is exactly 299.15 is virtually 0, but the sample mean is a good estimate of the population mean μ.

▶ So, the mean number of liked songs for all teen users of the platform is about 299.

In-Class Practice
Self-Assessment

1. The data from another random sample of 30 teen users of the music platform are shown. Do you expect the sample mean be the same as in Example 1? Use this sample to estimate the population mean μ.

Number of Liked Songs

305	237	261	374	341	313
257	243	352	330	189	315
297	418	275	288	307	263
295	288	341	322	271	299
209	164	363	228	390	285

 I don't understand yet.
 I can do it with help.
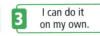 I can do it on my own.
 I can teach someone.

Not every random sample results in the same estimate of a population parameter; there will be some sampling variability. Larger sample sizes, however, tend to produce more accurate estimates.

EXAMPLE 2 **Estimating Population Proportions**

Two candidates, A and B, are running for office. Eight reporters conduct surveys of randomly selected residents. The residents are asked whether they will vote for Candidate A. The results are shown.

Sample Size	Number of Votes for Candidate A in the Sample	Percentage of Votes for Candidate A in the Sample
5	2	40%
12	4	33.3%
20	12	60%
50	29	58%
125	73	58.4%
150	88	58.7%
200	118	59%

a. Based on the results of the first two sample surveys, do you think Candidate A will win the election?

The first two survey results show that fewer than 50% of the residents will vote for Candidate A. More than 50% of the votes are needed to win.

▶ Based on these surveys, you can predict Candidate A will not win the election.

b. Based on all the sample surveys, do you think Candidate A will win the election?

As the sample sizes increase, the percent of votes approaches 59%.

▶ Because 59% of the votes are more than the 50% needed to win, you should feel confident that Candidate A will win the election.

In-Class Practice

Self-Assessment

2. Two candidates are running for class president. The results of four surveys of randomly selected students in the class are shown. The students are asked whether they will vote for the incumbent. Do you think the incumbent will be reelected?

Sample Size	Number of "Yes" Responses	Percentage of Votes for Incumbent
10	7	70%
20	11	55%
30	13	43.3%
40	17	42.5%

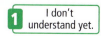 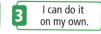

Analyzing Estimated Population Parameters

EXAMPLE 3 Analyzing an Estimated Population Proportion

A polling company claims 34% of U.S. adults say mathematics is the most valuable school subject. You survey a random sample of 50 adults.

a. **What can you conclude about the accuracy of the company's claim (hypothesis) that the population proportion is 0.34 when 15 adults in your survey say mathematics is the most valuable subject?**

To analyze the claim, simulate choosing 80 random samples of size 50 using a random number generator with numbers from 1 to 100 for each sample. Let numbers 1 through 34 represent adults who say math. Find the sample proportions and make a dot plot showing the distribution.

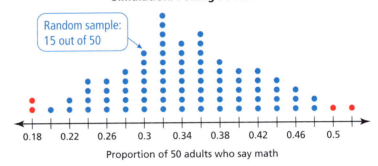

Note that 15 out of 50 corresponds to a sample proportion of $\frac{15}{50} = 0.3$. In the simulation, this result occurred in 7 of the 80 random samples. It is not unusual for 15 adults out of 50 to say that math is the most valuable subject when the true population percentage is 34%.

▶ So, you can conclude the company's claim is probably accurate.

b. **Assume that the true population proportion is 0.34. Estimate the variation among sample proportions using samples of size 50.**

The dot plot shows that the distribution is approximately normal. So, about 95% of the possible sample proportions will lie within two standard deviations of 0.34. Excluding the two least and two greatest sample proportions, represented by red dots ● in the dot plot, leaves 76 of 80, or 95%, of the sample proportions. These 76 proportions range from 0.2 to 0.48.

▶ So, 95% of the time, a sample proportion should lie in the interval from 0.2 to 0.48.

In-Class Practice

Self-Assessment

3. **WHAT IF?** In Example 3, what can you conclude about the accuracy of the company's claim when 25 adults in your survey say mathematics is the most valuable subject?

  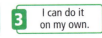

Finding Margins of Error for Surveys

The **margin of error** is the maximum expected difference between a sample result and the population parameter it is estimating. With data that is approximately normal, 95% of the data is within 2 standard deviations of the mean. You can use this two standard deviation distance as the margin of error.

EXAMPLE 4 Finding and Analyzing a Margin of Error

Use the simulation data from Example 3. The distribution has a standard deviation of about 0.07.

a. Find and interpret the margin of error.

The margin of error is 2 • 0.07 = 0.14, so 95% of the sample proportions should be within 0.14 of the population proportion, 0.34.

b. Use the simulator online to determine what happens to the margin of error as the sample size increases.

Simulate choosing random samples of different sizes.

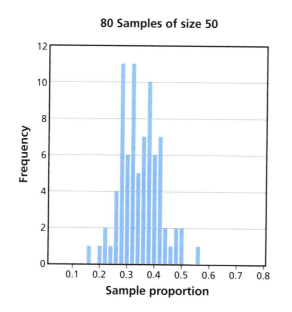
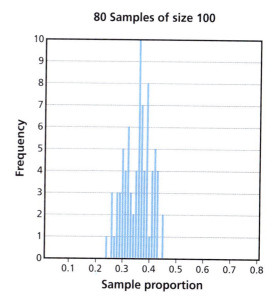

As the sample size increases, the interval in which most of the data lie decreases.

▶ So, the margin of error decreases as the sample size increases.

In-Class Practice

Self-Assessment

4. A distribution of sample proportions has a standard deviation of about 0.05. Find and interpret the margin of error.

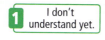 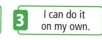

Finding Margins of Error for a Population Proportion

> **Key Concept**
>
> **Margin of Error for a Population Proportion**
>
> When a random sample of size n is taken from a large population, the margin of error for a population proportion can be approximated by
>
> $$\text{Margin of error} = \pm \frac{1}{\sqrt{n}}.$$
>
> You can use the results of the sample and the margin of error to write an interval in which the population parameter likely lies (with 95% confidence). If the percentage of the sample responding a certain way is p (expressed as a decimal), then the percentage of the population who would respond the same way is likely to be between
>
> $$p - \frac{1}{\sqrt{n}} \text{ and } p + \frac{1}{\sqrt{n}}.$$

EXAMPLE 5   **Finding a Margin of Error Using a Formula**

In a survey of 2,537 U.S. adults, 7% said that most of the food they eat is organic. Give an interval that is likely to contain the exact percentage of U.S. adults who eat mostly organic foods.

Use the formula to approximate the margin of error.

$\text{Margin of error} = \pm \dfrac{1}{\sqrt{n}}$ Write formula.

$= \pm \dfrac{1}{\sqrt{2{,}537}}$ Substitute 2,537 for n.

$\approx \pm 0.02$ Use technology.

The margin of error for the survey is about $\pm 2\%$. To find the interval, subtract and add 2% to the percentage of adults surveyed who said that most of the food they eat is organic, 7%.

$7\% - 2\% = 5\%$ $7\% + 2\% = 9\%$

▶ It is likely that the exact percentage of U.S. adults who eat mostly organic foods is between 5% and 9%.

In-Class Practice

Self-Assessment

5. In a survey of 1,316 U.S. teenagers, 53% said that online bullying is a major problem among their peers. Give an interval that is likely to contain the exact percentage of U.S. teenagers who think that online bullying is a major problem among their peers.

  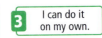

8.5 Practice

1. The numbers of text messages sent and received in one day by a random sample of 30 teen cell phone users are shown. Estimate the population mean μ. (See Example 1.)

Number of Text Messages				
35	65	64	88	46	62
42	71	68	65	97	65
58	47	52	37	84	75
58	85	46	56	90	96
78	76	74	36	74	72

2. Use the data in Exercise 1 to answer each question.

   a. Estimate the population proportion p of teen cell phone users who send and receive more than 70 text messages each day.

   b. Estimate the population proportion p of teen cell phone users who send and receive fewer than 50 text messages each day.

3. When the President of the United States vetoes a bill, Congress can override the veto by a two-thirds majority vote in each House. Five news organizations conduct individual random surveys of U.S. Senators. The senators are asked whether they will vote to override the veto. The results are shown. (See Example 2.)

Sample Size	Number of Votes to Override Veto	Percentage of Votes to Override Veto
7	6	85.7%
22	16	72.7%
28	21	75%
31	17	54.8%
49	27	55.1%

   a. Based on the results of the first two surveys, explain whether you think the Senate will vote to override the veto.

   b. Based on the results in the table, explain whether you think the Senate will vote to override the veto.

4. A senior class consisting of 292 students votes on whether they want their class trip to take place at an amusement park or a Broadway play. In a random sample of 50 seniors, 64% are in favor of an amusement park. How confident are you that the class trip will take place at an amusement park?

▶ **5.** A national polling company claims that 17% of U.S. public school teachers have a second job. You survey a random sample of 100 U.S. public school teachers. (See Example 3.)

   a. What can you conclude about the accuracy of the claim that the population proportion is 0.17 when 32 teachers in your survey have a second job?

   b. What can you conclude about the accuracy of the claim that the population proportion is 0.17 when 14 teachers in your survey have a second job?

   c. Assume that the true population proportion is 0.17. Estimate the variation among sample proportions for samples of size 100.

6. A national polling company claims that 54% of U.S. adults are married. You survey a random sample of 40 adults. Assume that the true population proportion is 0.54. Estimate the variation among sample proportions for samples of size 40.

▶ **7.** A distribution of data simulated for Exercise 5(c) has a standard deviation of about 0.05. Find and interpret the margin of error. (See Example 4.)

Find the margin of error for a survey that has the given sample size.

8. 260   **9.** 1,000   **10.** 2,024

▶ **11.** In a survey of 10,260 adults, 26% said that driverless passenger vehicles are a good idea. Give an interval that is likely to contain the exact percentage of all adults who think driverless passenger vehicles are a good idea. (See Example 5.)

12. In a survey of 7,578 U.S. homeowners, 8% had installed solar panels at their home. Give an interval that is likely to contain the exact percentage of all U.S. homeowners who have installed solar panels at their home.

13. A developer claims that the percentage of city residents who favor building a splash pad at a local park is likely between 72.3% and 81.7%. About how many residents were surveyed?

14. The figure shows the distribution of the sample proportions from three simulations using different sample sizes. Which simulation has the least margin of error? the greatest?

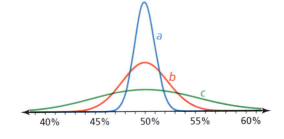

15. A random sample of size *n* produces a margin of error of ±*E*. Write an expression in terms of *n* for the sample size needed to reduce the margin of error to $\pm\frac{1}{2}E$. By how many times must the sample size be increased to cut the margin of error in half?

16. **SMP.2** A survey reports that 47% of the voters surveyed, or about 235 voters, said they voted for Candidate A and the remainder said they voted for Candidate B.

    a. How many voters were surveyed?
    b. What is the margin of error for the survey?
    c. For each candidate, find an interval that is likely to contain the exact percentage of all voters who voted for the candidate.
    d. Based on your intervals in part (c), can you be confident that Candidate B won? If not, how many people in the sample would need to vote for Candidate B for you to be confident that Candidate B won?

17. Consider a large population of which *p* percent (in decimal form) have a certain characteristic. To be reasonably sure that you are choosing a sample that is representative of a population, you should choose a random sample of *n* people where

    $$n > 1{,}500p(1 - p).$$

    Find *n* for several values of *p*. Explain how the percent of a population that has the characteristic affects the size of the sample needed.

18. To estimate the margin of error for a population mean, you can use the formula

    $$\text{Margin of error} = \pm\frac{2\sigma}{\sqrt{n}}$$

    where σ is the standard deviation of the sample data and *n* is the sample size. To estimate the number of times cell phone users check their phone each day, a polling company surveys a random sample of 2,000 cell phone users. The sample has a mean of 52 checks per day and a standard deviation of 11 checks per day.

    a. Find and interpret the margin of error.
    b. Give an interval that is likely to contain the actual population mean.

19. **SMP.1 DIG DEEPER** In a survey, 52% of the respondents said they prefer sports drink X and 48% said they prefer sports drink Y. Explain how many people you have to survey to be confident that sports drink X is truly preferred to sports drink Y.

20. **PERFORMANCE TASK** Write a statistical question about teenagers at your school. Use your question to survey a random sample of at least 50 teenagers at your school. Use the results of your survey to write a report. Your report should include any statistics found in your survey, the sample size, the margin of error, and any conclusions you can draw from the data.

Interpreting Data

MARGIN OF ERROR Randomness, sample size, and the method of data collection are important when conducting an experiment or observational study. The sample size affects the margin of error, which can be used to draw further conclusions from the experiment or study.

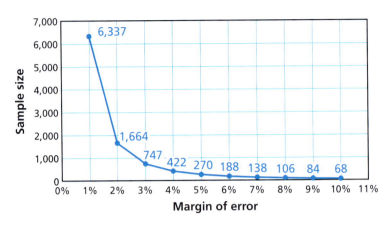

21. Describe the relationship between sample size and margin of error.

22. In a survey of 10,211 U.S. adults, 67% do not answer a phone call when they do not know who the caller is. Explain how this could affect the validity of telephone surveys.

Review & Refresh

23. Find the inverse of the function.

    $y = \log_6 x - 1$

24. Determine whether the graph represents an arithmetic sequence or a geometric sequence. Then write a rule for the nth term.

    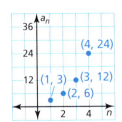

25. Multiply.

    $$\frac{x^2 - 3x - 4}{x^2 - 8x + 12} \cdot \frac{2x^2 - 12x}{x^2 - 4x}$$

26. Determine whether the study is a randomized comparative experiment. If it is, describe the treatment, the treatment group, and the control group. If it is not, explain why not and discuss whether the conclusions drawn from the study are valid.

    Salt Rock Lamps Lower Stress

    A recent study claims that using a Himalayan salt rock lamp for at least 1 hour each day reduces stress levels. One hundred twenty people who used a salt rock lamp for at least 1 hour each day were monitored for a month, as were one hundred twenty people who did not use a salt rock lamp at all. After a month, the stress levels of the people who used a salt rock lamp were 16% lower.

27. Graph the function.

    $g(x) = 2|x - 3|$

8.6 Making Inferences from Experiments

Learning Target: Understand how to make inferences from experiments.

Success Criteria:
- I can analyze data from an experiment.
- I can explain how to resample data.
- I can use resampling to make inferences about a treatment.

INVESTIGATE Analyzing Data

Work with a partner. A randomized comparative experiment tests whether a new training program affects the 100-meter dash times of runners on track teams. The table shows the results.

Times (seconds)	
Control Group	Treatment Group
11.1	11.0
11.3	11.2
11.4	11.5
11.2	10.9
11.0	11.1
11.7	11.4
11.8	10.8
11.1	10.9
11.1	11.3
11.8	11.6

1. Find the mean time of the control group and the mean time of the treatment group. Find and interpret the difference of the means.

2. Write the times from the table on pieces of paper.

   a. Place the pieces in a bag and randomly draw 10 pieces. Call this the "control" group, and call the 10 pieces in the bag the "treatment" group. Repeat Exercise 1 using the new groups and return the pieces to the bag. Perform this *resampling* experiment five times.

   b. How does the difference in the means of the original control and treatment groups compare with the differences resulting from chance?

3. Collect all the resampling differences of means in Exercise 2 for the whole class. Explain whether you should *affirm* or *reject* the following hypothesis.

   The new training program has no effect on the 100-meter dash times.

Experiments with Two Samples

EXAMPLE 1 Analyzing Data from an Experiment

A randomized comparative experiment tests whether a soil supplement affects the total yield (in kilograms) of cherry tomato plants. The table shows the results.

Total Yield of Cherry Tomato Plants (kilograms)										
Control Group	1.2	1.3	0.9	1.4	2.0	1.2	0.7	1.9	1.4	1.7
Treatment Group	1.4	0.9	1.5	1.8	1.6	1.8	2.4	1.9	1.9	1.7

a. Find the experimental difference of the mean yield of the treatment group, $\bar{x}_{treatment}$, and the mean yield of the control group, $\bar{x}_{control}$.

$$\bar{x}_{control} = \frac{13.7}{10} = 1.37 \qquad \bar{x}_{treatment} = \frac{16.9}{10} = 1.69$$

$$\bar{x}_{treatment} - \bar{x}_{control} = 1.69 - 1.37 = 0.32$$

▶ The experimental difference of the means is 0.32 kilogram.

b. Display the data in a double dot plot.

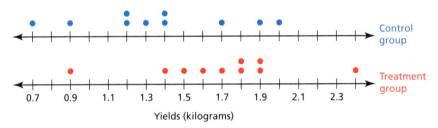

c. What can you conclude from parts (a) and (b)?

Because both data sets are fairly symmetric, the mean is a suitable measure of center. The mean yield of the treatment group is 0.32 kilogram more than the control group.

▶ So, the supplement might be slightly effective, but the sample size is small and the difference could be due to chance.

In-Class Practice
Self-Assessment

1. A randomized comparative experiment tests whether a supplement affects resting heart rate. Repeat Example 1 using the results of the experiment.

Heart Rate (beats per minute)										
Control Group	88	72	72	63	66	74	81	76	71	74
Treatment Group	74	81	83	81	84	76	90	82	81	83

 I don't understand yet.   I can do it with help.   I can do it on my own.   I can teach someone.

Resampling Data

The samples in Example 1 are too small to make meaningful inferences about the treatment. Statisticians have developed a method called *resampling* to overcome this problem.

EXAMPLE 2 **Resampling Data Using a Simulation**

Resample the data in Example 1. Use the mean yields of the new control and treatment groups to calculate the difference of the means.

Combine the measurements from both groups and assign a number to each value. Let the numbers 1 through 10 represent the data in the original control group, and let the numbers 11 through 20 represent the data in the original treatment group.

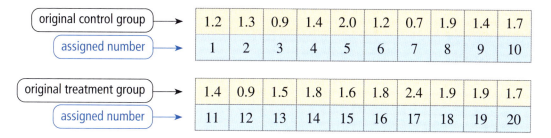

Use a random number generator to randomly generate 20 numbers from 1 through 20 *without repeating a number*. The table shows the results.

14	19	4	3	18	9	5	15	2	7
1	17	20	16	6	8	13	12	11	10

Use the first 10 numbers to make a new control group, and the next 10 to make a new treatment group.

Resample of Cherry Tomato Plant Yields (kilograms)										
New Control Group	1.8	1.9	1.4	0.9	1.9	1.4	2.0	1.6	1.3	0.7
New Treatment Group	1.2	2.4	1.7	1.8	1.2	1.9	1.5	0.9	1.4	1.7

Find the mean yields of the new control and treatment groups.

$$\overline{x}_{\text{new control}} = \frac{14.9}{10} = 1.49 \qquad \overline{x}_{\text{new treatment}} = \frac{15.7}{10} = 1.57$$

▶ So, $\overline{x}_{\text{new treatment}} - \overline{x}_{\text{new control}} = 1.57 - 1.49 = 0.08$. This is less than the experimental difference found in Example 1.

In-Class Practice

Self-Assessment

2. Resample the data in Exercise 1 using a simulation. Use the mean yields of the new control and treatment groups to calculate the difference of the means.

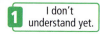

8.6 Making Inferences from Experiments

Making Inferences About a Treatment

To perform an analysis of the data in Example 1, you will need to resample the data many times.

EXAMPLE 3 **Making Inferences About a Treatment**

To conclude that the treatment in Example 1 is responsible for the difference in yield, analyze this hypothesis:

The supplement has no effect on the yield of the cherry tomato plants.

Simulate 200 resamplings of the data in Example 1. Compare the experimental difference of 0.32 from Example 1 with the resampling differences. What can you conclude about the hypothesis?

The histogram shows the results of a simulation. The shape of the histogram shows that the differences have an approximately normal distribution.

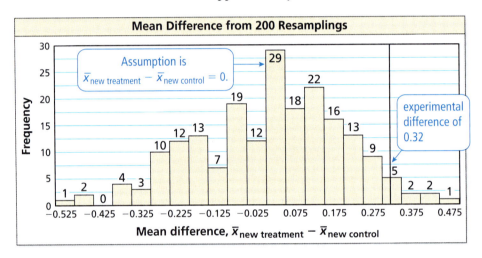

- The hypothesis assumes that the difference of the mean yields is 0.
- From the graph, there are about 5 to 10 values that are greater than 0.32, which is at most 5% of the values.
- The experimental difference falls outside the middle 90% of the resampling differences. This means it is unlikely to get a difference this large when you assume that the difference is 0.

▶ The experimental difference of 0.32 is significant in this situation. Because the experimental difference falls in the extreme values of the resampling distribution, you can conclude that the hypothesis is likely false, and that the supplement *does* have an effect on the yield. Because the mean difference is positive, the treatment *increases* the yield.

In-Class Practice

Self-Assessment

3. Explain how you can determine whether an experimental difference in measures of center is significant.

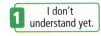   

8.6 Practice

1. A randomized comparative experiment tests whether music therapy affects the anxiety scores of high school students. Greater scores indicate greater anxiety. The tables show the results. (See Example 1.)

	Anxiety Score						
Control Group	49	45	43	47	46	45	47	46
Treatment Group	39	40	39	37	41	40	42	43

   a. Find the experimental difference of the mean of the treatment group and the mean of the control group.

   b. Display the data in a double dot plot.

   c. What can you conclude from parts (a) and (b)?

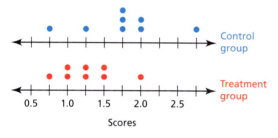

2. **SMP.7** Without calculating, explain whether the experimental difference, $\bar{x}_{treatment} - \bar{x}_{control}$, in the double dot plot is *positive*, *negative*, or *zero*.

3. Resample the data in Exercise 1. Use the means of the new control and treatment groups to calculate the difference of the means. (See Example 2.)

4. **SMP.6** You assign the numbers 1–16 to the values in Exercise 1. The output of a random number generator is shown. Explain whether the numbers shown will produce a reliable resampling.

2	11	3	5	8	9	6	13
12	14	16	10	4	1	3	15

5. The histogram shows the results from 200 resamplings of the data in Exercise 1. Analyze the hypothesis:

   Music therapy has no effect on the anxiety score.

   Compare the experimental difference in Exercise 1 with the resampling differences. What can you conclude about the hypothesis? (See Example 3.)

6. **SMP.3** Your friend states that the mean of the resampling differences should be close to 0 as the number of resamplings increases. Explain whether your friend is correct.

Interpreting Data

HISPANIC POPULATION IN THE U.S. A pollster considers the demographics of the United States. The map shows the Hispanic or Latino population density in the U.S.

Hispanic or Latino Population Density
(Persons per square kilometer)

0–1
1–2
2–3
3–5
5+

7. Describe the shading of the map.

8. Why might the Hispanic or Latino population density vary from one state to another?

9. Why do people who work in polling companies need to be familiar with cultural origins?

Review & Refresh

10. Determine whether the sample below is biased.

    Your student council randomly surveys five students from each grade about the school media center.

11. Graph the function. Label the vertex and axis of symmetry.

    $f(x) = (x - 1)^2$

12. Determine whether the research topic below is best investigated through an experiment or an observational study.

    You want to know whether adults have better vision with larger or smaller smartphone screens.

13. The prices from a random sample of 9 solar balloons are shown in the table. Estimate the population mean μ.

Prices of a Solar Balloon (dollars)		
15.50	16.35	17.00
13.53	15.00	12.77
15.85	12.55	18.25

14. Simplify the expression. Write your answer as a power.

    $(2z^2)^{-3}$

15. Solve $\sqrt{7x + 8} = 6$.

8 Chapter Review with CalcChat

Rate your understanding of each section.

1 I don't understand yet. **2** I can do it with help. **3** I can do it on my own. **4** I can teach someone.

8.1 Using Normal Distributions (pp. 399–406)
◉ **Learning Target:** Understand normal distributions.

Vocabulary
normal distribution
normal curve
standard normal distribution
z-score

1. A normal distribution has mean μ and standard deviation σ. An *x*-value is randomly selected from the distribution. Find $P(x \leq \mu - 3\sigma)$.

2. The times drivers spend waiting in a curbside pickup zone are normally distributed with a mean of 8 minutes and a standard deviation of 2 minutes. The goal of the curbside pickup service is for about 97.5% of drivers to spend no more than 10 minutes waiting. Is the service meeting the goal?

3. The weights of objects created in a welding class are normally distributed with a mean of 11.2 pounds and a standard deviation of 2 pounds. What is the probability that a randomly selected object is at least 14 pounds?

8.2 Populations, Samples, and Hypotheses (pp. 407–414)
◉ **Learning Target:** Use random samples and simulations to make conclusions.

Vocabulary
population
sample
census
parameter
statistic
hypothesis

4. To estimate the average number of miles driven by U.S. motorists each year, a researcher conducts a survey of 1,000 drivers, records the number of miles they drive in a year, and then determines the average. Identify the population and the sample.

5. A pitcher throws 40 fastballs in a baseball game. An analyst records the speeds of 10 of the fastballs and finds that the mean speed is 92.4 miles per hour. Is the mean speed a parameter or a statistic?

6. A shelter features either a dog or a cat for adoption in a weekly newsletter. You suspect that the shelter features a dog more often. The shelter claims that they do not favor either type of animal. What should you conclude when a dog is featured in 17 out of 28 newsletters?

8.3 Collecting Data (pp. 415–422)

Learning Target: Describe sampling methods and recognize bias when collecting data.

Vocabulary
random sample
self-selected sample
systematic sample
stratified sample
cluster sample
convenience sample
bias
unbiased sample
biased sample
experiment
observational study
survey
simulation
biased question

7. You want to determine whether students in your school are interested in a first responder class. Identify the type of sample described.

   a. You list all the students alphabetically and choose every fifth student.

   b. You email surveys and use only the surveys that are returned.

   c. You ask all the students from your anatomy and physiology class.

8. An administrative assistant records whether students use a water bottle refilling station. Identify the method of data collection.

9. Explain why the question may be biased or otherwise introduce bias into the survey. Then describe a way to correct the flaw.

   "Should the city replace the outdated library systems it is using?"

8.4 Experimental Design (pp. 423–428)

Learning Target: Describe and analyze experiments and their designs.

Vocabulary
controlled experiment
treatment group
control group
placebo
randomization
randomized comparative experiment

10. Determine whether the study is a randomized comparative experiment. If it is, describe the treatment, the treatment group, and the control group. If it is not, explain why not and discuss whether the conclusions drawn from the study are valid.

> **New Car Wash Cleans Faster**
> To test the new design of a car wash, an engineer randomly selected and divided 80 customers into two groups. One group used the old design to wash their cars and one group used the new design to wash their cars. Users of the new car wash design were able to wash their cars 30% faster.

11. A restaurant manager wants to know which type of sandwich bread attracts the most repeat customers. Is the topic best investigated through an experiment or an observational study? Describe the design of the experiment or observational study.

12. A researcher wants to test the effectiveness of a sleeping pill. Identify a potential problem, if any, with the experimental design below. Then describe how you can improve it.

   The researcher selects 16 volunteers who have insomnia. Eight volunteers are given the sleeping pill and the other eight volunteers are given a placebo. Their sleep habits are recorded for 1 month.

8.5 Making Inferences from Sample Surveys (pp. 429–438)

Learning Target: Use sample surveys to make conclusions about populations.

Vocabulary
descriptive statistics
inferential statistics
margin of error

13. There are two candidates for homecoming king. The table shows the results from four random surveys of the students in the school. The students were asked whether they will vote for Candidate A. Do you think Candidate A will be the homecoming king?

Sample Size	Number of "Yes" Responses	Percentage of Votes
8	6	75%
22	14	63.6%
34	16	47.1%
62	29	46.8%

14. In a survey of 1,000 U.S. teenagers, 41% consider entrepreneurship as a career option. Give an interval that is likely to contain the exact percentage of U.S. teenagers who consider entrepreneurship as a career option.

8.6 Making Inferences from Experiments (pp. 439–444)

Learning Target: Understand how to make inferences from experiments.

15. A randomized comparative experiment tests whether a mentoring program affects number of absences from school. The control group has eight students and the treatment group, which participates in the mentoring program, has eight students. The table shows the results. Find the experimental difference of the mean of the treatment group, $\bar{x}_{\text{treatment}}$, and the mean of the control group, $\bar{x}_{\text{control}}$.

	Days Absent							
Control Group	6	8	8	8	7	9	12	4
Treatment Group	4	4	5	2	3	6	0	7

16. The histogram shows the results from 200 resamplings of the data in Exercise 15.

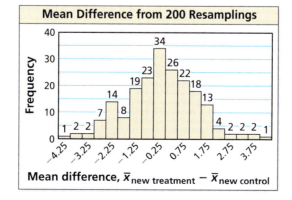

Analyze the hypothesis below. Then compare the experimental difference in Exercise 15 with the resampling differences. What can you conclude about the hypothesis?

The mentoring program has no effect on the number of absences from school.

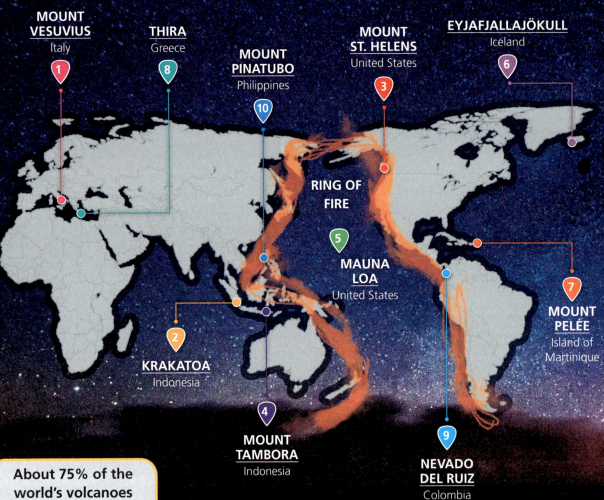

Analyzing Data

Use the information on the previous page to complete the following exercises.

1. Explain what is shown in the display. What do you notice? What do you wonder?

2. A survey asked 2,500 people who live in the Ring of Fire how concerned they are about an eruption on a scale of 1 to 10. The mean response was 7. Is the mean response a parameter or statistic?

3. A researcher uses the result of the survey in Exercise 2 to claim that the average person is concerned about a volcanic eruption. Explain why the researcher's claim might not be valid.

MONITORING VOLCANIC ACTIVITY

You work for an organization that monitors worldwide volcanic activity. The numbers of cases of volcanic activity each week in a recent year are normally distributed with a mean of 18.1 and a standard deviation of 2.9. Write a report that includes the following:

- a normal curve that represents the distribution
- several conclusions that can be made using the mean and standard deviation
- the probability that there are 25 or more cases of volcanic activity in a randomly selected week

Connecting Big Ideas

For use after Chapter 8.
SMP.7

After guessing a secret word in an online game, each letter turns green, yellow, or gray. Players continue to guess until every letter is green.

- 🟩 This is the correct letter in the correct location.

- 🟨 The letter is in the word, but is in a different location.

- ⬛ The letter is not in the word.

The amount of time it takes all players to guess a word correctly is normally distributed with a mean of 37 seconds and a standard deviation of 7 seconds.

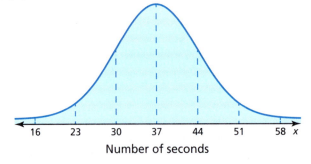

Number of seconds

450 Connecting Big Ideas

1. What do you notice? What do you wonder?

2. About what percentage of players guessed the word correctly in less than 30 seconds?

3. What is the probability that a randomly selected player guessed the word correctly in 40 seconds or more?

4. In a randomly selected group of 5,000 players, about how many do you expect to guess the word correctly in no more than 20 seconds?

5. You collect data from the first 200 players in a day. Is your sample likely to be representative of all players?

THINKING ABOUT THE BIG IDEAS

How can **Understanding Data Analysis** help you determine whether a sample is representative of a population?

Connecting Big Ideas

9 Trigonometric Ratios and Functions

- 9.1 Right Triangle Trigonometry
- 9.2 Angles and Radian Measure
- 9.3 Trigonometric Functions of Any Angle
- 9.4 Graphing Sine and Cosine Functions
- 9.5 Graphing Other Trigonometric Functions
- 9.6 Modeling with Trigonometric Functions
- 9.7 Using Trigonometric Identities
- 9.8 Using Sum and Difference Formulas

NATIONAL GEOGRAPHIC EXPLORER
Elizabeth Kapu'uwailani Lindsey — CULTURAL ANTHROPOLOGIST

Dr. Elizabeth Kapu'uwailani Lindsey is an award-winning filmmaker and anthropologist. She is committed to ethnographic rescue, the conservation of vanishing indigenous knowledge and tradition. Dr. Lindsey earned her doctorate studying and documenting the nearly lost traditions of the palu, Micronesian non-instrument navigators. Lindsey's expeditions now take her to some of the most remote regions of the world.

- Why is it important to document and conserve cultural traditions?
- What is ethnonavigation?
- Describe some ways to navigate without using modern instruments.

PERFORMANCE TASK
Most navigation today involves tools such as maps, compasses, and computers. In the Performance Task on pages 524 and 525, you will learn how bearings are used in navigation.

Ethnographic Rescue

Big Idea of the Chapter
Understanding Functions of Angles

Trigonometry is the branch of mathematics dealing with relationships between side lengths and angles of triangles. Six functions of angles are sine (sin), cosine (cos), tangent (tan), cotangent (cot), secant (sec), and cosecant (csc).

One of the goals of ethnographic rescue is to preserve languages, food, and customs of indigenous peoples. Early Polynesian navigators were skilled in using the Sun, stars, and other natural phenomena to navigate the seas. Because wind makes it nearly impossible to sail in a straight line, they also used their extensive knowledge of the wind and waves to navigate accurately.

1. You navigate a sailboat. The map shows one possible route that you can take to arrive at a port.

    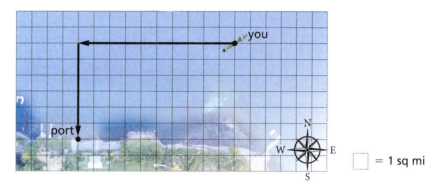

    a. Write precise instructions for how you should travel to arrive at the port using this route.

    b. You want to know how to arrive at the port using the shortest possible route. Draw the route. Then describe the information needed to give precise instructions for the route.

    c. Describe the direction and the distance that you should travel in part (b). Explain how you found this information.

    d. There is a strong wind blowing east. How might this affect your answer in part (c)?

2. Research other techniques that early Polynesians used to navigate.

Getting Ready for Chapter 9

Solving Linear Equations

EXAMPLE 1 Solve $-3 = \dfrac{x+8}{4}$.

$-3 = \dfrac{x+8}{4}$ Write the equation.

$4 \cdot (-3) = 4 \cdot \dfrac{x+8}{4}$ Multiplication Property of Equality

$-12 = x + 8$ Simplify.

$\underline{-8} \quad \underline{-8}$ Subtraction Property of Equality

$-20 = x$ Simplify.

▶ The solution is $x = -20$.

Solve the equation.

1. $\dfrac{x}{4} = 6$

2. $\dfrac{5+x}{3} = 2$

3. $3x - 7 = 11$

4. $-\dfrac{1}{2} = \dfrac{x-6}{4}$

5. $3.5 = 2x + 5$

6. $-\dfrac{4}{3} = -10x + \dfrac{1}{3}$

Pythagorean Theorem

EXAMPLE 2 Find the missing side length of the triangle.

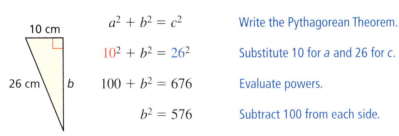

$a^2 + b^2 = c^2$ Write the Pythagorean Theorem.

$10^2 + b^2 = 26^2$ Substitute 10 for a and 26 for c.

$100 + b^2 = 676$ Evaluate powers.

$b^2 = 576$ Subtract 100 from each side.

$b = 24$ Take positive square root of each side.

▶ So, the missing side length is 24 centimeters.

Find the missing side length of the triangle.

7.

8. (triangle with b, 25 ft, 7 ft)

9.1 Right Triangle Trigonometry

> **Learning Target:** Understand the six trigonometric functions.
>
> **Success Criteria:**
> - I can define the six trigonometric functions.
> - I can evaluate trigonometric functions.
> - I can use trigonometric functions to find side lengths of right triangles.

INVESTIGATE Finding Ratios of Side Lengths of Right Triangles

Work with a partner. Consider a right triangle that has an acute angle θ (the Greek letter *theta*). The three sides of the triangle are the *hypotenuse*, the side *opposite* θ, and the side *adjacent* to θ.

1. Label the hypotenuse, opposite side, and adjacent side of the right triangle below.

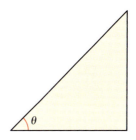

2. In each triangle shown, the measure of θ is 30°. Use a centimeter ruler to approximate the following ratios of side lengths. What do you notice?

$$\frac{\text{opposite}}{\text{hypotenuse}} \qquad \frac{\text{adjacent}}{\text{hypotenuse}} \qquad \frac{\text{opposite}}{\text{adjacent}}$$

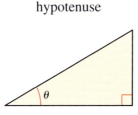 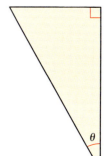

3. Explain whether the relationships you found in Exercise 2 are true for any right triangle with a 30° angle.

4. Construct right triangles with 45° angles. What do you notice about the ratios of the side lengths?

5. What do your results in Exercises 2–4 suggest about angles and ratios of side lengths in right triangles?

> **Vocabulary**
> sine
> cosine
> tangent
> cosecant
> secant
> cotangent

The Six Trigonometric Functions

Consider a right triangle that has an acute angle θ. The three sides of the triangle are the *hypotenuse*, the side *opposite* θ, and the side *adjacent* to θ.

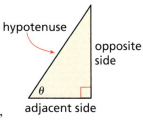

The side lengths of a right triangle are used to define the six trigonometric functions: **sine**, **cosine**, **tangent**, **cosecant**, **secant**, and **cotangent** (abbreviated sin, cos, tan, csc, sec, and cot, respectively).

Key Concept

Right Triangle Definitions of Trigonometric Functions

Let θ be an acute angle of a right triangle. The six trigonometric functions of θ are defined as shown.

$$\sin\theta = \frac{\text{opposite}}{\text{hypotenuse}} \qquad \cos\theta = \frac{\text{adjacent}}{\text{hypotenuse}} \qquad \tan\theta = \frac{\text{opposite}}{\text{adjacent}}$$

$$\csc\theta = \frac{\text{hypotenuse}}{\text{opposite}} \qquad \sec\theta = \frac{\text{hypotenuse}}{\text{adjacent}} \qquad \cot\theta = \frac{\text{adjacent}}{\text{opposite}}$$

The abbreviations *opp*, *adj*, and *hyp* are often used to represent the side lengths of the right triangle.

The ratios in the second row are reciprocals of the ratios in the first row.

$$\csc\theta = \frac{1}{\sin\theta} \qquad \sec\theta = \frac{1}{\cos\theta} \qquad \cot\theta = \frac{1}{\tan\theta}$$

EXAMPLE 1 Evaluating Trigonometric Functions

Evaluate the six trigonometric functions of the angle θ.

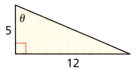

From the Pythagorean Theorem, the length of the hypotenuse is

$$\text{hyp} = \sqrt{5^2 + 12^2} = \sqrt{169} = 13.$$

Using adj = 5, opp = 12, and hyp = 13, the values are:

$$\sin\theta = \frac{\text{opp}}{\text{hyp}} = \frac{12}{13} \qquad \cos\theta = \frac{\text{adj}}{\text{hyp}} = \frac{5}{13} \qquad \tan\theta = \frac{\text{opp}}{\text{adj}} = \frac{12}{5}$$

$$\csc\theta = \frac{\text{hyp}}{\text{opp}} = \frac{13}{12} \qquad \sec\theta = \frac{\text{hyp}}{\text{adj}} = \frac{13}{5} \qquad \cot\theta = \frac{\text{adj}}{\text{opp}} = \frac{5}{12}$$

In-Class Practice

Self-Assessment

1. Evaluate the six trigonometric functions of the angle θ.

EXAMPLE 2 **Evaluating Trigonometric Functions**

In a right triangle, θ is an acute angle and $\sin \theta = \frac{4}{7}$. Evaluate the other five trigonometric functions of θ.

Draw a right triangle with acute angle θ such that the leg opposite θ has length 4 and the hypotenuse has length 7.

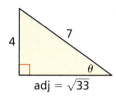

Find the length of the adjacent side. By the Pythagorean Theorem, the length of the other leg is

$$\text{adj} = \sqrt{7^2 - 4^2} = \sqrt{33}.$$

Find the values of the remaining five trigonometric functions.

Because $\sin \theta = \frac{4}{7}$, $\csc \theta = \frac{\text{hyp}}{\text{opp}} = \frac{7}{4}$. The other values are:

$$\cos \theta = \frac{\text{adj}}{\text{hyp}} = \frac{\sqrt{33}}{7} \qquad \tan \theta = \frac{\text{opp}}{\text{adj}} = \frac{4}{\sqrt{33}} = \frac{4\sqrt{33}}{33}$$

$$\sec \theta = \frac{\text{hyp}}{\text{adj}} = \frac{7}{\sqrt{33}} = \frac{7\sqrt{33}}{33} \qquad \cot \theta = \frac{\text{adj}}{\text{opp}} = \frac{\sqrt{33}}{4}$$

Key Concept

Trigonometric Values for Special Angles

The table gives the values of the six trigonometric functions for the angles 30°, 45°, and 60°, which occur frequently in trigonometry. You can obtain these values from the triangles shown.

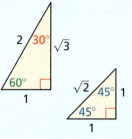

θ	$\sin \theta$	$\cos \theta$	$\tan \theta$	$\csc \theta$	$\sec \theta$	$\cot \theta$
30°	$\frac{1}{2}$	$\frac{\sqrt{3}}{2}$	$\frac{\sqrt{3}}{3}$	2	$\frac{2\sqrt{3}}{3}$	$\sqrt{3}$
45°	$\frac{\sqrt{2}}{2}$	$\frac{\sqrt{2}}{2}$	1	$\sqrt{2}$	$\sqrt{2}$	1
60°	$\frac{\sqrt{3}}{2}$	$\frac{1}{2}$	$\sqrt{3}$	$\frac{2\sqrt{3}}{3}$	2	$\frac{\sqrt{3}}{3}$

In-Class Practice

Self-Assessment

2. In a right triangle, θ is an acute angle and $\cos \theta = \frac{7}{10}$. Evaluate the other five trigonometric functions of θ.

Finding Side Lengths and Angle Measures

EXAMPLE 3 Finding an Unknown Side Length

Find the value of x for the right triangle.

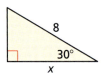

Write an equation using a trigonometric function that involves the ratio of x and 8. Solve the equation for x.

$\cos 30° = \dfrac{\text{adj}}{\text{hyp}}$ Write trigonometric equation.

$\dfrac{\sqrt{3}}{2} = \dfrac{x}{8}$ Substitute.

$4\sqrt{3} = x$ Multiply each side by 8.

▶ The length of the side is $x = 4\sqrt{3}$.

Finding all unknown side lengths and angle measures of a triangle is called *solving the triangle*. Solving right triangles with acute angles other than 30°, 45°, and 60° may require technology. Be sure to use *degree* mode.

EXAMPLE 4 Using Technology to Solve a Right Triangle

Solve $\triangle ABC$.

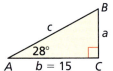

Because the triangle is a right triangle, A and B are complementary angles. So, $B = 90° - 28° = 62°$.

Next, write two equations using trigonometric functions, one that involves the ratio of a and 15, and one that involves c and 15. Solve the equations for a and c.

$\tan 28° = \dfrac{\text{opp}}{\text{adj}}$ Write trigonometric equation. $\sec 28° = \dfrac{\text{hyp}}{\text{adj}}$

$\tan 28° = \dfrac{a}{15}$ Substitute. $\sec 28° = \dfrac{c}{15}$

$15(\tan 28°) = a$ Multiply each side by 15. $15\left(\dfrac{1}{\cos 28°}\right) = c$

$7.98 \approx a$ Use technology. $16.99 \approx c$

▶ So, $B = 62°$, $a \approx 7.98$, and $c \approx 16.99$.

In-Class Practice

Self-Assessment

3. Find the value of x for the triangle to the right.

4. Solve $\triangle ABC$.

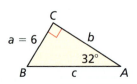

| 1 I don't understand yet. | 2 I can do it with help. | 3 I can do it on my own. | 4 I can teach someone. |

Connections to Real Life

An *angle of elevation* is an angle formed by a horizontal line and a line of sight *up* to an object. An *angle of depression* is an angle formed by a horizontal line and a line of sight *down* to an object.

EXAMPLE 5 Using an Angle of Elevation

A parasailer is attached to a boat with a rope that is 72 feet long. The angle of elevation from the boat to the parasailer is 28°. Estimate the parasailer's height above the boat.

Draw a diagram that represents the situation.

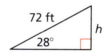

Write and solve an equation to estimate the height h.

$\sin 28° = \dfrac{h}{72}$ Write trigonometric equation.

$72(\sin 28°) = h$ Multiply each side by 72.

$33.8 \approx h$ Use technology.

▶ The height of the parasailer above the boat is about 33.8 feet.

STEM Video: Parasailing to Great Heights

In-Class Practice

Self-Assessment

5. WHAT IF? In Example 5, estimate the height of the parasailer above the boat when the angle of elevation is 38°.

 I don't understand yet.   I can do it with help.   I can do it on my own.   **4** I can teach someone.

9.1 Practice

Evaluate the six trigonometric functions of the angle θ. (See Example 1.)

1.
2.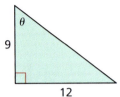
3.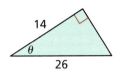

Let θ be an acute angle of a right triangle. Evaluate the other five trigonometric functions of θ. (See Example 2.)

4. $\sin \theta = \frac{7}{11}$
5. $\cos \theta = \frac{5}{12}$
6. $\csc \theta = \frac{15}{8}$
7. $\sec \theta = \frac{14}{9}$
8. $\tan \theta = \frac{7}{6}$
9. $\cot \theta = \frac{16}{11}$

10. **SMP.3 ERROR ANALYSIS** Describe and correct the error in finding $\csc \theta$, given that θ is an acute angle of a right triangle and $\cos \theta = \frac{7}{11}$.

Find the value of x for the right triangle. (See Example 3.)

11.
12.
13.

SMP.5 Use a tool to evaluate the trigonometric function.

14. $\tan 31°$
15. $\csc 59°$
16. $\sin 23°$

Solve △ABC using the diagram and the given measurements. (See Example 4.)

17. $B = 36°, a = 23$
18. $A = 27°, b = 9$
19. $B = 16°, b = 14$
20. $B = 31°, a = 23$
21. $B = 72°, c = 12.8$
22. $A = 64°, a = 7.4$

23. **CONNECTION TO REAL LIFE** A person whose eye level is 1.5 meters above the ground is standing 75 meters from the base of the Jin Mao Building in Shanghai, China. The person estimates the angle of elevation to the top of the building is about 80°. Estimate the height of the building.

460   Chapter 9   Trigonometric Ratios and Functions

24. **OPEN-ENDED** Write a real-life problem that can be solved using a right triangle. Then solve your problem.

▶ 25. **CONNECTION TO REAL LIFE** To measure the width of a river, you plant a stake on one side of the river, directly across from a boulder. You then walk 100 meters to the right of the stake and measure a 79° angle between the stake and the boulder. About how wide is the river? (See Example 5.)

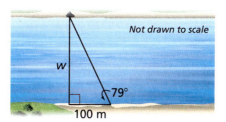

26. Evaluate the six trigonometric functions of the angle (90° − θ) in Exercise 2. Describe the relationships you notice.

27. Consider a semicircle with a radius of 1 unit, as shown below. Write the values of the six trigonometric functions of the angle θ.

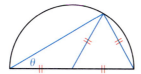

28. **SMP.7** Is it possible to draw a right triangle in which the values of the cosine function of the acute angles are equal?

29. A passenger in an airplane sees two towns directly to the left of the plane. Explain how to find the distance y between the two towns. Then find y.

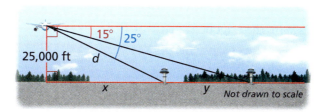

30. **SMP.1 DIG DEEPER** A procedure for approximating π based on the work of Archimedes is to inscribe a regular hexagon in a circle.

   a. Use the diagram to solve for x. What is the perimeter of the hexagon?

   b. Explain why a regular n-sided polygon inscribed in a circle of radius 1 has a perimeter of

   $$2n \cdot \sin\left(\frac{180}{n}\right)^\circ.$$

   c. Use the expression from part (b) to find an expression in terms of n that approximates π. Then evaluate the expression when n = 50.

Interpreting Data

RAINBOWS A rainbow is visible when sunlight passes through drops of water in the atmosphere. Some of the light in the drops is reflected, and different colors of light are reflected at slightly different angles.

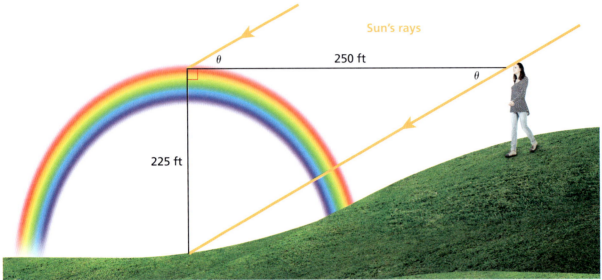

not drawn to scale

31. The person in the diagram can see the color red on the rainbow. Find and interpret θ.

32. Research the angles at which you can view the other 6 colors in a rainbow.

Review & Refresh

33. Graph the function.
$$y = 2(x - 3)^2 + 6$$

34. The number of concerts attended in one year by a random sample of 32 teenagers are shown in the table. Estimate the population mean μ.

Number of Concerts Attended							
3	2	0	4	2	0	2	14
3	4	2	17	1	28	0	1
4	4	0	5	9	12	9	1
0	0	1	0	1	0	6	23

35. Graph the function.
$$f(x) = e^{-x} + 8$$

36. A randomized comparative experiment tests whether a vitamin supplement increases human bone density. The control group has eight people and the treatment group, which receives the vitamin supplement, has eight people.

	Bone Density (g/cm²)			
Control Group	0.9	1.2	1.0	0.8
Treatment Group	1.2	1.0	0.9	1.1

Control Group	1.3	1.1	0.9	1.0
Treatment Group	1.1	0.9	1.3	1.2

Find the experimental difference of the mean yield of the treatment group, $\bar{x}_{treatment}$, and the mean yield of the control group, $\bar{x}_{control}$.

9.2 Angles and Radian Measure

Learning Target: Draw angles in standard position and understand radian measure.

Success Criteria:
- I can draw angles in standard position.
- I can explain the meaning of radian measure.
- I can convert between degrees and radians.
- I can use radian measure to find arc lengths and the area of a sector.

INVESTIGATE Using Radian Measure

Work with a partner. Consider a circle with radius r centered at the origin. Let the vertex of an angle be at the origin, with one side of the angle on the positive x-axis. When the other side of the angle intercepts an arc of length r, the measure of the angle is one *radian*.

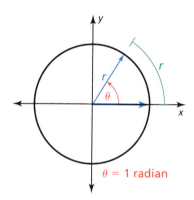

1. The circle below has a radius of 1 inch. The blue point corresponds to an angle of 1 radian. What is the length of the intercepted arc?

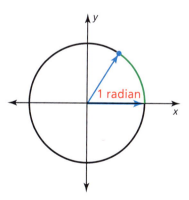

2. **SMP.5** Draw any circle.

    a. Plot points that correspond to angles of 1, 2, 3, 4, 5, and 6 radians.

    b. Estimate the angle measures (in degrees) that correspond to the points you plotted in part (a).

3. The circumference of a circle with radius r is $2\pi r$. How many radians are in a circle?

9.2 Angles and Radian Measure   463

Vocabulary
initial side
terminal side
standard position
coterminal
radian
sector
central angle

Drawing Angles in Standard Position

Key Concept

Angles in Standard Position

In a coordinate plane, an angle can be formed by fixing one ray, called the **initial side**, and rotating the other ray, called the **terminal side**, about the vertex.

An angle is in **standard position** when its vertex is at the origin and its initial side lies on the positive x-axis.

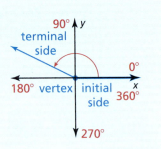

The measure of an angle is positive when the rotation of its terminal side is counterclockwise and negative when the rotation is clockwise. The terminal side of an angle can rotate more than 360°.

EXAMPLE 1 Drawing Angles in Standard Position

a. Draw a 240° angle in standard position.

Because 240° is 60° more than 180°, the terminal side is 60° counterclockwise past the negative x-axis.

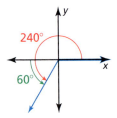

b. Draw a 500° angle in standard position.

Because 500° is 140° more than 360°, the terminal side makes one complete rotation 360° counterclockwise plus 140° more.

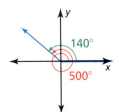

c. Draw a −50° angle in standard position.

Because −50° is negative, the terminal side is 50° clockwise from the positive x-axis.

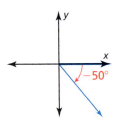

In-Class Practice

Self-Assessment

Draw an angle in standard position with the given measure.

1. 65°
2. −120°
3. −450°

Finding Coterminal Angles

In Example 1(b), the angles 500° and 140° are **coterminal** because their initial sides and terminal sides coincide. An angle coterminal with a given angle can be found by adding or subtracting multiples of 360°.

EXAMPLE 2 Finding Coterminal Angles

a. **Find one positive angle and one negative angle that are coterminal with −45°.**

You can add and subtract 360° to find coterminal angles.

$-45° + 360° = 315°$

$-45° - 360° = -405°$

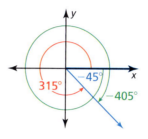

▶ So, a positive angle is 315° and a negative angle is −405°.

b. **Find one positive angle and one negative angle that are coterminal with 395°.**

You can add and subtract multiples of 360° to find coterminal angles.

$395° - 360° = 35°$

$395° - 2(360°) = -325°$

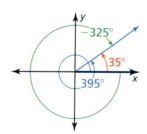

▶ So, a positive angle is 35° and a negative angle is −325°.

In-Class Practice

Self-Assessment

Find one positive angle and one negative angle that are coterminal with the given angle.

4. 80°

5. 230°

6. 740°

7. −135°

9.2 Angles and Radian Measure 465

Using Radian Measure

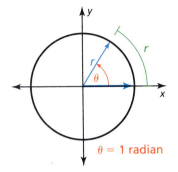

$\theta = 1$ radian

Angles can also be measured in *radians*. One **radian** is the measure of an angle whose sides intercept an arc of length r, where r is the radius.

Because the circumference of a circle is $2\pi r$, there are 2π radians in a full circle. So, degree measure and radian measure are related by the equation $360° = 2\pi$ radians, or $180° = \pi$ radians.

Degrees to radians: degree measure $\times \dfrac{\pi \text{ radians}}{180°}$

Radians to degrees: radian measure $\times \dfrac{180°}{\pi \text{ radians}}$

EXAMPLE 3 Converting Between Degrees and Radians

a. Convert $120°$ to radians.

$$120° = 120 \text{ degrees} \left(\dfrac{\pi \text{ radians}}{180 \text{ degrees}}\right)$$
$$= \dfrac{2\pi}{3}$$

b. Convert $-\dfrac{\pi}{12}$ to degrees.

$$-\dfrac{\pi}{12} = \left(-\dfrac{\pi}{12} \text{ radians}\right)\left(\dfrac{180°}{\pi \text{ radians}}\right)$$
$$= -15°$$

Concept Summary

Degree and Radian Measures of Special Angles

You may find it helpful to memorize the equivalent degree and radian measures for special angles from $0°$ to $90°$. All other special angles shown are multiples of these angles.

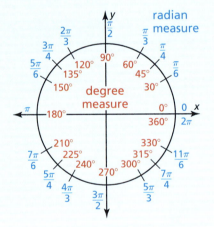

In-Class Practice

Self-Assessment

Convert the degree measure to radians or the radian measure to degrees.

8. $135°$

9. $-40°$

10. $\dfrac{5\pi}{4}$

1 I don't understand yet. **2** I can do it with help. **3** I can do it on my own. **4** I can teach someone.

Arc Lengths and Areas of Sectors

A **sector** is a region of a circle that is bounded by two radii and an arc of the circle. The **central angle** of a sector is the angle formed by the two radii. There are simple formulas for the arc length and area of a sector when the central angle is measured in radians.

Key Concept

Arc Length and Area of a Sector

The arc length s and area A of a sector with radius r and central angle θ (measured in radians) are as follows.

Arc length: $s = r\theta$

Area: $A = \frac{1}{2}r^2\theta$

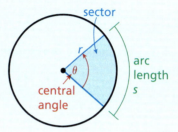

EXAMPLE 4 Finding an Arc Length and the Area of a Sector

A softball field forms a sector with the dimensions shown. Find the length of the outfield fence and the area of the field.

First convert the measure of the central angle to radians.

$$90° = 90 \text{ degrees} \left(\frac{\pi \text{ radians}}{180 \text{ degrees}}\right)$$

$$= \frac{\pi}{2} \text{ radians}$$

Use the radian measure to find the arc length and the area of the sector.

Arc length: $s = r\theta$

$= 200\left(\frac{\pi}{2}\right)$

$= 100\pi$

Area: $A = \frac{1}{2}r^2\theta$

$= \frac{1}{2}(200)^2\left(\frac{\pi}{2}\right)$

$= 10{,}000\pi$

▶ The length of the outfield fence is 100π, or about 314 feet. The area of the field is $10{,}000\pi$, or about 31,416 square feet.

In-Class Practice

Self-Assessment

11. **WHAT IF?** In Example 4, the outfield fence is 220 feet from home plate. Estimate the length of the outfield fence and the area of the field.

1 I don't understand yet.   **2** I can do it with help.   **3** I can do it on my own.   **4** I can teach someone.

9.2 Practice

Draw an angle in standard position with the given measure. (See Example 1.)

▶ 1. 110°

2. 450°

3. −900°

4. −10°

Find one positive angle and one negative angle that are coterminal with the given angle. (See Example 2.)

▶ 5. 70°

6. 255°

7. −125°

8. −800°

Convert the degree measure to radians or the radian measure to degrees. (See Example 3.)

9. 40°

10. $\dfrac{\pi}{9}$

▶ 11. −260°

12. $\dfrac{3\pi}{4}$

MATCHING Match the angle measure with the angle.

13. 600°

14. $-\dfrac{9\pi}{4}$

15. $\dfrac{5\pi}{6}$

16. −240°

A.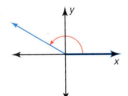

C.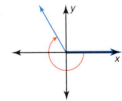

B.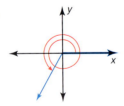

D.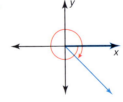

▶ 17. The observation deck of a building forms a sector with the dimensions shown. Find the length of the safety rail and the area of the deck. (See Example 4.)

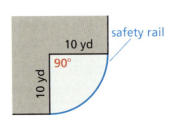

18. **SMP.3 ERROR ANALYSIS** Describe and correct the error in finding the area of a sector with a radius of 6 centimeters and a central angle of 40°.

$$A = \frac{1}{2}(6)^2(40)$$
$$= 720 \text{ cm}^2$$

19. **WIND ENERGY** A wind turbine rotates 15 times per minute. At that rate, through what angle does the tip of one of its blades rotate in one hour? Give your answer in both degrees and radians.

20. **SMP.7** Explain what happens to the length of an intercepted arc when the radius of a circle is doubled but the measure of the central angle remains the same.

21. **ANTHROPOLOGIST NAVIGATION** You use a navigation system on your boat to avoid an algae bloom. Your original course involved traveling along an arc with a central angle of 150° and a radius of 1 mile. Your new course involves traveling along an arc with a central angle of 170° and a radius of 2 miles. How much longer is the new course?

22. Explain your reasoning in finding the measure of θ.

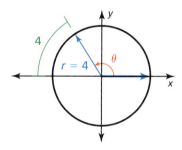

23. **SMP.6** There are 60 *minutes* in 1 degree of arc, and 60 *seconds* in 1 minute of arc. The notation 50° 30′ 10″ represents an angle with a measure of 50 degrees, 30 minutes, and 10 seconds.

   a. Write the angle measure 70.55° using the notation above.

   b. Write the angle measure 110° 45′ 30″ to the nearest hundredth of a degree.

   c. Write the angle measure 40° 15′ 45″ to the nearest tenth of a radian.

24. **SMP.1 DIG DEEPER** A dartboard has 20 identical sectors, each worth a point value from 1 to 20. The shaded regions double or triple this value. Explain your reasoning in finding the area of the triple region for the entire dartboard.

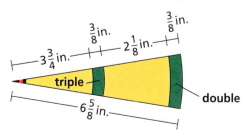

Interpreting Data

GREAT CIRCLE ROUTES A *great circle route* is the shortest route between two points on the surface of a sphere. Great circle routes are commonly used in long-distance air travel to save time and fuel.

25. **SMP.2** How can you use the formula

$$s = r\theta$$

to find the shortest flying distance from New York City to Madrid? What do r and θ represent in this situation?

26. Approximate the greatest flying distance between 2 locations on Earth. Assume a flight altitude of 35,000 feet.

Review & Refresh

27. Evaluate the six trigonometric functions of the angle θ.

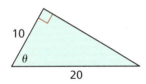

28. Estimate the margin of error for a survey that has a sample size of 770.

29. In the equation $\dfrac{y}{x} = 8$, tell whether x and y show *direct variation, inverse variation,* or *neither*.

30. Multiply $5i$ and $(2 - i)$.

31. Rewrite $5^0 = 1$ in logarithmic form.

Solve the equation.

32. $x^{3/4} - 8 = 0$

33. $7^{2x + 3} = 7^{6 - x}$

34. Use finite differences to determine the degree of the polynomial function that fits the data. Then use technology to find the polynomial function.

x	1	2	3	4	5	6
f(x)	6	14	25	40	60	86

35. Write a polynomial function f of least degree that has rational coefficients, a leading coefficient of 1, and zeros of 3 and $\sqrt{2}$.

470 Chapter 9 Trigonometric Ratios and Functions

9.3 Trigonometric Functions of Any Angle

Learning Target: Evaluate trigonometric functions of any angle.

Success Criteria:
- I can evaluate trigonometric functions given a point on an angle.
- I can evaluate trigonometric functions using the unit circle.
- I can find and use reference angles to evaluate trigonometric functions.

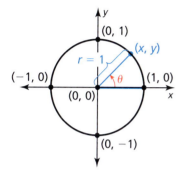

The *unit circle* is a circle in the coordinate plane with its center at the origin and a radius r of 1 unit. The equation of the unit circle is

$$x^2 + y^2 = 1. \qquad \text{Equation of unit circle}$$

As the point (x, y) starts at $(1, 0)$ and moves counterclockwise around the unit circle, the angle θ increases from 0° through 360°.

INVESTIGATE Writing Trigonometric Functions

Work with a partner. A right triangle with acute angle θ is inscribed inside the unit circle as shown.

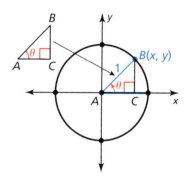

1. Explain how you can write the coordinates of $B(x, y)$ in terms of θ.

2. Find the exact coordinates of the point (x, y) on the unit circle when $\theta = 60°$. Then find the six trigonometric functions of θ.

3. Consider $\theta = 120°$ as shown. What do you notice about the acute angle formed by the terminal side of θ and the x-axis? Explain how you can use this information to find the exact coordinates of the point (x, y). Then find the six trigonometric functions of θ. What do you notice?

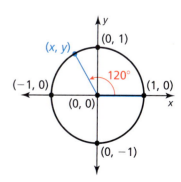

4. Explain how to use your results in Exercises 2 and 3 to find the exact coordinates of the point (x, y) when $\theta = 135°$.

Vocabulary
unit circle
quadrantal angle
reference angle

Trigonometric Functions of Any Angle

You can generalize the right-triangle definitions of trigonometric functions so that they apply to any angle in standard position.

Key Concept

General Definitions of Trigonometric Functions

Let θ be an angle in standard position, and let (x, y) be the point where the terminal side of θ intersects the circle $x^2 + y^2 = r^2$. The six trigonometric functions of θ are defined as shown.

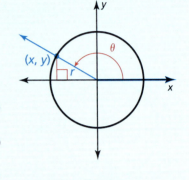

$$\sin \theta = \frac{y}{r} \qquad \csc \theta = \frac{r}{y}, y \neq 0$$

$$\cos \theta = \frac{x}{r} \qquad \sec \theta = \frac{r}{x}, x \neq 0$$

$$\tan \theta = \frac{y}{x}, x \neq 0 \qquad \cot \theta = \frac{x}{y}, y \neq 0$$

These functions are sometimes called *circular functions*.

EXAMPLE 1   Evaluating Trigonometric Functions Given a Point

Let $(-4, 3)$ be a point on the terminal side of an angle θ in standard position. Evaluate the six trigonometric functions of θ.

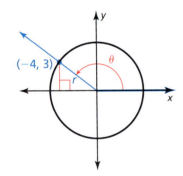

Use the Pythagorean Theorem to find the length of r.

$$r = \sqrt{x^2 + y^2} = \sqrt{(-4)^2 + 3^2} = \sqrt{25} = 5$$

Using $x = -4$, $y = 3$, and $r = 5$, the values of the six trigonometric functions of θ are:

$$\sin \theta = \frac{y}{r} = \frac{3}{5} \qquad \csc \theta = \frac{r}{y} = \frac{5}{3}$$

$$\cos \theta = \frac{x}{r} = -\frac{4}{5} \qquad \sec \theta = \frac{r}{x} = -\frac{5}{4}$$

$$\tan \theta = \frac{y}{x} = -\frac{3}{4} \qquad \cot \theta = \frac{x}{y} = -\frac{4}{3}$$

In-Class Practice

Self-Assessment

1. Evaluate the six trigonometric functions of θ.

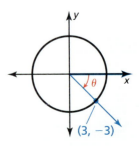

 I don't understand yet.   I can do it with help.   I can do it on my own.   I can teach someone.

Key Concept

The Unit Circle

The circle $x^2 + y^2 = 1$, which has center $(0, 0)$ and radius 1, is called the **unit circle**. The values of $\sin \theta$ and $\cos \theta$ are the y-coordinate and x-coordinate, respectively, of the point where the terminal side of θ intersects the unit circle.

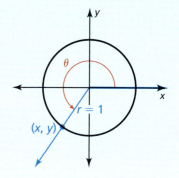

$$\sin \theta = \frac{y}{r} = \frac{y}{1} = y$$

$$\cos \theta = \frac{x}{r} = \frac{x}{1} = x$$

It is convenient to use the unit circle to evaluate trigonometric functions of *quadrantal angles*. A **quadrantal angle** is an angle in standard position whose terminal side lies on an axis. The measure of a quadrantal angle is always a multiple of $90°$, or $\frac{\pi}{2}$ radians.

EXAMPLE 2 Using the Unit Circle

Use the unit circle to evaluate the six trigonometric functions of $\theta = 270°$.

Draw a unit circle with the angle $\theta = 270°$ in standard position.

The terminal side of θ intersects the unit circle at $(0, -1)$.

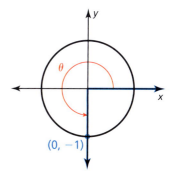

Find the values of the six trigonometric functions using $x = 0$ and $y = -1$.

$$\sin \theta = \frac{y}{r} = \frac{-1}{1} = -1 \qquad \csc \theta = \frac{r}{y} = \frac{1}{-1} = -1$$

$$\cos \theta = \frac{x}{r} = \frac{0}{1} = 0 \qquad \sec \theta = \frac{r}{x} = \frac{1}{0} \text{ undefined}$$

$$\tan \theta = \frac{y}{x} = \frac{-1}{0} \text{ undefined} \qquad \cot \theta = \frac{x}{y} = \frac{0}{-1} = 0$$

In-Class Practice

Self-Assessment

Use the unit circle to evaluate the six trigonometric functions of θ.

2. $\theta = 90°$
3. $\theta = 180°$
4. $\theta = 2\pi$

1 I don't understand yet. **2** I can do it with help. **3** I can do it on my own. **4** I can teach someone.

Reference Angles

Key Concept

Reference Angle Relationships

Let θ be an angle in standard position. The **reference angle** for θ is the acute angle θ' (theta prime) formed by the terminal side of θ and the x-axis. The relationship between θ and θ' is shown below for nonquadrantal angles θ with terminal sides in Quadrants II, III, and IV, such that $90° < \theta < 360°$ or, in radians, $\frac{\pi}{2} < \theta < 2\pi$.

Quadrant II

Quadrant III

Quadrant IV

Degrees: $\theta' = 180° - \theta$ Degrees: $\theta' = \theta - 180°$ Degrees: $\theta' = 360° - \theta$
Radians: $\theta' = \pi - \theta$ Radians: $\theta' = \theta - \pi$ Radians: $\theta' = 2\pi - \theta$

EXAMPLE 3   Finding Reference Angles

Find the reference angle θ' for each angle.

a. $\theta = \dfrac{5\pi}{3}$

b. $\theta = -130°$

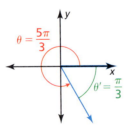

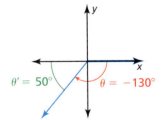

The terminal side of θ lies in Quadrant IV.

θ is coterminal with $230°$, whose terminal side lies in Quadrant III.

▶ So, $\theta' = 2\pi - \dfrac{5\pi}{3} = \dfrac{\pi}{3}$.

▶ So, $\theta' = 230° - 180° = 50°$.

In-Class Practice

Self-Assessment

Find the reference angle for the angle.

5. $210°$

6. $-260°$

7. $\dfrac{-7\pi}{9}$

1 I don't understand yet.   **2** I can do it with help.   **3** I can do it on my own.   **4** I can teach someone.

Reference angles allow you to evaluate a trigonometric function for any angle θ. The sign of a trigonometric function's value depends on the quadrant in which the terminal side of θ lies.

Key Concept

Evaluating Trigonometric Functions

Use these steps to evaluate a trigonometric function for any angle θ:

Step 1 Find the reference angle θ'.

Step 2 Evaluate the trigonometric function for θ'.

Step 3 Determine the sign of the trigonometric function value from the quadrant in which the terminal side of θ lies.

Signs of Function Values

Quadrant II
sin θ, csc θ : +
cos θ, sec θ : −
tan θ, cot θ : −

Quadrant I
sin θ, csc θ : +
cos θ, sec θ : +
tan θ, cot θ : +

Quadrant III
sin θ, csc θ : −
cos θ, sec θ : −
tan θ, cot θ : +

Quadrant IV
sin θ, csc θ : −
cos θ, sec θ : +
tan θ, cot θ : −

EXAMPLE 4   Using Reference Angles to Evaluate Functions

a. Evaluate tan(−240°).

The angle −240° is coterminal with 120°. The reference angle is

$$\theta' = 180° - 120° = 60°.$$

The tangent function is negative in Quadrant II, so

$$\tan(-240°) = -\tan 60° = -\sqrt{3}.$$

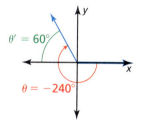

b. Evaluate $\csc \dfrac{17\pi}{6}$.

The angle $\dfrac{17\pi}{6}$ is coterminal with $\dfrac{5\pi}{6}$. The reference angle is

$$\theta' = \pi - \frac{5\pi}{6} = \frac{\pi}{6}.$$

The cosecant function is positive in Quadrant II, so

$$\csc \frac{17\pi}{6} = \csc \frac{\pi}{6} = 2.$$

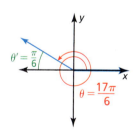

In-Class Practice

Self-Assessment

Evaluate the function without using technology.

8. sin 315°

9. cos(−210°)

10. $\sec \dfrac{11\pi}{4}$

9.3   Trigonometric Functions of Any Angle

9.3 Practice

Evaluate the six trigonometric functions of θ. (See Example 1.)

1.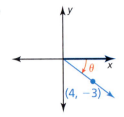
2.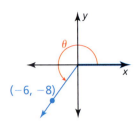
3.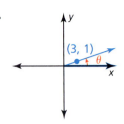

Use the unit circle to evaluate the six trigonometric functions of θ. (See Example 2.)

4. $\theta = 0°$
5. $\theta = \dfrac{\pi}{2}$
6. $\theta = 540°$
7. $\theta = \dfrac{7\pi}{2}$
8. $\theta = -270°$
9. $\theta = -2\pi$

Find the reference angle for the angle. (See Example 3.)

10. $150°$
11. $-100°$
12. $\dfrac{23\pi}{4}$
13. $\dfrac{8\pi}{3}$
14. $-370°$
15. $-\dfrac{19\pi}{6}$

16. **SMP.3 ERROR ANALYSIS** Describe and correct the error in finding a reference angle θ' for $\theta = 650°$.

θ is coterminal with 290°, whose terminal side lies in Quadrant IV.
So, $\theta' = 290° - 270° = 20°$.

Evaluate the function without using technology. (See Example 4.)

17. $\sec 135°$
18. $\cot 60°$
19. $\cos \dfrac{\pi}{4}$
20. $\csc(-420°)$
21. $\tan\left(-\dfrac{3\pi}{4}\right)$
22. $\cos \dfrac{7\pi}{4}$

23. **CONNECTION TO REAL LIFE** The horizontal distance d (in feet) traveled by an object launched at an angle θ and with an initial speed v (in feet per second) is given by

$$d = \dfrac{v^2}{32} \sin 2\theta.$$

You kick a football at an angle of 60° with an initial speed of 49 feet per second. Estimate the horizontal distance traveled by the football.

RESOURCES

24. A rock climber is using a rock climbing treadmill that is 10 feet long. The climber begins by lying horizontally on the treadmill, which is then rotated about its midpoint by 110° so that the rock climber is climbing toward the top. If the midpoint of the treadmill is 6 feet above the ground, how high above the ground is the top of the treadmill?

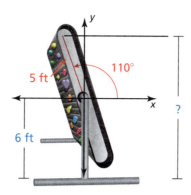

25. **SMP.2** A sprinkler at ground level is used to water a garden. The water leaving the sprinkler has an initial speed of 25 feet per second.

    a. Use the model for horizontal distance given in Exercise 23 to complete the table.

Angle of sprinkler, θ	30°	35°	40°	45°	50°	55°	60°
Horizontal distance water travels, d							

    b. Which value of θ appears to maximize the horizontal distance traveled by the water?

26. Use symmetry and the given information to label the coordinates of the other points corresponding to special angles on the unit circle shown at the right.

27. Describe all values of θ that satisfy each set of conditions.

    a. $\sin \theta > 0$, $\cos \theta < 0$, and $\tan \theta > 0$
    b. $\sin \theta > 0$, $\cos \theta < 0$, and $\tan \theta < 0$

28. Write $\tan \theta$ as the ratio of two other trigonometric functions. Use this ratio to explain why $\tan 90°$ is undefined but $\cot 90° = 0$.

29. **SMP.7** Explain whether $\theta = 60°$ is the only solution of the equation $\tan \theta = \sqrt{3}$.

30. An ozone molecule is made up of two oxygen atoms bonded to a third oxygen atom, as shown. Find the distance d (in picometers) between the centers of the two unbonded oxygen atoms.

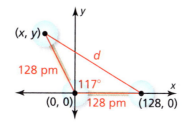

9.3 Trigonometric Functions of Any Angle

Interpreting Data

SUNDIALS A sundial is a device that uses the Sun to indicate the time. As the Sun changes position, the shadow cast by the gnomon (a thin rod) indicates the time. For example, the sundial shown to the right indicates a time of about 3:00 P.M. Think of a sundial like a unit circle, with a radius of 1 unit and 12 P.M. represents 0°. The display shows the degree of the shadow on such a sundial for 12 hours.

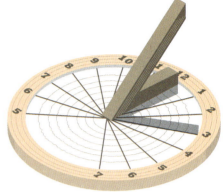

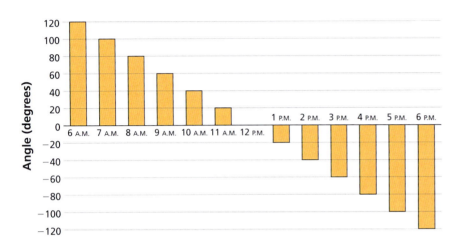

31. At what time(s) does the angle formed by the shadow fall in the fourth quadrant?

32. Find the six trigonometric functions of the angle corresponding to 8:30 A.M.

33. Explain why a sundial cannot be used to find every hour in a day.

Review & Refresh

34. Find $\dfrac{3x}{x-2} - \dfrac{6}{x-2}$.

35. Write an equation of the parabola in vertex form that passes through (0, 10) and has vertex (5, 25).

36. Let $f(x) = \sqrt{3x+7}$ and $g(x) = x^2 - 1$. Find $f(g(2))$.

37. Find the value of x for the right triangle.

38. Graph $f(x) = \sqrt{\tfrac{1}{2}x}$. Find the domain and range.

39. Using radian measure, give one positive angle and one negative angle that are coterminal with the angle shown.

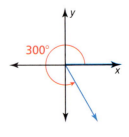

9.4 Graphing Sine and Cosine Functions

Learning Target: Describe and graph sine and cosine functions.

Success Criteria:
- I can identify characteristics of sine and cosine functions.
- I can graph transformations of sine and cosine functions.

INVESTIGATE   Graphing the Sine Function

Work with a partner.

1. Consider the function $y = \sin x$.

   a. Complete the table, where x is an angle measure in radians.

   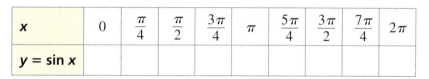

x	0	$\frac{\pi}{4}$	$\frac{\pi}{2}$	$\frac{3\pi}{4}$	π	$\frac{5\pi}{4}$	$\frac{3\pi}{2}$	$\frac{7\pi}{4}$	2π
y = sin x									

   b. Plot the points (x, y) from part (a). Draw a smooth curve through the points to sketch the graph of $y = \sin x$. Make several observations about the graph.

   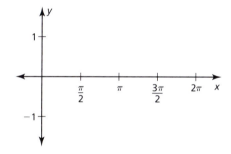

2. In the previous section, you learned how to use the unit circle in the coordinate plane to evaluate trigonometric functions of any angle. Use the graphing tool online to graph $y = \sin x$. Examine the graph when $x < 0$ and when $x > 2\pi$. What do you notice? Explain why the graph behaves this way.

   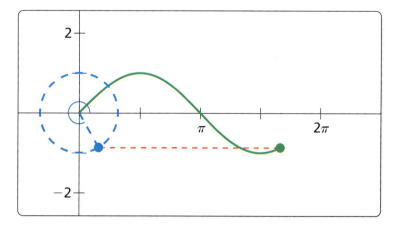

Vocabulary
amplitude
periodic function
cycle
period
phase shift
midline

Characteristics of Sine and Cosine Functions

Consider the parent functions $y = \sin x$ and $y = \cos x$.

x	-2π	$-\frac{3\pi}{2}$	$-\pi$	$-\frac{\pi}{2}$	0	$\frac{\pi}{2}$	π	$\frac{3\pi}{2}$	2π
$y = \sin x$	0	1	0	-1	0	1	0	-1	0
$y = \cos x$	1	0	-1	0	1	0	-1	0	1

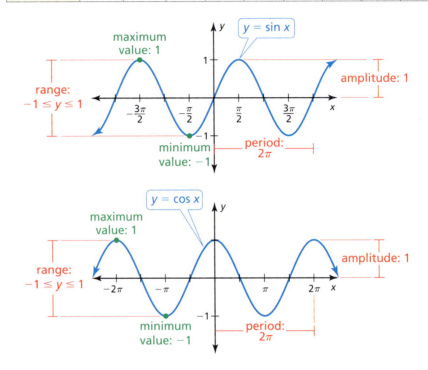

- The domain of each function is all real numbers.

- The range of each function is $-1 \le y \le 1$. So, the minimum value of each function is -1 and the maximum value is 1.

- The **amplitude** of the graph of each function is one-half of the difference of the maximum value and the minimum value, or $\frac{1}{2}[1 - (-1)] = 1$.

- Each function is **periodic**, which means that its graph has a repeating pattern. The shortest repeating portion is a **cycle**. The horizontal length of each cycle is the **period**. The graph of each function has a period of 2π.

- The x-intercepts for $y = \sin x$ occur at $x = 0, \pm\pi, \pm 2\pi, \pm 3\pi, \ldots$.

- The x-intercepts for $y = \cos x$ occur at $x = \pm\frac{\pi}{2}, \pm\frac{3\pi}{2}, \pm\frac{5\pi}{2}, \pm\frac{7\pi}{2}, \ldots$.

In-Class Practice

Self-Assessment

1. Explain why the periods of $y = \sin x$ and $y = \cos x$ are both 2π.

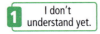

Stretching and Shrinking Sine and Cosine Functions

The graphs of $y = a \sin bx$ and $y = a \cos bx$ are transformations of the parent functions. The value of a indicates a vertical stretch or shrink. The value of b indicates a horizontal stretch or shrink.

Key Concept

Amplitude and Period

The amplitude and period of the graphs of $y = a \sin bx$ and $y = a \cos bx$, where a and b are nonzero real numbers, are as follows:

$$\text{Amplitude} = |a| \qquad \text{Period} = \frac{2\pi}{|b|}$$

Each graph below shows five key points that you can use to sketch the graphs of $y = a \sin bx$ and $y = a \cos bx$ for $a > 0$ and $b > 0$. These points partition the interval $0 \leq x \leq \frac{2\pi}{b}$ into four equal parts. The *x*-intercepts, maximum, and minimum occur at these points.

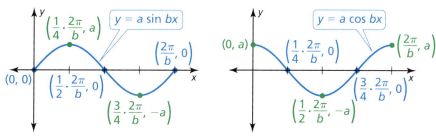

EXAMPLE 1 Graphing a Sine Function

Identify the amplitude and period of $g(x) = 4 \sin x$. Graph the function and describe the graph as a transformation of the graph of $f(x) = \sin x$.

The amplitude is $|a| = 4$ and the period is $\frac{2\pi}{|b|} = \frac{2\pi}{1} = 2\pi$.

x-Intercepts: $(0, 0)$; $\left(\frac{1}{2} \cdot 2\pi, 0\right) = (\pi, 0)$; $(2\pi, 0)$

Maximum: $\left(\frac{1}{4} \cdot 2\pi, 4\right) = \left(\frac{\pi}{2}, 4\right)$ Minimum: $\left(\frac{3}{4} \cdot 2\pi, -4\right) = \left(\frac{3\pi}{2}, -4\right)$

▶ The graph of g is a vertical stretch by a factor of 4 of the graph of f.

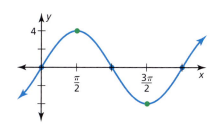

In-Class Practice

Self-Assessment

2. Identify the amplitude and period of $g(x) = 2 \sin \pi x$. Graph the function and describe the graph as a transformation of the graph of its parent function.

| 1 I don't understand yet. | 2 I can do it with help. | 3 I can do it on my own. | 4 I can teach someone. |

EXAMPLE 2 Graphing Cosine Functions

Identify the amplitude and period of g. Graph each function and describe each graph as a transformation of the graph of $f(x) = \cos x$.

a. $g(x) = \cos 2x$

The amplitude is $|a| = 1$ and the period is $\dfrac{2\pi}{|b|} = \dfrac{2\pi}{2} = \pi$.

x-Intercepts: $\left(\dfrac{1}{4} \cdot \pi, 0\right) = \left(\dfrac{\pi}{4}, 0\right); \left(\dfrac{3}{4} \cdot \pi, 0\right) = \left(\dfrac{3\pi}{4}, 0\right)$

Maximums: $(0, 1); (\pi, 1)$ Minimum: $\left(\dfrac{1}{2} \cdot \pi, -1\right) = \left(\dfrac{\pi}{2}, -1\right)$

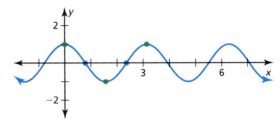

▶ The graph of g is a horizontal shrink by a factor of $\dfrac{1}{2}$ of the graph of f.

b. $g(x) = \dfrac{1}{2} \cos 2\pi x$

The amplitude is $|a| = \dfrac{1}{2}$ and the period is $\dfrac{2\pi}{|b|} = \dfrac{2\pi}{2\pi} = 1$.

x-Intercepts: $\left(\dfrac{1}{4} \cdot 1, 0\right) = \left(\dfrac{1}{4}, 0\right); \left(\dfrac{3}{4} \cdot 1, 0\right) = \left(\dfrac{3}{4}, 0\right)$

Maximums: $\left(0, \dfrac{1}{2}\right); \left(1, \dfrac{1}{2}\right)$ Minimum: $\left(\dfrac{1}{2} \cdot 1, -\dfrac{1}{2}\right) = \left(\dfrac{1}{2}, -\dfrac{1}{2}\right)$

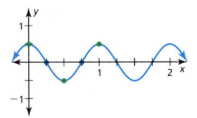

▶ The graph of g is a vertical shrink by a factor of $\dfrac{1}{2}$ and a horizontal shrink by a factor of $\dfrac{1}{2\pi}$ of the graph of f.

In-Class Practice

Self-Assessment

3. Identify the amplitude and period of $g(x) = \dfrac{1}{3} \cos \dfrac{1}{2}x$. Graph the function and describe the graph as a transformation of the graph of its parent function.

| 1 I don't understand yet. | 2 I can do it with help. | 3 I can do it on my own. | 4 I can teach someone. |

Translating Sine and Cosine Functions

The graphs of $y = a \sin b(x - h) + k$ and $y = a \cos b(x - h) + k$ represent translations h units left or right and k units up or down of $y = a \sin bx$ and $y = a \cos bx$. A horizontal translation of a periodic function is called a **phase shift**.

Key Concept

Graphing $y = a \sin b(x - h) + k$ and $y = a \cos b(x - h) + k$

You can graph $y = a \sin b(x - h) + k$ or $y = a \cos b(x - h) + k$, where $a > 0$ and $b > 0$, as follows:

- Identify the amplitude a, the period $\dfrac{2\pi}{b}$, the horizontal shift h, and the vertical shift k of the graph.

- Draw the horizontal line $y = k$, called the **midline** of the graph.

- Find the five key points by translating the key points of $y = a \sin bx$ or $y = a \cos bx$ horizontally h units and vertically k units.

- Draw the graph through the five translated key points.

EXAMPLE 3 Graphing a Translation

Graph $g(x) = 5 \cos \frac{1}{2}(x - 3\pi)$.

Identify the amplitude, period, horizontal shift, and vertical shift.

Amplitude: $a = 5$ Horizontal shift: $h = 3\pi$

Period: $\dfrac{2\pi}{b} = \dfrac{2\pi}{\frac{1}{2}} = 4\pi$ Vertical shift: $k = 0$

Draw the midline of the graph. Because $k = 0$, the midline is the x-axis.

Find the five key points.

On $y = k$: $(\pi + 3\pi, 0) = (4\pi, 0)$;
$(3\pi + 3\pi, 0) = (6\pi, 0)$

Maximums: $(0 + 3\pi, 5) = (3\pi, 5)$;
$(4\pi + 3\pi, 5) = (7\pi, 5)$

Minimum: $(2\pi + 3\pi, -5) = (5\pi, -5)$

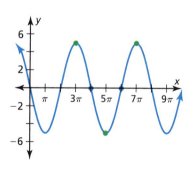

Draw the graph through the key points.

In-Class Practice

Self-Assessment

Graph the function.

4. $g(x) = \cos x + 4$

5. $g(x) = \dfrac{1}{2} \sin\left(x - \dfrac{\pi}{2}\right)$

1 I don't understand yet.   **2** I can do it with help.   **3** I can do it on my own.   **4** I can teach someone.

Reflecting Sine and Cosine Functions

When $a < 0$, the graphs of $y = a \sin b(x - h) + k$ and $y = a \cos b(x - h) + k$ are reflections of the graphs of $y = |a| \sin b(x - h) + k$ and $y = |a| \cos b(x - h) + k$, respectively, in the midline $y = k$.

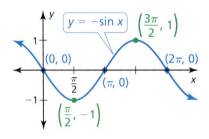
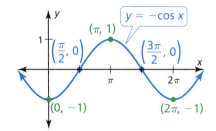

EXAMPLE 4 Graphing a Reflection

Graph $g(x) = -2 \sin \frac{2}{3}x + 1$.

Identify the amplitude, period, horizontal shift, and vertical shift.

Amplitude: $|a| = |-2| = 2$ Horizontal shift: $h = 0$

Period: $\frac{2\pi}{b} = \frac{2\pi}{\frac{2}{3}} = 3\pi$ Vertical shift: $k = 1$

Draw the midline of the graph, $y = 1$.

Find the five key points of $f(x) = |-2| \sin \frac{2}{3}x + 1$.

On $y = k$: $(0, 0 + 1) = (0, 1)$; $\left(\frac{3\pi}{2}, 0 + 1\right) = \left(\frac{3\pi}{2}, 1\right)$;

$(3\pi, 0 + 1) = (3\pi, 1)$

Maximum: $\left(\frac{3\pi}{4}, 2 + 1\right) = \left(\frac{3\pi}{4}, 3\right)$

Minimum: $\left(\frac{9\pi}{4}, -2 + 1\right) = \left(\frac{9\pi}{4}, -1\right)$

Reflect the graph. Because $a < 0$, the graph is reflected in the midline $y = 1$. So, $\left(\frac{3\pi}{4}, 3\right)$ becomes $\left(\frac{3\pi}{4}, -1\right)$ and $\left(\frac{9\pi}{4}, -1\right)$ becomes $\left(\frac{9\pi}{4}, 3\right)$.

Draw the graph through the key points.

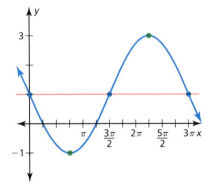

In-Class Practice

Self-Assessment

Graph the function.

6. $g(x) = -\cos\left(x + \frac{\pi}{2}\right)$

7. $g(x) = -3 \sin \frac{1}{2}x + 2$

1 I don't understand yet.   **2** I can do it with help.   **3** I can do it on my own.   **4** I can teach someone.

9.4 Practice

with Calc Chat and Calc View

Identify the amplitude and period of the function. Then graph the function and describe the graph of g as a transformation of the graph of its parent function. (See Examples 1 and 2.)

1. $g(x) = 3 \sin x$
2. $g(x) = \cos 4x$
3. $g(x) = \cos 3x$
4. $g(x) = \sin 2\pi x$
5. $g(x) = 3 \sin 2x$
6. $g(x) = \frac{1}{2} \cos 4\pi x$

Write an equation of the form $y = a \sin bx$ so that the graph has the given amplitude and period.

7. amplitude: 10 period: 4
8. amplitude: $\frac{1}{2}$ period: 3π

Graph the function. (See Example 3.)

9. $g(x) = \cos\left(x - \frac{\pi}{2}\right)$
10. $g(x) = \cos x - 4$
11. $g(x) = \sin x + 2$
12. $g(x) = 2 \cos x - 1$
13. $g(x) = \sin 2(x + \pi)$
14. $g(x) = \sin \frac{1}{2}(x + 2\pi) + 3$

15. **SMP.3 ERROR ANALYSIS** Describe and correct the error in finding the period of the function $y = \frac{1}{2} \sin 4x$.

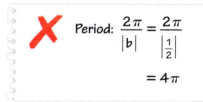

16. **SMP.3 ERROR ANALYSIS** Describe and correct the error in determining the point where the maximum value of the function $y = 2 \sin\left(x - \frac{\pi}{2}\right)$ occurs.

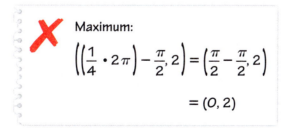

Graph the function. (See Example 4.)

17. $g(x) = -\cos x + 3$
18. $g(x) = -\sin x - 5$
19. $g(x) = -\sin \frac{1}{2}x - 2$
20. $g(x) = -\cos 2x + 1$
21. $g(x) = -4 \cos\left(x + \frac{\pi}{4}\right) - 1$
22. $g(x) = -5 \sin\left(x - \frac{\pi}{2}\right) + 3$

23. **SMP.7 MATCHING** Match each function with its graph. Explain your reasoning.

   a. $y = 3 + \sin x$

   b. $y = -3 + \cos x$

   c. $y = \sin 2\left(x - \dfrac{\pi}{2}\right)$

   d. $y = \cos 2\left(x - \dfrac{\pi}{2}\right)$

   A.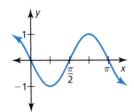

   C.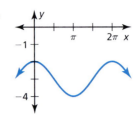

   B.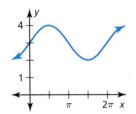

   D.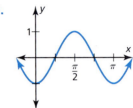

Write a rule for g that represents the indicated transformations of the graph of f.

24. $f(x) = 3 \sin x$; translation 2 units up and π units right

25. $f(x) = \dfrac{1}{3} \cos \pi x$; translation 1 unit down, followed by a reflection in the line $y = -1$

26. The population L (in thousands) of lynx and the population H (in thousands) of hares in a region can be modeled by the equations below, where t is time (in years).

    $$L = 11.5 + 6.5 \sin \dfrac{\pi}{5}t \qquad\qquad H = 27.5 + 17.5 \cos \dfrac{\pi}{5}t$$

    a. Determine the ratio of hares to lynx when $t = 0$, 2.5, 5, and 7.5 years.

    b. Use the graphs to explain how the changes in the two populations appear to be related.

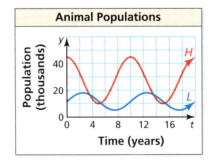

27. **CONNECTION TO REAL LIFE** On a Ferris wheel, your height h (in feet) above the ground after t (in seconds) is given by $h = 85 \sin \dfrac{\pi}{20}(t - 10) + 90$.

    a. Graph the function.

    b. How many cycles does the Ferris wheel make in 180 seconds? What are your maximum and minimum heights?

28. Find the average rate of change of each function over the interval $0 < x < \pi$.

   a. $y = 2 \cos x$

   b.
x	0	$\frac{\pi}{2}$	π	$\frac{3\pi}{2}$	2π
$f(x) = -\cos x$	-1	0	1	0	-1

   c.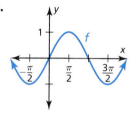

29. The portion of the moon visible from your home can be approximated by

    $f(t) = 0.5 \sin(0.214t + 0.4) + 0.5$

    where t is the number of days since January 1, 2023. Use technology to graph the function. On about which days of the year does a full moon occur?

30. The water depth d (in feet) in the Bay of Fundy on a given day can be modeled by

    $d = 35 - 14 \cos \frac{\pi}{6.2} t$

    where t is the time in hours and $t = 0$ represents midnight. Use technology to graph the function. At what time(s) is the water depth 21 feet? Explain.

31. **SMP.8** Write an expression in terms of the integer n that represents all the x-intercepts of the graph of the function $y = \cos 2x$. Justify your answer.

32. **SMP.7** Describe a transformation of the graph of $f(x) = \sin x$ that results in the graph of $g(x) = \cos x$.

33. **SMP.1 DIG DEEPER** For a person at rest, the blood pressure P (in millimeters of mercury) at time t (in seconds) is given by

    $P = 100 - 20 \cos \frac{8\pi}{3} t$.

    One cycle is equivalent to one heartbeat. Explain your reasoning in finding the heart rate (in beats per minute) of the person.

9.4 Graphing Sine and Cosine Functions

Interpreting Data

TEMPERATURE CHANGE THROUGHOUT THE YEAR Every location on Earth experiences periodic changes in temperature. The Earth is tilted 23.5 degrees on its axis. This affects the distribution of the Sun's energy across the surface of Earth. As a result, we have the four seasons of spring, summer, autumn, and winter.

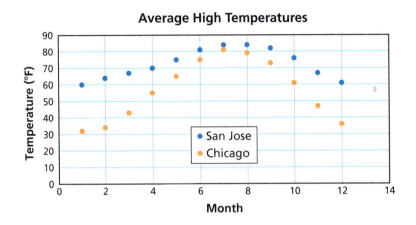

34. Describe the shape of the data for each city.

35. What type of function would you use to model each data set?

36. Approximate the amplitude of each graph.

Review & Refresh

37. Evaluate the six trigonometric functions of θ.

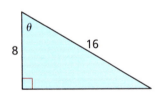

38. Solve $15x^2 - 8x + 1 = 0$.

Perform the operation.

39. $(-x^2 + 7x - 4)(2x^2 - x + 8)$

40. $(4x^3 - 9x^2 - 10) + (12x^2 - 8x - 5)$

41. $(x - 3)(x - 8)(3x + 1)$

42. $(5x^4 + 11x^3 - 10x + 4) - (8x^2 + 3 - 2x^3)$

Convert the degree measure to radians or the radian measure to degrees.

43. $72°$

44. $-\dfrac{5\pi}{6}$

Graph the system of quadratic inequalities.

45. $y > x^2 - 1$
$y \leq -x^2 - x + 6$

46. Evaluate the six trigonometric functions of θ.

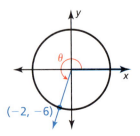

488   Chapter 9   Trigonometric Ratios and Functions

9.5 Graphing Other Trigonometric Functions

Learning Target: Describe and graph tangent, cotangent, secant, and cosecant functions.

Success Criteria:
- I can identify characteristics of tangent, cotangent, secant, and cosecant functions.
- I can graph tangent and cotangent functions.
- I can graph secant and cosecant functions.

INVESTIGATE Graphing the Tangent Function

Work with a partner.

1. Complete the table for $y = \tan x$, where x is an angle measure in radians. What do you notice? Why does this happen? How does this affect the graph of $y = \tan x$?

x	$-\frac{\pi}{6}$	0	$\frac{\pi}{6}$	$\frac{\pi}{4}$	$\frac{\pi}{3}$	$\frac{\pi}{2}$	$\frac{2\pi}{3}$	$\frac{3\pi}{4}$
$y = \tan x$								
x	$\frac{5\pi}{6}$	π	$\frac{7\pi}{6}$	$\frac{5\pi}{4}$	$\frac{4\pi}{3}$	$\frac{3\pi}{2}$	$\frac{5\pi}{3}$	2π
$y = \tan x$								

2. Plot the points (x, y) from Exercise 1. Then sketch the graph of $y = \tan x$. Make several observations about the graph.

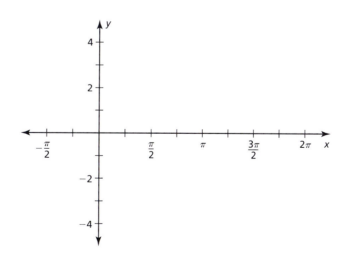

3. Use the graphing tool online to graph $y = \tan x$. Compare the graph with the graphs of $y = \sin x$ and $y = \cos x$.

Exploring Tangent and Cotangent Functions

Consider the parent functions $y = \tan x$ and $y = \cot x$.

⟵————— x approaches $-\frac{\pi}{2}$ —————⟶ ⟵————— x approaches $\frac{\pi}{2}$ —————⟶

x	$-\frac{\pi}{2}$	-1.57	-1.5	$-\frac{\pi}{4}$	0	$\frac{\pi}{4}$	1.5	1.57	$\frac{\pi}{2}$
$y = \tan x$	Undef.	$-1{,}256$	-14.10	-1	0	1	14.10	$1{,}256$	Undef.

⟵————— $\tan x$ approaches $-\infty$ —————⟶ ⟵————— $\tan x$ approaches $+\infty$ —————⟶

Because $\tan x = \dfrac{\sin x}{\cos x}$, $\tan x$ is undefined for x-values at which $\cos x = 0$, such as $x = \pm\dfrac{\pi}{2}$. The table indicates that the graph has asymptotes at these values.

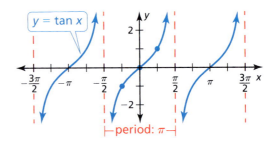

You can use a similar approach to graph $y = \cot x$. Because $\cot x = \dfrac{\cos x}{\sin x}$, $\cot x$ is undefined for x-values at which $\sin x = 0$, which are multiples of π. The graph has asymptotes at these values.

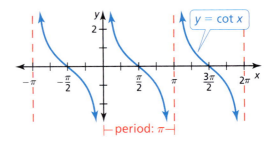

- The domain of $y = \tan x$ is all real numbers except odd multiples of $\dfrac{\pi}{2}$.
- The domain of $y = \cot x$ is all real numbers except multiples of π.
- The range of each function is $(-\infty, \infty)$. The period of each graph is π.
- The x-intercepts for $y = \tan x$ are at $x = 0, \pm\pi, \pm 2\pi, \pm 3\pi, \ldots$.
- The x-intercepts for $y = \cot x$ are at $x = \pm\dfrac{\pi}{2}, \pm\dfrac{3\pi}{2}, \pm\dfrac{5\pi}{2}, \pm\dfrac{7\pi}{2}, \ldots$.

In-Class Practice

Self-Assessment

1. Consider the graphs of $y = \tan x$ and $y = \cot x$. Describe the locations of the asymptotes.

1 I don't understand yet. **2** I can do it with help. 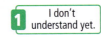 **3** I can do it on my own. **4** I can teach someone.

Graphing Tangent and Cotangent Functions

The graphs of $y = a \tan bx$ and $y = a \cot bx$ are transformations of the parent functions. The value of a indicates a vertical stretch or shrink. The value of b indicates a horizontal stretch or shrink.

- The period of the graph of each function is $\dfrac{\pi}{|b|}$.
- The vertical asymptotes for $y = a \tan bx$ occur at odd multiples of $\dfrac{\pi}{|2b|}$.
- The vertical asymptotes for $y = a \cot bx$ occur at multiples of $\dfrac{\pi}{|b|}$.

You can use five key x-values to sketch the graphs of $y = a \tan bx$ and $y = a \cot bx$ for $a > 0$ and $b > 0$. These are the x-intercept, the x-values where the asymptotes occur, and the x-values halfway between the x-intercept and the asymptotes. At each halfway point, the value of the function is either a or $-a$.

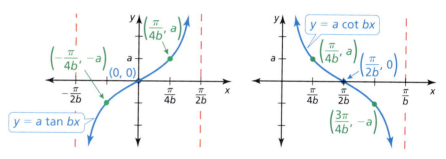

EXAMPLE 1 — Graphing a Tangent Function

Graph one period of $g(x) = 2 \tan 3x$. Describe the graph of g as a transformation of the graph of $f(x) = \tan x$.

Period: $\dfrac{\pi}{|b|} = \dfrac{\pi}{3}$ x-Intercept: $(0, 0)$

Asymptotes: $x = \dfrac{\pi}{|2b|}$, or $x = \dfrac{\pi}{6}$; $x = -\dfrac{\pi}{|2b|}$, or $x = -\dfrac{\pi}{6}$

Halfway points: $\left(\dfrac{\pi}{4b}, a\right) = \left(\dfrac{\pi}{12}, 2\right)$; $\left(-\dfrac{\pi}{4b}, -a\right) = \left(-\dfrac{\pi}{12}, -2\right)$

▶ The graph of g is a vertical stretch by a factor of 2 and a horizontal shrink by a factor of $\dfrac{1}{3}$ of the graph of f.

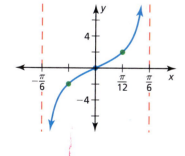

In-Class Practice

Self-Assessment

Graph one period of the function. Describe the graph of g as a transformation of the graph of its parent function.

2. $g(x) = \tan 2x$

3. $g(x) = 5 \tan \pi x$

| 1 I don't understand yet. | 2 I can do it with help. | 3 I can do it on my own. | 4 I can teach someone. |

9.5 Graphing Other Trigonometric Functions

EXAMPLE 2 — Graphing Cotangent Functions

Graph one period of g. Describe each graph as a transformation of the graph of $f(x) = \cot x$.

a. $g(x) = \cot \frac{1}{2} x$

Period: $\dfrac{\pi}{|b|} = 2\pi$

x-Intercept: $\left(\dfrac{\pi}{2b}, 0\right) = (\pi, 0)$

Asymptotes: $x = 0$; $x = \dfrac{\pi}{|b|}$, or $x = 2\pi$

Halfway points: $\left(\dfrac{\pi}{4b}, a\right) = \left(\dfrac{\pi}{2}, 1\right)$; $\left(\dfrac{3\pi}{4b}, -a\right) = \left(\dfrac{3\pi}{2}, -1\right)$

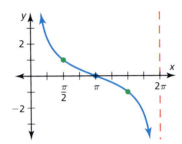

▶ The graph of g is a horizontal stretch by a factor of 2 of the graph of f.

b. $g(x) = \frac{1}{2} \cot 2x$

Period: $\dfrac{\pi}{|b|} = \dfrac{\pi}{2}$

x-Intercept: $\left(\dfrac{\pi}{2b}, 0\right) = \left(\dfrac{\pi}{4}, 0\right)$

Asymptotes: $x = 0$; $x = \dfrac{\pi}{|b|}$, or $x = \dfrac{\pi}{2}$

Halfway points: $\left(\dfrac{\pi}{4b}, a\right) = \left(\dfrac{\pi}{8}, \dfrac{1}{2}\right)$; $\left(\dfrac{3\pi}{4b}, -a\right) = \left(\dfrac{3\pi}{8}, -\dfrac{1}{2}\right)$

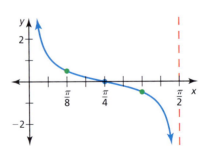

▶ The graph of g is a vertical shrink by a factor of $\frac{1}{2}$ and a horizontal shrink by a factor of $\frac{1}{2}$ of the graph of f.

In-Class Practice

Self-Assessment

4. Graph one period of $g(x) = 2 \cot 4x$. Describe the graph of g as a transformation of the graph of its parent function.

1 I don't understand yet.   **2** I can do it with help.   **3** I can do it on my own.   **4** I can teach someone.

Graphing Secant and Cosecant Functions

Consider the parent functions $y = \sec x$ and $y = \csc x$, which are shown below.

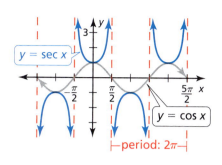
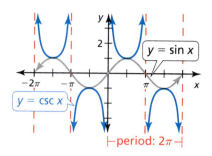

- The domain of $y = \sec x$ is all real numbers except odd multiples of $\frac{\pi}{2}$.
- The domain of $y = \csc x$ is all real numbers except multiples of π.
- The range of each function is $(-\infty, -1)$ and $(1, \infty)$. The period of each graph is 2π.

To graph $y = a \sec bx$ or $y = a \csc bx$, first graph $y = a \cos bx$ or $y = a \sin bx$, respectively. Then use the asymptotes and several points to sketch a graph of the function. The period of $y = a \sec bx$ and $y = a \csc bx$ is $\frac{2\pi}{|b|}$.

EXAMPLE 3 Graphing a Secant Function

Graph one period of $g(x) = 2 \sec x$. Describe the graph of g as a transformation of the graph of $f(x) = \sec x$.

Graph the function $y = 2 \cos x$. The period is $\frac{2\pi}{1} = 2\pi$.

Graph asymptotes of g. Because the asymptotes of g occur when $2 \cos x = 0$, graph $x = -\frac{\pi}{2}$, $x = \frac{\pi}{2}$, and $x = \frac{3\pi}{2}$.

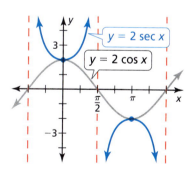

Plot points on g, such as $(0, 2)$ and $(\pi, -2)$. Then use the asymptotes to sketch the curve.

▶ The graph of g is a vertical stretch by a factor of 2 of the graph of f.

In-Class Practice

Self-Assessment

Graph one period of the function. Describe the graph of g as a transformation of the graph of its parent function.

5. $g(x) = \frac{1}{2} \sec x$

6. $g(x) = 2 \sec \pi x$

EXAMPLE 4 **Graphing Cosecant Functions**

Graph one period of g. Describe each graph as a transformation of the graph of $f(x) = \csc x$.

a. $g(x) = 3 \csc x$

Graph the function $y = 3 \sin x$. The period is $\frac{2\pi}{1} = 2\pi$.

Graph asymptotes of g. Because the asymptotes of g occur when $3 \sin x = 0$, graph $x = 0$, $x = \pi$, and $x = 2\pi$.

Plot points on g, such as $\left(\frac{\pi}{2}, 3\right)$ and $\left(\frac{3\pi}{2}, -3\right)$. Then use the asymptotes to sketch the curve.

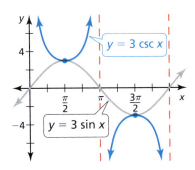

▶ The graph of g is a vertical stretch by a factor of 3 of the graph of f.

b. $g(x) = \frac{1}{2} \csc \pi x$

Graph the function $y = \frac{1}{2} \sin \pi x$. The period is $\frac{2\pi}{\pi} = 2$.

Graph asymptotes of g. Because the asymptotes of g occur when $\frac{1}{2} \sin \pi x = 0$, graph $x = 0$, $x = 1$, and $x = 2$.

Plot points on g, such as $\left(\frac{1}{2}, \frac{1}{2}\right)$ and $\left(\frac{3}{2}, -\frac{1}{2}\right)$. Then use the asymptotes to sketch the curve.

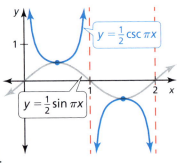

▶ The graph of g is a vertical shrink by a factor of $\frac{1}{2}$ and a horizontal shrink by a factor of $\frac{1}{\pi}$ of the graph of f.

In-Class Practice

Self-Assessment

Graph one period of the function. Describe the graph of g as a transformation of the graph of its parent function.

7. $g(x) = \csc 3x$

8. $g(x) = 2 \csc 2x$

1 I don't understand yet. **2** I can do it with help. **3** I can do it on my own. **4** I can teach someone.

494 Chapter 9 Trigonometric Ratios and Functions

9.5 Practice

Graph one period of the function. Describe the graph of g as a transformation of the graph of its parent function. (See Examples 1 and 2.)

1. $g(x) = 2 \tan x$

2. $g(x) = \cot 3x$

3. $g(x) = 3 \cot \frac{1}{4}x$

4. $g(x) = 4 \cot \frac{1}{2}x$

5. $g(x) = \frac{1}{2} \tan \pi x$

6. $g(x) = \frac{1}{3} \tan 2\pi x$

7. **SMP.3 ERROR ANALYSIS** Describe and correct the error in finding the period of $y = \cot 3x$.

$$\text{Period: } \frac{2\pi}{|b|} = \frac{2\pi}{3}$$

8. **SMP.3 ERROR ANALYSIS** Describe and correct the error in describing the transformation of $f(x) = \tan x$ represented by $g(x) = 2 \tan 5x$.

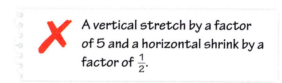

A vertical stretch by a factor of 5 and a horizontal shrink by a factor of $\frac{1}{2}$.

Graph one period of the function. Describe the graph of g as a transformation of the graph of its parent function. (See Examples 3 and 4.)

9. $g(x) = 3 \csc x$

10. $g(x) = \sec 4x$

11. $g(x) = \frac{1}{2} \sec \pi x$

12. $g(x) = \frac{1}{4} \sec 2\pi x$

13. $g(x) = 5 \csc \frac{1}{4}x$

14. $g(x) = 4 \csc \frac{1}{2}x$

Use the graph to write a function of the form $y = a \tan bx$.

15.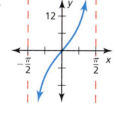

16.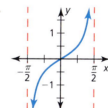

17.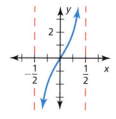

18.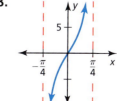

RESOURCES

9.5 Graphing Other Trigonometric Functions 495

19. SMP.7 MATCHING Match the equation with the correct graph. Explain your reasoning.

a. $g(x) = 4 \csc \pi x$
b. $g(x) = 4 \sec \pi x$
c. $g(x) = \sec 2x$
d. $g(x) = \csc 2x$

A.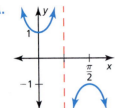

C.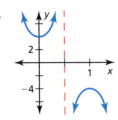

B.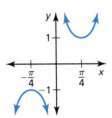

D.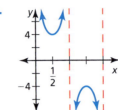

Graph one period of the function. Describe the graph of g as a transformation of the graph of its parent function.

20. $g(x) = \sec x + 3$

21. $g(x) = \csc x - 2$

22. $g(x) = \cot(x - \pi)$

23. $g(x) = -\tan x$

Write a rule for g that represents the indicated transformation of the graph of f.

24. $f(x) = \cot 2x$; translation 3 units up and $\dfrac{\pi}{2}$ units left

25. $f(x) = 2 \tan x$; translation π units right, followed by a horizontal shrink by a factor of $\dfrac{1}{3}$

26. $f(x) = 5 \sec(x - \pi)$; translation 2 units down, followed by a reflection in the x-axis

27. $f(x) = 4 \csc x$; vertical stretch by a factor of 2 and a reflection in the x-axis

28. Order the functions from the least average rate of change to the greatest average rate of change over the interval $-\dfrac{\pi}{4} < x < \dfrac{\pi}{4}$.

A.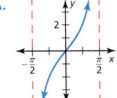

C.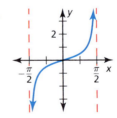

B.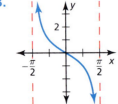

D.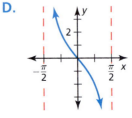

29. Determine which function has a greater local maximum value and which function has a greater local minimum value.

   A. $f(x) = \frac{1}{4} \csc \pi x$

   B.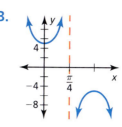

30. You stand on a bridge 140 feet above the ground. You look down at a car traveling away. The distance d (in feet) the car is from the base of the bridge can be modeled by $d = 140 \tan \theta$. Graph the function using technology. Describe what happens to θ as d increases.

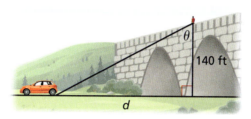

31. **SMP.2** You stand 120 feet from the base of a 260-foot building. You watch your friend go down the side of the building in an elevator.

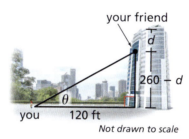

   a. Write an equation that gives the distance d (in feet) your friend is from the top of the building as a function of the angle of elevation θ.

   b. Graph the function found in part (a). Explain how the graph relates to this situation.

32. Rewrite $a \sec bx$ in terms of $\cos bx$. Use your results to explain the relationship between the local maximums and minimums of the cosine and secant functions.

33. **SMP.1 DIG DEEPER** A trigonometric equation that is true for all values of the variable for which both sides of the equation are defined is called a *trigonometric identity*. Write a trigonometric identity involving the function below. Explain your method.

$$y = \frac{1}{2}\left(\tan \frac{x}{2} + \cot \frac{x}{2}\right)$$

Interpreting Data

DEFORESTATION Deforestation is forest loss. Most deforestation in the United States occurred between 1800 and 1900. The forest area has been relatively stable for the last century.

34. How is the graph similar to the graph of a tangent function? How is it different?

35. What were some causes of deforestation from 1800 to 1900? Why has forest area remained stable over the last century?

Review & Refresh

36. Find one positive angle and one negative angle that are coterminal with 100°.

37. Find the amplitude and period of the graph of the function.

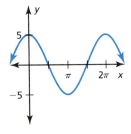

38. Evaluate sin 240° without using technology.

39. Solve $\dfrac{9}{5x-4} = \dfrac{2}{x-1}$.

40. Determine whether the data show an exponential relationship. Then write a function that models the data.

x	−2	−1	0	1	2	3
y	0.2	0.6	1.8	5.4	16.2	48.6

41. Use finite differences to determine the degree of the polynomial function that fits the data below. Then use technology to find the polynomial function.

$(-2, -2), (-1, 0), (0, 4), (1, 10), (2, 18)$

42. Solve $x^2 + 3x - 10 = 0$.

9.6 Modeling with Trigonometric Functions

> **Learning Target:** Write trigonometric functions.
>
> **Success Criteria:**
> - I can write and graph trigonometric functions using frequency.
> - I can write trigonometric functions for a given graph.
> - I can find a trigonometric model for a situation and for a set of data.

INVESTIGATE Modeling a Ferris Wheel

Work with a partner. You board a car at the bottom of a Ferris wheel, which is 2 meters above the ground. At the highest point, you are 80 meters above the ground. The Ferris wheel rotates at a constant speed and it takes 48 seconds to complete one cycle.

1. Sketch the circle shown below. Moving in a counterclockwise direction, plot and label points on the circle that represent your location on the Ferris wheel every 12 seconds for one full cycle, starting at $t = 0$ as shown.

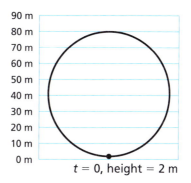

2. Complete the table of values that shows your heights h (in meters) above ground as a function of time t (in seconds).

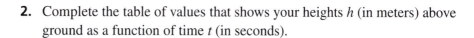

t	0	6	12	18	24	30	36	42	48
h									

3. Sketch a graph that shows your heights above ground during two full cycles. Make several observations about the graph.

4. Write an equation for your graph using a trigonometric function. Explain the type of trigonometric function you chose. Compare your results with your classmates.

5. Describe another real-life situation that can be modeled using a trigonometric function.

> **Vocabulary**
> frequency
> sinusoid

Frequency

The periodic nature of trigonometric functions makes them useful for modeling *oscillating* motions or repeating patterns that occur in real life. Some examples are sound waves, the motion of a pendulum, and temperature during the year. In such applications, the reciprocal of the period is called the **frequency**, which gives the number of cycles per unit of time.

EXAMPLE 1 Using Frequency

A sound consisting of a single frequency is called a *pure tone*. An audiometer produces pure tones to test a person's auditory functions. An audiometer produces a pure tone with a frequency f of 2,000 hertz (cycles per second). The tone causes changes in air pressure, increasing or decreasing it by up to 2 millipascals. Write and graph a sine model that gives the change in pressure P as a function of the time t (in seconds).

Find the values of a and b in the model $P = a \sin bt$. The maximum change in pressure is 2, so $a = 2$. Use the frequency f to find b.

$$\text{frequency} = \frac{1}{\text{period}} \qquad \text{Write relationship involving frequency and period.}$$

$$2{,}000 = \frac{b}{2\pi} \qquad \text{Substitute.}$$

$$4{,}000\pi = b \qquad \text{Multiply each side by } 2\pi.$$

The change in pressure P as a function of time t is given by $P = 2 \sin 4{,}000\pi t$.

Graph the model. The amplitude is $a = 2$ and the period is $\dfrac{1}{f} = \dfrac{1}{2{,}000}$.

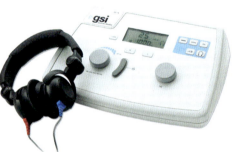

The key points are:

x-Intercepts: $(0, 0); \left(\dfrac{1}{2} \cdot \dfrac{1}{2{,}000}, 0\right) = \left(\dfrac{1}{4{,}000}, 0\right); \left(\dfrac{1}{2{,}000}, 0\right)$

Maximum: $\left(\dfrac{1}{4} \cdot \dfrac{1}{2{,}000}, 2\right) = \left(\dfrac{1}{8{,}000}, 2\right)$

Minimum: $\left(\dfrac{3}{4} \cdot \dfrac{1}{2{,}000}, -2\right) = \left(\dfrac{3}{8{,}000}, -2\right)$

▶ The graph of $P = 2 \sin 4{,}000\pi t$ is shown.

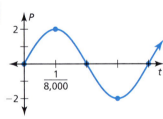

In-Class Practice

Self-Assessment

1. **WHAT IF?** In Example 1, how does the function change when the audiometer produces a pure tone with a frequency of 1,000 hertz?

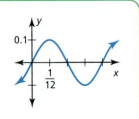

Writing Trigonometric Functions

Graphs of sine and cosine functions are called **sinusoids**. One method to write a sine or cosine function that models a sinusoid is to find the values of *a*, *b*, *h*, and *k* for

$$y = a \sin b(x - h) + k \quad \text{or} \quad y = a \cos b(x - h) + k$$

where $|a|$ is the amplitude, $\frac{2\pi}{b}$ is the period ($b > 0$), *h* is the horizontal shift, and *k* is the vertical shift.

EXAMPLE 2 Writing a Trigonometric Function

Write a function for the sinusoid shown.

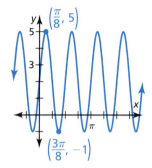

Find the maximum and minimum values. From the graph, the maximum value is 5 and the minimum value is -1.

Identify the vertical shift, *k*. The value of *k* is the mean of the maximum and minimum values.

$$k = \frac{(\text{maximum value}) + (\text{minimum value})}{2} = \frac{5 + (-1)}{2} = \frac{4}{2} = 2$$

Decide whether the graph should be modeled by a sine or cosine function. Because the graph crosses the midline $y = 2$ on the *y*-axis, the graph is a sine curve with no horizontal shift. So, $h = 0$.

The graph has a period of $\frac{\pi}{2}$. Find *b*.

$$\frac{\pi}{2} = \frac{2\pi}{b} \quad \Rightarrow \quad b = 4$$

The amplitude is

$$|a| = \frac{(\text{maximum value}) - (\text{minimum value})}{2} = \frac{5 - (-1)}{2} = \frac{6}{2} = 3.$$

The graph is not a reflection, so $a > 0$. Therefore, $a = 3$.

▶ The function is $y = 3 \sin 4x + 2$.

In-Class Practice

Self-Assessment

Write a function for the sinusoid.

2.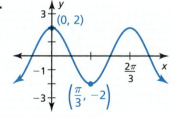

3.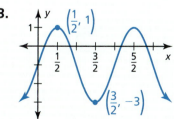

 I don't understand yet.   I can do it with help.   I can do it on my own. **4** I can teach someone.

9.6 Modeling with Trigonometric Functions

EXAMPLE 3   **Modeling Circular Motion**

Two people swing jump ropes. The highest and lowest points of the middle of each rope are shown. Each rope makes 2 revolutions per second. Write a model for the height h (in inches) of one of the ropes as a function of the time t (in seconds) given that the rope is at its lowest point when $t = 0$.

75 in. above ground

3 in. above ground

Not drawn to scale

A rope oscillates between 3 inches and 75 inches above the ground. So, a sine or cosine function may be an appropriate model for the height over time. The maximum height of a rope is 75 inches. The minimum height is 3 inches.

Find the vertical shift, k.

$$k = \frac{(\text{maximum value}) + (\text{minimum value})}{2} = \frac{75 + 3}{2} = 39$$

Decide whether the height should be modeled by a sine or cosine function. When $t = 0$, the height is at its minimum. So, use a cosine function whose graph is a reflection in the x-axis with no horizontal shift ($h = 0$).

Find the amplitude and period.

The amplitude is $|a| = \dfrac{(\text{maximum value}) - (\text{minimum value})}{2} = \dfrac{75 - 3}{2} = 36$.

Because the graph is a reflection in the x-axis, $a < 0$. So, $a = -36$.

Because a rope is rotating at a rate of 2 revolutions per second, one revolution is completed in 0.5 second. So, the period is $\dfrac{2\pi}{b} = 0.5$, and $b = 4\pi$.

▶ A model for the height of a rope is $h(t) = -36 \cos 4\pi t + 39$.

In-Class Practice

Self-Assessment

4. **WHAT IF?** Describe how the model in Example 3 changes when the lowest point of the rope is 5 inches above the ground and the highest point is 70 inches above the ground.

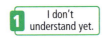 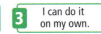

Using Technology to Find Trigonometric Models

EXAMPLE 4 Using Sinusoidal Regression

The table shows the numbers N of hours of daylight in Houston, Texas, on the 15th day of each month, where $t = 1$ represents January. Use technology to write a model that gives N as a function of t and interpret the period of its graph.

t	1	2	3	4	5	6	7	8	9	10	11	12
N	10.45	11.17	11.98	12.90	13.65	14.05	13.88	13.22	12.35	11.47	10.67	10.25

Enter the data from the table.

Make a scatter plot. The data appear sinusoidal.

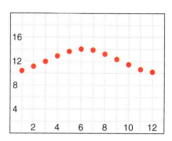

Perform a sinusoidal regression.

Graph the regression equation with the data.

$N = a \sin(bt + c) + d$

PARAMETERS
$a = -1.88305$ $b = -0.510834$
$c = 14.1597$ $d = 12.1231$

STATISTICS
$R^2 = 0.9993$

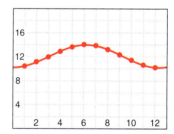

▶ The model appears to be a good fit. So, a model for the data is
$N = -1.88 \sin(-0.511t + 14.16) + 12.1$. The period, $\dfrac{2\pi}{|-0.511|} \approx 12$, makes sense because there are 12 months in a year and you expect this pattern to continue in the years to follow.

In-Class Practice
Self-Assessment

5. The table shows the average daily temperature T (in degrees Fahrenheit) for a city each month, where $m = 1$ represents January. Use technology to write a model that gives T as a function of m and interpret the period of its graph.

m	1	2	3	4	5	6	7	8	9	10	11	12
T	29	32	39	48	59	68	74	72	65	54	45	35

1 I don't understand yet. **2** I can do it with help. **3** I can do it on my own. **4** I can teach someone.

9.6 Practice

1. **CONNECTION TO REAL LIFE** Frequency is measured in *hertz*, or cycles per second. The lowest frequency of sounds that can be heard by humans is 20 hertz. The maximum pressure P produced from a sound with a frequency of 20 hertz is 0.02 millipascal. Write and graph a sine model that gives the pressure P as a function of the time t (in seconds). (See Example 1.)

2. **CONNECTION TO REAL LIFE** A middle-A tuning fork vibrates with a frequency f of 440 hertz (cycles per second). You strike a middle-A tuning fork with a force that produces a maximum pressure of 5 pascals. Write and graph a sine model that gives the pressure P as a function of the time t (in seconds).

Write a function for the sinusoid. (See Example 2.)

3.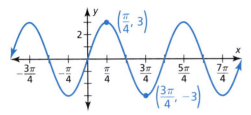

4.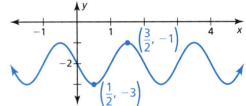

5. **ERROR ANALYSIS** Describe and correct the error in finding the amplitude of a sinusoid with a maximum point at (2, 10) and a minimum point at (4, −6).

$$|a| = \frac{(\text{maximum value}) + (\text{minimum value})}{2}$$
$$= \frac{10 + (-6)}{2}$$
$$= 2$$

6. **SMP.7** Explain whether you would use a sine or cosine function to model each sinusoid with the y-intercept described.

   a. The y-intercept occurs at the maximum value of the function.

   b. The y-intercept occurs at the minimum value of the function.

   c. The y-intercept occurs halfway between the maximum and minimum values of the function.

7. **SMP.4 CONNECTION TO REAL LIFE** You attach an LED light to the spokes of each of your bicycle wheels. On one wheel, the highest point of the light is 22 inches above the ground, and the lowest point is 4 inches. While riding your bike at a speed of 12 miles per hour, the wheel makes 2.5 revolutions per second. Write a model for the height h (in inches) of the light as a function of the time t (in seconds) given that the light is at its lowest point when $t = 0$. (See Example 3.)

8. **SMP.4 CONNECTION TO REAL LIFE** The Great Laxey Wheel, located on the Isle of Man, is the largest working water wheel in the world. The highest point of a bucket on the wheel is 70.5 feet above the viewing platform, and the lowest point is 2 feet below the viewing platform. The wheel makes a complete turn every 24 seconds. Write a model for the height h (in feet) of a bucket as a function of time t (in seconds) given that the bucket is at its lowest point when $t = 0$.

The time *t* is measured in months, where *t* = 1 represents January. Use technology to write a model that gives the average monthly high temperature *D* as a function of *t* and interpret the period of the graph. (See Example 4.)

9. Air Temperatures in Las Vegas, NV

t	1	2	3	4	5	6
D	58	63	70	78	89	99

t	7	8	9	10	11	12
D	104	102	94	81	67	57

10. Water Temperatures at Miami Beach, FL

t	1	2	3	4	5	6
D	71	73	75	78	81	85

t	7	8	9	10	11	12
D	86	85	84	81	76	73

11. CONNECTION TO REAL LIFE A circuit has an alternating voltage of 100 volts that peaks every 0.5 second. Write a sinusoidal model for the voltage *V* as a function of the time *t* (in seconds).

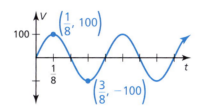

12. The graph shows the average daily temperature of Lexington, Kentucky. The average daily temperature of Louisville, Kentucky, is modeled by $y = -22\cos\frac{\pi}{6}t + 57$, where *y* is the temperature (in degrees Fahrenheit) and *t* is the number of months since January 1. Explain which city has the greater average daily temperature.

13. **SMP.7** During one cycle, a sinusoid has a minimum at $\left(\frac{\pi}{2}, 3\right)$ and a maximum at $\left(\frac{\pi}{4}, 8\right)$. Write a sine function *and* a cosine function for the sinusoid. Use technology to verify your answers.

14. The table shows the numbers of employees *N* (in thousands) at a retail store company each year for 11 years. The time *t* is measured in years, with *t* = 1 representing the first year.

t	1	2	3	4	5	6	7	8	9	10	11
N	20.8	22.7	24.6	23.2	20	17.5	16.7	17.8	21	22	24.1

a. Use sinusoidal regression to find a model that gives *N* as a function of *t*.

b. Predict the number of employees at the company in the 12th year.

Interpreting Data

VISIBLE LIGHT Visible light makes up only a small part of the electromagnetic (EM) spectrum. There is a huge range of EM radiation that humans cannot see. Radio waves, microwaves, and X-rays are all types of invisible EM radiation. The period of EM radiation is called its *wavelength*.

15. Describe the range of frequencies for each color.

16. Humans can hear sounds with frequencies between 20 hertz and 20,000 hertz. Compare the frequencies of audible sounds to the frequencies of colors.

17. Why do you think the quartz sphere in the photo produces different colors?

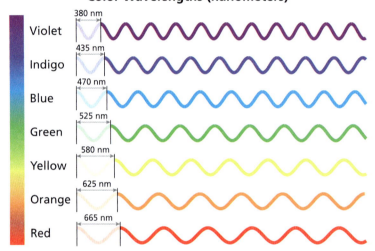

Color Wavelengths (nanometers)

Review & Refresh

Expand the logarithmic expression.

18. $\log_8 \frac{x}{7}$

19. $\ln 2x$

Simplify the expression.

24. $\frac{17}{\sqrt{2}}$

25. $\frac{3}{\sqrt{6} - 2}$

26. $\frac{8}{\sqrt{10} + 3}$

27. $\frac{13}{\sqrt{3} + \sqrt{11}}$

20. Use the unit circle to evaluate the six trigonometric functions of $\theta = -\frac{\pi}{2}$.

Graph one period of the function. Describe the graph of g as a transformation of the graph of its parent function.

21. $g(x) = 3 \tan 2x$

22. $g(x) = \csc 2\pi x$

Graph the function.

28. $g(x) = \sin 2\left(x - \frac{\pi}{2}\right)$

29. $g(x) = 3 \cos x - 5$

23. The mean age of all the students in a first aid class is 24 years. Is the mean age a parameter or a statistic?

30. Tell whether x and y show *direct variation*, *inverse variation*, or *neither*.

x	−2	−1	0	1	2
y	1	3	5	7	9

506 Chapter 9 Trigonometric Ratios and Functions

9.7 Using Trigonometric Identities

Learning Target: Verify and use trigonometric identities.

Success Criteria:
- I can evaluate trigonometric functions using trigonometric identities.
- I can simplify trigonometric expressions using trigonometric identities.
- I can verify trigonometric identities.

INVESTIGATE Writing a Trigonometric Identity

Work with a partner. In the diagram, the point (x, y) is on the unit circle. In Section 9.3, you wrote the coordinates of (x, y) in terms of θ, as shown.

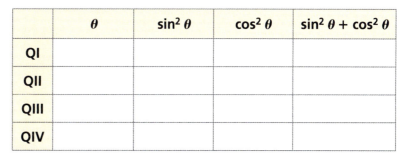

1. Write an equation in terms of θ that relates the side lengths of the inscribed triangle.

2. Complete the table to verify that the equation you wrote in Exercise 1 is valid for angles in each of the four quadrants.

	θ	$\sin^2 \theta$	$\cos^2 \theta$	$\sin^2 \theta + \cos^2 \theta$
QI				
QII				
QIII				
QIV				

3. Explain what it means for an equation to be an *identity*. The equation you wrote in Exercise 1 is called a *Pythagorean identity*. There are two other equivalent Pythagorean identities that use different trigonometric functions. Explain how you can derive them from your results above.

4. Use the diagram above to sketch the angle $-\theta$. Explain how you can write the coordinates of $(\cos(-\theta), \sin(-\theta))$.

5. Use your results in Exercise 4 to write trigonometric identities using each of the following.

   a. $\cos(-\theta)$
   b. $\sin(-\theta)$
   c. $\tan(-\theta)$

Vocabulary
trigonometric identity

Using Trigonometric Identities

Recall that when an angle θ is in standard position with its terminal side intersecting the unit circle at (x, y), then $x = \cos \theta$ and $y = \sin \theta$.

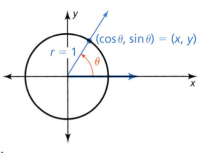

Because (x, y) is on a circle centered at the origin with radius 1, it follows that

> Note that $\sin^2 \theta$ represents $(\sin \theta)^2$ and $\cos^2 \theta$ represents $(\cos \theta)^2$.

$$x^2 + y^2 = 1 \quad \text{and} \quad \cos^2 \theta + \sin^2 \theta = 1.$$

The equation $\cos^2 \theta + \sin^2 \theta = 1$ is true for any value of θ. A trigonometric equation that is true for all values of the variable for which both sides of the equation are defined is called a **trigonometric identity**. In Section 9.1, you used reciprocal identities to find the values of the cosecant, secant, and cotangent functions. These and other fundamental trigonometric identities are listed below.

Key Concept

Fundamental Trigonometric Identities

Reciprocal Identities

$$\sin \theta = \frac{1}{\csc \theta} \qquad \cos \theta = \frac{1}{\sec \theta} \qquad \tan \theta = \frac{1}{\cot \theta}$$

$$\csc \theta = \frac{1}{\sin \theta} \qquad \sec \theta = \frac{1}{\cos \theta} \qquad \cot \theta = \frac{1}{\tan \theta}$$

Tangent and Cotangent Identities

$$\tan \theta = \frac{\sin \theta}{\cos \theta} \qquad \cot \theta = \frac{\cos \theta}{\sin \theta}$$

Pythagorean Identities

$$\sin^2 \theta + \cos^2 \theta = 1 \qquad 1 + \tan^2 \theta = \sec^2 \theta \qquad 1 + \cot^2 \theta = \csc^2 \theta$$

Cofunction Identities

$$\sin\left(\frac{\pi}{2} - \theta\right) = \cos \theta \qquad \cos\left(\frac{\pi}{2} - \theta\right) = \sin \theta \qquad \tan\left(\frac{\pi}{2} - \theta\right) = \cot \theta$$

Negative Angle Identities

$$\sin(-\theta) = -\sin \theta \qquad \cos(-\theta) = \cos \theta \qquad \tan(-\theta) = -\tan \theta$$

In-Class Practice

Self-Assessment

1. Describe the difference between a trigonometric identity and a trigonometric equation.

1 I don't understand yet. **2** I can do it with help. **3** I can do it on my own. **4** I can teach someone.

EXAMPLE 1 **Finding Values of Trigonometric Functions**

Given that $\sin \theta = \dfrac{4}{5}$ and $\dfrac{\pi}{2} < \theta < \pi$, find the values of the other five trigonometric functions of θ.

Find $\cos \theta$.

$$\sin^2 \theta + \cos^2 \theta = 1 \qquad \text{Write Pythagorean identity.}$$

$$\left(\dfrac{4}{5}\right)^2 + \cos^2 \theta = 1 \qquad \text{Substitute } \dfrac{4}{5} \text{ for } \sin \theta.$$

$$\cos^2 \theta = 1 - \left(\dfrac{4}{5}\right)^2 \qquad \text{Subtract } \left(\dfrac{4}{5}\right)^2 \text{ from each side.}$$

$$\cos^2 \theta = \dfrac{9}{25} \qquad \text{Simplify.}$$

$$\cos \theta = \pm\dfrac{3}{5} \qquad \text{Take square root of each side.}$$

$$\cos \theta = -\dfrac{3}{5} \qquad \text{Because } \theta \text{ is in Quadrant II, } \cos \theta \text{ is negative.}$$

Find the values of the other four trigonometric functions of θ using the values of $\sin \theta$ and $\cos \theta$.

$$\tan \theta = \dfrac{\sin \theta}{\cos \theta} = \dfrac{\frac{4}{5}}{-\frac{3}{5}} = -\dfrac{4}{3} \qquad \cot \theta = \dfrac{\cos \theta}{\sin \theta} = \dfrac{-\frac{3}{5}}{\frac{4}{5}} = -\dfrac{3}{4}$$

$$\csc \theta = \dfrac{1}{\sin \theta} = \dfrac{1}{\frac{4}{5}} = \dfrac{5}{4} \qquad \sec \theta = \dfrac{1}{\cos \theta} = \dfrac{1}{-\frac{3}{5}} = -\dfrac{5}{3}$$

EXAMPLE 2 **Simplifying Trigonometric Expressions**

Simplify (a) $\tan\left(\dfrac{\pi}{2} - \theta\right)\sin \theta$ and (b) $\sec \theta \tan^2 \theta + \sec \theta$.

a. $\tan\left(\dfrac{\pi}{2} - \theta\right)\sin \theta = \cot \theta \sin \theta$ Cofunction identity

$\qquad = \left(\dfrac{\cos \theta}{\sin \theta}\right)(\sin \theta)$ Cotangent identity

$\qquad = \cos \theta$ Simplify.

b. $\sec \theta \tan^2 \theta + \sec \theta = \sec \theta(\sec^2 \theta - 1) + \sec \theta$ Pythagorean identity

$\qquad = \sec^3 \theta - \sec \theta + \sec \theta$ Distributive Property

$\qquad = \sec^3 \theta$ Simplify.

In-Class Practice

Self-Assessment

2. Given that $\cos \theta = \dfrac{1}{6}$ and $0 < \theta < \dfrac{\pi}{2}$, find the values of the other five trigonometric functions of θ.

Simplify the expression.

3. $\sin x \cot x \sec x$

4. $\cos \theta - \cos \theta \sin^2 \theta$

5. $\dfrac{\tan x \csc x}{\sec x}$

9.7   Using Trigonometric Identities

Verifying Trigonometric Identities

You can use the fundamental identities from this chapter to verify new identities. To do so, use algebra and trigonometric properties to manipulate one side of the equation until it is identical to the other side.

EXAMPLE 3 **Verifying a Trigonometric Identity**

Verify the identity $\dfrac{\sec^2 \theta - 1}{\sec^2 \theta} = \sin^2 \theta$.

$$\dfrac{\sec^2 \theta - 1}{\sec^2 \theta} = \dfrac{\sec^2 \theta}{\sec^2 \theta} - \dfrac{1}{\sec^2 \theta} \qquad \text{Write as separate fractions.}$$

$$= 1 - \left(\dfrac{1}{\sec \theta}\right)^2 \qquad \text{Simplify.}$$

$$= 1 - \cos^2 \theta \qquad \text{Reciprocal identity}$$

$$= \sin^2 \theta \qquad \text{Pythagorean identity}$$

Verifying an identity is not the same as solving an equation because you cannot assume that the two sides are equal. So, you cannot use any properties of equality, such as adding the same quantity to each side of the equation.

EXAMPLE 4 **Verifying a Trigonometric Identity**

Verify the identity $\sec x + \tan x = \dfrac{\cos x}{1 - \sin x}$.

$$\sec x + \tan x = \dfrac{1}{\cos x} + \tan x \qquad \text{Reciprocal identity}$$

$$= \dfrac{1}{\cos x} + \dfrac{\sin x}{\cos x} \qquad \text{Tangent identity}$$

$$= \dfrac{1 + \sin x}{\cos x} \qquad \text{Add fractions.}$$

$$= \dfrac{1 + \sin x}{\cos x} \cdot \dfrac{1 - \sin x}{1 - \sin x} \qquad \text{Multiply by } \dfrac{1 - \sin x}{1 - \sin x}.$$

$$= \dfrac{1 - \sin^2 x}{\cos x(1 - \sin x)} \qquad \text{Simplify numerator.}$$

$$= \dfrac{\cos^2 x}{\cos x(1 - \sin x)} \qquad \text{Pythagorean identity}$$

$$= \dfrac{\cos x}{1 - \sin x} \qquad \text{Simplify.}$$

In-Class Practice

Self-Assessment

Verify the identity.

6. $\cot(-\theta) = -\cot \theta$

7. $\cos x \csc x \tan x = 1$

9.7 Practice

Find the values of the other five trigonometric functions of θ. (See Example 1.)

1. $\sin \theta = \dfrac{1}{3}, 0 < \theta < \dfrac{\pi}{2}$

2. $\tan \theta = -\dfrac{3}{7}, \dfrac{\pi}{2} < \theta < \pi$

3. $\cos \theta = -\dfrac{5}{6}, \pi < \theta < \dfrac{3\pi}{2}$

4. $\cot \theta = -3, \dfrac{3\pi}{2} < \theta < 2\pi$

Simplify the expression. (See Example 2.)

5. $\sin x \cot x$

6. $\cos \theta (1 + \tan^2 \theta)$

7. $\dfrac{\csc^2 x - \cot^2 x}{\sin(-x) \cot x}$

8. $\dfrac{\cos^2 x \tan^2(-x) - 1}{\cos^2 x}$

Verify the identity. (See Examples 3 and 4.)

9. $\cos\left(\dfrac{\pi}{2} - x\right) \cot x = \cos x$

10. $\sin\left(\dfrac{\pi}{2} - x\right) \tan x = \sin x$

11. $\dfrac{1 + \cos x}{\sin x} + \dfrac{\sin x}{1 + \cos x} = 2 \csc x$

12. $\dfrac{\sin x}{1 - \cos(-x)} = \csc x + \cot x$

Use transformations to describe why the identity is valid.

13. $\cos(x + \pi) = \cos(x - \pi)$

14. $3 + \tan x = 3 + \tan(x + \pi)$

15. **SMP.6** The graph of g is a translation of the graph of f. Explain whether $f(x) = g(x)$ is *sometimes*, *always*, or *never* an identity.

16. **SMP.7 CONNECT CONCEPTS** A function f is *odd* when $f(-x) = -f(x)$. A function f is *even* when $f(-x) = f(x)$. Which of the six trigonometric functions are odd? Which are even?

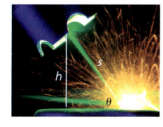

17. **CONNECTION TO REAL LIFE** A generator of a laser beam has height h. The length s of the laser beam measured from the generator to its target when the angle from the surface to the generator is θ can be modeled by the equation below. Show that the equation is equivalent to $s = h \csc \theta$.

$$s = \dfrac{h \cot \theta}{\sin(90° - \theta)}$$

18. Explain how you can use a trigonometric identity to find all the values of x for which $\sin x = \cos x$.

19. **SMP.2 DIG DEEPER** When light traveling in a medium (such as air) strikes the surface of a second medium (such as water) at an angle θ_1, the light begins to travel at a different angle θ_2. This change of direction is defined by Snell's law, $n_1 \sin \theta_1 = n_2 \sin \theta_2$, where n_1 and n_2 are the *indices of refraction* for the two mediums. Snell's law can be derived from

$$\dfrac{n_1}{\sqrt{\cot^2 \theta_1 + 1}} = \dfrac{n_2}{\sqrt{\cot^2 \theta_2 + 1}}.$$

Simplify the equation to derive Snell's law. If $\theta_1 = \theta_2$, then what must be true about the values of n_1 and n_2? When does this occur?

Interpreting Data

EULER'S IDENTITY *Euler's identity* shows a connection between five important numbers in mathematics: 0, 1, π, e, and i. This identity is derived from *Euler's formula* when $\theta = \pi$. Euler's formula uses trigonometric functions to describe the effects of imaginary exponents.

Euler's Formula
$e^{i\theta} = \cos \theta + i \sin \theta$

20. Use Euler's formula to verify Euler's identity, $e^{i\pi} + 1 = 0$.

21. The number e is named after Leonard Euler. Who was he?

22. Why was the Greek letter π used to represent the ratio of the circumference of a circle to its diameter? Who first used it? Who popularized its usage?

Review & Refresh

23. Graph one period of the function

    $g(x) = 5 \tan 2x$.

    Describe the graph of g as a transformation of the graph of its parent function.

24. A buoy bobs up and down as waves go past. The vertical displacement y (in feet) of the buoy with respect to sea level can be modeled by

    $y = 11.5 \cos \dfrac{\pi}{4} t$

    where t is the time (in seconds). Find and interpret the period and amplitude in the context of the problem. Then graph the function.

25. Simplify $10^{\log 4}$.

26. Write a function for the sinusoid.

    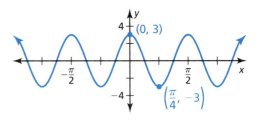

27. A normal distribution has a mean of 27 and a standard deviation of 3. Find the probability that a randomly selected x-value from the distribution is between 24 and 33.

28. Graph the function $f(x) = \dfrac{x+2}{x-1}$. Find the domain and range.

29. Evaluate $9^{5/2}$ without using technology.

9.8 Using Sum and Difference Formulas

Learning Target: Use sum and difference formulas to evaluate and simplify trigonometric expressions.

Success Criteria:
- I can evaluate trigonometric expressions using sum and difference formulas.
- I can simplify trigonometric expressions using sum and difference formulas.
- I can solve trigonometric equations using sum and difference formulas.

INVESTIGATE Deriving Sum and Difference Formulas

Work with a partner.

1. Use trigonometric ratios to help find the indicated missing angle measures and missing side lengths in terms of a and b in the diagram.

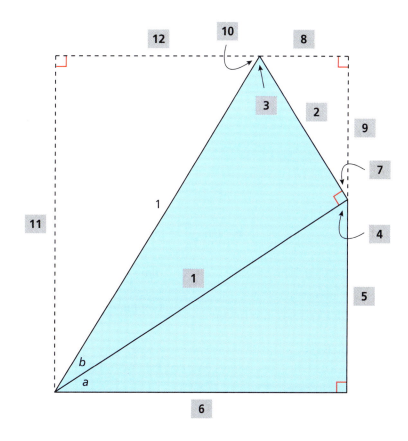

2. Explain what you can conclude about $\sin(a + b)$ and $\cos(a + b)$.

3. Use your results in Exercise 2 to write formulas for $\sin(a - b)$ and $\cos(a - b)$.

Using Sum and Difference Formulas

Key Concept

Sum and Difference Formulas

Sum Formulas	Difference Formulas
$\sin(a + b) = \sin a \cos b + \cos a \sin b$	$\sin(a - b) = \sin a \cos b - \cos a \sin b$
$\cos(a + b) = \cos a \cos b - \sin a \sin b$	$\cos(a - b) = \cos a \cos b + \sin a \sin b$
$\tan(a + b) = \dfrac{\tan a + \tan b}{1 - \tan a \tan b}$	$\tan(a - b) = \dfrac{\tan a - \tan b}{1 + \tan a \tan b}$

EXAMPLE 1 Evaluating Trigonometric Expressions

Find the exact value of (a) $\sin 15°$ and (b) $\tan \dfrac{7\pi}{12}$.

a. $\sin 15° = \sin(60° - 45°)$ — Substitute $60° - 45°$ for $15°$.

$= \sin 60° \cos 45° - \cos 60° \sin 45°$ — Difference formula for sine

$= \dfrac{\sqrt{3}}{2}\left(\dfrac{\sqrt{2}}{2}\right) - \dfrac{1}{2}\left(\dfrac{\sqrt{2}}{2}\right)$ — Evaluate.

$= \dfrac{\sqrt{6} - \sqrt{2}}{4}$ — Simplify.

▶ The exact value of $\sin 15°$ is $\dfrac{\sqrt{6} - \sqrt{2}}{4}$.

b. $\tan \dfrac{7\pi}{12} = \tan\left(\dfrac{\pi}{3} + \dfrac{\pi}{4}\right)$ — Substitute $\dfrac{\pi}{3} + \dfrac{\pi}{4}$ for $\dfrac{7\pi}{12}$.

$= \dfrac{\tan \dfrac{\pi}{3} + \tan \dfrac{\pi}{4}}{1 - \tan \dfrac{\pi}{3} \tan \dfrac{\pi}{4}}$ — Sum formula for tangent

$= \dfrac{\sqrt{3} + 1}{1 - \sqrt{3} \cdot 1}$ — Evaluate.

$= -2 - \sqrt{3}$ — Simplify.

▶ The exact value of $\tan \dfrac{7\pi}{12}$ is $-2 - \sqrt{3}$.

Check

$\tan\left(\dfrac{7\pi}{12}\right)$	$= -3.732050808$
$-2 - \sqrt{3}$	$= -3.732050808$

In-Class Practice

Self-Assessment

Find the exact value of the expression.

1. $\sin 105°$
2. $\cos 15°$
3. $\tan \dfrac{5\pi}{12}$

EXAMPLE 2 — Using a Difference Formula

Find $\cos(a - b)$ given that $\cos a = -\dfrac{4}{5}$ with $\pi < a < \dfrac{3\pi}{2}$ and $\sin b = \dfrac{5}{13}$ with $0 < b < \dfrac{\pi}{2}$.

Find $\sin a$ and $\cos b$.

Because $\cos a = -\dfrac{4}{5}$ and a is in Quadrant III, $\sin a = -\dfrac{3}{5}$, as shown in the figure.

Because $\sin b = \dfrac{5}{13}$ and b is in Quadrant I, $\cos b = \dfrac{12}{13}$, as shown in the figure.

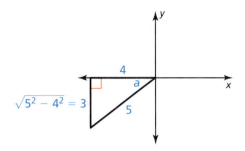 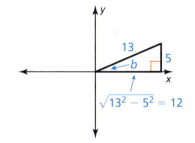

Use the difference formula for cosine to find $\cos(a - b)$.

$\cos(a - b) = \cos a \cos b + \sin a \sin b$ Difference formula for cosine

$= -\dfrac{4}{5}\left(\dfrac{12}{13}\right) + \left(-\dfrac{3}{5}\right)\left(\dfrac{5}{13}\right)$ Evaluate.

$= -\dfrac{63}{65}$ Simplify.

▶ The value of $\cos(a - b)$ is $-\dfrac{63}{65}$.

EXAMPLE 3 — Simplifying a Trigonometric Expression

Simplify the expression $\cos(x + \pi)$.

$\cos(x + \pi) = \cos x \cos \pi - \sin x \sin \pi$ Sum formula for cosine

$= (\cos x)(-1) - (\sin x)(0)$ Evaluate.

$= -\cos x$ Simplify.

In-Class Practice

Self-Assessment

4. Find $\sin(a - b)$ given that $\sin a = \dfrac{8}{17}$ with $0 < a < \dfrac{\pi}{2}$ and $\cos b = -\dfrac{24}{25}$ with $\pi < b < \dfrac{3\pi}{2}$.

Simplify the expression.

5. $\sin(x + \pi)$ **6.** $\cos(x - 2\pi)$ **7.** $\tan(x - \pi)$

1 I don't understand yet.   **2** I can do it with help.   **3** I can do it on my own.   **4** I can teach someone.

9.8 Using Sum and Difference Formulas

Solving Equations and Rewriting Formulas

EXAMPLE 4   **Solving a Trigonometric Equation**

Solve $\sin\left(x + \frac{\pi}{3}\right) + \sin\left(x - \frac{\pi}{3}\right) = 1$ for $0 \leq x < 2\pi$.

$$\sin\left(x + \frac{\pi}{3}\right) + \sin\left(x - \frac{\pi}{3}\right) = 1 \quad \text{Write equation.}$$

$$\sin x \cos \frac{\pi}{3} + \cos x \sin \frac{\pi}{3} + \sin x \cos \frac{\pi}{3} - \cos x \sin \frac{\pi}{3} = 1 \quad \text{Use formulas.}$$

$$\frac{1}{2}\sin x + \frac{\sqrt{3}}{2}\cos x + \frac{1}{2}\sin x - \frac{\sqrt{3}}{2}\cos x = 1 \quad \text{Evaluate.}$$

$$\sin x = 1 \quad \text{Simplify.}$$

▶ In the interval $0 \leq x < 2\pi$, the solution is $x = \frac{\pi}{2}$.

EXAMPLE 5   **Rewriting a Real-Life Formula**

The *index of refraction* of a transparent material is the ratio of the speed of light in a vacuum to the speed of light in the material. A triangular prism, like the one shown, can be used to measure the index of refraction using the formula shown. For $\alpha = 60°$, show that the formula can be rewritten as $n = \frac{\sqrt{3}}{2} + \frac{1}{2}\cot\frac{\theta}{2}$.

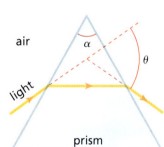

$$n = \frac{\sin\left(\frac{\theta}{2} + 30°\right)}{\sin\frac{\theta}{2}} \quad \text{Write formula with } \frac{\alpha}{2} = \frac{60°}{2} = 30°.$$

$$= \frac{\sin\frac{\theta}{2}\cos 30° + \cos\frac{\theta}{2}\sin 30°}{\sin\frac{\theta}{2}} \quad \text{Sum formula for sine}$$

$$= \frac{\left(\sin\frac{\theta}{2}\right)\left(\frac{\sqrt{3}}{2}\right) + \left(\cos\frac{\theta}{2}\right)\left(\frac{1}{2}\right)}{\sin\frac{\theta}{2}} \quad \text{Evaluate.}$$

$$= \frac{\frac{\sqrt{3}}{2}\sin\frac{\theta}{2}}{\sin\frac{\theta}{2}} + \frac{\frac{1}{2}\cos\frac{\theta}{2}}{\sin\frac{\theta}{2}} \quad \text{Write as separate fractions.}$$

$$= \frac{\sqrt{3}}{2} + \frac{1}{2}\cot\frac{\theta}{2} \quad \text{Simplify.}$$

In-Class Practice

Self-Assessment

8. Solve $\sin\left(\frac{\pi}{4} - x\right) - \sin\left(x + \frac{\pi}{4}\right) = 1$ for $0 \leq x < 2\pi$.

9.8 Practice

Find the exact value of the expression. (See Example 1.)

1. $\tan(-15°)$
2. $\sin(-165°)$
3. $\cos 105°$
4. $\cos \dfrac{11\pi}{12}$
5. $\tan \dfrac{17\pi}{12}$
6. $\sin\left(-\dfrac{7\pi}{12}\right)$

Evaluate the expression given that $\cos a = \dfrac{4}{5}$ with $0 < a < \dfrac{\pi}{2}$ and $\sin b = -\dfrac{15}{17}$ with $\dfrac{3\pi}{2} < b < 2\pi$. (See Example 2.)

7. $\sin(a + b)$
8. $\sin(a - b)$
9. $\tan(a - b)$

Simplify the expression. (See Example 3.)

10. $\tan(x + \pi)$
11. $\cos(x + 2\pi)$
12. $\sin\left(x - \dfrac{3\pi}{2}\right)$

Solve the equation for $0 \leq x < 2\pi$. (See Example 4.)

13. $2 \sin x - 1 = 0$
14. $\cos x + 1 = 0$
15. $\tan(x + \pi) - \tan(\pi - x) = 0$
16. $\sin\left(x + \dfrac{3\pi}{2}\right) - \sin\left(x - \dfrac{3\pi}{2}\right) = \sqrt{3}$

17. **SMP.7 CONNECTION TO REAL LIFE** A photographer is at a height h taking aerial photographs with a 35-millimeter camera. The ratio of the image length WQ to the length NA of the actual object is given by

$$\dfrac{WQ}{NA} = \dfrac{35 \tan(\theta - t) + 35 \tan t}{h \tan \theta}$$

where θ is the angle between the vertical line perpendicular to the ground and the line from the camera to point A and t is the tilt angle of the film. When $t = 45°$, show that the formula can be rewritten as $\dfrac{WQ}{NA} = \dfrac{70}{h(1 + \tan \theta)}$. (See Example 5.)

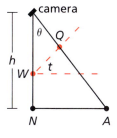

18. Derive the cofunction identity $\sin\left(\dfrac{\pi}{2} - \theta\right) = \cos \theta$ using the difference formula for sine.

19. **CONNECT CONCEPTS** Explain how to use the graph to solve $\sin\left(x + \dfrac{\pi}{4}\right) - \sin\left(\dfrac{\pi}{4} - x\right) = 0$ for $0 \leq x < 2\pi$. Then find the solutions.

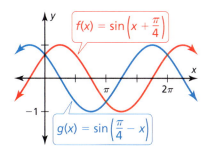

20. **DIG DEEPER** Write (a) $\sin 3x$ as a function of $\sin x$, (b) $\cos 3x$ as a function of $\cos x$, and (c) $\tan 3x$ as a function of $\tan x$.

Interpreting Data

APPROACHES TO TRIGONOMETRY In this chapter, you have studied trigonometry from the right triangle approach and from the unit circle approach.

21. Explain which approach is suggested by the graphic below.

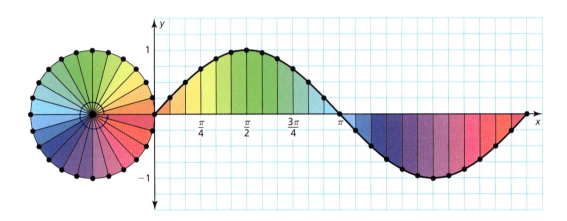

22. What is the connection between the unit circle and the graph?

23. Explain whether it is possible to draw a similar graphic that relates the unit circle with the graph of the tangent function.

Review & Refresh

Solve the equation.

24. $1 - \dfrac{9}{x-2} = -\dfrac{7}{2}$

25. $\dfrac{2x-3}{x+1} = \dfrac{10}{x^2-1} + 5$

26. Find the value of x for the right triangle.

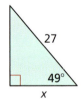

27. Simplify $(1 - \sin\theta)(1 + \sin\theta)$.

28. The owner of a restaurant asks 20 customers whether they are satisfied with the quality of their meals. Identify the method of data collection.

29. Graph one period of the function $g(x) = 4\sec x$. Describe the graph of g as a transformation of the graph of $f(x) = \sec x$.

30. The graph of $f(x) = b^x$ is shown. Describe the possible values of b.

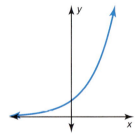

31. The highest point of the tip of a clock's second hand is 8 feet above the floor, and the lowest point is 7.5 feet. Write a model for the height h (in feet) of the tip of the second hand as a function of the time t (in minutes) given that the tip of the second hand is at its highest point when $t = 0$.

9 Chapter Review

Rate your understanding of each section.

1 I don't understand yet. **2** I can do it with help. **3** I can do it on my own. **4** I can teach someone.

9.1 Right Triangle Trigonometry (pp. 455–462)

⊙ **Learning Target:** Understand the six trigonometric functions.

Vocabulary
sine
cosine
tangent
cosecant
secant
cotangent

Evaluate the six trigonometric functions of the angle θ.

1.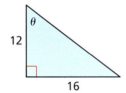

2.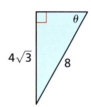

3. In a right triangle, θ is an acute angle and $\cos \theta = \frac{6}{11}$. Evaluate the other five trigonometric functions of θ.

Solve $\triangle ABC$.

4.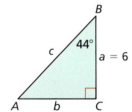

5.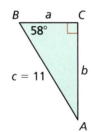

6. For a given angle θ, explain why $\sec \theta$ and $\csc \theta$ must both be greater than or equal to 1.

7. You fly a kite at an angle of 70°. The length of the string is 400 feet, and you hold the reel 4 feet above the ground.

   a. How high above the ground is the kite?

   b. A friend watching the kite estimates that the angle of elevation to the kite is 85°. How far from your friend are you standing?

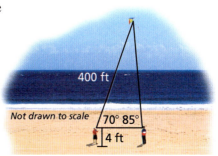

Not drawn to scale

9.2 Angles and Radian Measure (pp. 463–470)

Learning Target: Draw angles in standard position and understand radian measure.

Vocabulary
initial side
terminal side
standard position
coterminal
radian
sector
central angle

Convert the degree measure to radians or the radian measure to degrees.

8. 30°

9. 225°

10. $\dfrac{3\pi}{4}$

11. $\dfrac{5\pi}{3}$

12. Using radian measure, write one positive angle and one negative angle that are coterminal with 380°.

13. Find the value of θ. Then draw the angle in standard position.

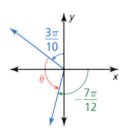

14. Find the arc length and area of a sector with a radius of 7 inches and a central angle of $\dfrac{\pi}{6}$.

15. A sprinkler system on a farm rotates 140° and sprays water up to 35 meters. Draw a diagram that shows the region that is irrigated by the sprinkler. Then find the area of the region.

9.3 Trigonometric Functions of Any Angle (pp. 471–478)

Learning Target: Evaluate trigonometric functions of any angle.

Vocabulary
unit circle
quadrantal angle
reference angle

Evaluate the six trigonometric functions of θ.

16.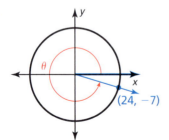

17.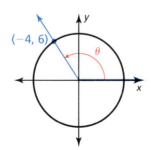

Evaluate the function without using a calculator.

18. $\tan 330°$

19. $\sec(-405°)$

20. $\sin \dfrac{13\pi}{6}$

21. $\sec \dfrac{11\pi}{3}$

9.4 Graphing Sine and Cosine Functions (pp. 479–488)

⊙ **Learning Target:** Describe and graph sine and cosine functions.

Vocabulary
amplitude
periodic function
cycle
period
phase shift
midline

Identify the amplitude and period of the function. Then graph the function and describe the graph of g as a transformation of the graph of its parent function.

22. $g(x) = 3 \sin x$

23. $g(x) = 8 \cos x$

24. $g(x) = 6 \sin \pi x$

25. $g(x) = \frac{1}{4} \cos 4x$

Use the graph to write a function of the form $y = a \sin bx$.

26.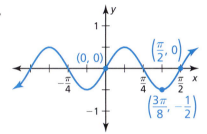

27.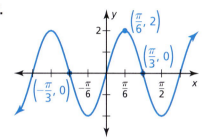

Graph the function.

28. $g(x) = \cos(x + \pi) + 2$

29. $g(x) = -\sin x - 4$

30. $g(x) = 2 \sin\left(x + \frac{\pi}{2}\right)$

31. $g(x) = \frac{1}{2} \cos\left(x - \frac{3\pi}{2}\right) + 1$

9.5 Graphing Other Trigonometric Functions (pp. 489–498)

⊙ **Learning Target:** Describe and graph tangent, cotangent, secant, and cosecant functions.

Graph one period of the function. Describe the graph of g as a transformation of the graph of its parent function.

32. $g(x) = 2 \cot x$

33. $g(x) = 4 \tan 3\pi x$

34. $g(x) = \sec \frac{1}{2} x$

35. $g(x) = \frac{1}{2} \csc \frac{\pi}{4} x$

36. The graph of $y = \sec bx$ has a period of $\frac{\pi}{3}$. Describe the asymptotes of the graph.

37. In 2017, Alex Honnold completed the first *free solo* climb of El Capitan in Yosemite National Park. Suppose a spectator stood 1,500 feet from the base of the 3,000-foot-tall rock wall. Write and graph an equation that represents the distance d (in feet) of Alex from the top of the wall as a function of the angle of elevation θ.

9.6 Modeling with Trigonometric Functions (pp. 499–506)

⊙ **Learning Target:** Write trigonometric functions.

Vocabulary
frequency
sinusoid

Write a function for the sinusoid.

38.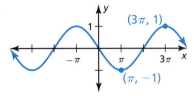

39.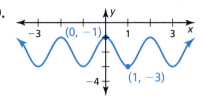

40. The sinusoid shown can be used to model the daily numbers of hours of daylight in Bozeman, Montana. Write a function for the model.

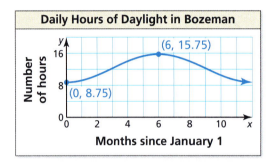

41. One of the largest sewing machines in the world has a *flywheel* (which turns as the machine sews) that is 5 feet in diameter. The highest point of the handle at the edge of the flywheel is 9 feet above the ground, and the lowest point is 4 feet. The wheel makes a complete turn every 2 seconds. Write a model for the height h (in feet) of the handle as a function of the time t (in seconds) given that the handle is at its lowest point when $t = 0$.

42. The table shows the monthly precipitation P (in inches) for Minneapolis, Minnesota, where the time t is measured in months and $t = 1$ represents January. Use technology to write a model that gives P as a function of t and interpret the period of its graph.

Time, t	Precipitation, P
1	0.87
2	0.75
3	1.89
4	2.64
5	3.35
6	4.25
7	4.02
8	4.29
9	3.07
10	2.40
11	1.73
12	1.14

9.7 Using Trigonometric Identities (pp. 507–512)

Learning Target: Verify and use trigonometric identities.

Vocabulary
trigonometric identity

Find the values of the other five trigonometric functions of θ.

43. $\cos\theta = \dfrac{3}{5}, 0 < \theta < \dfrac{\pi}{2}$

44. $\sin\theta = -\dfrac{5}{13}, \dfrac{3\pi}{2} < \theta < 2\pi$

45. $\sin\theta = \dfrac{1}{4}, \dfrac{\pi}{2} < \theta < \pi$

46. $\tan\theta = \dfrac{7}{2}, \pi < \theta < \dfrac{3\pi}{2}$

Simplify the expression.

47. $\cot^2 x - \cot^2 x \cos^2 x$

48. $\dfrac{(\sec x + 1)(\sec x - 1)}{\tan x}$

49. $\sin\left(\dfrac{\pi}{2} - x\right)\tan x$

50. $\dfrac{\sin x - \csc x}{\csc x}$

Verify the identity.

51. $\dfrac{\cos x \sec x}{1 + \tan^2 x} = \cos^2 x$

52. $\tan\left(\dfrac{\pi}{2} - x\right)\cot x = \csc^2 x - 1$

53. Your friend simplifies an expression and obtains $\sec x \tan x - \sin x$. You simplify the same expression and obtain $\sin x \tan^2 x$. Explain whether your answers are equivalent.

9.8 Using Sum and Difference Formulas (pp. 513–518)

Learning Target: Use sum and difference formulas to evaluate and simplify trigonometric expressions.

Find the exact value of the expression.

54. $\sin 75°$

55. $\tan(-45°)$

56. $\sin\dfrac{\pi}{12}$

57. $\cos\dfrac{7\pi}{12}$

58. Find $\tan(a + b)$, given that $\tan a = \dfrac{1}{4}$ with $\pi < a < \dfrac{3\pi}{2}$ and $\tan b = \dfrac{3}{7}$ with $0 < b < \dfrac{\pi}{2}$.

Simplify the expression.

59. $\sin\left(x - \dfrac{\pi}{2}\right)$

60. $\cos\left(x + \dfrac{\pi}{2}\right)$

61. $\tan\left(x - \dfrac{\pi}{2}\right)$

62. $\tan(x - 2\pi)$

Solve the equation for $0 \leq x < 2\pi$.

63. $\cos\left(x + \dfrac{3\pi}{4}\right) + \cos\left(x - \dfrac{3\pi}{4}\right) = 1$

64. $\tan(x + \pi) + \cos\left(x + \dfrac{\pi}{2}\right) = 0$

9 PERFORMANCE TASK
SMP.2 SMP.4

In navigation, *bearings* are used to indicate direction.

Smooth Sailing

The bearing of a line indicates the measure of the angle formed by the line and either the north or the south direction.

Bearings are written as either a north or a south direction, followed by a number of degrees in either the east or west direction.

Bearings are never greater than 90°. Navigators often use the terms *due north*, *due south*, *due east*, and *due west* to indicate a bearing of 0° or 90°.

Sailors use *nautical mile*s to measure distances and *knots* to measure speeds.

Nautical Mile:
A unit for distance based on the circumference of Earth
1 nautical mile ≈ 1.15 miles

Knot:
A knot is one nautical mile per hour.
1 knot ≈ 1.15 miles per hour

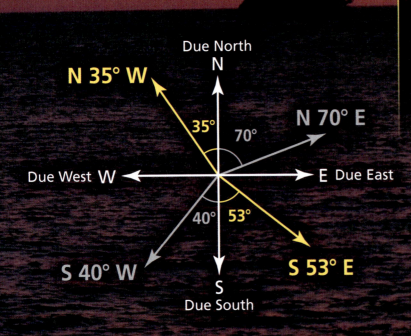

Analyzing Data

Use the information on the previous page to complete the following exercises.

1 Explain what is shown in the display. What do you notice? What do you wonder?

2 You sail a boat 8 nautical miles due north from your current location. You then sail 4 nautical miles due west and arrive at an island. At what bearing are you from your original location?

3 You take a direct route from your original location to the island in Exercise 2. How fast (in knots) must you sail to reach the island in under 45 minutes?

GET YOUR BEARINGS

You are navigating a boat to Port A, which is 5.2 nautical miles due east of Port B. You determine that the bearing from your current location to Port A is S 60° E and your bearing to Port B is S 30° W. You travel at an average speed of 24 knots. How long will it take you to reach your destination if you can take a direct route?

To avoid an island directly between your location and Port A, you travel due east until your new bearing to Port A is S 40° E. How does this affect your travel time? Justify your answer.

10 Sequences and Series

10.1 Defining and Using Sequences and Series
10.2 Analyzing Arithmetic Sequences and Series
10.3 Analyzing Geometric Sequences and Series
10.4 Finding Sums of Infinite Geometric Series
10.5 Using Recursive Rules with Sequences

NATIONAL GEOGRAPHIC EXPLORER
Barton Seaver CHEF

Barton Seaver is a chef who has dedicated his career to restoring the relationship we have with our ocean. It is his belief that the choices we make for dinner directly impact the ocean and its fragile ecosystems. He is the author of *For Cod and Country*, a book of recipes that inspires ocean conservation.

- Some of the most popular fish in the United States are salmon, tuna, tilapia, pollock, and pangasius. Are any of these endangered?
- What does it mean to *farm raise* fish?
- What percent of the meat eaten by Americans is fish? beef? chicken? pork?

PERFORMANCE TASK
Conservationists frequently monitor fish populations. In the Performance Task on pages 572 and 573, you will analyze a plan to stabilize a fish population.

Ocean Conservation

Big Idea of the Chapter
Use Sequences and Series

A sequence is an ordered list of numbers. Numbers in a sequence often follow a pattern that can be described by a rule. A series is an expression formed by adding the terms of a sequence.

The focus of ocean conservation is the protection of marine ecosystems. Conservationists try to prevent any negative effects of human activity. For ecosystems that are already damaged, the focus is on restoring the system so that vulnerable species can thrive. Ocean conservationists have training in fields such as biology, ecology, oceanography, and maritime law.

A conservationist estimates the number of salmon in a region each year for t years. The results are shown in the table.

Time, t (years)	1	2	3	4	5	6
Number of salmon, a_t (thousands)	800	823	846	869	892	915

1. Assuming the population continues to grow at this rate, estimate the number of salmon after 7 years, 8 years, and 9 years. Explain your reasoning.

2. Write and graph an equation that relates t and a_t.

3. Write an equation that relates a_t and a_{t-1}. Can you graph the relationship using only this equation? Explain.

Getting Ready for Chapter 10

Evaluating Functions

EXAMPLE 1 Evaluate the function $y = 2x^2 - 10$ for the values $x = 0, 1, 2, 3,$ and 4.

Input, x	$2x^2 - 10$	Output, y
0	$2(0)^2 - 10$	-10
1	$2(1)^2 - 10$	-8
2	$2(2)^2 - 10$	-2
3	$2(3)^2 - 10$	8
4	$2(4)^2 - 10$	22

Complete the table to evaluate the function.

1. $y = 3 - 2^x$

x	y
1	
2	
3	

2. $y = 5x^2 + 1$

x	y
2	
3	
4	

3. $y = -4x + 24$

x	y
5	
10	
15	

Solving Equations

EXAMPLE 2 Solve the equation $45 = 5(3)^x$.

$45 = 5(3)^x$ Write original equation.

$\dfrac{45}{5} = \dfrac{5(3)^x}{5}$ Division Property of Equality

$9 = 3^x$ Simplify.

$\log_3 9 = \log_3 3^x$ Take $\log_3$ of each side.

$2 = x$ Simplify.

Solve the equation.

4. $7x + 3 = 31$

5. $\dfrac{1}{16} = 4\left(\dfrac{1}{2}\right)^x$

6. $216 = 3(x + 6)$

7. $2^x + 16 = 144$

8. $\dfrac{1}{4}x - 8 = 17$

9. $8\left(\dfrac{3}{4}\right)^x = \dfrac{27}{8}$

10.1 Defining and Using Sequences and Series

Learning Target: Understand sequences and series.

Success Criteria:
- I can use rules to write terms of sequences.
- I can write rules for sequences.
- I can write and find sums of series.

INVESTIGATE Finding Terms of Sequences

Work with a partner.

1. For each pattern, find the number of objects in each figure. Then find the number of objects in the next figure.

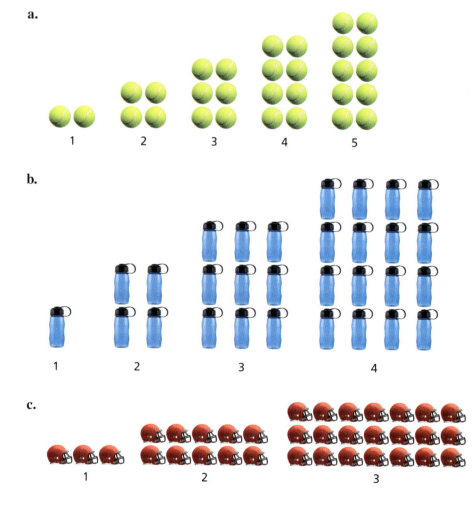

a.

b.

c.

2. For each pattern in Exercise 1, find the number of objects in the 10th figure. Explain how you found your answer.

10.1 Defining and Using Sequences and Series 529

Vocabulary
sequence
terms of a sequence
series
summation notation
sigma notation

Writing Terms of Sequences

A **sequence** is an ordered list of numbers. A *finite sequence* is a function that has a limited number of terms and whose domain is the finite set $\{1, 2, 3, \ldots, n\}$. The values in the range are called the **terms** of the sequence.

Domain: 1 2 3 4 $\ldots$ n   Relative position of each term
              ↓ ↓ ↓ ↓   ↓
Range: a_1 a_2 a_3 a_4 $\ldots$ a_n Terms of the sequence

An *infinite sequence* is a function that continues without stopping and whose domain is the set of positive integers.

Finite sequence: 2, 4, 6, 8

Infinite sequence: 2, 4, 6, 8, $\ldots$

A sequence can be specified by an equation, or *rule*. For example, both sequences above can be described by the rule $a_n = 2n$ or $f(n) = 2n$.

The domain of a sequence may begin with 0 instead of 1. When this is the case, the domain of a finite sequence is the set $\{0, 1, 2, 3, \ldots, n\}$ and the domain of an infinite sequence becomes the set of nonnegative integers. Unless otherwise indicated, assume the domain of a sequence begins with 1.

EXAMPLE 1   Writing the Terms of Sequences

Write the first six terms of (a) $a_n = 2n + 5$ and (b) $f(n) = (-3)^{n-1}$.

a. $a_1 = 2(1) + 5 = 7$ 1st term   b. $f(1) = (-3)^{1-1} = 1$

 $a_2 = 2(2) + 5 = 9$ 2nd term $f(2) = (-3)^{2-1} = -3$

 $a_3 = 2(3) + 5 = 11$ 3rd term $f(3) = (-3)^{3-1} = 9$

 $a_4 = 2(4) + 5 = 13$ 4th term $f(4) = (-3)^{4-1} = -27$

 $a_5 = 2(5) + 5 = 15$ 5th term $f(5) = (-3)^{5-1} = 81$

 $a_6 = 2(6) + 5 = 17$ 6th term $f(6) = (-3)^{6-1} = -243$

▶ The first six terms are 7, 9, 11, 13, 15, 17.

▶ The first six terms are 1, -3, 9, -27, 81, -243.

In-Class Practice

Self-Assessment

Write the first six terms of the sequence.

1. $a_n = n + 4$

2. $f(n) = (-2)^{n-1}$

3. $a_n = \dfrac{n}{n+1}$

530   Chapter 10   Sequences and Series

Writing Rules for Sequences

EXAMPLE 2 **Writing Rules for Sequences**

Describe the pattern, write the next term, and write a rule for the nth term of the sequence (a) $-1, -8, -27, -64, \ldots$ and (b) $0, 2, 6, 12, \ldots$.

a. You can write the terms as $(-1)^3, (-2)^3, (-3)^3, (-4)^3, \ldots$. The next term is $a_5 = (-5)^3 = -125$. A rule for the nth term is $a_n = (-n)^3$.

b. You can write the terms as $0(1), 1(2), 2(3), 3(4), \ldots$. The next term is $f(5) = 4(5) = 20$. A rule for the nth term is $f(n) = (n-1)n$.

EXAMPLE 3 **Graphing a Sequence**

You work in a grocery store and stack apples in the shape of a square pyramid with 7 layers. Write a rule for the number of apples in each layer. Then graph the sequence.

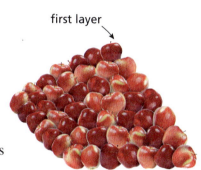
first layer

Make a table showing the numbers of apples in the first 3 layers. Let a_n represent the number of apples in layer n.

Layer, n	1	2	3
Number of apples, a_n	$1 = 1^2$	$4 = 2^2$	$9 = 3^2$

Write a rule for the number of apples in each layer. From the table, you can see that $a_n = n^2$.

Plot the points $(1, 1), (2, 4), (3, 9), (4, 16),$ $(5, 25), (6, 36),$ and $(7, 49)$.

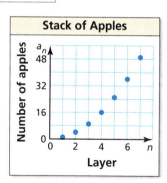

Stack of Apples

In-Class Practice

Self-Assessment

Describe the pattern, write the next term, graph the first five terms, and write a rule for the nth term of the sequence.

4. $3, 5, 7, 9, \ldots$

5. $1, -2, 4, -8, \ldots$

6. $2, 5, 10, 17, \ldots$

7. **WHAT IF?** In Example 3, there are 9 layers of apples. How many apples are in the 9th layer?

Writing Rules for Series

When the terms of a sequence are added together, the resulting expression is a **series**. A series can be finite or infinite.

Finite series: $2 + 4 + 6 + 8$

Infinite series: $2 + 4 + 6 + 8 + \cdots$

You can use **summation notation** to write a series. For example, the two series above can be written in summation notation as follows.

Finite series: $2 + 4 + 6 + 8 = \sum_{i=1}^{4} 2i$

Infinite series: $2 + 4 + 6 + 8 + \cdots = \sum_{i=1}^{\infty} 2i$

For both series, the *index of summation* is i and the *lower limit of summation* is 1. The *upper limit of summation* is 4 for the finite series and ∞ (infinity) for the infinite series. Summation notation is also called **sigma notation** because it uses the uppercase Greek letter *sigma*, written Σ.

EXAMPLE 4   Writing Series Using Summation Notation

Write each series using summation notation.

a. $25 + 50 + 75 + \cdots + 250$

Notice that the first term is 25(1), the second is 25(2), the third is 25(3), and the last is 25(10). So, the terms of the series can be written as

$a_i = 25i$, where $i = 1, 2, 3, \ldots, 10$.

The lower limit of summation is 1 and the upper limit of summation is 10.

▶ The summation notation for the series is $\sum_{i=1}^{10} 25i$.

b. $\dfrac{1}{2} + \dfrac{2}{3} + \dfrac{3}{4} + \dfrac{4}{5} + \cdots$

Notice that for each term, the denominator of the fraction is 1 more than the numerator. So, the terms of the series can be written as

$a_i = \dfrac{i}{i+1}$, where $i = 1, 2, 3, 4, \ldots$.

The lower limit of summation is 1 and the upper limit of summation is infinity.

▶ The summation notation for the series is $\sum_{i=1}^{\infty} \dfrac{i}{i+1}$.

In-Class Practice

Self-Assessment

Write the series using summation notation.

8. $5 + 10 + 15 + \cdots + 100$

9. $6 + 36 + 216 + 1{,}296 + \cdots$

1 I don't understand yet.   **2** I can do it with help.   **3** I can do it on my own.   **4** I can teach someone.

The index of summation for a series does not have to be i—any letter can be used. Also, the index does not have to begin at 1.

EXAMPLE 5 Finding the Sum of a Series

Find the sum $\sum_{k=4}^{8} (3 + k^2)$.

$$\sum_{k=4}^{8} (3 + k^2) = (3 + 4^2) + (3 + 5^2) + (3 + 6^2) + (3 + 7^2) + (3 + 8^2)$$
$$= 19 + 28 + 39 + 52 + 67$$
$$= 205$$

Finding sums of series by adding the terms can be tedious. Below are formulas you can use to find the sums of three special types of series.

Key Concept

Formulas for Special Series

Sum of n terms of 1: $\sum_{i=1}^{n} 1 = n$

Sum of first n positive integers: $\sum_{i=1}^{n} i = n(n + 1)/2$

Sum of squares of first n positive integers: $\sum_{i=1}^{n} i^2 = \dfrac{n(n + 1)(2n + 1)}{6}$

EXAMPLE 6 Using a Formula to Find a Sum

How many apples are in the stack in Example 3?

From Example 3, you know that the ith term of the series is given by $a_i = i^2$, where $i = 1, 2, 3, \ldots, 7$. Using summation notation and the third formula listed above, you can find the total number of apples as follows:

$$1^2 + 2^2 + \cdots + 7^2 = \sum_{i=1}^{7} i^2 = \dfrac{7(7 + 1)(2 \cdot 7 + 1)}{6} = \dfrac{7(8)(15)}{6} = 140$$

▶ There are 140 apples in the stack.

In-Class Practice

Self-Assessment

Find the sum.

10. $\sum_{i=1}^{5} 8i$ **11.** $\sum_{i=1}^{34} 1$ **12.** $\sum_{k=1}^{6} k$

13. You begin to make a display of baseballs in the shape of a square pyramid, similar to the pyramid in Example 3. The pyramid will have 10 layers. You run out of baseballs after making the bottom 6 layers. How many baseballs did you use?

10.1 Practice

Write the first six terms of the sequence. (See Example 1.)

1. $a_n = n + 2$
2. $f(n) = n^3 + 2$
3. $f(n) = 4^{n-1}$
4. $a_n = -n^2$
5. $a_n = (n+3)^2$
6. $f(n) = \dfrac{2n}{n+2}$

Describe the pattern, write the next term, and write a rule for the nth term of the sequence. (See Example 2.)

7. $1, 6, 11, 16, \ldots$
8. $3.1, 3.8, 4.5, 5.2, \ldots$
9. $-4, 8, -12, 16, \ldots$
10. $\dfrac{1}{10}, \dfrac{3}{20}, \dfrac{5}{30}, \dfrac{7}{40}, \ldots$
11. $\dfrac{2}{3}, \dfrac{2}{6}, \dfrac{2}{9}, \dfrac{2}{12}, \ldots$
12. $2, 9, 28, 65, \ldots$

13. **CONNECTION TO REAL LIFE** Rectangular tables are placed together along their short edges, as shown in the diagram. Write a rule for the number of people who can be seated around n tables arranged in this manner. Then graph the sequence. (See Example 3.)

14. **CONNECTION TO REAL LIFE** A city worker earns $33,000 for the first year of employment. The worker receives raises of $2,400 each year. Write a rule for the salary of the worker each year. Then graph the sequence.

Write the series using summation notation. (See Example 4.)

15. $7 + 10 + 13 + 16 + 19$
16. $-1 + 2 + 7 + 14 + \cdots$
17. $\dfrac{1}{3} + \dfrac{1}{9} + \dfrac{1}{27} + \dfrac{1}{81} + \cdots$
18. $-2 + 4 - 8 + 16 - 32$

Find the sum. (See Examples 5 and 6.)

19. $\displaystyle\sum_{i=1}^{6} 2i$
20. $\displaystyle\sum_{k=1}^{4} 3k^2$
21. $\displaystyle\sum_{k=3}^{6} (5k - 2)$
22. $\displaystyle\sum_{i=10}^{25} i$
23. $\displaystyle\sum_{i=1}^{35} 1$
24. $\displaystyle\sum_{n=1}^{18} n^2$

25. Write a rule for the total number of green squares in the nth figure of each pattern.

a.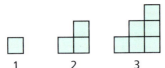

b.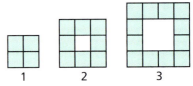

26. **ERROR ANALYSIS** Describe and correct the error in finding the sum of the series.

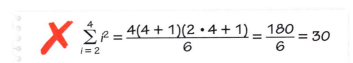

$$\sum_{i=2}^{4} i^2 = \dfrac{4(4+1)(2 \cdot 4 + 1)}{6} = \dfrac{180}{6} = 30$$

534 Chapter 10 Sequences and Series

27. You want to save $500 for a new tablet. You begin by saving a penny on the first day. You save an additional penny each day after that.

    a. How much money will you have saved after 100 days?

    b. Use a series to determine how many days it takes you to save $500.

28. **SMP.7** Use the diagram to determine the sum of the series. Explain your method.

$$1+3+5+7+9+\cdots+(2n-1)=?$$

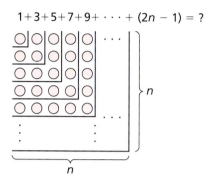

29. Is there a way to use the formula for the sum of the first n positive integers to evaluate $\sum_{i=3}^{1,659} i$? If so, explain how to use it. If not, explain why not.

30. **CONNECT CONCEPTS** For a regular n-sided polygon, the measure a_n of an interior angle is given by $a_n = \dfrac{180(n-2)}{n}$.

    a. Write a rule for the sequence where T_n is the sum of the measures of the interior angles of a regular n-sided polygon.

    b. Use your rule in part (a) to find the sum of the interior angle measures of the Guggenheim Museum skylight, which is a regular dodecagon.

31. **SMP.6** Determine whether each statement is true. If so, show that it is true. If not, provide a counterexample.

    a. $\sum_{i=1}^{n} ca_i = c\sum_{i=1}^{n} a_i$

    b. $\sum_{i=1}^{n} (a_i + b_i) = \sum_{i=1}^{n} a_i + \sum_{i=1}^{n} b_i$

    c. $\sum_{i=1}^{n} a_i b_i = \sum_{i=1}^{n} a_i \sum_{i=1}^{n} b_i$

    d. $\sum_{i=1}^{n} (a_i)^c = \left(\sum_{i=1}^{n} a_i\right)^c$

32. **SMP.8 DIG DEEPER** Write a formula for the sum of the cubes of the first n positive integers.

33. **SMP.4** You are trying to move rings from one peg and stack them in order on another peg. A move consists of moving exactly one ring, which cannot be placed on top of a smaller ring. The minimum number a_n of moves needed to move n rings is 1 for 1 ring, 3 for 2 rings, 7 for 3 rings, 15 for 4 rings, and 31 for 5 rings. Use a rule to find the minimum number of moves required to move 8 rings.

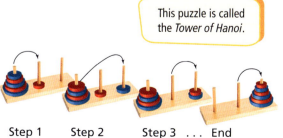

This puzzle is called the *Tower of Hanoi*.

Interpreting Data

COMMON NAILS The *penny size* of a common nail is determined by its length. A nail of the smallest size, 2d, is 1 inch long. For the sizes 2d through 10d, each increase of 1d corresponds to an increase in length of $\frac{1}{4}$ inch. A nail of size 20d is 4 inches long, and for sizes 20d to 60d, each increase of 10d corresponds to an increase in length of $\frac{1}{2}$ inch.

Length (inches)	Diameter (inches)
1	0.072
2	0.120
3	0.148
4	0.203
5	0.238
6	0.284

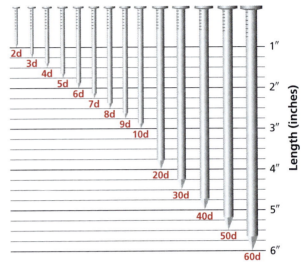

34. Write a rule for the length a_n (in inches) of a nail of penny size nd, where $2 \leq n \leq 10$.

35. Sketch a graph that shows the relationship between length and diameter. Explain whether the quantities show a linear relationship.

36. Why is the word penny used to describe the size of a common nail?

Review & Refresh

Simplify the expression.

37. $\dfrac{\sin(-\theta)}{\csc \theta}$

38. $\tan\left(x - \dfrac{3\pi}{2}\right)$

Find the sum or difference.

39. $\dfrac{5}{8x} + \dfrac{3}{8x}$

40. $\dfrac{6}{x+2} - \dfrac{2}{x-2}$

41. Evaluate the six trigonometric functions of θ.

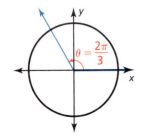

42. Write a function for the sinusoid.

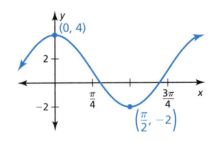

Solve the system.

43. $2x - y - 3z = 6$
$x + y + 4z = -1$
$3x - 2z = 8$

44. $2x - 3y + z = 4$
$x - 2z = 1$
$y + z = 2$

10.2 Analyzing Arithmetic Sequences and Series

> **Learning Target:** Analyze arithmetic sequences and series.
>
> **Success Criteria:**
> - I can identify arithmetic sequences.
> - I can write rules for arithmetic sequences.
> - I can find sums of finite arithmetic series.

In an *arithmetic sequence*, the difference of consecutive terms, called the *common difference*, is constant. For example, in the arithmetic sequence 1, 4, 7, 10, . . . , the common difference is 3.

INVESTIGATE — Finding the Sum of an Arithmetic Sequence

Work with a partner. When German mathematician Carl Friedrich Gauss (1777–1855) was young, one of his teachers asked him to find the sum of the whole numbers from 1 through 100. To the astonishment of his teacher, Gauss came up with the answer after only a few moments. Here is what Gauss did:

$$
\begin{array}{cccccccccc}
1 & + & 2 & + & 3 & + & \cdots & + & 100 \\
100 & + & 99 & + & 98 & + & \ldots & + & 1 \\
\hline
101 & + & 101 & + & 101 & + & \cdots & + & 101
\end{array}
$$

$$\frac{100 \times 101}{2} = 5{,}050$$

1. **SMP.8** Explain Gauss's thought process. Then write a formula for the sum S_n of the first n terms of an arithmetic sequence.

2. Show that the numbers of shoes in the figures below form an arithmetic sequence. Then find the total number of shoes in the first 8 figures by (a) writing the number of shoes in each figure and adding, and (b) using the formula you found in Exercise 1.

1   2   3   4

3. Explain why Gauss's method works for any arithmetic sequence.

Vocabulary
arithmetic sequence
common difference
arithmetic series

Identifying Arithmetic Sequences

In an **arithmetic sequence**, the difference of consecutive terms is constant. This constant difference is called the **common difference**.

EXAMPLE 1 **Identifying Arithmetic Sequences**

Explain whether each sequence is arithmetic.

a. $-9, -2, 5, 12, 19, \ldots$

Find the differences of consecutive terms.

$a_2 - a_1 = -2 - (-9) = 7$

$a_3 - a_2 = 5 - (-2) = 7$

$a_4 - a_3 = 12 - 5 = 7$

$a_5 - a_4 = 19 - 12 = 7$

Position	1	2	3	4	5
Term	-9	-2	5	12	19

$+7 \quad +7 \quad +7 \quad +7$ ← Each term is 7 greater than the previous term.

▶ The differences are constant, so the sequence is arithmetic.

b. $23, 15, 9, 5, 3, \ldots$

Find the differences of consecutive terms.

$a_2 - a_1 = 15 - 23 = -8$

$a_3 - a_2 = 9 - 15 = -6$

$a_4 - a_3 = 5 - 9 = -4$

$a_5 - a_4 = 3 - 5 = -2$

Position	1	2	3	4	5
Term	23	15	9	5	3

$+(-8) \quad +(-6) \quad +(-4) \quad +(-2)$

▶ The differences are not constant, so the sequence is not arithmetic.

In-Class Practice

Self-Assessment

Explain whether the sequence is arithmetic.

1. $15, 9, 3, -3, -9, \ldots$
2. $8, 4, 2, 1, \frac{1}{2}, \ldots$

Writing Rules for Arithmetic Sequences

Key Concept

Rule for an Arithmetic Sequence

Algebra The nth term of an arithmetic sequence with first term a_1 and common difference d is given by

$$a_n = a_1 + (n-1)d.$$

Example The nth term of an arithmetic sequence with a first term of 3 and a common difference of 2 is given by

$$a_n = 3 + (n-1)2, \text{ or } a_n = 2n + 1.$$

EXAMPLE 2 Writing a Rule for the nth Term

Write a rule for the nth term of each sequence. Then find a_{15}.

a. 3, 8, 13, 18, ...

The sequence is arithmetic with first term $a_1 = 3$, and common difference $d = 8 - 3 = 5$. So, a rule for the nth term is

$$a_n = a_1 + (n-1)d \qquad \text{Write general rule.}$$
$$= 3 + (n-1)5 \qquad \text{Substitute 3 for } a_1 \text{ and 5 for .}$$
$$= 5n - 2. \qquad \text{Simplify.}$$

▶ A rule is $a_n = 5n - 2$, and the 15th term is $a_{15} = 5(15) - 2 = 73$.

b. 55, 47, 39, 31, ...

The sequence is arithmetic with first term $a_1 = 55$, and common difference $d = 47 - 55 = -8$. So, a rule for the nth term is

$$a_n = a_1 + (n-1)d \qquad \text{Write general rule.}$$
$$= 55 + (n-1)(-8) \qquad \text{Substitute 55 for } a_1 \text{ and } -8 \text{ for } d.$$
$$= -8n + 63. \qquad \text{Simplify.}$$

▶ A rule is $a_n = -8n + 63$, and the 15th term is
$a_{15} = -8(15) + 63 = -57$.

In-Class Practice

Self-Assessment

Write a rule for the nth term of the sequence. Then find a_{15}.

3. 7, 11, 15, 19, ...

4. $-1, -\frac{1}{3}, \frac{1}{3}, 1, \ldots$

EXAMPLE 3 **Writing a Rule Given a Term and Common Difference**

One term of an arithmetic sequence is $a_{19} = -45$. The common difference is $d = -3$. Write a rule for the nth term. Then graph the first six terms.

Use the general rule to find the first term.

$a_n = a_1 + (n - 1)d$	Write general rule.
$a_{19} = a_1 + (19 - 1)d$	Substitute 19 for n.
$-45 = a_1 + 18(-3)$	Substitute -45 for a_{19} and -3 for d.
$9 = a_1$	Solve for a_1.

Write a rule for the nth term.

$a_n = a_1 + (n - 1)d$	Write general rule.
$= 9 + (n - 1)(-3)$	Substitute 9 for a_1 and -3 for d.
$= -3n + 12$	Simplify.

Use the rule to create a table of values for the sequence. Then plot the points.

n	1	2	3	4	5	6
a_n	9	6	3	0	-3	-6

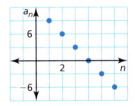

EXAMPLE 4 **Writing a Rule Given Two Terms**

Two terms of an arithmetic sequence are $a_7 = 17$ and $a_{26} = 93$. Write a rule for the nth term.

Write and solve a system of equations using $a_n = a_1 + (n - 1)d$. Substitute 26 for n to write Equation 1. Substitute 7 for n to write Equation 2.

$a_{26} = a_1 + (26 - 1)d$ ➡ $93 = a_1 + 25d$ Equation 1

$a_7 = a_1 + (7 - 1)d$ ➡ $17 = a_1 + 6d$ Equation 2

Subtracting Equation 2 from Equation 1 gives $76 = 19d$. So, $d = 4$. Substituting 4 for d in Equation 1 gives $93 = a_1 + 100$. So, $a_1 = -7$.

Write a rule for a_n:

$a_n = a_1 + (n - 1)d$	Write general rule.
$= -7 + (n - 1)4$	Substitute for a_1 and d.
$= 4n - 11$	Simplify.

In-Class Practice

Self-Assessment

Write a rule for the nth term of the sequence. Then find a_{15} and graph the first six terms of the sequence.

5. $a_{11} = 50, d = 7$

6. $a_7 = 71, a_{16} = 26$

1 I don't understand yet.   **2** I can do it with help.   **3** I can do it on my own.   **4** I can teach someone.

Finding Sums of Finite Arithmetic Series

The expression formed by adding the terms of an arithmetic sequence is called an **arithmetic series**. The sum of the first n terms of an arithmetic series is denoted by S_n. To find a rule for S_n, you can write S_n in two different ways and add the results.

$$S_n = a_1 \;\;\;\;\;\;\;\; + (a_1 + d) + (a_1 + 2d) + \cdots + a_n$$
$$\underline{S_n = a_n \;\;\;\;\;\;\;\; + (a_n - d) + (a_n - 2d) + \cdots + a_1}$$
$$2S_n = \underbrace{(a_1 + a_n) + (a_1 + a_n) + (a_1 + a_n) + \cdots + (a_1 + a_n)}$$

$(a_1 + a_n)$ is added n times.

You can conclude that $2S_n = n(a_1 + a_n)$, which leads to the following result.

Key Concept

The Sum of a Finite Arithmetic Series

The sum of the first n terms of an arithmetic series is

$$S_n = n\left(\frac{a_1 + a_n}{2}\right).$$

In words, S_n is the mean of the first and nth terms, multiplied by the number of terms.

EXAMPLE 5 Finding the Sum of an Arithmetic Series

Find the sum $\sum_{i=1}^{20} (3i + 7)$.

Find the first and last terms.

$a_1 = 3(1) + 7 = 10$ Find first term.

$a_{20} = 3(20) + 7 = 67$ Find last term.

Find the sum.

$S_{20} = 20\left(\dfrac{a_1 + a_{20}}{2}\right)$ Write rule for S_{20}.

$\;\;\;\;\;\; = 20\left(\dfrac{10 + 67}{2}\right)$ Substitute 10 for a_1 and 67 for a_{20}.

$\;\;\;\;\;\; = 770$ Evaluate.

In-Class Practice

Self-Assessment

Find the sum.

7. $\sum_{i=1}^{10} 9i$ **8.** $\sum_{k=1}^{12} (7k + 2)$ **9.** $\sum_{n=1}^{20} (-4n + 6)$

1 I don't understand yet.   **2** I can do it with help.   **3** I can do it on my own.   **4** I can teach someone.

10.2 Practice

Explain whether the sequence is arithmetic. (See Example 1.)

1. $1, -1, -3, -5, -7, \ldots$

2. $5, 8, 13, 20, 29, \ldots$

3. $36, 18, 9, \frac{9}{2}, \frac{9}{4}, \ldots$

4. $\frac{1}{2}, \frac{3}{4}, 1, \frac{5}{4}, \frac{3}{2}, \ldots$

Write a rule for the nth term of the sequence. Then find a_{20}. (See Example 2.)

5. $12, 20, 28, 36, \ldots$

6. $86, 79, 72, 65, \ldots$

7. $-2, -\frac{5}{4}, -\frac{1}{2}, \frac{1}{4}, \ldots$

8. $2.3, 1.5, 0.7, -0.1, \ldots$

9. What can you conclude about the terms of an arithmetic sequence when $d > 0$? $d < 0$?

10. **SMP.3 ERROR ANALYSIS** Describe and correct the error in writing a rule for the nth term of the arithmetic sequence

    $22, 9, -4, -17, -30, \ldots$

    > The first term is 22 and the common difference is -13.
    > $a_n = -13 + (n - 1)(22)$
    > $a_n = -35 + 22n$

Write a rule for the nth term of the sequence. Then graph the first six terms of the sequence. (See Example 3.)

11. $a_{11} = 43, d = 5$

12. $a_{13} = 42, d = 4$

13. $a_{20} = -27, d = -2$

14. $a_{17} = -5, d = -\frac{1}{2}$

Write a rule for the nth term of the arithmetic sequence. (See Example 4.)

15. $a_6 = -8, a_{15} = -62$

16. $a_7 = 58, a_{11} = 94$

17. $a_{18} = -59, a_{21} = -71$

18. $a_8 = 12, a_{16} = 22$

Write a rule for the sequence with the given terms.

19.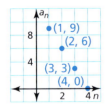

20.
n	4	5	6	7	8
a_n	31	39	47	55	63

Find the sum. (See Example 5.)

21. $\sum_{i=1}^{33} (6 - 2i)$

22. $\sum_{i=1}^{20} (2i - 3)$

23. $\sum_{i=1}^{41} (-2.3 + 0.1i)$

24. Find the sum of the first 19 terms of the sequence $9, 2, -5, -12, \ldots$.

25. Find the sum of the first 22 terms of the sequence $17, 9, 1, -7, \ldots$.

26. **SMP.4 CONNECTION TO REAL LIFE** Domestic bees make their honeycomb by starting with a single hexagonal cell, then forming ring after ring of hexagonal cells around the initial cell, as shown. The numbers of cells in successive rings forms an arithmetic sequence.

Initial cell   1 ring   2 rings

   a. Write a rule for the number of cells in the nth ring.
   b. How many cells are in the honeycomb after the ninth ring is formed?

27. Does the sum of a series double when the common difference is doubled, and the first term and number of terms remain unchanged? Explain why or why not.

28. **CONNECT CONCEPTS** A quilt is made up of strips of cloth, starting with an inner square surrounded by rectangles to form successively larger squares. The inner square and the rectangles have a width of 1 foot. Write and evaluate an expression using summation notation that gives the sum of the areas of the strips of cloth used to make the quilt shown.

29. **SMP.7** Find the sum of the positive odd integers less than 300. Explain your method.

30. Find the value of n for $\sum_{i=1}^{n}(3i+5)=544$.

31. A theater has n rows of seats, and each row has d more seats than the row in front of it. There are x seats in the last (nth) row and a total of y seats in the theater. Write an expression for the number of seats in the front row.

32. **SMP.1 DIG DEEPER** One of the major sources of our knowledge of Egyptian mathematics is the Ahmes papyrus, which is a scroll copied in 1650 B.C. by an Egyptian scribe. The following problem is from the Ahmes papyrus.

    Divide 10 hekats of barley among 10 men so that the common difference is $\frac{1}{8}$ of a hekat of barley.

    Use what you know about arithmetic sequences and series to determine what portion of a hekat each man should receive. Explain your method.

33. The expressions $3 - x$, x, and $1 - 3x$ are the first three terms of an arithmetic sequence. Find the value of x and the next term of the sequence.

Interpreting Data

THEATER OF DIONYSUS The Theater of Dionysus was an ancient Greek theater in Athens. It could seat an audience of up to 17,000.

34. Use the photo to estimate the number of rows in the theater.

35. **SMP.2** Write an arithmetic sequence that models a full audience at the theater. Use your sequence to verify that the theater could seat an audience of about 17,000.

Dionysus
Greek God of Theater

Theater of Dionysus

Review & Refresh

36. The graph of a polynomial function is shown. Is the degree of the function *odd* or *even*? Is the leading coefficient of the function *positive* or *negative*?

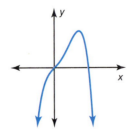

37. You and your friend enter a drawing to win tickets to a play. From 35 entries, 2 winners are randomly selected. What is the probability that you and your friend win?

38. Simplify $\cos\left(x - \frac{3\pi}{2}\right)$.

39. Explain whether functions f and g are inverses.

x	−1	0	1	2	3
f(x)	2	4	6	8	10

x	−1	0	1	2	3
g(x)	$\frac{1}{2}$	$\frac{1}{4}$	$\frac{1}{6}$	$\frac{1}{8}$	$\frac{1}{10}$

40. Find the sum $\sum_{k=1}^{4} (k^2 + 2)$.

41. Given that $\cos \theta = \frac{15}{17}$ and $\frac{3\pi}{2} < \theta < 2\pi$, find the values of the other five trigonometric functions of θ.

10.3 Analyzing Geometric Sequences and Series

> **Learning Target:** Analyze geometric sequences and series.
>
> **Success Criteria:**
> - I can identify geometric sequences.
> - I can write rules for geometric sequences.
> - I can find sums of finite geometric series.

INVESTIGATE **Finding the Sum of a Geometric Sequence**

Work with a partner. In a *geometric sequence*, the ratio of any term to the previous term, called the *common ratio*, is constant. You can write the nth term of a geometric sequence with first term a_1 and common ratio r as

$$a_n = a_1 r^{n-1}.$$

So, you can write the sum S_n of the first n terms of a geometric sequence as

$$S_n = a_1 + a_1 r + a_1 r^2 + a_1 r^3 + \cdots + a_1 r^{n-1}.$$

This sum may have many terms that can be tedious to add.

1. A student wants to find a way to write S_n concisely by doing something Gauss may have tried. A portion of the student's work is shown below.

   a. Explain what the student did.

   $$S_n = a_1 + a_1 r + a_1 r^2 + a_1 r^3 + \cdots + a_1 r^{n-1}$$
   $$-rS_n = - a_1 r - a_1 r^2 - a_1 r^3 - \cdots - a_1 r^{n-1} - a_1 r^n$$

   b. Continue the student's work by completing the statement.

   $$S_n - rS_n = \underline{}$$

   c. Show how you can solve for S_n in part (b).

2. Show that the numbers of fish in the figures below form a geometric sequence. Then find the total number of fish in the first 10 figures by (a) writing the number of fish in each figure and adding, and (b) using the formula you wrote in Exercise 1(c).

1   2   3   4

Vocabulary
geometric sequence
common ratio
geometric series

Geometric Sequences

In a **geometric sequence**, the ratio of any term to the previous term is constant. This constant ratio is called the **common ratio** and is denoted by r.

EXAMPLE 1 Identifying Geometric Sequences

Explain whether each sequence is geometric.

a. 6, 12, 20, 30, 42, . . .

$$\frac{a_2}{a_1} = \frac{12}{6} = 2 \qquad \frac{a_3}{a_2} = \frac{20}{12} = \frac{5}{3} \qquad \frac{a_4}{a_3} = \frac{30}{20} = \frac{3}{2} \qquad \frac{a_5}{a_4} = \frac{42}{30} = \frac{7}{5}$$

▶ The ratios are not constant, so the sequence is not geometric.

b. 256, 64, 16, 4, 1, . . .

$$\frac{a_2}{a_1} = \frac{64}{256} = \frac{1}{4} \qquad \frac{a_3}{a_2} = \frac{16}{64} = \frac{1}{4} \qquad \frac{a_4}{a_3} = \frac{4}{16} = \frac{1}{4} \qquad \frac{a_5}{a_4} = \frac{1}{4}$$

▶ The ratios are constant, so the sequence is geometric.

Key Concept

Rule for a Geometric Sequence

The nth term of a geometric sequence with first term a_1 and common ratio r is given by

$$a_n = a_1 r^{n-1}.$$

EXAMPLE 2 Writing a Rule for the nth Term

Write a rule for the nth term of 5, 15, 45, 135, ... Then find a_8.

The sequence is geometric with first term $a_1 = 5$, and common ratio $r = \frac{15}{5} = 3$. So, a rule for the nth term is

$a_n = a_1 r^{n-1}$ Write general rule.

$ = 5(3)^{n-1}.$ Substitute values.

▶ A rule is $a_n = 5(3)^{n-1}$, and the 8th term is $a_8 = 5(3)^{8-1} = 10{,}935$.

In-Class Practice

Self-Assessment

Explain whether the sequence is geometric.

1. $27, 9, 3, 1, \frac{1}{3}, \ldots$

2. $2, 6, 24, 120, 720, \ldots$

3. Write a rule for the nth term of the sequence 3, 15, 75, 375, ... Then find a_9.

1 I don't understand yet. **2** I can do it with help. **3** I can do it on my own. **4** I can teach someone.

EXAMPLE 3 **Writing a Rule Given a Term and Common Ratio**

One term of a geometric sequence is $a_4 = 12$. The common ratio is $r = 2$. Write a rule for the nth term. Then graph the first six terms of the sequence.

$a_n = a_1 r^{n-1}$ Write general rule.

$a_4 = a_1 r^{4-1}$ Substitute 4 for n.

$12 = a_1 (2)^3$ Substitute 12 for a_4 and 2 for r.

$1.5 = a_1$ Solve for a_1.

So, $a_n = 1.5(2)^{n-1}$. Use the rule to create a table of values for the sequence. Then plot the points.

n	1	2	3	4	5	6
a_n	1.5	3	6	12	24	48

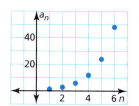

EXAMPLE 4 **Writing a Rule Given Two Terms**

Two terms of a geometric sequence are $a_2 = 12$ and $a_5 = -768$. Write a rule for the nth term.

Write a system of equations using $a_n = a_1 r^{n-1}$. Substitute 2 for n to write Equation 1. Substitute 5 for n to write Equation 2.

$a_2 = a_1 r^{2-1}$ ➡ $12 = a_1 r$ Equation 1

$a_5 = a_1 r^{5-1}$ ➡ $-768 = a_1 r^4$ Equation 2

Solve the system.

$\dfrac{12}{r} = a_1$ Solve Equation 1 for a_1.

$-768 = \dfrac{12}{r}(r^4)$ Substitute for a_1 in Equation 2.

$-768 = 12r^3$ Simplify.

$-4 = r$ Solve for r.

$12 = a_1(-4)$ Substitute for r in Equation 1.

$-3 = a_1$ Solve for a_1.

▶ So, a rule is $a_n = -3(-4)^{n-1}$.

In-Class Practice

Self-Assessment

Write a rule for the nth term of the sequence. Then graph the first six terms of the sequence.

4. $a_6 = -96$, $r = -2$ **5.** $a_1 = -4$, $a_5 = -2{,}500$

1 I don't understand yet.   **2** I can do it with help.   **3** I can do it on my own.   **4** I can teach someone.

Finding Sums of Finite Geometric Series

The expression formed by adding the terms of a geometric sequence is called a **geometric series**. The sum of the first n terms of a geometric series is denoted by S_n. You can develop a rule for S_n as follows.

$$S_n = a_1 + a_1 r + a_1 r^2 + a_1 r^3 + \cdots + a_1 r^{n-1}$$
$$-rS_n = \quad\quad - a_1 r - a_1 r^2 - a_1 r^3 - \cdots - a_1 r^{n-1} - a_1 r^n$$
$$\overline{S_n - rS_n = a_1 + \; 0 \; + \; 0 \; + \; 0 \; + \cdots + \; 0 \quad\quad - a_1 r^n}$$
$$S_n(1 - r) = a_1(1 - r^n)$$

When $r \neq 1$, you can divide each side of this equation by $1 - r$ to obtain the following rule for S_n.

Key Concept

The Sum of a Finite Geometric Series

The sum of the first n terms of a geometric series with common ratio $r \neq 1$ is

$$S_n = a_1\left(\frac{1 - r^n}{1 - r}\right).$$

EXAMPLE 5 Finding the Sum of a Geometric Series

Find the sum $\sum_{k=1}^{10} 4(3)^{k-1}$.

Find the first term and identify the common ratio.

$a_1 = 4(3)^{1-1} = 4$ Find first term.

$r = 3$ Identify common ratio.

Find the sum.

$S_{10} = a_1\left(\dfrac{1 - r^{10}}{1 - r}\right)$ Write rule for S_{10}.

$= 4\left(\dfrac{1 - 3^{10}}{1 - 3}\right)$ Substitute 4 for a_1 and 3 for r.

$= 118{,}096$ Evaluate.

▶ The sum is 118,096.

Check

$\sum_{k=1}^{10} 4(3)^{k-1} = 118{,}096$

In-Class Practice

Self-Assessment

Find the sum.

6. $\sum_{k=1}^{8} 5^{k-1}$

7. $\sum_{i=1}^{12} 6(-2)^{i-1}$

Connections to Real Life

EXAMPLE 6 Finding the Sum of a Geometric Series

You post a link about a volunteer program on social media. Six of your friends repost the link, then six of each of their friends repost the link, and so on. Find the total number of people who reposted the link after the seventh round.

After the first round, 6 people reposted the link. There are 7 rounds. So, use $a_1 = 6$, $r = 6$, and $n = 7$ to find the sum.

$$S_7 = a_1\left(\frac{1-r^7}{1-r}\right) \quad \text{Write rule for } S_7.$$

$$= 6\left(\frac{1-6^7}{1-6}\right) \quad \text{Substitute 6 for } a_1 \text{ and 6 for } r.$$

$$= 335{,}922 \quad \text{Evaluate.}$$

▶ So, 335,922 people reposted the link after the seventh round.

EXAMPLE 7 Calculating a Loan Payment

$$M = \frac{L}{\sum_{k=1}^{t}\left(\frac{1}{1+i}\right)^k}$$

You can find the monthly payment M (in dollars) for a loan using the formula shown, where L is the loan amount (in dollars), i is the monthly interest rate (in decimal form), and t is the term (in months). Find the monthly payment on a 5-year loan for $20,000 with an annual interest rate of 6%.

Substitute for L, i, and t. The loan amount is $L = 20{,}000$, the monthly interest rate is $i = \frac{0.06}{12} = 0.005$, and the term is $t = 5(12) = 60$.

$$M = \frac{20{,}000}{\sum_{k=1}^{60}\left(\frac{1}{1+0.005}\right)^k}$$

Notice that the denominator is a geometric series with first term $\frac{1}{1.005}$ and common ratio $\frac{1}{1.005}$. Use technology to find the monthly payment.

$$\frac{20{,}000}{\left(\sum_{k=1}^{60}\left(\frac{1}{1+0.005}\right)^k\right)} = 386.656030589$$

▶ So, the monthly payment is $386.66.

In-Class Practice

Self-Assessment

8. You post an image on social media. Four of your friends repost the image, then four of each of their friends repost the image, and so on. Find the total number of people who reposted the image after the sixth round.

9. **WHAT IF?** In Example 7, how does the monthly payment change when the annual interest rate is 5%? By how much does it change?

10.3 Practice

Explain whether the sequence is geometric. (See Example 1.)

1. 96, 48, 24, 12, 6, . . .
2. 729, 243, 81, 27, 9, . . .
3. 2, 4, 6, 8, 10, . . .
4. 5, 20, 35, 50, 65, . . .
5. 0.3, −1.5, 7.5, −37.5, 187.5, . . .
6. $\frac{1}{2}, \frac{1}{6}, \frac{1}{18}, \frac{1}{54}, \frac{1}{162}, \ldots$

Write a rule for the nth term of the sequence. Then find a_7. (See Example 2.)

7. 6, 24, 96, 384, . . .
8. 375, 75, 15, 3, . . .
9. $4, 6, 9, \frac{27}{2}, \ldots$
10. 1.3, −3.9, 11.7, −35.1, . . .

Write a rule for the nth term of the sequence. Then graph the first six terms of the sequence. (See Example 3.)

11. $a_3 = 4, r = 2$
12. $a_2 = 30, r = \frac{1}{2}$
13. $a_4 = -192, r = 4$
14. $a_5 = 3, r = -\frac{1}{3}$

SMP.3 ERROR ANALYSIS Describe and correct the error in writing a rule for the nth term of the geometric sequence described.

15. 4, 12, 36, 108, . . .

16. $a_2 = 48, r = 6$

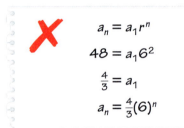

Write a rule for the sequence with the given terms.

17.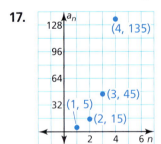

18.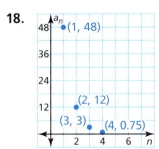

19.
n	2	3	4	5
a_n	−12	24	−48	96

20.
n	2	3	4	5
a_n	−21	63	−189	567

Write a rule for the nth term of the geometric sequence. (See Example 4.)

21. $a_2 = 28,\ a_5 = 1{,}792$

22. $a_2 = -72,\ a_6 = -\frac{1}{18}$

▶ 23. $a_1 = -6,\ a_5 = -486$

24. $a_2 = -48,\ a_5 = \frac{3}{4}$

Find the sum. (See Example 5.)

▶ 25. $\sum_{i=1}^{9} 6(7)^{i-1}$

26. $\sum_{i=1}^{10} 7(4)^{i-1}$

27. $\sum_{i=1}^{10} 4\left(\frac{3}{4}\right)^{i-1}$

28. $\sum_{i=0}^{9} 9\left(-\frac{3}{4}\right)^{i}$

▶ 29. **CONNECTION TO REAL LIFE** You share a link for a movie trailer in a chat. Three of your friends repost the link, then three of each of their friends repost the link, and so on. Find the total number of people who reposted the link after the sixth round. (See Example 6.)

CONNECTION TO REAL LIFE Use the monthly payment formula given in Example 7. (See Example 7.)

30. You take out a 3-year personal loan for $1,300 to pay for a trip. The annual interest rate of the loan is 4.5%. Calculate the monthly payment.

▶ 31. You are buying a used car. You take out a 5-year loan for $15,000. The annual interest rate of the loan is 4%. Calculate the monthly payment.

32. **OCEAN CONSERVATION TROUT POPULATION** A hatchery raises trout to maintain wild populations for commercial fishing. There are 6,400 unhatched eggs at first. Each day, this number decreases by 25% as the eggs hatch. How long will it be until only 2,025 unhatched eggs remain?

33. **PERFORMANCE TASK** Brainstorm an idea for a small business that you could own and operate. Describe the goods or services your business would provide.

   a. How much money would you need to start?
   b. Research loans for covering the startup costs. Explain which option you prefer.
   c. Show a sample repayment plan.

34. **SMP.1 DIG DEEPER** The first four iterations of the fractal called the *Koch snowflake* are shown below. Find the perimeter and area of each iteration. Explain whether the perimeters and areas form geometric sequences.

35. **SMP.7** Use the rule for the sum of a finite geometric series to write $3x + 6x^3 + 12x^5 + 24x^7$ as a rational expression.

Interpreting Data

ARCHIMEDES PARABOLA Archimedes explored topics in modern calculus using the concept of the *infinitely small* and the *method of exhaustion*. Using this method, he was able to find areas of regions bounded by curves.

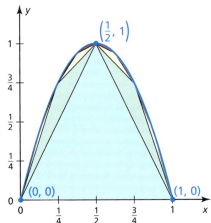

36. Find the area of the blue triangle.

37. Each green triangle has $\frac{1}{8}$ the area of the blue triangle. Each yellow triangle has $\frac{1}{8}$ the area of each green triangle. Compare the area of each yellow triangle to the area of the blue triangle.

38. **SMP.8** Show how to use a finite geometric series to approximate the area bounded by the x-axis and the parabola.

Review & Refresh

39. Determine whether the study is a randomized comparative experiment. If it is, describe the treatment, the treatment group, and the control group. If it is not, explain why not and discuss whether the conclusions drawn from the study are valid.

> **Physical Health**
> **Bananas Improve Flexibility**
> On a cross country team, students can choose a banana or another snack after each practice. Fifty-five athletes who chose a banana were monitored for the season, as were 55 athletes who chose other snacks. At the end of the season, students in the "banana" group had 5% greater flexibility than students in the other group.

40. Describe the transformation of $f(x) = 2^x$ represented by $g(x) = 2^x + 3$.

41. Simplify the expression $\tan(x - 6\pi)$.

42. Find the sum $\sum_{k=2}^{6} (3k - 1)$.

43. Find the difference $\frac{5}{2x} - \frac{3}{5x}$.

44. Write a rule for the sequence with the given terms.

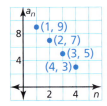

45. Find the discriminant of $x^2 - 4x + 1 = 0$ and describe the number and type of solutions of the equation.

10.4 Finding Sums of Infinite Geometric Series

Learning Target: Find partial sums and sums of infinite geometric series.

Success Criteria:
- I can find partial sums of infinite geometric series.
- I can find sums of infinite geometric series.
- I can solve real-life problems using infinite geometric series.

INVESTIGATE Finding Sums of Infinite Geometric Series

Work with a partner. Use the grid shown that represents 1 square unit.

1. Shade one half of the grid. Then shade one half of the grid that remains. Record how much area of the original grid you shade at each step. Explain why these areas form a geometric sequence. Repeat this until you find it too difficult to shade one half of the grid that remains.

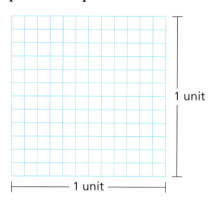

2. Complete the table.

Number of shaded regions	1	2	3	4	5	6	...
Combined area of shaded regions	$\frac{1}{2}$	$\frac{3}{4}$					...

What number is the combined area of the shaded regions approaching?

3. In the previous lesson, you learned that the sum of the first n terms of a finite geometric series with first term a_1 and common ratio $r \neq 1$ is

$$S_n = a_1\left(\frac{1-r^n}{1-r}\right).$$

Write a rule for the combined area in Exercise 1 after n regions are shaded. Explain what happens when n approaches infinity. What does this mean?

4. Use your results in Exercise 3 to write a formula for the sum of an infinite geometric series when $-1 < r < 1$.

5. In Exercise 1, each successive region you shaded is *one half* the area of the previous shaded region. Assume that you begin with the entire square unit shaded, and you continuously shade a region that is *twice* the area of the previous shaded region. Can you determine what the combined area might be?

> **Vocabulary**
> partial sum

Partial Sums of Infinite Geometric Series

The sum S_n of the first n terms of an infinite series is called a **partial sum**. The partial sums of an infinite geometric series may approach a limiting value.

EXAMPLE 1 Finding Partial Sums

Consider the infinite geometric series

$$\frac{1}{2} + \frac{1}{8} + \frac{1}{32} + \frac{1}{128} + \frac{1}{512} + \cdots.$$

Find and graph the partial sums S_n for $n = 1, 2, 3, 4,$ and 5. Then describe what happens to S_n as n increases.

Find the partial sums.

$S_1 = \frac{1}{2} = 0.5$

$S_2 = \frac{1}{2} + \frac{1}{8} = 0.625$

$S_3 = \frac{1}{2} + \frac{1}{8} + \frac{1}{32} \approx 0.656$

$S_4 = \frac{1}{2} + \frac{1}{8} + \frac{1}{32} + \frac{1}{128} \approx 0.664$

$S_5 = \frac{1}{2} + \frac{1}{8} + \frac{1}{32} + \frac{1}{128} + \frac{1}{512} \approx 0.666$

Plot the points (1, 0.5), (2, 0.625), (3, 0.656), (4, 0.664), and (5, 0.666).

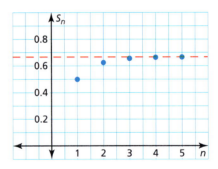

▶ From the graph, S_n appears to approach $\frac{2}{3}$ as n increases.

In-Class Practice

Self-Assessment

1. Consider the infinite geometric series

$$\frac{2}{5} + \frac{4}{25} + \frac{8}{125} + \frac{16}{625} + \frac{32}{3,125} + \cdots.$$

Find and graph the partial sums S_n for $n = 1, 2, 3, 4,$ and 5. Then describe what happens to S_n as n increases.

1 I don't understand yet. **2** I can do it with help. **3** I can do it on my own. **4** I can teach someone.

Sums of Infinite Geometric Series

In Example 1, you can understand why S_n approaches $\frac{2}{3}$ as n increases by considering the rule for the sum of a finite geometric series.

$$S_n = a_1\left(\frac{1-r^n}{1-r}\right) = \frac{1}{2}\left(\frac{1-\left(\frac{1}{4}\right)^n}{1-\frac{1}{4}}\right) = \frac{1}{2}\left(\frac{1-\left(\frac{1}{4}\right)^n}{\frac{3}{4}}\right) = \frac{2}{3}\left[1-\left(\frac{1}{4}\right)^n\right]$$

As n increases, $\left(\frac{1}{4}\right)^n$ approaches 0, so S_n approaches $\frac{2}{3}$. Therefore, $\frac{2}{3}$ is defined to be the sum of the infinite geometric series in Example 1. Generally, as n increases for *any* infinite geometric series with common ratio r between -1 and 1, the value of S_n approaches

$$S_n = a_1\left(\frac{1-r^n}{1-r}\right) \approx a_1\left(\frac{1-0}{1-r}\right) = \frac{a_1}{1-r}.$$

Key Concept

The Sum of an Infinite Geometric Series

The sum of an infinite geometric series with first term a_1 and common ratio r is given by $S = \dfrac{a_1}{1-r}$ provided $|r| < 1$. If $|r| \geq 1$, then the sum does not exist.

EXAMPLE 2 Finding Sums of Infinite Geometric Series

Find the sum of each infinite geometric series, if it exists.

a. $\sum_{i=1}^{\infty} 3(0.7)^{i-1}$

For this series, $a_1 = 3(0.7)^{1-1} = 3$ and $r = 0.7$. The sum of the series is

$S = \dfrac{a_1}{1-r}$ Formula for sum of an infinite geometric series

$= \dfrac{3}{1-0.7}$ Substitute 3 for a_1 and 0.7 for r.

$= 10.$ Simplify.

b. $1 + 3 + 9 + 27 + \cdots$

For this series, $a_1 = 1$ and $a_2 = 3$. So, the common ratio is $r = \frac{3}{1} = 3$. Because $|3| \geq 1$, the sum does not exist.

In-Class Practice

Self-Assessment

Find the sum of the infinite geometric series, if it exists.

2. $\sum_{n=1}^{\infty} \left(-\frac{1}{2}\right)^{n-1}$ **3.** $\sum_{n=1}^{\infty} 3\left(\frac{5}{4}\right)^{n-1}$ **4.** $3 + \frac{3}{4} + \frac{3}{16} + \frac{3}{64} + \cdots$

10.4 Finding Sums of Infinite Geometric Series

EXAMPLE 3 **Finding a Sum in Real Life**

A pendulum that is released and swings freely travels 18 inches on the first swing. On each successive swing, the pendulum travels 75% of the distance of the previous swing. What is the total distance it travels?

Write an infinite geometric series to represent the problem. The pendulum travels 18 inches on the first swing, so the first term is 18. On successive swings, it travels $18(0.75)$ inches, $18(0.75)^2$ inches, $18(0.75)^3$ inches, and so on. So, the total distance traveled by the pendulum is given by

$$18 + 18(0.75) + 18(0.75)^2 + 18(0.75)^3 + \cdots.$$

For this series, $a_1 = 18$ and $r = 0.75$. The sum of the series is

$S = \dfrac{a_1}{1-r}$ Formula for sum of an infinite geometric series

$= \dfrac{18}{1-0.75}$ Substitute 18 for a_1 and 0.75 for r.

$= 72.$ Simplify.

▶ The pendulum travels a total distance of 72 inches, or 6 feet.

EXAMPLE 4 **Writing a Repeating Decimal as a Fraction**

Write $0.242424\ldots$ as a fraction in simplest form.

Write the repeating decimal as an infinite geometric series.

$$0.242424\ldots = 0.24 + 0.0024 + 0.000024 + 0.00000024 + \cdots$$

For this series, $a_1 = 0.24$ and $r = \dfrac{0.0024}{0.24} = 0.01$. Find the sum of the series.

$S = \dfrac{a_1}{1-r}$ Formula for sum of an infinite geometric series

$= \dfrac{0.24}{1-0.01}$ Substitute 0.24 for a_1 and 0.01 for r.

$= \dfrac{0.24}{0.99}$ Simplify.

$= \dfrac{24}{99}$ Write as a quotient of integers.

$= \dfrac{8}{33}$ Simplify.

In-Class Practice

Self-Assessment

5. A pendulum that is released and swings freely travels 10 inches on its first swing. On each successive swing, the pendulum travels 90% of the distance of the previous swing. What is the total distance the pendulum travels?

6. Write $0.555\ldots$ as a fraction in simplest form.

10.4 Practice

Consider the infinite geometric series. Find and graph the partial sums S_n for $n = 1, 2, 3, 4,$ and 5. Then describe what happens to S_n as n increases. (See Example 1.)

▶ 1. $\dfrac{1}{2} + \dfrac{1}{6} + \dfrac{1}{18} + \dfrac{1}{54} + \dfrac{1}{162} + \cdots$

2. $\dfrac{2}{3} + \dfrac{1}{3} + \dfrac{1}{6} + \dfrac{1}{12} + \dfrac{1}{24} + \cdots$

3. $4 + \dfrac{12}{5} + \dfrac{36}{25} + \dfrac{108}{125} + \dfrac{324}{625} + \cdots$

4. $2 + \dfrac{2}{6} + \dfrac{2}{36} + \dfrac{2}{216} + \dfrac{2}{1,296} + \cdots$

Find the sum of the infinite geometric series, if it exists. (See Example 2.)

▶ 5. $\displaystyle\sum_{n=1}^{\infty} 8\left(\dfrac{1}{5}\right)^{n-1}$

6. $\displaystyle\sum_{i=1}^{\infty} \dfrac{2}{5}\left(\dfrac{5}{3}\right)^{i-1}$

7. $-5 - 2 - \dfrac{4}{5} - \dfrac{8}{25} - \cdots$

8. $\dfrac{1}{2} - \dfrac{5}{3} + \dfrac{50}{9} - \dfrac{500}{27} + \cdots$

9. **CONNECTION TO REAL LIFE** You push a tire swing one time and then allow it to swing freely. On the first swing, the tire travels a distance of 14 feet. On each successive swing, the tire travels 75% of the distance of the previous swing. What is the total distance the tire travels? (See Example 3.)

Write the repeating decimal as a fraction in simplest form. (See Example 4.)

10. $0.222\ldots$

▶ 11. $0.161616\ldots$

12. $32.323232\ldots$

13. **OPEN-ENDED** Write two infinite geometric series that each have a sum of 6. Justify your answers.

14. **SMP.2 CONNECT CONCEPTS** The *Sierpinski triangle* is a fractal created using equilateral triangles. The process involves removing smaller triangles from larger triangles by joining the midpoints of the sides of the larger triangles as shown. Assume that the initial triangle has an area of 1 square foot.

Stage 1   Stage 2   Stage 3

a. Let a_n be the total area of the triangles that are removed at Stage n. Write a rule for a_n.

b. Find $\displaystyle\sum_{n=1}^{\infty} a_n$. Interpret your answer in the context of this situation.

15. **SMP.6** Is $0.999\ldots$ equal to 1? Justify your answer.

16. **DIG DEEPER** Archimedes used the sum of an infinite geometric series to compute the area enclosed by a parabola and a straight line. He proved that the area of the region is $\dfrac{4}{3}$ the area of the inscribed triangle. The first term of the series for the parabola shown is represented by the area of the blue triangle, and the second term is represented by the total area of the red triangles. Use Archimedes's result to find the area of the region. Then write the area as the sum of an infinite geometric series.

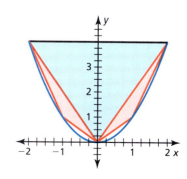

Interpreting Data

BOUNCING BALL The height at which a ball bounces depends on the height from which it is dropped, its composition, and the composition of the surface it bounces off. You drop a ball from a height of 10 feet. The heights of the first few bounces are shown.

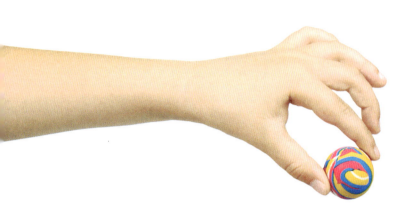
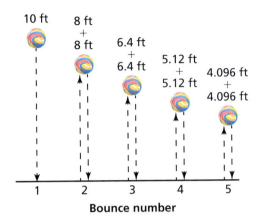

17. Find the total distance traveled by the ball through the 5th bounce.

18. Use an infinite geometric series to find the total distance the ball travels.

19. Does the ball bounce an infinite number of times? Does this make the solution of Exercise 18 meaningless? Explain why or why not.

Review & Refresh

Determine whether the sequence is *arithmetic*, *geometric*, or *neither*.

20. $-8, -2, 4, 10, 16, \ldots$

21. $0, -1, -3, -7, -15, \ldots$

22. $13.5, 40.5, 121.5, 364.5, \ldots$

23. Determine the type of function represented by the table.

x	0	4	8	12	16
y	−7	−1	2	2	−1

Solve the equation.

24. $4^x = 12$

25. $\dfrac{10}{x+3} - 6 = \dfrac{1}{x}$

26. Find the sum $\sum_{i=2}^{6} \dfrac{3}{i}$.

27. Divide $x^3 + 3x^2 - 1$ by $x + 4$.

28. A group of students is arranged in rows for a yearbook photograph. The first row has five students, and each subsequent row has two more students than the previous row.

   a. Write a rule for the number of students in the *n*th row.

   b. There are a total of eight rows. How many students are in the group?

29. The graph of g is a transformation of the graph of $f(x) = 0.5^x$. Write a rule for g.

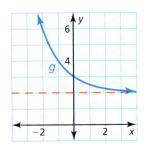

10.5 Using Recursive Rules with Sequences

Learning Target: Write and use recursively defined sequences.

Success Criteria:
- I can write terms of recursively defined sequences.
- I can write recursive rules for sequences.
- I can translate between recursive rules and explicit rules.
- I can use recursive rules to solve real-life problems.

INVESTIGATE Writing a Recursive Equation

Work with a partner. You use a ride-sharing service to visit friends. You enter your destination and obtain the fare estimate shown.

1. The actual fare depends on how long the ride takes. Your fare is $12.20 plus $0.35 per minute. Use a spreadsheet to repeatedly add $0.35 to the cost. How much time was used to calculate the fare estimate?

2. A *recursive equation* tells how a term of a sequence is related to one or more preceding terms.

   a. Write a recursive equation for the sequence in Exercise 1 that relates a term a_n to the preceding term a_{n-1}.

   b. Find and interpret a_{15}.

   c. The actual ride takes 23 minutes. What is your total fare?

> **Vocabulary**
> explicit rule
> recursive rule

Evaluating Recursive Rules

So far in this chapter, you have worked with explicit rules for the nth term of a sequence, such as $a_n = 3n - 2$ and $a_n = 7(0.5)^n$. An **explicit rule** gives a_n as a function of the term's position number n in the sequence.

In this section, you will learn another way to define a sequence—by a *recursive rule*. A **recursive rule** gives the beginning term(s) of a sequence and a *recursive equation* that tells how a_n is related to one or more preceding terms.

EXAMPLE 1 Evaluating Recursive Rules

Write the first six terms of each sequence.

a. $a_0 = 1, a_n = a_{n-1} + 4$

$a_0 = 1$	1st term
$a_1 = a_0 + 4 = 1 + 4 = 5$	2nd term
$a_2 = a_1 + 4 = 5 + 4 = 9$	3rd term
$a_3 = a_2 + 4 = 9 + 4 = 13$	4th term
$a_4 = a_3 + 4 = 13 + 4 = 17$	5th term
$a_5 = a_4 + 4 = 17 + 4 = 21$	6th term

▶ The first six terms are 1, 5, 9, 13, 17, and 21.

b. $f(1) = 1, f(n) = 3 \cdot f(n - 1)$

$f(1) = 1$	1st term
$f(2) = 3 \cdot f(1) = 3(1) = 3$	2nd term
$f(3) = 3 \cdot f(2) = 3(3) = 9$	3rd term
$f(4) = 3 \cdot f(3) = 3(9) = 27$	4th term
$f(5) = 3 \cdot f(4) = 3(27) = 81$	5th term
$f(6) = 3 \cdot f(5) = 3(81) = 243$	6th term

▶ The first six terms are 1, 3, 9, 27, 81, and 243.

In-Class Practice

Self-Assessment

Write the first six terms of the sequence.

1. $a_1 = 3, a_n = a_{n-1} - 7$

2. $a_0 = 162, a_n = 0.5a_{n-1}$

3. $f(0) = 1, f(n) = f(n - 1) + n$

4. $a_1 = 4, a_n = 2a_{n-1} - 1$

5. Explain the difference between an explicit rule and a recursive rule for a sequence.

Writing Recursive Rules

In part (a) of Example 1, the *differences* of consecutive terms of the sequence are constant, so the sequence is arithmetic. In part (b), the *ratios* of consecutive terms are constant, so the sequence is geometric. In general, rules for arithmetic and geometric sequences can be written recursively as follows.

> **Key Concept**
>
> **Recursive Equations for Arithmetic and Geometric Sequences**
> **Arithmetic Sequence** $a_n = a_{n-1} + d$, where d is the common difference
> **Geometric Sequence** $a_n = r \cdot a_{n-1}$, where r is the common ratio

EXAMPLE 2 Writing Recursive Rules

Write a recursive rule for each sequence.

a. 3, 13, 23, 33, 43, ...

n	1	2	3	4	5
a_n	3	13	23	33	43

+10 +10 +10 +10

The sequence is arithmetic with first term $a_1 = 3$ and common difference $d = 10$.

$a_n = a_{n-1} + d$ Recursive equation for arithmetic sequence
$ = a_{n-1} + 10$ Substitute 10 for d.

▶ A recursive rule for the sequence is $a_1 = 3$, $a_n = a_{n-1} + 10$.

b. 16, 40, 100, 250, 625, ...

n	1	2	3	4	5
a_n	16	40	100	250	625

$\times \frac{5}{2}$ $\times \frac{5}{2}$ $\times \frac{5}{2}$ $\times \frac{5}{2}$

The sequence is geometric with first term $a_1 = 16$ and common ratio $r = \frac{5}{2}$.

$a_n = r \cdot a_{n-1}$ Recursive equation for geometric sequence
$ = \frac{5}{2} a_{n-1}$ Substitute $\frac{5}{2}$ for r.

▶ A recursive rule for the sequence is $a_1 = 16$, $a_n = \frac{5}{2} a_{n-1}$.

In-Class Practice

Self-Assessment

Write a recursive rule for the sequence.

6. 2, 14, 98, 686, 4,802, ...

7. 11, 22, 33, 44, 55, ...

 I don't understand yet.   I can do it with help.   I can do it on my own.   I can teach someone.

Translating Between Recursive and Explicit Rules

EXAMPLE 3 **Translating from Explicit Rules to Recursive Rules**

a. **Write a recursive rule for $a_n = -6 + 8n$.**

The explicit rule represents an arithmetic sequence with first term $a_1 = -6 + 8(1) = 2$ and common difference $d = 8$.

$a_n = a_{n-1} + d$ Recursive equation for arithmetic sequence

$a_n = a_{n-1} + 8$ Substitute 8 for d.

▶ A recursive rule for the sequence is $a_1 = 2$, $a_n = a_{n-1} + 8$.

b. **Write a recursive rule for $a_n = -3\left(\frac{1}{2}\right)^{n-1}$.**

The explicit rule represents a geometric sequence with first term $a_1 = -3\left(\frac{1}{2}\right)^0 = -3$ and common ratio $r = \frac{1}{2}$.

$a_n = r \cdot a_{n-1}$ Recursive equation for geometric sequence

$a_n = \frac{1}{2} a_{n-1}$ Substitute $\frac{1}{2}$ for r.

▶ A recursive rule for the sequence is $a_1 = -3$, $a_n = \frac{1}{2} a_{n-1}$.

EXAMPLE 4 **Translating from Recursive Rules to Explicit Rules**

a. **Write an explicit rule for $a_1 = -5$, $a_n = a_{n-1} - 2$.**

The recursive rule represents an arithmetic sequence with first term $a_1 = -5$ and common difference $d = -2$.

$a_n = a_1 + (n-1)d$ Explicit rule for arithmetic sequence

$a_n = -5 + (n-1)(-2)$ Substitute -5 for a_1 and -2 for d.

$a_n = -3 - 2n$ Simplify.

▶ An explicit rule for the sequence is $a_n = -3 - 2n$.

b. **Write an explicit rule for $a_1 = 10$, $a_n = 2a_{n-1}$.**

The recursive rule represents a geometric sequence with first term $a_1 = 10$ and common ratio $r = 2$.

$a_n = a_1 r^{n-1}$ Explicit rule for geometric sequence

$a_n = 10(2)^{n-1}$ Substitute 10 for a_1 and 2 for r.

▶ An explicit rule for the sequence is $a_n = 10(2)^{n-1}$.

In-Class Practice

Self-Assessment

8. Write a recursive rule for $a_n = 17 - 4n$.

9. Write an explicit rule for $a_1 = 2$, $a_n = -6a_{n-1}$.

1 I don't understand yet.   2 I can do it with help.   3 I can do it on my own.   4 I can teach someone.

Connections to Real Life

EXAMPLE 5 **Using a Recursive Rule**

A lake initially contains 5,200 fish. Each year, the population declines 30% due to fishing and other causes, so the lake is restocked with 400 fish.

STEM Video: Setting Fishery Limits

a. **Write a recursive rule for the number a_n of fish at the start of the nth year.**

The initial value is 5,200. Because the population declines 30% each year, 70% of the fish remain in the lake from one year to the next. Also, 400 fish are added each year. Use a verbal model to write a recursive equation.

| Fish at start of year n | = 0.7 • | Fish at start of year $n-1$ | + | New fish added |

$$a_n = 0.7 \cdot a_{n-1} + 400$$

▶ A recursive rule is $a_1 = 5{,}200$, $a_n = 0.7a_{n-1} + 400$.

b. **Find the number of fish at the start of the fifth year.**

Use technology to enter 5,200 (the value of a_1). Then enter the rule

$$.7 \times \text{ans} + 400$$

to find a_2. Press enter three more times to find $a_5 \approx 2{,}262$.

```
5200
.7 · [5200] + 400    = 4040
.7 · [4040] + 400    = 3228
.7 · [3228] + 400    = 2659.6
.7 · [2659.6] + 400  = 2261.72
```

▶ There are about 2,262 fish in the lake at the start of the fifth year.

c. **Describe what happens to the population of fish over time.**

Continue pressing enter to determine what happens to the population of fish over time. The screen at the right shows the fish populations for Years 46 to 50. The population of fish appears to approach 1,333.

```
.7 · [1333.33...] + 400 = 1333.333747
.7 · [1333.33...] + 400 = 1333.333623
.7 · [1333.33...] + 400 = 1333.333536
.7 · [1333.33...] + 400 = 1333.333475
.7 · [1333.33...] + 400 = 1333.333433
```

▶ Over time, the population of fish in the lake stabilizes at about 1,333 fish.

In-Class Practice

Self-Assessment

10. WHAT IF? In Example 5, 75% of the fish remain each year. What happens to the population of fish over time?

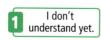

EXAMPLE 6 **Calculating the Balance of a Loan**

A homebuyer borrows $150,000 at 6% annual interest compounded monthly for 30 years. The monthly payment is $899.33.

- Find the balance after the third payment.
- Due to rounding in the calculations, the last payment is often different from the original payment. Find the amount of the last payment.

Write a recursive equation that gives the balance after each payment. Because the monthly interest rate is $\frac{0.06}{12} = 0.005$, the balance increases by a factor of 1.005 each month, and then the payment of $899.33 is subtracted.

$$\boxed{\text{Balance after payment}} = 1.005 \cdot \boxed{\text{Balance before payment}} - \boxed{\text{Payment}}$$

$$a_n = 1.005 \cdot a_{n-1} - 899.33$$

Use a spreadsheet and the recursive equation to find the balance after the third payment and after the 359th payment.

	A	B	
1	Payment number	Balance after payment	
2	1	149850.67	B2 = Round(1.005*150000 − 899.33, 2)
3	2	149700.59	B3 = Round(1.005*B2 − 899.33, 2)
4	3	149549.76	.
358	357	2667.38	.
359	358	1781.39	.
360	359	890.97	B360 = Round(1.005*B359 − 899.33, 2)

▶ The balance after the third payment is $149,549.76. The balance after the 359th payment is $890.97, so the final payment is 1.005(890.97) = $895.42.

Check By continuing the spreadsheet for the 360th payment using the original monthly payment of $899.33, the balance is −3.91.

| 361 | 360 | −3.91 | B361 = Round(1.005*B360 − 899.33, 2) |

This shows an overpayment of $3.91. So, it is reasonable that the last payment is $899.33 − $3.91 = $895.42.

In-Class Practice

Self-Assessment

11. WHAT IF? How do the answers in Example 6 change when the annual interest rate is 7.5% and the monthly payment is $1,048.82?

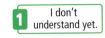 I don't understand yet.
 I can do it with help.
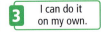 I can do it on my own.
 I can teach someone.

10.5 Practice with Calc Chat and Calc View

Write the first six terms of the sequence. (See Example 1.)

1. $a_1 = 1$
   $a_n = a_{n-1} + 3$

2. $f(0) = 10$
   $f(n) = \frac{1}{2} \cdot f(n-1)$

3. $a_1 = 2$
   $a_n = (a_{n-1})^2 + 1$

4. $f(1) = 2, f(2) = 3$
   $f(n) = f(n-1) \cdot f(n-2)$

Write a recursive rule for the sequence. (See Example 2.)

5. $21, 14, 7, 0, -7, \ldots$

6. $54, 43, 32, 21, 10, \ldots$

7. $4, -12, 36, -108, \ldots$

8. $44, 11, \frac{11}{4}, \frac{11}{16}, \frac{11}{64}, \ldots$

Write a recursive rule for the sequence shown in the graph.

9.

10.

11. **SMP.3 ERROR ANALYSIS** Describe and correct the error in writing a recursive rule for the sequence $3, 12, 48, 192, 768, \ldots$.

> Beginning with the second term of the sequence, each term a_n equals $4a_{n-1}$. So, a recursive rule is given by $a_n = 4a_{n-1}$.

Write a recursive rule for the sequence. (See Example 3.)

12. $a_n = 12(11)^{n-1}$

13. $a_n = 3 + 4n$

14. $a_n = 2.5 - 0.6n$

15. $a_n = -\frac{1}{2}\left(\frac{1}{4}\right)^{n-1}$

16. You save money to buy a video game console. The explicit rule $a_n = 30n + 82$ gives the amount saved after n months. Write a recursive rule for the amount you have saved n months from now.

Write an explicit rule for the sequence. (See Example 4.)

17. $a_1 = 3, a_n = a_{n-1} - 6$

18. $a_1 = 13, a_n = 4a_{n-1}$

19. $a_1 = -4, a_n = 0.65a_{n-1}$

20. $a_1 = 5, a_n = a_{n-1} - \frac{1}{3}$

21. The value of a car is given by the recursive rule

    $a_1 = 25{,}600,\ a_n = 0.86 a_{n-1}$

    where n is the number of years since the car was new. Write an explicit rule for the value of the car after n years.

22. In 1202, the mathematician Leonardo Fibonacci wrote *Liber Abaci*, in which he used a sequence to describe the growth of a hypothetical rabbit population. Write a recursive rule for the sequence.

    1, 1, 2, 3, 5, 8, 13, . . .   Fibonacci sequence

▶ 23. **SMP.5 CONNECTION TO REAL LIFE** A streaming service initially has 50,000 members. Each year, the company loses 20% of its current members and gains 5,000 new members. (See Example 5.)

   a. Write a recursive rule for the number a_n of members at the start of the nth year.

   b. Find the number of members at the start of the fifth year.

   c. Use a tool to describe what happens to the number of members over time.

24. **SMP.2 OPEN-ENDED** Give an example of a real-life situation that you can represent with a recursive rule. Then write the rule.

25. **OPEN-ENDED** Give an example of a sequence in which each term after the third term is a function of the three preceding terms. Write a recursive rule for the sequence and find its first eight terms.

26. **CONNECTION TO REAL LIFE** You borrow $2,000 to travel. The loan has a 9% annual interest rate that is compounded monthly for 2 years. The monthly payment is $91.37. (See Example 6.)

   a. Find the balance after the fifth payment.

   b. Find the amount of the last payment.

27. A tree farm initially has 9,000 trees. Each year, 10% of the trees are harvested and 800 seedlings are planted.

   a. Write a recursive rule for the number a_n of trees on the tree farm at the beginning of the nth year.

   b. What happens to the number of trees after an extended period of time?

28. A fractal tree starts with a single branch (the trunk). At each stage, each new branch from the previous stage grows two more branches, as shown.

Stage 1   Stage 2   Stage 3   Stage 4

a. List the number of new branches in each of the first seven stages. What type of sequence do these numbers form?

b. Write an explicit rule and a recursive rule for the sequence in part (a).

29. **SMP.7** The graph shows the first six terms of the sequence $a_1 = p$, $a_n = ra_{n-1}$.

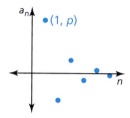

a. Describe what happens to the terms of the sequence as n increases.

b. Describe the set of possible values of r.

30. Let $a_1 = 34$. Write the terms of the sequence until you discover a pattern.

$$a_{n+1} = \begin{cases} \frac{1}{2}a_n, & \text{if } a_n \text{ is even} \\ 3a_n + 1, & \text{if } a_n \text{ is odd} \end{cases}$$

Do the same for $a_1 = 25$. What can you conclude?

31. **SMP.1 DIG DEEPER** The first four triangular numbers T_n and the first four square numbers S_n are represented by the numbers of points in the diagrams.

a. Write an explicit rule and a recursive rule for each sequence.

b. Write a rule for the square numbers in terms of the triangular numbers. Use diagrams to explain the rule.

32. **SMP.8 CONNECT CONCEPTS** The recursive rule for a sequence is as follows.

$f(1) = 3, f(2) = 10, f(n) = 4 + 2 \cdot f(n-1) - f(n-2)$

a. Use finite differences to find a pattern in the terms of the sequence. What type of relationship do the terms of the sequence show?

b. Write an explicit rule for the sequence.

Interpreting Data

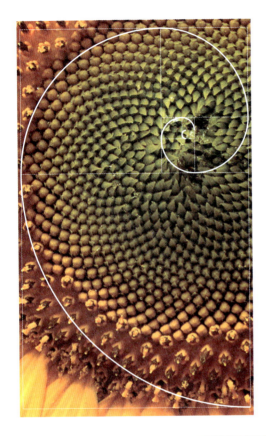

FIBONACCI SEQUENCE In the Fibonacci sequence, each number is the sum of the two preceding numbers.

$$1, 1, 2, 3, 5, 8, 13, \ldots$$

33. The Fibonacci sequence can be used to describe the arrangement of seeds on the face of a sunflower. Describe another situation in nature in which the Fibonacci sequence is used.

34. Continue the pattern shown below in Pascal's Triangle. Explain what this pattern represents.

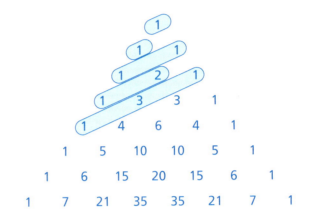

Review & Refresh

Solve the equation.

35. $\sqrt{x} + 2 = 7$

36. $2\sqrt[3]{x} - 13 = -5$

37. Find the value of x for the right triangle.

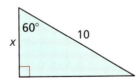

Find the sum of the infinite geometric series, if it exists.

38. $\sum_{i=1}^{\infty} 6(0.5)^{i-1}$

39. $1, -\frac{3}{2}, \frac{9}{4}, -\frac{27}{8}, \frac{81}{16}, \ldots$

Graph the function.

40. $f(x) = \left(\frac{5}{2}\right)^x$

41. $f(x) = 2\log_3 x - 3$

42. The table shows the numbers of tickets sold for various baseball games in a league over a season. Display the data in a histogram. Do the data fit a normal distribution?

Tickets sold	Frequency
150–189	1
190–229	2
230–269	4
270–309	8
310–349	8
350–389	7

Solve the system using any method.

43. $y = -x + 1$
$y = (x - 2)^2 - 3$

44. $x^2 + 3x = 4 - y$
$y = 4$

10 Chapter Review

Rate your understanding of each section.
1. I don't understand yet.
2. I can do it with help.
3. I can do it on my own.
4. I can teach someone.

10.1 Defining and Using Sequences and Series (pp. 529–536)

Learning Target: Understand sequences and series.

Vocabulary
sequence
terms of a sequence
series
summation notation
sigma notation

Write the first six terms of the sequence.

1. $a_n = 3n - 1$
2. $f(n) = (-2)^{n+1}$

3. Describe the pattern shown in the figure. Then write a rule for the nth layer of the figure, where $n = 1$ represents the top layer.

Write the series using summation notation.

4. $7 + 10 + 13 + \cdots + 40$
5. $0 + 2 + 6 + 12 + \cdots$

Find the sum.

6. $\sum_{i=2}^{7}(9 - i^3)$
7. $\sum_{i=1}^{46} i$
8. $\sum_{i=1}^{12} i^2$

10.2 Analyzing Arithmetic Sequences and Series (pp. 537–544)

Learning Target: Analyze arithmetic sequences and series.

Vocabulary
arithmetic sequence
common difference
arithmetic series

9. Determine whether the sequence $12, 4, -4, -12, -20, \ldots$ is arithmetic.

Write a rule for the nth term of the sequence. Then find a_{15} and graph the first six terms of the sequence.

10. $2, 8, 14, 20, \ldots$
11. $a_{14} = 42, d = 3$
12. $a_6 = -12, a_{12} = -36$

13. Find the sum $\sum_{i=1}^{36}(2 + 3i)$.

14. Part of a pile of chalk is shown. The bottom row has 15 pieces of chalk, and the top row has 6 pieces of chalk. Each row has one less piece of chalk than the row below. Use an arithmetic series to find the number of pieces of chalk in the pile.

10.3 Analyzing Geometric Sequences and Series (pp. 545–552)

⊙ **Learning Target:** Analyze geometric sequences and series.

Vocabulary
geometric sequence
common ratio
geometric series

15. Determine whether the sequence 7, 14, 28, 56, 112, . . . is geometric.

Write a rule for the nth term of the geometric sequence. Then graph the first six terms of the sequence.

16. $25, 10, 4, \frac{8}{5}, \ldots$

17. $a_5 = 162, r = -3$

18. $a_3 = 16, a_5 = 256$

Write a rule for the sequence with the given terms.

19.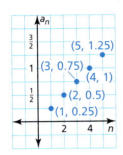

20.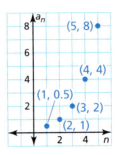

Find the sum.

21. $\sum_{i=1}^{9} 5(-2)^{i-1}$

22. $\sum_{k=1}^{5} 11(-3)^{k-2}$

23. $\sum_{i=1}^{12} -4\left(\frac{1}{2}\right)^{i+3}$

24. A job as an environmental engineer pays a salary of $65,000 the first year. After the first year, the salary increases by 3.5% per year.

  a. Write a rule giving the salary a_n during the nth year of employment.

  b. What is the salary during the fifth year of employment?

  c. An employee works 10 years for the company. What are the total earnings?

10.4 Finding Sums of Infinite Geometric Series (pp. 553–558)

⊙ **Learning Target:** Find partial sums and sums of infinite geometric series.

Vocabulary
partial sum

25. Consider the infinite geometric series $1 + \left(-\frac{1}{4}\right) + \frac{1}{16} + \left(-\frac{1}{64}\right) + \frac{1}{256} + \cdots$. Find and graph the partial sums S_n for $n = 1, 2, 3, 4,$ and 5. Then describe what happens to S_n as n increases.

Find the sum of the infinite geometric series, if it exists.

26. $\sum_{n=1}^{\infty} 3\left(\frac{1}{5}\right)^{n-1}$

27. $\sum_{n=1}^{\infty} \frac{1}{2}\left(\frac{5}{3}\right)^{n-1}$

28. $-2 + \frac{1}{2} - \frac{1}{8} + \frac{1}{32} + \cdots$

29. Write the repeating decimal 0.1212 . . . as a fraction in simplest form.

30. On an amusement park ride, you swing back and forth from a harness. You travel 250 feet on the first swing. On each subsequent swing, you travel 70% of the distance of the previous swing. What is the total distance that you travel?

10.5 Using Recursive Rules with Sequences (pp. 559–568)

Learning Target: Write and use recursively defined sequences.

Vocabulary
explicit rule
recursive rule

Write the first six terms of the sequence.

31. $a_1 = 7, a_n = a_{n-1} + 11$

32. $a_1 = 6, a_n = 4a_{n-1}$

33. $f(0) = -2, f(n) = -f(n-1) + 5$

34. $f(0) = 4, f(n) = f(n-1) + 2n$

Write a recursive rule for the sequence.

35. $9, 6, 4, \frac{8}{3}, \frac{16}{9}, \ldots$

36. $4, 11, 18, 25, 32, \ldots$

37. Write a recursive rule for $a_n = 105\left(\frac{3}{5}\right)^{n-1}$.

Write an explicit rule for the sequence.

38. $a_1 = -4, a_n = a_{n-1} + 26$

39. $a_1 = 8, a_n = -5a_{n-1}$

40. $a_1 = 26, a_n = \frac{2}{5}a_{n-1}$

41. The graph shows the expected population of a city n years after 2020. Write a recursive rule for the population P_n of the city.

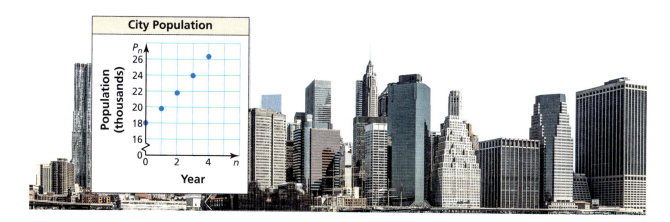

42. The first five hexagonal numbers are represented by the numbers of points in the diagrams.

   a. Write a recursive rule for the nth hexagonal number.

   b. Use your rule in part (a) to find the next 3 hexagonal numbers.

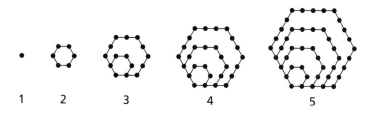

10 PERFORMANCE TASK
SMP.4 SMP.8

Walleye Stocking

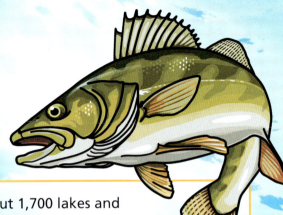

Walleye occupy about 1,700 lakes and 100 streams in Minnesota. About 900 of these lakes are stocked by the Minnesota Department of Natural Resources.

WALLEYE IS THE STATE FISH OF:

MINNESOTA

SOUTH DAKOTA

VERMONT

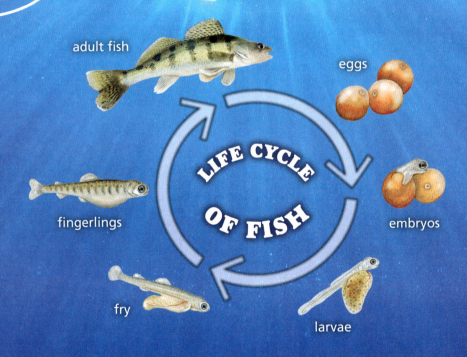

LIFE CYCLE OF FISH

adult fish — eggs — embryos — larvae — fry — fingerlings

In Minnesota, lakes that are stocked with walleye receive about 1,000 fry per littoral acre or 1 pound of fingerlings per littoral acre.

A littoral acre is a measure of the surface area of a lake where the depth of the water is less than 15 feet.

572 Chapter 10 Sequences and Series

Analyzing Data

Use the information on the previous page to complete the following exercises.

1. Explain what is shown in the display. What do you notice? What do you wonder?

2. Write a sequence that represents the number of walleye that are stocked in Minnesota lakes as the number of littoral acres increases.

3. Determine whether your sequence in Exercise 2 is *arithmetic*, *geometric*, or *neither*. Then write a rule for the *n*th term of the sequence.

CONSERVATION PLAN

A lake in Minnesota covers about 10,000 littoral acres and contains about 700,000 walleye that are at least 14 inches long. Researchers estimate that this population declines about 15% each year. Starting this year, the Department of Natural Resources (DNR) plans to stock the lake with fry every year. About 1% of the fry are expected to survive to reach a length of 14 inches, which takes about 4 years.

The DNR wants to stabilize this population at a minimum of 650,000 walleye. Analyze the DNR's plan to determine whether this goal will be achieved. Justify your answer.

11 Matrices

11.1 Basic Matrix Operations
11.2 Multiplying Matrices
11.3 Determinants and Cramer's Rule
11.4 Inverse Matrices

NATIONAL GEOGRAPHIC EXPLORER
Ronan M. Donovan — PHOTOGRAPHER

Ronan M. Donovan is a photographer. While researching chimpanzees in Uganda's Kibale National Park, he captured the images that helped him establish a career in conservation photography, using images to advocate for conservation outcomes. Part of his work involved climbing fig trees to create a series of photographs of the primates from above.

- If you were a conservation photographer, what species of endangered animals would be of interest to you?
- There are 4 types of great apes: gorillas, orangutans, bonobos, and chimpanzees. Find an interesting fact about each type of great ape.

PERFORMANCE TASK
An important part of conservation is understanding relationships among animals in a food chain. In the Performance Task on pages 614 and 615, you will analyze a food web to see how animals are interdependent.

Conservation Photography

Big Idea of the Chapter
Use Matrices

A matrix is a rectangular array of numbers. You can add, subtract, and multiply matrices in much the same way that you add, subtract, and multiply numbers. You can also multiply a matrix by a number.

Conservation photography uses photos of nature to advocate for wildlife and Earth's ecosystem. It is a powerful tool to show the beauty of the environment, as well as threats to it. When capturing images, photographers concentrate on the story they are telling, as well as the purpose they want their images to serve. They often work with other conservationists, advocates, and environmentalists.

The table shows the numbers of gorillas, bonobos, and orangutans at three zoos.

	Zoo A	Zoo B	Zoo C
Gorillas	6	10	20
Bonobos	5	7	9
Orangutans	4	6	5

1. For each zoo, the number of each type of primate can be represented by a *matrix*, as shown.

$$A = \begin{bmatrix} 6 \\ 5 \\ 4 \end{bmatrix} \qquad B = \begin{bmatrix} 10 \\ 7 \\ 6 \end{bmatrix} \qquad C = \begin{bmatrix} 20 \\ 9 \\ 5 \end{bmatrix}$$

Use technology to perform each of the following operations. Then interpret the results.

   a. $A + B$
   b. $A + B + C$
   c. $C - A$
   d. $\frac{1}{3}(A + B + C)$

2. Explain how to perform each of the operations in Exercise 1 without using technology.

Getting Ready for Chapter 11

Solving Linear Equations

EXAMPLE 1 Solve $2x = 6x - 14$.

$2x = 6x - 14$		Write original equation.
$2x = 6x - 14$		Subtraction Property of Equality
$\underline{-6x \quad -6x}$		
$-4x = -14$		Simplify.
$\dfrac{-4x}{-4} = \dfrac{-14}{-4}$		Division Property of Equality
$x = \dfrac{7}{2}$		Simplify.

▶ The solution is $x = \dfrac{7}{2}$.

Solve the equation.

1. $4x - 3 = 10x$
2. $-2x = 5x - 5$
3. $\dfrac{2}{3}(x - 9) = x + 1$

Solving Linear Systems

EXAMPLE 2 Solve the system. $5x - 2y = -5$ Equation 1
                                      $x + 2y = 11$ Equation 2

Because the coefficients of the *y*-terms are the same, you can solve by elimination without multiplying either equation by a constant.

Add the equations to eliminate the *y*-terms.

$5x - 2y = -5$	Equation 1
$\underline{x + 2y = 11}$	Equation 2
$6x = 6$	Add the equations.

Solve for *x*.

$6x = 6$	Write equation.
$x = 1$	Divide each side by 6.

Substitute 1 for *x* in one of the original equations and solve for *y*.

$x + 2y = 11$	Equation 2
$1 + 2y = 11$	Substitute 1 for *x*.
$y = 5$	Simplify.

▶ The solution is $(1, 5)$.

Solve the system.

4. $-x + 3y = 12$
   $x - 7y = -20$

5. $4x - y = 7$
   $y = 3x - 3$

6. $\dfrac{1}{2}x - 6y = -1$
   $3x - 8y = 8$

11.1 Basic Matrix Operations

Learning Target: Perform basic operations involving matrices.

Success Criteria:
- I can add and subtract matrices.
- I can multiply matrices by scalars.
- I can solve matrix equations.
- I can represent data in a matrix to solve real-life problems.

INVESTIGATE Analyzing Matrices

Work with a partner. A *matrix* is a rectangular array of numbers. The plural of matrix is *matrices*. The matrices below represent the T-shirt inventories at four stores.

Store A

$$A = \begin{bmatrix} 65 & 40 \\ 52 & 60 \\ 46 & 46 \end{bmatrix} \begin{matrix} \text{Small} \\ \text{Medium} \\ \text{Large} \end{matrix}$$

Short Sleeve / Long Sleeve

Store B

$$B = \begin{bmatrix} 38 & 44 & 58 \\ 34 & 28 & 30 \\ 48 & 40 & 52 \end{bmatrix} \begin{matrix} \text{Small} \\ \text{Medium} \\ \text{Large} \end{matrix}$$

Sleeveless / Short Sleeve / Long Sleeve

Store C

$$C = \begin{bmatrix} 55 & 39 \\ 50 & 40 \\ 32 & 36 \end{bmatrix} \begin{matrix} \text{Small} \\ \text{Medium} \\ \text{Large} \end{matrix}$$

Short Sleeve / Long Sleeve

Store D

$$D = \begin{bmatrix} 25 & 24 & 27 \\ 30 & 28 & 21 \\ 15 & 18 & 20 \end{bmatrix} \begin{matrix} \text{Small} \\ \text{Medium} \\ \text{Large} \end{matrix}$$

Sleeveless / Short Sleeve / Long Sleeve

1. Describe the matrices. How are they similar? How are they different?

2. How can you describe the *dimensions* of each matrix?

3. **SMP.2** Find and interpret each of the following, if possible.

   a. $A + C$
   b. $B - D$
   c. $A + B$
   d. $C - B$
   e. $2A$
   f. $\frac{1}{2}B$

4. Use your results in Exercise 3 to describe how to add matrices, subtract matrices, and multiply a matrix by a real number.

5. Explain why $C + A$ gives the same result as $A + C$.

Vocabulary
matrix
dimensions of a matrix
elements of a matrix
equal matrices
scalar
scalar multiplication

Adding and Subtracting Matrices

A **matrix** is a rectangular array of numbers. The **dimensions** of a matrix with m rows and n columns are $m \times n$ (read "m by n"). So, the dimensions of matrix A are 2×3. The numbers in the matrix are its **elements**.

$$A = \begin{bmatrix} -1 & 0 & 3 \\ 6 & 5 & 2 \end{bmatrix} \} \text{ 2 rows}$$

The element in the first row and third column is 3.

3 columns

Two matrices are **equal** when their dimensions are the same *and* the elements in corresponding positions are equal.

Key Concept

Adding and Subtracting Matrices

To add or subtract two matrices, add or subtract their corresponding elements. You can add or subtract matrices only when they have the same dimensions.

Adding Matrices
$$\begin{bmatrix} a & b \\ c & d \end{bmatrix} + \begin{bmatrix} e & f \\ g & h \end{bmatrix} = \begin{bmatrix} a+e & b+f \\ c+g & d+h \end{bmatrix}$$

Subtracting Matrices
$$\begin{bmatrix} a & b \\ c & d \end{bmatrix} - \begin{bmatrix} e & f \\ g & h \end{bmatrix} = \begin{bmatrix} a-e & b-f \\ c-g & d-h \end{bmatrix}$$

EXAMPLE 1 Adding and Subtracting Matrices

Perform the indicated operation, if possible.

a. $\begin{bmatrix} 2 & -3 \\ 5 & 4 \\ -2 & 8 \end{bmatrix} - \begin{bmatrix} -1 & 2 \\ 7 & 8 \\ -5 & 6 \end{bmatrix}$

$\begin{bmatrix} 2 & -3 \\ 5 & 4 \\ -2 & 8 \end{bmatrix} - \begin{bmatrix} -1 & 2 \\ 7 & 8 \\ -5 & 6 \end{bmatrix} = \begin{bmatrix} 2-(-1) & -3-2 \\ 5-7 & 4-8 \\ -2-(-5) & 8-6 \end{bmatrix} = \begin{bmatrix} 3 & -5 \\ -2 & -4 \\ 3 & 2 \end{bmatrix}$

b. $\begin{bmatrix} -8 & 1 & 3 \\ 5 & -4 & 9 \end{bmatrix} + \begin{bmatrix} 6 & -1 \\ 2 & 7 \end{bmatrix}$

The dimensions of the matrices are 2×3 and 2×2. Because the matrices have different dimensions, the sum is undefined.

In-Class Practice

Self-Assessment

Perform the indicated operation, if possible. If not possible, explain why not.

1. $\begin{bmatrix} -3 & 4 \\ 9 & 6 \end{bmatrix} + \begin{bmatrix} 4 & 0 \\ -5 & 7 \end{bmatrix}$

2. $\begin{bmatrix} -5 & 1 \end{bmatrix} - \begin{bmatrix} 0 \\ -3 \end{bmatrix}$

1 I don't understand yet. **2** I can do it with help. **3** I can do it on my own. **4** I can teach someone.

Scalar Multiplication and Properties of Matrices

Key Concept

Scalar Multiplication and Properties of Matrix Operations

In operations with matrices, numbers are usually referred to as **scalars**. To multiply a matrix by a scalar, multiply each element in the matrix by the scalar. This process is called **scalar multiplication**.

Multiplying a Matrix by a Scalar, k $\quad k\begin{bmatrix} a & b \\ c & d \end{bmatrix} = \begin{bmatrix} ka & kb \\ kc & kd \end{bmatrix}$

Let A, B, and C be matrices with the same dimensions, and let k be a scalar.

Associative Property of Addition $\quad (A + B) + C = A + (B + C)$

Commutative Property of Addition $\quad A + B = B + A$

Distributive Property $\quad k(A + B) = kA + kB$
$\quad k(A - B) = kA - kB$

EXAMPLE 2 Multiplying Matrices by Scalars

Perform the indicated operation(s).

a. $2\begin{bmatrix} 3 & -2 \\ 1 & 5 \\ 2 & 0 \end{bmatrix}$

$$2\begin{bmatrix} 3 & -2 \\ 1 & 5 \\ 2 & 0 \end{bmatrix} = \begin{bmatrix} 2(3) & 2(-2) \\ 2(1) & 2(5) \\ 2(2) & 2(0) \end{bmatrix} = \begin{bmatrix} 6 & -4 \\ 2 & 10 \\ 4 & 0 \end{bmatrix}$$

b. $-3\begin{bmatrix} 5 & 0 \\ -2 & 4 \end{bmatrix} + \begin{bmatrix} -1 & 7 \\ 3 & 2 \end{bmatrix}$

$$-3\begin{bmatrix} 5 & 0 \\ -2 & 4 \end{bmatrix} + \begin{bmatrix} -1 & 7 \\ 3 & 2 \end{bmatrix} = \begin{bmatrix} -3(5) & -3(0) \\ -3(-2) & -3(4) \end{bmatrix} + \begin{bmatrix} -1 & 7 \\ 3 & 2 \end{bmatrix}$$

$$= \begin{bmatrix} -15 & 0 \\ 6 & -12 \end{bmatrix} + \begin{bmatrix} -1 & 7 \\ 3 & 2 \end{bmatrix}$$

$$= \begin{bmatrix} -15 + (-1) & 0 + 7 \\ 6 + 3 & -12 + 2 \end{bmatrix}$$

$$= \begin{bmatrix} -16 & 7 \\ 9 & -10 \end{bmatrix}$$

In-Class Practice

Self-Assessment

Perform the indicated operation(s).

3. $-7\begin{bmatrix} 2 & 3 & -2 \\ -7 & 4 & 7 \\ -2 & 5 & -6 \end{bmatrix}$

4. $4\begin{bmatrix} 3 & 5 \\ 4 & 2 \\ 0 & -2 \end{bmatrix} - \begin{bmatrix} 9 & 7 \\ -6 & 5 \\ 2 & -3 \end{bmatrix}$

1 I don't understand yet. **2** I can do it with help. **3** I can do it on my own. **4** I can teach someone.

Solving Matrix Equations

You can use what you know about matrix operations and matrix equality to solve equations involving matrices.

EXAMPLE 3 **Using Equality of Matrices**

Solve the matrix equation for $a, b, c,$ and d.

$$\begin{bmatrix} a & b \\ 2c & d+4 \end{bmatrix} = \begin{bmatrix} 4 & -7 \\ 8 & 6 \end{bmatrix}$$

Equate corresponding elements and solve the resulting equations, if necessary.

$a = 4$ $\quad\quad$ $b = -7$ $\quad\quad$ $2c = 8$ $\quad\quad$ $d + 4 = 6$
$\quad\quad\quad\quad\quad\quad\quad\quad\quad\quad\quad\quad$ $c = 4$ $\quad\quad\quad$ $d = 2$

▶ The solution is $a = 4, b = -7, c = 4,$ and $d = 2$.

EXAMPLE 4 **Solving a Matrix Equation**

Solve the matrix equation for $a, b, c,$ and d.

$$4\left(\begin{bmatrix} -2a & 5 \\ -4 & 2 \end{bmatrix} + \begin{bmatrix} 3 & -6 \\ 7c & 1 \end{bmatrix}\right) = \begin{bmatrix} -28 & b \\ 40 & d \end{bmatrix}$$

Simplify the left side of the equation.

$4\left(\begin{bmatrix} -2a & 5 \\ -4 & 2 \end{bmatrix} + \begin{bmatrix} 3 & -6 \\ 7c & 1 \end{bmatrix}\right) = \begin{bmatrix} -28 & b \\ 40 & d \end{bmatrix}$ $\quad$ Write original equation.

$4\begin{bmatrix} -2a+3 & -1 \\ 7c-4 & 3 \end{bmatrix} = \begin{bmatrix} -28 & b \\ 40 & d \end{bmatrix}$ $\quad$ Add matrices inside parentheses.

$\begin{bmatrix} -8a+12 & -4 \\ 28c-16 & 12 \end{bmatrix} = \begin{bmatrix} -28 & b \\ 40 & d \end{bmatrix}$ $\quad$ Perform scalar multiplication.

Equate corresponding elements and solve the resulting equations, if necessary.

$-8a + 12 = -28$ $\quad$ $-4 = b$ $\quad$ $28c - 16 = 40$ $\quad$ $12 = d$
$\quad\quad -8a = -40$ $\quad\quad\quad\quad\quad\quad\quad\quad$ $28c = 56$
$\quad\quad\quad a = 5$ $\quad\quad\quad\quad\quad\quad\quad\quad\quad$ $c = 2$

▶ The solution is $a = 5, b = -4, c = 2,$ and $d = 12$.

In-Class Practice

Self-Assessment

Solve the matrix equation for $a, b, c,$ and d.

5. $\begin{bmatrix} a & b \\ c-2 & 4d \end{bmatrix} = \begin{bmatrix} -5 & 4 \\ 3 & 8 \end{bmatrix}$

6. $3\left(\begin{bmatrix} 2 & 4 \\ 2c & 2d \end{bmatrix} - \begin{bmatrix} 8 & 0 \\ c & 5 \end{bmatrix}\right) = \begin{bmatrix} a & b \\ 9 & 9 \end{bmatrix}$

1 I don't understand yet. $\quad$ **2** I can do it with help. $\quad$ **3** I can do it on my own. $\quad$ **4** I can teach someone.

Connections to Real Life

Matrices are useful for organizing data and for performing the same operations on multiple data values simultaneously.

EXAMPLE 5 **Using Matrices in Real Life**

The tables show the amounts (in inches) of snow that each of three cities received in January and February of 2023 and 2024.

Organize the data using two matrices, one for each year. Then find and interpret a matrix that gives the average amounts (in feet) of snow from 2023 to 2024 by month for each city.

Snow Totals

Jan.

City	2023	2024
A	18	16
B	23	25
C	16	12

Feb.

City	2023	2024
A	21	15
B	22	18
C	24	18

Organize the data using two 3 × 2 matrices.

$$A = \begin{bmatrix} 18 & 21 \\ 23 & 22 \\ 16 & 24 \end{bmatrix} \begin{matrix} \text{City A} \\ \text{City B} \\ \text{City C} \end{matrix} \quad\quad B = \begin{bmatrix} 16 & 15 \\ 25 & 18 \\ 12 & 18 \end{bmatrix} \begin{matrix} \text{City A} \\ \text{City B} \\ \text{City C} \end{matrix}$$

(2023: Jan. Feb.) (2024: Jan. Feb.)

To find the average amounts of snow for 2023 and 2024 by month for each city, add matrix A and matrix B, and then multiply the result by $\frac{1}{2}$.

$$\frac{1}{2}(A + B) = \frac{1}{2}\left(\begin{bmatrix} 18 & 21 \\ 23 & 22 \\ 16 & 24 \end{bmatrix} + \begin{bmatrix} 16 & 15 \\ 25 & 18 \\ 12 & 18 \end{bmatrix}\right)$$

$$= \frac{1}{2}\begin{bmatrix} 34 & 36 \\ 48 & 40 \\ 28 & 42 \end{bmatrix}$$

$$= \begin{bmatrix} 17 & 18 \\ 24 & 20 \\ 14 & 21 \end{bmatrix}$$

▶ The average amounts of snow in January for Cities A, B, and C, were 17 inches, 24 inches, and 14 inches, respectively. In February, the average amounts were 18 inches, 20 inches, and 21 inches, respectively.

In-Class Practice

Self-Assessment

7. Find and interpret a matrix that gives the change in the amounts (in feet) of snow from 2023 to 2024 by month for each city.

 1 I don't understand yet.   2 I can do it with help.   3 I can do it on my own.   4 I can teach someone.

11.1 Basic Matrix Operations 581

11.1 Practice

Perform the indicated operation, if possible. If not possible, explain why not. (See Example 1.)

1. $\begin{bmatrix} 4 & -1 \\ 3 & -2 \end{bmatrix} + \begin{bmatrix} 6 & -7 \\ 3 & -5 \end{bmatrix}$

2. $\begin{bmatrix} 14 \\ 13 \\ -5 \end{bmatrix} - \begin{bmatrix} 12 \\ -17 \\ 9 \end{bmatrix}$

3. $\begin{bmatrix} 1 & 9 \\ 3 & -4 \\ -7 & 2 \end{bmatrix} - \begin{bmatrix} -1 & 1 & 12 \\ 7 & -3 & 10 \end{bmatrix}$

4. $\begin{bmatrix} -5 & 3 & 1 \\ -4 & 6 & 0 \\ 10 & -2 & 7 \end{bmatrix} + \begin{bmatrix} 9 & 7 & 12 \\ -1 & 5 & -3 \\ -6 & 11 & -8 \end{bmatrix}$

SMP.3 ERROR ANALYSIS Describe and correct the error in adding the matrices.

5.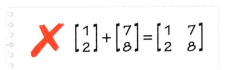

6.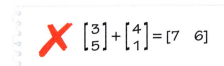

Perform the indicated operation(s). (See Example 2.)

7. $\dfrac{1}{2}\begin{bmatrix} 4 & -6 \\ 8 & 12 \\ 2 & 22 \end{bmatrix}$

8. $6\begin{bmatrix} 1 & 3 & 2 \\ -2 & 4 & -1 \end{bmatrix} + \begin{bmatrix} 5 & 7 & -1 \\ 6 & -4 & 7 \end{bmatrix}$

9. $\begin{bmatrix} -7 & 8 & 11 \\ 12 & -5 & 16 \end{bmatrix} - 3\begin{bmatrix} -4 & 4 & 6 \\ 5 & -2 & 7 \end{bmatrix}$

10. $-2\left(\begin{bmatrix} 3 & -6 \\ 5 & -7 \\ 12 & 8 \end{bmatrix} + \begin{bmatrix} 6 & 9 \\ -8 & 1 \\ 10 & -3 \end{bmatrix}\right)$

Solve the matrix equation for a, b, c, and d. (See Examples 3 and 4.)

11. $\begin{bmatrix} a & b \\ 3 & -4 \end{bmatrix} = \begin{bmatrix} 6 & 2 \\ c & d \end{bmatrix}$

12. $\begin{bmatrix} 7 & d \\ 5 & b \end{bmatrix} = \begin{bmatrix} c & 4 \\ a & 17 \end{bmatrix}$

13. $\begin{bmatrix} 30 & b \\ a+6 & -9 \\ c & 4d \end{bmatrix} = \begin{bmatrix} 30 & 21 \\ 16 & -9 \\ -5 & 44 \end{bmatrix}$

14. $\begin{bmatrix} 18-a & -2 & 5b \\ 14 & -d & c \end{bmatrix} = \begin{bmatrix} 5 & -2 & 500 \\ 14 & 64 & 112 \end{bmatrix}$

15. $2\left(\begin{bmatrix} 3a & 11 \\ 4 & 6 \end{bmatrix} + \begin{bmatrix} -7 & -6 \\ 11 & 5d \end{bmatrix}\right) = \begin{bmatrix} 22 & b \\ c & 52 \end{bmatrix}$

16. $-3\left(\begin{bmatrix} 7 & 2b \\ 8c & 8 \end{bmatrix} - \begin{bmatrix} 4 & 4b \\ 5 & d \end{bmatrix}\right) = \begin{bmatrix} a & 54 \\ 63 & d \end{bmatrix}$

17. **CONNECTION TO REAL LIFE** The table shows the numbers of dogs and cats at a shelter by age group adopted in May and June. Organize the data using two matrices, one for each month. Then find and interpret a matrix that gives the average numbers of dogs and cats adopted by month for each age group. (See Example 5.)

Adoptions

Age Group	Dogs		Cats	
	May	June	May	June
< 1 year	6	12	13	7
1–6 years	7	9	5	3
> 6 years	4	2	1	3

18. **PHOTOGRAPHER** **ENDANGERED SPECIES** The table shows the numbers of species from five groups in the United States and in the world listed as endangered or threatened in 2023. Organize the data using two matrices, one for the United States and one for the world. Then find and interpret a matrix that gives the numbers of species in each group listed as endangered or threatened that are not in the United States.

Endangered and Threatened Species

Group	Endangered		Threatened	
	U.S.	World	U.S.	World
Mammals	67	329	29	52
Birds	77	294	23	45
Reptiles	17	87	29	54
Amphibians	23	31	16	17
Fishes	94	121	78	87

Hawksbill Turtle: Critically endangered

Find the matrix X that makes the equation true.

19. $X + \begin{bmatrix} 5 & 0 \\ -2 & 3 \end{bmatrix} = \begin{bmatrix} 6 & 3 \\ 1 & 0 \end{bmatrix}$

20. $2X + \begin{bmatrix} 5 & 0 \\ 8 & -2 \end{bmatrix} = \begin{bmatrix} 9 & -8 \\ 4 & 4 \end{bmatrix}$

21. **SMP.6** One important property of addition of real numbers is that the number 0 is the additive identity. That is, $a + 0 = a$ for any real number a. For any $m \times n$ matrix A, is there a matrix O such that $A + O = A$? If so, describe matrix O. If not, explain why not.

22. **CONNECT CONCEPTS** Let matrix $B = \begin{bmatrix} 2 & 2 & 2 \\ -1 & -1 & -1 \end{bmatrix}$.

    a. Write a 2×3 matrix A where the columns represent the vertices of the triangle shown and the first row represents the x-coordinates.

    b. Add matrices A and B. Then draw the triangles represented by the matrices A and $A + B$ in the same coordinate plane. How are the triangles related?

    c. Multiply matrix A by 3. Then draw the triangles represented by the matrices A and $3A$ in the same coordinate plane. How are the triangles related?

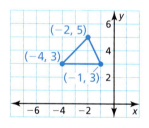

23. Use matrices A, B, and C, defined as shown, to show that each property is true for 2×2 matrices.

    $A = \begin{bmatrix} a & b \\ c & d \end{bmatrix} \quad B = \begin{bmatrix} e & f \\ g & h \end{bmatrix} \quad C = \begin{bmatrix} p & q \\ r & s \end{bmatrix}$

    a. Commutative Property of Addition
    b. Associative Property of Addition
    c. Distributive Property

24. **DIG DEEPER** Write two matrices A and B such that

    $A + B = \begin{bmatrix} 2 & 6 & 5 \\ -5 & -7 & -8 \\ 3 & 14 & 4 \end{bmatrix}$ and $A - B = \begin{bmatrix} -6 & -8 & 11 \\ -1 & -5 & 10 \\ -3 & 4 & -12 \end{bmatrix}$.

Interpreting Data

COMPUTER GRAPHICS In computer graphics, an image is stored as a large matrix of pixel values. Each pixel value indicates the location and color of the pixel on a computer screen.

25. A computer screen has 96 pixels per inch (PPI). How many pixels does the screen have in 1 square inch?

26. An image displayed on the screen covers a rectangle that is 1 inch by 2 inches. How many pixels are in the rectangle?

27. If you double the size of a computer image, what would you expect to happen to the matrix of pixel values?

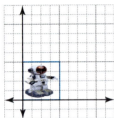
$k_x = 1, k_y = 1$ (Unscaled)

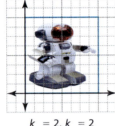

$k_x = 2, k_y = 2$

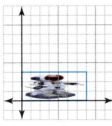
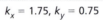
$k_x = 1.75, k_y = 0.75$

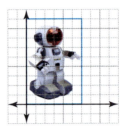
$k_x = 1.5, k_y = 2.25$

Review & Refresh

28. Write the first six terms of the sequence.

    $a_1 = 15, a_n = a_{n-1} - 3$

Find the product.

29. $(x + 2)(3x^2 - 2x - 5)$

30. $(4t - 1)^3$

31. $\dfrac{x^2 - 2x - 15}{2x} \cdot \dfrac{2x^2 - 14x}{x^2 - 10x + 21}$

32. Write a rule for the sequence with the given terms.

n	2	3	4	5	6
a_n	−2	6	−18	54	−162

33. A city official records whether people litter in a park before and after more garbage cans are added. Identify the method of data collection.

34. The rear windshield wiper of a car rotates 120°, as shown. Find the area cleared by the wiper.

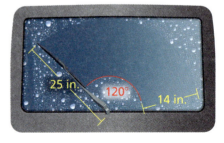

35. Find the sum of the infinite geometric series.

    $16 + 4 + 1 + \dfrac{1}{4} + \cdots$

11.2 Multiplying Matrices

Learning Target: Understand how to multiply matrices.

Success Criteria:
- I can determine whether a product of matrices is defined.
- I can multiply matrices.
- I can use matrix multiplication to solve real-life problems.

INVESTIGATE Multiplying Matrices

Work with a partner. In the 11.1 Investigate, you used matrices to represent the T-shirt inventories at several stores.

Store A

	Short Sleeve	Long Sleeve	
$A =$	65	40	Small
	52	60	Medium
	46	46	Large

Store B

	Sleeveless	Short Sleeve	Long Sleeve	
$B =$	38	44	58	Small
	34	28	30	Medium
	48	40	52	Large

1. Store A charges $10 for each short-sleeve shirt and $15 for each long-sleeve shirt. What is the total value of the inventory for each size? Explain your reasoning.

2. **SMP.2** Matrix P represents the cost per shirt at Store A.

    Store A
    Dollars
    $$P = \begin{bmatrix} 10 \\ 15 \end{bmatrix} \begin{array}{l} \text{Short Sleeve} \\ \text{Long Sleeve} \end{array}$$

    Use technology to find $A \times P$. Interpret the results. Then explain how to find $A \times P$ without using technology.

3. **SMP.2** Matrix Q represents the cost per shirt at Store B.

    Store B
    Dollars
    $$Q = \begin{bmatrix} 8 \\ 12 \\ 20 \end{bmatrix} \begin{array}{l} \text{Sleeveless} \\ \text{Short Sleeve} \\ \text{Long Sleeve} \end{array}$$

    Find and interpret $B \times Q$ without using technology. Explain your method.

RESOURCES

Multiplying Matrices

The product of two matrices A and B is defined provided the number of columns in A is equal to the number of rows in B.

$$\underset{m \times n}{A} \cdot \underset{n \times p}{B} = \underset{m \times p}{AB}$$

$\uparrow \text{equal} \uparrow$

dimensions of AB

EXAMPLE 1 Describing Matrix Products

Determine whether each product AB is defined. If so, state the dimensions of AB.

a. $A = \begin{bmatrix} 5 & 0 & -1 \\ 3 & -6 & 7 \end{bmatrix}, B = \begin{bmatrix} 5 & 10 & -7 & -3 \\ -2 & 3 & 2 & 6 \\ 0 & 9 & 8 & 1 \end{bmatrix}$

Because A is a 2×3 matrix and B is a 3×4 matrix, the number of columns in A is equal to the number of rows in B. So, the product AB is defined and is a 2×4 matrix.

b. $A = \begin{bmatrix} 6 & -5 & 0 \\ 1 & 2 & -1 \end{bmatrix}, B = \begin{bmatrix} -3 & 11 & 9 \\ 8 & -1 & 2 \end{bmatrix}$

Because A and B are 2×3 matrices, the number of columns in A does not equal the number of rows in B. So, the product AB is not defined.

Key Concept

Multiplying Matrices

Words To find the element in the ith row and jth column of the product matrix AB, multiply each element in the ith row of A by the corresponding element in the jth column of B, then add the products.

Algebra $\overset{A}{\begin{bmatrix} a & b \\ c & d \end{bmatrix}} \cdot \overset{B}{\begin{bmatrix} e & f \\ g & h \end{bmatrix}} = \overset{AB}{\begin{bmatrix} ae + bg & af + bh \\ ce + dg & cf + dh \end{bmatrix}}$

In-Class Practice

Self-Assessment

Determine whether the product AB is defined. If so, state the dimensions of AB.

1. $A = \begin{bmatrix} 3 \\ -1 \\ 1 \end{bmatrix}, B = \begin{bmatrix} -7 & 8 \end{bmatrix}$

2. $A = \begin{bmatrix} 1 & 0 \\ -2 & 8 \\ 6 & 10 \end{bmatrix}, B = \begin{bmatrix} 12 & -2 & 5 \end{bmatrix}$

1 I don't understand yet. **2** I can do it with help. **3** I can do it on my own. **4** I can teach someone.

EXAMPLE 2 **Finding the Product of Two Matrices**

Find AB when $A = \begin{bmatrix} 3 & 2 \\ -7 & 8 \end{bmatrix}$ and $B = \begin{bmatrix} -1 & 4 \\ 6 & 5 \end{bmatrix}$.

A is a 2×2 matrix and B is a 2×2 matrix. So, AB is a 2×2 matrix.

Multiply the numbers in the first row of A by the numbers in the first column of B, add the products, and put the result in the first row, first column of AB.

$$\begin{bmatrix} 3 & 2 \\ -7 & 8 \end{bmatrix}\begin{bmatrix} -1 & 4 \\ 6 & 5 \end{bmatrix} = \begin{bmatrix} 3(-1) + 2(6) & \end{bmatrix}$$

Multiply the numbers in the first row of A by the numbers in the second column of B, add the products, and put the result in the first row, second column of AB.

$$\begin{bmatrix} 3 & 2 \\ -7 & 8 \end{bmatrix}\begin{bmatrix} -1 & 4 \\ 6 & 5 \end{bmatrix} = \begin{bmatrix} 3(-1) + 2(6) & 3(4) + 2(5) \end{bmatrix}$$

Multiply the numbers in the second row of A by the numbers in the first column of B, add the products, and put the result in the second row, first column of AB.

$$\begin{bmatrix} 3 & 2 \\ -7 & 8 \end{bmatrix}\begin{bmatrix} -1 & 4 \\ 6 & 5 \end{bmatrix} = \begin{bmatrix} 3(-1) + 2(6) & 3(4) + 2(5) \\ -7(-1) + 8(6) & \end{bmatrix}$$

Multiply the numbers in the second row of A by the numbers in the second column of B, add the products, and put the result in the second row, second column of AB.

$$\begin{bmatrix} 3 & 2 \\ -7 & 8 \end{bmatrix}\begin{bmatrix} -1 & 4 \\ 6 & 5 \end{bmatrix} = \begin{bmatrix} 3(-1) + 2(6) & 3(4) + 2(5) \\ -7(-1) + 8(6) & -7(4) + 8(5) \end{bmatrix}$$

▶ Simplifying the product matrix gives $AB = \begin{bmatrix} 9 & 22 \\ 55 & 12 \end{bmatrix}$.

In Example 2, notice that the product BA is not the same as the product AB.

$$BA = \begin{bmatrix} -1 & 4 \\ 6 & 5 \end{bmatrix}\begin{bmatrix} 3 & 2 \\ -7 & 8 \end{bmatrix} = \begin{bmatrix} -31 & 30 \\ -17 & 52 \end{bmatrix} \neq AB$$

In general, matrix multiplication is *not* commutative.

In-Class Practice
Self-Assessment

Find the product.

3. $\begin{bmatrix} 6 & 4 \\ 0 & -5 \end{bmatrix}\begin{bmatrix} 0 & 2 \\ -3 & 1 \end{bmatrix}$

4. $\begin{bmatrix} 3 & -4 \\ 6 & 5 \\ 1 & 0 \end{bmatrix}\begin{bmatrix} -1 & 7 & -2 \\ -6 & 2 & 4 \end{bmatrix}$

1 I don't understand yet.   **2** I can do it with help.   **3** I can do it on my own.   **4** I can teach someone.

EXAMPLE 3 Using Matrix Operations

Use the given matrices to perform the operation.

$$A = \begin{bmatrix} 5 & 7 \\ 3 & 1 \\ -4 & 2 \end{bmatrix}, B = \begin{bmatrix} 0 & 1 \\ 3 & -6 \end{bmatrix}, C = \begin{bmatrix} 2 & -3 \\ -1 & 5 \end{bmatrix}$$

a. $A(B + C)$

$$A(B + C) = \begin{bmatrix} 5 & 7 \\ 3 & 1 \\ -4 & 2 \end{bmatrix} \left(\begin{bmatrix} 0 & 1 \\ 3 & -6 \end{bmatrix} + \begin{bmatrix} 2 & -3 \\ -1 & 5 \end{bmatrix} \right)$$

$$= \begin{bmatrix} 5 & 7 \\ 3 & 1 \\ -4 & 2 \end{bmatrix} \begin{bmatrix} 2 & -2 \\ 2 & -1 \end{bmatrix}$$

$$= \begin{bmatrix} 24 & -17 \\ 8 & -7 \\ -4 & 6 \end{bmatrix}$$

b. $AB + AC$

$$AB + AC = \begin{bmatrix} 5 & 7 \\ 3 & 1 \\ -4 & 2 \end{bmatrix} \begin{bmatrix} 0 & 1 \\ 3 & -6 \end{bmatrix} + \begin{bmatrix} 5 & 7 \\ 3 & 1 \\ -4 & 2 \end{bmatrix} \begin{bmatrix} 2 & -3 \\ -1 & 5 \end{bmatrix}$$

$$= \begin{bmatrix} 21 & -37 \\ 3 & -3 \\ 6 & -16 \end{bmatrix} + \begin{bmatrix} 3 & 20 \\ 5 & -4 \\ -10 & 22 \end{bmatrix}$$

$$= \begin{bmatrix} 24 & -17 \\ 8 & -7 \\ -4 & 6 \end{bmatrix}$$

Key Concept

Properties of Matrix Multiplication

Let A, B, and C be matrices and let k be a scalar.

Associative Property of Matrix Multiplication $A(BC) = (AB)C$

Left Distributive Property $A(B + C) = AB + AC$

Right Distributive Property $(A + B)C = AC + BC$

Associative Property of Scalar Multiplication $k(AB) = (kA)B = A(kB)$

In-Class Practice

Self-Assessment

5. Use the matrices in Example 3 to evaluate $A(B - C)$.

1 I don't understand yet. **2** I can do it with help. **3** I can do it on my own. **4** I can teach someone.

Connections to Real Life

Matrix multiplication is useful in business applications. An *inventory* matrix, when multiplied by a *cost per item* matrix, results in a *total cost* matrix.

$$\begin{bmatrix} \text{Inventory} \\ \text{matrix} \end{bmatrix} \cdot \begin{bmatrix} \text{Cost per item} \\ \text{matrix} \end{bmatrix} = \begin{bmatrix} \text{Total cost} \\ \text{matrix} \end{bmatrix}$$

$$m \times n \qquad n \times p \qquad m \times p$$

The column labels for the inventory matrix must match the row labels for the cost per item matrix for the total cost matrix to be meaningful.

EXAMPLE 4 · Using an Inventory Matrix

Students in two classes submit meal choices for a banquet. Each chicken meal costs \$6, each beef meal costs \$8, and each vegetarian meal costs \$4. Use matrix multiplication to find the total cost of the meals for each class.

Meal Selections

CLASS A
10 Chicken Meals
12 Beef Meals
8 Vegetarian Meals

CLASS B
11 Chicken Meals
14 Beef Meals
7 Vegetarian Meals

Write the meal selections and the costs per meal in matrix form. To use matrix multiplication, set up the matrices so that the columns of the meal selection matrix match the rows of the cost matrix.

Meal Selection

$$\begin{array}{c} \\ \text{Class A} \\ \text{Class B} \end{array} \begin{array}{ccc} \text{Chicken} & \text{Beef} & \text{Vegetarian} \\ \begin{bmatrix} 10 & 12 & 8 \\ 11 & 14 & 7 \end{bmatrix} \end{array}$$

Cost

$$\begin{array}{c} \\ \text{Chicken} \\ \text{Beef} \\ \text{Vegetarian} \end{array} \begin{array}{c} \text{Dollars} \\ \begin{bmatrix} 6 \\ 8 \\ 4 \end{bmatrix} \end{array}$$

To find the total cost of the meals for each class, multiply the meal selection matrix by the cost matrix. The meal selection matrix is 2×3 and the cost matrix is 3×1. So, their product is a 2×1 matrix.

$$\begin{bmatrix} 10 & 12 & 8 \\ 11 & 14 & 7 \end{bmatrix} \begin{bmatrix} 6 \\ 8 \\ 4 \end{bmatrix} = \begin{bmatrix} 10(6) + 12(8) + 8(4) \\ 11(6) + 14(8) + 7(4) \end{bmatrix}$$

$$= \begin{bmatrix} 188 \\ 206 \end{bmatrix}$$

The labels for the product matrix are shown below.

Total Cost

$$\begin{array}{c} \\ \text{Class A} \\ \text{Class B} \end{array} \begin{array}{c} \text{Dollars} \\ \begin{bmatrix} 188 \\ 206 \end{bmatrix} \end{array}$$

▶ The total cost of the meals for Class A is \$188, and the total cost for Class B is \$206.

In-Class Practice

Self-Assessment

6. WHAT IF? What is the total cost for each class in Example 4 when a chicken meal costs \$5, a beef meal costs \$6, and a vegetarian meal costs \$3?

11.2 Multiplying Matrices

11.2 Practice

Determine whether the product AB is defined. If so, state the dimensions of AB. (See Example 1.)

▶ 1. $A = \begin{bmatrix} 6 & 8 & 7 \end{bmatrix}$, $B = \begin{bmatrix} 8 \\ -1 \\ -5 \end{bmatrix}$

2. $A = \begin{bmatrix} -1 & 3 & -7 \\ 4 & 2 & -2 \end{bmatrix}$, $B = \begin{bmatrix} 1 & -5 \\ -6 & 2 \end{bmatrix}$

3. $A = \begin{bmatrix} 5 & -8 & 10 \\ -6 & 3 & -2 \end{bmatrix}$, $B = \begin{bmatrix} 1 \\ -7 \end{bmatrix}$

4. $A = \begin{bmatrix} 5 & 8 & -3 & 2 \\ 3 & 0 & -9 & 6 \end{bmatrix}$, $B = \begin{bmatrix} -1 & 0 \\ 8 & 3 \\ -5 & 4 \\ 7 & 2 \end{bmatrix}$

Find the product. (See Example 2.)

5. $\begin{bmatrix} -2 & 3 \end{bmatrix} \begin{bmatrix} 4 & 0 \\ 2 & 1 \end{bmatrix}$

6. $\begin{bmatrix} 2 & 7 \\ 0 & -2 \end{bmatrix} \begin{bmatrix} 5 & -1 \\ 1 & 3 \end{bmatrix}$

▶ 7. $\begin{bmatrix} 3 & -1 \\ -2 & 6 \\ 2 & -3 \end{bmatrix} \begin{bmatrix} 1 & 0 \\ 4 & -4 \end{bmatrix}$

8. $\begin{bmatrix} 9 & -2 & 3 \\ 0 & 5 & -1 \\ 4 & 1 & 6 \end{bmatrix} \begin{bmatrix} -6 & 4 & 5 \\ 1 & -5 & 2 \\ 0 & 9 & 7 \end{bmatrix}$

9. **SMP.3 ERROR ANALYSIS** Describe and correct the error in finding the element in the first row and first column of the product matrix.

$$\begin{bmatrix} -2 & 3 \\ 5 & 1 \end{bmatrix} \begin{bmatrix} 4 & 2 \\ 7 & 0 \end{bmatrix} = \begin{bmatrix} -2(4) + 3(2) & \end{bmatrix}$$
$$= \begin{bmatrix} -2 & \end{bmatrix}$$

Use the given matrices to evaluate the expression. (See Example 3.)

$A = \begin{bmatrix} 4 & 1 \\ -3 & 0 \end{bmatrix}$, $B = \begin{bmatrix} 5 & -2 \\ 6 & -1 \end{bmatrix}$, $C = \begin{bmatrix} 3 & 0 \\ -1 & 8 \end{bmatrix}$

10. $AC + BC$

▶ 11. $A(B - C)$

12. $(AB)C$

13. $\frac{1}{2}(AB)$

14. Solve for x and y.

$$\begin{bmatrix} 2 & x & 1 \\ 3 & -1 & 4 \end{bmatrix} \begin{bmatrix} -3 & 8 \\ 1 & 4 \\ 5 & 2 \end{bmatrix} = \begin{bmatrix} -7 & -6 \\ y & 28 \end{bmatrix}$$

15. **CONNECTION TO REAL LIFE** A softball coach buys equipment for two teams. The coach buys 4 bats, 36 softballs, and 12 uniforms for Team A and 6 bats, 45 softballs, and 15 uniforms for Team B. Each bat costs $80, each softball costs $4, and each uniform costs $20. Use matrix multiplication to find the total cost of the equipment for each team. (See Example 4.)

16. **PHOTOGRAPHER PRINTS** A conservation photographer prints photographs of different animals. The table shows the numbers of each photograph size (in inches) printed. Each 5 × 7 costs $2.25, each 8 × 10 costs $4.50, and each 11 × 14 costs $11.00. Use matrix multiplication to find the total cost of the photographs for each animal.

	5 × 7	8 × 10	11 × 14
Bonobos	8	4	1
Elephants	6	5	3
Sea lions	10	4	1

17. **SMP.6 CONNECT CONCEPTS** Use the matrices and the graph of the triangle shown.

$A = \begin{bmatrix} 1 & 0 \\ 0 & -1 \end{bmatrix}$

$B = \begin{bmatrix} 0 & -1 \\ 1 & 0 \end{bmatrix}$

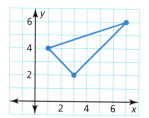

a. Write a 2 × 3 matrix C whose columns represent the vertices of the triangle.

b. Find AC and draw the resulting triangle. How are the triangles related?

c. Find BC and draw the resulting triangle. How are the triangles related?

d. Make a hypothesis about matrices A and B.

18. **SMP.1 PERFORMANCE TASK** As a teacher, you assign your students' total grades using a weighted system of four components: homework, quizzes, tests, and projects.

Student	Homework	Quizzes	Tests	Projects
A	82	90	84	85
B	71	77	94	89
C	90	88	93	90
D	92	84	86	88
E	83	85	72	78

a. Assign a weight to each component. Use matrix multiplication to find the total grades of the students shown in the table.

b. Choose one student and write a letter to a parent/guardian explaining the student's total grade in your class.

19. **SMP.1 SMP.7 DIG DEEPER** A *diagonal matrix* is a square matrix in which each element not on the main diagonal (from top left to bottom right) is zero. Consider two diagonal matrices A and B with the same dimensions where $A \neq B$. Write a rule that can be used to find AB without using traditional matrix multiplication. Justify your answer.

Interpreting Data

MULTIPLICATION OF LARGE MATRICES Two types of processing units in a computer are the central processing unit (CPU) and the graphics processing unit (GPU). The graph shows the amounts of time it takes for each processing unit in a certain computer to multiply $n \times n$ matrices.

20. Describe the shape of each graph.

21. Use what you know about matrix multiplication to explain why each graph is nonlinear.

22. Research the difference between these two types of processing units.

Review & Refresh

Graph the function.

23. $g(x) = \frac{1}{2} \sin 2\pi x$

24. $h(x) = -\cos(x - \pi) + 4$

25. You borrow $8,000 to buy a car. The loan has a 4.5% annual interest rate that is compounded monthly for 5 years. The monthly payment is $149.14.

    a. Find the balance after the sixth payment.

    b. Find the amount of the last payment.

Solve the equation.

26. $x^2 + 9 = 5$

27. $2x^2 - 6 = -24$

28. Consider the infinite geometric series $\frac{1}{4} + \frac{1}{8} + \frac{1}{16} + \frac{1}{32} + \frac{1}{64} + \cdots$. Find and graph the partial sums S_n for $n = 1, 2, 3, 4,$ and 5. Then describe what happens to S_n as n increases.

Perform the indicated operation(s).

29. $-4 \begin{bmatrix} 0 & 6 \\ -4 & -1 \end{bmatrix} + \begin{bmatrix} -9 & 3 \\ 4 & -2 \end{bmatrix}$

30. $\begin{bmatrix} 4 & 0 & -2 \\ -7 & 9 & 6 \end{bmatrix} - \begin{bmatrix} -6 & 8 & -2 \\ -1 & 5 & 1 \end{bmatrix}$

Let $f(x) = \sqrt{x - 2}$ and $g(x) = x^2 - 5$. Find the indicated value.

31. $f(g(4))$

32. $g(f(6))$

11.3 Determinants and Cramer's Rule

Learning Target: Find and use determinants of matrices.

Success Criteria:
- I can find the determinant of a square matrix.
- I can use determinants to find areas of triangles.
- I can use determinants to solve systems of equations.

INVESTIGATE Finding the Determinant

Work with a partner. Consider the unit square shown.

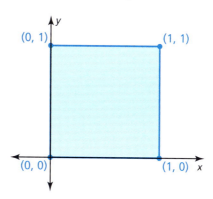

1. Form 2×1 matrices, $\begin{bmatrix} x \\ y \end{bmatrix}$, using the coordinates of each vertex.

2. Multiply $\begin{bmatrix} a & b \\ c & d \end{bmatrix}$ by each matrix in Exercise 1. How does the diagram below correspond to your products?

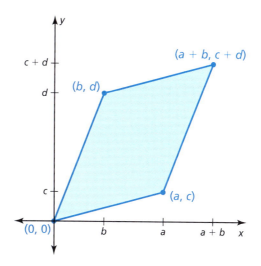

3. The area of the shaded parallelogram in Exercise 2 is called the *determinant* of $\begin{bmatrix} a & b \\ c & d \end{bmatrix}$. Find the determinant of $\begin{bmatrix} a & b \\ c & d \end{bmatrix}$.

Vocabulary
determinant
Cramer's Rule
coefficient matrix

Evaluating Determinants

Associated with each square ($n \times n$) matrix is a real number called its **determinant**. The determinant of a square matrix A is denoted by det A or by $|A|$.

Key Concept

The Determinant of a Matrix

Determinant of a 2 × 2 Matrix

$$\det\begin{bmatrix} a & b \\ c & d \end{bmatrix} = \begin{vmatrix} a & b \\ c & d \end{vmatrix} = ad - cb$$

The determinant of a 2 × 2 matrix is the difference of the products of the elements on the diagonals in the order shown.

Determinant of a 3 × 3 Matrix

Repeat the first two columns to the right of the determinant. Subtract the sum of the red products from the sum of the blue products.

$$\det\begin{bmatrix} a & b & c \\ d & e & f \\ g & h & i \end{bmatrix} = \begin{vmatrix} a & b & c \\ d & e & f \\ g & h & i \end{vmatrix} \begin{matrix} a & b \\ d & e \\ g & h \end{matrix} = (aei + bfg + cdh) - (gec + hfa + idb)$$

EXAMPLE 1 Evaluating Determinants

Evaluate the determinant of each matrix.

a. $\begin{bmatrix} 2 & 5 \\ 1 & 4 \end{bmatrix}$

b. $\begin{bmatrix} 3 & 4 & -1 \\ 2 & 0 & 6 \\ -2 & -3 & 1 \end{bmatrix}$

a. $\begin{vmatrix} 2 & 5 \\ 1 & 4 \end{vmatrix} = 2(4) - 1(5) = 8 - 5 = 3$

b. $\begin{vmatrix} 3 & 4 & -1 \\ 2 & 0 & 6 \\ -2 & -3 & 1 \end{vmatrix} \begin{matrix} 3 & 4 \\ 2 & 0 \\ -2 & -3 \end{matrix} = (0 + (-48) + 6) - (0 + (-54) + 8)$

$= -42 - (-46)$

$= 4$

In-Class Practice

Self-Assessment

Evaluate the determinant of the matrix.

1. $\begin{bmatrix} 6 & -2 \\ 3 & 5 \end{bmatrix}$

2. $\begin{bmatrix} 2 & -3 & 4 \\ 1 & 6 & 0 \\ 3 & -1 & 5 \end{bmatrix}$

You can use a determinant to find the area of a triangle whose vertices are points in a coordinate plane.

> ### Key Concept
>
> **Area of a Triangle**
>
> The area of a triangle with vertices (x_1, y_1), (x_2, y_2), and (x_3, y_3) is given by
>
> $$\text{Area} = \pm \frac{1}{2} \begin{vmatrix} x_1 & y_1 & 1 \\ x_2 & y_2 & 1 \\ x_3 & y_3 & 1 \end{vmatrix}$$
>
> where the symbol $\pm$ indicates that the appropriate sign should be chosen to yield a positive value.

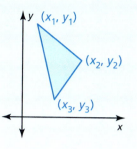

EXAMPLE 2 Finding the Area of a Triangle

Find the area of the triangle.

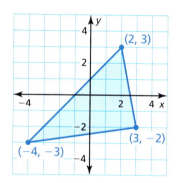

$$\text{Area} = \pm \frac{1}{2} \begin{vmatrix} 2 & 3 & 1 \\ 3 & -2 & 1 \\ -4 & -3 & 1 \end{vmatrix}$$

$$= \pm \frac{1}{2} \begin{vmatrix} 2 & 3 & 1 & 2 & 3 \\ 3 & -2 & 1 & 3 & -2 \\ -4 & -3 & 1 & -4 & -3 \end{vmatrix}$$

$$= \pm \tfrac{1}{2}[(-4 - 12 - 9) - (8 - 6 + 9)]$$

$$= \pm \tfrac{1}{2}(-25 - 11)$$

$$= \pm(-18)$$

▶ So, the area of the triangle is 18 square units.

In-Class Practice

Self-Assessment

3. Find the area of the triangle with vertices $(3, 6)$, $(8, -1)$, and $(-4, 5)$.

1 I don't understand yet.   **2** I can do it with help.   **3** I can do it on my own.   **4** I can teach someone.

Cramer's Rule

You can use determinants to solve a system of linear equations. The method, called **Cramer's Rule** and named after Swiss mathematician Gabriel Cramer (1704–1752), uses the **coefficient matrix** of the linear system.

Linear System

$ax + by = e$
$cx + dy = f$

Coefficient Matrix

$\begin{bmatrix} a & b \\ c & d \end{bmatrix}$

Key Concept

Cramer's Rule for a 2 × 2 System

Let A be the coefficient matrix of the linear system $\begin{array}{l} ax + by = e \\ cx + dy = f \end{array}$.

If $\det A \neq 0$, then the system has exactly one solution. The solution is

$$x = \frac{\begin{vmatrix} e & b \\ f & d \end{vmatrix}}{\det A} \quad \text{and} \quad y = \frac{\begin{vmatrix} a & e \\ c & f \end{vmatrix}}{\det A}.$$

Notice that the numerators for x and y are the determinants of the matrices formed by replacing the values of the x and y coefficient columns, respectively, with the column of the constant values.

EXAMPLE 3 Using Cramer's Rule for a 2 × 2 System

Use Cramer's Rule to solve the system $\begin{array}{l} 3x - 2y = 7 \\ 5x + 4y = -3 \end{array}$.

Evaluate the determinant of the coefficient matrix.

$$\begin{vmatrix} 3 & -2 \\ 5 & 4 \end{vmatrix} = 12 - (-10) = 22$$

Apply Cramer's Rule because the determinant is not 0.

$$x = \frac{\begin{vmatrix} 7 & -2 \\ -3 & 4 \end{vmatrix}}{22} \qquad y = \frac{\begin{vmatrix} 3 & 7 \\ 5 & -3 \end{vmatrix}}{22}$$

$$= \frac{28 - 6}{22} = \frac{22}{22} = 1 \qquad = \frac{-9 - 35}{22} = \frac{-44}{22} = -2$$

▶ The solution is $(1, -2)$.

In-Class Practice

Self-Assessment

Use Cramer's Rule to solve the linear system.

4. $7x - 2y = 20$
   $3x + 4y = -6$

5. $5x + 6y = 14$
   $-2x - 3y = -8$

1 I don't understand yet. **2** I can do it with help. **3** I can do it on my own. **4** I can teach someone.

Key Concept

Cramer's Rule for a 3 × 3 System

Let A be the coefficient matrix of the linear system shown below.

Linear System

$ax + by + cz = j$
$dx + ey + fz = k$
$gx + hy + iz = l$

Coefficient Matrix

$$A = \begin{bmatrix} a & b & c \\ d & e & f \\ g & h & i \end{bmatrix}$$

If $\det A \neq 0$, then the system has exactly one solution. The solution is

$$x = \frac{\begin{vmatrix} j & b & c \\ k & e & f \\ l & h & i \end{vmatrix}}{\det A}, \quad y = \frac{\begin{vmatrix} a & j & c \\ d & k & f \\ g & l & i \end{vmatrix}}{\det A}, \quad \text{and} \quad z = \frac{\begin{vmatrix} a & b & j \\ d & e & k \\ g & h & l \end{vmatrix}}{\det A}.$$

EXAMPLE 4 Using Cramer's Rule for a 3 × 3 System

Use Cramer's Rule to solve the system.

$2x - 3y + 5z = 12$
$x + 4y - 3z = -5$
$3x - 2y - z = -23$

Evaluate the determinant of the coefficient matrix.

$$\begin{vmatrix} 2 & -3 & 5 \\ 1 & 4 & -3 \\ 3 & -2 & -1 \end{vmatrix} \begin{matrix} 2 & -3 \\ 1 & 4 \\ 3 & -2 \end{matrix} = (-8 + 27 - 10) - (60 + 12 + 3) = -66$$

Apply Cramer's Rule because the determinant is not 0.

$$x = \frac{\begin{vmatrix} 12 & -3 & 5 \\ -5 & 4 & -3 \\ -23 & -2 & -1 \end{vmatrix}}{-66} \qquad y = \frac{\begin{vmatrix} 2 & 12 & 5 \\ 1 & -5 & -3 \\ 3 & -23 & -1 \end{vmatrix}}{-66} \qquad z = \frac{\begin{vmatrix} 2 & -3 & 12 \\ 1 & 4 & -5 \\ 3 & -2 & -23 \end{vmatrix}}{-66}$$

$$= \frac{198}{-66} \qquad\qquad = \frac{-264}{-66} \qquad\qquad = \frac{-396}{-66}$$

$$= -3 \qquad\qquad\quad = 4 \qquad\qquad\quad = 6$$

▶ The solution is $(-3, 4, 6)$.

In-Class Practice

Self-Assessment

Use Cramer's Rule to solve the linear system.

6. $5x - 2y + 3z = -2$
$4x + 7y - z = 0$
$2x - 6y + 5z = -7$

7. $-2x + 3y - 2z = -20$
$6x - 2y - 3z = 23$
$3x + 2y + z = 2$

Connections to Real Life

EXAMPLE 5 Using the Determinant of a Matrix

The molecular mass of a compound is the sum of the atomic masses of the atoms it contains. The molecular masses (in atomic mass units) of three compounds are shown. Use a linear system and Cramer's Rule to find the atomic masses of bromine (Br), nitrogen (N), and fluorine (F).

> Subscripts in a chemical formula indicate the number of atoms of each element in one molecule of the compound. No subscript indicates there is 1 atom of that element.

Compound	Formula	Molecular Mass
Bromine azide	BrN_3	122
Bromine trifluoride	BrF_3	137
Nitrogen trifluoride	NF_3	71

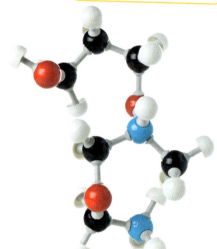

Write a linear system using the formula for each compound. Let B, N, and F represent the atomic masses of bromine, nitrogen, and fluorine.

$B + 3N = 122$ BrN_3: 1 bromine atom and 3 nitrogen atoms
$B + 3F = 137$ BrF_3: 1 bromine atom and 3 fluorine atoms
$ N + 3F = 71$ NF_3: 1 nitrogen atom and 3 fluorine atoms

Evaluate the determinant of the coefficient matrix.

$$\begin{vmatrix} 1 & 3 & 0 \\ 1 & 0 & 3 \\ 0 & 1 & 3 \end{vmatrix} \begin{matrix} 1 & 3 \\ 1 & 0 \\ 0 & 1 \end{matrix} = (0 + 0 + 0) - (0 + 3 + 9) = -12$$

Apply Cramer's Rule because the determinant is not 0.

$$B = \frac{\begin{vmatrix} 122 & 3 & 0 \\ 137 & 0 & 3 \\ 71 & 1 & 3 \end{vmatrix}}{-12} \qquad N = \frac{\begin{vmatrix} 1 & 122 & 0 \\ 1 & 137 & 3 \\ 0 & 71 & 3 \end{vmatrix}}{-12} \qquad F = \frac{\begin{vmatrix} 1 & 3 & 122 \\ 1 & 0 & 137 \\ 0 & 1 & 71 \end{vmatrix}}{-12}$$

$$= \frac{-960}{-12} \qquad\qquad = \frac{-168}{-12} \qquad\qquad = \frac{-228}{-12}$$

$$= 80 \qquad\qquad\quad = 14 \qquad\qquad\quad = 19$$

▶ The atomic masses (in atomic mass units) of bromine, nitrogen, and fluorine are 80, 14, and 19, respectively.

In-Class Practice

Self-Assessment

8. The table shows the molecular masses (in atomic mass units) of three compounds. Use a linear system and Cramer's Rule to find the atomic masses of carbon (C), hydrogen (H), and oxygen (O).

Compound	Formula	Molecular Mass
Acetone	C_3H_6O	58
Butanoic acid	$C_4H_8O_2$	88
Citric acid	$C_6H_8O_7$	192

11.3 Practice

Evaluate the determinant of the matrix. (See Example 1.)

▶1. $\begin{bmatrix} 3 & 1 \\ 2 & 4 \end{bmatrix}$

2. $\begin{bmatrix} -5 & 9 \\ 7 & -2 \end{bmatrix}$

3. $\begin{bmatrix} -8 & -9 \\ 14 & 12 \end{bmatrix}$

4. $\begin{bmatrix} 1 & 0 & 5 \\ 6 & 2 & 0 \\ 3 & 8 & 9 \end{bmatrix}$

▶5. $\begin{bmatrix} -2 & 7 & 0 \\ -3 & 1 & 4 \\ 5 & 0 & -6 \end{bmatrix}$

6. $\begin{bmatrix} -9 & 0 & 1 \\ 2 & 4 & 8 \\ -3 & -4 & -6 \end{bmatrix}$

SMP.3 ERROR ANALYSIS Describe and correct the error in evaluating the determinant of the matrix.

7.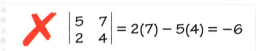
$\begin{vmatrix} 5 & 7 \\ 2 & 4 \end{vmatrix} = 2(7) - 5(4) = -6$

8.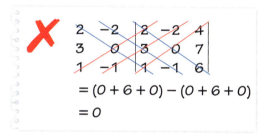

9. For what value of k is the determinant of $\begin{bmatrix} 0 & 2 & 0 \\ k & 9 & 2 \\ 5 & 4 & 2 \end{bmatrix}$ equal to 0?

Find the area of the triangle. (See Example 2.)

10.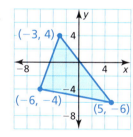

▶11.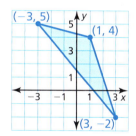

12.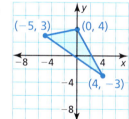

13. **CONNECTION TO REAL LIFE** A researcher of *Lyme disease* tests ticks from the triangular region shown below. Find the area of the triangular region.

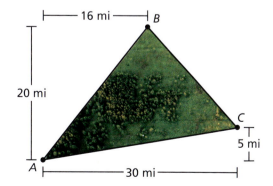

11.3 Determinants and Cramer's Rule 599

14. **SMP.7** Find a positive value of y such that a triangle with vertices $(-4, 3)$, $(0, 1)$, and $(1, y)$ has an area of 5 square units.

Use Cramer's Rule to solve the linear system. (See Examples 3 and 4.)

15. $4x + 3y = 5$
    $3x + 2y = 4$

16. $2x + 5y = 11$
    $4x + 8y = 20$

17. $-x + y - 4z = -7$
    $3x + 5y - 6z = -5$
    $2x - 3y + 5z = 12$

18. $2x - 4y + 7z = -1$
    $-3x + 5y - z = 26$
    $x - 6y + z = -24$

19. **SMP.4 CONNECTION TO REAL LIFE** There are x occupied floor seats and y occupied balcony seats at a concert with 6,700 total attendees. The tickets cost $40 per floor seat and $25 per balcony seat. The total revenue is $185,500. Write and solve a system to determine the number of occupied seats of each type at the concert.

The table shows the molecular masses (in atomic mass units) of three compounds. Use a linear system and Cramer's Rule to find the atomic masses of the indicated elements. (See Example 5.)

20. phosphorus (P), selenium (Se), iodine (I)

Compound	Formula	Molecular Mass
Diphosphorus pentaselenide	P_2Se_5	457
Phosphorus triiodide	PI_3	412
Selenium diiodide	SeI_2	333

21. sulfur (S), chlorine (Cl), calcium (Ca)

Compound	Formula	Molecular Mass
Sulfur dichloride	SCl_2	103
Calcium chloride	$CaCl_2$	111
Calcium sulfide	CaS	72

22. **CONNECTION TO REAL LIFE** When tin is melted down, it can be combined with other metals. An artist creates bronze jewelry using aluminum, copper, and tin. The costs of each metal are shown in the table. The artist orders a total of 10 pounds of metals for a cost of $32.70. The artist orders seven times as much copper as tin. How many pounds of tin does the artist order?

Metal	Price Per Pound
Aluminum	$0.75
Copper	$2.75
Tin	$7.75

STEM Video: Tin Jewelry

23. A system of pulleys is loaded with 128-pound and 32-pound weights, as shown. The tensions t_1 and t_2 (in pounds) in the ropes and the acceleration a (in feet per second squared) of the 32-pound weight are represented by the system

$$\begin{aligned} t_1 - 2t_2 &= 0 \\ t_1 - 2a &= 128. \\ t_2 + a &= 32 \end{aligned}$$

Find t_1, t_2, and a.

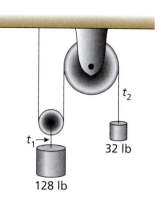

The points (x_1, y_1), (x_2, y_2), and (x_3, y_3) lie on the same line only when

$$\begin{vmatrix} x_1 & y_1 & 1 \\ x_2 & y_2 & 1 \\ x_3 & y_3 & 1 \end{vmatrix} = 0.$$

Determine whether the points lie on the same line.

24. $(0, 1), (2, 4), (3, 6)$

25. $(-5, -4), (-2, -1), (3, 4)$

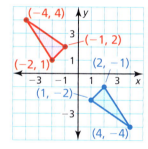

26. **OPEN-ENDED** Compare the area of the red triangle to the area of the blue triangle using two methods. Explain which method you prefer.

27. Solve the equation.

$$\begin{vmatrix} x+3 & x \\ 4 & x-1 \end{vmatrix} = 5$$

28. **SMP.8** Consider 3 × 3 square matrices in which the elements are consecutive integers, such as the one at the right. Find the determinants of four matrices of this type. Make a conjecture based on the results.

$$\begin{bmatrix} 2 & 3 & 4 \\ 5 & 6 & 7 \\ 8 & 9 & 10 \end{bmatrix}$$

29. A community organizer requests a triangular plot of land with an area of 5,000 square feet for an urban garden. On a blueprint, one vertex is at $(0, 0)$ and another is at $(100, 50)$. The y-coordinate of the final vertex is 120. Find the possible locations of the final vertex.

30. Consider the equation for the determinant of a 3 × 3 matrix,

$$\begin{vmatrix} a & b & c \\ d & e & f \\ g & h & i \end{vmatrix} = (aei + bfg + cdh) - (gec + hfa + idb).$$

How can you rewrite the determinant of a 3 × 3 matrix using determinants of 2 × 2 matrices? Show that your equation is equivalent to the equation above.

31. **SMP.1 DIG DEEPER** Consider the system consisting of $ax + by = e$ and $cx + dy = f$.

   a. Solve the system by finding rational expressions for x and y.

   b. Explain the relationship between determinants and your answers in part (a).

Interpreting Data

VOLTAGE You can find the currents (in amperes) in a circuit by using *Kirchoff's Laws* to write a system of linear equations, such as the one shown.

$5i_1 + 1(i_1 - i_2) + 8(i_1 - i_3) = 60$
$1(i_2 - i_1) + 6i_2 + 4(i_2 - i_3) = 0$
$8(i_3 - i_1) + 4(i_3 - i_2) + 2i_3 = 0$

Current Flow in Branches of Circuit

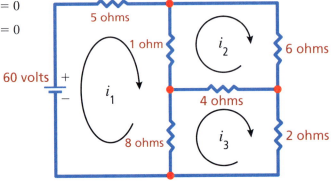

32. Rewrite the system to find its coefficient matrix.

33. Use Cramer's Rule to find each current.

34. Use a different method to find the currents. Explain which method you prefer.

Review & Refresh

35. Solve the equation for a, b, c, and d.

$$\begin{bmatrix} 8-a & 5b \\ c & -2d \end{bmatrix} = \begin{bmatrix} 4 & 20 \\ 22 & 14 \end{bmatrix}$$

36. Find the product $\begin{bmatrix} 0 & 2 \\ -1 & 3 \end{bmatrix} \begin{bmatrix} 0 & -9 \\ 7 & 1 \end{bmatrix}$.

37. Write a recursive rule for the sequence.

5, 10, 30, 120. . .

38. Find the value of x for the right triangle.

39. Find all the real zeros of

$f(x) = 4x^3 - 10x^2 - 8x + 6$.

40. Verify the identity $\sin\left(\dfrac{3\pi}{2} - x\right)\tan x = -\sin x$.

41. Find the inverse of the function $f(x) = 9x^2$, $x \leq 0$. Then graph the function and its inverse.

42. Find the value of c. Then write an expression represented by the diagram.

43. Graph the function $y = e^{x+4}$. Then find the domain and range.

44. Find the sum.

$$\dfrac{3}{x+1} + \dfrac{2x}{x+2}$$

11.4 Inverse Matrices

Learning Target: Understand the relationship between a matrix and its inverse.

Success Criteria:
- I can find the inverse of a matrix.
- I can solve linear systems using inverse matrices.
- I can solve real-life problems using inverse matrices.

INVESTIGATE Describing Matrices and Their Inverses

Work with a partner.

1. Each matrix shown below has an *inverse*. Find the determinant of each matrix. Then use technology to find the inverse of each matrix. How is each matrix related to its inverse?

$$A = \begin{bmatrix} 3 & 7 \\ 2 & 5 \end{bmatrix} \qquad B = \begin{bmatrix} 2 & 1 \\ 5 & 2 \end{bmatrix}$$

$$C = \begin{bmatrix} -4 & 2 \\ 2 & -2 \end{bmatrix} \qquad D = \begin{bmatrix} -4 & -2 \\ -2 & -2 \end{bmatrix}$$

2. Use technology to find the inverse of each matrix. What do you notice? Why does this happen?

$$E = \begin{bmatrix} 6 & 3 \\ 4 & 2 \end{bmatrix} \qquad F = \begin{bmatrix} -4 & -2 \\ -10 & -5 \end{bmatrix}$$

3. Use your results in Exercises 1 and 2 to describe how you can find the inverse of a 2 × 2 matrix.

4. Find the product of each matrix in Exercise 1 and its inverse. What do you notice?

5. The matrix below is called the 2 × 2 *identity matrix I*.

$$I = \begin{bmatrix} 1 & 0 \\ 0 & 1 \end{bmatrix} \qquad \text{2 × 2 identity matrix}$$

Explore the relationship between a matrix, its inverse, and the identity matrix. Make several observations.

Vocabulary
identity matrix
inverse matrices
matrix of variables
matrix of constants

Finding Inverse Matrices

The $n \times n$ **identity matrix** is a matrix that consists of 1's on its main diagonal (from top left to bottom right) and 0's for all other elements. If A is any $n \times n$ matrix and I is the $n \times n$ identity matrix, then $AI = A$ and $IA = A$.

2 × 2 Identity Matrix

$$I = \begin{bmatrix} 1 & 0 \\ 0 & 1 \end{bmatrix}$$

3 × 3 Identity Matrix

$$I = \begin{bmatrix} 1 & 0 & 0 \\ 0 & 1 & 0 \\ 0 & 0 & 1 \end{bmatrix}$$

Two $n \times n$ matrices A and B are **inverses** of each other when their products are the $n \times n$ identity matrix; that is, $AB = I$ and $BA = I$. An $n \times n$ matrix A has an inverse if and only if $\det A \neq 0$. The inverse of A is denoted by A^{-1}.

Key Concept

The Inverse of a 2 × 2 Matrix

The inverse of the matrix $A = \begin{bmatrix} a & b \\ c & d \end{bmatrix}$ is

$$A^{-1} = \frac{1}{\det A} \begin{bmatrix} d & -b \\ -c & a \end{bmatrix} = \frac{1}{ad - cb} \begin{bmatrix} d & -b \\ -c & a \end{bmatrix} \text{ when } \det A \neq 0.$$

EXAMPLE 1 Finding the Inverse of a 2 × 2 Matrix

Find the inverse of each matrix, if possible.

a. $A = \begin{bmatrix} 4 & 7 \\ 3 & 5 \end{bmatrix}$
b. $B = \begin{bmatrix} 5 & 3 \\ 4 & 2 \end{bmatrix}$
c. $C = \begin{bmatrix} -6 & 9 \\ 2 & -3 \end{bmatrix}$

a. $A^{-1} = \dfrac{1}{20 - 21}\begin{bmatrix} 5 & -7 \\ -3 & 4 \end{bmatrix} = -1\begin{bmatrix} 5 & -7 \\ -3 & 4 \end{bmatrix} = \begin{bmatrix} -5 & 7 \\ 3 & -4 \end{bmatrix}$

b. $B^{-1} = \dfrac{1}{10 - 12}\begin{bmatrix} 2 & -3 \\ -4 & 5 \end{bmatrix} = -\dfrac{1}{2}\begin{bmatrix} 2 & -3 \\ -4 & 5 \end{bmatrix} = \begin{bmatrix} -1 & \frac{3}{2} \\ 2 & -\frac{5}{2} \end{bmatrix}$

c. $C^{-1} = \dfrac{1}{18 - 18}\begin{bmatrix} -3 & -9 \\ -2 & -6 \end{bmatrix} = \dfrac{1}{0}\begin{bmatrix} -3 & -9 \\ -2 & -6 \end{bmatrix}$

Because the determinant of matrix C is 0, C does not have an inverse.

In-Class Practice

Self-Assessment

Find the inverse of the matrix, if possible.

1. $\begin{bmatrix} 2 & 9 \\ 1 & 5 \end{bmatrix}$
2. $\begin{bmatrix} 1 & 4 \\ 2 & 7 \end{bmatrix}$
3. $\begin{bmatrix} 6 & 8 \\ 2 & 3 \end{bmatrix}$

EXAMPLE 2 **Solving a Matrix Equation**

Solve the matrix equation $AX = B$ for the 2×2 matrix X.

$$\overbrace{\begin{bmatrix} 2 & 7 \\ 1 & 4 \end{bmatrix}}^{A} X = \overbrace{\begin{bmatrix} 2 & 8 \\ 1 & 5 \end{bmatrix}}^{B}$$

Begin by finding the inverse of A: $A^{-1} = \dfrac{1}{8-7}\begin{bmatrix} 4 & -7 \\ -1 & 2 \end{bmatrix} = \begin{bmatrix} 4 & -7 \\ -1 & 2 \end{bmatrix}$

To solve the equation for X, multiply both sides of $AX = B$ by A^{-1} on the left.

$\begin{bmatrix} 4 & -7 \\ -1 & 2 \end{bmatrix}\begin{bmatrix} 2 & 7 \\ 1 & 4 \end{bmatrix} X = \begin{bmatrix} 4 & -7 \\ -1 & 2 \end{bmatrix}\begin{bmatrix} 2 & 8 \\ 1 & 5 \end{bmatrix}$ $A^{-1}AX = A^{-1}B$

$\begin{bmatrix} 1 & 0 \\ 0 & 1 \end{bmatrix} X = \begin{bmatrix} 1 & -3 \\ 0 & 2 \end{bmatrix}$ $IX = A^{-1}B$

$X = \begin{bmatrix} 1 & -3 \\ 0 & 2 \end{bmatrix}$ $X = A^{-1}B$

EXAMPLE 3 **Finding the Inverse of a 3 × 3 Matrix Using Technology**

Use technology to find the inverse of A. Then use technology to verify your result.

$$A = \begin{bmatrix} 2 & 1 & -2 \\ -1 & -1 & 2 \\ -3 & -1 & 3 \end{bmatrix}$$

Enter matrix A and calculate A^{-1}.

$A = \begin{bmatrix} 2 & 1 & -2 \\ -1 & -1 & 2 \\ -3 & -1 & 3 \end{bmatrix}$

$A^{-1} = \begin{bmatrix} 1 & 1 & 0 \\ 3 & 0 & 2 \\ 2 & 1 & 1 \end{bmatrix}$

Check

Calculate AA^{-1} and $A^{-1}A$ to verify that you obtain the 3×3 identity matrix.

$AA^{-1} = \begin{bmatrix} 1 & 0 & 0 \\ 0 & 1 & 0 \\ 0 & 0 & 1 \end{bmatrix}$ ✓

$A^{-1}A = \begin{bmatrix} 1 & 0 & 0 \\ 0 & 1 & 0 \\ 0 & 0 & 1 \end{bmatrix}$ ✓

In-Class Practice

Self-Assessment

Solve the matrix equation.

4. $\begin{bmatrix} 2 & 3 \\ 5 & 0 \end{bmatrix} X = \begin{bmatrix} 3 & 12 \\ 0 & 15 \end{bmatrix}$

5. $\begin{bmatrix} 4 & -1 \\ 2 & 6 \end{bmatrix} X = \begin{bmatrix} 11 & -10 \\ 12 & 8 \end{bmatrix}$

Use technology to find the inverse of A. Then use technology to verify your result.

6. $A = \begin{bmatrix} 2 & -2 & 5 \\ 0 & -1 & 1 \\ 1 & -1 & 2 \end{bmatrix}$

7. $A = \begin{bmatrix} -1 & 3 & -3 \\ 1 & 0 & 1 \\ 3 & 4 & 0 \end{bmatrix}$

Using Inverse Matrices to Solve Linear Systems

> **Key Concept**
>
> **Using an Inverse Matrix to Solve a Linear System**
> - Write the system as a matrix equation $AX = B$. The matrix A is the coefficient matrix, X is the **matrix of variables**, and B is the **matrix of constants**.
> - Find the inverse of matrix A.
> - Multiply each side of $AX = B$ by A^{-1} on the left to find the solution $X = A^{-1}B$.

EXAMPLE 4 Solving a Linear System

Use an inverse matrix to solve the linear system.

$2x + 5y = 3$ Equation 1
$x + 3y = 2$ Equation 2

Write the linear system as a matrix equation $AX = B$.

$$\underset{\text{matrix }(A)}{\underset{\text{coefficient}}{\begin{bmatrix} 2 & 5 \\ 1 & 3 \end{bmatrix}}} \cdot \underset{\text{variables }(X)}{\underset{\text{matrix of}}{\begin{bmatrix} x \\ y \end{bmatrix}}} = \underset{\text{constants }(B)}{\underset{\text{matrix of}}{\begin{bmatrix} 3 \\ 2 \end{bmatrix}}}$$

Find the inverse of matrix A.

$$A^{-1} = \frac{1}{6-5}\begin{bmatrix} 3 & -5 \\ -1 & 2 \end{bmatrix} = \begin{bmatrix} 3 & -5 \\ -1 & 2 \end{bmatrix}$$

Check

Equation 1

$2(-1) + 5(1) \stackrel{?}{=} 3$

$3 = 3$ ✓

Equation 2

$-1 + 3(1) \stackrel{?}{=} 2$

$2 = 2$ ✓

Multiply each side of $AX = B$ by A^{-1} on the left.

$\begin{bmatrix} 3 & -5 \\ -1 & 2 \end{bmatrix}\begin{bmatrix} 2 & 5 \\ 1 & 3 \end{bmatrix}X = \begin{bmatrix} 3 & -5 \\ -1 & 2 \end{bmatrix}\begin{bmatrix} 3 \\ 2 \end{bmatrix}$ $A^{-1}AX = A^{-1}B$

$\begin{bmatrix} 1 & 0 \\ 0 & 1 \end{bmatrix}X = \begin{bmatrix} -1 \\ 1 \end{bmatrix}$ $IX = A^{-1}B$

$X = \begin{bmatrix} -1 \\ 1 \end{bmatrix}$ $X = A^{-1}B$

▶ The solution of the system is $(-1, 1)$.

In-Class Practice

Self-Assessment

Use an inverse matrix to solve the linear system.

8. $6x + 7y = 5$
$7x + 8y = 6$

9. $2x - 3y = 1$
$-4x + 5y = 1$

EXAMPLE 5 Using a Matrix Equation in Real Life

A company sells three sizes of fruit baskets. What is the cost of each type of fruit?

Small basket $5.99
Contains 2 apples, 2 grapefruits, and 1 peach

Medium basket $9.27
Contains 3 apples, 2 grapefruits, and 3 peaches

Large basket $13.76
Contains 5 apples, 3 grapefruits, and 4 peaches

Write and solve a system of linear equations that represents the problem.

Words
$2 \cdot$ (Cost of apple) $+ 2 \cdot$ (Cost of grapefruit) $+$ (Cost of peach) $= \$5.99$

$3 \cdot$ (Cost of apple) $+ 2 \cdot$ (Cost of grapefruit) $+ 3 \cdot$ (Cost of peach) $= \$9.27$

$5 \cdot$ (Cost of apple) $+ 3 \cdot$ (Cost of grapefruit) $+ 4 \cdot$ (Cost of peach) $= \$13.76$

Variables Let x be the cost (in dollars) of an apple, let y be the cost (in dollars) of a grapefruit, and let z be the cost (in dollars) of a peach.

System
$2x + 2y + z = 5.99$ Equation 1
$3x + 2y + 3z = 9.27$ Equation 2
$5x + 3y + 4z = 13.76$ Equation 3

Rewrite the system as a matrix equation.

$$\begin{bmatrix} 2 & 2 & 1 \\ 3 & 2 & 3 \\ 5 & 3 & 4 \end{bmatrix} \begin{bmatrix} x \\ y \\ z \end{bmatrix} = \begin{bmatrix} 5.99 \\ 9.27 \\ 13.76 \end{bmatrix}$$

Use technology to enter the coefficient matrix A and the matrix of constants B. Then find the solution $X = A^{-1}B$.

$A = \begin{bmatrix} 2 & 2 & 1 \\ 3 & 2 & 3 \\ 5 & 3 & 4 \end{bmatrix}$

$B = \begin{bmatrix} 5.99 \\ 9.27 \\ 13.76 \end{bmatrix}$

$A^{-1}B = \begin{bmatrix} 0.9 \\ 1.5 \\ 1.19 \end{bmatrix}$

▶ The solution is (0.9, 1.5, 1.19). So, an apple costs $0.90, a grapefruit costs $1.50, and a peach costs $1.19.

Check
Small basket: $2(0.90) + 2(1.50) + 1.19 = \$5.99$ ✓
Medium basket: $3(0.90) + 2(1.50) + 3(1.19) = \$9.27$ ✓
Large basket: $5(0.90) + 3(1.50) + 4(1.19) = \$13.76$ ✓

In-Class Practice

Self-Assessment

10. The company in Example 5 introduces three new fruit baskets. A small basket that costs $5.20 contains 2 oranges and 3 pears. A medium basket that costs $7.55 contains 3 oranges, 2 pears, and 2 plums. A large basket that costs $11.70 contains 4 oranges, 3 pears, and 4 plums. What is the cost of each type of fruit?

11.4 Practice

Find the inverse of the matrix, if possible. (See Example 1.)

1. $\begin{bmatrix} 4 & 3 \\ 9 & 7 \end{bmatrix}$

2. $\begin{bmatrix} 3 & 5 \\ 4 & 7 \end{bmatrix}$

3. $\begin{bmatrix} 6 & -3 \\ 4 & -2 \end{bmatrix}$

4. $\begin{bmatrix} 3 & 9 \\ 5 & 15 \end{bmatrix}$

5. $\begin{bmatrix} 5 & -3 \\ -11 & 7 \end{bmatrix}$

6. $\begin{bmatrix} -6 & 2 \\ -14 & 5 \end{bmatrix}$

SMP.3 ERROR ANALYSIS Describe and correct the error in finding the inverse of the matrix.

7.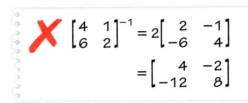

8.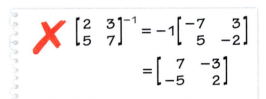

Solve the matrix equation. (See Example 2.)

9. $\begin{bmatrix} 2 & 5 \\ 7 & 3 \end{bmatrix} X = \begin{bmatrix} 12 & 9 \\ 13 & 17 \end{bmatrix}$

10. $\begin{bmatrix} -1 & 4 \\ 6 & 3 \end{bmatrix} X = \begin{bmatrix} -8 & 17 \\ 21 & -21 \end{bmatrix}$

11. $\begin{bmatrix} -1 & 5 \\ 0 & -2 \end{bmatrix} X = \begin{bmatrix} 3 & -1 & 0 \\ 6 & 8 & 4 \end{bmatrix}$

12. $\begin{bmatrix} -5 & 2 \\ -9 & 3 \end{bmatrix} X = \begin{bmatrix} 4 & 5 & 0 \\ 3 & 1 & 6 \end{bmatrix}$

Use technology to find the inverse of A. Then use technology to verify your result. (See Example 3.)

13. $A = \begin{bmatrix} 1 & -1 & -2 \\ 0 & 1 & 2 \\ 3 & 0 & 1 \end{bmatrix}$

14. $A = \begin{bmatrix} 2 & 1 & 1 \\ 1 & 0 & 2 \\ -2 & 1 & -6 \end{bmatrix}$

15. $A = \begin{bmatrix} 2 & -2 & 1 \\ -1 & 1 & 0 \\ 2 & 0 & 2 \end{bmatrix}$

16. $A = \begin{bmatrix} 1 & 5 & -2 \\ 2 & 3 & -6 \\ -1 & 4 & 4 \end{bmatrix}$

Use an inverse matrix to solve the linear system. (See Example 4.)

17. $x + 2y = 1$
    $3x + 7y = 2$

18. $-9x + 8y = 1$
    $5x - 6y = -13$

19. $-7x + 2y = 29$
    $5x - 3y = -27$

20. $-x - 7y = 37$
    $4x - 2y = 32$

Use an inverse matrix and technology to solve the linear system.

21. $x - y - 3z = 2$
    $5x + 2y + z = -17$
    $-3x - y = 8$

22. $-3x + y - 8z = 18$
    $x - 2y + z = -11$
    $2x - 2y + 5z = -17$

23. **CONNECTION TO REAL LIFE** A bouquet of 2 roses, 6 carnations, and 2 tulips costs $23. A bouquet of 4 roses, 4 carnations, and 2 tulips costs $30. A bouquet of 3 roses, 2 carnations, and 5 tulips costs $28. What is the cost of each type of flower? (See Example 5.)

24. The table shows the amounts of nuts in snack bags. Bag A costs $13.98, bag B costs $13.79, and bag C costs $13.81. What is the cost per ounce of each type of nut?

	walnuts	pecans	cashews
Bag A	6 oz	4 oz	6 oz
Bag B	7 oz	3 oz	6 oz
Bag C	5 oz	4 oz	7 oz

SMP.6 Explain whether the statement is *always*, *sometimes*, or *never* true.

25. Multiplication of a matrix and its inverse is commutative.

26. If the product of two matrices is an identity matrix, then the matrices are inverses.

27. A 3 × 2 matrix has an inverse.

28. **SMP.8 CONNECT CONCEPTS** The *zero matrix*, denoted O, is an $m \times n$ matrix consisting entirely of 0's. Find the products of several $k \times m$ matrices and $m \times n$ zero matrices. What do you notice? How is multiplying a matrix A by O similar to multiplying a real number a by 0?

29. You write the matrix equation shown to represent a linear system. Explain how p and q are related when the system has (a) infinitely many solutions and (b) no solution.

$$\begin{bmatrix} 2m & 2n \\ m & n \end{bmatrix} \cdot \begin{bmatrix} x \\ y \end{bmatrix} = \begin{bmatrix} p \\ q \end{bmatrix}$$

30. **CONNECTION TO REAL LIFE** You can use matrix multiplication and inverses to encode and decode words. Let the numbers 1 to 26 represent the corresponding letters in the alphabet, where 1 = A and 26 = Z.

   a. Convert each letter in the word "CAT" to a number and write the result as a 1 × 3 matrix.

   b. You can produce a coded matrix by multiplying the 1 × 3 matrix from part (a) by a 3 × 3 matrix that has an inverse, called the encoding matrix. Let matrix A be the encoding matrix. Find the coded matrix.

   $$A = \begin{bmatrix} -4 & -1 & 1 \\ 3 & 1 & -1 \\ 2 & -2 & 1 \end{bmatrix}$$

   c. Repeat parts (a) and (b) using a different three-letter word. Then exchange coded matrices with a partner and find your partner's word.

31. **DIG DEEPER** Let $A = \begin{bmatrix} x & 0 \\ y & z \end{bmatrix}$. For what values of x, y, and z does $A = A^{-1}$? Justify your answer.

32. **DIG DEEPER** Let $A = \begin{bmatrix} a & b \\ c & d \end{bmatrix}$ where det $A \neq 0$. Verify that $A^{-1} = \dfrac{1}{ad - bc} \begin{bmatrix} d & -b \\ -c & a \end{bmatrix}$.

Interpreting Data

INVERSE OF A 3 × 3 MATRIX One way to find the inverse of a 3 × 3 matrix with a nonzero determinant is to use the formula shown below.

$$A^{-1} = \frac{1}{|A|} \begin{bmatrix} \begin{vmatrix} a_{22} & a_{23} \\ a_{32} & a_{33} \end{vmatrix} & \begin{vmatrix} a_{13} & a_{12} \\ a_{33} & a_{32} \end{vmatrix} & \begin{vmatrix} a_{12} & a_{13} \\ a_{22} & a_{23} \end{vmatrix} \\ \begin{vmatrix} a_{23} & a_{21} \\ a_{33} & a_{31} \end{vmatrix} & \begin{vmatrix} a_{11} & a_{13} \\ a_{31} & a_{33} \end{vmatrix} & \begin{vmatrix} a_{13} & a_{11} \\ a_{23} & a_{21} \end{vmatrix} \\ \begin{vmatrix} a_{21} & a_{22} \\ a_{31} & a_{32} \end{vmatrix} & \begin{vmatrix} a_{12} & a_{11} \\ a_{32} & a_{31} \end{vmatrix} & \begin{vmatrix} a_{11} & a_{12} \\ a_{21} & a_{22} \end{vmatrix} \end{bmatrix}$$

The digits of each subscript refer to a specific row and column of A. For example, a_{13} means row 1 column 3.

33. Use the formula to find the inverse of $A = \begin{bmatrix} 6 & -2 & 1 \\ -4 & 1 & -1 \\ 1 & 0 & 1 \end{bmatrix}$.

34. Verify that the product of A and A^{-1} is equal to the identity matrix.

35. **SMP.5** Use a different method to find the inverse of A. Explain which method you prefer.

Review & Refresh

36. Find the domain and range of the function.

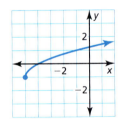

37. Let $f(x) = 5x^{1/2}$ and $g(x) = -3x^{1/2}$. Find $(f + g)(x)$ and $(f - g)(x)$ and state the domain of each. Then evaluate $(f + g)(16)$ and $(f - g)(16)$.

38. Evaluate the determinant of the matrix.

$$\begin{bmatrix} 3 & 1 & -1 \\ -2 & -4 & 0 \\ 4 & 7 & 5 \end{bmatrix}$$

Evaluate the function without using technology.

39. $\sec \dfrac{7\pi}{3}$

40. $\tan(-210°)$

41. Determine the type of function represented by the table.

x	−3	−2	−1	0	1
y	0.5	1.5	4.5	13.5	40.5

42. Use the given matrices to evaluate $B(A + C)$.

$$A = \begin{bmatrix} 2 & -6 \\ 5 & 8 \end{bmatrix}, B = \begin{bmatrix} 4 & 3 \\ -6 & -2 \\ -1 & 2 \end{bmatrix},$$

$$C = \begin{bmatrix} 1 & 10 \\ -7 & 3 \end{bmatrix}$$

43. The shaded region represents 68% of the area under a normal curve. What are the mean and standard deviation of the normal distribution?

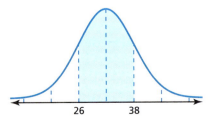

11 Chapter Review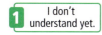

Rate your understanding of each section.
1. I don't understand yet.
2. I can do it with help.
3. I can do it on my own.
4. I can teach someone.

11.1 Basic Matrix Operations (pp. 577–584)

Learning Target: Perform basic operations involving matrices.

Vocabulary
matrix
dimensions of a matrix
elements of a matrix
equal matrices
scalar
scalar multiplication

Perform the indicated operation(s).

1. $\begin{bmatrix} 4 & -5 \\ 2 & 3 \end{bmatrix} + \begin{bmatrix} -1 & 3 \\ -7 & 4 \end{bmatrix}$

2. $\begin{bmatrix} -2 & 3 & 5 \\ -1 & 6 & -2 \end{bmatrix} - \begin{bmatrix} -4 & 7 & 5 \\ -8 & 0 & -9 \end{bmatrix}$

3. $-3\begin{bmatrix} 5 & -2 \\ 3 & 6 \end{bmatrix}$

4. $8\begin{bmatrix} 8 & 4 & 5 \\ -1 & 6 & -2 \end{bmatrix}$

5. $2\begin{bmatrix} 4 & 2 \\ 1 & -3 \\ 0 & -3 \end{bmatrix} + \begin{bmatrix} -1 & 2 \\ 6 & 5 \\ 3 & 7 \end{bmatrix}$

6. $\frac{1}{3}\begin{bmatrix} 0 & 12 \\ 3 & -9 \\ 6 & 0 \end{bmatrix} - \frac{3}{4}\begin{bmatrix} -4 & -8 \\ -12 & 0 \\ 4 & -8 \end{bmatrix}$

Solve the matrix equation for a, b, c, and d.

7. $\begin{bmatrix} -a+3 & 2b \\ c-1 & d \end{bmatrix} = \begin{bmatrix} 9 & 6 \\ 7 & -3 \end{bmatrix}$

8. $\begin{bmatrix} 6 & b+4 \\ -c & 12 \end{bmatrix} = \begin{bmatrix} a-4 & 1 \\ 1 & 4d \end{bmatrix}$

9. $\begin{bmatrix} 2 & b \\ c-5 & d+1 \end{bmatrix} + \begin{bmatrix} -3 & 7 \\ 4 & -2 \end{bmatrix} = \begin{bmatrix} a & 9 \\ -6 & -3 \end{bmatrix}$

10. An orchard sells apples and peaches. The tables show the numbers of pounds of fruit sold during July, August, and September for two years. Organize the data using two matrices, one for each year. Then find and interpret a matrix that gives the average numbers of pounds of apples and peaches sold in each month.

Apples

	Year 1	Year 2
July	450	510
August	530	650
September	1,050	990

Peaches

	Year 1	Year 2
July	960	930
August	1,130	1,260
September	720	580

11.2 Multiplying Matrices (pp. 585–592)

⊙ **Learning Target:** Understand how to multiply matrices.

Find the product, if possible. If not possible, explain why not.

11. $\begin{bmatrix} -1 & -1 \end{bmatrix} \begin{bmatrix} 8 & 2 \\ -6 & -9 \end{bmatrix}$

12. $\begin{bmatrix} -2 & 5 \\ 0 & 3 \end{bmatrix} \begin{bmatrix} 6 & -3 & 5 \\ 2 & 0 & -1 \end{bmatrix}$

13. $\begin{bmatrix} -2 & 3 \\ 3 & 1 \end{bmatrix} \begin{bmatrix} 2 & -3 \\ -1 & 0 \\ 4 & 5 \end{bmatrix}$

14. $\begin{bmatrix} 4 & -2 & 3 \\ -1 & 0 & 5 \end{bmatrix} \begin{bmatrix} 2 & -6 \\ 0 & 5 \\ -3 & 1 \end{bmatrix}$

Use the given matrices to evaluate the expression.

$$A = \begin{bmatrix} 4 & -1 \\ 2 & -3 \end{bmatrix}, B = \begin{bmatrix} -5 & 0 \\ 6 & -4 \end{bmatrix}, C = \begin{bmatrix} -8 & 4 \\ 6 & 0 \\ 0 & 2 \end{bmatrix}$$

15. $AB + B$

16. $C(A + B)$

17. A company manufactures three models of virtual reality headsets. The matrices show the numbers of units shipped to each of two warehouses and the prices of the models. Write a matrix that gives the total value of the headsets in each warehouse.

Shipping Location

	Model A	Model B	Model C
Warehouse 1	5,000	6,000	8,000
Warehouse 2	4,000	10,000	5,000

Cost

	Dollars
Model A	199
Model B	399
Model C	499

11.3 Determinants and Cramer's Rule (pp. 593–602)

⊙ **Learning Target:** Find and use determinants of matrices.

Vocabulary
determinant
Cramer's Rule
coefficient matrix

Evaluate the determinant of the matrix.

18. $\begin{bmatrix} -4 & 2 \\ 5 & 8 \end{bmatrix}$

19. $\begin{bmatrix} 3 & 0 & 2 \\ 1 & -6 & 3 \\ 2 & 4 & -1 \end{bmatrix}$

20. Find two ways to complete the matrix so that the determinant is 1.

$$\begin{bmatrix} 1 & & \\ -2 & 0 & -5 \\ 1 & 1 & 3 \end{bmatrix}$$

21. You sketch a large triangular pennant for your school football team. In a coordinate plane, the vertices of the triangle are (0, 0), (0, 50), and (70, 20), where the coordinates are measured in inches. How many square *feet* of material do you need to make the pennant?

11.4 Inverse Matrices (pp. 603–610)

Learning Target: Understand the relationship between a matrix and its inverse.

Vocabulary
identity matrix
inverse matrices
matrix of variables
matrix of constants

Find the inverse of the matrix, if possible.

22. $\begin{bmatrix} 1 & 2 \\ 4 & 5 \end{bmatrix}$

23. $\begin{bmatrix} -3 & -2 \\ 5 & -2 \end{bmatrix}$

24. $\begin{bmatrix} 4 & -8 \\ -3 & -6 \end{bmatrix}$

25. $\begin{bmatrix} 2 & 4 \\ -7 & -14 \end{bmatrix}$

Solve the matrix equation.

26. $\begin{bmatrix} -3 & 2 \\ -7 & 5 \end{bmatrix} X = \begin{bmatrix} 6 & 3 \\ -4 & 1 \end{bmatrix}$

27. $\begin{bmatrix} 6 & 4 \\ 4 & 3 \end{bmatrix} X = \begin{bmatrix} 1 & 1 \\ 2 & 3 \end{bmatrix}$

28. $\begin{bmatrix} -8 & 2 \\ 2 & -1 \end{bmatrix} X = \begin{bmatrix} 4 & -8 \\ 2 & 16 \end{bmatrix}$

29. $\begin{bmatrix} -4 & -2 \\ 6 & 4 \end{bmatrix} X = \begin{bmatrix} 8 & -6 \\ 2 & 4 \end{bmatrix}$

Use an inverse matrix to solve the linear system.

30. $x + 4y = 11$
    $2x - 5y = 9$

31. $3x + y = -1$
    $-x + 2y = 12$

32. $3x + 2y = -11$
    $4x - 3y = 8$

33. $-x + 5y = 1$
    $3x - 8y = 4$

34. Find the inverse of matrix A, where $n \neq 0$.

$$A = \begin{bmatrix} n & 0 & 0 \\ 0 & n & 0 \\ 0 & 0 & n \end{bmatrix}$$

35. A diner sells three different breakfast platters. Find the cost of one pancake, the cost of one egg, and the cost of one sausage link.

Breakfast Platters

RISE 'N SHINE	STOMACH GROWLER	BREAKFAST BONANZA
2 pancakes, 1 egg, 1 sausage link	3 pancakes, 1 egg, 2 sausage links	4 pancakes, 3 eggs, 3 sausage links
$6.50	$10	$15

11 PERFORMANCE TASK
SMP.2 SMP.4

Food Webs

A food web is a visual representation of the food chains in an ecosystem. A partial food web for an ecosystem is shown.

Arrows represent the flow of energy.
- Monkeys eat insects, so an arrow indicates that energy flows from insects to monkeys.

A food web shows **direct** and **indirect** food sources.
- Eagles eat parrots. So, parrots are a direct food source for eagles.
- Pythons eat chimpanzees, and chimpanzees eat insects. So, insects are an indirect food source (through one intermediary) for pythons.

Analyzing Data

Use the information on the previous page to complete the following exercises.

Explain what is shown in the display. What do you notice? What do you wonder?

The food web below shows the relationships among chimpanzees, insects, and monkeys in the region described on the previous page. These relationships are also represented in matrix A. Explain how the matrix is related to the food web.

$$A = \begin{array}{c} \\ C \\ I \\ M \end{array} \begin{array}{c} \begin{array}{ccc} C & I & M \end{array} \\ \left[\begin{array}{ccc} 0 & 1 & 1 \\ 0 & 1 & 0 \\ 0 & 1 & 0 \end{array} \right] \end{array}$$

Find and interpret A^2 in the matrix in Exercise 2.

IDENTIFYING FOOD SOURCES

Local government officials plan to use an insecticide to drastically reduce the insect population. Create a matrix B to represent the entire food web on the previous page. Then find and interpret B^2 and B^3. Use the matrices to explain the potential impact of this plan. (*Hint*: Make sure the animals represented by the rows and columns of your matrix are listed in the same order.)

Connecting Big Ideas

For use after Chapter 11.
SMP.2

WORLD POPULATION

1 Gumball
20 million people

Births per Year
≈ 140 million

World Population
≈ 8 billion

Deaths per Year
≈ 60 million

Past Historic Population
≈ 117 billion

 What do you notice? What do you wonder?

About what percent of the *total* historic population is alive today?

 What method of data collection do you think was used to determine the numbers of births and deaths per year?

Write an explicit rule and a recursive rule to represent the world population over time, assuming the birth rate and death rate remain constant.

 Estimate the total historic population in 100 years.

THINKING ABOUT THE BIG IDEAS

How can you **Use Sequences and Series** to model how the total historic population changes over time?

Connecting Big Ideas

Selected Answers

Chapter 1
Getting Ready for Chapter 1
1. 47
2. −46
3. $3\frac{3}{5}$
4. 4
5. 13
6. 0
7.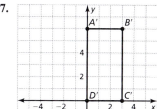
8.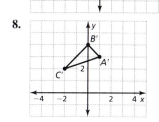

1.1 Practice
1. absolute value; The graph is a vertical stretch with a translation 2 units left and 8 units down; The domain of each function is all real numbers, but the range of f is $y \geq -8$, and the range of the parent function is $y \geq 0$.
3. linear; The graph is a vertical stretch and a translation 2 units down; The domain and range of each function is all real numbers.
5. 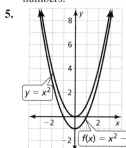 ; The graph of f is a vertical translation 1 unit down of the graph of the parent quadratic function.
7. 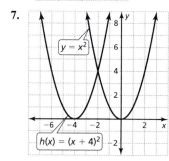 ; The graph of h is a horizontal translation 4 units left of the graph of the parent quadratic function.
9. 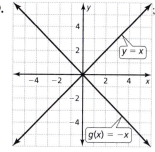 ; The graph of g is a reflection in the x-axis of the graph of the parent linear function.
11. The graph of g is a horizontal translation 3 units left of the graph of f, not 3 units right.
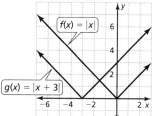
13. 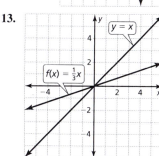 ; The graph of f is a vertical shrink by a factor of $\frac{1}{3}$ of the graph of the parent linear function.
15. 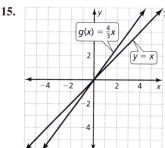 ; The graph of g is a vertical stretch by a factor of $\frac{4}{3}$ of the graph of the parent linear function.
17. 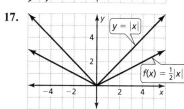 ; The graph of f is a vertical shrink by the factor of $\frac{1}{2}$ of the graph of the parent absolute value function.
19. 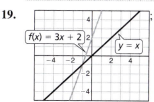 ; The graph of f is a vertical stretch by a factor of 3 followed by a translation 2 units up of the graph of the parent linear function.

21. 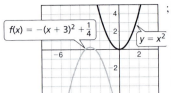 ; The graph of f is a reflection in the x-axis followed by a translation 3 units left and $\frac{1}{4}$ unit up of the graph of the parent quadratic function.

23. $A'(-1, -3), B'(1, -3), C'(-1, -1), D'(-3, -1)$

25. a. Sample answer: $y = \begin{cases} 2x + 10, & \text{if } 0 \leq x \leq 2 \\ -6x + 26, & \text{if } 2 < x \leq 3 \\ 8, & 3 < x \leq 5 \\ 4x - 12, & x > 5 \end{cases}$

piecewise function

b. yes; The arrow at the end of the last piece on the graph means that portion continues into the future.

c. $1,000; The graph would be a vertical translation 10 units up.

27. a. 1 **b.** 2 **c.** −1 **d.** 0

For part (c), the value −1 is the only value that makes the graph intersect the x-axis. The graph intersects the x-axis at $x = -1$ and $x = 1$.

For part (d), the value 0 is the only value that makes the graph intersect the x-axis, and it intersects the x-axis at all points.

For part (a), the values −1 and 1 make the graph intersect the x-axis. Because −1 was used for part (c), use 1 which makes the graph intersect the x-axis at $x = \frac{1}{3}$.

For part (b), the values 0, 1, and 2 make the graph intersect the x-axis. Because 0 was used for part (d) and 1 was used for part (a), use 2 which makes the graph intersect the x-axis at $x = 2$ and $x = 4$.

29. Sample answer: quadratic

1.1 Review & Refresh

30. yes
31. x-intercept: −2; y-intercept: 2
32. x-intercept: 8; y-intercept: −4
33. 6 **34.** no
35. $160\pi \approx 502.65$ in.^{3} **36.** $18\pi \approx 56.55$ cm^3
37. $(x - 6)(x + 5)$ **38.** $3(x + 1)(x + 4)$
39. Lines a and b are perpendicular.

1.2 Practice

1. $g(x) = x - 1$ **3.** $g(x) = |4x + 3|$
5. f could be translated 3 units up or 3 units right.
7. $g(x) = 5x - 2$ **9.** $g(x) = -3 + |x + 11|$
11. $g(x) = 5x + 10$ **13.** $g(x) = |\frac{1}{4}x + 3|$
15. A **17.** B
19. $g(x) = |\frac{1}{2}x - 2|$ **21.** $g(x) = |x - 3|$
23. $21.56
25. The graph has been reflected in the x-axis; 16 square units
27. The graph is decreasing from about 30.5° to 33.5°, and then increases from about 33.5° to 34.6°; The incubation period decreases as the average nest temperature increases.

1.2 Review & Refresh

29. 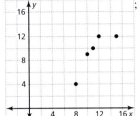 ; positive linear correlation

30. a.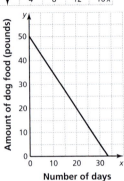

domain: $0 \leq x \leq 33\frac{1}{3}$, range: $0 \leq y \leq 50$

b. The slope of −1.5 represents a decrease of 1.5 pounds of dog food each day. The y-intercept of 50 means that the initial amount of dog food in the bag is 50 pounds, and the x-intercept of $33\frac{1}{3}$ means after $33\frac{1}{3}$ days the bag is empty.

31. $(-1, 6)$
32. quadratic; The graph is a vertical stretch by a factor of 2 followed by a translation 1 unit left of the parent quadratic function.

1.3 Practice

1. $y = \frac{1}{5}x$; The tip increases $0.20 for each dollar spent on the meal.
3. $y = 50x + 100$; The balance increases $50 each week.
5. Carrier A; 10 months
7. yes; Sample answer: $y = 4.25x + 1.75$; 65.5 calories
9. $y = 723.3x + 21,538$; The average annual tuition and fees is increasing by about $723 each year since 2009-2010 academic year when it was about $21,538; $32,388
11. a–b. Check students' work.
13. For the location where the price was $1.70, the supply was less than the demand. For the location where the price was $0.60, the supply was greater than the demand.

1.3 Review & Refresh

14. 17 **15.** infinitely many solutions
16. $(2, -2)$
17. $y < -2x + 1, y \geq \frac{1}{3}x - 2$
18. $x = \frac{1}{2}z - 2y - 4$ **19.** 56%
20. $5x^2 - 5x - 2$ **21.** $-5n^3 - 5n^2 - 16n + 13$
22. $g(x) = 2x + 4$ **23.** $g(x) = -\frac{3}{2}|x - 4|$

1.4 Practice

1. no solution **3.** one solution
5. $(1, 2, -1)$ **7.** no solution
9. $(x, 1, x + 1)$ or $(z - 1, 1, z)$

11. $\left(x, \dfrac{-x+1}{2}, \dfrac{x-9}{2}\right)$ or $(-2y+1, y, -y-4)$ or $(2z+9, -z-4, z)$

13. The entire first equation should be multiplied by 3, not just the left side; $15x + 2z = -10$

15. $(4, -3, 2)$

17. $\left(x, \dfrac{13}{3}x, \dfrac{-5x+3}{3}\right)$ or $\left(\dfrac{3}{13}y, y, \dfrac{-5y-13}{13}\right)$ or $\left(\dfrac{-3z+3}{5}, \dfrac{-13z+13}{5}, z\right)$

19. $\ell + m + n = 65$, $n = \ell + m - 15$, $\ell = \tfrac{1}{3}m$; $\ell = 10$ ft, $m = 30$ ft, $n = 25$ ft

21. a. Sample answer: $a = -1, b = -1, c = -1$
   b. Sample answer: $a = 4, b = 4, c = 5$
   c. Sample answer: $a = 5, b = 5, c = 5$

23. 5 tangerines; Sample answer: Using the scales, you can write the following system.
$t + a = g$
$t + b = a$
$2g = 3b$
You can rewrite Equation 3 as $b = \tfrac{2}{3}g$. Substitute this into Equation 2 and then add Equation 1 to this to get $t = \tfrac{1}{6}g$. Substituting this into Equation 1 produces $a = \tfrac{5}{6}g$. So, $5t = \tfrac{5}{6}g = a$, which means 5 tangerines have the same weight as an apple.

1.4 Review & Refresh

25. $g(x) = |x+2| - 5$ **26.** $g(x) = 3|x| - 15$
27. $x^2 - 4x + 4$ **28.** $9m^2 + 6m + 1$
29. $x = 39$
30. $w > -21$
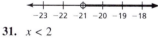
31. $x < 2$

32. $-\tfrac{5}{2} < h < -\tfrac{1}{2}$
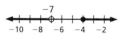
33. $t < -7$ or $t \geq -4$

34. linear; 13,800 mi **35.** $x = 2.5$
36. Check students' work.
37. $\dfrac{1}{b^3}$ **38.** $64c^6$

Chapter 1 Review

1. 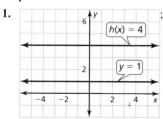 ; The graph of h is a vertical translation 3 units up of the graph of the parent constant function.

2. 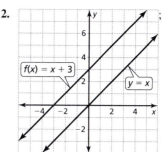 ; The graph of f is a vertical translation 3 units up of the graph of the parent linear function.

3. 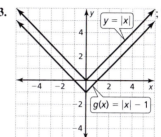 ; The graph of g is a vertical translation 1 unit down of the graph of the parent absolute value function.

4. 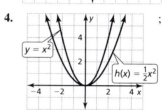 ; The graph of h is a vertical shrink by a factor of $\tfrac{1}{2}$ of the graph of the parent quadratic function.

5.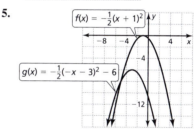

6. The graph of g is a horizontal translation 2 units left and a vertical translation 1 unit down of the graph of f.
7. linear; 570 mi **8.** $g(x) = 3x$
9. $g(x) = -|x+4|$ **10.** $g(x) = 3x + 1$
11. $g(x) = \tfrac{1}{2}|x+1| + 1$ **12.** $50
13. $y = 55x$; The distance traveled is 55 miles per hour.
14. $y = -20x + 700$; The hot air balloon descends 20 meters per minute.
15. Babysitter A; 8 h
16. yes; Sample answer: $y = 1.5x + 12$; 102 ice cream cones
17. $y = 3.5x + 223$; Sample answer: The slope of 3.5 means that the number of tickets sold at a movie theater increases by 3,500 each year. The y-intercept of 223 means that 223,000 tickets were sold initially; 265,000 tickets
18. no; Because 0.3 is closer to 0 than it is 1, the correlation is weak.
19. $(4, -2, 1)$ **20.** $\left(-\tfrac{4}{3}, -\tfrac{17}{3}, \tfrac{26}{3}\right)$
21. $\left(x, \dfrac{x-9}{4}, \dfrac{-5x+17}{4}\right)$ or $(9 + 4y, y, -7 - 5y)$ or $\left(\dfrac{-4z+17}{5}, \dfrac{-z-7}{5}, z\right)$
22. no solution **23.** $(-11, -8, 3)$
24. $(-16, 12, 10)$

25. 200 student tickets, 350 adult tickets, and 50 children under 12 tickets
26. Sample answer: $-2, -1, 1, 4, -4, 2$; $(x, 4x + 2, 6x)$
27. Party A candidate: 50 million votes, Party B candidate: 40 million votes, Other candidates: 10 million votes
28. no; It is possible for a point (x, y, z) to satisfy two equations but not the third.

Chapter 2
Getting Ready for Chapter 2
1. -3.6
2. 5
3. 8
4. $\sqrt{40}$
5. $\sqrt{5}$
6. 10

2.1 Practice
1. The graph of g is a translation 6 units left and 2 units down of the graph of f.

3. The graph of g is a translation 7 units right and 1 unit up of the graph of f.

5. A
7. C
9. The graph of g is a vertical stretch by a factor of 3 of the graph of f.

11. The graph of g is a horizontal shrink by a factor of $\frac{1}{2}$, followed by a reflection in the x-axis of the graph of f.

13. $g(x) = -4x^2 + 2$; $(0, 2)$
15. $h(x) = -0.03(x - 14)^2 + 10.99$
17. Sample answer: The graph of g is a horizontal stretch by a factor of $\sqrt{6}$ of the graph of f; about 1.67 ft
19. $g(x) = 2x^2 - 4$; $(0, -4)$
21. a vertical shrink by a factor of $\frac{7}{16}$
23. no

2.1 Review & Refresh
25. $(-6, 3, -5)$
26. $x > -7$
27. $8x^3(x - 5)$
28. $-27, -39, -51$
29. 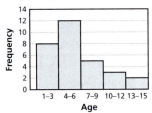 ; skewed right

30. $97
31. $\frac{5\sqrt{7}}{7}$

2.2 Practice
1.
3.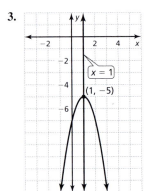
5. C
7. B
9.

11.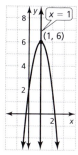

13. The formula is missing the negative sign; The x-coordinate of the vertex is
$x = -\dfrac{b}{2a} = -\dfrac{24}{2(4)} = -3.$

15. The maximum value is 2. The domain is all real numbers and the range is $y \leq 2$. The function is increasing when $x < -2$ and decreasing when $x > -2$.

17. The minimum value is -18. The domain is all real numbers and the range is $y \geq -18$. The function is decreasing when $x < 3$ and increasing when $x > 3$.

19. a. about 3,093 rev/min; about 74.68 ft-lbs
    b. The torque increases as the speed increases until the speed reaches about 3,093 revolutions per minute, then the torque begins to decrease.

21.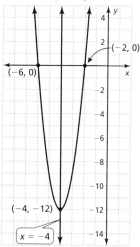

23.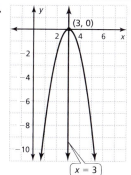

25. $A = w(20 - w) = -w^2 + 20w$; The maximum area is 100 square units.

27. You cannot use these points to find the axis of symmetry. You can only determine the axis of symmetry if the y-coordinates of the two points are the same, because the axis of symmetry would lie halfway between the two points.

29. 160 ft; about 1.5 ft   31. no

33. The y-intercept is apq.

35. $\dfrac{n^2}{16}$ ft²; The perimeter can be represented by $n = 2\ell + 2w$, so $\ell = \dfrac{n}{2} - w$. The area can then be represented by
$A(w) = \left(\dfrac{n}{2} - w\right)w = -w^2 + \dfrac{n}{2}w.$ So, the w-coordinate of the vertex is $-\dfrac{n}{2} \div 2(-1) = \dfrac{n}{4}$ and $A\left(\dfrac{n}{4}\right) = \dfrac{n^2}{16}.$

37. Sample answer: about 10 ft 4 in.

39. Sample answer: 53°; The ball is less likely to bounce off the rim when approaching from a steeper angle.

2.2 Review & Refresh

40. $x = 8$ 41. no solution

42. The graph is a vertical shrink by a factor of $\tfrac{1}{4}$, followed by a translation 2 units up of the parent quadratic function.

43. $(1.32, -1.72, 8.24)$ 44. $x = -25, x = 3$
45. 168 ft³   46. exponential decay; 14%
47. $-2 < n \leq 10$

2.3 Practice

1. $y = \tfrac{1}{4}x^2$

3. $x = -\tfrac{1}{28}y^2$ 5. $y = -\tfrac{3}{32}x^2$

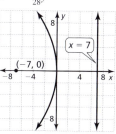   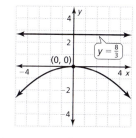

7. $y = -\tfrac{1}{36}(x - 2)^2 + 3$ 9. $x = (y + 1)^2 + 1$

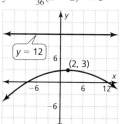   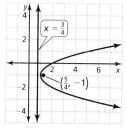

11. The vertex is (3, 2). The focus is (3, 4). The directrix is $y = 0$. The axis of symmetry is $x = 3$. The graph is a vertical shrink by a factor of $\tfrac{1}{2}$, followed by a translation 3 units right and 2 units up.

13. $y = \tfrac{1}{32}x^2$

15. $y = \tfrac{1}{6.8}x^2$; The domain is $-2.9 \leq x \leq 2.9$, and the range is $0 \leq y \leq \tfrac{841}{680}$; The domain represents the width of the trough, and the range represents the depth of the trough.

17. a. B is the vertex, C is the focus, and A is a point on the directrix.
    b. The focus and directrix will both be shifted down 3 units.

19. Check students' work.

21. It is 2,205 feet above the vertex.

2.3 Review & Refresh

23. $y = -2x + 6$

24. Compared to h, the average rate of change of g over the interval $0 \le x \le 3$ is $1 \div \frac{\sqrt[3]{9/2}}{3} \approx 1.8$ times greater.
25. when $x > -3$; when $x < -3$
26. nonlinear
27. $x = 7$
28. 3 one-point free throws, 5 two-point shots, and 3 three-point shots
29.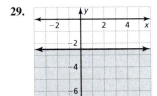

2.4 Practice

1. $y = -3(x + 2)^2 + 6$
3. $y = 0.06(x - 3)^2 + 2$
5. $y = -4(x - 2)(x - 4)$
7. $y = \frac{1}{10}(x - 12)(x + 6)$
9. The x-intercepts were substituted incorrectly.
   $y = a(x - p)(x - q)$
   $4 = a(3 + 1)(3 - 2)$
   $a = 1$
   $y = (x + 1)(x - 2)$
11. $S(C) = 180C^2$; 18,000 lb
13. $y = 0.026x^2 - 0.02x + 1.6$; about 27,600 users
15. The number of tiles in each figure is 1, 5, 11, and 19, which have constant second differences of 2; 155 tiles
17. *Sample answer:* The data shows an increase in efficiency from 0°C to about 13°C, then efficiency decreases as temperatures continue to increase.
19. about 13°C

2.4 Review & Refresh

20. yes
21.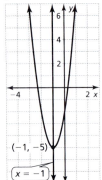
22. $m \ge 4$

23. $n > 21$
24. $p > 2$
25. $q \ge -12$
26. $3(x - 4)(x - 1)$

27. The focus is $(-3, 0)$, the directrix is $x = 3$, and the axis of symmetry is the x-axis.
    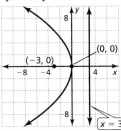
28. The focus is $(0, 4)$, the directrix is $y = -4$, and the axis of symmetry is the y-axis.
    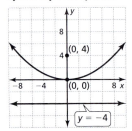
29. exponential
30. $y = \frac{3}{2}x + \frac{5}{2}$

Chapter 2 Review

1. The graph is a translation 4 units left of the parent quadratic function.
   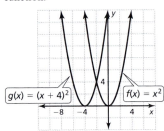
2. The graph is a vertical shrink by a factor of $\frac{1}{5}$ and a reflection in the x-axis of the graph of f.
   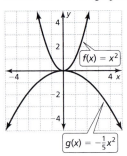
3. The graph is a translation 7 units right and 2 units up of the parent quadratic function.
   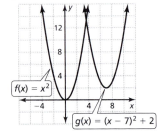

4. The graph is a vertical stretch by a factor of 3, followed by a reflection in the x-axis and a translation 2 units left and 1 unit down of the parent quadratic function.

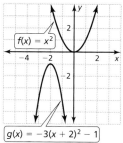

5. a. h is negative. k is zero.
   b. h is positive. k is negative.
   c. h is zero. k is negative.
   d. h is positive. k is positive.

6. $y = -\frac{2}{75}(x - 30)^2 + 24$

7. The minimum value is -8; The function is decreasing when $x < -5$ and increasing when $x > -5$.

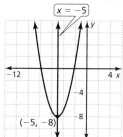

8. The minimum value is -4; The function is decreasing when $x < 1$ and increasing when $x > 1$.

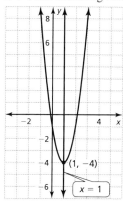

9. The maximum value is 35; The function is increasing when $x < 4$ and decreasing when $x > 4$.

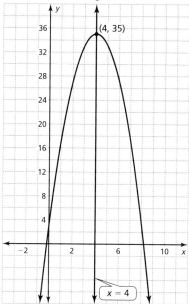

10. The minimum value is -25; The function is decreasing when $x < -2$ and increasing when $x > -2$.

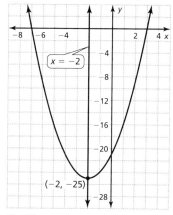

11. $(4, 13)$
12. Sample answer: $y = x^2 + 10x + 3$
13. the first kick; the second kick
14. $x = -\frac{1}{8}y^2$
15. $y = -\frac{1}{16}(x - 2)^2 + 6$
16. The focus is $(0, 9)$, the directrix is $y = -9$, and the axis of symmetry is $x = 0$.

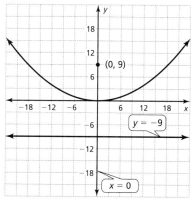

Selected Answers A7

17. The focus is $(-2, 0)$, the directrix is $x = 2$, and the axis of symmetry is $y = 0$.

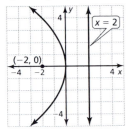

18. $y = \frac{1}{4}(x - 2)^2 - 4$
19. The microphone is $1\frac{5}{6}$ inches below the opening of the parabolic dish.
20. $y = \frac{16}{81}(x - 10)^2 - 4$ 21. $y = -\frac{3}{5}(x + 1)(x - 5)$
22. $y = 4x^2 + 5x + 1$
23. a. $y = -\frac{1}{640}(x - 80)^2 + 30$
    b. 20 ft
24. The y-values have constant second differences of -8; $y = -16x^2 + 150$; about 3.06 sec
25. a. $0.045x^2 + 2.4x + 1$
    b. about 200 ft

Chapter 3
Getting Ready for Chapter 3

1. $3\sqrt{3}$ 2. $-4\sqrt{7}$ 3. $\frac{\sqrt{11}}{8}$
4. $\frac{3\sqrt{2}}{7}$ 5. $-\frac{\sqrt{65}}{11}$ 6. $-4\sqrt{5}$
7. $(x - 6)(x + 6)$ 8. $(x - 3)(x + 3)$
9. $(2x - 5)(2x + 5)$ 10. $(x - 11)^2$
11. $(x + 14)^2$ 12. $(7x + 15)^2$

3.1 Practice

1. $x = -1$ and $x = -2$ 3. $x = 1$
5. $z = 1$ and $z = 11$ 7. $x = -2 \pm \frac{\sqrt{26}}{2}$
9. The square of a real number cannot be -4; The equation has no real solution.
11. $x = 6$ and $x = 2$ 13. $p = -4$ and $p = \frac{1}{3}$
15. no real solution   17. $x = -1.5$ and $x = 1.5$
19. $x = -2$ and $x = -4$ 21. $x = -7$ and $x = -12$
23. $x = -\frac{1}{2}$ and $x = \frac{4}{5}$ 25. $5.75; 1,983.75
27. a. $h(t) = -16t^2 + 196$; $-16t^2$ represents the change in height (in feet) of the rock after t seconds and 196 represents the initial height (in feet) of the rock; 3.5 sec
    b. -75; The rock falls 75 feet between 1.25 seconds and 2.5 seconds.
29. $x = 3$
31. a. 36 ft   b. 1.5 sec
33. 0.5 ft or 6 in.

35.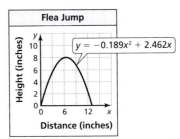

The vertex is approximately (6.5, 8.0) and indicates that the flea's maximum jump height of about 8 inches occurs about 6.5 inches away from the starting point. The zeros $x \approx 13$ and $x = 0$ mean flea jumped a horizontal distance of about 13 inches.

37. 7 ft
39. a. positive   b. yes
41. Sample answer: $x^4 - 5x^2 + 4 = 0$; Factor the trinomial as $(x^2 - 1)(x^2 - 4) = 0$. Then factor the differences of squares as $(x + 1)(x - 1)(x + 2)(x - 2) = 0$. Set each factor equal to 0 and solve for x.
43. $x = -1$
45. Sample answer: nose of an airplane, parabolic antenna

3.1 Review & Refresh

46. $-3x^3 + 7x^2 - 15x + 9$ 47. $y = -\frac{1}{3}(x + 3)^2 - 2$
48. $-44x^3 + 33x^2 + 88x$
49. $|n - 3| > 9$; $n < -6$ or $n > 12$
50. a.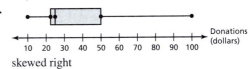

    skewed right
    b. yes; $100 is an outlier.
51. maximum: 10; domain: all real numbers; range: $y \leq 10$; increasing: $x < -2$; decreasing: $x > -2$.

3.2 Practice

1. $3i\sqrt{2}$ 3. $-21i$
5. $x = -2$ and $y = 4$ 7. $x = -4$ and $y = -3$
9. $9 + 11i$ 11. $-2 - 20i$
13. a. $-4 + 5i$ b. $2\sqrt{2} + 10i$
15. $14 - 5i$ 17. $-27 - 36i$
19. i^2 can be simplified; $17 + 7i$
21. 20   23. 82
25. $2i(-5 + 9i) = -18 - 10i$ 27. $(12 + 2i)$ ohms
29. $(14 - i)$ ohms   31. $x = \pm i\sqrt{7}$
33. $x = \pm 3i\sqrt{6}$ 35. $x = \pm 6i$
37. $x = \pm 4i\sqrt{3}$
39. Method 1 distributes $4i$ to each term, then simplifies. Method 2 factors $4i$ out of each term, combines like terms, and then distributed $4i$ to each term and simplifies; Check students' work.
41. f and g; h; Functions f and g have real zeros because their graphs touch the x-axis. Function h has imaginary zeros because its graph does not touch the x-axis.
43. no; $\sqrt{a}\sqrt{b} = \sqrt{ab}$ only for $a \geq 0$ and $b \geq 0$.
45. $\frac{\sqrt{2}}{2} + \frac{\sqrt{2}}{2}i$ 47. Sample answer: π

3.2 Review & Refresh

49. 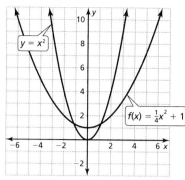 ; The graph of f is a vertical shrink by a factor of $\frac{1}{4}$, followed by a vertical translation 1 unit up of the graph of the parent quadratic function.

50. 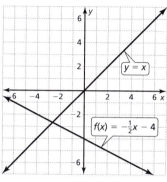 ; The graph of f is a reflection in the x-axis, followed by a vertical shrink by a factor of $\frac{1}{2}$ and a vertical translation 4 units down of the graph of the parent linear function.

51. $y = -\frac{1}{8}x^2$ **52.** $x = \frac{1}{12}(y+4)^2 + 5$

53. 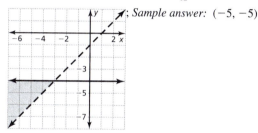 ; Sample answer: $(-5, -5)$

54. $x > -2$ **55.** $x \leq 9$ **56.** $x = 5$

3.3 Practice

1. $x^2 + 10x + 25$; $(x+5)^2$ **3.** $x^2 + 9x + \frac{81}{4}$; $\left(x + \frac{9}{2}\right)^2$

5. The added value should have been squared to complete the square; $x^2 + 30x + 225$

7. 36; $(x+6)^2$ **9.** $x = -3 \pm \sqrt{6}$

11. $r = \dfrac{-1 \pm i\sqrt{7}}{2}$ **13.** $s = -1 \pm i\sqrt{2}$

15. $y = (x-4)^2 + 3$; $(4, 3)$

17. $f(x) = 2(x-2)^2 - 21$; $(2, -21)$

19. $y = \frac{1}{8}(x+1)^2 + 9$; parabola

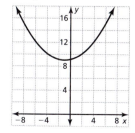

21. $x = -\frac{1}{20}(y+5)^2 + 2$; parabola

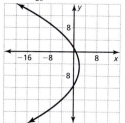

23. $(x+9)^2 + y^2 = 100$; circle

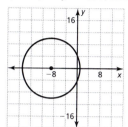

25. a. 17 ft   **b.** $\dfrac{\sqrt{17}}{4} + 1 \approx 2$ sec

27. $x = -3 + \sqrt{57}$ **29.** $x = -1 + \sqrt{11}$

31. $x^2 + 2hx$

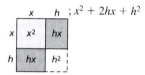 ; $x^2 + 2hx + h^2$

33. a. Sample answer: $g(x) = x^2 + 4x + 1$; The graph of g is a vertical shrink of the graph of f, and vertical shrinks do not affect the x-intercepts.

b. $x = -2 \pm \sqrt{3}$; Sample answer:

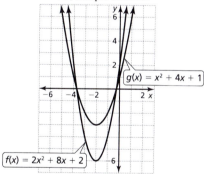

35. $x = \dfrac{-b \pm \sqrt{b^2 - 4c}}{2}$; the Quadratic Formula when $a = 1$

37. a–b. Check students' work.

39.

As the ball travels up and to the right at point A, air resistance pushes down and to the left. As the ball travels to the right at point B, air resistance pushes to the left. As the ball travels down and to the right at point C, air resistance pushes up and to the left.

3.3 Review & Refresh
41. $x < 4$
42. $y \leq -1$
43. $n > -15$
44. $s \geq -20$
45. absolute value; The graph of g is a translation 1 unit left and 2 units down of the graph of the parent absolute value function.
46. $-2 + 8i$
47. $2 + 16i$
48. $14 - 22i$
49. $m = -\frac{3}{2}; m = \frac{2}{3}$
50. $y = 5x^2 - 2x + 6$

3.4 Practice
1. $x = 3$ and $x = 1$
3. $x = 7$
5. $x = \dfrac{-1 \pm i\sqrt{14}}{3}$
7. $x = \dfrac{3 \pm \sqrt{89}}{8}$
9. $w = \dfrac{7 \pm i\sqrt{47}}{8}$
11. 0; one real solution
13. -135; two imaginary solutions
15. -47; two imaginary solutions
17. D
19. B
21. Sample answer: $a = 1$ and $c = 5$; $x^2 + 4x + 5 = 0$
23. Sample answer: $a = 2$ and $c = 4$; $2x^2 - 8x + 4 = 0$
25. yes; no
27. Sample answer: $-5x^2 + 8x - 12 = 0$
29. $x = \pm 2\sqrt{2}$; Check students' work.
31. $x = \dfrac{-1 \pm 3i}{4}$; Check students' work.
33. $x = 6$
35. Sample answer: $a = \frac{13}{2}, c = \frac{13}{2}; \frac{13}{2}x^2 - 13x + \frac{13}{2} = 0$
37. a. about 0.97 sec b. the first bird
39. a. 2009
    b. The average rate of change is -2.5. So, between the years 2005 and 2020, the amount of nuclear energy decreased by about 2.5 billion kilowatt hours each year.
    c. no; According to the model, the amount of nuclear energy generated in 2040 would be about the same as the amount of nuclear energy generated in 1981, which is unlikely.
41. Add the solutions from the Quadratic Formula to get $\dfrac{-b}{a}$. Then divide the result by 2 to get $-\dfrac{b}{2a}$; Because the graph is symmetric, the vertex of a parabola is halfway between the two x-intercepts and the x-coordinate of the vertex is $-\dfrac{b}{2a}$.
43. yes; $x = \pm\frac{1}{2}, x = \pm 3i$
45. Check students' work.

3.4 Review & Refresh
46. $x = -2 \pm 2i$
47. $(4, 5)$
48. $x = 2$ and $x = -4$
49. $x = 2$ and $y = -6$
50. $-1.5 < x \leq 2.5$
51. $x = 2, x = 3$
52. 20%

3.5 Practice
1. $(0, 2)$ and $(-2, 0)$
3. no real solution
5. no real solution
7. $(4, -2)$
9. $(2, 1)$ and $(-1, -2)$
11. no real solution
13. The terms $2x^2$ and $-x$ were added, but they are not like terms; $x = -4$ or $x = \frac{9}{2}$
15. $x = 0$
17. $x = -3$ and $x = -5$
19. When the graphs intersect at a point (a, b), then $b = f(a)$ and $b = g(a)$, so $f(x) = g(x)$ when $x = a$.
21. Sample answers:
    a. $m = 1$
    b. $m = 0$
    c. $m = -1$

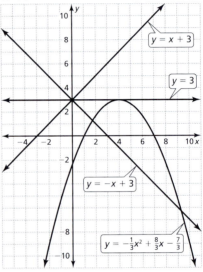

23. a. $(0, -1)$; The y-intercept of each line is one unit away from the center of the circle, which has a radius of one.
    b. System A: $\left(\frac{3}{5}, \frac{4}{5}\right)$, System B: $\left(\frac{8}{17}, \frac{15}{17}\right)$, System C: $\left(\frac{5}{13}, \frac{12}{13}\right)$; The two numbers in the numerator and the number in the denominator form a Pythagorean Triple.
25. $\sqrt{2} \approx 1.41$ mi; Oak Lane can be represented by $y = -\frac{1}{7}x + \frac{5}{7}$ and the area in which a student can live and not be eligible for a parking pass can be represented by $x^2 + y^2 = 1$. The graphs of these equations intersect at $(-0.6, 0.8)$ and $(0.8, 0.6)$, and the distance between these points is $\sqrt{2}$.
27. $14.50; $22

3.5 Review & Refresh
29. $y \geq -x + 1$
30. $y < x - 2$
31. [graph]; domain: all real numbers, range: $y > 1$
32. no

33. The graph of g is a translation 5 units right and 3 units down of the graph of f.

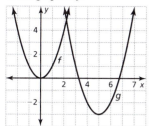

34. The graph of g is a vertical stretch by a factor of $\frac{1}{4}$ and a translation 2 units left of the graph of f.

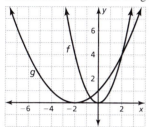

35. ±18

36. $y = -1.0x + 19$; $r = -0.9915$ indicates that there is a strong negative correlation and the equation closely models the data.

3.6 Practice

1.

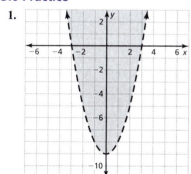

3.

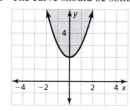

5. The curve should be solid, not dashed.

7.

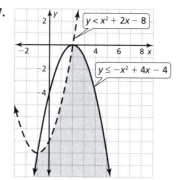

9.

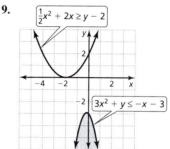

11. $x \leq 4$ or $x \geq 7$ **13.** $x < -2$ or $x > 4$

15. $0.382 < x < 2.618$

17. at least 70 ft and at most 130 ft

19. a. $x_1 < x < x_2$, $x < x_1$ or $x > x_2$
b. $x_1 < x < x_2$

21. a. $\frac{32}{3} \approx 10.67$ square units
b. $\frac{256}{3} \approx 85.33$ square units

23. a. Sample answer: (2, 0) and (3, 1)
b. no
c. no; Because both points are points of intersection, they are either both solutions or both not solutions.

25. Check students' work; Yes, the shape approximates the curve of a parabola.

3.6 Review & Refresh

27. $(-1, -2)$ and $(1, 2)$ **28.** $\left(\frac{114}{89}, -\frac{286}{89}, \frac{398}{89}\right)$

29. $y = -3x + 4$ **30.** $a_n = 2(3)^n$; $a_8 = 13{,}122$

31. a. The cost of renting the pavilion is $30 per hour with an initial fee of $50.
b. $0 < x \leq 24$; The domain is continuous.

Chapter 3 Review

1. $x = \pm 5$ **2.** $x = \pm 2$
3. $x = 2$ and $x = -8$ **4.** $x = 6$ and $x = 2.5$
5. $h(t) = -16t^2 + 3$; about 0.43 sec
6. a. yes **b.** no
    c. no **d.** yes
7. length: 45 ft, width: 28 ft **8.** $x = 9$ and $y = -3$
9. $5 - 3i$ **10.** $11 + 10i$
11. $-62 + 11i$ **12.** 68
13. $(7 + 3i)$ ohms **14.** $x = \pm i\sqrt{3}$
15. $x = \pm 4i$ **16.** $x = -8 \pm \sqrt{47}$
17. $x = 3 \pm 3\sqrt{2}$

18. $x = (y + 6)^2 + 4$; parabola

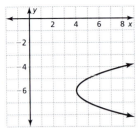

19. $(x - 1)^2 + (y + 4)^2 = 81$; circle

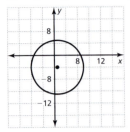

20. $y = (x - 1)^2 + 19$; $(1, 19)$

21. 94 ft **22.** $x = \dfrac{5 \pm \sqrt{17}}{2}$

23. $x = 0.5$ and $x = -3$ **24.** $x = \dfrac{3}{2}$

25. $x = \dfrac{6 \pm i\sqrt{3}}{3}$ **26.** 0; one real solution

27. 40; two real solutions
28. Sample answer: $a = 6, c = 6$
29. about 929 m and about 2,046 m
30. $(-4, 1)$ **31.** $(1, 4)$ and $(9, 4)$
32. $(-2, 6)$ and $(1, 0)$ **33.** $(4, 5)$
34. $x \approx -0.14$ and $x \approx 1.77$ **35.** $x = 0$ and $x = \dfrac{9}{2}$

36.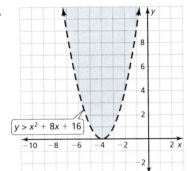

37.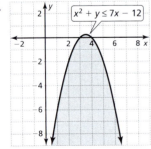

38.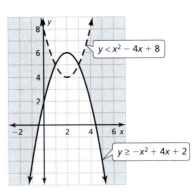

39.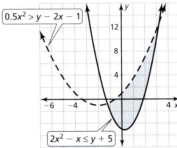

40. $x \leq -5$ or $x \geq 4$ **41.** $\dfrac{2}{3} \leq x \leq 1$

42. a. $>$ or $\geq$; $4(-1)^2 - 3(-1) > (-1) + 6$, $7 > 5$
   b. $<$ or $\leq$; $4(1)^2 - 3(1) < (-4) + 6$, $1 < 2$
   c. $\geq$ or $\leq$; $4(2)^2 - 3(2) \geq (4) + 6$, $10 \geq 10$; $4(2)^2 - 3(2) \leq (4) + 6$, $10 \leq 10$

Chapter 4

Getting Ready for Chapter 4

1. $x + 4$ **2.** $z - 4$ **3.** $5x$
4. $6x^2 + 4x + 5$ **5.** 64 in.^{3}
6. $\dfrac{32\pi}{3} \approx 33.51$ ft^3 **7.** 48 ft^3
8. $45\pi \approx 141.37$ cm^3

4.1 Practice

1. polynomial function; $f(x) = 5x^3 - 6x^2 - 3x + 2$; degree: 3 (cubic); leading coefficient: 5
3. not a polynomial function
5. $f(-4) = -192$ **7.** $h(-2) = -46$
9. The function is not in standard form so the wrong term was used to classify the function; f is a polynomial function. The degree is 5. The leading coefficient is 7. $f(x) \to -\infty$ as $x \to -\infty$. $f(x) \to +\infty$ as $x \to +\infty$.
11. $f(x) \to +\infty$ as $x \to -\infty$ and $f(x) \to +\infty$ as $x \to +\infty$
13. $f(x) \to +\infty$ as $x \to -\infty$ and $f(x) \to -\infty$ as $x \to +\infty$
15.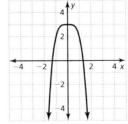

17.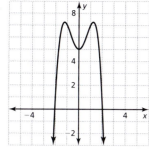

19. a. $x < -1$ and $x > 1$
   b. $-1 < x < 1$
   c. $x > 2$
   d. $x < -1$ and $-1 < x < 2$

21. 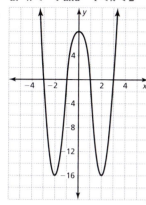; The degree is even and the leading coefficient is positive.

23. a. 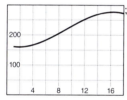; The number of tigers decreases slightly from Year 1 to Year 2, increases from Year 2 to Year 16, and decreases from Year 16 to Year 18.
   b. about 7 tigers per year
   c. no; Eventually the number of tigers becomes negative.

25. -480; Substituting the two given points into the function $f(x) = 2x^3 + bx^2 + cx - 5$ results in the system of equations $2 + b + c - 5 = 0$ and $16 + 4b + 2c - 5 = 3$. Solving for b and c gives $f(x) = 2x^3 - 7x^2 + 10x - 5$, and $f(-5) = -480$.

27. no; Eventually the number of sea otter strandings becomes negative.

4.1 Review & Refresh

29. $12kz - 4kw$
30. $g(x) = -|x - 2| - 1$
31. $-\frac{1}{2} \leq x \leq 4$
32. $\frac{5 - \sqrt{37}}{6} < x < \frac{5 + \sqrt{37}}{6}$

33. The graph of g is a horizontal translation 5 units left of the graph of f.

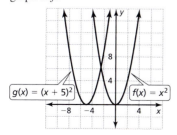

34. The graph of g is a vertical stretch by a factor of $\frac{3}{2}$ and a reflection in the x-axis of the graph of f.

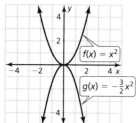

35. yes
36. $x < -3$ or $x > 12$

4.2 Practice

1. $x^2 + x + 1$
3. $12x^5 + 5x^4 - 3x^3 + 6x - 4$
5. $-2x^3 - 14x^2 + 7x - 4$
7. $-10x^5 + 8x^4 - 7x^3 - 20x^2 - x + 18$
9. The negative was not distributed through the entire second polynomial; $= -x^3 + x^2 - 10x + 6$
11. $-44x^8 - 8x^7 - 36x^6 - 4x^5$
13. $x^4 - 5x^3 - 3x^2 + 22x + 20$
15. $4x^6 - 8x^5 + 10x^4 - 8x^3 - 38x^2 - 8x$
17. $12x^3 - 29x^2 + 7x + 6$
19. $30x^3 - 19x^2 - 14x + 8$
21. $(a + b)(a - b) = a^2 - ab + ab - b^2$
$= a^2 - b^2$
23. $x^2 - 81$
25. $8k^3 + 72k^2 + 216k + 216$
27. $p^3q^3 - 6p^2q^2 + 12pq - 8$
29. $36m^2 + 24m + 4$
31. $16q^4 - 96q^3 + 216q^2 - 216q + 81$
33. $y^5z^5 + 5y^4z^4 + 10y^3z^3 + 10y^2z^2 + 5yz + 1$
35. $2x^3 + 10x^2 + 14x + 6$
37. a. $5{,}000(1 + r)^3 + 1{,}000(1 + r)^2 + 4{,}000(1 + r)$
   b. $7{,}000r^3 + 25{,}000r^2 + 34{,}000r + 16{,}000$; 7,000 is the total amount of money that gained interest for three years, 25,000 is the total amount of money that gained interest for two years, 34,000 is the total amount of money that gained interest for one year, and 16,000 is the total amount of money invested.
39. a. $(x^2 - y^2)^2 + (2xy)^2 = x^4 - 2x^2y^2 + y^4 + 4x^2y^2$
$= x^4 + 2x^2y^2 + y^4$
$(x^2 + y^2)^2 = x^4 + 2x^2y^2 + y^4$
   b. The Pythagorean triple is 11, 60, and 61;
$(11)^2 + (60)^2 = (61)^2$
$121 + 3{,}600 = 3{,}721$
$3{,}721 = 3{,}721$
41. cube of a binomial

4.2 Review & Refresh

43. $x = -\frac{1}{24}y^2$
44. $f(x) \to +\infty$ as $x \to -\infty$ and $f(x) \to -\infty$ as $x \to +\infty$
45. $y = 0.25$
46.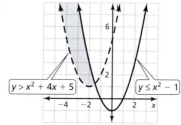
47. $9 - 2i$
48. 350 ft^2

4.3 Practice

1. $x + 1 + \dfrac{2x+3}{x^2-1}$
3. $2 + \dfrac{-2x^2 + x + 7}{4x^3 + x^2 - 2x - 3}$
5. $x^2 - 3x + 5 - \dfrac{9}{x+3}$
7. $3x^2 - 2x - 2 - \dfrac{4}{x-1}$
9. The quotient should be one degree less than the dividend and the remainder is written incorrectly;
$= x^2 + 2x - 1 + \dfrac{1}{x-2}$
11. $f(2) = 11$
13. $f(5) = -752$
15. no; The Remainder Theorem states that $f(a) = 25$.
17. $-0.525x^3 + 7.19x^2 - 29.8x + 213$

4.3 Review & Refresh

19. $10x\sqrt{3x}$
20. $y = -\frac{1}{4}(x+6)^2 - 3$
21. $64k^3 + 144k^2 + 108k + 27$
22.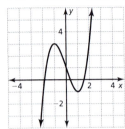
23. $x = -9$ and $x = -5$
24. at least 5 ft and at most 20 ft

4.4 Practice

1. $x(x-6)(x+4)$
3. $q^2(2q-3)(q+6)$
5. $(x+4)(x^2-4x+16)$
7. $4h^6(h-4)(h^2+4h+16)$
9. $x^2 + 9$ is not a factorable binomial because it is not the difference of two squares; $3x(x^2+9)$
11. $(y^2+6)(y-5)$
13. $(x-2)(x+2)(x-8)$
15. $(c^2+5)(c^2+4)$
17. $(2z-5)(2z+5)(4z^2+25)$
19. factor
21. not a factor
23.
$\begin{array}{r|rrrr} -4 & 1 & -1 & -20 & 0 \\ & & -4 & 20 & 0 \\ \hline & 1 & -5 & 0 & 0 \end{array}$
$g(x) = x(x+4)(x-5)$
25.
$\begin{array}{r|rrrrr} 6 & 1 & -6 & 0 & -8 & 48 \\ & & 6 & 0 & 0 & -48 \\ \hline & 1 & 0 & 0 & -8 & 0 \end{array}$
$f(x) = (x-6)(x-2)(x^2+2x+4)$
27. a. D   b. C
    c. A   d. B
29. $(c-d)(c+d)(7a+b)$
31. $(a^3-b^2)(ab+1)^2$
33. a. If the volume of the missing block is included, the volume of the diagram is a^3 because the length, width, and height are all a. Because the length, width, and height of the missing piece are b, the volume of the missing block is b^3. Subtracting the volume of the missing block from the entire volume gives $a^3 - b^3$.
    b. I: $a^2(a-b)$, II: $ab(a-b)$, III: $b^2(a-b)$
    c. $a^3 - b^3 = a^2(a-b) + ab(a-b) + b^2(a-b)$
    $= (a-b)(a^2+ab+b^2)$
35. The price of the stock increases from Week 0 to Week 13, decreases from Week 13 to Week 32, and increases for weeks after Week 32.

37. Find $g(25)$ by substitution or by synthetic division. If $g(25) = 0$, then $(x-25)$ is a factor; The weeks at which the price of the stock is $20.30

4.4 Review & Refresh

38. $-x^2 + 3x - 8$
39. area: $3x^2 + 7x + 3$; perimeter: $8x + 8$
40. polynomial function; $f(x) = -3x^4 - x^3 + 2x^2 - 2x + 5$; degree: 4 (quartic); leading coefficient: -3
41. exponential decay function
42.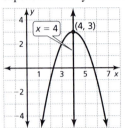
43.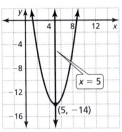
44.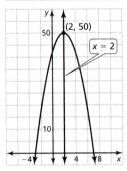
45. $n + 8.5 \leq 17$

4.5 Practice

1. $z = -3, z = 0,$ and $z = 4$
3. $v = -4, v = 2,$ and $v = 4$
5. $c = 0, c = 3,$ and $c = \pm\sqrt{6}$
7. $x = -3, x = 0,$ and $x = 2$
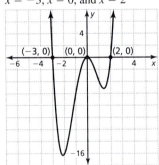
9. $x = -5, x = 0,$ and $x = 3$
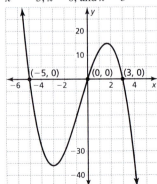

11. no; The graph crosses through the x-axis at each x-intercept.
13. $x = -5, x = 1,$ and $x = 3$ 15. $x = -1, x = 5,$ and $x = 6$
17. -1 and 2
19. $-4, 1.5,$ and 3
21. $1, \dfrac{-1 + \sqrt{17}}{2},$ and $\dfrac{-1 - \sqrt{17}}{2}$
23. $-\dfrac{3}{4}$ and $\dfrac{1}{2}$
25. The factors were listed as $\dfrac{q}{p}$ instead of $\dfrac{p}{q}$;
    $\pm 1, \pm 2, \pm 4, \pm 8, \pm \dfrac{1}{3}, \pm \dfrac{2}{3}, \pm \dfrac{4}{3}, \pm \dfrac{8}{3}$
27. $f(x) = x^3 - 10x - 12$
29. $f(x) = x^4 + 5x^3 - 33x^2 - 85x$
31. length: 8 ft, width: 4 ft, height: 4 ft
33. $k = 60$
35. $k = 6$
37. $10,849.20

4.5 Review & Refresh
39. $4b^2 - 9$
40. $25x^2 + 80x + 64$
41. $x^3 + 7x^2 + 11x + 5$
42. $y = -\dfrac{1}{2}x^2 + 3x + 8$
43. $f(x) = \left(x + \dfrac{7}{2}\right)^2 + \dfrac{3}{4}; \left(-\dfrac{7}{2}, \dfrac{3}{4}\right)$
44. $x = \pm 2i$
45. $x = 4 \pm \sqrt{30}$
46. 30 million grips
47. $y = \dfrac{1}{8}x^2 + 3$
48. $g(x) = -\dfrac{2}{3}x - 9$

4.6 Practice
1. $3; -5, -2,$ and 3
3. $5; 0, 0, 0, 1 - \dfrac{i\sqrt{2}}{2},$ and $1 + \dfrac{i\sqrt{2}}{2}$
5. $4; -1, 2, \dfrac{1}{2} - \dfrac{i\sqrt{3}}{2},$ and $\dfrac{1}{2} + \dfrac{i\sqrt{3}}{2}$
7. $-1, 1, 2,$ and 4
9. $-5, -2,$ and 2
11. $-4, -1, 2, i\sqrt{2},$ and $-i\sqrt{2}$
13. 2
15. 2
17. $f(x) = x^3 + 4x^2 - 7x - 10$
19. $f(x) = x^3 - 11x^2 + 41x - 51$
21. $f(x) = x^5 - 8x^4 + 23x^3 - 32x^2 + 22x - 4$
23. *Sample answer:* $y = x^6 - 4x^4 - x^2 + 4$
25. The conjugate of the given imaginary zero was not included; $f(x) = x^3 - 4x^2 + 6x - 4$

27.
Positive real zeros	Negative real zeros	Imaginary zeros	Total zeros
1	1	2	4

29.
Positive real zeros	Negative real zeros	Imaginary zeros	Total zeros
2	1	0	3
0	1	2	3

31.
Positive real zeros	Negative real zeros	Imaginary zeros	Total zeros
2	1	4	7
0	1	6	7

33. 5th year
35. $x \approx 4.2577$
37. no; The Fundamental Theorem of Algebra applies to functions of degree greater than zero. Because the function $f(x) = 2$ is equivalent to $f(x) = 2x^0$, it has degree 0, and does not fall under the Fundamental Theorem of Algebra.

39. a. If the function is of degree n, the sum of the zeros is equal to the opposite of the coefficient of the $(n-1)$th term.
    b. The product of the zeros is equal to the constant term of the polynomial function.

41. a.
Deposit	Year 1	Year 2	Year 3	Year 4
1st Deposit	1,000	$1,000g$	$1,000g^2$	$1,000g^3$
2nd Deposit	—	1,000	$1,000g$	$1,000g^2$
3rd Deposit	—	—	1,000	$1,000g$
4th Deposit	—	—	—	1,000

   b. about 4.84%

43. *Sample answer:* The number of registered motor vehicles per person in 1990 was about 0.76 vehicles and in 2020 was about 0.83 vehicles.

4.6 Review & Refresh
44. f
45. $1\dfrac{3}{5}$ cups of Solution A and $\dfrac{2}{5}$ cup of Solution B
46. $g(x) = -(x - 2)^2 + 7$
47. $2x + 5$

4.7 Practice
1. The graph of g is a translation 3 units up of the graph of f.

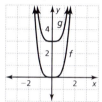

3. The graph of g is a translation 2 units right and 1 unit down of the graph of f.

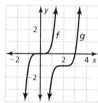

5. The graph of g is a vertical stretch by a factor of 5, followed by a translation 1 unit up of the graph of f.

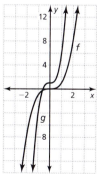

7. $g(x) = (x + 2)^4 + 1$

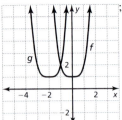

; The graph of g is a translation 2 units left of the graph of f.

9. $g(x) = -x^3 + x^2 - 3$

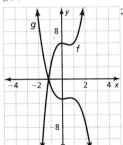

; The graph of g is a vertical shrink by a factor of $\frac{1}{2}$, followed by a reflection in the x-axis of the graph of f.

11. The graph has been translated horizontally to the right 2 units instead of to the left 2 units.

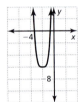

13. $g(x) = -x^3 + 9x^2 - 27x + 21$

15. *Sample answer:* If the function is translated up and then reflected in the x-axis, the order is important; If the function is translated left and then reflected in the x-axis, the order is not important; Reflecting a graph in the x-axis does not affect its x-coordinate, but it does affect its y-coordinate. So, the order is only important if the translation is vertical.

17. The corners of the cardboard should be cut so that squares with side lengths of 5 inches are removed.

19. Check students' work.

4.7 Review & Refresh

20. minimum: -7; domain: all real numbers; range: $y \geq -7$; increasing: $x > -5$; decreasing: $x < -5$

21. maximum: 1; domain: all real numbers; range: $y \leq 1$; increasing: $x < 1$; decreasing: $x > 1$

22. $y \geq x^2 - x - 2$

23.

; The graph of g is a horizontal translation 3 units left of the graph of the parent absolute value function.

24.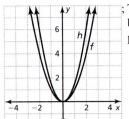

; The graph of h is a vertical stretch by a factor of $\frac{3}{2}$ of the graph of the parent quadratic function.

25. 4; $-1, 1, 3i,$ and $-3i$ 26. $13 - 5i$
27. $9 + 6i$ 28. $21 + 35i$ 29. $26 + 58i$

4.8 Practice

1.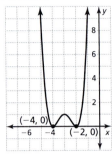

3.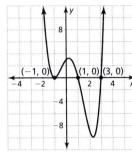

5. Because 0 is a repeated zero with an even power, the graph should only touch the x-axis at 0, not cross it. Because 3 is a repeated zero with an odd power, the graph should cross the x-axis at 3.

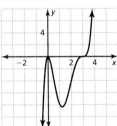

7. $-4, -\frac{1}{2},$ and 1   9. $-1, -\frac{1}{4}, \frac{1}{3}, \frac{3}{2}$

11.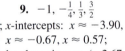

; x-intercepts: $x \approx -3.90$, $x \approx -0.67, x \approx 0.57$; local maximum: $(-2.67, 15.96)$; local minimum: $(0, -3)$; increasing: $x < -2.67$ and $x > 0$; decreasing: $-2.67 < x < 0$

13.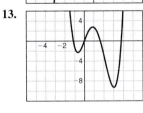

; x-intercepts: $x \approx -1.15, x = 0$, $x \approx 1.64, x \approx 3.79$; local maximum: $(0.87, 2.78)$; local minimums: $(-0.68, -2.31)$ $(3.02, -9.30)$; increasing: $-0.68 < x < 0.87$ and $x > 3.02$; decreasing: $x < -0.68$ and $0.87 < x < 3.02$

15. 5
17. yes; $f(x) = x^3$ has no turning points because its graph is always increasing.
19. even   21. neither   23. even
25. **a.** The zeros of the function are -3 and 0. The local maximum is $(-2, 4)$ and the local minimum is $(0, 0)$.
b. The x-intercepts of the graphs of $y = f(x)$ and $y = -f(x)$ are the same.

c. The minimum value of $y = f(x)$ is the opposite of the maximum value of $y = -f(x)$, and the maximum value of $y = f(x)$ is the opposite of the minimum value of $y = -f(x)$.

27. no; Let f and g be two odd functions. Then $f(-x) = -f(x)$ and $g(-x) = -g(x)$.
$f(-x) \cdot g(-x) = [-f(x)] \cdot [-g(x)] = f(x) \cdot g(x)$
So, the product of two odd functions is an even function.

29. The carbon dioxide level increases from January to mid-May, decreases from mid-May to October, and increases from November to December.

31. Check students' work.

4.8 Review & Refresh

32. $9z^2 - 16$
33. $-2, -2, 1, -3i, 3i$
34. The graph of g is a translation 2 units left and 5 units down of the graph of f.

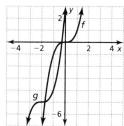

35. quadratic
36. $n = -3, n = 0, n = 2$
37. $x = 4$ and $x = 2$
38. a. 14 ft   b. 1.5 sec

4.9 Practice

1. $f(x) = (x + 1)(x - 1)(x - 2)$
3. $3; f(x) = \frac{2}{3}x^3 + 4x^2 - \frac{1}{3}x - 4$
5. about 248 passengers using the quintic model
7. Sample answer: $f(x) = -\frac{1}{12}x^4$

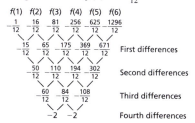

9. Sample answer:
$f(x) = 0.0001x^4 - 0.008x^3 + 0.16x^2 - 1.33x + 71.3$

11. Sample answer: increased awareness of the harmful affects of smoking and regulations

4.9 Review & Refresh

12. The degree is even, and the leading coefficient is negative.
13. The degree is odd, and the leading coefficient is positive.
14. $(2, 1)$
15. $\left(\frac{1}{2}, \frac{7}{4}\right)$ and $(2, 1)$
16. focus: $\left(0, c + \frac{1}{4a}\right)$; directrix: $y = c - \frac{1}{4a}$

17.

Positive real zeros	Negative real zeros	Imaginary zeros	Total zeros
3	2	0	5
3	0	2	5
1	2	2	5
1	0	4	5

18. $4x^3 + 2x^2 - 4x - 2$

19.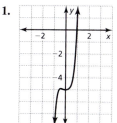
; x-intercepts: $x \approx -1.24$, $x = 0$, $x = 2$, $x \approx 3.24$;
local maximums: $(-0.73, 4)$, $(2.73, 4)$;
local minimum: $(1, -5)$;
increasing: $x < -0.73$ and $1 < x < 2.73$;
decreasing: $-0.73 < x < 1$ and $x > 2.73$

Chapter 4 Review

1.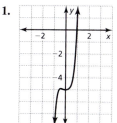
2.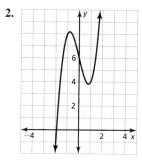

3.
4.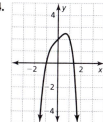

5. a.
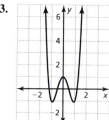
; The life expectancy increases from 2000 to about 2014 and decreases from about 2014 to 2016.

b. about 0.1252 year per year
c. no; After 2014, the model decreases for all future years, which is not likely.

6. $4x^3 - 4x^2 - 4x - 8$
7. $3x^4 + 3x^3 - x^2 - 3x + 15$
8. $2x^2 + 11x + 1$
9. $2y^3 + 10y^2 + 5y - 21$
10. $8m^3 + 12m^2n + 6mn^2 + n^3$
11. $s^3 + 3s^2 - 10s - 24$
12. $m^4 + 16m^3 + 96m^2 + 256m + 256$
13. $243s^5 + 810s^4 + 1{,}080s^3 + 720s^2 + 240s + 32$
14. $z^6 + 6z^5 + 15z^4 + 20z^3 + 15z^2 + 6z + 1$
15. $x - 1 + \dfrac{4x - 3}{x^2 + 2x + 1}$
16. $x^2 + 2x - 10 + \dfrac{7x + 43}{x^2 + x + 4}$
17. $-2x^2 - 4x - 5 - \dfrac{15}{x - 2}$
18. $f(5) = 546$

19. $f(-3) = -18$
20. $-3, 2, -2, -39; 2x^3 + x^2 - 2x + 4, x + 3,$
$2x^2 - 5x + 13 - \dfrac{35}{x+3}$
21. about 303,000 overnight stays
22. $8(2x - 1)(4x^2 + 2x + 1)$ **23.** $y^3(5y + 2)(25y^2 - 10y + 4)$
24. $2z(z^2 - 5)(z - 1)(z + 1)$ **25.** $(a - 2)(a + 2)(2a - 7)$
26.
$$\begin{array}{r|rrrrr} -2 & 1 & 2 & 0 & -27 & -54 \\ & & -2 & 0 & 0 & 54 \\ \hline & 1 & 0 & 0 & -27 & 0 \end{array}$$
$f(x) = (x + 2)(x - 3)(x^2 + 3x + 9)$
27. *Sample answer:* $(x + 8)$ inches by $(x + 6)$ inches by $(x - 1)$ inches
28. about 2,732,000 copies **29.** $x = -4, x = -2,$ and $x = 3$
30. $x = -4, x = -3,$ and $x = 2$
31. -2 and 0 **32.** -3 and 3

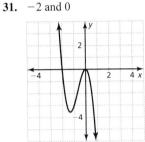 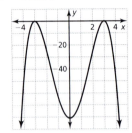

33. $f(x) = x^3 - 5x^2 + 5x - 1$
34. $f(x) = x^4 - 9x^3 + 11x^2 + 51x - 30$
35. a. length: 3 in., width: 3 in., height: 58 in.
   b. 8,156,250 ft³
36. $-3, -1, -1, -i,$ and i
37. $f(x) = x^4 - x^3 + 14x^2 - 16x - 32$
38. $f(x) = x^4 + 7x^3 + 6x^2 - 4x + 80$
39.

Positive real zeros	Negative real zeros	Imaginary zeros	Total zeros
2	0	2	4
0	0	4	4

40.

Positive real zeros	Negative real zeros	Imaginary zeros	Total zeros
1	3	0	4
1	1	2	4

41. May and September
42. The graph of g is a reflection in the y-axis, followed by a translation 2 units up of the graph of f.

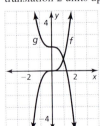

43. The graph of g is a reflection in the x-axis, followed by a translation 9 units left of the graph of f.

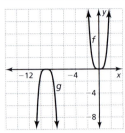

44. $g(x) = \dfrac{1}{1{,}024}(x - 3)^5 + \dfrac{3}{4}(x - 3) - 5$
45. $g(x) = x^4 + 2x^3 - 7$
46. C **47.** B **48.** A **49.** D
50. $V(x) = 3\pi x^2(x + 3); W(x) = \dfrac{\pi}{3}x^2\left(\dfrac{1}{3}x + 3\right);$
$W(3) = 12\pi \approx 37.70;$ When x is 3 feet, the volume of the cone is about 37.70 cubic yards.
51. ; x-intercept: $x \approx 1.68$; local maximum: $(0, -1)$; local minimum: $(-1, -2)$; increasing: $-1 < x < 0$; decreasing: $x < -1$ and $x > 0$
52. ; x-intercepts: $x \approx 0.25, x \approx 1.34$; local maximum: $(-1.13, 7.06)$; local minimums: $(-2, 6),$ $(0.88, -3.17)$; increasing: $-2 < x < -1.13$ and $x > 0.88$; decreasing: $x < -2$ and $-1.13 < x < 0.88$
53. odd **54.** even **55.** neither
56. The domains of both odd-degree and even-degree polynomial functions is all real numbers. The range of odd-degree functions is all real numbers, but the range of even-degree functions is $y \geq k$ or $y \leq k$, where k is the minimum or maximum of the function.
57. $y = x(x - 2)(x - 5)$
58. $f(x) = \dfrac{3}{16}(x + 4)(x - 4)(x - 2)$
59. $3; f(x) = 2x^3 - 7x^2 - 6x$
60. $4; f(x) = -0.125x^4 + x^3 - 8x + 4$
61. $y = 1.765t^3 - 19.75t^2 + 203.9t + 439;$ about 2,300 moose

Chapter 5

Getting Ready for Chapter 5

1. y^7 **2.** n **3.** $\dfrac{1}{x^3}$
4. $3x^3$ **5.** $\dfrac{8w^9}{z^6}$ **6.** $\dfrac{m^{10}}{z^4}$
7. $y = 2 - 4x$ **8.** $y = 3 + 3x$ **9.** $y = \dfrac{8x - 3}{4x}$

5.1 Practice

1. 2 **3.** ± 4 **5.** 2 **7.** 125
9. The negative cube root of 27 is -3; $(-27)^{5/3} = ((-27)^{1/3})^5 = (-3)^5 = -243$
11. 0.34 **13.** 0.02
15. $x \approx -7.66$ **17.** $x \approx \pm 1.68$

19. potatoes: 0.047 or 4.7%, oranges: 0.043 or 4.3%, ground beef: 0.037 or 3.7%
21. 1.12 m/sec; 1.47 m/sec; 2.15 m/sec; The equation that relates particle mass to the speed of the river is $m = ks^6$, where m is the mass of the particle, s is the speed of the river, and k is a constant. When the mass is doubled, multiply each side of the formula by 2 and rewrite. $2m = 2ks^6$, $2m = k \cdot 2s^6$, $2m = k(2^{1/6}s)^6$. So, the speed of the river must be $2^{1/6} \approx 1.12$ times faster for a particle double the mass to be transported, or about 1.12 meters per second. Similarly, for a particle 10 times the mass, the speed needs to be $10^{1/6} \approx 1.47$ times faster, or about 1.47 meters per second, and for a particle 100 times the mass, the speed needs to be $100^{1/6} \approx 2.15$ times faster, or about 2.15 meters per second.
23. about 3 astronomical units

5.1 Review & Refresh
24. 4; $f(x) = -x^4 + 2x^3 + 5x^2 - 6x + 1$
25. $y = \frac{1}{4}(x-8)^2 + 5$
26.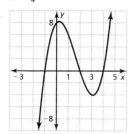
27. linear; 3.0 mi

5.2 Practice
1. $9^{2/3}$
3. $\frac{5}{4}$
5. 4
7. 12
9. 3
11. 6
13. $3\sqrt[4]{7}$
15. $\frac{\sqrt[3]{10}}{2}$
17. $\frac{\sqrt[3]{14}}{2}$
19. The square root was taken instead of the cube root; $2\sqrt[3]{13}$
21. $\frac{15 + 5\sqrt{2}}{7}$
23. $\frac{9\sqrt{3} - 9\sqrt{7}}{-4}$
25. $\frac{3\sqrt{2} + \sqrt{30}}{-2}$
27. $12\sqrt[3]{11}$
29. $5\sqrt[5]{7}$
31. $6(3^{1/3})$
33. $3y^2$
35. $\frac{m^2}{n}$
37. $\frac{|g|}{|h|}$
39. Sample answer: $\sqrt[6]{x^6} = |x|$; $\sqrt[6]{x^{12}} = x^2$
41. $\frac{2m\sqrt[5]{5mn^3}}{n^2}$
43. $21\sqrt[3]{y}$
45. $4w^2\sqrt{w}$
47. $P = 12x^{1/3}$
    $A = 6x^{2/3}$
49. a. $r = \sqrt[3]{\frac{3V}{4\pi}}$

    b. $S = 4\pi\left(\sqrt[3]{\frac{3V}{4\pi}}\right)^2$
    $S = \frac{4\pi(3V)^{2/3}}{(4\pi)^{2/3}}$
    $S = (4\pi)^{3/3 - 2/3}(3V)^{2/3}$
    $S = (4\pi)^{1/3}(3V)^{2/3}$

    c. The surface area of the larger balloon is $2^{2/3} \approx 1.59$ times as large as the surface area of the smaller balloon.
51. $f: y = \sqrt{x}$, $g: y = \sqrt[3]{x}$; $h: y = \sqrt[4]{x}$; $k: y = \sqrt[5]{x}$
53. $y = \sqrt[3]{x}$ and $y = \sqrt[5]{x}$

5.2 Review & Refresh
54. 25
55. The focus is $\left(0, \frac{1}{8}\right)$. The directrix is $y = -\frac{1}{8}$. The axis of symmetry is $x = 0$.

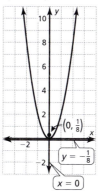

56. $y = \frac{1}{4}(x-2)(x+3)(x-4)$
57. $g(x) = 16x^4 + 16x^3 - 16x^2$; The graph of g is a horizontal shrink by a factor of $\frac{1}{2}$ of the graph of f.
58. a. $h(t) = -16t^2 + 25$; 1.25 sec
    b. $h(0.25) - h(1) = 15$; The sunglasses fell 15 feet between 0.25 second and 1 second.
59. neither

5.3 Practice
1. 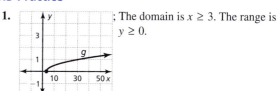 ; The domain is $x \geq 3$. The range is $y \geq 0$.

3. 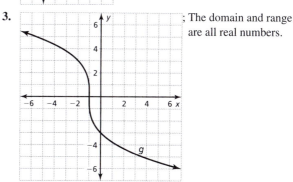 ; The domain and range are all real numbers.

5. The graph of g is a reflection in the x-axis, followed by a translation 1 unit down of the graph of f.

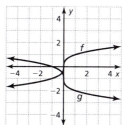

7. The graph of g is a vertical shrink by a factor of $\frac{1}{4}$, followed by a reflection in the y-axis of the graph of f.

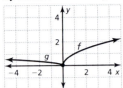

9. 24 ft per sec
11. $g(x) = 2\sqrt{x} + 8$
13. $g(x) = 2\sqrt{x + 1}$
15. $g(x) = -\frac{1}{3}\sqrt{x - 1} + 9$

17.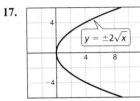
(0, 0), right

19.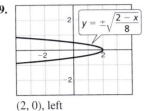
(2, 0), left

21.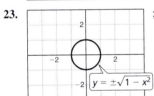
; The radius is 3 units. The x-intercepts are ± 3. The y-intercepts are ± 3.

23.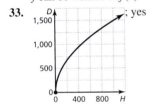
; The radius is 1 unit. The x-intercepts are ± 1. The y-intercepts are ± 1.

25. always
27. always
29. about 3.2 ft
31. Sample answer: $g(x) = \sqrt{-x + 2} + 1$, $h(x) = -\sqrt{x - 1} + 2$; f can be written as $f(x) = \sqrt{-x + 4}$ or $f(x) = -\sqrt{x - 3} + 1$.

33. ; yes

5.3 Review & Refresh

34. $6p^3$
35. $\frac{2\sqrt[5]{m^2}}{m}$
36. $8n\sqrt[4]{q}$
37. $7a^{2/3}bc^{1/4}$
38. 3; $y = \frac{1}{2}x^3 + \frac{3}{2}x^2 + 2x - 1$
39. 4.64
40. $x = 1$ and $x = -\frac{7}{3}$
41. $x = -\frac{10}{3}$ and $x = 6$
42. $y = \begin{cases} \frac{1}{2}x - 1, & \text{if } x \le -2 \\ x + 2, & \text{if } x > -2 \end{cases}$
43. $(-3, 1, 4)$

5.4 Practice

1. $x = 7$
3. $x = -\frac{1,000}{3}$
5. Only one side of the equation was cubed;
$\sqrt[3]{3x - 8} = 4$
$(\sqrt[3]{3x - 8})^3 = 4^3$
$3x - 8 = 64$
$x = 24$

7. $x = 12$
9. $x = \frac{1}{2}$
11. $x = 3$
13. $x = \pm 8$
15. $x = 3$
17. When raising each side to an exponent, the 8 was not included;
$8x^{3/2} = 1,000$
$(8x^{3/2})^{2/3} = 1,000^{2/3}$
$4x = 100$
$x = 25$
19. $x > 25$
21. $x \ge 0$
23. $x = 5$
25. a. The greatest stopping distance is 450 feet on ice. On wet asphalt, the stopping distance is 112.5 feet. On snow, the stopping distance is 225 feet. The least stopping distance is 90 feet on dry asphalt.
    b. about 272.2 ft
27. the data is increasing

5.4 Review & Refresh

29. $x^5 + 2x^4 + 5x^3 + 11x^2 + 5$
30. $3|m|n^2$
31. $g(x) = \sqrt{-x}$
32. $(-6, 4, 9)$
33. F3

5.5 Practice

1. $(f + g)(x) = 14\sqrt[4]{x}$ and the domain is $x \ge 0$; $(f - g)(x) = -24\sqrt[4]{x}$ and the domain is $x \ge 0$; $(f + g)(16) = 28$; $(f - g)(16) = -48$
3. $(f + g)(x) = -7x^3 + 5x^2 + x$ and the domain is all real numbers; $(f - g)(x) = -7x^3 - 13x^2 + 11x$ and the domain is all real numbers; $(f + g)(-1) = 11$; $(f - g)(-1) = -17$
5. $(fg)(x) = 2x^{10/3}$ and the domain is all real numbers; $\left(\frac{f}{g}\right)(x) = 2x^{8/3}$ and the domain is $x \ne 0$; $(fg)(-27) = 118,098$; $\left(\frac{f}{g}\right)(-27) = 13,122$
7. $(fg)(x) = 36x^{3/2}$ and the domain is $x \ge 0$; $\left(\frac{f}{g}\right)(x) = \frac{4}{9}x^{1/2}$ and the domain is $x > 0$; $(fg)(9) = 972$; $\left(\frac{f}{g}\right)(9) = \frac{4}{3}$
9. Because the functions have an even index, the domain is restricted; The domain of $(fg)(x)$ is $x \ge 0$.
11. about 2,541.04; about 2,458.96; about 102,598.56; about 60.92
13. a. -21 b. -1
    c. 0   d. 2
15. $(H + L)(x) = -0.191x^3 + 15.937x^2 - 79.02x + 215.6$; the total number of snowshoe hare and lynx pelts purchased by the Hudson Bay Company of Canada; $(H + L)(8) = 505.616$ represents the total number of snowshoe hare and lynx pelts purchased by the Hudson Bay Company of Canada in 1903.

5.5 Review & Refresh

17. The graph of g is a reflection in the x-axis, followed by a translation 2 units left of the graph of f.

18. linear   19. $-4\sqrt[3]{9}$ 20. $x = -4$
21. a. 2017
    b. The number of commercial drones sold increased by 68,000 each year from 2016 to 2018.
    c. no

5.6 Practice

1. 2   3. 30
5. a. $f(g(x)) = |x + 2| - 9$; all real numbers
   b. $g(f(x)) = |x - 7|$; all real numbers
   c. $f(f(x)) = x - 18$; all real numbers
7. a. $f(g(x)) = 3\sqrt{x + 7} - 7; x \geq -7$
   b. $g(f(x)) = \sqrt{3x}; x \geq 0$
   c. $f(f(x)) = 9x - 28$; all real numbers
9. $p(d(t)) = 1.8t + 1; p(d(1.5)) = 3.7$; After 1.5 minutes, the pressure is 3.7 atmospheres.
11. a. 4   b. 1
    c. 0   d. -3
13. $g(p(q(h(x)))) = g(p(q(x - 2))) = g(p(\sqrt{x - 2}))$
    $= g(\sqrt{x - 2} + 9) = \frac{1}{3}(\sqrt{x - 2} + 9) = \frac{1}{3}\sqrt{x - 2} + 3$
15. $r(s(16)) \approx 1.94$; A 16-year-old who gets the amount of sleep they need spends about 1.9 hours in REM sleep.

5.6 Review & Refresh

16. a. The function is increasing when $x < 2$ and decreasing when $x > 2$.
    b. $1 < x < 3$ c. $x < 1$ and $x > 3$
17. $(-2, 5), (-1, 3)$ 18. $\left(\frac{7}{2}, -\frac{9}{4}\right)$
19. $0 \leq x < 16$ 20. $x \geq -217$
21. $8\pi \approx 25.1$ cm^3
22. $(fg)(x) = -16x^{9/2}$, domain: $x \geq 0$; $\left(\frac{f}{g}\right)(x) = -4x^{3/2}$,
    domain: $x > 0$; $(fg)(4) = -8,192$; $\left(\frac{f}{g}\right)(4) = -32$

5.7 Practice

1. $x = \frac{y - 5}{3}; -\frac{8}{3}$ 3. $x = \sqrt[3]{\frac{y}{3}}; -1$
5. $f^{-1}(x) = \frac{1}{6}x$

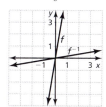

7. $f^{-1}(x) = \frac{x - 5}{-2}$

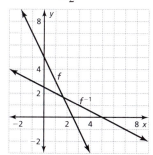

9. When switching x and y, the negative should not be switched with the variables;
   $y = -x + 3$
   $x = -y + 3$
   $-x + 3 = y$
   So, $f^{-1}(x) = -x + 3$.
11. no
13. $f^{-1}(x) = \sqrt{x} + 3$ 15. $f^{-1}(x) = -\sqrt{\frac{x + 2}{2}} - 5$

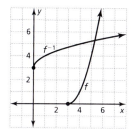 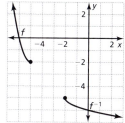

17. no   19. function; $f^{-1}(x) = \sqrt[3]{x + 1}$
21. function; $f^{-1}(x) = x^2 - 4, x \geq 0$
23. function; $f^{-1}(x) = \sqrt[3]{-\frac{5}{2}x - 10} + 2$
25. $f^{-1}(7.5) \approx 31.3$; A boat with a maximum hull speed of approximately 7.5 knots has a waterline length of 31.3 feet.
27. $f^{-1}(-2) = -1$ 29. all n such that $n \neq 5, 1, -6$
31. no   33. yes   35. B   37. A
39. a. $C^{-1}(x) = \frac{9}{5}x + 32$; The equation converts temperatures in Celsius to Fahrenheit.
    b. start: 41°F; end: 14°F
41. Check students' work.
43. As the BMI increases, body fat percentage also increases.

5.7 Review & Refresh

45. The function is increasing when $x < -1.15$ and $x > 1.15$ and decreasing when $-1.15 < x < 1.15$. The function is positive when $-2 < x < 0$ and $x > 2$ and negative when $x < -2$ and $0 < x < 2$.
46. $x = \frac{1}{6}$ and $y = 2$
47. $(f + g)(x) = 6x^2 + 7x + 8$, all real numbers;
    $(f - g)(x) = -2x^2 + 7x - 14$, all real numbers;
    $(f + g)(3) = 83, (f - g)(3) = -11$
48. $V = 12x^3 + 86x^2 + 182x + 120$
49. $y = \frac{1}{12}(x - 3)^2 + 1$
50. $f(g(x)) = \frac{12}{x} - 2$; all real numbers except $x = 0$

Chapter 5 Review

1. ± 6 2. -4 3. 243   4. $\frac{1}{9}$
5. $x = 3$ 6. $x = -10$ and $x = -6$
7. $3^{1.45} < 3^{1.5}$ and $3^{3/2} = \sqrt{3^3} = \sqrt{27} < \sqrt{36} = 6$. So, $3^{1.45} < 6$.
8. 7.0 mm   9. $6^{3/5}$ 10. $-\frac{2 + \sqrt{7}}{3}$ 11. $7\sqrt{3}$
12. $5^{1/3} \cdot 2^{3/4}$ 13. $\frac{(2z)^{1/4}}{6}$ 14. $-z^2\sqrt{10z}$

15. The graph of g is a vertical stretch by a factor of 2, followed by a reflection in the x-axis of the graph of f.

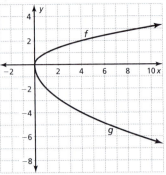

16. The graph of g is a reflection in the y-axis, followed by a translation 6 units down of the graph of f.

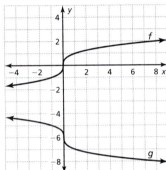

17.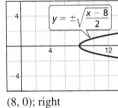
(8, 0); right

18.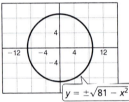
The radius is 9. The x-intercepts are ±9. The y-intercepts are ±9.

19. 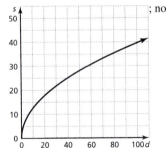 ; no

20. $x = 2$ and $x = 10$ 21. $x = \pm 36$
22. $8 \leq x < 152$ 23. $x \geq 30$ 24. 4,082 m
25. $(fg)(x) = 8(3-x)^{5/6}$ and the domain is $x \leq 3$;
$\left(\dfrac{f}{g}\right)(x) = \dfrac{1}{2}(3-x)^{1/6}$ and the domain is $x < 3$; $(fg)(2) = 8$;
$\left(\dfrac{f}{g}\right)(2) = \dfrac{1}{2}$

26. $(f+g)(x) = 3x^2 + x + 5$ and the domain is all real numbers;
$(f-g)(x) = 3x^2 - x - 3$ and the domain is all real numbers;
$(f+g)(-5) = 75$; $(f-g)(-5) = 77$

27. sometimes   28. always   29. 5
30. 100   31. 3   32. 9
33. $f(g(x)) = \dfrac{2}{x^2} - 5$; all real numbers except $x = 0$
34. $h(f(x)) = 6x - 11$; all real numbers
35. $g(h(x)) = \dfrac{1}{(3x+4)^2}$; all real numbers except $x = -\dfrac{4}{3}$
36. $g(g(x)) = x^4$; all real numbers except $x = 0$
37. radical function   38. the 10% coupon
39. $f^{-1}(x) = -2x + 20$

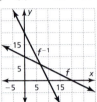

40. $f^{-1}(x) = \sqrt{x-8}$

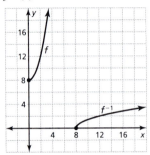

41. $f^{-1}(x) = \sqrt[3]{-x-9}$

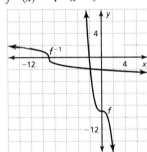

42. $f^{-1}(x) = \dfrac{1}{9}(x-5)^2$, $x \geq 5$

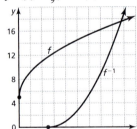

43. no   44. yes
45. $d^{-1}(100) = 128.7$; 100 U.S. dollars is equal to 128.7 British pounds.

Chapter 6

Getting Ready for Chapter 6

1. 6   2. $-32n^5$ 3. $\dfrac{81w^4}{16x^4}$ 4. $48g$

5. domain: $-5 \leq x \leq 5$, range: $0 \leq y \leq 5$
6. domain: $-2, -1, 0, 1$, range: $3, 1, -1, -3$

6.1 Practice

1.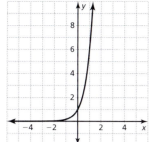

3.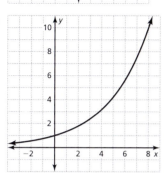

5.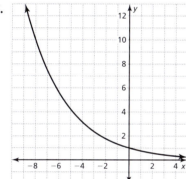

7. $b = 3$
9. a. exponential decay
   b. 35% decrease
11. about 0.01%
13. $y \approx a(1 + 0.2599)^t$; about 25.99% growth; $y \to 0$ as $t \to -\infty$ and $y \to +\infty$ as $t \to +\infty$
15. $5,593.60   **17.** $3,982.92   **19.** $3,774.71
21. The initial principal deposited in the account; the interest gained after t years; no; no
23. about 222 people per year
25. $V \approx 1,300(0.6782)^t$
27. It is an example of exponential decay because the dependent variable decreases as the independent variable increases.

6.1 Review & Refresh

28. x^{11} **29.** $216x^{18}$ **30.** $16x^8$
31. $3 + 5x$ **32.** yes   **33.** no
34. $f(g(x)) = \frac{1}{4}x^2 - 5x + 19$; all real numbers
35. $h(f(x)) = \dfrac{4}{x^2 - 6}$; all real numbers except $x = \pm\sqrt{6}$
36. $(fg)(x) = -4x^{7/2}, x \geq 0; \left(\dfrac{f}{g}\right)(x) = -\dfrac{x^{5/2}}{4}, x > 0$;
$(fg)(4) = -512, \left(\dfrac{f}{g}\right)(4) = -8$

37. a. when $x < -2$ and $x > 0$
   b. when $-2 < x < 0$
   c. when $x > 1$
   d. when $x < -2$ and $-2 < x < 1$
38. $x \leq -2$ or $x \geq 8$

6.2 Practice

1. e^8 **3.** $\dfrac{64}{e^{6x}}$ **5.** $2e^{4x}$

7. exponential growth

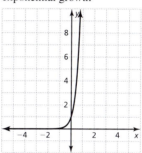

9. exponential growth

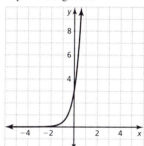

11. exponential decay

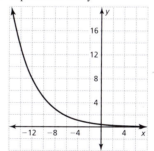

13. $y \approx (1 - 0.528)^t$; about 52.8% decay
15. $y \approx 0.5(1 + 1.226)^t$; about 122.6% growth
17. about 47 bacteria
19.

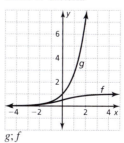

$g; f$

6.2 Review & Refresh

21. $y = -\frac{1}{5}(x - 1)(x + 5)(x - 4)$

22. $y = x^2 - 6, x \geq 0$

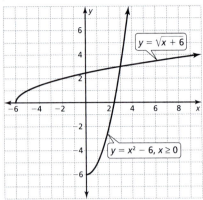

23. exponential growth

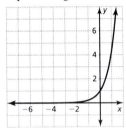

24. a. $f(t(x)) = 146.25x$; You earn $146.25 each week.
   b. $f(t(12)) = 1{,}755$; After 12 weeks you earn $1,755.

6.3 Practice

1. $3^2 = 9$ **3.** $\left(\frac{1}{2}\right)^{-4} = 16$ **5.** $\log_{16} \frac{1}{16} = -1$
7. 4   **9.** -3 **11.** -1.099 **13.** -2.079
15. x **17.** $2x$ **19.** $9x$
21. -3 and $\frac{1}{64}$ are in the wrong position; $\log_4 \frac{1}{64} = -3$
23. $y = 2^x$ **25.** $f^{-1}(x) = \frac{1}{3} \ln x$
27. $y = 10^{x-13}$

29.

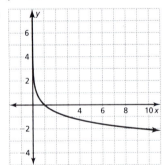

31.

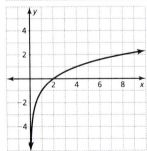

33. 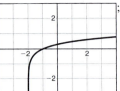 ; domain: $x > -2$, range: all real numbers, asymptote: $x = -2$

35. 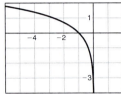 ; domain: $x < 0$, range: all real numbers, asymptote: $x = 0$

37. b, c, a, d
39. When $b = 1$, the function $f(x) = b^x = 1^x = 1$ for all values of x. Because the graph of f is a horizontal line, its inverse cannot be a function. Excluding a base of 1 from the definition of a logarithm ensures that all logarithmic functions of the form $g(x) = \log_b x$ are inverses of exponential functions.
41. Sample answer: $f(x) = \log(x + 1) - 3$

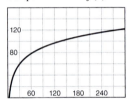

43. $\frac{y}{0.48} = e^{3.7725}$; $\ln \frac{y}{0.48} = 3.7725$

6.3 Review & Refresh

44. $-e^{11}$ **45.** $\frac{1}{5e^2}$ **46.** $16e^{4x}$ **47.** $2e^{4x}$
48. $x = -11$ and $x = -1$ **49.** $n = 0$ and $n = 1$
50. exponential decay   **51.** exponential growth

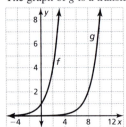

52. function; $f^{-1}(x) = \sqrt[3]{\dfrac{x-2}{3}}$
53. function; $f^{-1}(x) = x^2 - 1, x \geq 0$
54. 60 ft

6.4 Practice

1. The graph of g is a translation 7 units right of the graph of f.

3. The graph of g is a translation 6 units up of the graph of f.

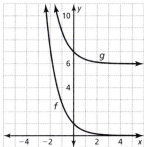

5. The graph of g is a horizontal shrink by a factor of $\frac{1}{2}$ of the graph of f.

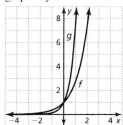

7. The graph of g is a horizontal shrink by a factor of $\frac{1}{5}$, followed by a translation 2 units up of the graph of f.

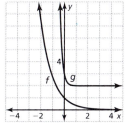

9. The graph of g is a vertical stretch by a factor of 3, followed by a translation 5 units down of the graph of f.

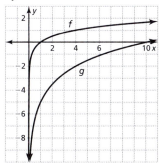

11. The graph of g is a reflection in the x-axis, followed by a translation 7 units right of the graph of f.

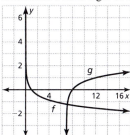

13. a. A   **b.** D
    c. C   **d.** B
15. $g(x) = 5^{-x} - 2$ **17.** $g(x) = 6\log_6 x - 5$

19. The graph of g is a translation 13 units up of the graph of f; $x = 0$

21. $g(x) = \log_4\left(\frac{1}{4}x\right)$ represents a horizontal stretch by a factor of 4, $h(x) = \frac{1}{4}\log_4 x$ represents a vertical shrink by a factor of $\frac{1}{4}$, and $g(x) \neq h(x)$. So, the transformations are different.

23. *Sample answer:* $f(x) = 1.5(2)^{x+1} + 2$

25. The graph of g is a reflection in the y-axis, horizontal stretch by a factor of $\frac{500}{7}$, and vertical stretch by a factor of 68.5 of the graph of f.

6.4 Review & Refresh

26. x **27.** 9   **28.** $2x$ **29.** $x - 3$

30. $y = \frac{1}{30}x + 1.9$; about 2,433

31. $x = -4, x = 0, x = 3$

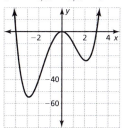

32. $x = \frac{1}{8}(y - 2)^2 - 1$ **33.** $x = 7$

34. $y = a(1 + 0.189)^t$; The growth rate is about 18.9%; $y \to 0$ as $x \to -\infty$ and $y \to +\infty$ as $x \to +\infty$

35. $y = a\left(1 - \frac{8}{9}\right)^t$; The decay rate is about 88.9%; $y \to +\infty$ as $x \to -\infty$ and $y \to 0$ as $x \to +\infty$

6.5 Practice

1. B   **3.** A   **5.** 0.565
7. 1.424   **9.** -0.712 **11.** $\log_3 2 + \log_3 x$
13. $1 + 5 \log x$ **15.** $\log_7 5 + \frac{1}{2}\log_7 x$
17. Only x is raised to the third power, not $7x$; $\ln 7x^3 = \ln 7 + 3 \ln x$

19. $\ln x^6 y^4$ **21.** $\ln \frac{64}{y^4}$ **23.** $\log_3 x$

25. about 1.404   **27.** about 1.232
29. about 1.581   **31.** about -0.860
33. 10 decibels
35. a. $2 \ln 2 \approx 1.39$ knots
    b.
$$s(h) = 2 \ln 100h$$
$$s(h) = \ln(100h)^2$$
$$e^{s(h)} = e^{\ln(100h)^2}$$
$$e^{s(h)} = (100h)^2$$
$$\log e^{s(h)} = \log(100h)^2$$
$$s(h) \log e = 2 \log(100h)$$
$$s(h) \log e = 2(\log 100 + \log h)$$
$$s(h) \log e = 2(2 + \log h)$$
$$s(h) = \frac{2}{\log e}(\log h + 2)$$

37. It is not true because by the Product Property, $\log_b M + \log_b N = \log_b(MN)$. If $\log_b(M + N) = \log_b(MN)$, then $M + N = M \cdot N$ which is not always true.

39. *Sample answer:* The graph of g could be a translation 1 unit up of the graph of f. The graph of g could be a horizontal shrink by a factor of $\frac{1}{100}$, followed by a translation 1 unit down of the graph of f. The graph of g could be a horizontal shrink by a factor of $\frac{1}{10}$ of the graph of f.

41. about 87.16%

6.5 Review & Refresh
43. $y = \frac{3}{4}(x+1)^2 - 2$
44. small: $2.50, medium: $2.80, large: $3.40
45. $x \approx -0.76$ and $x \approx 2.36$
46. e^6
47. $g(x) = 3^x - 4$

6.6 Practice
1. $x = -1$
3. $x = -\frac{5}{3}$
5. about 17.6 years old
7. $x = 3$
9. $x = \frac{1+\sqrt{41}}{2} \approx 3.7$ and $x = \frac{1-\sqrt{41}}{2} \approx -2.7$
11. $x = 4$
13. $x = -2$ and $x = -8$
15. 3 quarters into the 39th year; about halfway through the 5th month of the 39th year
17. $x \approx 3.6$
19. $x < 3$
21. $x > 3$
23. $x \geq 20.086$
25. about 50 min
27. $x \approx 1.23$
29. 36 cm footprint: about 11.7 years old;
    32 cm footprint: about 7.6 years old;
    28 cm footprint: about 4.6 years old;
    24 cm footprint: about 2.2 years old
31. $x \approx 10.61$
33. $x = 0$ and $x \approx 2.58$
35. *Sample answer:* The graph is nonlinear and decreases at a decreasing rate.

6.6 Review & Refresh
37. $x = -1$ and $x = 3$
38. about 6.99 decibels
39. $x = \frac{-3 \pm \sqrt{53}}{2}$
40. The graph of g is a translation 1 unit left, followed by a vertical stretch by a factor of 2 of the graph of f.

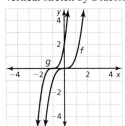

41. $\frac{m^5}{n}$
42. $6x^3 - 5x^2 + 3x - 1$
43. 6

6.7 Practice
1. exponential
3. Data are linear when the first differences are constant; The outputs have a common ratio of 3, so the data represents an exponential function.
5. $y = 2\left(\frac{1}{2}\right)^x$
7. $y = 0.25(2)^x$
9. *Sample answer:* $y = 7.20(1.39)^x$
11.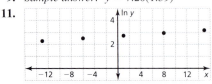

yes; $y = 14.73(1.03)^x$
13. $y = 6.70(1.41)^x$; about 208 electric scooters
15. $t = 12.59 - 2.55 \ln d$; about 2.6 h

17. a. *Sample answer:* The population has increased at relatively linear rate since 1950.
    b. $y = 2.67(1.016)^x$
    c. about 13 billion; no; The 70-year trend in the data is consistent, but a prediction for an additional 30 years is unlikely to be accurate.

6.7 Review & Refresh
18. yes
19. no
20. yes
21. about 2.727
22. about -0.632
23. The focus is $(2, 0)$, the directrix is $x = -2$, and the axis of symmetry is $y = 0$.

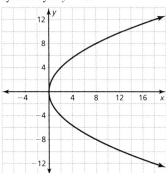

24. $g(x) = \log_3(x-2) + 1$
25. $x = 3$
26. $x = 11$
27.
$$-5 \begin{array}{|rrrr} 1 & -2 & -23 & 60 \\ & -5 & 35 & -60 \\ \hline 1 & -7 & 12 & 0 \end{array}$$

$f(x) = (x+5)(x-3)(x-4)$
28. $x^2 - 4x + 4$; $(x-2)^2$

Chapter 6 Review
1.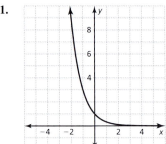

2.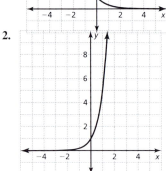

3.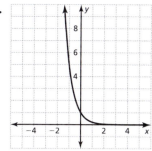

4. $1,725.39
5. a. always **b.** sometimes
6. about 15 g **7.** e^{15}
8. $\dfrac{2}{e^3}$ **9.** $\dfrac{9}{e^{10x}}$
10. exponential growth

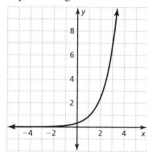

11. exponential decay

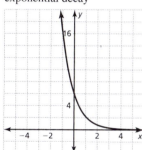

12. exponential decay

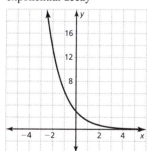

13. $74.08 **14.** sodium-22; tritium
15. 3 **16.** -2
17. $g(x) = \log_8 x$ **18.** $y = e^x + 4$
19.

20. 7.9

21. The graph of g is a horizontal shrink by a factor of $\tfrac{1}{5}$, followed by a translation 8 units down of the graph of f.

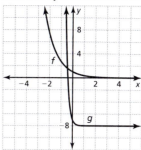

22. The graph of g is a vertical shrink by a factor of $\tfrac{1}{2}$, followed by a translation 5 units left of the graph of f.

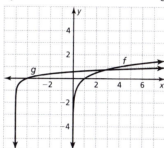

23. $g(x) = 3e^{x+6} + 3$ **24.** $g(x) = \log(-x) - 2$
25. $1 + 3\log x + \log y$ **26.** $\ln 4x^2$
27. about 3.32 **28.** about 1.13
29. $x \approx 1.29$ **30.** $x \approx 3.59$
31. $x > 1.39$ **32.** $0 < x \le 8{,}103.08$
33. 27 **34.** about 42.5 min
35. $y = 64\left(\tfrac{1}{2}\right)^x$ **36.** $y = \tfrac{1}{2}(6)^x$
37.

yes; $y = 2.29(1.45)^x$
38. $s = 3.95 + 27.48 \ln t$; about 53 pairs

Chapter 7
Getting Ready for Chapter 7
1. $\tfrac{1}{3}$ **2.** $1\tfrac{4}{15}$ **3.** $-\tfrac{17}{42}$
4. $\tfrac{11}{12}$ **5.** $-\tfrac{3}{7}$ **6.** $-\tfrac{1}{20}$

7.1 Practice
1. direct variation **3.** inverse variation
5. direct variation **7.** $y = -\dfrac{20}{x}; y = -\dfrac{20}{3}$
9. $y = \dfrac{21}{x}; y = 7$
11. The equation for direct variation was used; $y = \dfrac{40}{x}$
13. direct; $xy = a$, so $y = \dfrac{a}{x}$; $yz = b$, so $y = \dfrac{b}{z}$; $\dfrac{a}{x} = \dfrac{b}{z}, az = bx, x = \dfrac{a}{b}z$
15. The graph is a curve and is decreasing.
17. $2,500

7.1 Review & Refresh

18. $x = -3$
19. $x = 1$
20. Power Property and Quotient Property
21. 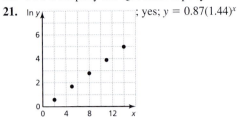 ; yes; $y = 0.87(1.44)^x$

22. $x - 9$
23. quadratic function; 15 in.
24. $8^{7/4}$
25. 3

7.2 Practice

1. 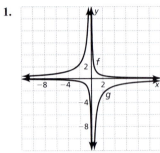 ; The graph of g lies farther from the axes and is reflected over the x-axis. Both graphs have the same asymptotes, domain, and range.

3. 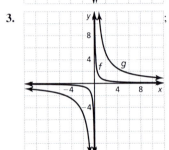 ; The graph of g lies farther from the axes. Both graphs lie in the first and third quadrants and have the same asymptotes, domain, and range.

5. 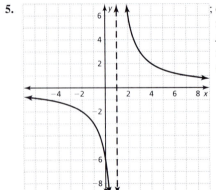 ; domain: all real numbers except $x = 1$; range: all real numbers except $y = 0$

7. 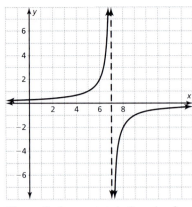 ; domain: all real numbers except $x = 7$; range: all real numbers except $y = 0$

9. The vertical asymptote is the value for x that makes the denominator 0; The vertical asymptote is $x = -6$.

11. 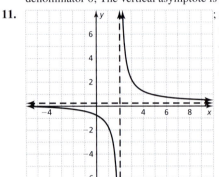 ; domain: all real numbers except $x = 2$; range: all real numbers except $y = \frac{1}{4}$

13. 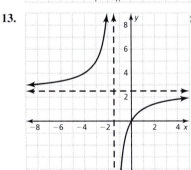 ; domain: all real numbers except $x = -\frac{3}{2}$; range: all real numbers except $y = \frac{5}{2}$

15. $g(x) = \dfrac{6}{x - 5} + 2$

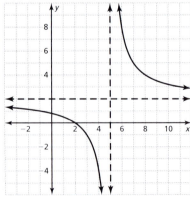 ; The graph of g is a translation 5 units right and 2 units up of the graph of $f(x) = \dfrac{6}{x}$.

17. $g(x) = \dfrac{-66}{x+7} + 9$

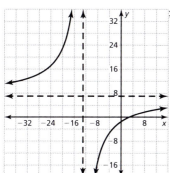

; The graph of g is a translation 7 units left and 9 units up of the graph of $f(x) = \dfrac{-66}{x}$.

19. a. about 23°C   b. about -0.005 sec/°C

21. 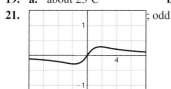 ; odd

23. provider B; provider A; provider A

25.

27. a. decreasing: $(-\infty, 0), (0, \infty)$
    b. increasing: $(-\infty, 0), (0, \infty)$

29. yes; a translation down

7.2 Review & Refresh

30. $(x-7)(2x^2+5)$ 31. 28, 25
32. -12; two imaginary solutions
33. $x = 16$ 34. exponential   35. $2^{11/10}$

7.3 Practice

1. $\dfrac{2x}{3x-4}, x \ne 0$ 3. simplified form

5. You cannot divide out common factors of the coefficients. The polynomials need to be factored first, and then the common factors can divide out; $\dfrac{x+12}{x+4}$

7. $(x-3)(x+3), x \ne 0, x \ne 2$

9. $\dfrac{2x(x+4)}{(x+2)(x-3)}, x \ne 1$

11. $(x+3)(x-2), x \ne -4, x \ne 4$

13. $\dfrac{256x^7}{y^{14}}, x \ne 0$ 15. $2, x \ne -2, x \ne 0, x \ne 3$

17. $\dfrac{x+4}{(x+2)(x-9)}$ 19. about $11.96

21. $x - 5$

23. a. $x \ne 1$ b. $x \ne -4, x \ne 1$

25. $f(x) = \dfrac{x(x-1)}{x+2}, g(x) = \dfrac{x(x+2)}{x-1}$

27. $y = \dfrac{1{,}600}{n}$

29. domain: $1 \le n \le 16$, range: $100 \le y \le 1{,}600$; The number of games n in a round is between 1 and 16 and the attendance per game in a round is between 100 and 1,600 people.

7.3 Review & Refresh

30. 5 years   31. exponential

32. 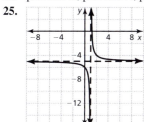 ; domain: all real numbers except $x = 1$; range: all real numbers except $y = 1$

33. ; domain: all real numbers except $x = 10$; range: all real numbers except $y = 2$

34. $y = 4^x$

7.4 Practice

1. $\dfrac{5}{x}$ 3. $\dfrac{9-2x}{x+1}$

5. $3x(x-2)$ 7. $2(x-3)(x+3)(x+4)$

9. $\dfrac{37}{30x}$ 11. $\dfrac{2(x+7)}{(x+4)(x+6)}$

13. The numerators and denominators were added, instead of first writing the fractions using the LCD and then adding; $\dfrac{2(x+10)}{5x^2}$

15. $g(x) = \dfrac{-2}{x-1} + 5$

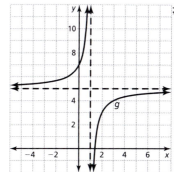

; The graph of g is a translation 1 unit right and 5 units up of the graph of $f(x) = \dfrac{-2}{x}$.

17. $g(x) = \dfrac{20}{x-3} + 3$

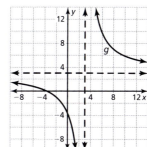

; The graph of g is a translation 3 units right and 3 units up of the graph of $f(x) = \dfrac{20}{x}$.

19. $\dfrac{x(x-18)}{6(5x+2)}, x \neq 0$ 21. $\dfrac{3x}{4(x-1)}, x \neq -2, x \neq 2$

23. **a.** sometimes; When the denominators have no common factors, the product of the denominators is the LCD. When the denominators have common factors, use the LCM to find the LCD.
   b. always; The LCD is the product of the highest power of each factor that appears in any of the denominators.

25. yes; Check students' work.

27. $A = \dfrac{391t^2 + 0.112}{0.218t^4 + 0.991t^2 + 1}$
   $+ \dfrac{391(t-1)^2 + 0.112}{0.218(t-1)^4 + 0.991(t-1)^2 + 1}$;
   The time at which the second dose is taken can be represented by $t - 1$ because it is in the bloodstream for one hour less than the first does. So, substitute $t - 1$ in for t in the original equation. The sum of the two doses is the amount of aspirin in the bloodstream after the second dose is taken.

29. Check student's work.

7.4 Review & Refresh

30. direct variation   31. $\dfrac{x^2}{y}, x \neq 0$ 32. $5.50

33. $x = -9$ and $x = 9$ 34. $y = \dfrac{1}{8}x^2$

35.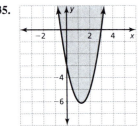

7.5 Practice

1. $x = 4$ 3. $x = -5, x = 7$
5. about 45.45 oz   7. $x = 2$ 9. $x = 2$
11. no solution   13. $x = 0, x = 7$
15. Each term of the equation should be multiplied by the LCD;
   $(2x+5)(3x) \cdot \dfrac{(7x+1)}{2x+5} + (2x+5)(3x) \cdot 4 =$
   $\dfrac{10x-3}{3x} \cdot (2x+5)(3x)$

17. yes; $f^{-1}(x) = \dfrac{7}{x} - 6$ 19. yes; $f^{-1}(x) = \dfrac{3}{x+2}$

21. no; $y = \pm \dfrac{1}{\sqrt{x-4}}$

23. **a.** about 190.6 ft   **b.** about 190.6 ft

25. **a.** yes; *Sample answer:* $\dfrac{1}{x} = \dfrac{1}{x+1}, 1 \neq 0$, no solution
   b. yes; *Sample answer:* $\dfrac{2}{x} = \dfrac{4}{x+3}, x = 3$
   c. yes; *Sample answer:* $\dfrac{1}{x} = \dfrac{x}{3-2x}, x = -3$ and $x = 1$
   d. yes; *Sample answer:* $\dfrac{1}{x+1} = \dfrac{3}{3x+3}, 0 = 0$, infinitely many solutions

27. $f^{-1}(x) = \dfrac{4x+1}{x-3}$ 29. $f^{-1}(x) = \dfrac{b-dx}{cx-a}$

31. To find an oblique asymptote, rewrite the rational function using long division. The non-remainder portion is the oblique asymptote; $y = \dfrac{x^2-9}{2x-4} = \dfrac{1}{2}x + 1 - \dfrac{5}{2x-4}$, so the oblique asymptote is $y = \dfrac{1}{2}x + 1$.

7.5 Review & Refresh

32. $f(g(8)) = 13, g(f(-2)) = 3$
33. 3   34. 28
35. $x - 2, x \neq -2$ 36. $-\dfrac{x+4}{2(x+6)}, x \neq 3$
37. $\dfrac{x}{2}, x \neq -7, x \neq 0, x \neq 2$
38. $x - 3, x \neq -2, x \neq 0, x \neq 5$
39. D   40. C   41. A   42. B

Chapter 7 Review

1. inverse variation   2. direct variation
3. direct variation   4. neither
5. direct variation   6. inverse variation
7. $y = \dfrac{5}{x}; y = -\dfrac{5}{3}$ 8. $y = \dfrac{24}{x}; y = -8$
9. $y = \dfrac{45}{x}; y = -15$ 10. $y = -\dfrac{8}{x}; y = \dfrac{8}{3}$

11. 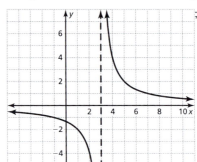 ; domain: all real numbers except $x = 3$; range: all real numbers except $y = 0$

12. 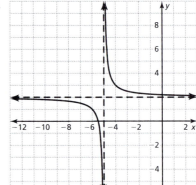 ; domain: all real numbers except $x = -5$; range: all real numbers except $y = 2$

13. 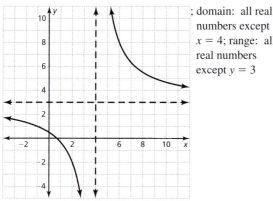 ; domain: all real numbers except $x = 4$; range: all real numbers except $y = 3$

14. 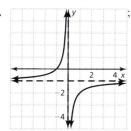 ; domain: all real numbers except $x = 0$; range: all real numbers except $y = -1$

15. a. 20 stands
b. The average cost per stand approaches $2.

16. $\dfrac{16x^3}{y^2}, x \neq 0$

17. $\dfrac{3(x+4)}{x+3}, x \neq 3, x \neq 4$

18. $\dfrac{3x(4x-1)}{(x-4)(x-3)}, x \neq 0, x \neq \dfrac{1}{4}$

19. $\dfrac{1}{(x+3)^2}, x \neq 5, x \neq 8$

20. -1

21. all real numbers except $x = -2$ and $x = 2$

22. $\dfrac{3x^2 + 26x + 36}{6x(x+3)}$

23. $\dfrac{5x^2 - 11x - 9}{(x+8)(x-3)}$

24. $\dfrac{-2(2x^2 + 3x + 3)}{(x-3)(x+3)(x+1)}$

25. $\dfrac{2x^2 + x + 6}{2(x-2)}$

26. $g(x) = \dfrac{16}{x-3} + 5$

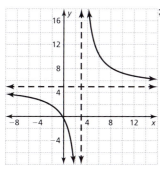 ; The graph of g is a translation 3 units right and 5 units up of the graph of $f(x) = \dfrac{16}{x}$.

27. $g(x) = \dfrac{-26}{x+7} + 4$

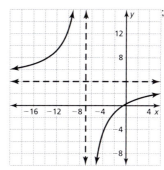 ; The graph of g is a translation 7 units left and 4 units up of the graph of $f(x) = \dfrac{-26}{x}$.

28. $\dfrac{3(x-3)}{3x+7}, x \neq -5, x \neq 3$

29. $\dfrac{140x^2 - 600x - 500}{x(x-10)(x+5)}$

30. $x = 5$
31. $x = 0$
32. no solution
33. $x = \pm\sqrt{3}$

34. yes; $f^{-1}(x) = \dfrac{3}{x} - 6$

35. yes; $f^{-1}(x) = \dfrac{10}{x} + 7$

36. yes; $f^{-1}(x) = \dfrac{1}{x-8}$

37. yes; $f^{-1}(x) = \dfrac{x}{1+x}$

38. $x = -3$
39. 8 consecutive expert ratings
40. 10 people
41. $x = 6$; When $x = 6$, $\dfrac{1}{x-6}$ is undefined.
42. $x \approx 1.26$

Chapter 8

Getting Ready for Chapter 8

1. about 77.2, 82.5, 82; median or mode
2. about 19.8, 16, 44; median
3. about 3.85; The typical data value differs from the mean by about 3.85 units.
4. about 7.09; The typical data value differs from the mean by about 7.09 units.

8.1 Practice

1. 50%
3. about 16%
5. about 68%
7. **a.** 81.5% **b.** 0.15%
9. **a.** 0.0968 **b.** 0.2681
11. no
13. about 0.0035
15. about 0.0538
17. no; When the mean is greater than the median, the distribution is skewed right.
19. about 0.617
21. The graph is approximately symmetric.
23. *Sample answer:* sizes 14 and smaller

8.1 Review & Refresh

24.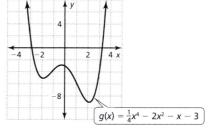

x-intercepts: about -2.84 and about 3.22; local maximum: $(-0.25, -2.87)$; local minimums: $(-1.86, -5.07)$ and $(2.11, -9.06)$; increasing when $-1.86 < x < -0.25$ and $x > 2.11$; decreasing when $x < -1.86$ and $-0.25 < x < 2.11$

25. no real solution
26. direct variation
27. about 0.845
28. $-2 - 18i$
29. $y = \frac{1}{4}(x - 5)^2 + 1$
30. $x = 15$

8.2 Practice

1. population: every adult in the United States; sample: 1,502 adults who were surveyed
3. statistic
5. 56%
7. a. The maker's claim is most likely true.
   b. The maker's claim is most likely false.
9. simulation 2; Because more samples are taken, simulation 2 gives a better indication of outcomes that are not likely to occur by chance.
11. a. *Sample answer:*

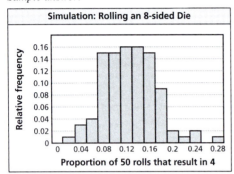

   b. The maker's claim is most likely false; The maker's claim is most likely true.
13. yes; no; The sample mean is an estimate of the population mean, and 5 hours is not close to 8 hours. But it is possible that the 200 people selected were not representative of the population.
15. The percentage of the population that is 65+ is increasing. The percentage of the population that is 15–64 is about the same. The percentage of the population that is 0–14 is decreasing.
17. *Sample answer:* The birth rate in the United States is decreasing. As the number of young people decreases, the portion of the population that is 65+ increases.

8.2 Review & Refresh

18. $x = 5 \pm \sqrt{29}$
19. $n = -1 \pm i$
20. no
21. about 56%
22. a. -1 b. 4
23. $\frac{1}{3x}, y \neq 0$

8.3 Practice

1. self-selected sample
3. random sample
5. convenience sample; Dog owners probably have strong opinions about an off-leash area for dogs.
7. cluster sample; Booth holders in section 5 are likely to have a different opinion than booth holders in other sections about the location of their booth.
9. *Sample answer:* Assign each student in the school a different integer from 1 to 1,225. Generate 250 unique random integers from 1 to 1,225 using the random number function in a spreadsheet program. Choose the 250 students who correspond to the 250 integers generated.
11. simulation
13. experiment

15. By using the phrase "isn't it true", it encourages a yes response; *Sample answer:* Reword the question as "Should the budget of our city be cut?"
17. It addresses more than one issue; *Sample answer:* Ask questions about color selection and quality separately.
19. a. stratified sample
    b. Because the counties are very different in population, selecting the same number of people from each county will underrepresent people living in counties with a large population, and overrepresent people living in counties with a small population.
21. It is not likely that the sample was a random sample because only 3.8% of the population speak "Other Indo-European Languages" at home. So the probability that all five people speak German at home is very small.

8.3 Review & Refresh

23. parameter
24. 4^7 or 16,384
25. $\frac{\sqrt[3]{18}}{18}$
26. 4
27. 3
28. 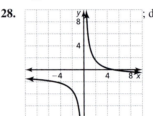 ; domain: $x \neq 0$; range: $y \neq -1$

29. about 16%
30. about 81.5%
31. $\log_2 4 + \log_2 x - \log_2 y$
32. $\ln x + 6 \ln y$
33. -8
34. 9

8.4 Practice

1. The study is a randomized comparative experiment; The treatment is the drug for improving sleep. The treatment group is the individuals who received the drug. The control group is the individuals who received the placebo.
3. experiment; *Sample answer:* Randomly select the same number of strawberry plants to be put in each of two groups. Use the new fertilizer on the plants in one group, and use the regular fertilizer on plants in the other group. Keep all other variables constant and record the weight of the fruit produced by each plant.
5. *Sample answer:* Because the heart rates are monitored for two different types of exercise, the groups cannot be compared. Running on a treadmill may have a different effect on heart rate than lifting weights; Check the heart rates of all the athletes after the same type of exercise.
7. The number of cases increased drastically from 1940 to 1952, and then declined to 0 a couple of years after 1960.
9. Field trials are carried out in the subjects' normal environments, as opposed to other experiments that may take place in a laboratory, hospital, or research facility; The double-blind method prevents the researcher from inadvertently introducing bias into the trial.

8.4 Review & Refresh

10. By referring to the cell phone model as outdated, it encourages a yes response; *Sample answer:* Reword the question as "Should the manufacturer change its cell phone model?"

11. 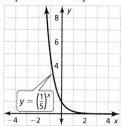 ; bell-shaped and symmetric

12. 6 strikes **13.** about 2

14. exponential decay

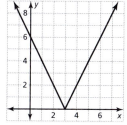

8.5 Practice

1. 65.4
3. a. yes
  b. no; As the sample size increases, the percentage of votes approaches 55%, which is not enough to override the veto.
5. a. The claim is probably not accurate.
  b. The claim is probably accurate.
  c. *Sample answer:* 0.11 to 0.25
7. 0.1; 95% of the sample proportions should be within 0.1 of the population proportion, 0.17.
9. about ±3.2%   **11.** between 25% and 27%
13. about 453 residents   **15.** $4n$; 4 times
17. *Sample answer:* $\rho = 0.5$: $n > 375$, $\rho = 0.6$: $n > 360$, $\rho = 0.8$: $n > 240$; The closer the percentage of a large population that have a certain characteristic is to 50%, the larger the sample must be to reasonably represent the population.
19. more than 2,500; To be confident that sports drink X is preferred, the margin of error needs to be less than 2%.
21. The margin of error increases as the sample size decreases.

8.5 Review & Refresh

23. $y = 6^{x+1}$ **24.** geometric; $a_n = 3(2)^{n-1}$
25. $\dfrac{2x+2}{x-2}, x \neq 0, x \neq 4, x \neq 6$
26. The study is not a randomized comparative experiment. The people were not randomly assigned to a control group and a treatment group. The conclusion that using a Himalayan salt rock lamp for at least 1 hour each day reduced stress levels may or may not be valid. There may be other reasons why stress levels were lower for the group that used salt lamps.
27.

8.6 Practice

1. a. -5.875
  b.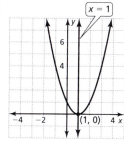
  c. The music therapy may be effective in reducing anxiety scores of college students, but the sample size is small and the difference could be due to chance.
3. Check students' work.
5. The experimental difference -5.875 lies on the left tail, beyond all the resampling differences. So, the experimental difference is significant and the hypothesis is most likely false.
7. A lighter shade of blue indicates a lower population density and a darker shade of blue indicates a higher population density.
9. *Sample answer:* Knowing about cultural origins may help people who work in polling companies to produce more representative samples for surveys.

8.6 Review & Refresh

10. no
11.

12. observational study   **13.** 15.2
14. $\dfrac{1}{8z^6}$ **15.** $x = 4$

Chapter 8 Review

1. about 0.15%   **2.** no   **3.** 0.0808
4. population: all U.S. motorists, sample: the 1,000 drivers surveyed
5. statistic
6. The shelter's claim is most likely true.
7. a. systematic sample
  b. self-selected sample
  c. convenience sample
8. observational study
9. By referring to the library systems as outdated, it encourages a yes response; *Sample answer:* Reword the question as "Should the city replace the library systems it is currently using?"
10. The study is a randomized comparative experiment; The treatment is using the new design of the car wash. The treatment group is the individuals who use the new design of the car wash. The control group is the individuals who use the old design of the car wash.

11. observational study; *Sample answer:* Record which type of bread customers choose. Then record how many customers who chose each type of bread return to the restaurant.
12. *Sample answer:* Volunteers may not be representative of the population; Randomly select from members of the population for the study.
13. no
14. between 37.8% and 44.2%
15. -3.875
16. The experimental difference -3.875 lies on the left tail, beyond the middle 95% of the resampling differences. So, the experimental difference is significant and the hypothesis is most likely false.

Chapter 9

Getting Ready for Chapter 9
1. $x = 24$
2. $x = 1$
3. $x = 6$
4. $x = 4$
5. $x = -0.75$
6. $x = \frac{1}{6}$
7. 13 m
8. 24 ft

9.1 Practice
1. $\sin \theta = \frac{5}{7}$, $\cos \theta = \frac{2\sqrt{6}}{7}$, $\tan \theta = \frac{5\sqrt{6}}{12}$, $\csc \theta = \frac{7}{5}$, $\sec \theta = \frac{7\sqrt{6}}{12}$, $\cot \theta = \frac{2\sqrt{6}}{5}$
3. $\sin \theta = \frac{2\sqrt{30}}{13}$, $\cos \theta = \frac{7}{13}$, $\tan \theta = \frac{2\sqrt{30}}{7}$, $\csc \theta = \frac{13\sqrt{30}}{60}$, $\sec \theta = \frac{13}{7}$, $\cot \theta = \frac{7\sqrt{30}}{60}$
5. $\sin \theta = \frac{\sqrt{119}}{12}$, $\tan \theta = \frac{\sqrt{119}}{5}$, $\csc \theta = \frac{12\sqrt{119}}{119}$, $\sec \theta = \frac{12}{5}$, $\cot \theta = \frac{5\sqrt{119}}{119}$
7. $\sin \theta = \frac{\sqrt{115}}{14}$, $\cos \theta = \frac{9}{14}$, $\tan \theta = \frac{\sqrt{115}}{9}$, $\csc \theta = \frac{14\sqrt{115}}{115}$, $\cot \theta = \frac{9\sqrt{115}}{115}$
9. $\sin \theta = \frac{11\sqrt{377}}{377}$, $\cos \theta = \frac{16\sqrt{377}}{377}$, $\tan \theta = \frac{11}{16}$, $\csc \theta = \frac{\sqrt{377}}{11}$, $\sec \theta = \frac{\sqrt{377}}{16}$
11. $x = 6$
13. $x = 7$
15. about 1.17
17. $A = 54°$, $b \approx 16.71$, $c \approx 28.43$
19. $A = 74°$, $a \approx 48.82$, $c \approx 50.79$
21. $A = 18°$, $a \approx 3.96$, $b \approx 12.17$
23. about 427 m
25. about 514 m
27. $\sin \theta = \frac{1}{2}$, $\cos \theta = \frac{\sqrt{3}}{2}$, $\tan \theta = \frac{\sqrt{3}}{3}$, $\csc \theta = 2$, $\sec \theta = \frac{2\sqrt{3}}{3}$, $\cot \theta = \sqrt{3}$
29. Use the tangent function to find the horizontal distance, $x + y$, from the airplane to the second town. Then use the tangent function to find the horizontal distance x from the airplane to the first town. Lastly, find the distance between the two towns; about 39,689 ft
31. about 42°; The color red on a rainbow is formed when sunlight is reflected in a water droplet at an angle of about 42°.

9.1 Review & Refresh
33.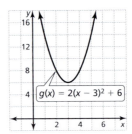
34. about 5
35.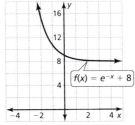
36. 0.0625 g/cm²

9.2 Practice
1.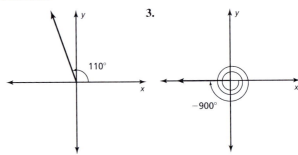
3.
5. *Sample answer:* 430°, $-290°$
7. *Sample answer:* 235°, $-485°$
9. $\frac{2\pi}{9}$
11. $-\frac{13\pi}{9}$
13. B
15. A
17. length: $5\pi \approx 15.7$ yd, area: $25\pi \approx 78.5$ yd²
19. 324,000°, or $1,800\pi$
21. $\frac{19\pi}{18} \approx 3.32$ mi
23. a. 70° 33′   b. 110.76°   c. 0.7 rad
25. θ represents the angle from the center of Earth to a given point and r represents the radius of Earth.

9.2 Review & Refresh
27. $\sin \theta = \frac{\sqrt{3}}{2}$, $\cos \theta = \frac{1}{2}$, $\tan \theta = \sqrt{3}$, $\csc \theta = \frac{2\sqrt{3}}{3}$, $\sec \theta = 2$, $\cot \theta = \frac{\sqrt{3}}{3}$
28. about ±3.6%
29. direct variation
30. $5 + 10i$
31. $\log_5 1 = 0$
32. $x = 16$
33. $x = 1$
34. 3; $f(x) = \frac{1}{6}x^3 + \frac{1}{2}x^2 + \frac{16}{3}x$
35. $f(x) = x^3 - 3x^2 - 2x + 6$

9.3 Practice
1. $\sin \theta = -\frac{3}{5}$, $\cos \theta = \frac{4}{5}$, $\tan \theta = -\frac{3}{4}$, $\csc \theta = -\frac{5}{3}$, $\sec \theta = \frac{5}{4}$, $\cot \theta = -\frac{4}{3}$

3. $\sin\theta = \frac{\sqrt{10}}{10}$, $\cos\theta = \frac{3\sqrt{10}}{10}$, $\tan\theta = \frac{1}{3}$, $\csc\theta = \sqrt{10}$, $\sec\theta = \frac{\sqrt{10}}{3}$, $\cot\theta = 3$

5. $\sin\theta = 1$, $\cos\theta = 0$, $\tan\theta =$ undefined, $\csc\theta = 1$, $\sec\theta =$ undefined, $\cot\theta = 0$

7. $\sin\theta = -1$, $\cos\theta = 0$, $\tan\theta =$ undefined, $\csc\theta = -1$, $\sec\theta =$ undefined, $\cot\theta = 0$

9. $\sin\theta = 0$, $\cos\theta = 1$, $\tan\theta = 0$, $\csc\theta =$ undefined, $\sec\theta = 1$, $\cot\theta =$ undefined

11. $80°$ 13. $\frac{\pi}{3}$ 15. $\frac{\pi}{6}$

17. $-\sqrt{2}$ 19. $\frac{\sqrt{2}}{2}$ 21. 1   23. about 65 ft

25. a.

Angle of sprinkler, θ	Horizontal distance water travels, d
30°	16.9
35°	18.4
40°	19.2
45°	19.5
50°	19.2
55°	18.4
60°	16.9

b. 45°

27. a. not possible   b. $90° < \theta < 180°$

29. no; $\theta = 240°$ is also a solution, and any angles coterminal with 60° and 240° are also solutions.

31. after 12 P.M. and before 4:30 P.M.

33. The sundial cannot measure the time after sunset or before sunrise.

9.3 Review & Refresh

34. 3, $x \neq 2$ 35. $y = -\frac{3}{5}(x-5)^2 + 25$

36. $f(g(2)) = 4$ 37. $x = 11$

38. 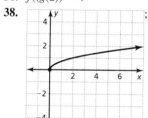 ; domain: $x \geq 0$; range: $y \geq 0$

39. Sample answer: $\frac{11\pi}{3}, -\frac{\pi}{3}$

9.4 Practice

1. amplitude: 3, period: 2π

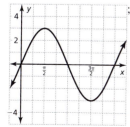 ; The graph of g is a vertical stretch by a factor of 3 of the graph of $f(x) = \sin x$.

3. amplitude: 1, period: $\frac{2\pi}{3}$

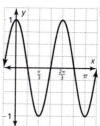 ; The graph of g is a horizontal shrink by a factor of $\frac{1}{3}$ of the graph of $f(x) = \cos x$.

5. amplitude: 3, period: π

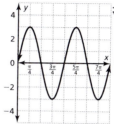 ; The graph of g is a horizontal shrink by a factor of $\frac{1}{2}$ and a vertical stretch by a factor of 3 of the graph of $f(x) = \sin x$.

7. $y = 10 \sin \frac{\pi}{2}x$

9. 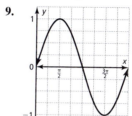   11.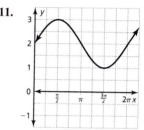

13.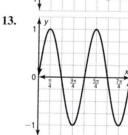

15. The value of a was substituted instead of the value of b; period: $\frac{\pi}{2}$

17. 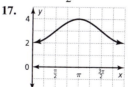   19.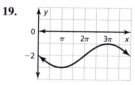

21.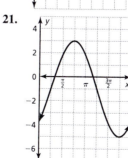

23. a. B; *Sample answer:* The graph of $y = \sin x$ has been translated 3 units up.
    b. C; *Sample answer:* The graph of $y = \cos x$ has been translated 3 units down.
    c. A; *Sample answer:* The graph of $y = \sin x$ has been shrunk horizontally by a factor of $\frac{1}{2}$ then translated $\frac{\pi}{2}$ units right.
    d. D; *Sample answer:* The graph of $y = \cos x$ has been shrunk horizontally by a factor of $\frac{1}{2}$ then translated $\frac{\pi}{2}$ units right.

25. $g(x) = -\frac{1}{3}\cos \pi x - 1$

27. a.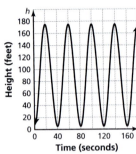
    b. 4.5 cycles; maximum: 175 ft, minimum: 5 ft

29. 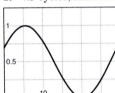; January 6, February 4, March 6, April 4, May 3, June 2, July 1, July 30, August 29, September 27, October 27, November 25, December 24

31. $(2n + 1)\frac{\pi}{4}$; The x-intercepts occur when $x = \pm\frac{\pi}{4}, \pm\frac{3\pi}{4}, \pm\frac{5\pi}{4}, \ldots$.

33. 80 beats per minute; The period is $\frac{3}{4}$, so there is one heartbeat every $\frac{3}{4}$ second and $\frac{1 \text{ beat}}{\frac{3}{4} \text{ sec}} \cdot \frac{60 \text{ sec}}{1 \text{ min}} = 80$ beats/min.

35. *Sample answer:* sine function for each city

9.4 Review & Refresh

37. $\sin \theta = \frac{\sqrt{3}}{2}, \cos \theta = \frac{1}{2}, \tan \theta = \sqrt{3}, \csc \theta = \frac{2\sqrt{3}}{3}$, $\sec \theta = 2, \cot \theta = \frac{\sqrt{3}}{3}$

38. $x = \frac{1}{5}$ and $x = \frac{1}{3}$

39. $-2x^4 + 15x^3 - 23x^2 + 60x - 32$

40. $4x^3 + 3x^2 - 8x - 15$ 41. $3x^3 - 32x^2 + 61x + 24$

42. $5x^4 + 13x^3 - 8x^2 - 10x + 1$

43. $\frac{2\pi}{5}$ 44. $-150°$

45.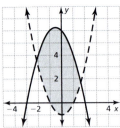

46. $\sin \theta = -\frac{3\sqrt{10}}{10}, \cos \theta = -\frac{\sqrt{10}}{10}, \tan \theta = 3, \csc \theta = -\frac{\sqrt{10}}{3}, \sec \theta = -\sqrt{10}, \cot \theta = \frac{1}{3}$

9.5 Practice

1. 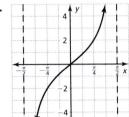; The graph of g is a vertical stretch by a factor of 2 of the graph of $f(x) = \tan x$.

3.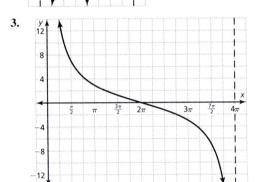
The graph of g is a horizontal stretch by a factor of 4 and a vertical stretch by a factor of 3 of the graph of $f(x) = \cot x$.

5. 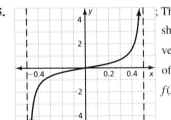; The graph of g is a horizontal shrink by a factor of $\frac{1}{\pi}$ and a vertical shrink by a factor of $\frac{1}{2}$ of the graph of $f(x) = \tan x$.

7. To find the period, use the expression $\frac{\pi}{|b|}$; Period: $\frac{\pi}{3}$

9. 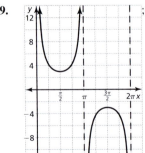; The graph of g is a vertical stretch by a factor of 3 of the graph of $f(x) = \csc x$.

11. 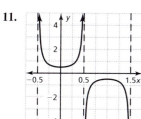 ; The graph of g is a horizontal shrink by a factor of $\frac{1}{\pi}$ and a vertical shrink by a factor of $\frac{1}{2}$ of the graph of $f(x) = \sec x$.

13. 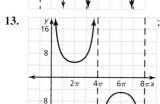 ; The graph of g is a horizontal stretch by a factor of 4 and a vertical stretch by a factor of 5 of the graph of $f(x) = \csc x$.

15. $y = 6 \tan x$ 17. $y = 2 \tan \pi x$

19. **a.** D; *Sample answer:* The parent function is the cosecant function and the graph has an asymptote at $x = 1$.
    b. C; *Sample answer:* The parent function is the secant function and the graph has an asymptote at $x = \frac{1}{2}$.
    c. A; *Sample answer:* The parent function is the secant function and the graph has an asymptote at $x = \frac{\pi}{4}$.
    d. B; *Sample answer:* The parent function is the cosecant function and the graph has an asymptote at $x = \frac{\pi}{2}$.

21. 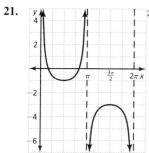 ; The graph of g is a translation 2 units down of the graph of $f(x) = \csc x$.

23. 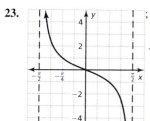 ; The graph of g is a reflection in the x-axis of the graph of $f(x) = \tan x$.

25. $g(x) = 2 \tan(3x - \pi)$ 27. $g(x) = -8 \csc x$
29. maximum: Function A; minimum: Function B
31. **a.** $d = 260 - 120 \tan \theta$
    b. 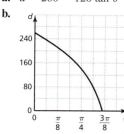 ; As the angle gets larger, the distance from your friend to the top of the building gets smaller. As the angle gets smaller, the distance from your friend to the top of the building gets larger.

33. *Sample answer:* $\csc x = \frac{1}{2}\left(\tan \frac{x}{2} + \cot \frac{x}{2}\right)$; Graphing the function produces the same graph as the cosecant function with asymptotes at $0, \pm\pi, \pm 2\pi, \ldots$.

35. *Sample answer:* industrialization; conservation efforts

9.5 Review & Refresh

36. *Sample answer:* $460°, -260°$
37. amplitude: 5; period: 2π
38. $-\frac{\sqrt{3}}{2}$ 39. $x = -1$
40. yes; $y = 1.8(3)^x$ 41. quadratic; $y = x^2 + 5x + 4$
42. $x = -5$ and $x = 2$

9.6 Practice

1. $P = 0.02 \sin 40\pi t$

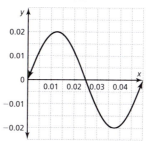

3. *Sample answer:* $y = 3 \sin 2x$
5. To find the amplitude, take half of the difference between the maximum and the minimum; $|a| = 8$
7. $h = -9 \cos 5\pi t + 13$
9. $D = 22.90 \sin(0.542t - 2.25) + 80.9$; The period of the graph represents the amount of time it takes for the temperature to complete one cycle, which is about 11.6 months.
11. *Sample answer:* $V = 100 \sin 4\pi t$
13. $y = 2.5 \sin 4\left(x - \frac{\pi}{8}\right) + 5.5$; $y = -2.5 \cos 4x + 5.5$
15. *Sample answer:* Violet has the highest frequency and red has the lowest frequency, with the other colors shown in increasing order of their frequencies.
17. *Sample answer:* The light reflects off the sphere at many different angles causing different wavelengths.

9.6 Review & Refresh

18. $\log_8 x - \log_8 7$ 19. $\ln 2 + \ln x$
20. $\sin \theta = -1$, $\cos \theta = 0$, $\tan \theta =$ undefined, $\csc \theta = -1$, $\sec \theta =$ undefined, $\cot \theta = 0$

21. 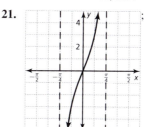 ; The graph of g is a horizontal shrink by a factor of $\frac{1}{2}$ and a vertical stretch by a factor of 3 of the graph of $f(x) = \tan x$.

22. ; The graph of g is a horizontal shrink by a factor of $\frac{1}{2\pi}$ of the graph of $f(x) = \csc x$.

23. parameter   24. $\frac{17\sqrt{2}}{2}$ 25. $\frac{6 + 3\sqrt{6}}{2}$

26. $-24 + 8\sqrt{10}$

27. $\dfrac{13\sqrt{11} - 13\sqrt{3}}{8}$

28.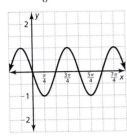

29.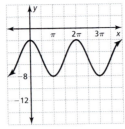

30. neither

9.7 Practice

1. $\cos\theta = \dfrac{2\sqrt{2}}{3}$, $\tan\theta = \dfrac{\sqrt{2}}{4}$, $\csc\theta = 3$, $\sec\theta = \dfrac{3\sqrt{2}}{4}$, $\cot\theta = 2\sqrt{2}$

3. $\sin\theta = -\dfrac{\sqrt{11}}{6}$, $\tan\theta = \dfrac{\sqrt{11}}{5}$, $\csc\theta = -\dfrac{6\sqrt{11}}{11}$, $\sec\theta = -\dfrac{6}{5}$, $\cot\theta = \dfrac{5\sqrt{11}}{11}$

5. $\cos x$

7. $-\sec x$

9. $\cos\left(\dfrac{\pi}{2} - x\right)\cot x = \sin x \cdot \dfrac{\cos x}{\sin x}$
$= \cos x$

11. $\dfrac{1+\cos x}{\sin x} + \dfrac{\sin x}{1+\cos x} = \dfrac{1+\cos x}{\sin x} + \dfrac{\sin x(1-\cos x)}{(1+\cos x)(1-\cos x)}$
$= \dfrac{1+\cos x}{\sin x} + \dfrac{\sin x(1-\cos x)}{1-\cos^2 x}$
$= \dfrac{1+\cos x}{\sin x} + \dfrac{\sin x(1-\cos x)}{\sin^2 x}$
$= \dfrac{1+\cos x}{\sin x} + \dfrac{1-\cos x}{\sin x}$
$= \dfrac{1+\cos x + 1 - \cos x}{\sin x}$
$= \dfrac{2}{\sin x}$
$= 2\csc x$

13. The cosine function has a period of 2π and $y = \cos(x - \pi)$ is a horizontal translation 2π units right of the graph of $y = \cos(x + \pi)$.

15. sometimes; $f(x) = g(x)$ only if the translation is a horizontal translation by an integer multiple of the period.

17. $s = \dfrac{h\cot\theta}{\sin(90° - \theta)}$
$= \dfrac{h\cot\theta}{\cos\theta}$
$= \dfrac{h\cos\theta}{\sin\theta\cos\theta}$
$= \dfrac{h}{\sin\theta}$
$= h\csc\theta$

19. $n_1\sin\theta_1 = n_2\sin\theta_2$; $n_1 = n_2$; This situation occurs when the mediums have the same index of refraction.

21. *Sample answer:* a Swiss mathematician and physicist

9.7 Review & Refresh

23. 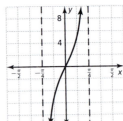 ; The graph of g is a horizontal shrink by a factor of $\dfrac{1}{2}$ and a vertical stretch by a factor of 5 of the graph of $f(x) = \tan x$.

24. The period is 8 and represents the amount of time, in seconds, that it takes for the buoy to bob up and down and return to the same position. The amplitude is 11.5 and represents the maximum distance, in feet, the buoy will be from its midline.

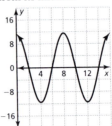

25. 4

26. *Sample answer:* $y = 3\cos 4x$

27. 81.85%

28. 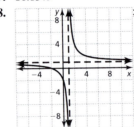 ; domain: all real numbers except $x = 1$; range: all real numbers except $y = 1$

29. 243

9.8 Practice

1. $\sqrt{3} - 2$

3. $\dfrac{\sqrt{2} - \sqrt{6}}{4}$

5. $\sqrt{3} + 2$

7. $-\dfrac{36}{85}$

9. $-\dfrac{84}{13}$

11. $\cos x$

13. $x = \dfrac{\pi}{6}$ and $\dfrac{5\pi}{6}$

15. $x = 0$ and π

17. $\dfrac{WQ}{NA} = \dfrac{35\tan(\theta - 45°) + 35\tan 45°}{h\tan\theta}$
$= \dfrac{35\left(\dfrac{\tan\theta - \tan 45°}{1 + \tan\theta\tan 45°}\right) + 35\tan 45°}{h\tan\theta}$
$= \dfrac{35\left(\dfrac{\tan\theta - 1}{1 + \tan\theta}\right) + 35}{h\tan\theta}$
$= \dfrac{35(\tan\theta - 1) + 35(1 + \tan\theta)}{h\tan\theta(1 + \tan\theta)}$
$= \dfrac{35\tan\theta - 35 + 35 + 35\tan\theta}{h\tan\theta(1 + \tan\theta)}$
$= \dfrac{70\tan\theta}{h\tan\theta(1 + \tan\theta)}$
$= \dfrac{70}{h(1 + \tan\theta)}$

19. Any point where the two graphs intersect on the interval $0 \leq x < 2\pi$ is a solution because if $f(x) = g(x)$ then $f(x) - g(x) = 0$; $x = 0$ and $x = \pi$

21. unit circle

23. no; The graph of the tangent function has vertical asymptotes at multiples of $\dfrac{\pi}{2}$ and the heights won't match the unit circle because tangent is the ratio of y to x.

9.8 Review & Refresh

24. $x = 4$ **25.** $x = -\dfrac{2}{3}$ **26.** $x \approx 17.7$

27. $\cos^2 \theta$ **28.** survey

29. 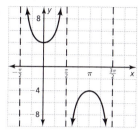 ; The graph of g is a vertical stretch by a factor of 4 of the graph of $f(x) = \sec x$.

30. $b > 1$ **31.** $h(t) = \dfrac{1}{4}\cos 2\pi t + 7.75$

Chapter 9 Review

1. $\sin \theta = \dfrac{4}{5}$, $\cos \theta = \dfrac{3}{5}$, $\tan \theta = \dfrac{4}{3}$, $\csc \theta = \dfrac{5}{4}$, $\sec \theta = \dfrac{5}{3}$, $\cot \theta = \dfrac{3}{4}$

2. $\sin \theta = \dfrac{\sqrt{3}}{2}$, $\cos \theta = \dfrac{1}{2}$, $\tan \theta = \sqrt{3}$, $\csc \theta = \dfrac{2\sqrt{3}}{3}$, $\sec \theta = 2$, $\cot \theta = \dfrac{\sqrt{3}}{3}$

3. $\sin \theta = \dfrac{\sqrt{85}}{11}$, $\tan \theta = \dfrac{\sqrt{85}}{6}$, $\csc \theta = \dfrac{11\sqrt{85}}{85}$, $\sec \theta = \dfrac{11}{6}$, $\cot \theta = \dfrac{6\sqrt{85}}{85}$

4. $A = 46°$, $b \approx 5.79$, $c = 8.34$

5. $A = 32°$, $a \approx 5.83$, $b = 9.33$

6. $\cos \theta$ and $\sin \theta$ are always less than or equal to 1, so their inverses must be greater than or equal to 1.

7. a. about 380 ft   **b.** about 170 ft

8. $\dfrac{\pi}{6}$ **9.** $\dfrac{5\pi}{4}$ **10.** $135°$ **11.** $300°$

12. Sample answer: $\dfrac{\pi}{9}$, $-\dfrac{17\pi}{9}$

13. $\dfrac{37\pi}{60}$

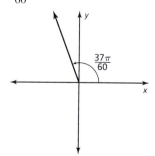

14. $\dfrac{7\pi}{6} \approx 3.7$ in.; $\dfrac{49\pi}{12} \approx 12.8$ in.^{2}

15. 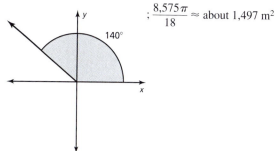 ; $\dfrac{8{,}575\pi}{18} \approx$ about 1,497 m^2

16. $\sin \theta = -\dfrac{7}{25}$, $\cos \theta = \dfrac{24}{25}$, $\tan \theta = -\dfrac{7}{24}$, $\csc \theta = -\dfrac{25}{7}$, $\sec \theta = \dfrac{25}{24}$, $\cot \theta = -\dfrac{24}{7}$

17. $\sin \theta = \dfrac{3\sqrt{13}}{13}$, $\cos \theta = -\dfrac{2\sqrt{13}}{13}$, $\tan \theta = -\dfrac{3}{2}$, $\csc \theta = \dfrac{\sqrt{13}}{3}$, $\sec \theta = -\dfrac{\sqrt{13}}{2}$, $\cot \theta = -\dfrac{2}{3}$

18. $-\dfrac{\sqrt{3}}{3}$ **19.** $\sqrt{2}$ **20.** $\dfrac{1}{2}$ **21.** 2

22. amplitude: 3, period: 2π
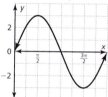
; The graph of g is a vertical stretch by a factor of 3 of the graph of $f(x) = \sin x$.

23. amplitude: 8, period: 2π
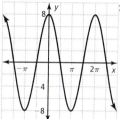
; The graph of g is a vertical stretch by a factor of 8 of the graph of $f(x) = \cos x$.

24. amplitude: 6, period: 2
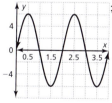
; The graph of g is a horizontal shrink by a factor of $\dfrac{1}{\pi}$ and a vertical stretch by a factor of 6 of the graph of $f(x) = \sin x$.

25. amplitude: $\dfrac{1}{4}$, period: $\dfrac{\pi}{2}$
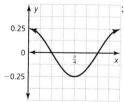
; The graph of g is a horizontal shrink by a factor of $\dfrac{1}{4}$ and a vertical shrink by a factor of $\dfrac{1}{4}$ of the graph of $f(x) = \cos x$.

26. $y = \dfrac{1}{2}\sin 4x$ **27.** $y = 2\sin 3x$

28.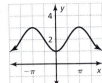
29.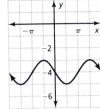
30.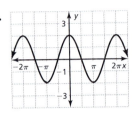
31.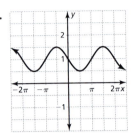

32. 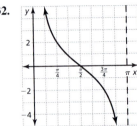 ; The graph of g is a vertical stretch by a factor of 2 of the graph of $f(x) = \cot x$.

33. 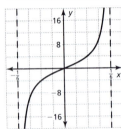 ; The graph of g is a horizontal shrink by a factor of $\frac{1}{3\pi}$ and a vertical stretch by a factor of 4 of the graph of $f(x) = \tan x$.

34. 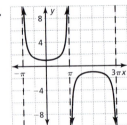 ; The graph of g is a horizontal stretch by a factor of 2 of the graph of $f(x) = \sec x$.

35. 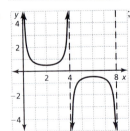 ; The graph of g is a horizontal stretch by a factor of $\frac{4}{\pi}$ and a vertical shrink by a factor of $\frac{1}{2}$ of the graph of $f(x) = \csc x$.

36. The asymptotes are at $x = \frac{n\pi}{12}$, where n is an odd integer.

37. $d = 3{,}000 - 1{,}500 \tan \theta$

38. Sample answer: $y = -\sin \frac{1}{2}x$

39. Sample answer: $y = \cos \pi x - 2$

40. $y = -3.5 \cos \frac{\pi}{6} x + 12.25$

41. $h = -2.5 \cos \pi t + 6.5$

42. $P = 1.71 \sin(0.527t - 2.08) + 2.55$; The period of the graph represents the amount of time it takes for the weather to complete one cycle, which is about 12 months.

43. $\sin \theta = \frac{4}{5}$, $\tan \theta = \frac{4}{3}$, $\csc \theta = \frac{5}{4}$, $\sec \theta = \frac{5}{3}$, $\cot \theta = \frac{3}{4}$

44. $\cos \theta = \frac{12}{13}$, $\tan \theta = -\frac{5}{12}$, $\csc \theta = -\frac{13}{5}$, $\sec \theta = \frac{13}{12}$, $\cot \theta = -\frac{12}{5}$

45. $\cos \theta = -\frac{\sqrt{15}}{4}$, $\tan \theta = -\frac{\sqrt{15}}{15}$, $\csc \theta = 4$, $\sec \theta = -\frac{4\sqrt{15}}{15}$, $\cot \theta = -\sqrt{15}$

46. $\sin \theta = -\frac{7\sqrt{53}}{53}$, $\cos \theta = -\frac{2\sqrt{53}}{53}$, $\csc \theta = -\frac{\sqrt{53}}{7}$, $\sec \theta = -\frac{\sqrt{53}}{2}$, $\cot \theta = \frac{2}{7}$

47. $\cos^2 x$ 48. $\tan x$ 49. $\sin x$ 50. $\cos^2 x$

51. $\dfrac{\cos x \sec x}{1 + \tan^2 x} = \dfrac{\cos x \sec x}{\sec^2 x}$
$= \dfrac{\cos x}{\sec x}$
$= \cos x \cos x$
$= \cos^2 x$

52. $\tan\left(\dfrac{\pi}{2} - x\right) \cot x = \cot x \cot x$
$= \cot^2 x$
$= \csc^2 x - 1$

53. yes; $\sec x \tan x - \sin x = \dfrac{1}{\cos x} \cdot \dfrac{\sin x}{\cos x} - \sin x$
$= \dfrac{\sin x}{\cos^2 x} - \sin x$
$= \sec^2 x \sin x - \sin x$
$= \sin x(\sec^2 x - 1)$
$= \sin x \tan^2 x$

54. $\dfrac{\sqrt{2} + \sqrt{6}}{4}$ 55. -1 56. $\dfrac{\sqrt{6} - \sqrt{2}}{4}$

57. $\dfrac{\sqrt{2} - \sqrt{6}}{4}$ 58. $\dfrac{19}{25}$ 59. $-\cos x$

60. $-\sin x$ 61. $-\cot x$ 62. $\tan x$

63. $x = \dfrac{3\pi}{4}$ and $x = \dfrac{5\pi}{4}$ 64. $x = 0$ and $x = \pi$

Chapter 10

Getting Ready for Chapter 10

1. $1, -1, -5$ 2. $21, 46, 81$ 3. $4, -16, -36$
4. $x = 4$ 5. $x = 6$ 6. $x = 66$
7. $x = 7$ 8. $x = 100$ 9. $x = 3$

10.1 Practice

1. $3, 4, 5, 6, 7, 8$ 3. $1, 4, 16, 64, 256, 1{,}024$
5. $16, 25, 36, 49, 64, 81$
7. The terms can be written as $5(1) - 4$, $5(2) - 4$, $5(3) - 4$, $5(4) - 4$; $a_5 = 21$; $a_n = 5n - 4$
9. The terms can be written as $-4(1), 4(2), -4(3), 4(4)$; $a_5 = -20$; $a_n = (-1)^n 4n$

11. The terms can be written as $\frac{2}{3(1)}, \frac{2}{3(2)}, \frac{2}{3(3)}, \frac{2}{3(4)}$; $a_5 = \frac{2}{15}$; $a_n = \frac{2}{3n}$

13. $a_n = 4n + 2$

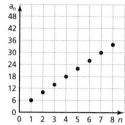

15. $\sum_{i=1}^{5} (3i + 4)$ **17.** $\sum_{i=1}^{\infty} \frac{1}{3^i}$ **19.** 42

21. 82   **23.** 35

25. a. $a_n = \frac{n(n+1)}{2}$ **b.** $a_n = 4n$

27. a. \$50.50   **b.** 316 days

29. yes; Use the formula for $i = 1$ and $n = 1{,}659$. The sum of the first 1,659 positive integers is 1,376,970. Then subtract $1 + 2 = 3$ from the sum. So, the sum of the series is 1,376,967.

31. a. true;
$$\sum_{i=1}^{n} ca_i = ca_1 + ca_2 + ca_3 + \cdots + ca_n$$
$$= c(a_1 + a_2 + a_3 + \cdots + a_n)$$
$$= c\sum_{i=1}^{n} a_i$$

b. true;
$$\sum_{i=1}^{n}(a_i + b_i) = (a_1 + b_1) + (a_2 + b_2) + \cdots + (a_n + b_n)$$
$$= a_1 + a_2 + \cdots + a_n + b_1 + b_2 + \cdots + b_n$$
$$= \sum_{i=1}^{n} a_i + \sum_{i=1}^{n} b_i$$

c. false; Sample answer: $\sum_{i=1}^{2}(2i)(3i) = 30$, $\left(\sum_{i=1}^{2} 2i\right)\left(\sum_{i=1}^{2} 3i\right) = 54$

d. false; Sample answer: $\sum_{i=1}^{2}(2i)^2 = 20$, $\left(\sum_{i=1}^{2} 2i\right)^2 = 36$

33. 255 moves

35. 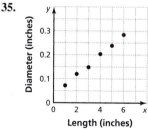 ; The relationship is approximately linear.

10.1 Review & Refresh

37. $-\sin^2 \theta$ **38.** $-\cot x$

39. $\frac{1}{x}$ **40.** $\frac{4x - 16}{(x+2)(x-2)}$

41. $\sin \theta = \frac{\sqrt{3}}{2}$, $\cos \theta = -\frac{1}{2}$, $\tan \theta = -\sqrt{3}$, $\csc \theta = \frac{2\sqrt{3}}{3}$, $\sec \theta = -2$, $\cot \theta = \frac{-\sqrt{3}}{3}$

42. Sample answer: $y = 3 \cos 2x + 1$

43. $(2, 1, -1)$ **44.** $(3, 1, 1)$

10.2 Practice

1. arithmetic; The common difference is -2.

3. not arithmetic; The differences are not constant.

5. $a_n = 8n + 4$; $a_{20} = 164$ **7.** $a_n = \frac{3}{4}n - \frac{11}{4}$; $a_{20} = \frac{49}{4}$

9. When $d > 0$, the terms increase. When $d < 0$, the terms decrease.

11. $a_n = 5n - 12$ **13.** $a_n = -2n + 13$

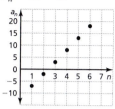

15. $a_n = -6n + 28$ **17.** $a_n = -4n + 13$

19. $a_n = -3n + 12$ **21.** -924

23. -8.2 **25.** $-1{,}474$

27. no; Sample answer: Consider a sequence with two terms. The sum is $a_1 + (a_1 + d) = 2a_1 + d$. Twice this sum is equal to $4a_1 + 2d$. Doubling the difference gives a sum of $a_1 + (a_1 + 2d) = 2a_1 + 2d$.

29. 22,500; The sequence of positive odd integers can be represented by $2i - 1$. So, find the sum $\sum_{i=1}^{150} (2i - 1)$.

31. $\frac{2y}{n} - x$ **33.** $x = \frac{2}{3}$; $-\frac{8}{3}$

35. Sample answer: 50, 85, 120, 155, 190, 225, 260, 295, 330, 365, 400, 435, 470, 505, 540, 575, 610, 645, 680, 715, 750, 785, 820, 855, 890, 925, 960, 995, 1,030, 1,065; $\sum_{n=1}^{30}(15 + 35n) = 16{,}725 \approx 17{,}000$

10.2 Review & Refresh

36. even; negative   **37.** $\frac{1}{595}$, or about 0.17%

38. $-\sin x$

39. no; $f(-1) = 2$, so $f^{-1}(2) = -1$, but $g(2) \neq -1$.

40. 38

41. $\sin \theta = -\frac{8}{17}$, $\tan \theta = -\frac{8}{15}$, $\csc \theta = -\frac{17}{8}$, $\sec \theta = \frac{17}{15}$, $\cot \theta = -\frac{15}{8}$

10.3 Practice

1. geometric; The common ratio is $\frac{1}{2}$.

3. not geometric; The ratios are not constant.

5. geometric; The common ratio is -5.

7. $a_n = 6(4)^{n-1}$; $a_7 = 24{,}576$

9. $a_n = 4\left(\frac{3}{2}\right)^{n-1}$; $a_7 = \frac{729}{16}$

11. $a_n = 2^{n-1}$ **13.** $a_n = -3(4)^{n-1}$

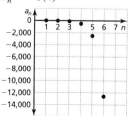

15. The difference of the first two terms was used instead of the ratio; $a_n = 4(3)^{n-1}$
17. $a_n = 5(3)^{n-1}$
19. $a_n = 6(-2)^{n-1}$
21. $a_n = 7(4)^{n-1}$
23. $a_n = -6(3)^{n-1}$ or $a_n = -6(-3)^{n-1}$
25. 40,353,606
27. $\frac{989,527}{65,536} \approx 15.10$
29. 1,092 people
31. $276.25
33. Check students' work.
35. $\frac{3x - 48x^9}{1 - 2x^2}$
37. Each yellow triangle is $\frac{1}{64}$ the area of the blue triangle.

10.3 Review & Refresh

39. no; Subjects are not randomly assigned to control groups and treatment groups. The conclusion may or may not be valid. There may be other reasons why students who chose bananas had greater flexibility.
40. The graph of g is a vertical translation 3 units up of the graph of f.
41. $\tan x$
42. 55
43. $\frac{19}{10x}$
44. $a_n = -2n + 11$
45. 12; 2 real solutions

10.4 Practice

1. 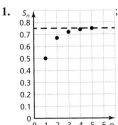 ; $S_1 = 0.5, S_2 = 0.67, S_3 \approx 0.72$, $S_4 \approx 0.74, S_5 \approx 0.75$; S_n appears to approach $\frac{3}{4}$.

3. ; $S_1 = 4, S_2 = 6.4, S_3 = 7.84, S_4 \approx 8.70$, $S_5 \approx 9.22$; S_n appears to approach 10.

5. 10
7. $-\frac{25}{3}$
9. 56 ft
11. $\frac{16}{99}$
13. Sample answer: $\sum_{i=1}^{\infty} 3\left(\frac{1}{2}\right)^{i-1}$; $\sum_{i=1}^{\infty} 2\left(\frac{2}{3}\right)^{i-1}$; $\frac{3}{1 - \frac{1}{2}} = 6$ and $\frac{2}{1 - \frac{2}{3}} = 6$
15. yes; $\sum_{i=1}^{\infty} 9(0.1)^i = 1$
17. 57.232 ft
19. no; no; The distance traveled on each bounce approaches zero as the number of bounces approaches infinity.

10.4 Review & Refresh

20. arithmetic
21. neither
22. geometric
23. quadratic
24. $x = \frac{\ln 12}{\ln 4} \approx 1.79$
25. $x = -1$ and $x = -\frac{1}{2}$
26. $4\frac{7}{20}$
27. $x^2 - x + 4 - \frac{17}{x + 4}$
28. a. $a_n = 2n + 3$ b. 96 students
29. $g(x) = 0.5^x + 2$

10.5 Practice

1. 1, 4, 7, 10, 13, 16
3. 2, 5, 26, 677, 458,330, 210,066,388,901
5. $a_1 = 21, a_n = a_{n-1} - 7$
7. $a_1 = 4, a_n = -3a_{n-1}$
9. $f(1) = 1, f(n) = f(n-1) + 1$
11. The recursive rule needs to give the first term; $a_1 = 3$, $a_n = 4a_{n-1}$
13. $a_1 = 7, a_n = a_{n-1} + 4$
15. $a_1 = -\frac{1}{2}, a_n = \frac{1}{4}a_{n-1}$
17. $a_n = -6n + 9$
19. $a_n = -4(0.65)^{n-1}$
21. $a_n = 25,600(0.86)^{n-1}$
23. a. $a_1 = 50,000, a_n = 0.8a_{n-1} + 5,000$
    b. 35,240 members
    c. The number of members stabilizes at 25,000.
25. Check students' work.
27. a. $a_1 = 9,000, a_n = 0.9a_{n-1} + 800$
    b. The number of members stabilizes at 8,000 trees.
29. a. The values alternate between positive and negative and get closer to zero.
    b. $-1 < r < 0$; The sign of a_n alternates between positive and negative and the absolute value decreases.
31. a. Explicit rules: $T_n = \frac{1}{2}n^2 + \frac{1}{2}n$, $S_n = n^2$;
    Recursive rules: $T_1 = 1, T_n = T_{n-1} + n$,
    $S_1 = 1, S_n = S_{n-1} + 2n - 1$
    b. $S_n = T_{n-1} + T_n$

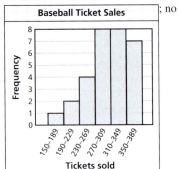

33. Check students' work.

10.5 Review & Refresh

35. $x = 25$
36. $x = 64$
37. $x = 5$
38. 12
39. The sum does not exist.
40.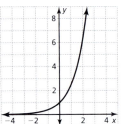
41. 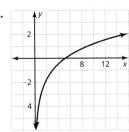 ; no
42.
43. $(0, 1), (3, -2)$
44. $(-3, 4), (0, 4)$

Chapter 10 Review

1. 2, 5, 8, 11, 14, 17
2. 4, −8, 16, −32, 64, −128
3. Each layer has n rows of blocks and $n + 1$ columns of blocks; $a_n = n^2 + n$

4. $\sum_{i=1}^{12}(3i+4)$
5. $\sum_{i=1}^{\infty}(i^2-i)$
6. -729
7. $1{,}081$
8. 650
9. arithmetic
10. $a_n=6n-4;\ a_{15}=86$
11. $a_n=3n;\ a_{15}=45$

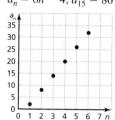
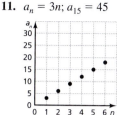

12. $a_n=-4n+12;\ a_{15}=-48$

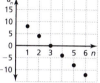

13. $2{,}070$
14. 105 pieces of chalk
15. geometric
16. $a_n=25\left(\dfrac{2}{5}\right)^{n-1}$
17. $a_n=2(-3)^{n-1}$

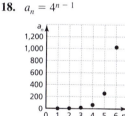

18. $a_n=4^{n-1}$ or $a_n=(-4)^{n-1}$

19. $a_n=\dfrac{1}{4}n$
20. $a_n=\dfrac{1}{2}(2)^{n-1}$
21. 855
22. $-223\dfrac{2}{3}$
23. $-\dfrac{4{,}095}{8{,}192}\approx 0.50$
24. a. $a_n=65{,}000(1.035)^{n-1}$
    b. about $\$74{,}589$
    c. about $\$762{,}541$
25. $S_1=1,\ S_2=0.75,\ S_3\approx 0.81,$ $S_4\approx 0.80,\ S_5\approx 0.80;$ S_n approaches 0.80.
26. $\dfrac{15}{4}$
27. The sum does not exist.
28. -1.6
29. $\dfrac{4}{33}$
30. $833\dfrac{1}{3}$ ft
31. $7, 18, 29, 40, 51, 62$
32. $6, 24, 96, 384, 1{,}536, 6{,}144$
33. $-2, 7, -2, 7, -2, 7$
34. $4, 6, 10, 16, 24, 34$
35. $a_1=9,\ a_n=\dfrac{2}{3}a_{n-1}$
36. $a_1=4,\ a_n=a_{n-1}+7$
37. $a_1=105,\ a_n=\dfrac{3}{5}a_{n-1}$
38. $a_n=26n-30$
39. $a_n=8(-5)^{n-1}$
40. $a_n=26\left(\dfrac{2}{5}\right)^{n-1}$
41. Sample answer: $P_0=18,\ P_n=1.1P_{n-1}$
42. a. $a_1=1,\ a_n=a_{n-1}+4n-3$
    b. $66, 91, 120$

Chapter 11

Getting Ready for Chapter 11

1. $x=-\dfrac{1}{2}$
2. $x=\dfrac{5}{7}$
3. $x=-21$
4. $(-6, 2)$
5. $(4, 9)$
6. $\left(4, \dfrac{1}{2}\right)$

11.1 Practice

1. $\begin{bmatrix}10 & -8\\ 6 & -7\end{bmatrix}$
3. not possible; The matrices have different dimensions.
5. Corresponding elements were not added together; $\begin{bmatrix}8\\10\end{bmatrix}$
7. $\begin{bmatrix}2 & -3\\ 4 & 6\\ 1 & 11\end{bmatrix}$
9. $\begin{bmatrix}5 & -4 & -7\\ -3 & 1 & -5\end{bmatrix}$
11. $a=6, b=2, c=3, d=-4$
13. $a=10, b=21, c=-5, d=11$
15. $a=6, b=10, c=30, d=4$
17.

	May Dogs Cats	June Dogs Cats	Average Dogs Cats
< 1 yr	$\begin{bmatrix}6 & 13\\ 7 & 5\\ 4 & 1\end{bmatrix}$	$\begin{bmatrix}12 & 7\\ 9 & 3\\ 2 & 3\end{bmatrix}$	$\begin{bmatrix}9 & 10\\ 8 & 4\\ 3 & 2\end{bmatrix}$
1– 6 yr			
> 6yr			

Over the two months, the monthly average number of adoptions were 9 dogs under 1 year old, 10 cats under 1 year old, 8 dogs between 1 and 6 years old, 4 cats between 1 and 6 years old, 3 dogs over 6 years old, and 2 cats over 6 years old.

19. $X=\begin{bmatrix}1 & 3\\ 3 & -3\end{bmatrix}$
21. yes; The dimension of matrix O is $m\times n$ and every element in it is 0.
23. a. $A+B=\begin{bmatrix}a & b\\ c & d\end{bmatrix}+\begin{bmatrix}e & f\\ g & h\end{bmatrix}$
    $=\begin{bmatrix}a+e & b+f\\ c+g & d+h\end{bmatrix}$
    $=\begin{bmatrix}e+a & f+b\\ g+c & h+d\end{bmatrix}$
    $=\begin{bmatrix}e & f\\ g & h\end{bmatrix}+\begin{bmatrix}a & b\\ c & d\end{bmatrix}$
    $=B+A$

b. $(A + B) + C = \left(\begin{bmatrix} a & b \\ c & d \end{bmatrix} + \begin{bmatrix} e & f \\ g & h \end{bmatrix}\right) + \begin{bmatrix} p & q \\ r & s \end{bmatrix}$

$= \begin{bmatrix} a+e & b+f \\ c+g & d+h \end{bmatrix} + \begin{bmatrix} p & q \\ r & s \end{bmatrix}$

$= \begin{bmatrix} a+e+p & b+f+q \\ c+g+r & d+h+s \end{bmatrix}$

$= \begin{bmatrix} a+(e+p) & b+(f+q) \\ c+(g+r) & d+(h+s) \end{bmatrix}$

$= \begin{bmatrix} a & b \\ c & d \end{bmatrix} + \begin{bmatrix} e+p & f+q \\ g+r & h+s \end{bmatrix}$

$= \begin{bmatrix} a & b \\ c & d \end{bmatrix} + \left(\begin{bmatrix} e & f \\ g & h \end{bmatrix} + \begin{bmatrix} p & q \\ r & s \end{bmatrix}\right)$

$= A + (B + C)$

c. $k(A + B) = k\left(\begin{bmatrix} a & b \\ c & d \end{bmatrix} + \begin{bmatrix} e & f \\ g & h \end{bmatrix}\right)$

$= k\begin{bmatrix} a+e & b+f \\ c+g & d+h \end{bmatrix}$

$= \begin{bmatrix} k(a+e) & k(b+f) \\ k(c+g) & k(d+h) \end{bmatrix}$

$= \begin{bmatrix} ka+ke & kb+kf \\ kc+kg & kd+kh \end{bmatrix}$

$= \begin{bmatrix} ka & kb \\ kc & kd \end{bmatrix} + \begin{bmatrix} ke & kf \\ kg & kh \end{bmatrix}$

$= k\begin{bmatrix} a & b \\ c & d \end{bmatrix} + k\begin{bmatrix} e & f \\ g & h \end{bmatrix}$

$= kA + kB$

25. 9,216 pixels

27. Each entry in the matrix would be multiplied by 4.

11.1 Review & Refresh

28. 15, 12, 9, 6, 3, 0

29. $3x^3 + 4x^2 - 9x - 10$

30. $64t^3 - 48t^2 + 12t - 1$

31. $\dfrac{x^2 - 2x - 15}{x - 3},\ x \neq 0, x \neq 7$

32. $a_n = \dfrac{2}{3}(-3)^{n-1}$

33. observational study

34. $168\pi \approx 527.8$

35. $\dfrac{64}{3}$

11.2 Practice

1. defined; 1×1

3. not defined

5. $[-2 \quad 3]$

7. $\begin{bmatrix} -1 & 4 \\ 22 & -24 \\ -10 & 12 \end{bmatrix}$

9. Each element in the first row of the first matrix is multiplied by the corresponding element in the first column of the second matrix instead of the first row of the second matrix; $\begin{bmatrix} 13 & \ \end{bmatrix}$

11. $\begin{bmatrix} 15 & -17 \\ -6 & 6 \end{bmatrix}$

13. $\begin{bmatrix} 13 & -\frac{9}{2} \\ -\frac{15}{2} & 3 \end{bmatrix}$

15. Team A: $704, Team B: $960

17. a. Sample answer: $C = \begin{bmatrix} 1 & 3 & 7 \\ 4 & 2 & 6 \end{bmatrix}$

b. Sample answer: $AC = \begin{bmatrix} 1 & 3 & 7 \\ -4 & -2 & -6 \end{bmatrix}$

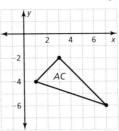

Triangle AC is a reflection in the x-axis of the triangle C.

c. Sample answer: $BC = \begin{bmatrix} -4 & -2 & -6 \\ 1 & 3 & 7 \end{bmatrix}$

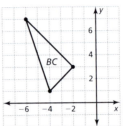

Triangle BC is a rotation 90° counterclockwise about the origin of triangle C.

d. Sample answer: Multiplying any $2 \times m$ matrix, which represents the vertices of a figure, by A reflects the figure in the x-axis. Multiplying any $2 \times m$ matrix, which represents the vertices of a figure, by B rotates the figure 90° counterclockwise about the origin.

19. The product AB is a diagonal matrix where each element along the diagonal is the product of the two corresponding elements in the matrices A and B.

21. The number of products involved in computing the product increases nonlinearly as the value of n increases.

11.2 Review & Refresh

23.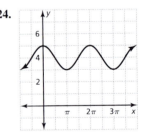

24.

25. a. $7,278.42   **b.** $149.42

26. $x = \pm 2i$

27. $x = \pm 3i$

28. $S_1 = 0.25,\ S_2 \approx 0.38,\ S_3 \approx 0.44,\ S_4 \approx 0.47,\ S_5 \approx 0.48$; S_n appears to approach $\dfrac{1}{2}$.

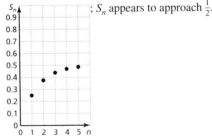

29. $\begin{bmatrix} -9 & -21 \\ 20 & 2 \end{bmatrix}$

30. $\begin{bmatrix} 10 & -8 & 0 \\ -6 & 4 & 5 \end{bmatrix}$

31. 3

32. -1

11.3 Practice

1. 10
3. 30
5. 26
7. The products were subtracted in the wrong order; 6
9. $k = 5$
11. 11 units^2
13. 260 mi^2
15. $(2, -1)$
17. $(2, -1, 1)$
19. $x + y = 6,700$
    $40x + 25y = 185,500$
    1,200 floor seats, 5,500 balcony seats
21. sulfur: 32; chlorine: 35.5; calcium: 40
23. $t_1 = 96$ lb, $t_2 = 48$ lb, $a = -16$ ft/sec^2
25. yes
27. $x = -2$ and $x = 4$
29. $(40, 120)$ or $(440, 120)$
31. a. $x = \dfrac{ed - bf}{ad - bc}, y = \dfrac{af - ce}{ad - bc}$
    b. The expressions for x and y are equivalent to those given by Cramer's Rule for a 2×2 system.
33. $i_1 = 7.2$ amperes, $i_2 = 2.4$ amperes, $i_3 = 4.8$ amperes

11.3 Review & Refresh

35. $a = 4, b = 4, c = 22, d = -7$
36. $\begin{bmatrix} 14 & 2 \\ 21 & 12 \end{bmatrix}$
37. $a_1 = 5, a_n = na_{n-1}$
38. $x = \dfrac{11}{2}$
39. $x = -1, x = \dfrac{1}{2},$ and $x = 3$
40. $\sin\left(\dfrac{3\pi}{2} - x\right) \tan x = \left(\sin\dfrac{3\pi}{2} \cos x - \cos\dfrac{3\pi}{2} \sin x\right) \tan x$
    $= [(-1)\cos x - (0)\sin x] \tan x$
    $= -\cos x \tan x$
    $= -\cos x \left(\dfrac{\sin x}{\cos x}\right)$
    $= -\sin x$
41. $f^{-1}(x) = -\dfrac{1}{3}\sqrt{x}$

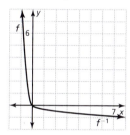

42. $c = 9; (x + 3)^2 = x^2 + 6x + 9$
43.

domain: all real numbers; range: $y > 0$

44. $\dfrac{2x^2 + 5x + 6}{(x + 1)(x + 2)}$

11.4 Practice

1. $\begin{bmatrix} 7 & -3 \\ -9 & 4 \end{bmatrix}$
3. The inverse does not exist.
5. $\begin{bmatrix} \dfrac{7}{2} & \dfrac{3}{2} \\ \dfrac{11}{2} & \dfrac{5}{2} \end{bmatrix}$

7. The second matrix is multiplied by the determinant instead of the reciprocal of the determinant;
$\begin{bmatrix} 1 & -\dfrac{1}{2} \\ -3 & 2 \end{bmatrix}$

9. $X = \begin{bmatrix} 1 & 2 \\ 2 & 1 \end{bmatrix}$
11. $X = \begin{bmatrix} -18 & -19 & -10 \\ -3 & -4 & -2 \end{bmatrix}$

13. $A^{-1} = \begin{bmatrix} 1 & 1 & 0 \\ 6 & 7 & -2 \\ -3 & -3 & 1 \end{bmatrix}$
15. $A^{-1} = \begin{bmatrix} -1 & -2 & \dfrac{1}{2} \\ -1 & -1 & \dfrac{1}{2} \\ 1 & 2 & 0 \end{bmatrix}$

17. $(3, -1)$
19. $(-3, 4)$
21. $(-9, 19, -10)$
23. rose: $5, carnation: $1.50, tulip: $2
25. always; The product is always the identity matrix.
27. never; The inverse is only defined for a square matrix.
29. a. $p = 2q$ b. $p \neq 2q$
31. $x = \pm 1, z = \pm 1, y = 0$ when x and z have the same sign, y is any real number when x and z have different signs;
Set each element of A equal to the corresponding element of A^{-1} using the inverse of a 2×2 matrix formula. Solve the resulting equations and test values of x and z to determine the values of y.

33. $A^{-1} = \begin{bmatrix} -1 & -2 & -1 \\ -3 & -5 & -2 \\ 1 & 2 & 2 \end{bmatrix}$
35. Check students' work.

11.4 Review & Refresh

36. domain: $x \geq 5$, range: $y \geq -1$
37. $(f + g)(x) = 2x^{1/2}$, domain: $x \geq 0$;
    $(f - g)(x) = 8x^{1/2}$, domain: $x \geq 0$;
    $(f + g)(16) = 8; (f - g)(16) = 32$
38. -52
39. 2
40. $-\dfrac{\sqrt{3}}{3}$
41. exponential
42. $\begin{bmatrix} 6 & 49 \\ -14 & -46 \\ -7 & 18 \end{bmatrix}$
43. $\mu = 32; \sigma = 6$

Chapter 11 Review

1. $\begin{bmatrix} 3 & -2 \\ -5 & 7 \end{bmatrix}$
2. $\begin{bmatrix} 2 & -4 & 0 \\ 7 & 6 & 7 \end{bmatrix}$
3. $\begin{bmatrix} -15 & 6 \\ -9 & -18 \end{bmatrix}$
4. $\begin{bmatrix} 64 & 32 & 40 \\ -8 & 48 & -16 \end{bmatrix}$
5. $\begin{bmatrix} 7 & 6 \\ 8 & -1 \\ 3 & 1 \end{bmatrix}$
6. $\begin{bmatrix} 3 & 10 \\ 10 & -3 \\ -1 & 6 \end{bmatrix}$
7. $a = -6, b = 3, c = 8, d = -3$
8. $a = 10, b = -3, c = -1, d = 3$
9. $a = -1, b = 2, c = -5, d = -2$

10.
$$\begin{array}{c} \text{Year 1} \\ \text{Apples Peaches} \\ \begin{bmatrix} 450 & 960 \\ 530 & 1{,}130 \\ 1{,}050 & 720 \end{bmatrix} \end{array} \begin{array}{c} \text{Year 2} \\ \text{Apples Peaches} \\ \begin{bmatrix} 510 & 930 \\ 650 & 1{,}260 \\ 990 & 580 \end{bmatrix} \end{array} \begin{array}{l} \text{July} \\ \text{August} \\ \text{September} \end{array}$$

$$\begin{array}{c} \text{Average} \\ \text{Apples Peaches} \\ \begin{bmatrix} 480 & 945 \\ 590 & 1{,}195 \\ 1{,}020 & 650 \end{bmatrix} \end{array} \begin{array}{l} \text{July} \\ \text{August} \\ \text{September} \end{array}$$

Over the two years, the average amounts of apples sold were 480 pounds in July, 590 pounds in August, and 1,020 pounds in September, and the average amounts of peaches sold were 945 pounds in July, 1,195 pounds in August, and 650 pounds in September.

11. $[-2 \;\; 7]$

12. $\begin{bmatrix} -2 & 6 & -15 \\ 6 & 0 & -3 \end{bmatrix}$

13. not possible; The product is not defined.

14. $\begin{bmatrix} -1 & -31 \\ -17 & 11 \end{bmatrix}$

15. $\begin{bmatrix} -31 & 4 \\ -22 & 8 \end{bmatrix}$

16. $\begin{bmatrix} 40 & -20 \\ -6 & -6 \\ 16 & -14 \end{bmatrix}$

17. $\begin{bmatrix} 7{,}381{,}000 \\ 7{,}281{,}000 \end{bmatrix}$

18. -42

19. 14

20. *Sample answer:* $0, 2; -4, 0$

21. about 12.15 ft^2

22. $\begin{bmatrix} -\frac{5}{3} & \frac{2}{3} \\ \frac{4}{3} & -\frac{1}{3} \end{bmatrix}$

23. $\begin{bmatrix} -\frac{1}{8} & \frac{1}{8} \\ -\frac{5}{16} & -\frac{3}{16} \end{bmatrix}$

24. $\begin{bmatrix} \frac{1}{8} & -\frac{1}{6} \\ -\frac{1}{16} & -\frac{1}{12} \end{bmatrix}$

25. The inverse does not exist.

26. $X = \begin{bmatrix} -38 & -13 \\ -54 & -18 \end{bmatrix}$

27. $X = \begin{bmatrix} -\frac{5}{2} & -\frac{9}{2} \\ 4 & 7 \end{bmatrix}$

28. $X = \begin{bmatrix} -2 & -6 \\ -6 & -28 \end{bmatrix}$

29. $X = \begin{bmatrix} -9 & 4 \\ 14 & -5 \end{bmatrix}$

30. $(7, 1)$

31. $(-2, 5)$

32. $(-1, -4)$

33. $(4, 1)$

34. $A^{-1} = \begin{bmatrix} \frac{1}{n} & 0 & 0 \\ 0 & \frac{1}{n} & 0 \\ 0 & 0 & \frac{1}{n} \end{bmatrix}$

35. pancake: $2.25, egg: $0.75, sausage link: $1.25

English-Spanish Glossary

English | Spanish

A

amplitude *(p. 480)* One-half the difference of the maximum value and the minimum value of the graph of a trigonometric function

amplitud *(p. 480)* La mitad de la diferencia del valor máximo y el valor mínimo del gráfico de una función trigonométrica

arithmetic sequence *(p. 538)* A sequence in which the difference of consecutive terms is constant

secuencia aritmética *(p. 538)* Una secuencia en la que la diferencia de términos consecutivos es constante

arithmetic series *(p. 541)* An expression formed by adding the terms of an arithmetic sequence

serie aritmética *(p. 541)* Una expresión formada al sumar los términos de una secuencia aritmética

asymptote *(p. 290)* A line that a graph approaches more and more closely

asíntota *(p. 290)* Una recta a la que una gráfica se acerca cada vez más

axis of symmetry *(p. 52)* A line that divides a parabola into mirror images and passes through the vertex

eje de simetría *(p. 52)* Una recta que divide una parábola en imágenes reflejo y que pasa a través del vértice

B

bias *(p. 417)* An error that results in a misrepresentation of a population

sesgo *(p. 417)* Un error que da como resultado una representación errónea de una población

biased question *(p. 419)* A question that is flawed in a way that leads to inaccurate results

pregunta sesgada *(p. 419)* Una pregunta imperfecta que lleva a obtener resultados inexactos

biased sample *(p. 417)* A sample that overrepresents or underrepresents part of a population

muestra sesgada *(p. 417)* Una muestra que representa excesiva o insuficientemente parte de una población

Binomial Theorem *(p. 163)* For any positive integer n, the binomial expansion of $(a + b)^n$ is
$(a + b)^n = {}_nC_0 a^n b^0 + {}_nC_1 a^{n-1} b^1 + {}_nC_2 a^{n-2} b^2 + \cdots + {}_nC_n a^0 b^n.$

teorema del binomio *(p. 163)* Por cada número entero positivo n, la expansión del binomio de $(a + b)^n$ es
$(a + b)^n = {}_nC_0 a^n b^0 + {}_nC_1 a^{n-1} b^1 + {}_nC_2 a^{n-2} b^2 + \cdots + {}_nC_n a^0 b^n.$

C

census *(p. 408)* Data from an entire population

censo *(p. 408)* Datos de toda una población

central angle *(p. 467)* The angle measure of a sector of a circle formed by two radii

ángulo central *(p. 467)* La medida del ángulo de un sector de un círculo formado por dos radios

cluster sample *(p. 416)* A sample in which a population is divided into groups, called clusters, and all of the members in one or more of the clusters are randomly selected

muestra de cluster *(p. 416)* Una muestra en la que una población se divide en grupos, llamados cluster en inglés, y todos los miembros de uno o más de los cluster son seleccionados en forma aleatoria

coefficient matrix *(p. 596)* A matrix consisting of the coefficients of a linear system

matriz de coeficiente *(p. 596)* Una matriz que consiste en los coeficientes de un sistema lineal

English-Spanish Glossary A47

common difference *(p. 538)* The constant difference d between consecutive terms of an arithmetic sequence

common logarithm *(p. 305)* A logarithm with base 10, denoted as $\log_{10}$ or simply by log

common ratio *(p. 546)* The constant ratio r between consecutive terms of a geometric sequence

completing the square *(p. 106)* To add a term c to an expression of the form $x^2 + bx$ such that $x^2 + bx + c$ is a perfect square trinomial

complex conjugates *(p. 98)* Pairs of complex numbers of the forms $a + bi$ and $a - bi$, where $b \neq 0$

complex fraction *(p. 379)* A fraction that contains a fraction in its numerator or denominator

complex number *(p. 96)* A number written in the form $a + bi$, where a and b are real numbers

composition *(p. 266)* A combination of functions where the output of one function is used as the input of another function

constant of variation *(p. 354)* A constant that describes the relationship between a pair of variables that show direct variation or inverse variation

control group *(p. 424)* The group that is not subjected to the treatment during an experiment

controlled experiment *(p. 424)* An experiment in which groups are studied under the same conditions with the exception of one or more variables of interest

convenience sample *(p. 416)* A sample in which only members of a population who are easy to reach are selected

correlation coefficient *(p. 23)* A number r from -1 to 1 that measures how well a line fits a set of data pairs (x, y)

cosecant *(p. 456)* A trigonometric function for an acute angle θ of a right triangle, denoted by
$$\csc \theta = \frac{\text{hypotenuse}}{\text{opposite}}$$

cosine *(p. 456)* A trigonometric function for an acute angle θ of a right triangle, denoted by
$$\cos \theta = \frac{\text{adjacent}}{\text{hypotenuse}}$$

cotangent *(p. 456)* A trigonometric function for an acute angle θ of a right triangle, denoted by
$$\cot \theta = \frac{\text{adjacent}}{\text{opposite}}$$

diferencia común *(p. 538)* La diferencia constante d entre términos consecutivos de una secuencia aritmética

logaritmo común *(p. 305)* Un logaritmo de base 10, denotado como $\log_{10}$ o simplemente como log

razón común *(p. 546)* La razón constante r entre términos consecutivos de una secuencia geométrica

completando el cuadrado *(p. 106)* Agregar un término c a una expresión de la forma $x^2 + bx$ para que $x^2 + bx + c$ sea un trinomio de cuadrado perfecto

conjugados complejos *(p. 98)* Pares de números complejos de las formas $a + bi$ y $a - bi$, donde $b \neq 0$

fracción compleja *(p. 379)* Una fracción que contiene una fracción en su numerador o denominador

número complejo *(p. 96)* Un número escrito en la forma $a + bi$, donde a y b son números reales

composición *(p. 266)* Una combinación de funciones en las que el resultado de una función se usa como la entra de otra función

constante de variación *(p. 354)* Una constante que describe la relación entre un par de variables que muestran una variación directa o una variación inversa

grupo de control *(p. 424)* El grupo que no se ve sometido a tratamiento durante un experimento

experimento controlado *(p. 424)* Un experimento en el que grupos son estudiados bajo las mismas condiciones con la excepción de una o más variables de interés

muestra de conveniencia *(p. 416)* Una muestra en la que únicamente se seleccionan los miembros de una población a los que es fácil de llegar

coeficiente de correlación *(p. 23)* Un número r de -1 a 1 que mide cuán bien ajusta una recta a un conjunto de pares de datos (x, y)

cosecante *(p. 456)* Una ecuación trigonométrica de un ángulo agudo θ de un triángulo recto, denotado por
$$\csc \theta = \frac{\text{hipotenusa}}{\text{opuesto}}$$

coseno *(p. 456)* Una ecuación trigonométrica de un ángulo agudo θ de un triángulo recto, denotado por
$$\cos \theta = \frac{\text{adyacente}}{\text{hipotenusa}}$$

cotangente *(p. 456)* Una ecuación trigonométrica de un ángulo agudo θ de un triángulo recto, denotado por
$$\cot \theta = \frac{\text{adyacente}}{\text{opuesto}}$$

coterminal *(p. 465)* Two angles whose initial sides and terminal sides coincide

Cramer's Rule *(p. 596)* A method of using determinants to solve a system of linear equations

cycle *(p. 480)* The shortest repeating portion of the graph of a periodic function

coterminal *(p. 465)* Dos ángulos cuyos lados iniciales y lados terminales coinciden

Regla de Cramer *(p. 596)* Un método de uso de determinantes para resolver un sistema de ecuaciones lineales

ciclo *(p. 480)* La porción más corta que se repite en el gráfico de una función periódica

decay factor *(p. 291)* The value of b in an exponential decay function of the form $y = ab^x$, where $a > 0$ and $0 < b < 1$

descriptive statistics *(p. 430)* The branch of statistics that involves the organization, summarization, and display of data

determinant *(p. 594)* A real number associated with each square ($n \times n$) matrix

dimensions of a matrix *(p. 578)* The number of rows and columns in a matrix

direct variation *(p. 354)* Two variables x and y show direct variation when $y = ax$, where $a \neq 0$.

directrix *(p. 62)* A fixed line perpendicular to the axis of symmetry, such that the set of all points (x, y) of the parabola are equidistant from the focus and the directrix

discriminant *(p. 118)* The expression $b^2 - 4ac$ in the Quadratic Formula

factor de decaimiento *(p. 291)* El valor de b en una función de decaimiento exponencial de la forma $y = ab^x$, donde $a > 0$ y $0 < b < 1$

estadística descriptiva *(p. 430)* La rama de la estadística que implica la organización, resumen y presentación de datos

determinante *(p. 594)* Un número real asociado con cada matriz cuadrada ($n \times n$)

dimensiones de una matriz *(p. 578)* El número de filas y columnas de una matriz

variación directa *(p. 354)* Dos variables x e y muestra una variación directa cuando $y = ax$, donde $a \neq 0$.

directriz *(p. 62)* Una recta fija perpendicular al eje de simetría de modo tal, que el conjunto de todos los puntos (x, y) de la parábola sean equidistantes del foco y la directriz

discriminante *(p. 118)* La expresión $b^2 - 4ac$ en la Fórmula Cuadrática

elements of a matrix *(p. 578)* The numbers in a matrix

end behavior *(p. 153)* The behavior of the graph of a function as x approaches positive infinity or negative infinity

equal matrices *(p. 578)* Matrices with the same dimensions and with equal elements in corresponding positions

even function *(p. 209)* For a function $f, f(-x) = f(x)$ for all x in its domain

experiment *(p. 418)* A method that imposes a treatment on individuals in order to collect data on their response to the treatment

elementos de una matriz *(p. 578)* Los números en una matriz

comportamiento final *(p. 153)* El comportamiento del gráfico de una función a medida que x se aproxima al infinito positivo o negativo

matrices iguales *(p. 578)* Matrices con las mismas dimensiones y con elementos iguales en posiciones correspondientes

función par *(p. 209)* Para una función $f, f(-x) = f(x)$ para toda x en su dominio

experimento *(p. 418)* Un método que impone un tratamiento a individuos para recoger datos con respecto a su respuesta al tratamiento

explicit rule *(p. 560)* A rule that gives a_n as a function of the term's position number n in the sequence

exponential decay function *(p. 291)* A function of the form $y = ab^x$, where $a > 0$ and $0 < b < 1$

exponential equations *(p. 328)* Equations in which variable expressions occur as exponents

exponential function *(p. 290)* A function of the form $y = ab^x$, where $a \neq 0$ and the base b is a positive real number other than 1

exponential growth function *(p. 290)* A function of the form $y = ab^x$, where $a > 0$ and $b > 1$

extraneous solutions *(p. 253)* Solutions that are not solutions of the original equation

regla explícita *(p. 560)* Una regla que da a_n como una función del número de posición n del término en la secuencia

función de decaimiento exponencial *(p. 291)* Una función de la forma $y = ab^x$, donde $a > 0$ y $0 < b < 1$

ecuaciones exponenciales *(p. 328)* Ecuaciones en donde las expresiones de una variable ocurren como exponentes

función exponencial *(p. 290)* Una función de la forma $y = ab^x$, donde $a \neq 0$ y la base b es un número real positivo distinto de 1

función de crecimiento exponencial *(p. 290)* Una función de la forma $y = ab^x$, dónde $a > 0$ y $b > 1$

soluciones externas *(p. 253)* Soluciones que no son soluciones de la ecuación original

factor by grouping *(p. 175)* A method of factoring a polynomial by grouping pairs of terms that have a common monomial factor

factored completely *(p. 174)* A polynomial written as a product of unfactorable polynomials with integer coefficients

finite differences *(p. 215)* The differences of consecutive y-values in a data set when the x-values are equally spaced

focus *(p. 62)* A fixed point in the interior of a parabola, such that the set of all points (x, y) of the parabola are equidistant from the focus and the directrix

frequency *(p. 500)* The number of cycles per unit of time, which is the reciprocal of the period

factorización por agrupación *(p. 175)* Un método de factorización de un polinomio al agrupar pares de términos que tienen un factor monomio común

factorizado completamente *(p. 174)* Un polinomio escrito como un producto de polinomios no factorizables con coeficientes de números enteros

diferencias finitas *(p. 215)* Las diferencias de valores consecutivos y en un conjunto de datos cuando los valores x están igualmente espaciados

foco *(p. 62)* Un punto fijo en el interior de una parábola, de tal forma que el conjunto de todos los puntos (x, y) de la parábola sean equidistantes del foco y la directriz

frecuencia *(p. 500)* El número de ciclos por unidad de tiempo, que es el recíproco del período

geometric sequence *(p. 546)* A sequence in which the ratio of any term to the previous term is constant

geometric series *(p. 548)* The expression formed by adding the terms of a geometric sequence

growth factor *(p. 290)* The value of b in an exponential growth function of the form $y = ab^x$, where $a > 0$ and $b > 1$

secuencia geométrica *(p. 546)* Una secuencia en donde la razón de cualquier término con respecto al término anterior es constante

serie geométrica *(p. 548)* La expresión formada al sumar los términos de una secuencia geométrica

factor de crecimiento *(p. 290)* El valor de b en una función de crecimiento exponencial de la forma $y = ab^x$, donde $a > 0$ y $b > 1$

H

hypothesis *(p. 411)* A claim about a characteristic of a population

hipótesis *(p. 411)* Una declaración acerca de una característica de una población

I

identity matrix *(p. 604)* An $n \times n$ matrix that consists of 1's on its main diagonal (from top left to bottom right) and 0's for all other elements

marcas de identidad *(p. 604)* Una matriz de $n \times n$ que consiste en 1 en su diagonal principal (desde el extremo superior izquierdo al extremo inferior derecho) y 0 en todos los demás elementos

imaginary number *(p. 96)* A number written in the form $a + bi$, where a and b are real numbers and $b \neq 0$

número imaginario *(p. 96)* Un número escrito de la forma $a + bi$, donde a y b son números reales y $b \neq 0$

imaginary unit *i* *(p. 96)* The square root of -1, denoted $i = \sqrt{-1}$

unidad imaginaria *i* *(p. 96)* La raíz cuadrada de -1, denotado $i = \sqrt{-1}$

index of a radical *(p. 230)* The value of n in the radical $\sqrt[n]{a}$

índice de un radical *(p. 230)* El valor de n en el radical $\sqrt[n]{a}$

inferential statistics *(p. 430)* The branch of statistics that involves using a sample to draw conclusions about a population

estadística inferencial *(p. 430)* La rama de la estadística que implica el uso de una muestra para sacar conclusiones acerca de una población

initial side *(p. 464)* The fixed ray of an angle in standard position in a coordinate plane

lado inicial *(p. 464)* El rayo fijo de un ángulo en posición normal en un plano coordenado

intercept form *(p. 55)* A quadratic function written in the form $f(x) = a(x - p)(x - q)$, where $a \neq 0$

forma de intersección *(p. 55)* Una ecuación cuadrática escrita en la forma $f(x) = a(x - p)(x - q)$, donde $a \neq 0$

inverse functions *(p. 272)* Functions that undo each other

funciones inversas *(p. 272)* Funciones que se anulan entre sí

inverse matrices *(p. 604)* Two $n \times n$ matrices whose product is the $n \times n$ identity matrix

matrices inversas *(p. 604)* Dos matrices $n \times n$ cuyo producto es la matriz de identidad $n \times n$

inverse variation *(p. 354)* Two variables x and y show inverse variation when $y = \dfrac{a}{x}$, where $a \neq 0$.

variación inversa *(p. 354)* Dos variables x e y muestran variación inversa cuando $y = \dfrac{a}{x}$, donde $a \neq 0$.

L

like radicals *(p. 238)* Radical expressions with the same index and radicand

radicales semejantes *(p. 238)* Expresiones radicales con el mismo índice y radicando

line of best fit *(p. 23)* A line that best models a set of data and lies as close as possible to all of the data points in a scatter plot

recta de mejor ajuste *(p. 23)* Una recta que modela mejor un conjunto de datos y que se acerca lo más posible a todos los puntos de datos en un diagrama de disperión

line of fit *(p. 22)* A line that models data in a scatter plot

recta de ajuste *(p. 22)* Una recta que modela datos en un diagrama de dispersión

English-Spanish Glossary

linear equation in three variables *(p. 28)* An equation of the form $ax + by + cz = d$, where x, y, and z are variables and a, b, and c are not all zero

local maximum *(p. 208)* The y-coordinate of a turning point of a function when the point is higher than all nearby points

local minimum *(p. 208)* The y-coordinate of a turning point of a function when the point is lower than all nearby points

logarithm of y with base b *(p. 304)* The function $\log_b y = x$ if and only if $b^x = y$, where $b > 0$, $y > 0$, and $b \neq 1$

logarithmic equations *(p. 329)* Equations that involve one or more logarithms of variable expressions

ecuación lineal en tres variables *(p. 28)* Una ecuación de la forma $ax + by + cz = d$, donde x, y, y z son variables y a, b, y c no son todas cero

máximo local *(p. 208)* La coordenada y de un punto de inflexión de una función cuando el punto es mayor que todos los puntos cercanos

mínimo local *(p. 208)* La coordenada y de un punto de inflexión de una función cuando el punto es menor que todos los puntos cercanos

logaritmo de y con base b *(p. 304)* La función $\log_b y = x$ si y solo si $b^x = y$, donde $b > 0$, $y > 0$, y $b \neq 1$

ecuaciones logarítmicas *(p. 329)* Ecuaciones que implican uno o más logaritmos de expresiones variables

---

M

---

margin of error *(p. 433)* The maximum expected difference between a sample result and the population parameter it is estimating

matrix *(p. 578)* A rectangular array of numbers

matrix of constants *(p. 606)* A matrix consisting of the constants of a linear system

matrix of variables *(p. 606)* A matrix consisting of the variables of a linear system

maximum value *(p. 54)* The y-coordinate of the vertex of the quadratic function $f(x) = ax^2 + bx + c$, where $a < 0$

midline *(p. 483)* The horizontal line $y = k$ in which the graph of a periodic function oscillates

minimum value *(p. 54)* The y-coordinate of the vertex of the quadratic function $f(x) = ax^2 + bx + c$, where $a > 0$

margen de error *(p. 433)* La máxima diferencia que se espera entre el resultado de una muestra y el parámetro de población que está estimando

matriz *(p. 578)* Una disposición rectangular de números

matriz de constantes *(p. 606)* Una matriz que consiste en las constantes de un sistema lineal

matriz de variables *(p. 606)* Una matriz que consiste en las variables de un sistema lineal

valor máximo *(p. 54)* La coordenada y del vértice de la función cuadrática $f(x) = ax^2 + bx + c$, cuando $a < 0$

línea media *(p. 483)* La línea horizontal $y = k$ en la que oscila el gráfico de una función periódica

valor mínimo *(p. 54)* La coordenada y del vértice de la función cuadrática $f(x) = ax^2 + bx + c$, cuando $a > 0$

---

natural base e *(p. 298)* An irrational number approximately equal to 2.71828…

natural logarithm *(p. 305)* A logarithm with base e, denoted by $\log_e$ or $\ln$

normal curve *(p. 400)* The graph of a normal distribution that is bell-shaped and is symmetric about the mean

base natural e *(p. 298)* Un número irracional aproximadamente equivalente a 2.71828…

logaritmo natural *(p. 305)* Un logaritmo con base e, denotado como $\log_e$ o $\ln$

curva normal *(p. 400)* El gráfico de una distribución normal con forma acampanada y es simétrica con respecto a la media

normal distribution *(p. 400)* A type of probability distribution in which the graph is a bell-shaped curve that is symmetric about the mean

nth root of a *(p. 230)* For an integer n greater than 1, if $b^n = a$, then b is an nth root of a.

distribución normal *(p. 400)* Un tipo de distribución de probabilidades en la que el gráfico es una curva acampanada que es simétrica con respecto a la media

raíz de orden n de a *(p. 230)* Para un número entero n mayor que 1, si $b^n = a$, entonces b es una raíz de orden n de a.

O

observational study *(p. 418)* Individuals are observed and variables are measured without controlling the individuals or their environment.

odd function *(p. 209)* For a function $f, f(-x) = -f(x)$ for all x in its domain

ordered triple *(p. 28)* A solution of a system of three linear equations represented by (x, y, z)

estudio de observación *(p. 418)* Se observan individuos y se miden variables sin controlar a los individuos o a su entorno.

función impar *(p. 209)* Para una función $f, f(-x) = -f(x)$ para toda x en su dominio

triple ordenado *(p. 28)* Un solución de un sistema de tres ecuaciones lineales representadas por (x, y, z)

P

parabola *(p. 44)* The U-shaped graph of a quadratic function

parameter *(p. 409)* A numerical description of a population characteristic

parent function *(p. 4)* The most basic function in a family of functions

partial sum *(p. 554)* The sum S_n of the first n terms of an infinite series

Pascal's Triangle *(p. 163)* A triangular array of numbers such that the numbers in the nth row are the coefficients of the terms in the expansion of $(a + b)^n$ for whole number values of n

period *(p. 480)* The horizontal length of each cycle of a periodic function

periodic function *(p. 480)* A function whose graph has a repeating pattern

phase shift *(p. 483)* A horizontal translation of a periodic function

placebo *(p. 424)* A harmless, fake treatment that is similar to the actual treatment

polynomial *(p. 152)* A monomial or a sum of monomials

polynomial function *(p. 152)* A function of the form $f(x) = a_n x^n + a_{n-1} x^{n-1} + \cdots + a_1 x + a_0$, where $a_n \neq 0$, the exponents are all whole numbers, and the coefficients are all real numbers

parábola *(p. 44)* El gráfico en forma de "U" de una función cuadrática

parámetro *(p. 409)* Una descripción numérica de una característica de la población

función principal *(p. 4)* La función más básica en una familia de funciones

sumatoria parcial *(p. 554)* La sumatoria parcial S_n de los primeros términos n de una serie infinita

triángulo de Pascal *(p. 163)* Una disposición triangular de números, de tal manera que los números en la fila n son los coeficientes de los términos en la expansión de $(a + b)^n$ para los valores de números enteros de n

período *(p. 480)* La longitud horizontal de cada ciclo de una función periódica

función periódica *(p. 480)* Una función cuyo gráfico tiene un patrón de repetición

desplazamiento de fase *(p. 483)* Una traslación horizontal de una función periódica

placebo *(p. 424)* Un tratamiento falso que es similar al tratamiento real

polinomio *(p. 152)* Un monomio o una suma de monomios

función polinómica *(p.152)* Una función de la forma $f(x) = a_n x^n + a_{n-1} x^{n-1} + \cdots + a_1 x + a_0$, donde $a_n \neq 0$, todos los exponentes son números enteros y todos los coeficientes son números reales

polynomial long division (p. 168) A method to divide a polynomial $f(x)$ by a nonzero divisor $d(x)$ to yield a quotient polynomial $q(x)$ and a remainder polynomial $r(x)$

population (p. 408) The collection of all data, such as responses, measurements, or counts, that are of interest

pure imaginary number (p. 96) A number written in the form $a + bi$, where $a = 0$ and $b \neq 0$

división larga de polinomios (p. 168) Un método para dividir un polinomio $f(x)$ por un divisor distinto de cero $d(x)$ para obtener un polinomio de cociente $q(x)$ y un polinomio de resto $r(x)$

población (p. 408) La recolección de datos, tales como respuestas, medidas o conteos que son de interés

número imaginario puro (p. 96) Un número escrito en la forma $a + bi$, donde $a = 0$ y $b \neq 0$

Q

quadrantal angle (p. 473) An angle in standard position whose terminal side lies on an axis

quadratic equation in one variable (p. 86) An equation that can be written in the standard form $ax^2 + bx + c = 0$, where a, b, and c are real numbers and $a \neq 0$

quadratic form (p. 175) An expression of the form $au^2 + bu + c$, where u is an algebraic expression

Quadratic Formula (p. 116) The solutions of the quadratic equation $ax^2 + bx + c = 0$ are
$$x = \frac{-b \pm \sqrt{b^2 - 4ac}}{2a},$$
where a, b, and c are real numbers and $a \neq 0$

quadratic function (p. 44) A function that can be written in the form $f(x) = a(x - h)^2 + k$, where $a \neq 0$

quadratic inequality in one variable (p. 136) An inequality of the form $ax^2 + bx + c < 0$, $ax^2 + bx + c > 0$, $ax^2 + bx + c \leq 0$, or $ax^2 + bx + c \geq 0$, where a, b, and c are real numbers and $a \neq 0$

quadratic inequality in two variables (p. 134) An inequality of the form $y < ax^2 + bx + c$, $y > ax^2 + bx + c$, $y \leq ax^2 + bx + c$, or $y \geq ax^2 + bx + c$, where a, b, and c are real numbers and $a \neq 0$

ángulo cuadrantal (p. 473) Un ángulo en posición estándar cuyo lado terminal descansa en un eje

ecuación cuadrática en una variable (p. 86) Una ecuación que puede escribirse en la forma estándar $ax^2 + bx + c = 0$, donde a, b, y c son números reales y $a \neq 0$

forma cuadrática (p. 175) Una expresión de la forma $au^2 + bu + c$, donde u es una expresión algebraica

Formula Cuadrática (p. 116) Las soluciones reales de la expresión cuadrática $ax^2 + bx + c = 0$ son
$$x = \frac{-b \pm \sqrt{b^2 - 4ac}}{2a},$$
donde a, b, y c son números reales y $a \neq 0$

función cuadrática (p. 44) Una función que puede escribirse en la forma $f(x) = a(x - h)^2 + k$, donde $a \neq 0$

desigualdad cuadrática en una variable (p. 136) Una desigualdad de la forma $ax^2 + bx + c < 0$, $ax^2 + bx + c > 0$, $ax^2 + bx + c \leq 0$, o $ax^2 + bx + c \geq 0$, donde a, b, y c son números reales y $a \neq 0$

desigualdad cuadrática en dos variables (p. 134) Una desigualdad de la forma $y < ax^2 + bx + c$, $y > ax^2 + bx + c$, $y \leq ax^2 + bx + c$, o $y \geq ax^2 + bx + c$, donde a, b, y c son números reales y $a \neq 0$

R

radian (p. 466) For a circle with radius r, the measure of an angle in standard position whose terminal side intercepts an arc of length r is one radian.

radical equation (p. 252) An equation with a radical that has a variable in the radicand

radical function (p. 244) A function that contains a radical expression with the independent variable in the radicand

radián (p. 466) Para un círculo con radio r, la medida de un ángulo en posición estándar cuyo lado terminal intercepta un arco de longitud r es un radián

ecuación radical (p. 252) Una ecuación con un radical que tiene una variable en el radicando

función radical (p. 244) Una función que contiene una expresión radical con la variable independiente en el radicando

random sample *(p. 416)* A sample in which each member of a population has an equal chance of being selected

randomization *(p. 424)* A process of randomly assigning subjects to different treatment groups

randomized comparative experiment *(p. 424)* An experiment in which subjects are randomly assigned to the control group or the treatment group

rational expression *(p. 368)* A fraction whose numerator and denominator are nonzero polynomials

rational function *(p. 360)* A function that has the form $f(x) = \dfrac{p(x)}{q(x)}$, where $p(x)$ and $q(x)$ are polynomials and $q(x) \neq 0$

recursive rule *(p. 560)* A rule that gives the beginning term(s) of a sequence and a recursive equation that tells how a_n is related to one or more preceding terms

reference angle *(p. 474)* The acute angle formed by the terminal side of an angle in standard position and the *x*-axis

reflection *(p. 5)* A transformation that flips a graph over the line of reflection

repeated solution *(p. 182)* A solution of an equation that appears more than once

root of an equation *(p. 86)* A solution of an equation

muestra aleatoria *(p. 416)* Una muestra en la que cada miembro de una población tiene igual posibilidad de ser seleccionado

aleatorización *(p. 424)* Un proceso de asignación aleatoria de sujetos a distintos grupos de tratamiento

experimento comparativo aleatorizado *(p. 424)* Un experimento en el que los sujetos son asignados aleatoriamente al grupo de control o al grupo de tratamiento

expresión racional *(p. 368)* Una fracción cuyo numerador y denominador son polinomios distintos a cero

función racional *(p. 360)* Una función que tiene la forma $f(x) = \dfrac{p(x)}{q(x)}$, donde $p(x)$ y $q(x)$ son polinomios y $q(x) \neq 0$

regla recursiva *(p. 560)* Una regla para definir el(los) primer(os) término(s) de una secuencia y una ecuación recursiva que indica cómo se relaciona a_n a uno o más términos precedentes

ángulo de referencia *(p. 474)* El ángulo agudo formado por el lado terminal de un ángulo en posición normal y el eje *x*

reflexión *(p. 5)* Una transformación que voltea un gráfico sobre una recta de reflexión

solución repetida *(p. 182)* Una solución de una ecuación que aparece más de una vez

raíz de una ecuación *(p. 86)* Una solución de una ecuación

sample *(p. 408)* A subset of a population

scalar *(p. 579)* A number used in operations with matrices

scalar multiplication *(p. 579)* The process of multiplying each element in a matrix by a scalar

secant *(p. 456)* A trigonometric function for an acute angle θ of a right triangle, denoted by $\sec \theta = \dfrac{\text{hypotenuse}}{\text{adjacent}}$

sector *(p. 467)* A region of a circle that is bounded by two radii and an arc of the circle

muestra *(p. 408)* Un subconjunto de una población

escalar *(p. 579)* Un número que se usa en operaciones con matrices

multiplicaión escalar *(p. 579)* El proceso de multiplicar cada elemento en la matriz por un escalar

secante *(p. 456)* Una ecuación trigonométrica de un ángulo agudo θ de un triángulo recto, denatado por $\sec \theta = \dfrac{\text{hipotenusa}}{\text{adyacente}}$

sector *(p. 467)* Una región de un círculo conformada por dos radios y un arco del círculo

English-Spanish Glossary

self-selected sample *(p. 416)* A sample in which members of a population can volunteer to be in the sample

sequence *(p. 530)* An ordered list of numbers

series *(p. 532)* The sum of the terms of a sequence

sigma notation *(p. 532)* For any sequence $a_1, a_2, a_3, \ldots$, the sum of the first k terms may be written as $\sum_{n=1}^{k} a_n = a_1 + a_2 + a_3 + \cdots + a_k$, where k is an integer.

simplest form of a radical *(p. 237)* An expression involving a radical with index n that has no radicands with perfect nth powers as factors other than 1, no radicands that contain fractions, and no radicals that appear in the denominator of a fraction

simplified form of a rational expression *(p. 368)* A rational expression whose numerator and denominator have no common factors (other than ± 1)

simulation *(p. 418)* The use of a model to reproduce the conditions of a situation or process so that the simulated outcomes closely match the real-world outcome

sine *(p. 456)* A trigonometric function for an acute angle θ of a right triangle, denoted by
$\sin \theta = \dfrac{\text{opposite}}{\text{hypotenuse}}$

sinusoid *(p. 501)* The graph of a sine or cosine function

solution of a system of three linear equations *(p. 28)* An ordered triple (x, y, z) whose coordinates make each equation true

standard form *(p. 53)* A quadratic function written in the form $f(x) = ax^2 + bx + c$, where $a \neq 0$

standard normal distribution *(p. 402)* The normal distribution with mean 0 and standard deviation 1

standard position *(p. 464)* An angle in a coordinate plane such that its vertex is at the origin and its initial side lies on the positive x-axis

statistic *(p. 409)* A numerical description of a sample characteristic

muestra autoseleccionada *(p. 416)* Una muestra en la que los miembros de una población pueden ofrecerse voluntariamente para formar parte de la misma

secuencia *(p. 530)* Una lista ordenada de números

serie *(p. 532)* La suma de los términos de una secuencia

notación sigma *(p. 532)* Para cualquier secuencia $a_1, a_2, a_3, \ldots$, la suma de los primeros términos k puede escribirse como $\sum_{n=1}^{k} a_n = a_1 + a_2 + a_3 + \cdots + a_k$, donde k es un número entero.

mínima expresión de un radical *(p. 237)* Una expresión que conlleva un radical con índice n que no tiene radicandos con potencias perfectas de orden n como factores distintos a 1, que no tiene radicandos que contengan fracciones y que no tiene radicales que aparezcan en el denominador de una fracción

forma simplificada de una expresión racional *(p. 368)* Una expresión racional cuyo numerador y denominador no tienen factores comunes (distintos a ± 1)

simulación *(p. 418)* El uso de un modelo para reproducir las condiciones de una situación o proceso, de tal manera que los resultados posibles simulados coincidan en gran medida con los resultados del mundo real

seno *(p. 456)* Una ecuación trigonométrica de un ángulo agudo θ de un triángulo recto, denotado por
$\sin \theta = \dfrac{\text{opuesto}}{\text{hipotenusa}}$

sinusoide *(p. 501)* El gráfico de una función seno o coseno

solución de un sistema de tres ecuaciones lineales *(p. 28)* Un triple ordenado (x, y, z) cuyas coordenadas hacen verdadera cada ecuación

forma estándar *(p. 53)* Una función cuadrática escrita en la forma $f(x) = ax^2 + bx + c$, donde $a \neq 0$

distribución normal estándar *(p. 402)* La distribución normal con una media de 0 y desviación estándar 1

posición estándar *(p. 464)* Un ángulo en un plano coordenado de tal manera que su vértice esté en el origen y que su lado inicial descanse en el eje x positivo

estadística *(p. 409)* Una descripción numérica de una característica de la muestra

stratified sample *(p. 416)* A sample in which a population is divided into smaller groups that share a similar characteristic and a sample is then randomly selected from each group

summation notation *(p. 532)* For any sequence $a_1, a_2, a_3, \ldots$, the sum of the first k terms may be written as $\sum_{n=1}^{k} a_n = a_1 + a_2 + a_3 + \cdots + a_k$, where k is an integer.

survey *(p. 418)* An investigation of one or more characteristics of a population

synthetic division *(p. 169)* A shortcut method to divide a polynomial by a binomial of the form $x - k$

system of nonlinear equations *(p. 126)* A system of equations where at least one of the equations is nonlinear

system of quadratic inequalities *(p. 135)* A set of two or more quadratic inequalities in the same variables

system of three linear equations *(p. 28)* A set of three equations of the form $ax + by + cz = d$, where x, y, and z are variables and a, b, and c are not all zero

systematic sample *(p. 416)* A sample in which a rule is used to select members of a population

muestra estratificada *(p. 416)* Una muestra en la que una población se divide en grupos más pequeños que comparten una característica similar, y una muestra se selecciona en forma aleatoria de cada grupo

notación de sumatoria *(p. 532)* Para cualquier secuencia $a_1, a_2, a_3, \ldots$, la sumatoria de los primeros términos k puede escribirse como $\sum_{n=1}^{k} a_n = a_1 + a_2 + a_3 + \cdots + a_k$, donde k es un número entero.

encuesta *(p. 418)* Una investigación de una o más características de una población

división sintética *(p. 169)* Un método abreviado para dividir un polinomio por un binomio de la forma $x - k$

sistema de ecuaciones no lineales *(p. 126)* Un sistema de ecuaciones en donde al menos una de las ecuaciones no es lineal

sistema de desigualdades cuadráticas *(p. 135)* Un conjunto de dos o más desigualdades cuadráticas en las mismas variables

sistema de tres ecuaciones lineales *(p. 28)* Un conjunto de tres ecuaciones de la forma $ax + by + cz = d$, donde x, y, y z son variables y a, b, y c no son todos cero

muestra sistemática *(p. 416)* Una muestra en la que se usa una regla para seleccionar miembros de una población

tangent *(p. 456)* A trigonometric function for an acute angle θ of a right triangle, denoted by $\tan \theta = \dfrac{\text{opposite}}{\text{adjacent}}$

terminal side *(p. 464)* A ray of an angle in standard position that has been rotated about the vertex in a coordinate plane

terms of a sequence *(p. 530)* The values in the range of a sequence

transformation *(p. 5)* A change in the size, shape, position, or orientation of a graph

translation *(p. 5)* A transformation that shifts a graph horizontally and/or vertically but does not change its size, shape, or orientation

treatment group *(p. 424)* The group that is subjected to the treatment in an experiment

tangente *(p. 456)* Una ecuación trigonométrica de un ángulo agudo θ de un triángulo recto, denotado por $\tan \theta = \dfrac{\text{opuesto}}{\text{adyacente}}$

lado terminal *(p. 464)* Un rayo de un ángulo en posición normal que ha sido rotado con respecto al vértice en un plano coordenado

términos de una secuencia *(p. 530)* Los valores en el rango de una secuencia

transformación *(p. 5)* Un cambio en el tamaño, forma, posición u orientación de un gráfico

traslación *(p. 5)* Una transformación que desplaza un gráfico horizontal y/o verticalmente, pero no cambia su tamaño, forma u orientación

grupo de tratamiento *(p. 424)* El grupo que está sometido al tratamiento en un experimento

trigonometric identity *(p. 508)* A trigonometric equation that is true for all values of the variable for which both sides of the equation are defined

identidad trigonométrica *(p. 508)* Una ecuación trigonométrica verdadera para todos los valores de la variable por la cual se definen ambos lados de la ecuación

unbiased sample *(p. 417)* A sample that is representative of a population

muestra no sesgada *(p. 417)* Una muestra que es representativa de la población

unit circle *(p. 473)* The circle $x^2 + y^2 = 1$, which has center $(0, 0)$ and radius 1

círculo unitario *(p. 473)* El círculo $x^2 + y^2 = 1$, que tiene como centro $(0, 0)$ y radio 1

vertex form *(p. 46)* A quadratic function written in the form $f(x) = a(x - h)^2 + k$, where $a \neq 0$

fórmula de vértice *(p. 46)* Una función cuadrática escrita en la forma $f(x) = a(x - h)^2 + k$, donde $a \neq 0$

vertex of a parabola *(p. 46)* The lowest point on a parabola that opens up or the highest point on a parabola that opens down

vértice de una parábola *(p. 46)* El punto más bajo de una parábola que se abre hacia arriba o el punto más alto de una parábola que se abre hacia abajo

vertical shrink *(p. 6)* A transformation that causes the graph of a function to shrink toward the x-axis when all the y-coordinates are multiplied by a factor k, where $0 < k < 1$

reducción vertical *(p. 6)* Una transformación que hace que el gráfico de una función se reduzca hacia el eje x cuando todas las coordenadas y se multiplican por un factor k, donde $0 < k < 1$

vertical stretch *(p. 6)* A transformation that causes the graph of a function to stretch away from the x-axis when all the y-coordinates are multiplied by a factor k, where $k > 1$

ampliación vertical *(p. 6)* Una transformación que hace que el gráfico de una función se amplíe desde el eje x cuando todas las coordenadas y se multiplican por un factor k, donde $k > 1$

z-score *(p. 402)* The z-value for a particular x-value which is the number of standard deviations the x-value lies above or below the mean

puntaje z *(p. 402)* El valor z para un valor particular x que es el número de desviaciones estándar que el valor x tiene por encima o por debajo de la media

zero of a function *(p. 88)* An x-value of a function f for which $f(x) = 0$

cero de una función *(p. 88)* Un valor x de una función f para el cual $f(x) = 0$

Index

A

Abbreviations
  for sides of right triangles, 456
  for trigonometric functions, 456
Absolute value functions
  defined, 4
  family of, 4
  identifying, 3–4
  parent function for
    identifying, 3–4
    transforming, 11
  transformations of, 11–18
    combinations of, 7, 15
    stretches and shrinks, 6, 14
    translations and reflections, 12–13
Addition
  of algebraic expressions, 150
  Associative Property of, 579
  Commutative Property of, 579
  of complex numbers, 97
  of functions, 259–260
  of like radicals and roots, 238
  of matrices, 578
  of polynomials, 159–166
  of rational expressions, 375–382
    with like denominators, 376
    with unlike denominators, 377
  of rational numbers, 352
Algebra, Fundamental Theorem of, 189–198
Algebra tiles, completing the square using, 105
Algebraic expressions, adding and subtracting, 150
Amplitude, of sine and cosine graphs, 480
Angles
  central, 467
  coterminal, 465
  degree measure of, 466
  of depression, 459
  of elevation, 459
  quadrantal, 473
  radian measure of, 463–470
    converting between degree and, 466
    defined, 463, 466
    of special angles, 466
    using, 463, 466
  reference, 474–475
    defined, 474
    evaluating trigonometric functions using, 474–475
    finding, 474
  of right triangles, finding measures of, 458
  special
    degree and radian measures of, 466
    trigonometric values for, 457
  in standard position, 464
  trigonometric functions of, 471–478
Arc length, of circle sectors, 467
Archimedes, 552
Area
  of circles, sectors of, 467
  under normal curves, 400
  of triangles, 595
Arithmetic sequences, 537–544
  defined, 537–538
  finding sums of, 537
  identifying, 538
  recursive equations for, 560
  rules for
    defined, 539
    explicit, 560
    recursive, 560–561
    writing, 539–540
Arithmetic series, 537–544
  defined, 541
  finite, finding sums of, 541
Associative Property of Addition, 579
Associative Property of Matrix Multiplication, 588
Associative Property of Scalar Multiplication, 588
Asymptotes
  defined, 290
  of exponential functions, 290
  of logarithmic functions, 307
  oblique, 390
  of rational functions, 362
  of trigonometric functions, 490–494
Axis of symmetry
  defined, 52
  finding, 52
  graphing quadratic functions using, 52–53
  horizontal, 63–64, 247
  vertical, 63–64

B

Bar graphs, 410. *See also* Histograms
Bell-shaped histograms, 399–400, 403
Bias, defined, 417
Biased questions, 419
Biased sampling, 417
  defined, 417
  recognizing, 417
Binomial(s)
  cube of a binomial pattern, 162
  dividing polynomials by, 167, 169
  expanding, 159
    using Binomial Theorem, 163
    using Pascal's Triangle, 159, 163
  linear, as factors, 176
  multiplying
    by monomials, 161
    three, 161
  square of a binomial pattern, 162
  sum and difference pattern, 162
Binomial Theorem, 163

C

Causality, vs. correlation, 425
Censuses, 408
Center, measures of, 398
Central angles, 467
Change-of-Base Formula, 322
Circles
  angle measures in (*See* Radian measure)
  equation of, 109, 473
  graphing, 247
  sectors of
    arc length of, 467
    area of, 467
    defined, 467
    solving nonlinear systems involving, 128
  unit
    defined, 471, 473
    equation of, 471
    using, 473
Circular functions, 472
Circular motion, 502
Cluster samples, 416
Coefficient(s)
  correlation, 23
  of polynomial functions
    Descartes's Rule of Signs on, 193–194
    leading, 152–153
Coefficient matrix, 596–597
Cofunction identities, 508
Common difference
  defined, 537–538

Index **A59**

writing rules given term and, 540
Common logarithms
   Change-of-Base Formula with, 322
   defined, 305
   evaluating, 305
Common ratio
   defined, 545–546
   writing rules given term and, 547
Commutative Property of Addition, 579
Comparative experiments
   causality in, 425
   randomized, 424, 439–440
Comparing linear equations, 21
Completing the square, 105–114
   with algebra tiles, 105
   defined, 106
   deriving Quadratic Formula by, 115
   solving quadratic equations by, 106–107
   writing equations of circles and parabolas using, 109
Complex conjugates, 192
   Complex Conjugates Theorem on, 192
   defined, 98, 192
   multiplying, 98
Complex fractions, 379
Complex numbers, 95–104
   in complex conjugates, 98, 192
   defined, 95–96
   equality of two, 97
   imaginary unit i, 96
   operations with, 97–98
   set of, 95
   as solutions to quadratic equations, 100
   standard form of, 96
   using, 95
Complex plane, 102
Compositions of functions, 265–270
   defined, 266
   evaluating, 266
   finding, 265, 267
Compound interest, 293, 300, 564
Conjugates, 238
Constant(s)
   matrices of, 606
   of variation, 354
Constant functions
   defined, 4, 152
   family of, 4
   identifying, 3–4
   parent function for, 3
Constant terms, of polynomial functions, 152
Continuously compound interest, 300

Control groups
   defined, 424
   resampling, 441
Controlled experiments, 424
Convenience samples, 416
Cooling, Newton's Law of, 331
Coordinate plane. *See also* **Graphing**
   complex, 102
   finding distances in, 42
Corollary to the Fundamental Theorem of Algebra, 190
Correlation, vs. causality, 425
Correlation coefficient, 23
Cosecant function
   characteristics of, 493
   definitions of
     general, 472
     right-triangle, 456
   evaluating, 456–457
     using point, 472
     using reference angles, 475
     using unit circle, 473
   graphing, 489–498
   parent function for, 493
Cosine function
   characteristics of, 480
   definitions of
     general, 472
     right-triangle, 456
   evaluating, 456–457
     using point, 472
     using reference angles, 475
     using unit circle, 473
   graphing, 479–488
     transformations of, 481–484
   parent function for, 480
Cost per item matrices, 589
Cotangent function
   characteristics of, 490
   definitions of
     general, 472
     right-triangle, 456
   evaluating, 456–457
     using point, 472
     using reference angles, 475
     using unit circle, 473
   graphing, 489–498
   parent function for, 490
Cotangent identities, 508
Coterminal angles, 465
Cramer, Gabriel, 596
Cramer's Rule, 593–602
   defined, 596
   solving systems of linear equations using, 596–598
Critical values, 136

Cross multiplying, solving rational equations by, 384
Cube of a binomial pattern, 162
Cube root functions, 244
Cube Roots, Product Property of, 235
Cubic functions
   defined, 152
   graphing
     identifying graphs, 151
     transformations of, 199
     writing functions from, 214
   identifying, 151
   in intercept form, 214
   inverses of, 275
   writing, 214
Cubic regression, 215–216
Cycles, of sine and cosine graphs, 480

D

Data
   classifying, 355
   hypotheses based on, 407–414
Data collection, 415–422. *See also* specific methods
   methods of, 415–418
     analyzing, 418
     defined, 418
     identifying, 418
Data distributions
   normal, 399–406
   skewed, 403
   symmetric, 400, 403
Data modeling
   with exponential functions, 292–293, 335–342
   with linear functions, 19–26
   with logarithmic functions, 335–342
   with polynomial functions, 155, 202, 213–218
   with quadratic functions, 69–79
   with trigonometric functions, 499–506
   writing equations for, 72–73
Data samples. *See* **Sample(s)**
Decay. *See* **Exponential decay**
Decay factors, 291
Decimals, repeating, writing as fractions, 556
Degree(s)
   of polynomial functions, 152–153, 208
   of polynomials, 168, 190
Degree measure
   converting between radian measure and, 466
   of special angles, 466

Denominators
  adding or subtracting rational expressions with like and unlike, 376–377
  least common
    adding or subtracting rational expressions with, 376–377
    simplifying complex fractions with, 379
    solving rational equations with, 385–386

Depreciation
  annual, 232
  straight line, 19

Depression, angle of, 459

Descartes, René, 193

Descartes's Rule of Signs, 193–194

Descriptive statistics, 430

Determinants
  of matrices, 593–602
    defined, 594
    evaluating, 594–595
    finding, 593
    finding area of triangle using, 595
    solving systems of linear equations using, 596–598
  as property of linear systems, 596

Deviation, standard
  defined, 399
  finding, 398

Diagonal matrices, 591

Difference(s)
  common
    defined, 537–538
    writing rules given term and, 540
  finite, 215
    defined, 215
    identifying functions using, 336
    writing functions using, 215
  first, 72, 215, 336
  second, 72, 215, 336
  third, 215

Difference formulas, 513–518
  defined, 514
  deriving, 513
  using, 514–515

Difference of two cubes pattern, 174

Difference of two squares pattern, 174

Dimensions, of matrices, 578

Direct variation, 353–355
  classifying, 354–355
  defined, 354
  describing, 353

Directrix, of parabolas
  defined, 62

  writing quadratic equations using, 62–64

Discriminant, of Quadratic Formula, 118–120

Distances, finding in coordinate plane, 42

Distributions. *See* Data distributions; Normal distributions

Distributive Property, 579
  Left, 588
  Right, 588
  using, 238

Division
  of functions, 259–261
  of polynomials, 167–172
    by binomials, 167, 169
    with long division, 168
    rational expressions by, 370
    Remainder Theorem on, 170
    with synthetic division, 169–170
  with rational exponents, 236
  of rational expressions, 367–374

Domain
  of functions, 288
  of rational expressions, 368
  of sequences, 530

Dot plots, 432, 440

Double-blind method, 428

E

e. *See* Natural base *e*

Elements, of matrices, 578

Elevation, angle of, 459

Elimination, systems of nonlinear equations solved by, 127

End behavior of functions, 153

Equality
  of matrices
    defined, 578
    using, 580
  of two complex numbers, 97

Equality for Exponential Equations, Property of, 328

Equality for Logarithmic Equations, Property of, 329

Equations. *See also* specific types of equations
  roots of, 86
  solving, 528

Euler's formula, 512

Euler's identity, 512

Even functions, 209

Exhaustion, method of, 552

Experiments
  analyzing data from, 439–440
  comparative, 424–425, 439–440
  controlled, 424

  correlation in, 425
  defined, 418
  design of, 423–428
    analyzing, 423, 426
    describing, 424
    evaluating, 424
    randomization in, 424–426
    types of, 424
  identifying, 418
  making inferences from, 439–444

Explicit rules
  defined, 560
  translating between recursive rules and, 562

Exponent(s). *See also* Rational exponents
  properties of, 235
    and properties of logarithms, 319–320
    using, 228, 288

Exponential decay functions, 289–296
  defined, 291
  graphing, 291
  identifying, 292
  modeling with, 292–293
  natural base, 299
  parent function for, 291
  rewriting, 292

Exponential equations
  defined, 328
  Property of Equality for, 328
  rewriting, 304
  solving, 327–334

Exponential form, of logarithm of y with base b, 304

Exponential functions. *See also* Exponential decay functions; Exponential growth functions
  defined, 290
  graphing transformations of, 311–318
    identifying graphs, 311
    translations, 312–313
  identifying, 3, 292
  logarithmic functions as inverse of, 306–307
  models of, 335–342
    choosing, 336
    using, 292–293
    writing, 292, 337–338
  natural base, 299, 313
  parent function for, 3
  writing, 335, 337–338
    models of, 292, 337–338
    rewriting, 292
    transformed, 315

from two points, 337
Exponential growth, describing, 289
Exponential growth functions,
    289–296
  defined, 290
  graphing, 290
  identifying, 292
  modeling with, 292–293
  natural base, 299
  parent function for, 290
Exponential inequalities, 330
Exponential Property of Inequality, 330
Exponential regression, 339
Expressions. *See also specific types of expressions*
  evaluating, 2
Extraneous solutions
  defined, 253
  to logarithmic equations, 329
  to radical equations, 253–254
  to rational equations, 386

F

Factor Theorem, 176
Factoring
  polynomial equations solved by, 182
  polynomials, 173–180
    completely, 174–175
    Factor Theorem on, 176
    by grouping, 175
    in quadratic form, 175
    special products, 84, 174
  quadratic equations solved by, 86, 88, 106
Families of functions, 4
Fibonacci sequence, 566, 568
Finite differences, 215
  defined, 215
  identifying functions using, 336
  writing functions using, 215
Finite sequences, 530
Finite series
  arithmetic, finding sums of, 541
  defined, 532
  geometric, finding sums of, 548–549
First differences, 72, 215, 336
Focus, of parabolas, 61–68
  defined, 62
  writing quadratic equations using, 62–64
Formulas. *See also* Quadratic Formula
  Change-of-Base, 322
  for compound interest, 293, 300
  for depreciation, 232
  Euler's, 512
  for inputs of functions, 272

  for margins of error, 434
  for monthly loan payments, 549
  rewriting, 516
  for special series, 533
  for standard normal distribution, 402
  sum and difference, 513–518
  for volume, 202
Fractions
  complex, 379
  denominators of (*See* Denominators)
  polynomials in (*See* Rational expressions)
  writing repeating decimals as, 556
Frequency, in trigonometric functions, 500
Function(s). *See also specific types of functions*
  compositions of, 265–270
    defined, 266
    evaluating, 266
    finding, 265, 267
  differences or ratios used for identifying, 336
  domain and range of, 288
  end behavior of, 153
  evaluating, 528
  families of, 4
  inverses of (*See* Inverse)
  performing operations on, 259–264
  zeros of (*See* Zeros of functions)
Function families, 4
Function notation
  for inverse functions, 273
  for transformations, 245, 312, 314
Fundamental Theorem of Algebra, 189–198

G

Gauss, Carl Friedrich, 537
Geometric sequences
  analyzing, 545–552
  defined, 545–546
  identifying, 546
  recursive equations for, 560
  rules for
    defined, 546
    recursive, 560–561
    writing, 546–547
Geometric series
  analyzing, 545–552
  defined, 548
  finite, finding sums of, 548–549
  infinite
    finding partial sums of, 554
    finding sums of, 553–558
Golden ratio, 389
Golden rectangles, 389

Graph of the system, 135
Graphing. *See also* Transformations
  circles, 247
  cubic functions, 151, 199, 214
  equations of parabolas, 63–64
  even functions, 209
  exponential decay functions, 291
  exponential growth functions, 290
  inverse functions, 273
  linear equations
    finding x-intercept of, 42
    writing from, 20
  logarithmic functions, 307
  natural base functions, 299
  nonlinear systems of equations, 125–126
  odd functions, 209
  operations on functions, 259
  parabolas
    analyzing graphs, 61
    from equations, 63–64
    from radical functions, 247
    using focus and directrix, 63–64
    using symmetry, 51–53
  parent functions, 3
  polynomial functions, 151–158
    analyzing, 205–212
    sketching, 154
    with tables of values, 154
    turning points of, 205, 208
    using x-intercepts, 206
  quadratic equations, solving by, 86, 129
  quadratic functions (*See also* Parabolas)
    identifying graphs, 43
    in intercept form, 55
    in standard form, 53
    with symmetry, 52–53
    with tables of values, 5–7, 44
    in vertex form, 52
    with x-intercepts, 55
  quadratic inequalities
    in one variable, 133
    systems of, 135
    in two variables, 134
  quartic functions, 151, 199
  radical functions, 243–250
  rational functions, 359–366
    other, 362–363
    rewriting and, 378
    simple, 359–361
  sequences, 531
  systems of nonlinear equations, 125–126
  systems of quadratic inequalities, 135

trigonometric functions
secant and cosecant, 489–498
sine and cosine, 479–488
tangent and cotangent, 489–498
Grouping, factoring by, 175
Growth
exponential (*See* Exponential growth)
logistic, 302
Growth factors, 290

H

Histograms
of normal distributions, 399–403
skewed, 403
Horizontal asymptotes, of rational functions, 362
Horizontal axis of symmetry, 63–64, 247
Horizontal Line Test, 275
Horizontal shrinks
defined, 14
of exponential functions, 312–313
of logarithmic functions, 314
of polynomial functions, 200–201
of quadratic functions, 44
of radical functions, 245–246
of trigonometric functions, 481–482
writing, 14
Horizontal stretches
defined, 14
of exponential functions, 312–313
of logarithmic functions, 314
of polynomial functions, 200
of quadratic functions, 44
of radical functions, 245
of trigonometric functions, 481–482
writing, 14
Horizontal translations
defined, 12
of exponential functions, 312–313
of linear functions, 12
of logarithmic functions, 314
of polynomial functions, 200
of quadratic functions, 44
of radical functions, 245
of trigonometric functions, 483
Hyperbolas, 360
Hypotenuse, 455–456
Hypotheses, 407–414
analyzing, 411
defined, 411

I

Identities
defined, 507

trigonometric
defined, 497, 508
fundamental, 508
using, 507–512
verifying, 510
writing, 507
Identity matrix
2×2, 603–604
3×3, 604
defined, 604
Imaginary numbers
in complex conjugates, 98, 192
defined, 95–96
imaginary unit i, 96
pure, 96
as solutions to quadratic equations, 96, 117–119
Imaginary zeros, of polynomial functions, 191–194
Index (indices)
of the radical, 230
of refraction, 511, 516
of summation, 532–533
Inequalities. *See specific types of inequalities*
Inequality
Exponential Property of, 330
Logarithmic Property of, 330
Inferences
defined, 430
from experiments, 439–444
from sample surveys, 429–438
Inferential statistics, 430
Infinite sequences, 530
Infinite series
defined, 532
geometric
finding partial sums of, 554
finding sums of, 553–558
Infinitely many solutions, systems of linear equations with, 28, 30
Infinitely small, 552
Initial side, 464
Inputs, of functions, writing formulas for, 272
Intercept. *See x-intercept*
Intercept form
of cubic functions, 214
of quadratic functions
defined, 55
finding minimum and maximum values using, 89
graphing, 55
writing quadratic equations using, 70–71
Interest, compound, 293, 300, 564
Inventory matrices, 589

Inverse, of functions, 271–280
defined, 272
describing, 271
exploring, 272–273
exponential and logarithmic functions as, 306–307
finding, 273–275
for exponential and logarithmic functions, 306
for linear functions, 273
for nonlinear functions, 274–275
for rational functions, 387
as functions vs. not functions, 274
graphing, 273
interpreting, 276
notation for, 273, 603
solving rational equations with, 387
Inverse matrices, 603–610
2×2, 604–605
3×3, 605
defined, 604
describing, 603
finding, 604–605
notation for, 603
Inverse variation, 353–359
classifying, 354–355
defined, 354
describing, 353
Inverse variation equations
using, 356
writing, 355–356
Irrational Conjugates Theorem, 185
Irrational numbers, natural base e as, 298

K

Kepler, Third Law of, 234
Kirchoff's Laws, 602
Koch snowflake, 551

L

Laws
Kirchoff's Laws, 602
Newton's Law of Cooling, 331
Third Law of Kepler, 234
LCD. *See* Least common denominator
LCM. *See* Least common multiple
Leading coefficients, 152–153
Least common denominator (LCD)
adding or subtracting rational expressions with, 376–377
simplifying complex fractions with, 379
solving rational equations with, 385–386

Least common multiple (LCM),
  finding, 376
Left Distributive Property, 588
Like denominators, adding or
  subtracting rational
  expressions with, 376
Like radicals
  adding and subtracting, 238
  defined, 238
Line of best fit
  defined, 23
  finding, 22–23
Line of fit
  best, 22–23
  defined, 22
  finding, 22–23
Line of reflection, 5, 273
Linear binomials, as factors, 176
Linear equations
  comparing, 21
  graphs of
    finding x-intercept of, 42
    writing from, 20
  in nonlinear systems of equations,
    126, 128
  point-slope form of, 20
  slope-intercept form of
    defined, 20
    writing, 20
  solving, 454, 576
  systems of (See Systems of linear
    equations)
  in three variables, defined, 28
  writing, 20
Linear functions
  defined, 1, 152
  family of, 4
  identifying, 3–4
  inverses of, 273
  modeling with, 19–26
    comparing linear equations in, 21
    lines of fit in, 22–23
    writing linear equations in, 20
  parent function for, 3–4
  transformations of, 11–18
    combinations of, 15
    describing and graphing, 5
    stretches and shrinks, 14
    translations and reflections,
      12–13
Linear regression, 23
Linear systems. See Systems of linear
  equations
Literal equations, rewriting, 228
Loan payments, monthly, 549, 564
Local maximum, of polynomial
  functions, 208

Local minimum, of polynomial
  functions, 208
Location Principle, 207
Logarithm(s), 303–310
  of b with base b, 305
  common
    Change-of-Base Formula with,
      322
    defined, 305
    evaluating, 305
  defined, 304
  evaluating expressions with, 305
  expanding and condensing
    expressions with, 321
  natural
    Change-of-Base Formula with,
      322
    defined, 305
    evaluating, 305
  of 1, 305
  properties of, 319–326
    deriving, 319
    using, 320
  of y with base b, 304
Logarithmic equations
  defined, 329
  Property of Equality for, 329
  rewriting, 304
  solving, 327–334
Logarithmic expressions
  evaluating, 305
  expanding and condensing, 321
Logarithmic form, of logarithm of y
  with base b, 304
Logarithmic functions, 303–310
  exponential functions as inverse of,
    306–307
  graphing, 307
    transformations of, 311–318
  modeling with, 335–342
  using, 323
Logarithmic inequalities, 330
Logarithmic Property of Inequality,
  330
Logarithmic regression, 339
Logistic function, 341
Logistic growth, 302
Long division, polynomial, 168
Lower limit of summation, 532

M

Margins of error, for surveys
  analyzing, 433
  defined, 433
  finding, 433–434
  formula for, 434

Matrices
  2×2
    determinants of, 594
    identity matrix, 603–604
    inverse of, 604–605
  3×3
    determinants of, 594
    identity matrix, 604
    inverse of, 605
  analyzing, 577
  coefficient, 596–597
  of constants, 606
  defined, 577–578
  determinants of, 593–602
    defined, 594
    evaluating, 594–595
    finding, 593
    finding area of triangle using, 595
    solving systems of linear
      equations using, 596–598
  diagonal, 591
  identity, 604
  inverse, 603–610
    defined, 604
    describing, 603
    finding, 604–605
    notation for, 603
  operations with, 577–584
    adding and subtracting, 578
    multiplying, 585–592
    multiplying by scalars, 579–580
    order of, 579, 587
    properties of, 579, 588
  of variables, 606
  zero, 609
Matrix equations, solving, 580, 605
Matrix Multiplication, Associative
  Property of, 588
Maximum values
  of polynomial functions, 208
  of quadratic functions, 54, 89
Mean
  estimating, 430
  standard deviation from, 399
Measures of center, 398
Method of exhaustion, 552
Midline, of sine and cosine graphs, 483
Minimum values
  of polynomial functions, 208
  of quadratic functions, 54, 89
Modeling
  with exponential functions,
    292–293, 335–342
  with linear functions, 19–26
  with logarithmic functions, 335–342
  with polynomial functions, 155, 202,
    213–218

with quadratic functions, 69–79
with trigonometric functions, 499–506
Monomials
defined, 152
finding common factors, 174
multiplying by binomials, 161
Monthly loan payments, 549, 564
Motion
circular, 502
oscillating, 500
Multiplication
of complex numbers, 98
cross, solving rational equations by, 384
of functions, 259–262
of matrices, 585–592
Associative Property of, 588
describing products, 586
properties of, 588
by scalars, 579–580
two, 587
of polynomials, 159–166
binomials by monomials, 161
by rational expressions, 369
three binomials, 161
with rational exponents, 236
of rational expressions, 367–374
scalar, 579–580
Associative Property of, 588

N

Natural base e, 297–302
approximating, 297
defined, 298
simplifying expressions with, 298
Natural base functions
defined, 299
graphing, 299
transformations of, 313
Natural logarithms
Change-of-Base Formula with, 322
defined, 305
evaluating, 305
Negative angle identities, 508
Negative Exponent Property, 236
Negative numbers, square roots of, 96
Negative real zeros, 193
Newton's Law of Cooling, 331
No solutions
systems of linear equations with, 28, 30
systems of nonlinear equations with, 126–128
Nonlinear functions, inverses of, 274–275

Nonlinear systems of equations
defined, 126
number of solutions of, 126–128
solving, 125–132
with circles, 128
by elimination, 127
by graphing, 125–126
by substitution, 127
Normal curves
area under, 400
defined, 400
Normal distributions, 399–406
analyzing, 399
defined, 399–400
interpreting, 401
recognizing, 403
vs. skewed distributions, 403
standard, 402–403
***n*th percentile,** 405
***n*th roots of *a*,** 229–234
defined, 230
finding, 230
solving equations using, 232
***n*th terms**
of arithmetic sequences, writing rules for, 539–540
of geometric sequences, writing rules for, 546–547
Numbers, types of, 95. *See also specific types of numbers*

O

Oblique asymptotes, 390
Observational studies
correlation in, 425
defined, 418
design of, 425
identifying, 418
Odd functions, 209
Operations. *See* Addition; Division; Multiplication; Subtraction
Order of operations, for matrix expressions, 579, 587
Ordered triples, 28
Origin
center at the, 247
symmetric about the, 209
Oscillating motion, 500

P

Parabolas
analyzing, 61
axis of symmetry of
defined, 52
graphing quadratic functions using, 52–53

horizontal, 63–64, 247
vertical, 63–64
defined, 44
directrix of
defined, 62
writing quadratic equations using, 62–64
equations of, 62–65
deriving, 62
graphing, 63–64
standard, 63–64
using, 65
writing, 62–64, 109
focus of, 61–68
defined, 62
writing quadratic equations using, 62–64
graphing
analyzing graphs, 61
from equations, 64
from radical functions, 247
using focus and directrix, 63–64
using symmetry, 51–53
properties of, 51–53
vertex of
defined, 46
writing equations using, 63–64, 70
Parabolic reflectors, 65
Parameters, population
analyzing, 432
defined, 409
estimating, 430–432
vs. statistics, 409
Parent functions, 3–10
absolute value
identifying, 3–4
transforming, 11
constant, 3
cube root, 244
defined, 4
exponential, 3
exponential decay, 291
exponential growth, 290
identifying, 3–4
linear, 3–4
quadratic, 3
simple rational, 360
square root, 3, 244
transformations of, 4, 11
trigonometric
secant and cosecant, 493
sine and cosine, 480
tangent and cotangent, 490
Partial sums, of infinite geometric series, 554

Pascal, Blaise, 163
Pascal's Triangle, 163
   defined, 163
   using, 159, 163
Patterns
   cube of a binomial, 162
   difference of two cubes, 174
   difference of two squares, 174
   square of a binomial, 162
   sum and difference of binomials, 162
   sum of two cubes, 174
Percentile, *n*th, 405
Perfect square trinomials, 106
Period
   of sine and cosine graphs, 480
   of tangent and cotangent graphs, 491
Periodic functions, 480
Phase shift, 483
Placebos, 424
Plane. *See* Coordinate plane
Points
   evaluating trigonometric functions using, 472
   finding distances between, 42
   writing exponential functions using, 337
   writing linear equations using, 20
   writing polynomial functions for sets of, 214
   writing quadratic equations using, 70–71
Point-slope form, writing equations in, 20
Polynomial(s). *See also* Binomial(s)
   adding, 159–166
   defined, 152
   degrees of, 168, 190
   dividing, 167–172
      by binomials, 167, 169
      with long division, 168
      rational expressions by, 370
      Remainder Theorem on, 170
      with synthetic division, 169–170
   factoring, 173–180
      completely, 174–175
      Factor Theorem on, 176
      by grouping, 175
      in quadratic form, 175
      special products, 84, 174
   in fractions (*See* Rational expressions)
   multiplying, 159–166
      binomials by monomials, 161
      by rational expressions, 369
      three binomials, 161
      perfect square trinomials, 106

      in quadratic form, 175
      special products of, 162
         factoring, 84, 174
   subtracting, 159–166
Polynomial equations
   solutions of
      Fundamental Theorem of Algebra on, 190
      number of, 190
      repeated, 181–182, 190
   solving, 181–188
      by factoring, 182
      Irrational Conjugates Theorem in, 185
      Rational Root Theorem in, 183
      with repeated solutions, 181–182
Polynomial functions
   coefficients of
      Descartes's Rule of Signs on, 193–194
      leading, 152–153
   defined, 152
   degrees of, 152–153, 208
   end behavior of, 153
   evaluating, 153
   factors of, defined, 206
   graphing, 151–158
      analyzing, 205–212
      sketching, 154
      with tables of values, 154
      transformations of, 199–204
      turning points of, 205, 208
      using x-intercepts, 206
   identifying, 151–152
   modeling with, 155, 202, 213–218
   solutions of, 206
   standard form of, 152
   types of, 152
   writing
      with finite differences, 215
      for sets of points, 214
      transformed, 201–202
      with zeros, 185, 192
   zeros of
      defined, 206
      finding, 182, 184, 189, 191, 207
      imaginary, 191–194
      rational, 184, 191
      real, 184, 191, 193–194, 207
      writing with, 185, 192
Polynomial long division, 168
Polynomial regression, 216
Population(s), 407–414
   censuses of, 408
   defined, 408
   hypotheses about, 411

   parameters of
      analyzing, 432
      defined, 409
      estimating, 430–432
   proportions of
      defined, 410
      estimating, 431
      finding margins of error for, 434
   vs. samples, 408
Population mean, estimating, 430
Positive real zeros, 193–194
Power. *See* Exponent(s)
Power of a Power Property, 236
Power of a Product Property, 236
Power of a Quotient Property, 236
Power Property of Logarithms, 319–320
Principal, 293
Principle, Location, 207
Probability distributions, normal, 399–406
Product of Powers Property, 236
Product Property of Cube Roots, 235
Product Property of Logarithms, 319–320
Product Property of Radicals, 237
Product Property of Square Roots, 235
Properties
   Associative Property of Addition, 579
   Associative Property of Matrix Multiplication, 588
   Associative Property of Scalar Multiplication, 588
   Commutative Property of Addition, 579
   Distributive Property, 579
      Left, 588
      Right, 588
      using, 238
   Equality for Exponential Equations, 328
   Equality for Logarithmic Equations, 329
   Exponential Property of Inequality, 330
   of exponents
      and properties of logarithms, 319–320
      rational, 235–242
      using, 228, 288
   Logarithmic Property of Inequality, 330
   of logarithms, 319–326
      deriving, 319
      using, 320

of matrix operations, 579, 588
Negative Exponent Property, 236
of parabolas, 52–53
Power of a Power Property, 236
Power of a Product Property, 236
Power of a Quotient Property, 236
Power Property of Logarithms, 319–320
Product of Powers Property, 236
Product Property of Cube Roots, 235
Product Property of Logarithms, 319–320
Product Property of Radicals, 237
Product Property of Square Roots, 235
Quotient of Powers Property, 236
Quotient Property of Logarithms, 319–320
Quotient Property of Radicals, 237
of radicals, 235–242
Zero Exponent Property, 236
Zero-Product Property, 88, 182

Proportions
population
defined, 410
estimating, 431
finding margins of error for, 434
sample
defined, 410
finding, 410, 432

Pure imaginary numbers, 96
Pure tone, 500
Pyramids, volume of, 202
Pythagorean identities, 507–508
Pythagorean Theorem, 42, 61, 454
Pythagorean triples, 165

Q

Quadrantal angles, 473
Quadratic equations
analyzing the discriminant of, 118–120
in nonlinear systems of equations, 126
in one variable, defined, 86
solutions of
complex, 100
imaginary, 96, 117–119
number of, 116–119
solving, 85–94
algebraically, 87–88
by completing the square, 106–107
by factoring, 86, 88, 106
by graphing, 86, 129
with Quadratic Formula, 115–117

with square roots, 86–87, 106
standard form of, 86
writing, 69–73
using point and vertex, 70
using point and x-intercepts, 70–71
using three points, 70, 72
Quadratic form of polynomials, 175
Quadratic Formula, 115–124
analyzing, 115
analyzing the discriminant with, 118–120
defined, 115–116
deriving, 115
solving equations using, 115–117
with imaginary solutions, 117–119
with one real solution, 117–118
with two real solutions, 116, 118
Quadratic functions
characteristics of, 51–60
defined, 4, 44
equations of (See Quadratic equations)
family of, 4
graphing (See also Parabolas)
identifying graphs, 43
in intercept form, 55
in standard form, 53
with symmetry, 52–53
with tables of values, 5–7, 44
in vertex form, 52
with x-intercepts, 55
identifying, 3–4, 43
intercept form of
defined, 55
finding minimum and maximum values using, 89
graphing, 55
writing quadratic equations using, 70–71
inverses of, 274
maximum and minimum values of, 54, 89
modeling with, 69–79
parent function for, 3
standard form of, 53
transformations of, 43–50
describing and graphing, 5–7, 44–45
reflections, 5
stretches and shrinks, 6, 44
translations, 44
using, 47
writing, 46
vertex form of
defined, 46

graphing, 52
using, 110
writing, 108
writing quadratic equations using, 70
writing
equations of, 70–73
transformed, 46
in vertex form, 108
zeros of, 88, 100
Quadratic inequalities, 133–140
in one variable
defined, 136
solving, 133, 136
systems of
defined, 135
graphing, 135
in two variables
defined, 134
graphing, 134
solving, 137
Quadratic regression, 73
Quartic functions
defined, 152
graphs of
identifying, 151
transforming, 199
Quartic regression, 216
Questions, biased, 419
Quotient of Powers Property, 236
Quotient Property of Logarithms, 319–320
Quotient Property of Radicals, 237

R

Radian measure, 463–470
converting between degree measure and, 466
defined, 463, 466
of special angles, 466
using, 463, 466
Radical(s)
adding and subtracting, 238
with exponents, 229
index of, 230
like, 238
properties of, 235–242
defined, 237
using, 237
simplifying expressions with, 237–238
solving equations with two, 254
Radical equations
defined, 252
solving, 251–258
with extraneous solutions, 253–254

Index **A67**

Radical expressions (continued)
  with radicals on both sides, 254
  with rational exponents, 254
Radical expressions
  simplest form of, 237–238
  simplifying, 237–238
  writing
    with exponents, 229
    in simplest form, 237–238
Radical functions
  cube root, 244
  defined, 244
  graphing, 243–250
    transformations of, 245–246
  inverses of, 275
  square root, 3, 244
Radical inequalities, solving, 251–258
Random samples, 416–417
  defined, 408, 416
  identifying, 416
  as unbiased, 417
Randomization
  in experimental design, 424–426
  in observational studies, 425
Randomized comparative experiments
  analyzing data from, 439–440
  defined, 424
  evaluating, 424
Range
  of functions, 288
  of sequences, 530
Ratio(s)
  common
    defined, 545–546
    writing rules given term and, 547
  golden, 389
  identifying functions using, 336
  of side lengths of right triangles, 455–456
Rational equations
  solving, 383–390
    by cross multiplying, 384
    with inverses of functions, 387
    with least common denominator, 385–386
  writing, 384
Rational exponents, 229–234
  approximating expressions with, 231
  defined, 231
  evaluating expressions with, 231
  multiplying and dividing with, 236
  properties of, 235–242
    defined, 236
    using, 236
  solving radical equations with, 254
  writing expressions with, 229

Rational expressions
  adding, 375–382
    with like denominators, 376
    with unlike denominators, 377
  defined, 368
  dividing, 367–374
    by polynomials, 370
  finding least common multiple of, 376
  multiplying, 367–374
    by polynomials, 369
  simplifying, 368
  subtracting, 375–382
    with like denominators, 376
    with unlike denominators, 377
Rational functions
  defined, 360
  graphing, 359–366
    other, 362–363
    rewriting and, 378
    simple, 359–361
    transformations of, 361
  inverses of, finding, 387
  rewriting, 362, 378
  simple, 359–361
    graphing, 359–361
    parent function for, 360
Rational numbers, adding and subtracting, 352
Rational Root Theorem, 183
Rational zeros, of polynomial functions, 184, 191
Real nth roots of a, 230
Real zeros, of polynomial functions, 191, 193–194, 207
Reciprocal identities, 508
Rectangles
  golden, 389
  transformations of, 2
Rectangular prism, volume of, 150
Recursive equations
  for arithmetic sequences, 560
  defined, 559–560
  for geometric sequences, 560
  writing, 559, 564
Recursive rules, 559–568
  for arithmetic sequences, 560–561
  defined, 560
  evaluating, 560
  for geometric sequences, 560–561
  translating between explicit rules and, 562
  writing, 561–563
Reference angles, 474–475
  defined, 474
  evaluating trigonometric functions using, 474–475

  finding, 474
Reflection, line of, 5, 273
Reflections
  of absolute value functions, 12–13
  defined, 5
  describing and graphing, 5
  of exponential functions, 312–313
  of inverse functions, 273
  of linear functions, 12–13
  of logarithmic functions, 314
  of polynomial functions, 200–201
  of quadratic functions, 5, 44
  of radical functions, 245
  of trigonometric functions, 484
  writing, 13
  in x-axis, 13, 44
  in y-axis, 13, 44
Refraction, indices of, 511, 516
Regression
  cubic, 215–216
  exponential, 339
  linear, 23
  logarithmic, 339
  polynomial, 216
  quadratic, 73
  quartic, 216
  sinusoidal, 503
Remainder Theorem, 170, 176
Repeated solutions, of polynomial equations, 181–182, 190
Repeating decimals, writing as fractions, 556
Resampling, 439–442
  making inferences based on, 442
  using simulations, 441
Rewriting
  exponential equations, 304
  exponential functions, 292
  formulas, 516
  literal equations, 228
  logarithmic equations, 304
  rational functions, 362, 378
Right Distributive Property, 588
Right triangles. *See also* Trigonometric functions
  angle measures of, finding, 458
  side lengths of
    abbreviations for, 456
    finding ratios of, 455
  solving, 458
Roots. *See also* Cube root; nth roots; Square root
  of equations, 86
Rules
  for arithmetic sequences
    defined, 539

writing, 539–540
explicit
  defined, 560
  translating between recursive rules and, 562
  for geometric sequences
    defined, 546
    writing, 546–547
  recursive, 559–568
    for arithmetic sequences, 560–561
    defined, 560
    evaluating, 560
    for geometric sequences, 560–561
    translating between explicit rules and, 562
    writing, 561–563
  for sequences
    defined, 530
    writing, 531
  for series, writing, 532, 541

Sample(s), 407–414
  defined, 408
  experiments with two, 440
  vs. populations, 408
  random, 408, 416–417
  recognizing bias in, 417
  types of, 416–417
Sample proportion
  defined, 410
  finding, 410, 432
Sample sizes
  defined, 426
  and margins of error, 433–434
Sample surveys
  making inferences from, 429–438
  variability in, 429
Sampling methods, 416–418
Scalar multiplication, 579–580
  Associative Property of, 588
Scalars, defined, 579
Scatter plots, line of fit in, 22–23
Secant function
  characteristics of, 493
  definitions of
    general, 472
    right-triangle, 456
  evaluating, 456–457
    using point, 472
    using unit circle, 473
  graphing, 489–498
  parent function for, 493
Second differences, 72, 215, 336

Sectors, of circles
  arc length of, 467
  area of, 467
  defined, 467
Self-selected samples, 416–417
Sequences. *See also* Arithmetic sequences; Geometric sequences
  defined, 530
  Fibonacci, 566, 568
  finding terms of, 529
  graphing, 531
  recursive rules for, 559–568
  using, 529–536
  writing rules for, 531
  writing terms of, 530
Series. *See also* Arithmetic series; Geometric series
  defined, 532
  finding sums of, 533
  special, formulas for, 533
  summation notation for, 532
  using, 529–536
  writing rules for, 532, 541
Sets, of complex numbers, 95
Shrinks
  of absolute value functions, 14
  defined, 6, 14
  describing and graphing, 6
  of exponential functions, 312–313
  of linear functions, 14
  of logarithmic functions, 314
  of polynomial functions, 200–201
  of quadratic functions, 44
  of radical functions, 245–246
  of trigonometric functions, 481–482
  writing, 14
Sierpinski triangle, 557
Sigma notation, 532
Signs, Descartes's Rule of, 193–194
Simple rational functions, 359–361
  graphing, 359–361
    transformations of, 361
  parent function for, 360
Simplest form
  of radical expressions, writing, 237–238
  of variable expressions, writing, 239
Simplified form, of rational expressions, 368
Simplifying expressions
  with complex fractions, 379
  with matrices, 580
  with natural base *e*, 298
  with radicals, 237–238
  rational, 368
  with square roots, 84

  trigonometric, 509, 515
  with variables, 239
Simulations
  defined, 418
  using, 407
    to analyze estimated population proportions, 432
    to analyze hypotheses, 411
    to resample data, 441
Sine function
  characteristics of, 480
  definitions of
    general, 472
    right-triangle, 456
  evaluating, 456–457
    using point, 472
    using reference angles, 475
    using unit circle, 473
  graphing, 479–488
    transformations of, 481–484
  parent function for, 480
Sinusoidal regression, 503
Sinusoids
  defined, 501
  modeling, 501–503
Skewed data distributions, 403
Slope-intercept form, of linear equations
  defined, 20
  writing equations in, 20
Small, infinitely, 552
Solutions
  exactly one, systems of linear equations with, 28–29
  extraneous
    defined, 253
    of logarithmic equations, 329
    of radical equations, 253
    of rational equations, 386
  infinitely many, systems of linear equations with, 28, 30
  no
    systems of linear equations with, 28, 30
    systems of nonlinear equations with, 126–128
  of polynomial equations
    Fundamental Theorem of Algebra on, 190
    number of, 190
    repeated, 181–182, 190
  of polynomial functions, 206
  of quadratic equations
    complex, 100
    imaginary, 96, 117–119
    number of, 116–119

repeated, of polynomial equations, 181–182, 190
of systems of nonlinear equations, number of, 126–128
of systems of three linear equations
  defined, 28
  number of, 28–30
  visualizing, 28
Special angles
  degree measure of, 466
  radian measure of, 466
  trigonometric values for, 457
Special products, of polynomials, 162
  factoring, 84, 174
Special series, formulas for, 533
Square of a binomial pattern, 162
Square root(s)
  of negative numbers, 96
  Product Property of, 235
  simplifying, 84
  solving quadratic equations with, 86–87, 106
Square root functions
  defined, 244
  graphing, 244
  identifying, 3
  parent function for, 3, 244
Standard deviation
  defined, 399
  finding, 398
Standard form
  of complex numbers, 96
  of equations of circles and parabolas, 109
  of polynomial functions, 152
  of quadratic equations, 86
  of quadratic functions, 53
Standard normal distributions, 402–403
Standard normal tables, 402
Standard position, angles in, 464
Statistics. *See also* Data
  defined, 409
  descriptive, 430
  inferential, 430
  vs. parameters, 409
Straight line depreciation, 19
Stratified samples, 416
Stretches
  of absolute value functions, 6, 14
  defined, 6, 14
  describing and graphing, 6
  of exponential functions, 312–313
  of linear functions, 14
  of logarithmic functions, 314
  of polynomial functions, 200–202
  of quadratic functions, 6, 44

of radical functions, 245
of trigonometric functions, 481–482
writing, 14
Subscripts, 598
Substitution, systems of nonlinear equations solved by, 127
Subtraction
  of algebraic expressions, 150
  of complex numbers, 97
  of functions, 259–261
  of like radicals and roots, 238
  of matrices, 578
  of polynomials, 159–166
  of rational expressions, 375–382
    with like denominators, 376
    with unlike denominators, 377
  of rational numbers, 352
Sum and difference pattern, 162
Sum formulas, 513–518
  defined, 514
  deriving, 513
  using, 514
Sum of two cubes pattern, 174
Summation
  index of, 532–533
  lower and upper limits of, 532
Summation notation, writing series using, 532
Surveys
  biased questions in, 419
  conducting, 415
  defined, 418
  margins of error for
    defined, 433
    finding, 433–434
  sample
    making inferences from, 429–438
    variability in, 429
Symmetry
  axis of
    defined, 52
    finding, 52
    graphing quadratic functions using, 52–53
  horizontal, 63–64, 247
  vertical, 63–64
  of data distributions, 400, 403
  about the origin, in odd functions, 209
  of parabolas, 51–53
  about the *y*-axis, in even functions, 209
Synthetic division, 169–170
Systematic samples, 416
Systems of linear equations
  solutions of
    defined, 28

number of, 28–30
visualizing, 28
solving, 576
  in three variables, 27–34
  using Cramer's Rule, 596–598
  using inverse matrices, 606–607
Systems of nonlinear equations
  defined, 126
  solutions of, number of, 126–128
  solving, 125–132
    with circles, 128
    by elimination, 127
    by graphing, 125–126
    by substitution, 127
Systems of quadratic inequalities
  defined, 135
  graphing, 135

T

Tables, standard normal, 402
Tables of values
  graphing absolute value functions with, 6
  graphing polynomial functions with, 154
  graphing quadratic functions with, 5–7, 44
Tangent function
  characteristics of, 490
  definitions of
    general, 472
    right-triangle, 456
  evaluating, 456–457
    using point, 472
    using reference angles, 475
    using unit circle, 473
  graphing, 489–498
  parent function for, 490
Tangent identities, 508
Terminal side, 464
Terms, of sequences
  arithmetic, 539–540
  defined, 530
  finding, 529
  geometric, 546–547
  writing, 530
Theorems
  Binomial Theorem, 163
  Complex Conjugates Theorem, 192
  Factor Theorem, 176
  Fundamental Theorem of Algebra, 189–198
  Irrational Conjugates Theorem, 185
  Pythagorean Theorem, 42, 61, 454
  Rational Root Theorem, 183
  Remainder Theorem, 170, 176
Third differences, 215

Three variables, linear equations in, 28

Three-variable systems of linear equations
  defined, 28
  solving, 27–34
    algebraically, 29–30
    writing and, 31
    visualizing solutions to, 28

Total cost matrices, 589

Transformations, 3–18. *See also* specific types
  of absolute value functions, 11–18
    combinations of, 7, 15
    describing, 6
    types of, 12–15
  combinations of, 7, 15
  of cubic functions, 199
  defined, 5
  of exponential functions, 311–318
    identifying, 311
    types of, 312–313
    writing, 315
  of figures, 2
  function notation for, 245, 312, 314
  of linear functions, 11–18
    combinations of, 15
    describing, 5
    types of, 12–15
  of logarithmic functions, 311–318
    identifying, 311
    types of, 314
    writing, 315
  of natural base functions, 313
  of parent functions, 4
  of polynomial functions, 199–204
    describing, 200–201
    writing, 201–202
  of quadratic functions, 43–50
    describing, 5–7, 44–45
    using, 47
    writing, 46
  of quartic functions, 199
  of radical functions, 245–246
    writing, 246
  of rational functions, 361
  of trigonometric functions
    secant and cosecant, 493–494
    sine and cosine, 481–484
    tangent and cotangent, 491–492
  types of, 5–6

Translations
  defined, 5, 12
  describing and graphing, 5
  of exponential functions, 312–313
  of linear functions, 5, 12–13
  of logarithmic functions, 314
  of parabolas, 64
  of polynomial functions, 200, 202
  of quadratic functions, 44
  of radical functions, 245
  of rational functions, 361
  of trigonometric functions, 483
  writing, 12

Treatment groups
  defined, 424
  resampling, 441–442

Triangles. *See also* Right triangles
  finding area of, 595
  Pascal's, 159, 163
  Sierpinski, 557
  solving, 458
  transformations of, 2

Trigonometric equations, solving, 516

Trigonometric expressions
  evaluating, 514
  simplifying, 509, 515

Trigonometric functions, 455–462
  of any angle, 471–478
  definitions of
    general, 472
    right-triangle, 456
  evaluating, 456–457
    using point, 472
    using reference angles, 474–475
    using sum and difference formulas, 513–518
    using trigonometric identities, 507–512
    using unit circle, 473
  graphing
    secant and cosecant, 489–498
    sine and cosine, 479–488
    tangent and cotangent, 489–498
  modeling with, 499–506
    frequency in, 500
    technology in, 503
  values for special angles in, 457
  writing, 471, 501

Trigonometric identities
  defined, 497, 508
  fundamental, 508
  using, 507–512
  verifying, 510
  writing, 507

Trinomials, perfect square, 106

Triples
  ordered, 28
  Pythagorean, 165

Turning points
  defined, 208
  of polynomial functions, 205, 208

U

Unbiased samples
  defined, 417
  selecting, 417

Unit circles
  defined, 471, 473
  equation of, 471
  using, 473

Unlike denominators, adding or subtracting rational expressions with, 377

Upper limit of summation, 532

V

Validity, of experiments, 426
Variability, in sample surveys, 429
Variable expressions, simplifying, 239
Variables
  matrices of, 606
  three, linear equations in, 28 (*See also* Three-variable systems)

Variation
  constant of, 354
  defined, 354
  describing types of, 353
  direct, 353–355
    classifying, 354–355
    defined, 354
    describing, 353
  inverse, 353–358
    classifying, 354–355
    defined, 354
    describing, 353

Vertex, of parabolas
  defined, 46
  writing equations using, 63–64, 70

Vertex form, of quadratic functions
  defined, 46
  graphing, 52
  using, 110
  writing, 108
  writing quadratic equations using, 70

Vertical asymptotes
  of logarithmic functions, 307
  of rational functions, 362
  of trigonometric functions, 491

Vertical axis of symmetry, 63–64

Vertical shrinks
  defined, 6
  describing and graphing, 6
  of exponential functions, 312–313
  of logarithmic functions, 314
  of polynomial functions, 200–201
  of quadratic functions, 6, 44
  of radical functions, 245
  of trigonometric functions, 481–482
  writing, 14

Vertical stretches
  of absolute value functions, 6

defined, 6
describing and graphing, 6
of exponential functions, 312–313
of logarithmic functions, 314
of polynomial functions, 200–202
of quadratic functions, 44
of radical functions, 245
of trigonometric functions, 481–482
writing, 14

Vertical translations
defined, 12
of exponential functions, 312–313
of linear functions, 12
of logarithmic functions, 314
of polynomial functions, 200
of quadratic functions, 44
of radical functions, 245
of trigonometric functions, 483

Volume
finding, 150
of pyramids, 202

Writing. *See also* Rewriting
cubic functions, 214
equations of circles, 109
equations of parabolas, 62–64, 109
exponential functions, 292, 335, 337–338
models of, 292, 337–338
transformed, 315
from two points, 337
formulas for inputs of functions, 272
geometric sequences, rules for, 546–547
inverse variation equations, 355–356
linear equations, 20
logarithmic functions, transformed, 315
polynomial functions

with finite differences, 215
for set of points, 214
transformed, 201–202
with zeros, 185, 192
quadratic equations, 69–73
to model data, 72–73
using point and vertex, 70
using point and *x*-intercepts, 70–71
using three points, 70, 72
quadratic functions
equations of, 70–73
transformed, 46
in vertex form, 108
radical expressions
with exponents, 229
in simplest form, 237–238
radical functions, transformed, 246
rational equations, 384
rational exponents, 229
recursive equations, 559, 564
recursive rules, 561–563
reflections of functions, 13
sequences
rules for, 531, 546–547
terms of, 530
series, rules for, 532, 541
stretches and shrinks of functions, 14
three-variable systems of linear equations, 31
translations of functions, 12
trigonometric functions, 471, 501
trigonometric identities, 507
variable expressions, in simplest form, 239

x-axis reflections
defined, 13

of quadratic functions, 44
x-intercept
graphing quadratic functions using, 55
of linear equations, finding, 42
of polynomial functions
defined, 206
graphing, 206
writing quadratic equations using, 70–71

y-axis, even functions as symmetric about the, 209
y-axis reflections
defined, 13
of quadratic functions, 44

Zero Exponent Property, 236
Zero matrix, 609
Zero-Product Property, 88, 182
Zeros of functions
defined, 88
polynomial
defined, 206
finding, 182, 184, 189, 191, 207
imaginary, 191–194
rational, 184, 191
real, 184, 191, 193–194, 207
writing functions using, 185, 192
quadratic, finding, 88, 100
z-scores, 402
defined, 402
using, 402

My Guide to the Standards for Mathematical Practice

SMP.1 Make Sense of Problems and Persevere in Solving Them
I can analyze the given information and find what the problem is asking to help plan a solution pathway.

SMP.2 Reason Abstractly and Quantitatively
I can represent a problem symbolically, or see relationships in numbers or symbols and draw conclusions about a concrete example.

SMP.3 Construct Viable Arguments and Critique the Reasoning of Others
I can make and justify conclusions and decide whether others' arguments are correct or flawed.

SMP.4 Model with Mathematics
I can apply the math I learned to a real-life problem and interpret mathematical results in the context of the situation.

SMP.5 Use Appropriate Tools Strategically
I can think about the tools that are available and how they might help solve a mathematical problem. I can use a tool for its advantages, while being aware of its limitations.

SMP.6 Attend to Precision
I can develop a habit of being careful of how I talk about concepts, label my work, and write my answers.

SMP.7 Look for and Make Use of Structure
I can see structure within a mathematical statement, or step back for an overview to see how individual parts make one single object.

SMP.8 Look for and Express Regularity in Repeated Reasoning
I can recognize patterns and make generalizations while evaluating the reasonableness of answers as I solve problems.

My Guide to Problem Solving

I can apply the mathematics I learn to model and solve real-life problems.

1 Understand the Problem

Before planning a solution, I read the problem carefully.

- What is the problem asking?
- What do I know?
- What do I need to find out?
- Is any information not needed?
- What are some possible entry points to a solution?

2 Make a Plan

I plan my solution pathway before jumping in to solve.

- What variables or relationships can I identify in the situation?
- Do I understand these in the real-life context?
- Are there any constraints that I need to consider?
- Have I solved a problem like this before?
- Which problem-solving strategy will I use?
  - Use a verbal model.
  - Draw a diagram.
  - Write an equation.
  - Solve a simpler problem.
  - Sketch a graph or number line.
  - Make a table.
  - Make a list.
  - Break the problem into parts.

3 Solve and Check

As I solve the problem, I monitor and evaluate my progress.

- How precise does my answer need to be?
- What tools can I use to help model and solve?
- How does my model help me analyze the relationships among the variables?
- How can I interpret my results in terms of the real-life situation?
- Are my answers reasonable mathematically? Do they make sense in the context?
- Am I willing to change course if necessary?
- How will I report on my conclusions and explain my reasoning?

Quick Reference

Properties

Properties of Exponents

Let a and b be real numbers and let m and n be rational numbers.

Zero Exponent
$a^0 = 1$, where $a \neq 0$

Negative Exponent
$a^{-n} = \dfrac{1}{a^n}$, where $a \neq 0$

Product of Powers Property
$a^m \cdot a^n = a^{m+n}$

Quotient of Powers Property
$\dfrac{a^m}{a^n} = a^{m-n}$, where $a \neq 0$

Power of a Power Property
$(a^m)^n = a^{mn}$

Power of a Product Property
$(ab)^m = a^m b^m$

Power of a Quotient Property
$\left(\dfrac{a}{b}\right)^m = \dfrac{a^m}{b^m}$, where $b \neq 0$

Rational Exponents
$a^{m/n} = (a^{1/n})^m = (\sqrt[n]{a})^m$
or $a^{m/n} = (a^m)^{1/n} = \sqrt[n]{a^m}$

Rational Exponents
$a^{-m/n} = \dfrac{1}{a^{m/n}} = \dfrac{1}{(a^{1/n})^m} = \dfrac{1}{(\sqrt[n]{a})^m}$, where $a \neq 0$

or $a^{-m/n} = \dfrac{1}{(a^m)^{1/n}} = \dfrac{1}{\sqrt[n]{a^m}}$, where $a \neq 0$

Properties of Radicals

Let a and b be real numbers and let n be an integer greater than 1.

Product Property of Radicals
$\sqrt[n]{ab} = \sqrt[n]{a} \cdot \sqrt[n]{b}$

Quotient Property of Radicals
$\sqrt[n]{\dfrac{a}{b}} = \dfrac{\sqrt[n]{a}}{\sqrt[n]{b}}$, where $b \neq 0$

Square Root of a Negative Number
1. If r is a positive real number, then $\sqrt{-r} = \sqrt{-1}\sqrt{r} = i\sqrt{r}$.
2. By the first property, it follows that $(i\sqrt{r})^2 = i^2 \cdot r = -r$.

Properties of Logarithms

Let b, m, and n be positive real numbers with $b \neq 1$.

Product Property
$\log_b mn = \log_b m + \log_b n$

Quotient Property
$\log_b \dfrac{m}{n} = \log_b m - \log_b n$

Power Property
$\log_b m^n = n \log_b m$

Other Properties

Zero-Product Property
If A and B are expressions and $AB = 0$, then $A = 0$ or $B = 0$.

Property of Equality for Exponential Equations
If $b > 0$ and $b \neq 1$, then $b^x = b^y$ if and only if $x = y$.

Property of Equality for Logarithmic Equations
If b, x, and y are positive real numbers with $b \neq 1$, then $\log_b x = \log_b y$ if and only if $x = y$.

Patterns

Square of a Binomial Pattern
$(a + b)^2 = a^2 + 2ab + b^2$
$(a - b)^2 = a^2 - 2ab + b^2$

Cube of a Binomial Pattern
$(a + b)^3 = a^3 + 3a^2b + 3ab^2 + b^3$
$(a - b)^3 = a^3 - 3a^2b + 3ab^2 - b^3$

Difference of Two Squares Pattern
$a^2 - b^2 = (a + b)(a - b)$

Sum of Two Cubes Pattern
$a^3 + b^3 = (a + b)(a^2 - ab + b^2)$

Sum and Difference Pattern
$(a + b)(a - b) = a^2 - b^2$

Completing the Square Pattern
$x^2 + bx + \left(\dfrac{b}{2}\right)^2 = \left(x + \dfrac{b}{2}\right)^2$

Perfect Square Trinomial Pattern
$a^2 + 2ab + b^2 = (a + b)^2$
$a^2 - 2ab + b^2 = (a - b)^2$

Difference of Two Cubes Pattern
$a^3 - b^3 = (a - b)(a^2 + ab + b^2)$

Theorems

The Remainder Theorem
If a polynomial $f(x)$ is divided by $x - k$, then the remainder is $r = f(k)$.

The Factor Theorem
A polynomial $f(x)$ has a factor $x - k$ if and only if $f(k) = 0$.

The Rational Root Theorem
If $f(x) = a_n x^n + \cdots + a_1 x + a_0$ has *integer* coefficients, then every rational solution of $f(x) = 0$ has the form
$$\dfrac{p}{q} = \dfrac{\text{factor of constant term } a_0}{\text{factor of leading coefficient } a_n}.$$

The Irrational Conjugates Theorem
Let f be a polynomial function with rational coefficients, and let a and b be rational numbers such that $\sqrt{b}$ is irrational. If $a + \sqrt{b}$ is a zero of f, then $a - \sqrt{b}$ is also a zero of f.

The Fundamental Theorem of Algebra

Theorem   If $f(x)$ is a polynomial of degree n where $n > 0$, then the equation $f(x) = 0$ has at least one solution in the set of complex numbers.

Corollary   If $f(x)$ is a polynomial of degree n where $n > 0$, then the equation $f(x) = 0$ has exactly n solutions provided each solution repeated twice is counted as 2 solutions, each solution repeated three times is counted as 3 solutions, and so on.

The Complex Conjugates Theorem
If f is a polynomial function with real coefficients, and $a + bi$ is an imaginary zero of f, then $a - bi$ is also a zero of f.

Descartes's Rule of Signs
Let $f(x) = a_n x^n + a_{n-1} x^{n-1} + \cdots + a_2 x^2 + a_1 x + a_0$ be a polynomial function with real coefficients.
- The number of positive real zeros of f is equal to the number of changes in sign of the coefficients of $f(x)$ or is less than this by an even number.
- The number of negative real zeros of f is equal to the number of changes in the sign of the coefficients of $f(-x)$ or is less than this by an even number.

The Binomial Theorem
$(a + b)^n = {}_nC_0 a^n b^0 + {}_nC_1 a^{n-1} b^1 + {}_nC_2 a^{n-2} b^2 + \cdots + {}_nC_n a^0 b^n$, where n is a positive integer.

Formulas

Algebra

Slope
$$m = \frac{y_2 - y_1}{x_2 - x_1}$$

Slope-intercept form
$$y = mx + b$$

Point-slope form
$$y - y_1 = m(x - x_1)$$

Standard form of a quadratic function
$f(x) = ax^2 + bx + c$, where $a \neq 0$

Vertex form of a quadratic function
$f(x) = a(x - h)^2 + k$, where $a \neq 0$

Intercept form of a quadratic function
$f(x) = a(x - p)(x - q)$, where $a \neq 0$

Quadratic Formula
$$x = \frac{-b \pm \sqrt{b^2 - 4ac}}{2a}, \text{ where } a \neq 0$$

Standard equation of a circle
$x^2 + y^2 = r^2$

Standard form of a polynomial function
$f(x) = a_n x^n + a_{n-1} x^{n-1} + \cdots + a_1 x + a_0$

Exponential growth function
$y = ab^x$, where $a > 0$ and $b > 1$

Exponential decay function
$y = ab^x$, where $a > 0$ and $0 < b < 1$

Logarithm of y with base b
$\log_b y = x$ if and only if $b^x = y$

Change-of-base formula
$$\log_c a = \frac{\log_b a}{\log_b c}, \text{ where } a, b, \text{ and } c \text{ are positive real numbers}$$
with $b \neq 1$ and $c \neq 1$.

Sum of n terms of 1
$$\sum_{i=1}^{n} 1 = n$$

Sum of first n positive integers
$$\sum_{i=1}^{n} i = \frac{n(n+1)}{2}$$

Sum of squares of first n positive integers
$$\sum_{i=1}^{n} i^2 = \frac{n(n+1)(2n+1)}{6}$$

Explicit rule for an arithmetic sequence
$a_n = a_1 + (n-1)d$

Sum of first n terms of an arithmetic series
$$S_n = n\left(\frac{a_1 + a_n}{2}\right)$$

Explicit rule for a geometric sequence
$a_n = a_1 r^{n-1}$

Sum of first n terms of a geometric series
$$S_n = a_1\left(\frac{1 - r^n}{1 - r}\right), \text{ where } r \neq 1$$

Sum of an infinite geometric series
$$S = \frac{a_1}{1 - r} \text{ provided } |r| < 1$$

Recursive equation for an arithmetic sequence
$a_n = a_{n-1} + d$, where d is the common difference

Recursive equation for a geometric sequence
$a_n = r \cdot a_{n-1}$, where r is the common ratio

Statistics

Sample mean
$$\bar{x} = \frac{\Sigma x}{n}$$

Standard deviation
$$\sigma = \sqrt{\frac{(x_1 - \mu)^2 + (x_2 - \mu)^2 + \cdots + (x_n - \mu)^2}{n}}$$

z-Score
$$z = \frac{x - \mu}{\sigma}$$

Margin of error for sample proportions
$$\pm \frac{1}{\sqrt{n}}$$

Trigonometry

General definitions of trigonometric functions

Let θ be an angle in standard position, and let (x, y) be the point where the terminal side of θ intersects the circle $x^2 + y^2 = r^2$. The six trigonometric functions of θ are defined as shown.

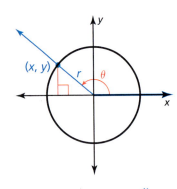

$$\sin \theta = \frac{y}{r} \qquad \cos \theta = \frac{x}{r} \qquad \tan \theta = \frac{y}{x}, x \neq 0$$

$$\csc \theta = \frac{r}{y}, y \neq 0 \qquad \sec \theta = \frac{r}{x}, x \neq 0 \qquad \cot \theta = \frac{x}{y}, y \neq 0$$

Conversion between degrees and radians

$180° = \pi$ radians

Arc length of a sector

$s = r\theta$

Area of a sector

$A = \frac{1}{2}r^2\theta$

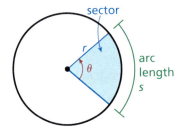

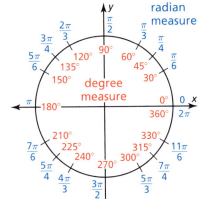

Reciprocal Identities

$$\sin \theta = \frac{1}{\csc \theta} \qquad \cos \theta = \frac{1}{\sec \theta} \qquad \tan \theta = \frac{1}{\cot \theta}$$

$$\csc \theta = \frac{1}{\sin \theta} \qquad \sec \theta = \frac{1}{\cos \theta} \qquad \cot \theta = \frac{1}{\tan \theta}$$

Tangent and Cotangent Identities

$$\tan \theta = \frac{\sin \theta}{\cos \theta} \qquad \cot \theta = \frac{\cos \theta}{\sin \theta}$$

Pythagorean Identities

$\sin^2 \theta + \cos^2 \theta = 1$
$1 + \tan^2 \theta = \sec^2 \theta$
$1 + \cot^2 \theta = \csc^2 \theta$

Negative Angle Identities

$\sin(-\theta) = -\sin \theta$
$\cos(-\theta) = \cos \theta$
$\tan(-\theta) = -\tan \theta$

Cofunction Identities

$$\sin\left(\frac{\pi}{2} - \theta\right) = \cos \theta$$

$$\cos\left(\frac{\pi}{2} - \theta\right) = \sin \theta$$

$$\tan\left(\frac{\pi}{2} - \theta\right) = \cot \theta$$

Sum Formulas

$\sin(a + b) = \sin a \cos b + \cos a \sin b$
$\cos(a + b) = \cos a \cos b - \sin a \sin b$
$$\tan(a + b) = \frac{\tan a + \tan b}{1 - \tan a \tan b}$$

Difference Formulas

$\sin(a - b) = \sin a \cos b - \cos a \sin b$
$\cos(a - b) = \cos a \cos b + \sin a \sin b$
$$\tan(a - b) = \frac{\tan a - \tan b}{1 + \tan a \tan b}$$

Probability

Standard Normal Table										
z	.0	.1	.2	.3	.4	.5	.6	.7	.8	.9
−3	.0013	.0010	.0007	.0005	.0003	.0002	.0002	.0001	.0001	.0000+
−2	.0228	.0179	.0139	.0107	.0082	.0062	.0047	.0035	.0026	.0019
−1	.1587	.1357	.1151	.0968	.0808	.0668	.0548	.0446	.0359	.0287
−0	.5000	.4602	.4207	.3821	.3446	.3085	.2743	.2420	.2119	.1841
0	.5000	.5398	.5793	.6179	.6554	.6915	.7257	.7580	.7881	.8159
1	.8413	.8643	.8849	.9032	.9192	.9332	.9452	.9554	.9641	.9713
2	.9772	.9821	.9861	.9893	.9918	.9938	.9953	.9965	.9974	.9981
3	.9987	.9990	.9993	.9995	.9997	.9998	.9998	.9999	.9999	1.0000−

Perimeter, Area, and Volume Formulas

Square

$P = 4s$
$A = s^2$

Rectangle
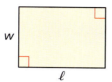

$P = 2\ell + 2w$
$A = \ell w$

Triangle
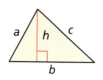

$P = a + b + c$
$A = \frac{1}{2}bh$

Circle
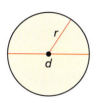

$C = \pi d$ or $C = 2\pi r$
$A = \pi r^2$

Parallelogram
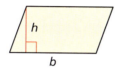

$A = bh$

Trapezoid
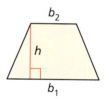

$A = \frac{1}{2}h(b_1 + b_2)$

Prism

$L = Ph$
$S = 2B + Ph$
$V = Bh$

Cylinder

$L = 2\pi rh$
$S = 2\pi r^2 + 2\pi rh$
$V = \pi r^2 h$

Pyramid
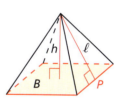

$L = \frac{1}{2}P\ell$
$S = B + \frac{1}{2}P\ell$
$V = \frac{1}{3}Bh$

Cone
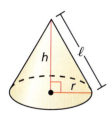

$L = \pi r \ell$
$S = \pi r^2 + \pi r \ell$
$V = \frac{1}{3}\pi r^2 h$

Sphere

$S = 4\pi r^2$
$V = \frac{4}{3}\pi r^3$

Other Formulas

Pythagorean Theorem
$a^2 + b^2 = c^2$

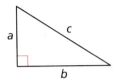

Simple Interest
$I = Prt$

Compound Interest
$A = P\left(1 + \dfrac{r}{n}\right)^{nt}$

Continuously Compounded Interest
$A = Pe^{rt}$

Distance
$d = rt$

Conversions

U.S. Customary
1 foot = 12 inches
1 yard = 3 feet
1 mile = 5,280 feet
1 mile = 1,760 yards
1 acre = 43,560 square feet
1 cup = 8 fluid ounces
1 pint = 2 cups
1 quart = 2 pints
1 gallon = 4 quarts
1 gallon = 231 cubic inches
1 pound = 16 ounces
1 ton = 2,000 pounds
1 cubic foot ≈ 7.5 gallons

Metric
1 centimeter = 10 millimeters
1 meter = 100 centimeters
1 kilometer = 1,000 meters
1 liter = 1,000 milliliters
1 kiloliter = 1,000 liters
1 milliliter = 1 cubic centimeter
1 liter = 1,000 cubic centimeters
1 cubic millimeter = 0.001 milliliter
1 gram = 1,000 milligrams
1 kilogram = 1,000 grams

U.S. Customary to Metric
1 inch = 2.54 centimeters
1 foot ≈ 0.3 meter
1 mile ≈ 1.61 kilometers
1 quart ≈ 0.95 liter
1 gallon ≈ 3.79 liters
1 cup ≈ 237 milliliters
1 pound ≈ 0.45 kilogram
1 ounce ≈ 28.3 grams
1 gallon ≈ 3,785 cubic centimeters

Metric to U.S. Customary
1 centimeter ≈ 0.39 inch
1 meter ≈ 3.28 feet
1 meter ≈ 39.37 inches
1 kilometer ≈ 0.62 mile
1 liter ≈ 1.06 quarts
1 liter ≈ 0.26 gallon
1 kilogram ≈ 2.2 pounds
1 gram ≈ 0.035 ounce
1 cubic meter ≈ 264 gallons

Time
1 minute = 60 seconds
1 hour = 60 minutes
1 hour = 3,600 seconds
1 year = 52 weeks

Temperature
$C = \dfrac{5}{9}(F - 32)$
$F = \dfrac{9}{5}C + 32$

Credits

Chapter 1
0 *top* ©Rebecca Drobis/National Geographic Image Collection; *bottom* Andrii Vodolazhskyi/Shutterstock.com; **1** Data from Google Scholar, https://scholar.google.com/, accessed March 14, 2023.; **3** Daniel M Ernst/Shutterstock.com; **9** Lightspring/Shutterstock.com; **10** Ljupco Smokovski/Shutterstock.com, My Sunnyday/Shutterstock.com, Data from Ingrid McNeely and Dylan Morgan, "Douglas Fir Biometrics," The Quantitative Environmental Learning Project, April 20, 2001, https://seattlecentral.edu/qelp/sets/076/076.html.; **15** MERCURY studio/Shutterstock.com; **17** Rob Wilson/Shutterstock.com; **18** 9MongKP/Shutterstock.com, Data from Mead R. Binhammer, Maddie Beange, and Randall Arauz, "Sand Temperature, Sex Ratios, and Nest Success in Olive Ridley Sea Turtles," Marine Turtle Newsletter 159, 2019, www.seaturtle.org/mtn/archives/mtn159/mtn159-2.shtml.; **19** Dragon Images/Shutterstock.com; **23** angelhell/iStock/Getty Images Plus; **26** Valentyn Volkov/Shutterstock.com, Data from "Avocado Prices: 2018 Weekly Retail Scan Data for Hass Avocados," Kaggle dataset, https://www.kaggle.com/datasets/neuromusic/avocado-prices, accessed May 17, 2023.; **27** cristovao/Shutterstock.com; **32** Harun Ozmen/Shutterstock.com, Valentyn Volkov/Shutterstock.com; **33** OvsiankaStudio/iStock/Getty Images Plus; **34** Rob Marmion/Shutterstock.com; **36** FootMade0525/Shutterstock.com; **38–39** ioat/Shutterstock.com

Chapter 2
40 *top* ©Jennifer W. Lopez; *bottom* Dotted Yeti/Shutterstock.com; **41** CHINE NOUVELLE/SIPA/Shutterstock.com; **43** Flashon Studio/Shuterstock.com; **47** serhii.suravikin/Shutterstock.com; **48** Freder/E+/Getty Images; **49** *top left* max dallocco/Shutterstock.com; *top right* Paitoon Pornsuksomboon/Shutterstock.com; *right* Valery Evlakhov/Shutterstock.com; *bottom* Tarzhanova/shutterstock.com; **50** volkova natalia/Shutterstock.com, Data from Bonnie Blanchard, "Size and Growth Patterns of Yellowstone National Park grizzly bear," Interagency Grizzly Bear Study Team, International Conference of Bear Research and Management 7, pp. 99-107, Table 3.; **51** wavebreakmedia/Shutterstock.com; **56** Aleksandr Lupin/Shutterstock.com; **58** Steve Mann/Shutterstock.com; **59** Alphotographic/iStock/Getty Images Plus; **60** *left* Ljupco Smokovski/Shutterstock.com; *right* mipan/Shutterstock.com; **61** Apollofoto/Shutterstock.com; **66** bekirevren/Shutterstock.com **68** *left* topseller/Shuttetstock.com; *right* Fit Ztudio/Shutterstock.com; **69** Alexander Raths/Shutterstock.com; **71** Minerva Studio/Shutterstock.com, Rainer Lesniewski/Shutterstock.com; **75** iVazoUSky/Shutterstock.com; **76** Sabphoto/Shutterstock.com, Adapted from J. A. Edwards and Ronald IL Smith, "Photosynthesis and respiration of Colobanthus quitensis and Deschampsia antarctica from the maritime Antarctic." British Antarctic Survey Bulletin 81 (1988), p. 47, Figure 2, https://nora.nerc.ac.uk/id/eprint/521557/1/Edwards.pdf.; **78** AlexLMX/shutterstock.com; **79** *top* NicolasMcComber/E+/Getty Images, Adam Fahey Designs/Shutterstock.com; *bottom* Dimitris Leonidas/Shutterstock.com; **80–81** solarseven/iStock/Getty Images Plus, EgudinKa/Shutterstock.com

Chapter 3
82 *top* ©Sora Devore/National Geographic Image Collection; *bottom* hornyak/Shutterstock.com; **83** Source: U.S. Energy Information Administration, Monthly Energy Review, Table 7.2a, January 2021, and Electric Power Monthly, February 2021., Data from U.S. Energy Information Administration, Monthly Energy Review, February 2023, https://www.eia.gov/totalenergy/data/monthly/pdf/sec8_3.pdf.; **85** all_about_people/Shutterstock.com; **89** *top* Krivosheev Vitaly/Shutterstock.com; *bottom* Jula Store/Shutterstock.com; **91** Asni Maryani/iStock/Getty Images; **92** *top* frentusha/iStock/Getty Images; *bottom* starets/iStock/Getty Images Plus; **93** dottedhippo/iStock/Getty Images Plus; **94** Nosyrevy/Shutterstock.com, Krishnavedala, "Paraboloid of Revolution" (https://commons.wikimedia.org/wiki/File:Paraboloid_of_Revolution.svg), https://creativecommons.org/licenses/by-sa/3.0/legalcode.; **95** Sinisa92/iStock/Getty Images Plus **104** DimaBerlin/Shutterstock.com; **105** Samuel Borges Photography/Shutterstock.com; **112** *top* Jiri Hera/Shutterstock.com; *bottom* makkayak/iStock/Getty Images Plus; **114** Andrey Yurlov/Shutterstock.com; **115** arekmalang/iStoc /Getty Images Plus; **120** Ljupco Smokovski/Shutterstock.com; **122** *top* Ben Haslam/iStock/Getty Images Plus; *bottom* Russell Watkins/Shutterstock.com; **123** chara_stagram/Shutterstock.com; **124** xpixel/Shutterstock.com; **125** stockyimages/Shutterstock.com; **132** Studio Romantic/Shutterstock.com; **133** Hugo Felix/Shutterstock.com; **139** Michael Shake/Shutterstock.com; **140** *left* Paolo Certo/Shutterstock.com; *right* Krakenimages.com/Shtutterstock.com; **142** Antagain/iStock/Getty Images Plus; **144–145** Holiday.Photo.Top/Shutterstock.com, Andris Torms/Shutterstock.com; **146–147** lovelyday12/Shutterstock.com, Maks Narodenko/Shutterstock.com, greenaperture/Shutterstock.com, Sascha Burkard/Shutterstock.com

Chapter 4
148 *top* ©Robert Lonsinger/National Geographic Image Collection; *bottom* Juniors Bildarchiv GmbH/Alamy Stock Photo; **149** tristan tan/Shutterstock.com, Johan Holmdahl/Shutterstock.com, Data from Florida Fish and Wildlife Conservation Commission, "Synoptic Aerial Surveys of manatees, East and West Coasts of Florida, 1991 to 2019," https://myfwc.com/research/manatee/research/population-monitoring/synoptic-surveys/, accessed March 16, 2023.; **151** Dean Drobot/Shutterstock.com; **155** Susan Schmitz/Shutterstock.com, GlobalP/iStock/Getty Images Plus; **157** GlobalP/iStock/Getty Images Plus; **158** Alyssa Golden/Shutterstock.com, U.S. Geological Survey, "Annual California Sea Otter Census - 1985-2014 Spring Census Summary," https://www.sciencebase.gov/catalog/item/5a32d390e4b08e6a89d88583. Accessed March 16, 2023.; **159** michaeljung/Shutterstock.com; **164** Arkhipenko Olga/Shutterstock.com; **166** Konstantin Chagin/Shutterstock.com; **167** oatintro/iStock/Getty Images Plus; **172** *left* Brian A Wolf/Shutterstock.com; *right* Maridav/Shutterstock.com; Data from California Condor Recovery Program: 2017 Annual Population Status, U.S. Department of the interior Fish and Wildlife Service, accessed 25 April 2023, https://nrm.dfg.ca.gov/FileHandler.ashx?DocumentID=83849&inline#:~:text=The%20total%20world%20population%20of,of%20the%20total%20wild%20population.; **173** Ebtikar/Shutterstock.com; **177** Allen.G/Shutterstock.com; **179** junyanjiang/Shutterstock.com; **180** EHStockphoto/Shutterstock.com; **181** Layland Masuda/Shutterstock.com; **187** Svitlana Unuchko/iStock/Getty Images Plus; **188** LifephotoN/Shutterstock.com; **189** *left* pikselstock/Shutterstock.com; *right* Julia Nikitina/Shutterstock.com; **194** *left* Suvorov_Alex/Shutterstock.com; *bottom right* New Africa/Shutterstock.com; **196** RLS Photo/Shutterstock.com; **198** Geobor/Shutterstock.com, Source of data: "Highway Statistics Series, Federal Highway Administration, US Department of Transportation, https://www.fhwa.dot.gov/policyinformation/statistics.cfm.; **199** aldomurillo/iStock/Getty Images Plus; **211** Darryl Brooks/Shutterstock.com; **212** Antonio Gravante/Shutterstock.com, Data from C. D. Keeling, S. C. Piper, R. B. Bacastow, M. Wahlen, T. P. Whorf, M. Heimann, and H. A. Meijer, "Exchanges of atmospheric CO2 and 13CO2 with the terrestrial biosphere and oceans from 1978 to 2000," I. Global aspects, SIO Reference Series, No. 01-06, San Diego: Scripps Institution of Oceanography, 2001, https://

scrippsco2.ucsd.edu/data/atmospheric_co2/mlo.html.; **213** *left* aldomurillo/iStock/Getty Images Plus; *right* oatintro/iStock/Getty Images Plus; **218** Graph is generic formatting of data sourced from a federally funded project: "30-day and Daily Cigarette Smoking Prevalence (percent), 1975-2018, United States 12th-grade Students," Monitoring the Future, University of Michigan, https://monitoringthefuture.org/data/Prevalence2021/Cigarettes.htm.; **220** pabradyphoto/iStock Editorial/Getty Images Plus; **221** tupungato/iStock Editorial/Getty Images Plus **223** drakuliren/iStock/Getty Images Plus; **224–225** BlueBarronPhoto/Shutterstock.com, photomaster/Shutterstock.com, Harry Collins Photography/Shutterstock.com

Chapter 5
226 *top* ©Benjamin Mirin/National Geographic Image Collection; *bottom* Steve Byland/Shutterstock.com; **227** Eric Isselee/Shutterstock.com, Data from R. R. Fay, Hearing in Vertebrates: a Psychophysics Databook (Winnetka, IL: Hill-Fay Associates, 1988; and D. Warfield, "The Study of Hearing in Animals," from W. Gay (ed.), Methods of Animal Experimentation, IV (London: Academic Press).; **229** Dean Drobot/Shutterstock.com; **232** AlexLMX/Shutterstock.com; **234** Dario Lo Presti/Shutterstock.com, David R. Williams, "Planetary Fact Sheet - Ratio to Earth Values," NASA Space Science Coordinated Archive, https://nssdc.gsfc.nasa.gov/planetary/factsheet/planet_table_ratio.html. Accessed March 17, 2023.; **235** DenisNata/Shutterstock.com; **242** ImageDB/iStock/Getty Images Plus; **243** hexvivo/iStock/Getty Images Plus; **250** Ground Picture/Shutterstock.com; **251** rui vale sousa/Shutterstock.com; **253** DNY59/iStock/Getty Images Plus; **257** J. S. Wolf Photography/Shutterstock.com; **258** belizar/Shutterstock.com, From Simon N. Chapman et al., "How Big Is It Really? Assessing the Efficacy of Indirect Estimates of Body Size in Asian Elephants," PLoS ONE 11, no. 3, March 2016, Figure 1a, https://doi.org/10.1371/journal.pone.0150533.; **262** *left* AaronAmat/iStock/Getty Images Plus; *bottom right* syabrin/iStock/Getty Images Plus; **264** *left* Geoffrey Kuchera/Shutterstock.com; *right* Volodymyr Burdiak/Shutterstock.com; Historical Hare and Lynx Population Data from Archives of Manitoba, Manitoba, Canada, https://www.gov.mb.ca/chc/archives/hbca/common_research_topics.html#furs,; **265** *left* Rido/Shutterstock.com; *right* Tomas Ragina/Shutterstock.com; **268** *top* tomazl/E+/Getty Images, amriphoto/E+/Getty Images; *bottom* DanielPrudek/iStock/Getty Images Plus; **271** williv/iStock/Getty Images Plus; **276** hudiemm/iStock/Getty Images Plus; **278** herreid/iStock/Getty Images Plus; **279** Maestrovideo/iStock/Getty Images Plus; **280** gresei/Shutterstock.com; **281** Pamela Toledo/Shutterstock.com; **284–285** Aleksandr Artt/Shutterstock.com, pialhovik/iStock/Getty Images Plus

Chapter 6
286 *top* ©Cengage Learning/National Geographic Learning; *bottom* marktucan/Shutterstock.com; **287** Tonkovic/Shutterstock.com; **289** antoniodiaz/Shutterstock.com; **294** Gena73/Shutterstock.com; **296** Josep Suria/Shutterstock.com; **301** Andrey_Popov/Shutterstock.com; **302** Ground Picture/Shutterstock.com; **303** ferlistockphoto/iStock/Getty Images Plus; **308** dzphotovideo/iStock/Getty Images Plus, German-skydiver/iStock/Getty Images Plus, Mauricio Graiki/iStock/Getty Images Plus, Serg_Velusceac/iStock/Getty Images Plus; **309** Robert Eastman/Shutterstock.com; **310** *top* cla78/Shutterstock.com; *bottom* Oliver Susemihl/iStock/Getty Images Plus; **311** Billion Photos/Shutterstock.com; **317** ozanuysal/iStock/Getty Images Plus; **318** EHStockphoto/Shutterstock.com; **323** Yuri Shevtsov/Shutterstock.com; **325** Maria Spb/Shutterstock.com; **326** Oleksandr Mazur/Shutterstock.com; **327** michaeljung/iStock/Getty Images Plus; **331** AS Foodstudio/Shutterstock.com; **332** abadonian/iStock/Getty Images Plus; **334** AshTproductions/Shutterstock.com **335** amenic181/iStock/Getty Images Plus; **340** Dean Drobot/Shutterstock.com; **341** AaronAmat/iStock/Getty Images Plus, VladimirFLoyd/iStock/Getty Images Plus, Ranta Images/iStock/Getty Images Plus, kemalbas/iStock/Getty Images Plus; **342** urfin/Shutterstock.com; **344** mrgao/iStock/Getty Images Plus; **345** naito29/Shutterstock.com; **346–347** Gam1983/iStock/Getty Images Plus, xpixel/Shutterstock.com; **348–349** Suri Sharma/Shutterstock.com, Kwangmoozaa/Shutterstock.com, Dan Kosmayer/Shutterstock.com, Trueffelpix/Shutterstock.com, photastic/Shutterstock.com, carmen2011/Shutterstock.com

Chapter 7
350 *top* ©Lynn Johnson/National Geographic Image Collection; *bottom* Zyabich/iStock/Getty Images Plus; **353** Dean Drobot/Shutterstock.com; **356** *top* Sofiaworld/Shutterstock.com; *bottom* BGStock72/Shutterstock.com; **358** Asier Romero/Shutterstock.com; **363** *left* aerogondo2/Shutterstock.com; *right* PhonlamaiPhoto/iStock/Getty Images Plus; **365** Africa Studio/Shutterstock.com; **366** Prostock-studio/Shutterstock.com, T. Tiwari et al., "Tetanus Surveillance: United States, 2001–2008," Morbidity and Mortality Weekly Report (MMWR), April 1, 2011, FIGURE. Annual rate of tetanus cases and tetanus deaths --- National Notifiable Diseases Surveillance System, United States, 1947—2008, https://www.cdc.gov/mmwr/preview/mmwrhtml/mm6012a1.htm#:~:text=In%201947%2C%20the%20first%20year,3.9%20per%201%20million%20population.; **367** Hugo Felix/Shutterstock.com; **373** nikolay100/iStock/Getty Images Plus, photomaru/iStock/Getty Images Plus; **374** nickp37/iStock/Getty Images Plus; **375** pikselstock/Shutterstock.com; **381** nicoolay/E+/Getty Images; **382** AYA images/Shutterstock.com, Data from Guillermo Chalar, "The Use of Phytoplankton Patterns of Diversity for Algal; Bloom Management," Limnologica 39, September 2009.; **383** Pixel-Shot/Shutterstock.com; **384** New Africa/Shutterstock.com; **388** Shuttertum/Shutterstock.com; **389** Artur Didyk/Shutterstock.com; **390** El Nariz/Shutterstock.com; **391** Vudhikul Ocharoen/iStock/Getty Images Plus; **393** Ljupco Smokovski/Shutterstock.com; **394–395** carloscastilla/iStock/Getty Images Plus, AlexLMX/iStock/Getty Images Plus, wir0man/iStock/Getty Images Plus

Chapter 8
396 *top* ©Arianna Soldati; *bottom* Lucie Petrikova/Shutterstock.com; **397** Trilok Sunny/Shutterstock.com; **399** Studio-Annika/iStock/Getty Images Plus; **401** Sean Locke Photography/Shutterstock.com; **402** New Africa/Shutterstock.com; **404** mimagephotography/Shutterstock.com; **405** ifong/Shutterstock.com, bigacis/Shutterstock.com, Evgeniya Khudyakova/Shutterstock.com; **406** Krakenimages.com/Shutterstock.com, Karen Julie Mickle et al., "Foot Shape of Older People: Implications for Shoe Design," Footwear Science 2, no. 3 (September 2010): Figure 3.; **407** chairoij/Shutterstock.com; **413** *top* Katrin_Timoff/iStock/Getty Images Plus; *bottom* Hayati Kayhan/Shutterstock.com; **414** fizkes/Shutterstock.com, Source: "Age distribution in the United States from 2011 to 2021," data from World Bank, World Development Indicators, accessed February 20, 2023, https://data.worldbank.org/country/united-states.; **415** Wavebreakmedia Ltd/Wavebreak Media/Getty Images Plus; **416** Rawpixel/iStock/Getty Images Plus, Boarding1Now/iStock/Getty Images Plus, SDI Productions/E+/Getty Images; **420** *top right* bsd studio/Shutterstock.com, Oleksiy Mark/Shutterstock.com; *middle* Master1305/Shutterstock.com; **422** ESB Professional/shutterstock.com, Adapted from "Population Ethnicity, and Language in the United States," GloBig, accessed February 20. 2023, https://platform.globig.co/knowledgebase/US/us-expansion/population-ethnicity-language-in-us. Data from U.S. Census Bureau.; **423** ahmetemre/iStock/Getty Images Plus; **425** Lammeyer/Shutterstock.com; **427** Ground Picture/Shutterstock.com; **428** Bernard Chantal/Shutterstock.com, Adapted from "Polio Case and Death Rates in the United States, 1910 to 2019," Our World in Data, accessed February 24, 2023, https://ourworldindata.org/grapher/prevalence-of-polio-rates-in-the-united-states.; **429** Anna Hoychuk/Shutterstock.com; **434** merve zengin/iStock/Getty Images Plus; **435** Christopher Sykes/Shutterstock.com; **436** scanrail/iStock/Getty Images Plus; **437** Civil/Shutterstock.com; **438** Damir Khabirov/Shutterstock.com; **439** wavebreakmedia/Shutterstock.com; **440** chengyuzheng/iStock/Getty Images Plus; **444** iodrakon/Shutterstock.com, "State Area Measurements and Internal Point Coordinates," U.S. Census Bureau, 2010, accessed February 20, 2023, https://www.census.gov/geographies/reference-files/2010/geo/state-area.html.; **445** GlobalP/iStock/Getty Images Plus; **446** *top* smartstock/iStock/Getty Images Plus; *bottom* Marta Martínez Photo/iStock/Getty Images Plus; **448–449** zuperia/Shutterstock.com, Rtstudio/shutterstock.com, Eachat/iStock/Getty Images Plus; **450–451** GE_4530/Shutterstock.com

Chapter 9

452 *top* ©Elizabeth Lindsey; *bottom* maloff/Shutterstock.com; **453** abriendomundo/iStock/Getty Images Plus; **455** Ustyujanin/Shutterstock.com; **459** *top* Glenn Young/Shutterstock.com; *bottom* Sergey Ginak/Shutterstock.com; **462** Lifestyle Graphic/Shutterstock.com, arda savasciogullari/Shutterstock.com, Kamenetskiy Konstantin/Shutterstock.com; **463** Sean Locke Photography/Shutterstock.com; **467** antpkr/Shutterstock.com; **470** *left* michaeljung/Shutterstock.com; *right* NPeter/Shutterstock.com; **476** Mike Flippo/Shutterstock.com; **478** smart_picture/Shutterstock.com; **479** ASDF_MEDIA/Shutterstock.com; **487** *top* Elena11/Shutterstock.com; *bottom* Henrik Dolle/Shutterstock.com; **488** Photobank.kiev.ua/Shutterstock.com; **489** 4x6/E+/Getty Images; **497** MyCreative/Shutterstock.com, Maxiphoto/iStock/Getty Images Plus; **498** Dietrich Leppert/Shutterstock.com; **499** michaeljung/Shutterstock.com; **500** Courtesy of Grason-Stadler; **502** davidf/E+/Getty Images; **503** railway fx/Shutterstock.com; **506** ju_see/Shutterstock.com; **507** rnl/Shutterstock.com; **511** DanBrandenburg/E+/Getty Images; **512** Dean Drobot/Shutterstock.com; **513** Antonio_Diaz/iStock/Getty Images Plus; **519** ChrisAt/iStock/Getty Images Plus, ©iStockphoto.com/4x6, ©iStockphoto.com/knape; **521** mama_mia/Shutterstock.com; **522** zimmytws/Shutterstock.com; **524–525** MakDill/Shutterstock.com, Lebazele/iStock/Getty Images Plus

Chapter 10

526 *top* ©Mark Thiessen/National Geographic Image Collection; *bottom* Rich Carey/Shutterstock.com; **527** *top* Vlad61/Shutterstock.com; *bottom* witoldkr1/iStock/Getty Images; **529** *left* B-D-S Piotr Marcinski/Shutterstock.com; *right* by_nicholas/iStock/Getty Images Plus, wwing/E+/Getty Images, DNY59/E+/Getty Images; **531** Halina Yakushevich/Shutterstock.com; **535** Evan-Amos, Vanamo Media, (https://commons.wikimedia.org/wiki/File:Solomon-R-Guggenheim-Museum-Skylight.jpg).; **537** *left* hexvivo/iStock/Getty Images Plus; *right* talevr/iStock/Getty Images Plus; **543** "Rhind Mathematical Papyrus" (ca. 1550 BCE), Ahmose, papyrus, 33 cm x 296 cm, The British Museum (https://commons.wikimedia.org/wiki/File:Rhind_Mathematical_Papyrus.jpg).; **544** *left* Eroshka/Shutterstock.com; *right* Aerial-motion/Shutterstock.com; **545** pomarinus/iStock/Getty Images Plus; **552** Viorel Sima/Shutterstock.com; **553** Kritchanut/iStock/Getty Images Plus; **556** FotoHelin/Shutterstock.com; **558** Purple Clouds/Shutterstock.com; **559** *left* Brian Mueller/Shutterstock.com; *right* MPFphotography/Shutterstock.com; **564** Skylines/Shutterstock.com; **565** luismmolina/E+/Getty Images; **566** *top* Eric Isselee/Shutterstock.com; *bottom* Leigh Prather/Shutterstock.com; **568** Ian 2010/Shutterstock.com; **571** spyarm/Shutterstock.com; **572–573** divedog/Shutterstock.com, Jean-Michel Girard/Shutterstock.com, annalisa e marina durante/Shutterstock.com, Evlakhov Valeriy/Shutterstock.com

Chapter 11

574 *top* ©Randall Scott/National Geographic Image Collection; *bottom* ©Ronan Donovan; **575** Fly_and_Dive/Shutterstock.com; **577** HomePixel/iStock/Getty Images Plus; **583** Rich Carey/Shutterstock.com; **584** ILIA BLIZNYUK/Shutterstock.com; **585** HomePixel/iStock/Getty Images Plus; **589** nitrub/iStock/Getty Images Plus; **590** aodaodaodaod/Shutterstock.com; **591** Eric Isselee/Shutterstock.com; **592** Rawpixel.com/Shutterstock.com; **593** Dean Drobot/Shutterstock.com; **598** Shawn Hempel/Shutterstock.com; **599** Sergey Gordienko/iStock Getty Images Plus; **600** Rtimages/iStock/Getty Images Plus; **601** Tim UR/Shutterstock.com; **602** Phovoir/Shutterstock.com; **603** pikselstock/Shutterstock.com; **607** Pektoral/iStock/Getty Images Plus, anna1311/iStock/Getty Images Plus, anna1311/iStock/Getty Images Plus; **608** dtv2/iStock/Getty Images Plus, WolfeLarry/iStock/Getty Images Plus, scisettialfio/iStock/Getty Images Plus; **609** Spalnic/Shutterstock.com; **611** Bronwyn Photo/Shutterstock.com, Twister40/iStock/ Getty Images Plus; **612** Mega Pixel/Shutterstock.com; **613** Fudio/iStock/Getty Images Plus, Hurst Photo/Shutterstock.com; **614–615** ESB Professional/Shutterstock.com, Agami Photo Agency/Shutterstock.com, cynoclub/iStock/Getty Images Plus, Nick Biemans/Shutterstock.com, samuelnielsen/iStock/Getty Images Plus, GlobalP/iStock/Getty Images Plus, Iuliia Morozova/iStock/Getty Images Plus; **616–617** 3d_kot/Shutterstock.com, NosorogUA/Shutterstock.com

Special thanks to Thurner Photography.